Lecture Notes in Computer Sci

Commenced Publication in 1973
Founding and Former Series Editors:
Gerhard Goos, Juris Hartmanis, and Jan van Leeuwen

David Eyers   Karsten Schwan (Eds.)

Middleware 2013

ACM/IFIP/USENIX
14th International Middleware Conference
Beijing, China, December 9-13, 2013
Proceedings

 Springer

Volume Editors

David Eyers
University of Otago
Department of Computer Science
PO Box 56, Dunedin, 9054, New Zealand
E-mail: dme@cs.otago.ac.nz

Karsten Schwan
Georgia Tech
College of Computing
266 Ferst Drive, Atlanta, GA 30332-0765, USA
E-mail: schwan@cc.gatech.edu

ISSN 0302-9743   e-ISSN 1611-3349
ISBN 978-3-642-45064-8   e-ISBN 978-3-642-45065-5
DOI 10.1007/978-3-642-45065-5
Springer Heidelberg New York Dordrecht London

Library of Congress Control Number: 2013953718

CR Subject Classification (1998): C.2, D.2, H.4, H.2, H.3, C.4, K.6.5, D.4

LNCS Sublibrary: SL 2 – Programming and Software Engineering

Typesetting: Camera-ready by author, data conversion by Scientific Publishing Services, Chennai, India

Printed on acid-free paper

Springer is part of Springer Science+Business Media (www.springer.com)

Preface

This edition marks the 14th ACM/IFIP/USENIX Middleware Conference. The conference has an increasingly long history, with the first event being held in 1998, in the Lake District of England. At that time, the growing significance of middleware technology was recognized, as was the need to support the active, rigorous, expanding, and evolving research discipline coupled with the middleware technology. The definition of the term "middleware" has also evolved significantly over time, but retains, at its core, the notion of different levels and layers of abstraction in distributed-computing systems. Cloud computing, and other topics connected to increasingly massive distributed systems, are helping maintain an increasing pace of middleware evolution. As always, the Middleware Conference aims to be a premier forum for the discussion of innovations and recent advances in all aspects of middleware systems.

The 2013 Middleware Conference included a variety of papers spanning the design, implementation, deployment, and evaluation of middleware for next-generation platforms such as cloud computing, social networks, and large-scale storage and distributed systems. The middleware solutions introduced provide features such as availability, efficiency, scalability, fault-tolerance, trustworthy operation, and support security and privacy needs.

The research track of the conference this year reflected a very strong technical program, with 24 papers accepted out of 189 submissions. The papers were judged based on originality, contribution, presentation quality, relevance to the conference, and potential impact on the field. The reviewing process again included an author feedback phase, which stimulated discussion within the Program Committee. We accepted "big ideas" and "systems and experience" papers as well as normal research submissions. This year, three of the accepted research track papers are "systems and experience" papers. The main program additionally included six high-quality submissions from the industry track. We were also delighted to provide an opportunity for a retrospective discussion from the authors of the paper deemed to have had highest impact from the program 10 years ago, in this case on the topic of peer-to-peer keyword searching.

The program also included workshops on topics such as adaptive/reflective middleware; cloud-enabled sensing; middleware modeling and evaluation; and cloud monitoring and management. Other important events within the conference included a significantly expanded poster and demonstration session, and a set of three tutorials. Finally, to help mentor the next generation of middleware researchers, the conference continued its long-running doctoral symposium.

It is our privilege to have had the opportunity to serve as the Program Chairs of the 2013 Middleware Conference and we would like to thank everyone who made the conference so successful. The Organizing Committee provided excellent support throughout the preparation of the conference—their many and varied roles are listed after this preface. The General Chairs, Gang Huang and Rick Schantz, consistently provided support that we greatly appreciated. The Program Committee did a thorough job of evaluating the submissions. The Steering Committee provided critical advice and insight, always provided in a timely manner—particular thanks is owed to the Steering Committee Chair, Gordon Blair. Last but not least, we would like to thank all of the authors—the outstanding quality of the papers within the 2013 ACM/IFIP/USENIX Middleware Conference represents significant, high-impact work that will provide an enduring contribution to the middleware research field.

December 2013   David Eyers
                                                       Karsten Schwan

Organization

Middleware 2013 was organized under the joint sponsorship of the Association for Computing Machinery (ACM), the International Federation for Information Processing (IFIP), and USENIX.

Organizing Committee

General Chairs

Gang Huang	Peking University, China
Rick Schantz	BBN Technologies, USA

Program Committee Chairs

David Eyers	University of Otago, New Zealand
Karsten Schwan	Georgia Institute of Technology, USA

Industry Chairs

Angelo Corsaro	PrismTech, UK
Tiancheng Liu	IBM Research China, China

Workshop and Tutorial Chairs

Laurent Réveillère	LaBRI, University of Bordeaux, France
Hailong Sun	Beihang University (BUAA), Beijing, China

Demo and Poster Chairs

Songlin Hu	Institute of Computing of CAS, China
Zibin Zheng	Chinese University of Hong Kong, China

Doctoral Symposium Chairs

Anders Andersen	University of Tromsø, Norway
Chang Xu	Nanjing University, China

Sponsorship Chairs

Xiaojun Ye	Tsinghua University, China
Teng Teng	Kingdee Middleware, China

Local Arrangements Chair

Xuanzhe Liu   Peking University, China

Web Chair

Ying Zhang   Peking University, China

Proceedings Chair

Dan O'Keeffe   Imperial College London, UK

Registration Chair

Yingfei Xiong   Peking University, China

Publicity Chairs

Tudor Dumitras   Symantec Research Labs, USA
Jatinder Singh   University of Cambridge, UK
Wenbo Zhang   Institute of Software of CAS, China

Steering Committee

Gordon Blair   Lancaster University, UK (Chair)
Jan De Meer   SmartSpaceLab, Germany
Fred Douglis   EMC Backup Recovery Systems, USA
Hans-Arno Jacobsen   University of Toronto, Canada
Cecilia Mascolo   University of Cambridge, UK
Indranil Gupta   University of Illinois at Urbana-Champaign,
                                       USA
Guruduth Banavar   IBM, USA
Anne-Marie Kermarrec   Inria, France
Fabio Kon   University of São Paulo, Brazil
Paulo Ferreira   INESC-ID, Portugal
Luís Veiga   INESC-ID, Portugal
Rui Oliveira   University of Minho, Portugal
Bettina Kemme   McGill University, Canada
Priya Narasimhan   Carnegie Mellon University, USA
Peter Triantafillou   University of Glasgow, UK

Program Committee

Lisa Amini   IBM Research, Ireland
Jean Bacon   University of Cambridge, UK
Ken Birman   Cornell University, USA

Gordon Blair	Lancaster University, UK
Rajkumar Buyya	The University of Melbourne, Australia
Roy Campbell	University of Illinois Urbana-Champaign, USA
Antonio Carzaniga	University of Lugano, Switzerland
António Casimiro	University of Lisbon, Portugal
Abhishek Chandra	University of Minnesota, USA
Lucy Cherkasova	HP Labs, USA
Brian Cooper	Google, USA
Dilma Da Silva	Qualcomm, USA
Sudipto Das	Microsoft Research, USA
Xavier Défago	JAIST, Japan
Tudor Dumitras	Symantec Research Labs, USA
Frank Eliassen	University of Oslo, Norway
Patrick Eugster	Purdue University, USA
Pascal Felber	University of Neuchatel, Switzerland
Paulo Ferreira	INESC ID / Technical University of Lisbon, Portugal
Jose Fortes	University of Florida, USA
Davide Frey	Inria, France
Xiaohui Gu	North Carolina State University, USA
Rachid Guerraoui	EPFL, Switzerland
Matti Hiltunen	AT&T Labs Research, USA
Kévin Huguenin	EPFL, Switzerland
Valerie Issarny	Inria, France
Arun Iyengar	IBM Research, USA
Hans-Arno Jacobsen	University of Toronto, Canada
Wouter Joosen	KU Leuven, Belgium
Vana Kalogeraki	AUEB, Greece
Bettina Kemme	McGill University, Canada
Anne-Marie Kermarrec	Inria, France
Fabio Kon	University of São Paulo, Brazil
Vibhore Kumar	IBM Research, USA
Ying Li	Peking University, China
Harry Li	Facebook, USA
Joseph Loyall	Raytheon BBN Technologies, USA
Sebastian Michel	Saarland University, Germany
Dejan Milojicic	HP Labs, USA
Elie Najm	Telecom-ParisTech, France
Priya Narasimhan	Carnegie Mellon University, USA
Nikos Ntarmos	University of Glasgow, UK
Adam Oliner	University of California, Berkeley, USA
Esther Pacitti	LIRMM and Inria, University of Montpellier 2, France
Peter Pietzuch	Imperial College London, UK

Padmanabhan Pillai   Intel Labs, USA
Rick Schlichting   AT&T Labs Research, USA
Douglas Schmidt   Vanderbilt University, USA
Swami Sivasubramanian   Amazon, USA
Mike Spreitzer   IBM Research, USA
Peter Triantafillou   University of Patras, Greece
Luís Veiga   INESC ID / Technical University of Lisbon,
                              Portugal
Nalini Venkatasubramanian   University of California Irvine, USA
Stratis Viglas   University of Edinburgh, UK
Spyros Voulgaris   VU University, The Netherlands
Dave Ward   Amazon, USA
Huaimin Wang   National University of Defense Technology,
                              China
Charles Zhang   The Hong Kong University of Science and
                              Technology, China
Xiaoyun Zhu   VMware, USA

Additional Reviewers

João Barreto   Luís Marques
Alysson Bessani   Ioannis Mpoutsis
Benjamin Billet   Navneet Kumar Pandey
Kelly Rosa Braghetto   Davy Preuveneers
Antorweep Chakravorty   Lucas Provensi
Daniel Cordeiro   Zhijing Qin
Fernando Costa   Reza Rahimi
William Culhane   Heverson Ribeiro
Wilfried Daniels   Remi Sharrock
Kashif Sana Dar   José Simão
Maarten Decat   Julian Stephen
Ngoc Do   Vinaitheerthan Sundaram
Stylianos Doudalis   Amir Taherkordi
Sérgio Esteves   Patrick Valduriez
Xavier Guerin   Bart Vanbrabant
Meng Han   Stefan Walraven
Benjamin Heintz   Long Wang
Danny Hughes   Peter Westerink
Arnaud Jegou   Nikos Zaheilas
Bert Lagaisse   Apostolos Zarras
Giljae Lee   Wenjie Zhang
Tongping Liu   Ye Zhao

Sponsoring Institutions

 International Federation for Information Processing
http://www.ifip.org

 Association for Computing Machinery
http://www.acm.org

 Advanced Computing Systems Association
http://www.usenix.org

 National Natural Science Foundation of China
http://www.nsfc.gov.cn

 Peking University
http://www.pku.edu.cn

Corporate Sponsors

 IBM
http://www.ibm.com

 Kingdee
http://kingdee.com

Table of Contents

Distributed Protocols

Cloud Computing

Storage

Services

Social Networks

Ten Year Best Paper

FastCast: A Throughput- and Latency-Efficient Total Order Broadcast Protocol

Gautier Berthou[1] and Vivien Quéma[2]

[1] Grenoble University
[2] Grenoble INP

Abstract. Many uniform total order broadcast protocols have been designed in the last 30 years. Unfortunately, none of them achieves both optimal throughput and low latency. Indeed, protocols achieving optimal throughput rely on a ring dissemination pattern, which induces high latencies. Protocols achieving low latency rely on IP multicast and fail to achieve good throughput because of message losses. In this paper, we describe *FastCast*, the first protocol that achieves both optimal throughput and low latency. To achieve low latency, *FastCast* relies on IP multicast. To achieve optimal throughput, *FastCast* defines a protocol responsible for dynamically computing the throughput at which processes can send IP multicast messages. Thanks to this dynamic bandwidth allocation protocol, *FastCast* allows multiple processes to simultaneously send messages, while avoiding message losses. An evaluation of *FastCast* on a cluster of 8 machines shows that it indeed achieves optimal throughput and a very low latency.

1 Introduction

State-machine replication [1] is a popular technique to ensure fault-tolerance in computer systems. The operating principle of state-machine replication is simple: several replicas of the same software object are maintained on different machines (also called processes). Each replica executes the same requests in the same order and is thus consistent with other replicas. Consequently, if one or more replicas fail, remaining replicas are consistent and guarantee accessibility to the object. To ensure that replicas execute requests in the same order, each replica broadcasts the requests it receives to other replicas using a *uniform total order broadcast* [2], and executes requests in the order in which they are delivered by the protocol. A uniform total order broadcast protocol ensures the following properties for all messages that are broadcast: (1) *Uniform agreement*: if a replica delivers a message m, then all correct replicas eventually deliver m; (2) *Strong uniform total order*: if some replica delivers some message m before message m', then a replica delivers m' only after it has delivered m.

Many uniform total order broadcast protocols have been designed in the last 30 years [3]. They can be classified into two categories: those targeting *low latency*, and those targeting *high throughput*. Latency measures the time required to complete a single message broadcast without contention, whereas throughput

D. Eyers and K. Schwan (Eds.): Middleware 2013, LNCS 8275, pp. 1–20, 2013.
© IFIP International Federation for Information Processing 2013

measures the number of broadcasts that the processes can complete per time unit when there is contention.

Protocols targeting low latency usually rely on IP multicast, a low-level networking protocol allowing senders to reach multiples destinations using a single message. These protocols do not achieve high throughput for the following reason: IP multicast messages are dropped when the network is congested. To limit congestion, protocols are designed in such a way that only one process at a time can send IP multicast messages. As we explain in Section 3.2, this does not allow achieving optimal throughput.

Protocols targeting high (actually *optimal*) throughput [4, 5] organize processes in a virtual ring topology: each process only communicates with its successor on the ring, using a reliable point-to-point communication protocol: TCP. These protocols achieve significantly higher throughput than protocols targeting low latency, e.g. +25% in a system comprising 4 processes. Nevertheless, these protocols have a significant drawback: because of the ring topology they rely on, latency linearly increases with the number of processes in the system.

In this paper, we present, *FastCast*, the first protocol that achieves both *optimal* throughput[1] and low latency. To achieve low latency, *FastCast* relies on IP multicast. To achieve optimal throughput, *FastCast* allows multiple processes to simultaneously send IP multicast messages. Message ordering is achieved by a fairly classical fixed-sequencer scheme [3]. The novelty in *FastCast* lies in a subprotocol executed by all processes that dynamically computes at which throughput each process can send IP multicast messages.

We have implemented *FastCast* in C++ and have compared its performance to that achieved by two recent state-of-the-art protocols: LCR [5] and RingPaxos [6]. The former achieves optimal throughput, whereas the latter aims at achieving both high throughput and low latency. Our evaluation on a cluster of 8 machines shows that *FastCast* achieves optimal throughput and very low latency. More precisely, *FastCast* achieves up to 86% faster throughput than RingPaxos, and up to 247% lower latency than LCR.

This paper is organized as follows. Section 2 gives a brief overview of the related work. Section 3 presents the *FastCast* protocol. A detailed performance evaluation is provided in Section 4, before concluding the paper in Section 5.

2   Related Work

Various total order broadcast protocols have been devised during the past 30 years [3]. We can distinguish two classes of protocols: those providing *uniform* agreement and those providing *non-uniform* agreement. In uniform agreement protocols, if a process delivers a message, then all correct processes will eventually deliver it. This is not necessarily the case in non-uniform protocols: if a node delivers a message and subsequently fail, the message might not be delivered by remaining (correct) processes. Total order broadcast protocols ensuring

---

[1] As proved in [5], a total order broacast protocol can only achieve optimal throughput if all processes simultaneously broadcast messages.

uniform agreement are more complex to implement and are often less efficient than non-uniform protocols. Nevertheless, they can be used for a much broader sets of applications. Consequently, the protocol we propose in this paper implements uniform agreement. In the remainder of this section, we do thus put more emphasis on uniform total order broadcast protocols.

Défago and Schiper have written an extensive survey on total order broadcast protocols [3]. They distinguish five types of total order broadcast protocols: fixed-sequencer, moving sequencer, privilege-based, communication history, and destination agreement. As is explained in the survey [3], "communication history" and "destination agreement" protocols [7–16] are less efficient than other types protocols. The three other types of protocols work as follows. In a *fixed sequencer* protocol [6, 17–23], a single process is elected as the sequencer and is responsible for the ordering of messages. The sequencer is unique, and another process is elected as a new sequencer only in the case of sequencer failure. *Moving sequencer* protocols [24–27] are based on the same principle as fixed sequencer protocols, but allow the role of the sequencer to be passed from one process to another (even in failure-free situations). This is achieved by a token which carries a sequence number and constantly circulates among the processes. The motivation is to distribute the load among sequencers, thus avoiding the bottleneck caused by a single sequencer. When a process p wants to broadcast a message m, it sends it to all other processes. Upon receiving m, processes store it into a *receive* queue. When the current token holder q has a message in its *receive* queue, q assigns a sequence number to the first message in the queue and broadcasts that message together with the token. For a message m to be delivered, it has to be acknowledged by all processes. Acks are gathered by the token. Finally, *privilege-based* protocols [28–33] rely on the idea that senders can broadcast messages only when they are granted the privilege to do so. The privilege to broadcast (and order) messages is granted to only one process at a time, but this privilege circulates from process to process in the form of a token. As with moving sequencer protocols, the throughput when all processes broadcast cannot be higher than when only one process broadcasts.

All the protocols mentioned above have been designed with the goal to ensure low broadcast latency. Latency measures the time required to complete a single message broadcast without contention. As shown in [5], above-mentioned protocols are far from sustaining optimal throughput. Throughput measures the number of broadcasts that the processes can complete per time unit. In some high load environments, e.g. database replication for e-commerce, throughput is often more important than latency. Indeed, under high load, the time spent by a message in a queue before being actually disseminated can grow indefinitely. A high throughput broadcast protocol reduces this waiting time. The authors of [5] prove that in a system comprising N nodes interconnected by a fully-switched network where each link has a bandwidth of B, the optimal throughput that can be achieved by a total order broadcast protocol is equal to $B * N/(N-1)$. For instance, in a system with 4 nodes interconnected by a gigabit ethernet switch (B=1Gb/s), each node can deliver messages at a throughput of 1,33Gb/s. The only protocol currently able to sustain that throughput is the LCR protocol [5]. In other protocols, the maximum throughput at which a node can deliver messages is B (1Gb/s in the example taken before). This is for instance the case of protocols known to be efficient such as Spread [33], RingPaxos [6], or the protocol designed by Chang and Maxemchuck [24]. The reason why these protocols do not achieve optimal throughput is that only one node at a time is allowed to broadcast a message. As explained in [5], optimal throughput can only be achieved when all nodes are allowed to simultaneously broadcast messages. Throughput-wise, LCR is thus much more efficient than other protocols. Nevertheless, the throughput-efficiency of LCR comes at a price: latency linearly increases with the number of nodes in the system. This comes from the fact that, in order to sustain high throughput, LCR uses a ring-based pipelining patterns: nodes are organized in a virtual ring. Each node only communicates with its successor in the ring. This pipelining pattern is efficient as it avoids message collisions, but it is not latency-efficient. In this paper, we propose a protocol that reaches optimal throughput, but that achieves a much lower latency than the LCR protocol.

3   The *FastCast* Protocol

In this section, we describe the *FastCast* protocol. We start by a description of the system model we consider. We then give an overview of *FastCast*, followed by a description of the three subprotocols that compose it.

3.1   System Model

We have designed the *FastCast* protocol for small clusters of homogeneous machines interconnected by a local area network. We assume that machines can only fail by crashing (i.e. Byzantine failures are out of the scope of this paper), that crashes are rare, and that each node is equipped with a *perfect* failure detector (P) [34]. A perfect failure detector outputs the list of alive processes and guarantees strong accuracy (correct machines are never suspected to have crashed) and strong completeness (every crash is eventually detected). In order to implement a perfect failure detector, each machine creates a TCP connection to all other machines and maintains this connection during the entire execution of the protocol (unless the machine fails). When a connection fails, the machine tries to re-establish it five times. If the machine does not succeed, it considers that the other machine crashed. This is a reasonable assumption provided that, on a cluster, the latency of the network interconnecting the machines is very low [35].

3.2   Overview

Our goal is to design a uniform total order broadcast protocol achieving optimal throughput, while guaranteeing a low latency. In order to ensure low latency, the best option is to use IP multicast. Indeed, using IP multicast, a process can reach all other processes in the system sending a single message. This choice is natural and most total order broadcast protocols rely on IP multicast. Unfortunately, IP multicast is not reliable: messages are dropped as soon as the network gets congested.

In order to reduce the ratio of message losses, most state-of-the-art total order broadcast protocols rely on a simple technique: only one process is allowed to send IP multicast messages. That way, it is easy to avoid network congestion by controlling the rate at which the sending process broadcasts IP multicast messages. Unfortunately, using one single sender is not enough to reach optimal throughput. To clarify that point, we depict in Figure 1 a system comprising 3 nodes interconnected by a 1Gb/s ethernet switch. On the left part of the Figure, only one node sends IP multicast messages. The maximum throughput at which nodes of the system can deliver messages in that configuration is 1Gb/s. On the right part of the Figure, we display a configuration where the 3 nodes simultaneously send IP multicast messages. Each node sends at a throughput of 500Mb/s. In that configuration, the maximum throughput at which nodes of the system can deliver messages is equal to 1,5Gb/s: each node delivers 500Mb/s that it produces itself, and 1Gb/s that are sent by other nodes. This is explained by two facts: (i) network cables and Network Interface Cards (NIC) are full-duplex (i.e. a node can simultaneously send and receive messages on the same network cable), and (ii) switches only forward IP multicast messages to nodes other than the source (i.e. a node does not receive its own messages via the network).

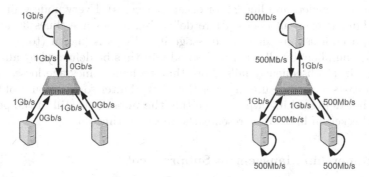

Fig. 1. Multicasting messages (one sender on the left, multiple senders on the right) in a system comprising 3 nodes

As the goal of *FastCast* is to reach optimal throughput while ensuring low latency, the protocol allows multiple processes to simultaneously send IP multicast messages. There are well-known algorithms for ensuring uniform total order of messages multicast by different senders [3]. In this paper, our goal is not to design a new one. Therefore, we take the simplest one, called *fixed-sequencer* protocol (see Sections 3.3 and 3.4 for a short description). Rather, we focus on designing a subprotocol in charge of synchronizing the various senders (see Section 3.5). More precisely, our protocol allows every sender to gather the bandwidth requirements of other senders and to adapt its bandwidth accordingly (using a max-min fair bandwidth allocation algorithm [36]). The idea implemented by the protocol is simple and, as we show in Section 4, yields excellent performance.

3.3   Ordering Subprotocol

FastCast is a uniform total order broadcast protocol exporting two primitives, utoBroadcast and utoDeliver, and ensuring the following four properties:

- **Validity**: if a correct process p_i utoBroadcasts a message m, then p_i eventually utoDelivers m.
- **Integrity**: for any message m, any correct process p_j utoDelivers m at most once, and only if m was previously utoBroadcast by some correct process p_i.
- **Uniform Agreement**: if any process p_i utoDelivers any message m, then every correct process p_j eventually utoDelivers m.
- **Total Order**: for any two messages m and m', if any process p_i utoDelivers m without having delivered m', then no process p_j utoDelivers m' before m.

The ordering subprotocol implementing these four properties is given in Figure 2. This is a fairly classical fixed-sequencer pattern [3]. One process is designated *leader*, and is in charge of assigning and broadcasting sequence numbers. It is important to notice that the leader is not in charge of forwarding content messages (named DATA message in Figure 2). Rather, these are processes that are in charge of sending their DATA messages to all other processes (line 10). In order to ensure uniform agreement on message delivery, every node acknowledges the reception of the messages and the sequence numbers associated with them (line 19 for the leader, and line 24 for other processes). Every node waits for an acknowledgment from all nodes before delivering a message (lines 30 and 31). That way, a node is sure that the message it delivers is known (together with its sequence number) by all other nodes and will thus be delivered by all correct nodes even if it subsequently fails. Note that to handle message losses, a node that broadcasts a message uses a timer (line 12). If after some amount of time, a node has not delivered its own message (i.e. the message is still in the pendings array as checked in line 35), it resends the message (line 36).

3.4   Membership Management Subprotocol

In order to handle nodes joining and leaving the system, the *FastCast* protocol is built on top of a group communication system [37] relying on a perfect failure detector [34]. Processes are organized into groups, which they can leave or join. When a process joins or leaves a group, this triggers a view change protocol. Thanks to the perfect failure detector, faulty processes are excluded from the group after crashing. Upon a membership change, processes agree on a new view: the current view v_r is replaced by a new view v_{r+1}.

The *view_change* procedure is detailed in Figure 3. Note that when a view change occurs, every process first completes the execution (if any) of all other procedures described in Figure 2. It then freezes those procedures and executes the view change procedure. The latter works as follows (Note that the view change functions make use of two primitives Rsend and Rreceive that implement reliable communication channels. In our implementation, these primitives are implemented using TCP): every process sends its pendings and seqnos arrays to

```
Procedures executed by any process p_i
 1: procedure initialize(initial_view)
 2:     pendings[] ← ∅
 3:     seqnos[] ← ∅
 4:     acks[][] ← ∅
 5:     snToDeliver ← 0
 6:     leader = p_0
 7:     sn ← 0

 8: procedure utoBroadcast(m)
 9:     id_m ← hash(p_i, m)
10:     Send ⟨DATA, id_m, m⟩ to all processes
11:     pendings[id_m] ← m
12:     SetTimeout ⟨id_m⟩

13: upon Receive ⟨DATA, id_m, m⟩ from p_j do
14:     if p_i = leader then
15:         if ∄ seqnos[id_m] then
16:             seqnos[id_m] ← sn
17:             sn ← sn + 1
18:             acks[id_m][p_i] = 1
19:             Send ⟨ACK, id_m, seqnos[id_m]⟩ to all processes
20:     pendings[id_m] ← m
21:     tryDeliver()

22: upon Receive ⟨ACK, id_m, sn_m⟩ from p_j do
23:     if p_j = leader and ∃ pendings[id_m] then
24:         Send ⟨ACK, id_m, sn_m⟩ to all processes
25:         acks[id_m][p_i] = 1
26:         seqnos[id_m] ← sn_m
27:     acks[id_m][p_j] = 1
28:     tryDeliver()

29: procedure tryDeliver()
30:     while ∃ id_m s.t. (seqnos[id_m] = snToDeliver and sum(acks[id_m]) = n) do
31:         utoDeliver(m)
32:         snToDeliver ← snToDeliver + 1
33:         pendings ← pendings − pendings[id_m]

34: upon Timeout⟨id_m⟩ do
35:     if ∃ pendings[id_m] then
36:         Send ⟨DATA, id_m, pendings[id_m]⟩ to all processes
37:         SetTimeout ⟨id_m⟩
```

Fig. 2. Pseudo-code of the ordering mechanism

all other processes (line 2). Upon receiving these arrays, every process updates its own pendings and seqnos arrays using those received from all other processes (lines 15 and 17). Then, the processes send back an ACK_RECOVER message (line 18). Processes wait until they receive ACK_RECOVER messages from all processes (line 3) before sending an END_RECOVERY message to all (line 4). When a process receives END_RECOVERY messages from all processes (line 5), it can deliver all the messages for which it has a sequence number (lines 19 to 24). Thus, at the end of the view change procedure, all processes belonging to the new view will have delivered the same messages in the same order. Each process then empties its pendings, seqnos and acks arrays (lines 8 to 10). Moreover, each process uses as new leader the first process in the new view (line 11).

Procedures executed by any process p_i

 1: **upon** view_change(new_view) **do**
 2:     Rsend $\langle$RECOVER, p_i, $pendings$, $seqnos\rangle$ to all $p_j \in new\_view$
 3:     Wait until received $\langle$ACK_RECOVER$\rangle$ from all $p_j \in new\_view$
 4:     Rsend $\langle$END_RECOVERY$\rangle$ to all $p_j \in new\_view$
 5:     Wait until received $\langle$END_RECOVERY$\rangle$ from all $p_j \in new\_view$
 6:     forceDeliver()
 7:     $view \leftarrow new\_view$
 8:     $pendings[] \leftarrow \emptyset$
 9:     $seqnos[] \leftarrow \emptyset$
10:     $acks[][] \leftarrow \emptyset$
11:     $leader$ = first process in $view$
12:     $sn \leftarrow nextToDeliver$

13: **upon** Rreceive $\langle$RECOVER, $pendings_{p_j}$, $seqnos_{p_j}\rangle$ from p_j **do**
14:     **for each** $[id_m] \in pendings_{p_j}$ **do**
15:         $pendings[id_m] \leftarrow pendings_{p_j}[id_m]$
16:         **if** $\exists\ seqnos_{p_j}[id_m]$ **then**
17:             $seqnos[id_m] \leftarrow seqnos_{p_j}[id_m]$
18:     Rsend $\langle$ACK_RECOVER$\rangle$ to p_j

19: **procedure** forceDeliver()
20:     **for each** $id_m \in seqnos[id_m]$, ordered by increasing sequence number **do**
21:         **if** $\exists\ pendings[id_m]$ and $seqnos[id_m] \geq snToDeliver$ **then**
22:             toDeliver($pendings[id_m]$)
23:             $pendings \leftarrow pendings - pendings[id_m]$
24:             $snToDeliver \leftarrow seqnos[id_m] + 1$
25:     **for each** $id_m \in keys(pending[id_m])$, ordered by increasing id_m **do**
26:         toDeliver($pendings[id_m]$)
27:         $pendings \leftarrow pendings - pendings[id_m]$

Fig. 3. Pseudo-code of the membership management subprotocol

3.5   Bandwidth Allocation Subprotocol

In this section, we describe the bandwidth allocation protocol implemented in *FastCast*. We start by describing the principles underlying its design. We then comment a detailed pseudo-code. Finally, we give an illustration of its behavior.

Principles. The goal of the bandwidth allocation protocol is to allocate bandwidth for each sending node in order to allow multiple nodes to simultaneously send IP multicast packets, while avoiding message losses. As explained before, having multiple senders is a requirement to ensure that the full network capability is used. If we assume that at a given time, all nodes know the bandwidth requirements of all other nodes, it is easy to allocate bandwidth using a max-min fair bandwidth allocation algorithm [36]. For instance, let us consider a system comprising 3 nodes interconnected by a 1Gb/s ethernet switch. Let us assume that each node knows that, e.g. node 1 requires 700Mb/s, node 2 requires 600Mb/s, and node 3 requires 300Mb/s. Each node can deterministically compute the following fair bandwidth allocation: 500Mb/s for nodes 1 and 2, and 300Mb/s for node 3. It is indeed not possible to allocate more than 500Mb/s to nodes 1 and 2. Otherwise, node 3 would have to receive messages at a higher throughput than 1Gb/s, which it cannot do. Indeed, the network link connecting node 3 to the switch has a capability of 1Gb/s.

It is possible to design a protocol allowing nodes to exchange their bandwidth requirements and ensuring that every node knows, at any time, the bandwidth requirements of other nodes. Such a protocol would nevertheless be costly and would require to force all nodes to synchronize whenever one node wants to change its bandwidth. Interestingly, it is possible to fairly allocate bandwidth with a weaker requirement: it is enough that every node receive the various bandwidth requirements from other nodes in the same order. This property can be easily achieved by leveraging the *FastCast* protocol itself. Each time a node wants to modify its allocated bandwidth (e.g. to increase it, or to decrease it), it sends a message to all other nodes using the *FastCast* protocol. That way, all nodes receive the bandwidth requirement messages in the same order.

The question that remains to answer is: when can nodes actually modify their bandwidth? A node behaves differently depending on whether it requires a decrease of its bandwidth or an increase of its bandwidth. In the case of a bandwidth decrease, the node actually decreases its bandwidth before sending the message notifying other nodes. That way, when other nodes receive its notification message, they know that the node already decreased its bandwidth and they can recompute the bandwidth allocation and possibly decide to increase their own bandwidth. In the case of a bandwidth increase, a node n cannot directly increase its bandwidth (otherwise, that could congest the network). The node does thus first send the message notifying others that it wants to increase its bandwidth. Upon receiving the notification that node n wants to increase its bandwidth, other nodes locally recompute the bandwidth allocation (based on the new bandwidth requirement sent by node n) and possibly reduce their own bandwidth. Then, each node sends an acknowledgement to node n. It is only after it has received acknowledgments from all other nodes that node n can actually increase its bandwidth (by locally computing the bandwidth allocation).

Detailed Pseudo-Code. Figure 4 gives the pseudo-code of the bandwidth allocation protocol. Every node stores the bandwidth requirements of other nodes in the bwRequirements array and its current bandwidth in the currentBW variable. The ongoing_increase, delivered_req, and acks fields are used when a node wants to increase its bandwidth: ongoing_increase stores the required increase (before being stored in bwRequirements when all other processes will have acknowledged it); the delivered_req field indicates whether the increase notification message has been delivered by the requiring node itself (if that is not the case, the requiring node cannot take its own request into account even if it received an acknowledgement from all other processes); finally, the acks field is used to count the number of acknowledgements that have been received for the ongoing bandwidth increase request.

Before going into the details of the protocol, let us remark that the BW_allocation function (lines 34 to 47) implements a classical max-min fair bandwidth allocation algorithm [36]. The only important point to mention is that it uses a variable, called availableBW, that represents the maximum capability of a network link. This capability is dependent from the average message size (it is well-known that the larger the messages, the higher the throughput that can be

```
Procedures executed by any process p_i
 1: procedure initialize(initial_view)
 2:     bwRequirements[] ← [0, · · · , 0]
 3:     currentBW ← 0
 4:     ongoing_increase ← 0
 5:     delivered_req ← false
 6:     acks ← 0

 7: procedure increase_BW(amount)
 8:     wait until ongoing_increase = 0
 9:     ongoing_increase ← amount
10:     utoBroadcast ⟨INCR, amount⟩ to all processes

11: upon utoDeliver ⟨INCR, amount⟩ from p_j ≠ p_i do
12:     bwRequirements[p_j] ← bwRequirements[p_j] + amount
13:     currentBW ← BW_allocation()
14:     Rsend ⟨ACK⟩ to p_j

15: upon utoDeliver ⟨INCR, amount⟩ from p_i do
16:     delivered_req ← true

17: upon Rreceive ⟨ACK⟩ from p_j do
18:     acks ← acks + 1
19:     if acks = N − 1 then
20:         wait until delivered_req = true
21:         bwRequirements[p_i] ← bwRequirements[p_i] + ongoing_increase
22:         currentBW ← BW_allocation()
23:         acks ← 0
24:         ongoing_increase ← 0
25:         delivered_req ← false

26: procedure decrease_BW(amount)
27:     wait until ongoing_increase = 0
28:     bwRequirements[p_i] ← bwRequirements[p_i] − amount
29:     currentBW ← BW_allocation()
30:     utoBroadcast ⟨DECR, amount⟩ to all processes

31: upon utoDeliver ⟨DECR, amount⟩ from p_j ≠ p_i do
32:     bwRequirements[p_j] ← bwRequirements[p_j] − amount
33:     currentBW ← BW_allocation()

34: function BW_allocation()
35:     nodes ← p_i and the (N-2) other iggest values in bwRequirements
36:     availableBW ← B
37:     do
38:     allocated = false
39:     for p_j in nodes do
40:         if bwRequirements[p_j] ≤ availableBW/size(nodes) then
41:             nodes ← nodes − p_j
42:             availableBW ← availableBW − bwRequirements[p_j]
43:             allocated = true
44:     while(nodes ≠ ∅ and allocated = true)
45:     if p_i ∈ nodes then
46:         return availableBW/size(nodes)
47:     return bwRequirements[p_i]
```

Fig. 4. Pseudo-code of the bandwidth allocation protocol

achieved by a communication protocol [5,6]). In our implementation, we use 4kB as the average message size and set the value of availableBW to the capability that the network links exhibit when used with 4kB messages (this capability is close to the optimal one). To be sure that this is the actual capability that network links will have at runtime, the *FastCast* protocols batches messages to ensure that sent messages are at least 4kB large (unless there is no contention, in which case small messages can be sent as the protocol does not need to sustain high throughput in such cases).

Let us now describe the bandwidth allocation subprotocol. A node can either ask to increase its bandwidth (using the increase_BW procedure at line 7) or to decrease it (using the decrease_BW procedure at line 26). Let us first describe what happens when a node wants to increase its bandwidth. The node calls the increase_BW procedure. Inside this procedure, the node utoBroadcasts

Table 1. A first example execution of the bandwidth allocation protocol

step	process	bwRequirements	currentBW	ongoing_increase	acks	delivered.req	
S1	p_0	$[0, 0, 0]$	0	0	0	-	
	p_1	$[0, 0, 0]$	0	0	0	-	Initial state
	p_2	$[0, 0, 0]$	0	0	0	-	
S2	p_0	$[0, 0, 0]$	0	800	0	-	
	p_1	$[0, 0, 0]$	0	300	0	-	p_0 calls increase_BW(800)
	p_2	$[0, 0, 0]$	0	0	0	-	p_1 calls increase_BW(300)
S3	p_0	$[0, 0, 0]$	0	800	0	-	
	p_1	$[0, 0, 0]$	0	300	0	-	p_2 utoDelivers $\langle \text{INCR}, 800 \rangle_{p_0}$
	p_2	$[800, 300, 0]$	0	0	0	-	p_2 utoDelivers $\langle \text{INCR}, 300 \rangle_{p_1}$
S4	p_0	$[0, 0, 0]$	0	800	1	-	
	p_1	$[0, 0, 0]$	0	300	1	-	p_0 Rreceives $\langle \text{ACK} \rangle_{p_2}$
	p_2	$[800, 300, 0]$	0	0	0	-	p_1 Rreceives $\langle \text{ACK} \rangle_{p_2}$
S5	p_0	$[0, \mathbf{300}, 0]$	0	800	1	✓	
	p_1	$[0, 0, 0]$	0	300	1	-	p_0 utoDelivers $\langle \text{INCR}, 800 \rangle_{p_0}$
	p_2	$[800, 300, 0]$	0	0	0	-	p_0 utoDelivers $\langle \text{INCR}, 300 \rangle_{p_1}$
S6	p_0	$[0, 300, 0]$	0	800	1	✓	
	p_1	$[0, 0, 0]$	0	300	$\mathbf{2}$	-	p_1 Rreceives $\langle \text{ACK} \rangle_{p_0}$
	p_2	$[800, 300, 0]$	0	0	0	-	
S7	p_0	$[0, 300, 0]$	0	800	1	✓	
	p_1	$[\mathbf{800, 300}, 0]$	$\mathbf{300}$	0	0	-	p_1 utoDelivers $\langle \text{INCR}, 800 \rangle_{p_0}$
	p_2	$[800, 300, 0]$	0	0	0	-	p_1 utoDelivers $\langle \text{INCR}, 300 \rangle_{p_1}$
S8	p_0	$[\mathbf{800}, 300, 0]$	$\mathbf{700}$	0	0	-	
	p_1	$[800, 300, 0]$	300	0	0	-	p_0 Rreceives $\langle \text{ACK} \rangle_{p_1}$
	p_2	$[800, 300, 0]$	0	0	0	-	

Table 2. A second example execution of the bandwidth allocation protocol

step	process	bwRequirements	currentBW	ongoing_increase	acks	delivered.req	
S9	p_0	$[800, 300, 0]$	700	0	0	-	Initial state
	p_1	$[800, 300, 0]$	300	0	0	-	(equal to S8 in Table 1)
	p_2	$[800, 300, 0]$	0	0	0	-	
S10	p_0	$[800, 300, 0]$	700	0	0	-	
	p_1	$[800, 300, 0]$	300	0	0	-	p_2 calls increase_BW(600)
	p_2	$[800, 300, 0]$	0	**600**	0	-	
S11	p_0	$[800, 300, \mathbf{600}]$	**500**	0	0	-	p_0 utoDelivers $\langle \text{INCR}, 600 \rangle_{p_2}$
	p_1	$[800, 300, \mathbf{600}]$	**300**	0	0	-	p_1 utoDelivers $\langle \text{INCR}, 600 \rangle_{p_2}$
	p_2	$[800, 300, 0]$	0	600	0	√	p_2 utoDelivers $\langle \text{INCR}, 600 \rangle_{p_2}$
S12	p_0	$[800, 300, 600]$	500	0	0	-	
	p_1	$[800, 300, 600]$	300	0	0	-	p_2 Rreceives $\langle \text{ACK} \rangle_{p_0}$
	p_2	$[800, 300, 0]$	0	600	1	√	
S13	p_0	$[800, 300, 600]$	500	0	0	-	
	p_1	$[800, 300, 600]$	300	0	0	-	p_2 Rreceives $\langle \text{ACK} \rangle_{p_1}$
	p_2	$[800, 300, \mathbf{600}]$	**500**	0	0	-	

an INCR message to all other processes (line 10). When delivering this message, other processes update their bwRequirements array (line 12), recompute the bandwidth allocation (line 13) using the BW_allocation function, and sends an ACK message back to the requiring process (line 14). When the requiring node has both received an acknowledgement from all other nodes and delivered its own increase request (line 16), it updates its bwRequirements array (line 21) and recompute the bandwidth allocation (line 22).

Let us now describe what happens when a node wants to decrease its bandwidth. The node calls the decrease_BW procedure. Inside this procedure, the node updates its bwRequirements array (line 28) and recompute the bandwidth allocation (line 29). The requiring node then utoBroadcasts a DECR message to all other processes (line 30). When delivering this message, other processes update their bwRequirements array (line 32) and recompute the bandwidth allocation (line 33), using the BW_allocation function.

Illustration. We provide three illustrations of the bandwidth allocation protocol in Table 1, Table 2, and Table 3. We consider a system with 3 processes interconnected by a 1Gb/s switch. In each table, we describe a set of steps that happen in the system and we illustrate how the different fields of the three processes are updated. Initially, the three processes have a null bandwidth (currentBW is equal to 0 in Table 1, step S1). In Table 1 we depicts what happens when from this initial

Table 3. A third example execution of the bandwidth allocation protocol

step	process	bwRequirements	currentBW	ongoing_increase	acks	delivered_req	
S14	p_0	$[800, 300, 600]$	500	0	0	-	Initial state
	p_1	$[800, 300, 600]$	300	0	0	-	(equal to S13 in Table 2)
	p_2	$[800, 300, 600]$	500	0	0	-	
S15	p_0	$[800, 300, 600]$	500	0	0	-	
	p_1	$[800, 300, 600]$	300	0	0	-	p_2 calls decrease_BW(500)
	p_2	$[800, 300, \mathbf{100}]$	**100**	0	0	-	
S16	p_0	$[800, 300, \mathbf{100}]$	**700**	0	0	-	p_0 utoDelivers $\langle \text{DECR}, 500 \rangle_{p_2}$
	p_1	$[800, 300, \mathbf{100}]$	**300**	0	0	-	p_1 utoDelivers $\langle \text{DECR}, 500 \rangle_{p_2}$
	p_2	$[800, 300, \mathbf{100}]$	100	0	0	-	p_2 utoDelivers $\langle \text{DECR}, 500 \rangle_{p_2}$

state, p_0 calls increase_BW(800) and p_1 calls increase_BW(300). Processes reach a state (step S8) in which p_0 has its currentBW variable equal to 700Mb/s and p_1 has its currentBW variable equal to 300Mb/s. From that state (also depicted in Table 2, step S9), Table 2 depicts what happens when p_2 calls increase_BW(600). Processes reach a state (step S13) in which p_0 and p_2 both have their currentBW variable equal to 500Mb/s, and p_1 has its currentBW variable equal to 300Mb/s. From that state (also depicted in Table 3, step S14), Table 3 depicts what happens when p_2 calls decrease_BW(500). Processes reach a state (step S16) in which p_0 has its currentBW variable equal to 700Mb/s, p_1 has its currentBW variable equal to 300Mb/s and p_2 has its currentBW variable equal to 100Mb/s.

4   Performance Evaluation

In this section, we assess the performance of the *FastCast* protocol and compare them to that achieved by two state-of-the-art protocols: LCR [5] and Ring-Paxos [6]. All three protocols ensure uniform total order delivery of messages. We chose LCR because it is the only existing protocol ensuring optimal throughput [5]. Moreover, the choice of RingPaxos is motivated by the fact, as shown in [6], it is the only protocol to *"achieve very high throughput while providing low latency"*. The experiments only evaluate the failure free case because failures are expected to be very rare in the targeted environment. Note that in the faulty case, the performance of *FastCast* would be very similar to that of LCR provided that both protocols implement almost similar recovery algorithms. LCR and *FastCast* relies on the use of a perfect failure detector, whereas RingPaxos assumes a bound on the number of faulty processes.

We start by a description of the experimental setup. We then assess the bandwidth allocation protocol of *FastCast*, and the throughput, the response time, and the latency of *FastCast*, LCR and RingPaxos. Our evaluation shows that *FastCast* is both throughput- and latency-efficient. More precisely, throughput-wise, *FastCast* is as efficient as LCR. Latency-wise, *FastCast* is more efficient than RingPaxos.

4.1   Experimental Setup

The experiments were run on a cluster comprising eight 8-core machines interconnected by a gigabit ethernet switch. Each core runs at 2.5GHz and is equipped with 16GB of RAM. Moreover, each machine runs a Linux 2.6.32 kernel. The raw bandwidth over IP between two machines (measured with Netperf [38]) is equal to 942Mb/s. In order to ensure that the evaluation is fair, we have implemented the *FastCast* and LCR protocols in C++, using the same code base as the RingPaxos protocol. Finally, all the presented experiments start with a warm-up phase, followed by a phase during which performance are measured. The measurement phase lasts 5 minutes.

4.2   Bandwidth Allocation Assessment

We first assess the bandwidth allocation protocol implemented in *FastCast*. For that purpose, we perform the following experiment. We deploy 4 nodes that send messages of variable sizes: from 1kB to 6kB. The bandwidth requirements of nodes vary during the experiment: initially all nodes require one fourth of the total available bandwidth. After $10s$, node 0 decreases its requirements, followed by node 1 at time $20s$. At time $30s$, node 2 increases its bandwidth requirement. Finally, at time $40s$, node 0 increases its bandwidth requirement, whereas node 2 decreases them. The results are depicted in Figure 5. The X axis represents the time, whereas the Y axis is used to represent the bandwidth requirements of the 4 nodes, as well as the achieved and optimal throughput. We observe that the achieved throughput is very close to the optimal one, thus confirming that the bandwidth allocation protocol works efficiently. Moreover, we have used that experiment to assess the time it takes for a node to increase its bandwidth, i.e. the time that elapses between the moment when the node notifies other nodes that it has new bandwidth requirements and the moment when the node is allowed to increase its bandwidth. We have run that experiment multiple times and the average time required by the different nodes to increase their bandwidth was $3.8ms$.

4.3   Throughput Assessment

To assess the throughput of the three protocols, we run the following benchmark: we deploy N nodes that broadcast messages at the maximum throughput they can sustain. The message size is fixed and set to 10kB, which allows reaching the best possible throughput for each studied protocol. Each process periodically computes the throughput at which it delivers messages. In this experiment, the

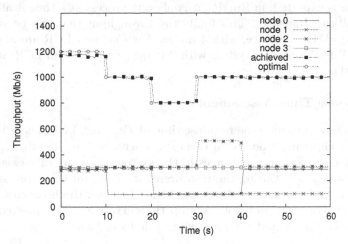

Fig. 5. Assessment of *FastCast*'s bandwidth allocation protocol

throughput is calculated as the ratio of delivered bytes over the time elapsed since the end of the warm-up phase. The plotted throughput is the average of the values computed by each process.

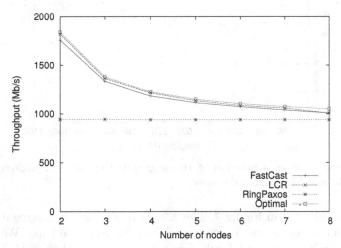

Fig. 6. Throughput as a function of the number of nodes in the system for the *FastCast*, LCR, and RingPaxos protocols

Figure 6 plots the throughput achieved by *FastCast*, LCR and RingPaxos when varying the number of nodes from 2 to 8. As reference, we plot the optimal throughput that can be achieved by $(N/(N-1))$ times the maximum link speed of 942Mb/s). We can make several observations. First, the throughput of *FastCast* and LCR is very close to optimal. As mentioned in the previous section, this confirms the fact that the bandwidth allocation algorithm works efficiently. Second, the throughput of RingPaxos is almost constant (at 939Mb/s). Again, this behavior is expected: in RingPaxos, only one process at a time is allowed to send IP multicast messages. This limits the throughput that can be sustained by the protocol. For instance, with 4 nodes, *FastCast* and LCR are about 25% faster than RingPaxos. In a system with 2 nodes, *FastCast* and LCR are about 86% faster than RingPaxos.

4.4   Response Time Assessment

In this section, we evaluate the response time of *FastCast*, LCR, and RingPaxos in a system comprising 8 nodes. In this experiment, we vary the throughput at which the nodes inject new messages in the system. The size of messages that are broadcast is 10kB. During the measurement phase, for every message m it broadcasts, a sender evaluates the elapsed time between the broadcast and the delivery of m. For each protocol, we stop the curve when the injected load is higher than the throughput the protocol is able to sustain.

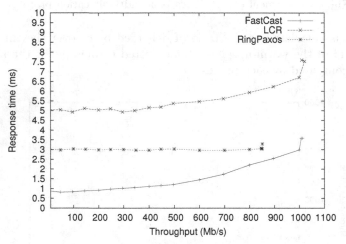

Fig. 7. Response time as a function of the aggregated sending throughput for the *FastCast*, LCR, and RingPaxos protocols

Results are depicted in Figure 7. The X axis represents the aggregated sending throughput, whereas the Y axis represents the response time. We observe that *FastCast* exhibits a consistently lower response time than both LCR and RingPaxos. More precisely, *FastCast* achieves an up to 400% lower response time than LCR and an up to 246% lower response time than RingPaxos. This comes from the fact that both LCR and RingPaxos rely on a ring topology for sending some of the messages that are exchanged among nodes: data messages in the case of LCR, and ordering messages in the case of RingPaxos (notice that, unlike in LCR, in RingPaxos, not all processes are organized in a ring [6]). The pipelining pattern introduced by a ring topology increases the time it takes to process each message with respect to a pure IP multicast protocol such as *FastCast* in which no pipelining pattern is used.

4.5   Latency Assessment

In this section, we evaluate the latency achieved by the *FastCast*, LCR, and RingPaxos protocols. We vary the size of the system from 2 to 8 nodes. Recall that latency is defined as the time required to complete a message broadcast when there is no contention. In order to measure the latency of the various protocols, we perform the following experiment: one node in the system broadcasts 10kB messages at a very low throughput (1Mb/s). The sending node evaluates the average time that elapses between the broadcast of each message and its delivery.

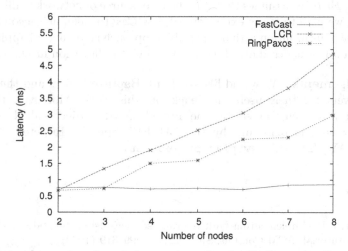

Fig. 8. Latency as a function of the number of nodes in the system for the *FastCast*, LCR, and RingPaxos protocols

Results are depicted in Figure 8. The X axis represents the number of nodes, whereas the Y axis represents the latency. We observe that *FastCast* exhibits a consistently lower latency than both LCR and RingPaxos. More precisely, *FastCast* achieves an up to 465% lower latency than LCR and an up to 247% lower latency than RingPaxos. Moreover, we observe that the latency of *FastCast* is constant, whereas that of RingPaxos and LCR increases with the number of nodes. This again comes from the fact that both LCR and RingPaxos rely on a ring topology for sending some of the messages. The reason why the curve for RingPaxos is not linear is that in RingPaxos only a majority of nodes need to be present in the ring. For instance, RingPaxos uses the same ring size (3) for systems comprising 4 and 5 nodes, whereas in LCR, the ring size linearly increases with the number of nodes in the system.

5   Conclusion

We have presented *FastCast*, a uniform total order broadcast protocol that achieves both optimal throughput and very low latency. Unlike previous throughput-optimal protocols, *FastCast* does not rely on a ring topology for message dissemination. Rather, *FastCast* uses IP multicast, a low-level communication protocol that allows reaching multiple processes using a single message. To avoid network congestion (and thus IP multicast packet drops), *FastCast* implements a subprotocol in charge of dynamically computing the throughput at which processes are allowed to send IP multicast messages. We have evaluated *FastCast* on a cluster of 8 machines and have compared its performance to that achieved by two recent state-of-the-art protocols: LCR and RingPaxos. The evaluation shows that *FastCast* achieves optimal throughput and very low latency.

Currently, *FastCast* assumes that it is the only source of network traffic. In our future work, we plan to study extensions of *FastCast* to take into account background traffic. Our intuition is that a possible approach is to have all applications running on a set of nodes share the same bandwidth allocation mechanism.

Acknowledgements. We would like to thank Baptiste Lepers and the anonymous reviewers for their useful feedback on this work. Moreover, the presented work has been funded by the French ANR project called SocEDA (http://www.soceda.org) and by the EU FP7 Specific Targeted Research Project "PLAY" (http://www.play-project.eu).

References

1. Schneider, F.B.: Implementing fault-tolerant services using the state machine approach: a tutorial. ACM Comput. Surv. 22(4), 299–319 (1990)
2. Hadzilacos, V., Toueg, S.: Fault-tolerant broadcasts and related problems, pp. 97–145 (1993)
3. Défago, X., Schiper, A., Urbán, P.: Total order broadcast and multicast algorithms: Taxonomy and survey. ACM Comput. Surv. 36(4), 372–421 (2004)
4. Guerraoui, R., Levy, R.R., Pochon, B., Quéma, V.: High Throughput Total Order Broadcast for Cluster Environments. In: IEEE International Conference on Dependable Systems and Networks (DSN 2006), Philadelphia, PA, USA (2006)
5. Guerraoui, R., Levy, R.R., Pochon, B., Quéma, V.: Throughput optimal total order broadcast for cluster environments. ACM Trans. Comput. Syst. 28(2), 5:1–5:32 (2010), http://doi.acm.org/10.1145/1813654.1813656
6. Marandi, P., Primi, M., Schiper, N., Pedone, F.: Ring paxos: A high-throughput atomic broadcast protocol. In: IEEE/IFIP International Conference on Dependable Systems and Networks (DSN), pp. 527–536 (2010)
7. Peterson, L., Buchholz, N., Schlichting, R.: Preserving and using context information in interprocess communication. ACM Trans. Comput. Syst. 7(3), 217–246 (1989)
8. Malhis, L., Sanders, W., Schlichting, R.: Numerical performability evaluation of a group multicast protocol. Distrib. Syst. Enj. J. 3(1), 39–52 (1996)
9. Ezhilchelvan, P., Macedo, R., Shrivastava, S.: Newtop: a fault-tolerant group communication protocol. In: Proceedings of the 15th International Conference on Distributed Computing Systems (ICDCS 1995). IEEE Computer Society, Washington, DC (1995)

10. Ng, T.: Ordered broadcasts for large applications. In: Proceedings of the 10th IEEE International Symposium on Reliable Distributed Systems (SRDS 1991), pp. 188–197. IEEE Computer Society, Pisa (1991)
11. Moser, L., Melliar-Smith, P., Agrawala, V.: Asynchronous fault-tolerant total ordering algorithms. SIAM J. Comput. 22(4), 727–750 (1993)
12. Chandra, T., Toueg, S.: Unreliable failure detectors for reliable distributed systems. J. ACM 43(2), 225–267 (1996)
13. Birman, K., Joseph, T.: Reliable communication in the presence of failures. ACM Trans. Comput. Syst. 5(1), 47–76 (1987)
14. Luan, S., Gligor, V.: A fault-tolerant protocol for atomic broadcast. IEEE Trans. Parallel Distrib. Syst. 1(3), 271–285 (1990)
15. Fritzke, U., Ingels, P., Mostefaoui, A., Raynal, M.: Consensus-based fault-tolerant total order multicast. IEEE Trans. Parallel Distrib. Syst. 12(2), 147–156 (2001)
16. Anceaume, E.: A lightweight solution to uniform atomic broadcast for asynchronous systems. In: Proceedings of the 27th International Symposium on Fault-Tolerant Computing (FTCS 1997). IEEE Computer Society, Washington, DC (1997)
17. Kaashoek, F., Tanenbaum, A.: An evaluation of the amoeba group communication system. In: Proceedings of the 16th International Conference on Distributed Computing Systems (ICDCS 1996). IEEE Computer Society, Washington, DC (1996)
18. Armstrong, S., Freier, A., Marzullo, K.: Multicast transport protocol. RFC 1301, IETF (1992)
19. Carr, R.: The tandem global update protocol. Tandem Syst. Rev. 1, 74–85 (1985)
20. Garcia-Molina, H., Spauster, A.: Ordered and reliable multicast communication. ACM Trans. Comput. Syst. 9(3), 242–271 (1991)
21. Birman, K., van Renesse, R.: Reliable Distributed Computing with the Isis Toolkit. IEEE Computer Society Press (1993)
22. Wilhelm, U., Schiper, A.: A hierarchy of totally ordered multicasts. In: Proceedings of the 14th Symposium on Reliable Distributed Systems. IEEE Computer Society, Washington, DC (1995)
23. Ban, B.: JGroups – A Toolkit for Reliable Multicast Communication (2007), http://www.jgroups.org
24. Chang, J.-M., Maxemchuk, N.: Reliable broadcast protocols. ACM Trans. Comput. Syst. 2(3), 251–273 (1984)
25. Whetten, B., Montgomery, T., Kaplan, S.: A high performance totally ordered multicast protocol. In: Birman, K.P., Mattern, F., Schiper, A. (eds.) Theory and Practice in Distributed Systems. LNCS, vol. 938, pp. 33–57. Springer, Heidelberg (1995)
26. Kim, J., Kim, C.: A total ordering protocol using a dynamic token-passing scheme. Distrib. Syst. Eng. J. 4(2), 87–95 (1997)
27. Cristian, F., Mishra, S., Alvarez, G.: High-performance asynchronous atomic broadcast. Distrib. Syst. Eng. J. 4(2), 109–128 (1997)
28. Friedman, T., Renesse, R.V.: Packing messages as a tool for boosting the performance of total ordering protocls. In: Proceedings of the 6th International Symposium on High Performance Distributed Computing (HPDC 1997). IEEE Computer Society, Washington, DC (1997)
29. Cristian, F.: Asynchronous atomic broadcast. IBM Technical Disclosure Bulletin 33(9), 115–116 (1991)

30. Ekwall, R., Schiper, A., Urban, P.: Token-based atomic broadcast using unreliable failure detectors. In: Proceedings of the 23rd IEEE International Symposium on Reliable Distributed Systems (SRDS 2004), pp. 52–65. IEEE Computer Society, Washington, DC (2004)

31. Amir, Y., Moser, L.E., Melliar-Smith, P.M., Agarwal, D.A., Ciarfella, P.: The Totem single-ring ordering and membership protocol. ACM Transactions on Computer Systems 13(4), 311–342 (1995)

32. Gopal, A., Toueg, S.: Reliable broadcast in synchronous and asynchronous environments (preliminary version). In: Bermond, J.-C., Raynal, M. (eds.) WDAG 1989. LNCS, vol. 392, pp. 110–123. Springer, Heidelberg (1989)

33. Amir, Y., Danilov, C., Miskin-Amir, M., Schultz, J., Stanton, J.: The spread toolkit: Architecture and performance. CNDS-2004-1, Johns Hopkins University, Tech. Rep. (2004)

34. Chandra, T., Toueg, S.: Unreliable failure detectors for reliable distributed systems. Journal of the ACM 43(2), 225–267 (1996)

35. Dunagan, J., Harvey, N.J.A., Jones, M.B., Kostic, D., Theimer, M., Wolman, A.: Fuse: Lightweight guaranteed distributed failure notification. In: Proceedings of 6th Symposium on Operating Systems Design and Implementation, OSDI 2004 (2004)

36. Le Boudec, J.-Y.: Rate adaptation, congestion control and fairness: A tutorial. Ecole Polytechnique Fédérale de Lausanne (2012)

37. Birman, K., Joseph, T.: Exploiting virtual synchrony in distributed systems. In: Proceedings of the Eleventh ACM Symposium on Operating Systems Principles (SOSP 1987), pp. 123–138. ACM Press, New York (1987)

38. Jones, R.: Netperf (2007), http://www.netperf.org/

VICINITY: A Pinch of Randomness Brings out the Structure

Spyros Voulgaris and Maarten van Steen

VU University, Amsterdam, The Netherlands
{spyros,steen}@cs.vu.nl

Abstract. Overlay networks are central to the operation of large-scale decentralized applications, be it Internet-scale P2P systems deployed in the wild or cloud applications running in a controlled—albeit large-scale—environment. A number of custom solutions exist for individual applications, each employing a tailor-made mechanism to build and maintain its specific structure. This paper addresses the role of randomness in developing and maintaining such structures. Taking VICINITY, a generic overlay management framework based on self-organization, we explore tradeoffs between deterministic and probabilistic decision-making for structuring overlays. We come to the conclusion that a pinch of randomness may even be needed in overlay construction, but also that much randomness or randomness alone is not good either.

1 Introduction

Does randomness matter? In this paper we claim it does, and, in fact, that incorporating randomness into distributed algorithms may even be necessary. We do not claim that randomness is necessary for all algorithms (which would clearly be wrong), but that for many large-scale distributed algorithms it is important to strive for simplicity through loose control. What is lost is determinism and the potential to formally prove correctness. Instead, at best only statistical properties can be shown to hold, but what can be achieved is that those properties emerge from very simple principles. A fundamental principle being that decisions concerning selection, of whatever kind, are sometimes random.

To substantiate our claim, we consider the influence of randomness in distributed gossiping algorithms. Gossiping is a well-known, and simple technique, widely deployed for a range of applications, including data replication, information dissemination, and system management. Gossiping is often deterministic: the rules for selecting whom to gossip with and what to gossip are strict, with no probabilistic element. On the other hand, there are also many gossiping algorithms that incorporate probabilistic decision-making, yet lack an examination of *why* such decision-making is so effective.

We have no general answer to where the effectiveness of randomness comes from, yet we believe such understanding is crucial for designing large-scale distributed systems. As a step toward such understanding, we concentrate in this paper on deploying a gossiping algorithm called VICINITY, for constructing overlay networks. It is not our purpose to advocate our solution to overlay construction. Instead, we use VICINITY as a framework to demonstrate how crucial incorporating randomness is. More specifically,

D. Eyers and K. Schwan (Eds.): Middleware 2013, LNCS 8275, pp. 21–40, 2013.

we show that there is a subtle balance to be sought between deterministic and probabilistic decision-making. A pinch of randomness is enough, too much randomness will spoil matters.

Our main contribution is systematically exploring the effect of randomness in gossip-based overlay construction. This brings us to the conclusion that such exploration can be crucial and that deciding in advance on the amount of randomness is difficult, if not impossible. As a side-effect of this exploration, we present VICINITY, a novel gossiping algorithm that can be deployed for a wide range of applications.

The rest of the paper is organized as follows. Section 2 defines our system model. Section 3 presents the VICINITY protocol, starting from its intuition, a baseline model, and the detailed design decisions that lead to the complete version of the protocol. Section 4 sheds some light on the individual roles of determinism and randomness. Section 5 offers an evaluation of VICINITY through two scenarios that portray the interplay between determinism and randomness and highlight their individual strengths and weaknesses. Section 6 discusses related work, and Section 7 communicates our overall conclusions from this work.

2 System Model

The Network. We consider a set of N nodes connected over a routed network infrastructure. Each node has a *profile*, containing some application-specific data of the node, determining the node's neighbors in the target structure. Such a profile could contain a node's geographic coordinates, a vector of preferences, social network information, or in general any other metric that the application uses for defining the target structure.

Knowledge regarding neighbors is stored and exchanged by means of node *descriptors*. The descriptor of a given node can be generated exclusively by that very node, but it can be freely handed by any third node to any other. The descriptor of a node is a tuple containing the following three fields:

1. the node's **address** (i.e., IP address and port)
2. the descriptor's **age** (a numeric field)
3. the node's application-specific **profile**

We consider that nodes are connected over a network that supports routing. That is, *any* node can send a message to *any* other, provided that the sender knows the receiver's *address* (i.e., IP address and port, on the Internet).

To enable communication with other nodes, each node maintains a small dynamic list of neighbors, called its *view*, V. A node view is essentially a list of descriptors of the node's neighbors. Node views have a small fixed length, ℓ. Their contents are dynamic, and are updated in an epidemic fashion through pairwise node communication. Although this is not binding, for simplicity we will consider that all nodes have the same view length.

The network is inherently dynamic and unreliable. Nodes can join, leave, or crash at any time and without prior notice. In particular, we make no distinction between node crashes and node leaves. Additionally, nodes are also free to dynamically update their profiles. Messages may be lost, or delayed. Byzantine behavior is beyond the scope of this work.

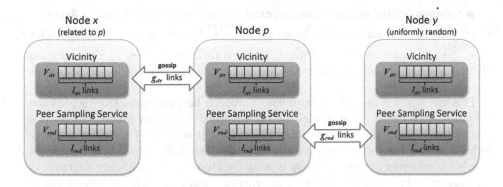

Fig. 1. The VICINITY framework

Finally, we consider that nodes participate in a *peer sampling service* [4], which provides them with a continuous stream of links to nodes picked uniformly at random among all *alive* nodes. Peer sampling protocols form a fundamental ingredient of many peer-to-peer applications nowadays, they are completely decentralized, and they have shown to be remarkably inexpensive.

As VICINITY strives for creating *structure*, we will be referring to its view as V_{str}, to its view's length as ℓ_{str}, and to its gossip length (i.e., the number of descriptors exchanged in each direction in a gossip interaction) as g_{str}. Likewise, as the peer sampling service is responsible for *randomness*, its view, view length, and gossip length will be referred to as V_{rnd}, ℓ_{rnd}, and g_{rnd}, respectively.

The Target Overlay. We also consider a *selection function* SELECT$(p, \mathcal{D}, k)$, that, given the descriptor of node p and a set $\mathcal{D}$ of node descriptors, returns the set of k descriptors (or all of them, if $|\mathcal{D}| < k$) that best approximate p's outgoing links in the target structure. The selection is based on node profiles. We assume function SELECT to be globally known by all nodes in the system.

The selection function essentially defines the target structure. Each node p aims at eventually establishing links to the "best" ℓ_{str} nodes, as defined by the outcome of SELECT$(p, \mathcal{D}_p^*, \ell_{str})$, where $\mathcal{D}_p^*$ is the set of descriptors of all nodes in the network excluding p.

Often, the selection function SELECT is based on a globally defined node proximity metric. That is, SELECT$(p, \mathcal{D}, k)$ sorts all descriptors in $\mathcal{D}$ with respect to their proximity to node p, and selects the k closest ones. Typical proximity metrics include semantic similarity, ID-based sorting, domain name proximity, geographic- or latency-based proximity, etc. Some applications may apply composite proximity metrics, combining two or more of the above. In certain cases, though, selecting appropriate neighbors involves more than a mere sorting based on some metric, typically when a node's significance as a neighbor depends not only on the its proximity to a given node, but also on which *other* nodes are being selected.

We assume that the selection function exhibits some sort of *transitivity*, in the sense that if node b is a "good" selection for node a ($a \xrightarrow{\text{SELECT}} b$), and c is a "good" selection for b ($b \xrightarrow{\text{SELECT}} c$), then c *tends* to be a "good" selection for a too ($a \xrightarrow{\text{SELECT}} c$). Generally, the "better" a selection node q is for node p, the more likely it is that q's "good" selections are also "good" for p.

This transitivity is essentially a correlation property between nodes sharing common neighbors, embodying the principle "my friend's friend is also my friend". Surely, this correlation is fuzzy and generally hard to quantify. It is more of a desired property rather than a hard requirement for our topology construction framework. The framework excels for networks exhibiting strong transitivity. However, its efficiency degrades as the transitivity becomes weaker. In the extreme case that no correlation holds between nodes with common neighbors, related nodes eventually discover each other through random encounters, although this may take a long time.

3   The VICINITY Protocol

3.1   VICINITY: The Intuition

The goal is to organize all VICINITY views so as to approximate the target structure as closely as possible. To this end, nodes regularly exchange node descriptors to gradually evolve their views towards the target. When gossiping, nodes send each other a subset of their views, of fixed small length g_{str}, known as the *gossip length*. The gossip length is the same for all nodes.

From our previous discussion, we are seeking a means to construct, for each node and with respect to the given selection function, the optimal view from all nodes currently in the system. There are two sides to this construction.

First, based on the assumption of transitivity in the selection function, SELECT, a node should explore the nearby nodes that its neighbors have found. In other words, if b is in a's VICINITY view, and c is in b's view, it makes sense to check whether c would also be suitable as a neighbor of a. Exploiting the transitivity in SELECT should then quickly lead to high-quality views. The way a node tries to improve its VICIN-ITY view resembles *hill-climbing* algorithms [9]. However, instead of trying to locate a single optimal node, here the objective is to optimize the selection of a whole set of nodes, namely the view. In that respect, VICINITY can be thought of as a distributed, collaborative hill-climbing algorithm.

Second, it is important that *all* nodes be examined. The problem with following transitivity alone is that a node will be eventually searching only in a single cluster of related nodes, possibly missing out on other clusters of also related—but still unknown—peers, in a way similar to getting locked in a local maximum in hill-climbing algorithms. Analogously to the special "long" links in small-world networks [12], a node needs to establish links outside its neighborhood's cluster. Likewise, when new nodes join the network, they should easily find an appropriate cluster to join. These issues call for a randomization of candidates for including in a view.

Active Thread (on node p)	Passive Thread (on node q)
1 **while** *true* **do**	1 **while** *true* **do**
2 $\quad$ wait(T time units)	2 $\quad$.
3 $\quad$ $q \leftarrow$ SELECTRANDOMNEIGHBOR()	3 $\quad$.
4 $\quad$ $buf_{snd} \leftarrow V_{str} \cup \{p\}$	4 $\quad$.
5 $\quad$ $buf_{snd} \leftarrow$ SELECT(q, buf_{snd}, g_{str})	5 $\quad$.
6 $\quad$ SEND(q, buf_{snd}) $\quad$ --→--→--→--→--→	6 $\quad$ $buf_{rcv} \leftarrow$ RECEIVE(p) // p can be any node
7 $\quad$.	7 $\quad$ $buf_{snd} \leftarrow V_{str} \cup \{q\}$
8 $\quad$.	8 $\quad$ $buf_{snd} \leftarrow$ SELECT(p, buf_{snd}, g_{str})
9 $\quad$ $buf_{rcv} \leftarrow$ RECEIVE(q) ←--←--←--←--←--	9 $\quad$ SEND(p, buf_{snd})
10 $\quad$ $buf_{rcv} \leftarrow buf_{rcv} \cup V_{str}$ // discard duplicates	10 $\quad$ $buf_{rcv} \leftarrow buf_{rcv} \cup V_{str}$ // discard duplicates
11 $\quad$ $V_{str} \leftarrow$ SELECT(p, buf_{rcv}, ℓ_{str})	11 $\quad$ $V_{str} \leftarrow$ SELECT(q, buf_{rcv}, ℓ_{str})

Fig. 2. Baseline version of the VICINITY protocol

In our design we decouple these two aspects by adopting a two-layered gossiping framework, as can be seen in Figure 1. The lower layer is the peer sampling service, responsible for maintaining a connected overlay and for periodically feeding the top-layer protocol with nodes uniformly randomly selected from the whole network. In its turn, the top-layer protocol, called VICINITY, is in charge of discovering nodes that are favored by the selection function. Each layer maintains its own, separate view, and communicates to the respective layer of other nodes.

3.2 VICINITY: Baseline Version

To better grasp the principal operation of the protocol, we first present a baseline version of VICINITY, shown in Figure 2. In this baseline version, each node periodically contacts a random node from its view, and the two nodes send each other the best—with respect to the receiver's profile—g_{str} neighbors they have in their views. Note that this baseline version of VICINITY is completely equivalent to the related T-MAN protocol [5].

As can be seen in the pseudocode of Figure 2, each node, p, periodically picks from its view a random node, q, to gossip with (line 3). It then applies the SELECT function to select the g_{str} nodes that are best for q, from the union of its own view and p itself (lines 4-5), and sends them to q (line 6). Upon reception of p's message, q selects the g_{str} best nodes for p among all nodes in its view and q itself (lines 7-8), and sends them back to p (line 9). Finally, each node updates its own view, by selecting the ℓ_{str} best neighbors out of its previous view and all received descriptors (line 11).

Note that the code for selecting and sending descriptors to the other side is symmetric for the two nodes (lines 4-6 vs. lines 7-9), as well as the code for merging the received descriptors to the current view (lines 11).

Each node essentially runs two threads. An *active* one, which periodically wakes up and initiates communication to another node, and a *passive* thread, which responds to the communication initiated by another node.

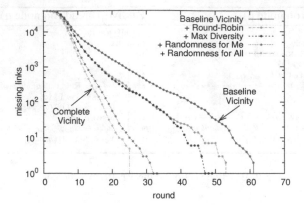

Fig. 3. Self-organization in a 100×100 torus, demonstrating the performance for different versions of VICINITY, ranging from the baseline to the complete one.

3.3   VICINITY: Fine-Tuning the Nuts and Bolts

A number of interesting design choices can substantially boost the performance of the baseline VICINITY protocol. In this section, we will motivate them and demonstrate them in parallel. For our demonstration we will consider a sample testbed, simulated on PeerNet [6], an open-source simulation and emulation framework for peer-to-peer networks written in Java, branching the popular PeerSim simulator [7].

Our testbed consists of a network of 10,000 nodes, assigned distinct 2D coordinates from a 100×100 grid, and whose aim is to self-organize in the respective torus overlay, starting from an arbitrary random topology. Nodes maintain a short view of $\ell_{str}=12$ descriptors each, which is initially filled with 12 neighbors picked uniformly at random from the whole network. When gossiping, nodes send $g_{str}=12$ descriptors to each other. The selection function selects, out of a given set, the k neighbors that are the closest to the reference node in Euclidean space. The goal of a node is to discover its four closest nodes out of the whole network, that is, to get their descriptors in its view. For example, the node with coordinates $(20,40)$ should get nodes $(19,40)$, $(21,40)$, $(20,39)$, and $(20,41)$ among its neighbors. We consider space to wrap around the edges of the grid, resulting in a torus topology. For example, the four closest nodes for node $(0,0)$ are $(99,0)$, $(1,0)$, $(0,99)$, and $(0,1)$.

Figure 3 plots the number of target links that are missing from all nodes' views, collectively. Initially, this accounts to 40,000 links, i.e., four for each of the 10,000 nodes. The red plot corresponds to the baseline version of VICINITY, detailed in the previous section. Clearly, target links are being discovered at exponential speed, and within 61 rounds nodes have self-organized to a complete torus structure. Nevertheless, as we see, the baseline is the slowest of all five versions shown.

Round-Robin Neighbor Selection. The first improvement concerns the policy for selecting which neighbor to gossip with. Rather than picking from one's view at random, we impose a *round robin* selection of gossip partners. The motivation behind this policy is twofold.

First, contacting one's neighbors in a round-robin order improves the node's chances to optimize its view faster, by increasing the number of *different* potentially good neighbors the node encounters. It is not hard to envisage that probing a single neighbor multiple times in a short time frame has little value, as the neighbor is unlikely to have new useful information to trade every time. In contrast, maximizing the intervals at which a given neighbor is probed, maximizes the potential utility of each gossip exchange. Given the rather static nature of a node's VICINITY view when converged, this is achieved by visiting neighbors in a round-robin fashion.

The second motivation for the round-robin policy is that, in the case of a dynamic network, it serves garbage collection of obsolete node descriptors. A descriptor may become obsolete as a result of network dynamics, if the node it points at is no longer alive. By picking neighbors in round-robin order, neighbors are being contacted in roughly uniform time periods, preventing any single—and possibly obsolete—descriptor from lingering indefinitely in a node's view.

The green plot of Figure 3 shows the evolution of the same experiment, with round-robin neighbor selection enabled. The improved performance over the baseline version is evident already from the early rounds of the experiment.

Maximize Descriptor Diversity. Another way to squeeze more benefit out of a single gossip exchange, is to increase the diversity of descriptors exchanged between the nodes. When responding to a node's gossip request, there is no value in sending back descriptors that were also included in that node's message. That node has these descriptors already. This can be very common especially when the network is in a converged or nearly converged state, in which case nodes are highly clustered. In that respect, a node's passive thread should *exclude* all received descriptors from the set of potential descriptors to send back.

The dark blue plot of Figure 3 presents the evolution of the experiment, this time applying both the round-robin and the diversity maximization policies. The plot confirms our reasoning, and shows that the discovery of target links is indeed accelerated, particularly at the stages closer to convergence, as anticipated.

Randomness for Me. Let us now take a ground-breaking twist in our design. All configurations considered so far have been too narrowly structure-oriented. They all exploit a single input channel of information for improving structure, and that channel is nothing more than other nodes' structure information. We have created a feedback loop on structure for structure! Or rather, a vicious cycle around structure.

Depending on the scenario, this can be a strength or a weakness. Once connected to some "good" neighbors, the chances to be introduced to additional "good" nodes increases. Once, however, connected exclusively to largely irrelevant nodes, navigating towards one's "neighborhood" can be slow, or in certain occasions impossible. We defer this discussion to Section 4.

With the intent of breaking the closed loop on structural information, we introduce *randomness* as a second input channel. Rather than having nodes discover new neighbors exclusively through their current neighbors' structural links, we also offer them the chance to sample nodes from the whole network *at random*.

To this end, we employ CYCLON [10] as a peer sampling protocol, to provide nodes with a stream of random neighbors. In each round, each node's active thread pulls the random descriptors provided by its CYCLON instance, merges them with its normal VICINITY view, and filters the union through the SELECT function to keep the best ℓ_{str} neighbors. This way, if CYCLON encounters a good neighbor by chance, that neighbor is picked up by VICINITY to improve its view.

For the sake of a fair comparison, we maintain the number of descriptors exchanged per round the same as in the baseline configuration, that is, 12 descriptors per round. However, now we exchange g_{str}=6 descriptors on behalf of VICINITY, and another six descriptors on behalf of CYCLON. This creates precisely the same bandwidth requirements as in the previous configurations, although distributed in a double number of half-sized packets.

The magenta plot of Figure 3 confirms that the configuration combining structure with randomness significantly outperforms all previous versions. It is worth emphasizing that the *rate* of discovering target links is significantly faster for the whole extent of the experiment, from its early stages until full convergence, despite the fact that only six links are exchanged per round by VICINITY as opposed to 12 in previous configurations.

Randomness for All. A final optization is to borrow the random links obtained through CYCLON not only to improve a node's own structure links, but also to improve the quality of links it sends to other nodes.

The dark blue plot of Figure 3 clearly shows that this optimization further improves performance. This last configuration constitutes the complete VICINITY protocol, and will be the one used by default for the rest of the paper, unless otherwise mentioned.

3.4   VICINITY: The Complete Protocol

The complete VICINITY protocol is presented—in pseudocode—in Figure 4. The rest of this section discusses the differences to the baseline protocol.

The round-robin neighbor selection policy is implemented by means of the *age* field in descriptors. The age of a descriptor gives an *approximate* estimation of how many rounds ago that descriptor either (i) was introduced in that node's VICINITY view, or (ii) was last used by the node for gossiping with the respective neighbor. Neighbors of higher age are given priority when choosing a neighbor for gossiping (line 3), and subsequently their age is zeroed, which results in a round-robin selection policy.

To approximate the number of rounds some descriptor has been in a node's view, any new descriptor entering a view is initialized with zero age (lines 9–active, 13–both), and the ages of all descriptors in the view are incremented by one once per round (line 5). Also, when a node is selected for gossiping (line 3), it is also *removed* from the view (line 4), as a means for garbage collection of descriptors. If that neighbor is still alive and responds, its fresh descriptor (with age zero) will be inserted anew to the view.

The role of randomness can be seen in lines 6–active and 9–passive, where random neighbors are also considered in the message to send to the other peer, as well as in line 10–active, where a node pulls "good" neighbors from its randomized view into its structured view.

Active Thread (on node p)	Passive Thread (on node q)
1 **while** *true* **do**	1 **while** *true* **do**
2 wait(T time units)	2
3 $q \leftarrow$ SELECTOLDESTNEIGHBOR $()$	3
4 $V_{str} \leftarrow V_{str} \setminus \{q\}$ *// for garbage collection*	4
5 INCAGE(V_{str})	5
6 $buf_{snd} \leftarrow V_{str} \cup V_{rnd} \cup \{p\}$	6
7 $buf_{snd} \leftarrow$ SELECT(q, buf_{snd}, g_{str})	7
8 SEND(q, buf_{snd}) $--\rightarrow--\rightarrow--\rightarrow--\rightarrow--\rightarrow$	8 $buf_{rcv} \leftarrow$ RECEIVE(p) *// p can be any node*
9 ZEROAGE(V_{rnd})	9 $buf_{snd} \leftarrow V_{str} \cup V_{rnd} \cup \{q\}$
10 $V_{str} \leftarrow$ SELECT(p, $V_{str} \cup V_{rnd}$, ℓ_{str})	10 $buf_{snd} \leftarrow buf_{snd} \setminus buf_{rcv}$ *// max diversity*
11 .	11 $buf_{snd} \leftarrow$ SELECT(p, buf_{snd}, g_{str})
12 $buf_{rcv} \leftarrow$ RECEIVE(q) $\leftarrow--\leftarrow--\leftarrow--\leftarrow--\leftarrow$	12 SEND(p, buf_{snd})
13 ZEROAGE(buf_{rcv})	13 ZEROAGE(buf_{rcv})
14 $buf_{rcv} \leftarrow V_{str} \cup buf_{rcv}$ *// duplicates: keep oldest*	14 $buf_{rcv} \leftarrow V_{str} \cup buf_{rcv}$ *// duplicates: keep oldest*
15 $V_{str} \leftarrow$ SELECT(p, buf_{rcv}, ℓ_{str})	15 $V_{str} \leftarrow$ SELECT(q, buf_{rcv}, ℓ_{str})

Fig. 4. The complete VICINITY protocol

From this point on, by VICINITY we will be referring to the complete version of the protocol, including all the design optimizations presented so far.

4 How Much Randomness Is Enough?

Randomness is good. At least for the specific scenario of the previous section. But how general can this claim be? How good is randomness in other scenarios? Just good, or rather necessary? How much randomness is "enough", and how much can it assist in structuring? Although it is infeasible to give a universal rule to quantitatively assess the value of randomness, in this section we aim at shedding some light at these questions.

To answer these questions, we delve into the principles governing self-organization, and we distinguish the specific roles of determinism and randomness in it.

4.1 The Role of Determinism

To explore the role of determinism, alone, isolated from the effects of randomness, let us consider self-organization without randomness, relying exclusively on structure. To further isolate our reasoning from the effects of randomness, including pseudo-randomness due to nodes continuously replacing their links *during* the process of convergence, it may help to think of fresh nodes joining an *already converged* network.

The whole operation of self-organization relies on the ability to periodically compare potential neighbors, and on being able to determine which ones are a step closer to your targets. We are looking, therefore, at some form of routing or orientation property in the target overlay.

For simplicity, let us consider a very trivial case. The whole network has converged, except for a single node, x. Node x has one target, z, and currently has exactly one neighbor, y. Imagine, for instance, a fresh node x joining an already converged network using an arbitrary node y as its bootstrap node. For self-organization to be successful, x should be able to reach z through y, y's neighbors, y's neighbors' neighbors, and so on. And this should be the case for *any* y and *any* z. This dictates the first required property for self-organization based exclusively on structure to be correct: *the target topology should form a strongly-connected graph.*

This, however, is not sufficient. Even if a directed path from y to z exists, say consisting of nodes $y_1, y_2, \ldots, y_k$, the selection function should be such that a call to SELECT$(x, Neighbors(y), g_{str})$ returns a subset of y's neighbors that contains y_1, then a call to SELECT$(x, Neighbors(y_1), g_{str})$ returns a set of nodes that contains y_2, and so on. We will refer to this property as *navigability*, and we state the second required property for correctness: *the given selection function should render the given target overlay navigable.*

Note that navigability is a property of the *combination* of (i) the target overlay and (ii) the selection function. Clearly, a strongly connected target overlay with a selection function that returns "bad" selections, will not let a network self-organize. The other way around, a selection function that works for some particular overlay will not necessarily be sufficient for any overlay. For instance the proximity-based selection function used in Section 3 is excellent for uniformly populated topologies, but it can get some nodes trapped in "local optima" in the presence of a U-shaped gap, a well known problem of greedy geographic routing protocols [1].

4.2 The Triple Role of Randomness

Having discussed the weaknesses of determinism in self-organization, it is not hard to imagine the benefits offered by randomization.

First, maintaining the whole overlay in a single connected partition is the cornerstone of any large-scale decentralized application. This need is even more pressuring in the case of a custom overlay management protocol, as the target overlay may per se consist of multiple distinct components. Keeping the whole overlay connected in a single component allows the joining of new nodes at arbitrary bootstrap points, and generally allows the reconfiguration of nodes in case of updates to their profiles.

Second, feeding nodes with neighbors picked uniformly at random from the whole overlay, prevents them from getting indefinitely stuck in local optima. Similarly to hill climbing algorithms, random sampling is crucial at helping nodes reach their global optimum.

Finally, even in target overlays and selection functions that guarantee a strongly connected, navigable target overlay, the diameter of that overlay is often large. When new nodes join a converged overlay at an arbitrary bootstrap node, it may take them long to gradually navigate to their optimal neighbors. Having a continuous stream of random samples from the whole network, however, gives them the opportunity to take a shortcut link close to their target, a well-known property of random, complex networks.

5 Evaluation

Given VICINITY's generic applicability, it is practically infeasible to provide an exhaustive evaluation of the framework. Instead, we will focus on the following two test cases that underline its two key components: its reliance on structure and its benefit from randomness:

Two-dimensional Torus. This is the same overlay structure we used in Section 3. Nodes are assigned two-dimensional coordinates, and their goal is to establish links to their closest neighbors. Building this target topology is primarily based on the Euclidean proximity heuristic. Informally speaking, the general idea is that nodes gradually improve their views with closer neighbors, which they then probe to find new, even closer ones, eventually reaching their closest neighbors. This emphasizes the utility of the deterministic component of VICINITY.

Clustering Nodes in Groups. In this test case, nodes are split up in uncorrelated groups. Each node's goal is to cluster with other nodes of the same group. The key difference with the previous test case is that nodes cannot gradually connect to groups "closer" to their own, as there is no notion of proximity between groups. The target overlay is explicitly clustered in non-connected components, therefore it is neither (strongly) connected nor navigable. Finding a node of the same group can be accomplished only by means of random encounters, which highlights the role of randomness. Once a node of the same group is found, though, the two nodes can grreatly assist each other by sharing their further knowledge of same group neighbors.

5.1   Two-Dimensional Torus

Overview. We consider a two-dimensional space. We assign each node (x,y) coordinates, such that they are (virtually) aligned in a regular square grid organization. A node's coordinates constitute its profile. Each node's goal is to establish links to its four closest neighbors, to the north, south, east, and west (wrapping around the grid's edges).

The natural choice of a selection function for such a target topology is one that gives preference to neighbors spatially closer to the reference node. More formally, we define the distance between two nodes a and b, with coordinates (x_a, y_a) and (x_b, y_b), respectively, to be their two-dimensional Euclidean distance, assuming that space wraps around the edges to form a torus:

$$dx = min\{|x_a - x_b|, \ width - |x_a - x_b|\}$$

$$dy = min\{|y_a - y_b|, \ height - |y_a - y_b|\}$$

$$dist(a,b) = \sqrt{dx^2 + dy^2}$$

The selection function SELECT$(p, \mathcal{D}, k)$ sorts all node descriptors in $\mathcal{D}$ by their distance to the reference node p, and returns the k closest ones.

Figure 5 graphically illustrates the self-organization of a "toy-size" network of 1024 nodes into a torus overlay, depicting snapshots of the overlay at different stages. Nodes' deterministic and randomized views have been set to a size of six, each. For clarity of the snapshots, only the best four outgoing links of each node are shown in the figure. Note the existence of either one or two lines between two connected nodes. This is because links are directed. A single line denotes a single link only from one node to the other (directionality not shown). A double line means that both nodes have established a link to each other. In the completed target topology (last snapshot) all links are double.

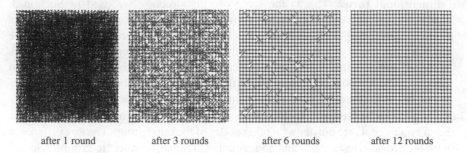

| after 1 round | after 3 rounds | after 6 rounds | after 12 rounds |

Fig. 5. Self-organization in a 32×32 torus topology

Experimental Analysis. Let us now observe the progress of self-organization for different network sizes and protocol configurations. Figure 6 plots the fraction of missing target links as a function of the experiment round, for networks of size 2^{12}, 2^{14}, and 2^{16} nodes, respectively. For each network size we present the progress of five different configurations. For a fair comparison, we have fixed the total number of descriptors exchanged in a single round by a node's active thread to 12.

The thick solid blue and green lines correspond to trading exclusively deterministic or randomized links, respectively. That is, all 12 links exchanged come either from the deterministic view or from the randomized view, respectively. The fine line of a given color corresponds to a very close configuration to its solid line counterpart, where just *one* link has been reserved for trading neighbors of the other view type. E.g., a fine blue line corresponds to the settings $g_{str}=11$ and $g_{rnd}=1$. Finally, the red line corresponds to an equally balanced use of determinism and randomness: six links are being traded per round for each view type.

A number of observations can be made from these graphs. Most importantly, we easily identify determinism as the primary component responsible for efficient self-organization. On the contrary, when randomness is used alone (solid green line), it performs several orders of magnitude worse than the other protocol configurations, whose performances are comparable to each other. This indicates that, for the given target topology, the crucial element accelerating self-organization is determinism.

It is not hard to see why using randomness alone is so inefficient. A node's only chance to find a target neighbor is if that neighbor shows up in its peer sampling service view, which is periodically refreshed with random nodes. In other words, a node is fishing for target neighbors blindly. As expected, its time to converge increases significantly as the size of the network grows, since the probability of spotting a target link at random diminishes.

Note that just a "pinch" of structure in a nearly random-only configuration (fine green line) brings a dramatic improvement to the outcome. This emphasizes the importance of structure, particularly in an overlay as navigable as a torus topology. In this scenario, a node has plenty of random input, while that single structured link deterministically brings it closer to its target neighborhood in each round.

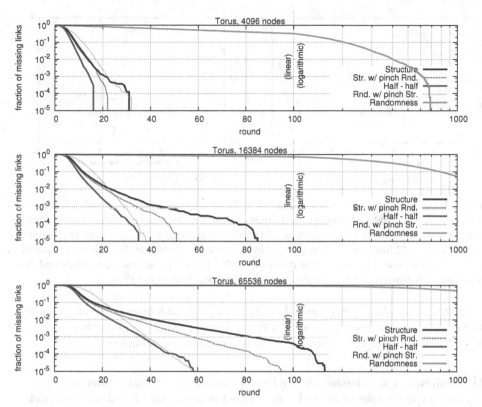

Fig. 6. Progress of self-organization in a torus overlay, for different configurations of VICINITY and a total gossip length ($g_{str}+g_{rnd}$) fixed to 12

When determinism is in exclusive control (blue line), convergence comes fast as node views deterministically improve in each round. An important observation, though, is that in all network sizes, the determinism-only experiment slows down when approaching complete convergence. This can be explained as follows. In these experiments nodes are initialized with a few random links all over the network, which are generally long-range links. Nodes that are priviledged to be initialized with links close to their target neighborhood, take a shortcut and converge very fast, replacing all their initial random links with very specific, short ones. Soon enough, the network becomes nearly converged, and nearly all long-range links have been replaced by local ones. This, however, creates an obstacle to nodes that have not managed to converge yet, as they can only navigate slowly, in small local steps, towards their target neighborhoods, "crawling" in an almost converged overlay.

The aforementioned issue is circumvented by adding a "pinch" of randomness in an otherwise fully-deterministic configuration (fine blue line). This provides nodes with an extra source of random, potentially long-range, links. In accordance to our explanation in the previous paragraph, this visibly accelerates the last few stages of convergence.

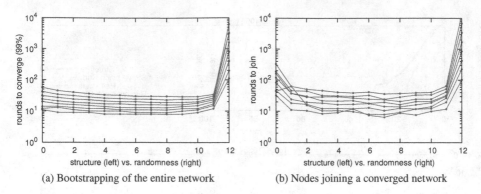

(a) Bootstrapping of the entire network   (b) Nodes joining a converged network

Fig. 7. Structure vs. Randomness in a torus topology. These graphs show the number of rounds it takes to reach the 99th percentile of convergence when bootstrapping an entire network (left), and the number of rounds for new nodes to join an already converged overlay (right). In all experiments, exactly 12 links are being exchanged by nodes when gossipping. Each line corresponds to a different network size (from 2^{10} at the bottom to 2^{17} at the top), and each dot corresponds to a different allocation of the 12 gossip slots to structured and randomized links.

Quite clearly, the balanced use of determinism and randomness (red line) outperforms all other configurations. This is a firm validation of our claim that both policies have distinct advantages to offer, which are best utilized in combination.

Determinism vs. Randomness Space Exploration. Having developed an understanding on the specific roles of determinism and randomness in self-organization in a torus topology, we now run an extensive set of experiments to create a complete picture of their interaction.

We considered eight different network sizes, namely 2^{10} (1024), 2^{11}, 2^{12}, 2^{13}, 2^{14}, 2^{15}, 2^{16}, and 2^{17} (131072), and for each network size we considered all possible combinations of deterministic and randomized gossip lengths, so that the total gossip length stays fixed and equal to 12. This accounts to 13 experiments per network size, that is, all combinations such that $g_{str} \in [0, 12]$ and $g_{rnd} = 12 - g_{str}$. For each experiment we recorded the number of rounds it took to establish 99% of the target links.

Figure 7(a) presents the results of these experiments. Each experiment is represented by a single dot, while dots corresponding to experiments on the same network size have been connected by lines. The lowest line corresponds to networks of 2^{10} nodes and the highest one to networks of 2^{17} nodes. The horizontal axis shows the specific combination of determinism and randomness used in each experiment. More specifically, the value on the horizontal axis corresponds to the g_{str} value of each configuration.

The first observation is that the dynamics of convergence follow the same patterns in all network sizes. It should be particularly noted that these results correspond to a single run per configuration, which prevents loss of information due to averaging.

The most distinguishing message from this graph is that the use of randomness alone (rightmost column) performs orders of magnitude worse than any other configuration. It can also be observed that the other extreme, that is, complete determinism (leftmost column) performs a bit worse than most other configurations that combine the two.

Node Joins. In addition to the experiments carried out so far, where all nodes start the VICINITY protocol at the same time, we also want to explore the behavior of VICINITY when nodes join an already converged overlay.

We considered the same combinations of network sizes and protocol configurations as the ones of Figure 7(a). In each experiment, we first let the network converge to the target topology, and then we inserted a new node initialized with exactly *one* neighbor picked at random, and we recorded how many rounds it took for that node to find its target neighbors.

Figure 7(b) shows the number of rounds it took a node to reach its target vicinity in networks of the aforementioned sizes and configurations.

As expected, purely randomized views result in slower convergence. However, we observe remarkably bad behavior also for determinism-only configurations. The explanation is that, as has also been discussed earlier, navigating in an already converged overlay in the absence of random long-range shortcuts is a slow process.

These graphs emphasize our claim, that neither of the two policies is sufficiently good on its own. Determinism and randomness appear to be complementary in creating structure.

5.2 Clustering Nodes in Groups

Overview. In this scenario, we assign each node a *group ID*, which constitutes its profile. The goal is to form clusters of nodes that share the same group IDs. From a node's perspective, the goal is to establish links to other nodes with the same group ID.

The only comparison operator defined on node profiles is equality of group IDs. By comparing their profiles, nodes can tell whether they belong to the same group or not. However, no other type of comparison or proximity metrics apply: any foreign group is "equally foreign", there is no notion of ranking or proximity. The target topology has been explicitly selected to form a non-connected, non-navigable graph, to shed light at the operation of VICINITY in such overlays.

The selection function $\text{SELECT}(p, \mathcal{D}, k)$ is simple and straightforward. It starts by selecting in a random sequence descriptors from $\mathcal{D}$ whose group ID is the same as p's. If these are fewer than k, it continues by selecting randomly from the rest of the descriptors.

Similarly to the torus scenario, Figure 8 provides a graphical illustration of an 1024-node network self-organizing into the target overlay. Again, nodes' deterministic and randomized views have been set to a size of six, each. Nodes are assigned group IDs such that a total of 16 groups exist, each having 64 nodes. Nodes are plotted in a layout that places members of the same group together, purely to make visualization intuitive. As far as the protocol operation is concerned, nodes do not have coordinates, but only their group ID. To avoid cluttering the graph, only two random outgoing links of each node's V_{str} view are shown, with links to foreign groups given higher priority. This way, when a node in Figure 8 appears to have no links to groups other than its own, it is guaranteed that *all* its V_{str} links point at nodes within its group.

Experimental Analysis. Figure 9 presents the progress of self-organization of the grouping scenario, for the same network sizes and protocol settings used in the torus

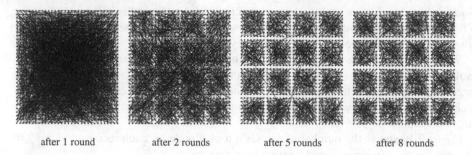

after 1 round   after 2 rounds   after 5 rounds   after 8 rounds

Fig. 8. Self-organization into 16 groups of 64 nodes each, in a 1024-node network

overlay. That is, network sizes of 2^{12}, 2^{14}, and 2^{16} have been considered, and the sum of the structured (g_{str}) and randomized (g_{rnd}) gossip length has been fixed to 12. Note that in this scenario, the group size is fixed to 64 nodes, therefore the networks of 4096, 16384, and 65536 nodes consist of 64, 256, and 1024 groups, respectively.

To better interpret the experimental results, we should build a good understanding of nodes' goals in this scenario. A node's task is divided in two steps: first, discover the right cluster; second, get well connected in it. The deterministic component of VICIN-ITY excels in the second. Through a single link to the target cluster, a node rapidly learns and becomes known to additional nodes in that cluster. It turns out that the crucial step in this test case is the first one: discovering the target cluster.

Returning now to the results of Figure 9, the most important observation is that, contrary to the torus scenario, randomness is clearly the key component for self-organization. Determinism alone (solid blue line) is consistently *unable* to let nodes find their group partners, indefinitely failing to build the target topology.

It is not hard to see why pure determinism fails. As nodes start clustering with other nodes of the same group, the pool of intergroup links in the network shrinks significantly. As explained above, once a node forms a link and gossips to one other node of its group, chances are it will acquire plenty of links to more nodes of the same group, rapidly trading its *intergroup* for *intragroup* links. In not so many rounds, most nodes end up having neighbors from their own groups exclusively. The problem comes with nodes that have not encountered nodes of their group early enough. If a node's neighbors are all from other groups, and these groups have already clustered into closed, self-contained clusters, the node has no chances whatsoever to be handed a link to a node of its own group, ever. A neighbor from such a self-contained foreign group can only provide alternative neighbors of that same, foreign group. The node, thus, finds itself in a dead end.

This demonstrates the need of a source of random, long-range links, to prevent such dead end scenarios. Indeed, just a "pinch" of randomness (fine blue line) is enough to save the day. It may not account for the most efficient configuration, but it clearly bridges the huge gap between dead end and convergence. This is a particularly significant observation, as it clearly demonstrates that involving randomness, even just a "pinch" of it, is not just a matter of performance, but a matter of *correctness*.

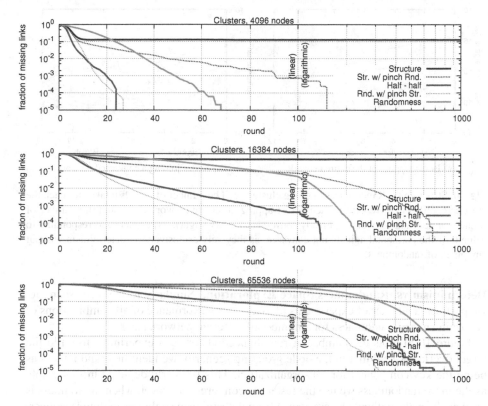

Fig. 9. Progress of self-organization in disjoint groups, for different configurations of VICINITY and a total gossip length ($g_{str}+g_{rnd}$) fixed to 12

When randomness acts on its own (solid green line), exposing each node to 12 random links in each round, convergence is certainly faster. However, in the lack of the deterministic component of VICINITY, a node should rely on randomness to discover *independently* each of the 12 target nodes of the same group.

Augmenting an almost complete randomness-based configuration with just a "pinch" of determinism (fine green line), gives the best achievable results. This was expected. Nodes, in this configuration, put nearly all of their communication quota on the hunt for same group nodes, through randomization. At the same time, this single link they reserve for targeted, deterministic communication, is sufficient to let them discover very fast all nodes of their group once they have discovered at least one of them.

Finally, the middleground configuration (red line), combining the deterministic and randomized components each with a gossip length of six descriptors, performs reasonably well in all cases, even if giving higher priority on randomness seems to improve things further for large networks.

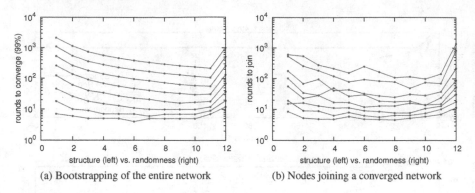

(a) Bootstrapping of the entire network   (b) Nodes joining a converged network

Fig. 10. Structure vs. Randomness in group clustering. The number of rounds it takes to reach the 99th percentile of convergence when bootstrapping an entire network (left), and the number of rounds for new nodes to join an already converged overlay (right). Experiments corresponding to value 0 of the horizontal axis do not converge, as they rely exclusively on determinism without any pinch of randomness.

Determinism vs. Randomness Space Exploration. Similarly to the torus scenario, we perform a number of experiments to assess the performance of all combinations of determinism and randomness for a number of different network sizes.

Figure 10(a) plots the number of rounds needed for each experiment to build the target overlay. Recall that in the node grouping scenario, we identified randomness as being the key component for self-organization. This is clearly depicted in this graph, as the more randomness we use the faster we converge. However, when randomness is used exclusively, without any assistance from determinism (rightmost column), convergence is slower.

Note that experiments corresponding to a determinism-only configuration (leftmost column) did *not* converge, hence they were omitted from the plots.

Node Joins. Finally, we want to assess the number of rounds it takes new nodes to find their location in the target overlay, when joining an already converged network.

Figure 10(b) presents the results of these experiments. In accordance with the number of rounds it takes a whole network to converge from scratch, the rounds it takes nodes to join already converged overlays is very comparable.

The clear message from this graph is that, as we have consistently experienced also in our previous experiments, the two extremes should be avoided. Pure determinism in the case of node grouping, with a non-connected target structure, should be avoided by all means, as it will fail to build the target overlay. Pure randomness should also be avoided, as it will provide poor performance.

Concluding our entire evaluation of self-organization, we can state that picking a configuration that balances determinism with randomness, is a safe option for a system that self-organizes the network efficiently and works for diverse topologies.

6 Related Work

The work most closely related to VICINITY is the T-MAN protocol, by Jelasity et. al. [2,3,5]. T-MAN is focused exclusively on the deterministic structuring aspect in self-organization of overlays. Although its design does employ a peer sampling service, this is used exclusively for providing nodes with random views *once*, during intialization, as well as for synchronizing nodes to start the topology building process together. As such, it is targeted at *bootstrapping* overlays, rather than maintaining them under dynamic network conditions. For example, garbage collection for stale descriptors and support for nodes joining an already converged overlay have not been considered in the design. The baseline version of VICINITY, shown in Figure 2, is nearly equivalent to the T-MAN protocol.

Earlier efforts for self-organization of overlays have led to solutions that are tailormade for specific applications, such as [11], which clusters users of a file-sharing application based on the content they share.

BuddyCast is a file recommendation mechanism embedded in the Tribler [8] BitTorrent client. Inspired by [11], it essentially constitutes a deployment of VICINITY in the real world, clustering users by their file content preferences, to provide them with relevant recommendations.

7 Conclusions

Does randomness matter? The main conclusion from our research is a clear affirmative answer. In some cases, having probabilistic decision-making is even necessary.

In our study, we have concentrated exclusively on overlay construction and maintenance. For this domain it is also clear that structure matters as well. Having only randomness may severely affect the behavior of our overlay-maintenance algorithm. What is striking, however, is that adding either a pinch of randomness accompanying an otherwise deterministic technique, or adding a pinch of structure to an otherwise fully random process can have dramatic effects. In our examples we have been able to trace with reasonable confidence why such pinches of randomness or structure helped, but there is still much research to be done when it comes to developing more general insights and to identifying which classes of algorithms and data structures benefit from randomness and which not.

The foundational question is why a *specific* mix of randomness and structure works so well, and how much of a pinch will indeed do the job. Our study sheds some light on this question, but also makes clear that much more work, and extended to other subfields, is necessary to come to a principled approach when dealing with designing large-scale distributed systems.

References

1. Cadger, F., Curran, K., Santos, J., Moffett, S.: A survey of geographical routing in wireless ad-hoc networks. IEEE Communications Surveys Tutorials 15(2), 621–653 (2013)
2. Jelasity, M., Babaoglu, O.: T-Man: Gossip-based Overlay Topology Management. In: Brueckner, S.A., Di Marzo Serugendo, G., Hales, D., Zambonelli, F. (eds.) ESOA 2005. LNCS (LNAI), vol. 3910, pp. 1–15. Springer, Heidelberg (2006)

3. Jelasity, M., Babaoglu, O.: T-Man: Gossip-based overlay topology management. In: Brueck-ner, S.A., Di Marzo Serugendo, G., Hales, D., Zambonelli, F. (eds.) ESOA 2005. LNCS (LNAI), vol. 3910, pp. 1–15. Springer, Heidelberg (2006)
4. Jelasity, M., Montresor, A., Babaoglu, O.: Gossip-based aggregation in large dynamic net-works. ACM Trans. Comp. Syst. 23(3), 219–252 (2005)
5. Jelasity, M., Montresor, A., Babaoglu, O.: T-man: Gossip-based fast overlay topology con-struction. Comput. Netw. 53(13), 2321–2339 (2009)
6. PeerNet, http://acropolis.cs.vu.nl/PeerNet
7. PeerSim, http://peersim.sourceforge.net
8. Pouwelse, J.A., Garbacki, P., Wang, J., Bakker, A., Yang, J., Iosup, A., Epema, D.H.J., Rein-ders, M., van Steen, M.R., Sips, H.J.: Tribler: a social-based peer-to-peer system: Research articles. Concurr. Comput.: Pract. Exper. 20(2), 127–138 (2008)
9. Russell, S., Norvig, P.: Artificial Intelligence: A Modern Approach, 3rd edn. Prentice Hall Press, Upper Saddle River (2009)
10. Voulgaris, S., Gavidia, D., van Steen, M.: Cyclon: Inexpensive membership management for unstructured p2p overlays. Journal of Network and Systems Management 13(2), 197–217 (2005)
11. Voulgaris, S., van Steen, M.: Epidemic-Style Management of Semantic Overlays for Content-Based Searching. In: Cunha, J.C., Medeiros, P.D. (eds.) Euro-Par 2005. LNCS, vol. 3648, pp. 1143–1152. Springer, Heidelberg (2005)
12. Watts, D.J.: Small Worlds, The Dynamics of Networks between Order and Randomness. Princeton University Press, Princeton (1999)

Experiences with Fault-Injection in a Byzantine Fault-Tolerant Protocol

Rolando Martins[1], Rajeev Gandhi[1], Priya Narasimhan[1], Soila Pertet[1],
António Casimiro[2], Diego Kreutz[2], and Paulo Veríssimo[2]

[1] Department of Electrical & Computer Engineering, Carnegie Mellon University
rolandomartins@cmu.edu, priya@cs.cmu.edu, {rgandhi,spertet}@ece.cmu.edu
[2] Departamento de Informática, Universidade de Lisboa, Faculdade de Ciências
{casim,pjv}@di.fc.ul.pt, kreutz@lasige.di.fc.ul.pt

Abstract. The overall performance improvement in Byzantine fault-tolerant state machine replication algorithms has made them a viable option for critical high-performance systems. However, the construction of the proofs necessary to support these algorithms are complex and often make assumptions that may or may not be true in a particular implementation. Furthermore, the transition from theory to practice is difficult and can lead to the introduction of subtle bugs that may break the assumptions that support these algorithms. To address these issues we have developed Hermes, a fault-injector framework that provides an infrastructure for injecting faults in a Byzantine fault-tolerant state machine. Our main goal with Hermes is to help practitioners in the complex process of debugging their implementations of these algorithms, and at the same time increase the confidence of possible adopters, e.g., systems researchers, industry, by allowing them to test the implementations. In this paper, we discuss our experiences with Hermes to inject faults in BFT-SMaRt, a high-performance Byzantine fault-tolerant state machine replication library.

Keywords: Byzantine fault-injector, failure diagnosis, cloud-computing, Byzantine fault-tolerance, intrusion-tolerance.

1 Introduction

Recent improvements in the performance of Byzantine Fault-Tolerant (BFT) protocols have made such protocols feasible for building fault- and intrusion-tolerant systems. Presently, there are multiple implementations of BFT protocols at disposal of system developers to make their own system fault/intrusion-tolerant without worrying about having to implement the functionality by themselves. However, as other research projects [1] have observed, while current state-of-the-art BFT protocol implementations have considerably improved the performance of the fault-free path, they often fail to properly handle all of the corner cases. The end result is that while many BFT implementations can efficiently handle the complexity of Byzantine failures, they often suffer from multiple orders of magnitude reductions in throughput and long periods of unavailability when in the

D. Eyers and K. Schwan (Eds.): Middleware 2013, LNCS 8275, pp. 41–61, 2013.

presence of non-independent faults, such as colluding malicious nodes. This often poses a dilemma for system programmers – on the one hand the use of a publicly available implementation of BFT protocol allows programmers to develop fault- and intrusion-tolerant systems without worrying about implementing these complicated aspects themselves while, on the other hand, there is a question about the ability of an implementation to actually handle complex as well as simple failures in an efficient manner.

System developers often need answers to multiple questions about a particular BFT protocol before they are able to select it and be confident that the implementation will actually meet all of their requirements. Questions can vary from performance to robustness and trustworthiness, such as the following examples. What kind of faults does the system tolerates? Does it really tolerates arbitrary faults? Or only more common faults, e.g. crash faults? What is the degradation of system throughput in the presence of faults? Are there thresholds for fault- arrival rates, beyond which the system breaks down? How does a BFT protocol compare with others?

Software fault injection is often used in software testing to quantitatively assess the impact of faults/bugs in the software. We use a similar approach to assess the performance of a BFT protocol and answer questions like the aforementioned ones that developers may have about the behavior of a protocol in the presence of faults. In this paper, we describe Hermes, our fault injection framework created to help BFT protocol developers in the strenuous task of testing the behavior of a BFT implementation under a diverse and broad range variety of faults. To show its usability, we used Hermes to assess the behavior of BFT-SMaRt [2], a well-known BFT protocol implementation.

Hermes allows system developers to get insight into the performance of a BFT protocol implementation by allowing them to inject faults and observe the behavior of the system. Hermes's fault injection architecture is flexible and allows protocol independent faults (like crash faults, network faults) as well as protocol dependent faults (like corrupt headers, forged signatures) to be injected into a BFT protocol. Our approach is clearly distinguished from existing ones by the fact that we provide a way to simultaneously inject faults across multiple nodes, allowing different type of faults to be injected in different nodes. Furthermore, by simply selecting the appropriate set of faults, the user can enforce a specific fault model, e.g., if collusion is outside the fault model, then no collusion faults can be used.

We built Hermes using AspectJ [3], for the JAVA runtime, and AspectC++ [4], for the C++ runtime, which allows it to seamlessly weave the fault-injecting infrastructure into the target protocol. The use of Aspect-Oriented Programming (AOP) was to avoid source-code modifications on the target system, especially in context-free faults, i.e., faults that do not modify or access any internal state of the protocol. We decided not to use dynamic weaving because it would introduce further complexity into the infrastructure. As such, the injection points are statically weaved and compiled into the target source code.

Hermes does not require a system developer to be familiar with the BFT protocol or its implementation for injecting protocol independent faults. On the other hand, protocol dependent faults, such as payload size corruption, require that the developer performs some modifications to the source code. A minimal amount of adaptation is unavoidable because it depends on the specific details of protocol in use. In our experience with BFT-SMaRt, it took us about two hours to inject protocol dependent faults.

2   Related Work

There has been considerable work done in developing fault injection systems [5–8] and analyzing the dependability of fault-tolerant systems [9–11]. Loki [5] is a fault injector for distributed systems that injects faults based on a partial view of the global system state. Loki allows the user to specify a state machine and a fault injection campaign in which faults are triggered by state changes. DBench Project [6] aimed to develop standards for creating dependability benchmarks for computer systems. This joint cooperation characterized benchmarks as representing an agreement that is widely accepted both by the computer industry and/or by the user community. Orchestra [9] is a fault injector that uses an interception approach similar to ours to inject communication faults into any layer in the protocol stack. The fault injection core provides the ability to filter, manipulate, and inject new messages. Ferrari [12] (Fault and Error Automatic Real-Time Injection) uses software traps to inject CPU, memory, and bus faults. The Fault Tolerance and Performance Evaluator (Ftape) [13] allows developers to inject faults into user mode registers in CPUs, memory locations, and the disk subsystem. Doctor [7] (Integrated Software Fault Injection Environment) allows developers to inject CPU faults, memory faults, and network communication faults in a system. Xception [14] takes advantage of the advanced debugging and performance monitoring features present in many modern processors to inject more realistic faults. Ballista [15] is a "black box" software testing tool that uses combinational tests of valid and invalid parameter values for subroutine calls, methods and functions. A good survey of fault injection techniques and tools for testing software dependability is provided in [16].

Some of the recent research has looked at the inefficiencies of BFT protocol implementations to handle Byzantine as well as benign faults. In [1], the authors provide a comparative in-depth analysis of several protocols, namely [17–20], in their pursuit to build Aardvark. Their assessment is based mainly in the use of flooding and packet delay (in both primary and non-primary nodes). Similarly, in Prime [21], the authors provide an evaluation of PBFT [17], a leader-based Byzantine fault-tolerant replication protocol, but mention that their approach should work well with all BFT protocols that are leader based, such as [19,22–26]. The experiments conducted in Prime were based on two attacks. The first involved delaying "pre-prepare" messages, while the second consisted in time-out manipulation, where the system would become stalled until large timeouts occurred.

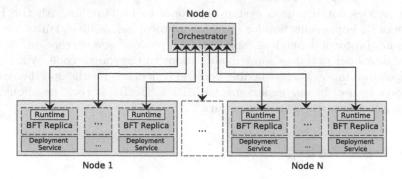

Fig. 1. Overview of the Hermes's architecture

3   Hermes's Overview

Our fault-injection platform, shown in Figure 1, is governed by a fault-injection orchestrator that enables the injection of multiple faults, simultaneous or not, across multiple remote nodes. The actual fault injection is performed by Hermes's runtime, which is incorporated into the BFT replica (through code-weaving). The initial deployment, i.e., the initial view, of both replicas and client is accomplished through the use of the deployment service. However, a BFT protcol can still reconfigure, e.g., adding a new replica, using its usual facilities without having to interact with the deployment service, because the runtime is able to transparently connect to Hermes's orchestrator.

We start by characterizing the types of faults we consider in this work, followed by the description of the orchestrator, runtime and deployment service.

3.1   Faults

We consider two types of faults, *context-free* faults and *context-dependent* faults. The first relates to faults that can be injected without any context information. For instance, for injecting CPU load it is not necessary to access any information on the protocol. The second, the context-dependent faults need to access data of the protocol being injected in the system. For example, corrupting a specific packet type for a given consensus instance, we need to access the data contained in the protocol header.

Context-Free Faults

- **CPU Load** - injects a specified amount of CPU load.
- **Crash** - crashes the runtime and associated BFT replica.
- **Sleep** - delays processing for a specified amount of time.
- **Drop packet** - induces a packet drop following a pre-defined policy (one-time or percentage-wise).

Context-Dependent Faults

- **Corrupt header** - corrupts a packet header with the main goal of breaking low-level protocol buffering, i.e., underflow and overflow.
- **Corrupt payload** - corrupts the payload of a packet with erroneous and random information.
- **Forge signatures** - substitutes part of the signature set with forged signatures, in an effort to convince correct nodes of an erroneous value.
- **DDOS** - causes the malicious nodes to start multicast messages to all correct nodes.

3.2   Orchestrator

The orchestrator is the main component of Hermes and its goal is to provide the orchestration between the various runtimes, that are built-in into the replicas and client, and act as a front-end to the developer. In Section 4, we provide an overview of the implementation and an example of its usage.

The interactions between the orchestrator and runtime are built on top of three communication primitives: *RemoteAction*, *Action* and *Notification*.

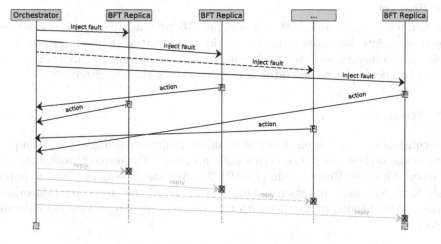

Fig. 2. Action operation overview

Action

An `Action` is used by the runtime to verify if the fault that is about to be injected into the replica is enabled and ready, or alternatively, if the fault is disabled. While this operation could be used to retrieve information from the overall execution of the injection protocol, its main purpose is to serve as synchronization barrier (shown in Figure 2) for the injection of simultaneous faults. For example, a fault is injected in the packet `send` procedure but it could only be run (injected) when all the malicious nodes reach the same fault. This allows us to test colluding among malicious nodes and also target specific test cases in order to explore specific and tricky/uncommon faults.

For achieving this, each active runtime calls an `Action` when it is about to inject the fault. Because it is a synchronous operation, the runtime waits for the reply from the orchestrator. This reply is only sent by the orchestrator when all the malicious nodes reach the synchronization point, that is, when all the runtimes have called the same `Action`. After receiving the reply, each runtime proceeds and injects the fault.

(a)   (b)

Fig. 3. RemoteAction (left) and Notification (right) operations

RemoteAction

The `RemoteAction`, shown in Figure 3a, is used by the orchestrator to perform remote procedure calls in the replicas's runtime, and it can be used to manipulate the state of the runtime, or to retrieve some portion of state from the replica.

Notification

The notification mechanism, shown in Figure 3b, provides an asynchronous message passing interface from a runtime to the orchestrator. Its main purpose is to avoid the overhead associated with synchronous operations, i.e. an `Action`, and is used to inform the orchestrator of the progress of the algorithm.

3.3 Runtime

The runtime's main responsibility is to inject faults accordingly to the indications of the orchestrator. The actual fault injection is achieved through the use of Aspect-Oriented Programming (AOP) [27]. We use aspects as a way to seamlessly introduce fault injection points, as well as all the necessary networking infrastructure needed to interact with the orchestrator. We provide more details in Section 4.

3.4 Deployment Service

The deployment service was built to allow remote bootstrap and closure of applications. While it is a general purpose deployment service, its main purpose is to launch replicas and clients to construct the initial view of the system. It should be noted that this does not represent an obstacle for any possible built-in reconfiguration mechanisms, e.g., adding or removing replicas, within the BFT protocol. All the necessary infrastructure to use Hermes is encapsulated inside the runtime, that in turn, is weaved into the replica's (and client) code. Thus, independently of how a replica is deployed, the runtime will perform all the necessary logistics.

4 Implementation

We have implemented the orchestrator in JAVA, while the runtime has implementations in both JAVA and C++. To avoid the complexity/overhead introduced by JAVA existing serialization mechanisms, we custom built a binary protocol that uses little endian encoding without padding. This also allowed us to easily extend Hermes runtime to C++, and in the future will allow to extend to other programming languages, such as python. The implementations are freely available as open-source projects (under an Apache license version 2) at:

- https://github.com/rolandomar/hermes (JAVA runtime and orchestration)
- https://github.com/rolandomar/hermesCPP (C++ runtime)

Bootstrap Process

It is assumed that each of the hosting nodes has the deployment service running. The orchestrator upon start-up uses the deployment service to create and bootstrap the target protocol nodes, which in this paper are BFT-SMaRt [2] replicas and clients. These nodes were previously weaved, with our runtime and faults, through the use of aspects (shown in Listings 1.3 and 1.4).

After its creation by the deployment service, the runtime within each protocol node bootstraps and connects back to the orchestrator. In turn, the orchestrator creates a barrier for synchronizing the start of all the nodes.

4.1 Orchestrator

An overview of the API provided by the orchestrator is shown in the appendix http://www.contrib.andrew.cmu.edu/~martinsr/middleware13/apA.eps. The faultInjection() and simultaneousFaultInjection() are the two most important operations offered by the orchestrator. They allow for a single and simultaneous fault injection, respectively. In order to provide further control over the activation of the faults, on the remote runtimes, we use the Action primitive.

```
1  public ActionResult onAction(
       OrchestrationNodeServerClient client, Action action)
2  switch (action.getSerialID()) {
3   case CheckFaultInjectionAction.SERIAL_ID: {
4   CheckFaultInjectionAction cfa =
       (CheckFaultInjectionAction) action;
5    String faultID = cfa.getFaultID();
6    /* omitted code */
7    return new CheckFaultInjectionActionResult(
       (cfa.getFaultContext().getRun() < 500));
8   }
9   /* omitted code */
10 }
```

Listing 1.1. Orchestration code for fine control over fault injection

When a runtime reaches a fault, it then uses the `Action` primitive to check if it should proceed with the injection. For example, we use it to only allow the faults to become active after the 500th invocation has taken place (shown in Listing 1.1). For now this value is fixed but can be easily ported as a parameter.

Listing 1.2 shows the code associated with *Attack 1* presented in our evaluation (Section 5). The attack simulates a simultaneous crash of a set of malicious nodes. It starts with the creation of a `CrashFault` associated with the specific injection point, given by `faultID`. In line 5, the orchestrator generates a simultaneous fault, in this case a crash fault. At this point, the orchestrator sends the fault information to the malicious nodes. The test run starts with the creation and bootstrap of a client (line 6-8), identified by `"1001"`, that with perform 1000 invocations, with each invocation incrementing the service counter by 1.

```
1  public void attack1(String[] malicious) {
2    String faultID =
        "2B4FA20ED54E4DA9B6B2A917D1FA723F";
3    HermesFault fault = new CrashFault(faultID);
4    try {
5    HermesFuture<Boolean> future =
        simultaneousFaultInjection(malicious, fault);
6    String command = HermesConfig.
        getClientCommandLaunch();
7    String[] args =
        new String[]command, "1001", "1", "1000";
8    launchHermesClient(command, args, 5000);
9    boolean ret = future.get(
        TIMEOUT, TimeUnit.MILLISECONDS);
10   if(!ret){
11     /* handle error */
12   }
13   } catch (Exception ex) {
14     /* handle error */
15   }
16 }
```

Listing 1.2. Orchestrator-side code for Attack 1

4.2   Runtime Code-Weaving

One of our goals was to make our approach as little intrusive as possible. For that purpose, and as previously explained we used AOP, through the use of AspectJ [3], for the JAVA runtime, and AspectC++ [4] for the C++ runtime. We use two distinct aspects, shown in Listings 1.3 and 1.4.

Runtime Startup Aspect

To seamlessly bootstrap Hermes's runtime into the replica's code, we use aspect **HermesStartupAspect** depicted in Listing 1.3. The aspect is executed before the actual execution of the **main()** procedure. It starts by retrieving the runtime identifier from the list of the application arguments (line 5-6). This identifier is then used to instantiate the singleton's instance (line 7-10). The bootstrap of the runtime is followed by the call to the actual application's **main()** (line 11).

```
1  @Aspect
2  public class HermesStartupAspect {
3   @Around("execution (* bftsmart.demo.counter.
       CounterServer.main*(..))")
4   public void advice(ProceedingJoinPoint jp)
        throws Throwable
5   String[] args = (String[]) jp.getArgs()[0];
6   String id = args[0];
7   HermesRuntime.getInstance().setID(id);
8   try {
9     HermesRuntime.getInstance().open();
10  } catch (Exception e) { /* handle error */}
11  jp.proceed();
12  }
```

Listing 1.3. Runtime bootstrap aspect for replicas and client

ServersCommunication Aspect

We needed to access the underlying communication infrastructure to inject low-level faults, such as payload corruption. For that purpose, we created the aspect shown in Listing 1.4. For the sake of simplicity and space we only shown the code associated with the payload corruption attack.

The initial portion of the aspect, lines 7-13, checks if the fault is active, and if so retrieves the information about the Paxos protocol, namely, the execution identifier and packet type, e.g., weak and strong packet types. If this information could not be retrieved, i.e., the message is not related to core Paxos protocol, but belongs to surrounding infrastructure such as state transfer, we bypass the fault injection and execute the target code (line 11). In line 14, we update the execution identifier within the fault's context. This information is later sent to the orchestrator in the fault validation, that is executed in line 19.

Because this is a context-dependent fault, the execution of the fault only triggers the verification of the fault's validity. The actual injection is performed in the **sendBytesFailureInjected()** procedure. This procedure is a duplicate of the original code with the added fault injection mechanisms. It was not possible to weave code around this procedure, because it was necessary to access the underlying infrastructure, i.e., in the packet formation we needed to corrupt payload but leave the header intact.

```
1  @Aspect
2  public class ServerConnectionAspect {
3   static public String faultID =
        "5B4FA20ED54E4DA9B6B2A917D1FA724F";
4   @Around("execution (* bftsmart.communication.
        server.ServersCommunicationLayer.send*(..))")
5  public void advice(ProceedingJoinPoint jp)
        throws Throwable {
6   HermesFault fault = HermesRuntime.getInstance().
        getFaultManager().getFault(faultID);
7   if (fault != null && fault.isEnabled()) {
8    byte[] msgData = (byte[]) jp.getArgs()[0];
9    PaxosInfo info = deserialize(msgData);
10   if (info == null) {
11    jp.proceed();
12    return;
13   }
14   fault.updateCtx("RUN", info.getRun());
15   try {
16    switch (fault.getSerialID()) {
17     case BFTForgePayloadFault.SERIAL_ID: {
18      BFTForgePayloadFault faultImpl =
          (BFTForgePayloadFault) fault;
19      faultImpl.execute();
20      int type = faultImpl.getType();
21      Integer attack =
          checkAttack(type,paxosInfo);
22      ServerConnection obj = (ServerConnection)
          jp.getTarget();
23      boolean useMac = (boolean) jp.getArgs()[1];
24      obj.sendBytesFailureInjected(
          attack,msgData,useMac);
25      return;
26     }
27     /* other faults omitted */
28    }
29   } catch (Exception ex) {
30     /* handle error case */}
31   }
32   jp.proceed();
33  }
34 }
```

Listing 1.4. ServerConnection aspect

5   Evaluation

Hardware Setup

We used a NUMA (Non-Uniform Memory Access) workstation with dual hexa-cores, for a total of 12 physical cores and 24 logical threads, with 32GB of RAM and 512GB of RAID-0 storage, comprising 2 SSDs with 256GB each.

For simulating a distributed environment we created 11 virtual machines (VMs), using QEMU/KVM, 10 of which were dedicated to run BFT replicas and 1 for the client. Each VM was allocated with 2GB of RAM and 2 virtual CPUs. The orchestrator ran on the host operating system. Both host the guests used Ubuntu 12.10 LTS as their operating system. Because the virtualized environment already introduces delay and jitter in the network stack (around 1ms latency while measuring with ICMP pings), we only constrained the total amount of bandwidth available (both in-bounding and out-bounding) in each VM to 100Mbit/s, and thus effectively creating a 100Mbit/s network. For the purpose, we used the *TC* command to manipulate the underlying network stacks, with the following commands:

```
tc qdisc add dev eth0 handle ffff: ingress
tc filter add dev eth0 parent ffff: protocol ip prio 50 /
    u32 match ip src 0.0.0.0/0 police rate 100mbit /
    burst 100mbit drop flowid :1
```

5.1   Experiments

Experimental Setup

In order to assess the resiliency of BFT-SMaRt, we performed 1000 invocations per run and injected the faults midpoint, i.e., in the 500th invocation. For such purpose, we devised the following attacks:

- **Attack 1** - *Simultaneous crash*: simultaneously crash all malicious nodes.
- **Attack 2** - *Payload forged with MAX_INT*: all malicious nodes forge their payload size, setting it to MAX_INT (2,147,483,647) bytes.
- **Attack 3** - *Delay Prepare messages below detection timeout*: all malicious nodes delay propose messages to 90% of the timeout used, e.g., for a timeout of 3s the resulting delay would be of 2.7s.
- **Attack 4** - *Delay Prepare messages above detection timeout*: all malicious nodes delay propose messages by 5 times the value of the timeout, e.g., with a timeout of 3s then the delay would be 15s.

Because of space constrains, we only show the results from attacks 1 to 4. The remaining (5 to 9) are available for consultation in the appendix at http://www.contrib.andrew.cmu.edu/~martinsr/middleware13/apA.eps.

For each attack, we tested it against 12 configurations, shown in Table 1, with *1f*, *2f* and *3f* standing for 1, 2 and 3 faults injected, respectively. *N* is the total number of replicas needed to enforce the $3f + 1$ requirement, while *M* is the set of identifiers for the malicious nodes used in a particular configuration. For example, $M = \{0\}$ stands for the set of malicious nodes only containing node "0", whereas $M = \{x, y\}$ represents a set with two randomly chosen identifiers.

Table 1. Configurations used in the attacks evaluation

Configurations					
1f, $|N| = 4$		2f, $|N| = 7$		3f, $|N| = 10$	
#	M	#	M	#	M
0	$\{0\}$	2	$\{0\}$	6	$\{0\}$
1	$\{x\}$	3	$\{x\}$	7	$\{x\}$
		4	$\{0, 1\}$	8	$\{0, 1\}$
		5	$\{x, y\}$	9	$\{x, y\}$
				10	$\{0, 1, 2\}$
				11	$\{x, y, z\}$

For each of these configurations we ran the attack 16 times, and computed the average and the 95% confidence intervals. Each run (a single test) is comprised of 1000 invocations. The maximum amount of time allowed for each run was 5 minutes. After this time, we considered that the run had failed, even if it was not completely stalled or aborted, but rather progressing very slowly.

In our evaluation we collected the following data:

Failed Runs (FR) - the number of failed runs, including stalled or aborted runs with a running time higher then 300s.

Fault-free Latency (LA) - the invocation latency before the fault was injected (in milliseconds).

Faulty Latency (LB) - the invocation latency after the fault was injected (in milliseconds).

Total Duration (D) - the total duration of the run. If the run timed out then the total duration is 300s (in seconds).

Recovery Time (R) - the invocation latency for the 500th and 501st invocations (in seconds).

Total Faulty Invocations (FI) - the number of successful invocations performed after the fault was injected. We only considered the faulty invocations from runs that produced at least 5 invocations after the 500th invocation (otherwise we considered them stalled without recovery).

The application that we chose to run was the `bftsmart.demo.counter`, a simple counter built on top of the BFT-SMaRt protocol. On each invocation we increment the counter by 1. After each successful invocation, the client sends a notification to the orchestrator to report the invocation number and latency. When the orchestrator receives the 1000th invocation from the client, it ends the test and calculates the duration of that run.

The experiments were run twice. We first performed the experiments using the default values and without any modification to the source code, whereas in the second time we tuned the timeout values and made modifications to the source code, of which we provide a detailed discussion on Section 5.3. The relevant parameters used in this work are shown in Table 2.

Table 2. Parameters considered in the evaluation

Parameters		
Parameter Name	Default (ms)	Tuned (ms)
SHORT_TIMEOUT	3000	2000
TOTAL_ORDER_TIMEOUT	10000	3000
CONNECTION_TIMEOUT	10000	3000
INVOCATION_TIMEOUT	40000	60000

For certain cases the SHORT_TIMEOUT is used to quickly trigger a reconfiguration, such as a voluntary exit from a group. The TOTAL_ORDER_TIMEOUT is the main timeout used in the implementation and is used to detect when a request was not processed and subsequently trigger the leader-change protocol. The CONNECTION_TIMEOUT controls the timeout associated with the establishment of a new connection to a replica. The last parameter, INVOCATION_TIMEOUT, is used by the client, more specifically through the ServiceProxy, to control the timeout associated with each invocation.

5.2 Results

In this section we will start to discuss the performance using the default parameters and without any modifications to the source code (left sub-table on the results tables 3 to 6). Later, using the knowledge gained throughout the first round of our evaluation, we show how it helped us to track the underlying issues and partially overcome them by tuning some of the system parameters (Table 2) and by applying a modification to the source code (right sub-table).

Generically, we can see throughout the results that the increase in the number of nodes in the system, from 4 to 10 nodes (*1f* to *3f*) results in a linear increase on the fault-free invocation latency, from 16ms to 20ms (see column **LA** in tables 3 to 6). In some cases, the faulty invocation latency drops after a fault has occurred. Because the number of nodes decreases, the latency (and overhead) associated with the protocol also decreases, except in attacks 3 and 4. The recovery time is higher when the leaders are attacked, going upwards to 30s in attack 3. We provide a discussion on the reasons beyond this high recovery time in Section 5.3.

Attack 1

Our goal with attack 1 was to evaluate the impact of simultaneously crashing multiple nodes in the system (for *2f* and *3f* configurations). The results from the single fault scenario (*1f* configurations) are presented to provide a baseline comparison. The results from our evaluation of attack 1 are shown in Table 3. In our initial evaluation, using the default values and implementation, we encountered some issues with configurations 4, 8 and 10. These issues seemed related with the change-leader protocol.

After a manual inspection of logs, we found that the problem was a composition of several issues. First, we found that 40s invocation timeout (from within the client's `ServiceProxy`) was too short, and it should be at least 60s. The stalls that we checked in the results were a direct result from this. When this timeout is triggered, the client aborts its execution and the run ends. This also hid the true values of the recovery time, that can reach roughly 60s (which we concluded after some additional experimentation with larger timeouts).

Overall, we found that the default timeout values (associated with the replicas) were too high for a LAN (Ethernet based network). But that did not account for the low performance that we detected in the protocol after the injections of the faults. After an inspection to the source code, we found a subtle bug in the timeout management that leads to problems in the change-leader protocol. We provide a better explanation to this problem later in Section 5.3.

Table 3. *Attack 1* with the default (left) and the tuned (right) configurations

	Attack 1 (Crash Fault)										
	Default						*Tuned*					
C	FR (%)	LB (ms)	LA (ms)	D (s)	R (s)	FI (#)	FR (%)	LB (ms)	LA (ms)	D (s)	R (s)	FI (#)
0	0	16±2	9±0	37±0	20±0	499±0	0	16±2	9±0	23±0	6±0	499±0
1	0	16±2	9±0	19±3	2±3	499±0	0	16±2	8±0	18±1	1±1	499±0
2	0	18±1	10±0	38±0	20±0	499±0	0	18±1	10±0	24±0	6±0	499±0
3	0	17±1	10±0	22±3	3±3	499±0	0	17±1	10±0	18±0	0±0	499±0
4	100	18±1	N/A	300±0	N/A	N/A	0	18±1	11±0	30±0	11±0	499±0
5	6	17±1	11±0	38±33	2±3	499±0	0	17±1	11±0	21±1	2±1	499±0
6	0	20±0	12±0	41±0	20±0	499±0	0	20±0	12±0	27±0	6±0	499±0
7	0	20±0	12±0	21±2	1±2	499±0	0	20±0	12±0	20±0	0±0	499±0
8	100	20±0	N/A	300±0	N/A	N/A	0	20±0	12±0	32±0	12±0	499±0
9	0	20±0	12±0	26±4	6±4	499±0	0	20±0	12±0	21±1	0±0	499±0
10	100	20±0	N/A	300±0	N/A	N/A	0	20±0	14±1	36±0	14±0	499±0
11	13	20±0	13±0	55±45	0±0	499±0	0	20±0	13±0	22±1	1±1	499±0

Attack 2

We designed attack 2 for assessing the impact of overflowing in the protocol. This was achieved by modifying the length field on the `PaxosMessage` packet. The results from our evaluation are show in Table 4.

The presence of failures indicates that the protocol is susceptible to the overflow attack (also to underflow and payload corruption, c.f. in appendix under attacks 6 and 7). Furthermore, the failure pattern from attack 2 closely resembles the pattern of attack 1, which indicates that the underlying causes should be the same or similar.

Using this insight, we were able to successfully track down the root of this behavior within the source code. We found that the crash (caused by the overflow or underflow) of the deliver thread in the low-level communication infrastructure is omitted from the overall leader module management. The same applies when

Table 4. *Attack 2* with the default (left) and the tuned (right) configurations

	Attack 2 (Value/Corruption Fault)										
	Default						Tuned				
C	FR (%)	LB (ms)	LA (ms)	D (s)	R (s)	FI (#)	FR (%)	LB (ms)	LA (ms)	D (s)	R (s)	FI (#)
0	0	16±2	8±0	36±0	20±0	499±0	0	16±2	8±0	23±0	6±0	499±0
1	0	16±2	8±0	21±4	5±4	499±0	0	16±2	8±0	17±0	0±0	499±0
2	0	18±1	10±0	38±0	20±0	499±0	0	17±1	10±0	24±0	6±0	499±0
3	0	17±1	10±0	23±4	5±4	499±0	0	17±1	10±0	18±0	0±0	499±0
4	100	18±1	N/A	300±0	N/A	N/A	0	18±1	11±0	27±0	9±0	499±0
5	13	17±1	11±0	63±43	11±5	499±0	0	17±1	11±0	20±1	1±1	499±0
6	0	20±0	13±0	40±0	20±0	499±0	0	20±0	13±0	26±0	6±0	499±0
7	0	20±0	13±0	22±2	1±2	499±0	0	20±0	13+0	21+0	0+0	499±0
8	100	20±0	N/A	300±0	N/A	N/A	0	20±0	13±0	30±0	9±0	499±0
9	6	20±0	14±0	42±32	4±4	499±0	6	20±0	13±0	39±32	1±1	499±0
10	100	20±0	N/A	300±0	N/A	N/A	0	20±0	15±0	34±0	12±0	499±0
11	0	20±0	15±0	31±4	10±4	499±0	0	20±0	15±0	24±1	2±1	499±0

we corrupt the payload of messages. The deliver thread detects the mismatch between the payload and the signature but silently ignores it. The protocol is able to recover because the timeout associated with the request is triggered forcing the leader-change sub-protocol to change the leader. It is important to note that BFT-SMaRt is implemented using the principle of decoupling the total ordering of requests from the actual consensus primitive [28]. The client sends its requests to every replica, not only the leader. This is done to prevent a malicious leader to stall the protocol. When a replica (non-leader) detects that the leader did not propose the request, it forwards the request to the current leader and activates a new timeout. If this fails, then a new regency is activated through the leader-change sub-protocol. Later in Section 5.3, we discuss the impact of this decision on the overall protocol performance.

Possibly it would be feasible to use information from the low-level communication layer to provide further knowledge to the leader module in order to speedup the recovery process when malicious nodes are in the role of the leader. We discuss a possible implementation of this approach later in Section 5.3.

Attack 3 and 4

The use of a leader in BFT protocols creates a potential attack point. This subject was previously explored by Prime [21], which shows the impact of the presence of a malicious leader. We devised attacks 3 and 4 for assessing the resilience of BFT-SMaRt to this kind of attack.

In certain cases, a reconfiguration can be triggered with a short timeout, that is about one third of the regular timeout (3s in the default configuration and 2s in our tuned configuration). To avoid detection, we delay conservatively the sending of prepare messages by 90% of the value of this timeout (2.7s for the default configuration and 1.8s for the tuned configuration). The results from attack 3 (Table 5) show that delay of the prepare messages by leader causes a increase of invocation latency to around 2.7s, as expected, causing the runs to fail as they take more than 300s to finish.

Alternatively, in attack 4 (Table 6) we used 5 times the value of the short timeout, resulting in a timeout of 15s, for the default configuration, and 10s for the tuned version. This clearly triggers the change-leader sub-protocol but eventually the protocol itself stalls when about 15 faulty invocations have been processed. Again, the failure pattern also shows some correlation with the failure pattern of attack 1.

Table 5. *Attack 3* with the default configuration (left) and the tuned version (right)

	Attack 3 (Timing Fault, Delay Below Timeout)										
	Default						Tuned				
C	FR (%)	LB (ms)	LA (ms)	D (s)	R (s)	FI (#)	FR (%)	LB (ms)	LA (ms)	D (s)	R (s)	FI (#)
0	100	16±2	2723±0	300±0	5±0	104±0	100	16±2	1822±0	300±0	3±0	157±0
1	13	16±2	86±10	51±46	0±0	449±63	19	16±2	130±10	69±54	0±0	434±65
2	100	18±1	2729±0	300±0	5±0	104±0	100	18±1	1828±0	300±0	3±0	156±0
3	13	17±1	88±10	53±45	0±0	449±64	6	17±1	46±5	35±33	0±0	477±40
4	100	18±1	2730±0	300±0	5±0	104±0	100	18±1	1828±0	300±0	3±0	156±0
5	25	17±1	186±16	88±59	1±1	400±83	38	17±1	296±16	123±66	1±0	370±81
6	100	20±0	2737±0	300±0	5±0	103±0	100	20±0	1835±0	300±0	3±0	154±0
7	6	20±0	49±7	38±33	0±0	474±46	13	20±0	89±8	55±45	0±0	456±55
8	100	20±0	2736±0	300±0	5±0	103±0	100	20±0	1835±0	300±0	3±0	154±0
9	19	20±0	136±13	73±53	1±1	424±75	19	20±0	134±10	72±53	0±0	434±65
10	100	20±0	2737±0	300±0	5±0	103±0	100	20±0	1836±0	300±0	3±0	154±0
11	38	20±0	312±22	126±66	2±1	350±93	50	20±0	444±21	160±68	1±0	327±84

Table 6. *Attack 4* with the default configuration (left) and the tuned version (right)

	Attack 4 (Timing Fault, Delay Above Timeout)										
	Default						Tuned				
C	FR (%)	LB (ms)	LA (ms)	D (s)	R (s)	FI (#)	FR (%)	LB (ms)	LA (ms)	D (s)	R (s)	FI (#)
0	56	16±2	915±117	252±35	30±0	228±116	0	16±2	8±0	22±0	6±0	499±0
1	13	16±2	102±28	66±46	9±6	438±77	0	16±2	8±0	17±1	0±0	499±0
2	19	17±1	353±55	187±38	30±0	408±91	0	17±1	10±0	24±0	6±0	499±0
3	0	17±1	53±18	45±32	5±5	499±0	0	17±1	10±0	19±1	1±1	499±0
4	100	18±1	16058±574	300±0	30±0	15±1	0	17±1	11±0	30±0	12±0	499±0
5	0	17±1	89±24	64±42	7±6	499±0	0	17±1	10±0	20±1	2±1	499±0
6	38	20±0	357±66	202±39	30±0	336±116	0	20±0	12±0	26±0	6±0	499±0
7	6	20±0	34±15	38±33	1±3	468±58	0	20±0	12±0	21±1	1±1	499±0
8	100	20±0	16196±640	300±0	30±0	13±2	0	20±0	13±0	32±0	12±0	499±0
9	19	20±0	101±31	73±53	5±5	408±92	0	20±0	13±0	23±1	2±1	499±0
10	100	20±0	15968±521	300±0	30±0	14±2	0	20±0	27±5	40±0	12±0	499±0
11	25	20±0	154±38	91±59	7±6	379±101	0	20±0	16±0	25±3	3±2	499±0

5.3   Lessons Learned

Although we are still in the process of analyzing all the data and logs that we have collected, we found some interesting issues within BFT-SMaRt implementation. Although the BFT-SMaRt is a leader-based BFT protocol we were surprised to verify the impact of simple crash faults on the system. While the implementation was able to sustain flawlessly single crash faults or even multiple random crash faults, it was vulnerable, performance wise, to the simultaneous injection of crash faults within the first elements of the nodes, i.e., the initial leaders.

1) After analyzing the code, we detected a misconfiguration of the client, which normally has a default 40s request timeout. When this timeout is triggered within the client, it aborts the execution of the run. This was the reason behind the stalls we detected while using the default timeout values and original implementation.

2) Because BFT-SMaRt is leader-based, faults in the leader have a high impact on the overall performance (and recovery) of the protocol. After increasing this timeout we were able to measure a recovery time around 60s. The high recovery time that we measured is only partially explained by the high timeout values. An analysis of the source code revealed that the protocol, in the presence of a request timeout, first tries to forward pending requests to the current leader. This was done to accommodate the possibility that the current leader did not propose the request because it might have been dropped by the underlying network infrastructure. However, in the presence of a single malicious leader, this in fact doubles the recovery time. This is because the request is first forwarded to the leader, and the change-leader sub-protocol only runs after this operation has timed out. On top of this, the leader-change protocol goes sequentially through the processes list to find the next leader (from the lowest to the highest identifier). Because we intentionally injected simultaneous faults in the nodes with the lowest identifiers (that are the first nodes to be elected as leaders), this resulted in the protocol having to go through all the malicious nodes. Furthermore, they immediately assume the roles of leaders, introducing further delays. To minimize this situation, we lowered the timeout values (shown in Table 2).

3) However, this alone did not fully explain the extensive recovery times. A closer inspection of the source code reveled a subtle implementation artifact. The timer used for failure detection (`RequestsTimer`) for all the pending requests present in the system gets its timeout value doubled each time the change-leader protocol is triggered (for example, when receiving a STOP and STOP_DATA messages from other nodes), but it is never reduced, even in the presence of more favorable system conditions, such as the absence of failures or timeouts. Given this, we introduced a modification to the original source code that consisted on only doubling the timeout within the same regency (i.e., the same leader) on the current view, otherwise the value is reset to the default value. Using our tuned parameters and correction to the source code (right sub-table on the results tables) we were able to almost avoid any failed runs, except in attack 3. Sporadically we got a failed run while using attack 2. We are in the process of analyzing the logs to determine the underlying issues associated with those failed runs.

4) Attack 3 was designed in light to previous work on Prime [21], and was designed to degrade overall performance of the system by delaying the sending of propose messages. The attack was designed so that the leader was not suspected by the other nodes, by limiting the amount of delay just below to the detection timeout value. By lowering the timeout value we were able to minimize the impact of this type of attack, although it is evident that a more proactive and structural approach has to be taken to solve this issue when using leader-based BFT protocols. While Prime provides a way to minimize this situation, it still does not provide a complete solution, because of the limitations derived from the use of Diffserv [29], because a flooding attack would compromise the measurements used to adapt the timeouts. We tried to perform a full evaluation of Prime but we discover after the initial tests that the protocol was not completely implemented. Therefore, we were unable to verify their results. To corroborate our findings, we can see in attack 4 that if a sufficiently small timeout is chosen then the attack is contained, with no apparent loss in performance (except for the recovery time associated with the election of the new leaders).

5) For Attack 2 we were able to manually verify the code and found a missing verification in the creation of the packet by the receiving thread (`ReceiverThread` in the `ServerConnection` class). Because it does not verify the size of the payload, it allows the attacker to crash the thread either with overflow or underflow attacks. While JAVA provides a managed memory system, some vulnerabilities have been found in the past that explore such cases.

6) Taking the knowledge gathered throughout our evaluation we implemented a second modification to the original protocol. As stated in the discussion of Attack 2, we make use of the low-level network events such as unexpected network errors (e.g., closing of TCP connections) or packet malformation (such as mismatched signatures) to trigger the change-leader sub-protocol. The results from this second modification are shown in the appendix, under section "Second Round of Corrections". We were able to cut roughly in half the recovery time from our first implementation modification (and timeout tuning). From the original implementation and timeout values we were able to provide up to a 10 fold improvement. Nevertheless, it should be noted that these modifications come at a price. Because we are assuming a more synchronous network layer and assuming that any type of fault we get from the network is malicious, we could be inducing false suspicion on nodes leading to unnecessary leader changes. However, this would only affect performance but not correctness.

BFT Limitations and Future Directions

It seems clear that leader-based BFT protocols have their weakest point in the leader and change-leader sub-protocol. The timeout settings also play an important role in the overall performance.

For situations without the presence of malicious node, the introduction of adaptive timeouts like in Adaptare-FD [30], could improve seamlessly the overall performance. However to efficiently deal with the presence of malicious nodes, current approaches [21] are still not able to deliver degradation-free performance. While making the assumption that the network is totally asynchronous makes a strong case from a standpoint of correctness and safety, we feel that in order to bridge theory and practice, stronger, yet realistic, assumptions must be made about underlying network infrastructure. The use of software-defined networking, for instance by OpenFlow [31], could allows us to improve on the current state-of-the-art, such as avoiding the issues related with flooding attacks [1].

6 Conclusions and Future Work

In this paper we presented a novel fault-injecting framework that enables the assessment of BFT implementations. Furthermore, we demonstrate the importance of providing support for non-independent faults. Using our approach we were able to detect 2 implementation bugs. The first, at the low communication level, allowed overflow and underflow attacks caused by a missing size verification on packet reception, whereas the second bug was related to a high level implementation artifact derived from the ever-increasing timeout values within the leader-change sub-protocol, that in certain cases would effectively stall the protocol for more than 60s in the presence of non-independent faults. Lastly, we proposed a second set of modifications to the source code, where we avoid forwarding messages to a possibly malicious leader prior to a change in regency and enhance it by using low-level networking exceptions/events, such as signature mismatch, to trigger a leader change when in the suspicion of the presence of a malicious leader.

Using our tuned parameters and source code modifications we were able to provide up to a 10 fold improvement over the original implementation and default parameters.

6.1 Future Work

We expect to enhance Hermes by providing the necessary infrastructure to support proof forging, by coordinating and distributing all the necessary keys across the malicious nodes. Furthermore, we want to expand the work accomplished in this paper, by introducing a visualization tool that continuously monitors and traces all the nodes present in the protocol with the goal of providing the initial support for debugging.

Acknowledgments. We thank Alysson Bessani and the conference reviewers for their feedback. This research was sponsored in part by the project CMUP-T/RNQ/0015/2009 (TRONE - Trustworthy and Resilient Operations in a Network Environment), and by Intel via the Intel Science and Technology Center for Cloud Computing (ISTC-CC).

References

1. Clement, A., Wong, E., Alvisi, L., Dahlin, M., Marchetti, M.: Making Byzantine Fault Tolerant Systems Tolerate Byzantine faults. In: Proceedings of the 6th USENIX Symposium on Networked Systems Design and Implementation, NSDI 2009, Berkeley, CA, USA, pp. 153–168. USENIX Association (2009)
2. BFT-SMaRt: High-Performance Byzantine Fault-tolerant State Machine Replication, http://code.google.com/p/bft-smart/ (accessed November 4, 2013)
3. Kiczales, G., Hilsdale, E.: Aspect-Oriented Programming. In: ACM SIGSOFT Software Engineering Notes, vol. 26, p. 313. ACM (2001)
4. Spinczyk, O., Gal, A., Schröder-Preikschat, W.: AspectC++: an Aspect-Oriented Extension to the C++ Programming Language. In: Proceedings of the 40th International Conference on Tools Pacific: Objects for Internet, Mobile and Embedded Applications, pp. 53–60. Australian Computer Society, Inc. (2002)
5. Chandra, R., Levefer, R.M., Cukier, M., Sanders, W.H.: Loki: A State-Driven Fault Injector for Distributed Systems. In: International Conference on Dependable Systems and Networks, pp. 237–242 (June 2000)
6. DBench Project Final Report (May 2004)
7. Han, S., Rosenberg, H.A., Shin, K.G.: Doctor: An integrated software fault injection environment. In: International Computer Performance and Dependability Symposium, pp. 204–213 (April 1995)
8. Alvarez, G.A., Cristian, F.: Centralized Failure Injection for Distributed, Fault-Tolerant Protocol Testing. In: International Conference on Distributed Computing Systems, pp. 78–85 (May 1997)
9. Dawson, S., Jahanian, F., Mitton, T., Tung, T.-L.: Testing of Fault-Tolerant and Real-Time Distributed Systems via Protocol Fault Injection. In: Symposium on Fault Tolerant Computing, pp. 404–414 (June 1996)
10. Looker, N., Xu, J.: Assessing the Dependability of OGSA Middleware by Fault Injection. In: Proceedings of the 22nd IEEE International Symposium on Reliable Distributed Systems, SRDS 2003, pp. 293–302 (October 2003)
11. Marsden, E., Fabre, J.-C.: Failure Analysis of an ORB in Presence of Faults. Technical report (October 2001)
12. Kanawati, G.A., Kanawati, N.A., Abraham, J.A.: FERRARI: A Flexible Software-Based Fault and Error Injection System. IEEE Transactions on Computers 44(2), 248–260 (1995)
13. Tsai, T.K., Iyer, R.K.: Measuring Fault Tolerance with the FTAPE Fault Injection Tool. In: Beilner, H., Bause, F. (eds.) MMB 1995 and TOOLS 1995. LNCS, vol. 977, pp. 26–40. Springer, Heidelberg (1995)
14. Carreira, J., Madeira, H., Silva, J.G.: Xception: Software Fault Injection and Monitoring in Processor Functional Units. In: Proceedings of the 5th Annual IEEE International Working Conference on Dependable Computing for Critical Applications, DCCA 1995, pp. 135–149 (1995)
15. DeVale, J., Koopman, P., Guttendorf, D.: The Ballista Software Robustness Testing Service. In: Proceedings of Testing Computer Software (1999)
16. Hsueh, M.-C., Tsai, T.K., Iyer, R.K.: Fault Injection Techniques and Tools. Computer 30(4), 75–82 (1997)
17. Castro, M., Liskov, B.: Practical Byzantine Fault Tolerance and Proactive Recovery. ACM Transactions on Computer Systems 20(4), 398–461 (2002)
18. Abd-El-Malek, M., Ganger, G.R., Goodson, G.R., Reiter, M.K., Wylie, J.J.: Fault-scalable Byzantine Fault-Tolerant Services. SIGOPS Operating Systems Review 39(5), 59–74 (2005)

19. Kotla, R., Alvisi, L., Dahlin, M., Clement, A., Wong, E.: Zyzzyva: Speculative byzantine fault folerance. In: Proceedings of 21st ACM SIGOPS Symposium on Operating Systems Principles, SOSP 2007, pp. 45–58. ACM, New York (2007)
20. Cowling, J., Myers, D., Liskov, B., Rodrigues, R., Shrira, L.: HQ Replication: A Hybrid Quorum Protocol for Byzantine Fault Tolerance. In: Proceedings of the 7th Symposium on Operating Systems Design and Implementation, SOSDI 2006, pp. 177–190. USENIX Association (2006)
21. Amir, U., Coan, B., Kirsch, J., Lane, J.: Prime: Byzantine Replication under Attack. IEEE Transactions on Dependable and Secure Computing 8(4), 564–577 (2011)
22. Amir, Y., Danilov, C., Dolev, D., Kirsch, J., Lane, J., Nita-Rotaru, C., Olsen, J., Zage, D.: Steward: Scaling Byzantine Fault-Tolerant Replication to Wide Area Networks. IEEE Transactions on Dependable and Secure Computing 7(1), 80–93 (2010)
23. Yin, J., Martin, J.-P., Venkataramani, A., Alvisi, L., Dahlin, M.: Separating Agreement From Execution for Byzantine Fault Tolerant Services. ACM SIGOPS Operating Systems Review 37(5), 253–267 (2003)
24. Martin, J.-P., Alvisi, L.: Fast byzantine consensus. IEEE Transactions on Dependable and Secure Computing 3(3), 202–215 (2006)
25. Amir, Y., Coan, B., Kirsch, J., Lane, J.: Customizable Fault Tolerance forWide-Area Replication. In: Proceedings of the 26th IEEE International Symposium on Reliable Distributed Systems, SRDS 2007, pp. 65–82. IEEE (2007)
26. Li, J., Mazieres, D.: Beyond One-Third Faulty Replicas in Byzantine Fault Tolerant Systems. In: Proceedings of the 4th USENIX Symposium on Networked Systems Design and Implementation, NSDI 2007 (2007)
27. Kiczales, G., Lamping, J., Mendhekar, A., Maeda, C., Lopes, C.V., Loingtier, J.-M., Irwin, J.: Aspect-oriented programming. In: Akşit, M., Matsuoka, S. (eds.) ECOOP 1997. LNCS, vol. 1241, pp. 220–242. Springer, Heidelberg (1997)
28. Sousa, J., Bessani, A.: From Byzantine Consensus to BFT State Machine Replication: A Latency-Optimal Transformation. In: Proceedings of the 9th European Dependable Computing Conference, EDCC 2012, pp. 37–48. IEEE Computer Society, Washington, DC (2012)
29. IETF. An Architecture for Differentiated Services, http://www.ietf.org/rfc/rfc2475.txt (accessed October 17, 2011)
30. Dixit, M., Casimiro, A., Lollini, P., Bondavalli, A., Verissimo, P.: Adaptare: Supporting Automatic and Dependable Adaptation in Dynamic Environments. ACM Transactions on Autonomous and Adaptive Systems (TAAS) 7(2), 18 (2012)
31. McKeown, N., Anderson, T., Balakrishnan, H., Parulkar, G., Peterson, L., Rexford, J., Shenker, S., Turner, J.: OpenFlow: Enabling Innovation in Campus Networks. ACM SIGCOMM Computer Communication Review 38(2), 69–74 (2008)

SplayNet: Distributed User-Space Topology Emulation

Valerio Schiavoni, Etienne Rivière, and Pascal Felber

University of Neuchâtel, Switzerland

Abstract. Network emulation allows researchers to test distributed applications on diverse topologies with fine control over key properties such as delays, bandwidth, congestion, or packet loss. Current approaches to network emulation require using dedicated machines and low-level operating system support. They are generally limited to one user deploying a single topology on a given set of nodes, and they require complex management. These constraints restrict the scope and impair the uptake of network emulation by designers of distributed applications. We propose a set of novel techniques for network emulation that operate only in user-space without specific operating system support. Multiple users can simultaneously deploy several topologies on shared physical nodes with minimal setup complexity. A modular network model allows emulating complex topologies, including congestion at inner routers and links, without any centralized orchestration nor dedicated machine. We implement our user-space network emulation mechanisms in SPLAYNET, as an extension of an open-source distributed testbed. Our evaluation with a representative set of applications and topologies shows that SPLAYNET provides accuracy comparable to that of low-level systems based on dedicated machines, while offering better scalability and ease of use.

Keywords: Topology emulation, large-scale networks, testbeds.

1 Introduction

A key aspect of distributed systems evaluation is the capacity to deterministically reproduce experiments and compare distributed applications in the same deployment context, and in particular when operating under the same network conditions. Distributed testbeds such as PlanetLab (`www.planet-lab.org`) allow testing applications in real-world conditions, by aggregating a large number of geographically distant machines. While extremely useful for large-scale systems evaluation, such testbeds cannot be reconfigured to expose a variety of network infrastructures or topologies. Furthermore, the high load and the unpredictable running conditions of shared testbeds are a hindrance for the reproducibility of evaluation results, or for the fair comparison of different applications.

Network emulation supports *controllable* and *reproducible* distributed systems evaluation. It allows running a distributed application on dedicated machines as if it were running on an arbitrary network topology, and observe the behavior of the application in various network conditions. The emulation of communication

D. Eyers and K. Schwan (Eds.): Middleware 2013, LNCS 8275, pp. 62–81, 2013.

links is based on an input *topology*, i.e., a graph representation of nodes, routers, and the properties of their connections. A cluster with a high-performance local network can typically support the execution of applications and the emulation of topologies.

The focus of this paper is on providing support for easy evaluation of networked applications (e.g., indexing [35], streaming [5], coding [15], data processing over non-standard topologies [11], etc.) under diverse yet reproducible networking conditions. Furthermore, we seek to provide support for concurrent deployments of emulated topologies and distributed applications, where the physical nodes of a cluster can be used for running multiple experiments with different topologies, without interference and loss of accuracy for any of the experiments. Finally, we posit that the uptake of network emulation mechanisms will be greater if the setup of such mechanisms remain simple and cross platform, and if they are integrated with a toolkit that facilitates distributed systems prototyping and evaluation, for researchers, students, and engineers. This requires mechanisms and tools for rapid development, deployment, observation, and control of distributed experiments. Note that our work focuses on the evaluation of networked applications on top of standard TCP and UDP connections, when presented with various end-to-end characteristics: bandwidth, delay, packet loss, and congestion. We do not consider the evaluation of the network stack itself, or the evaluation of low-level network characteristics and protocols, which is the focus of other tools [23].

Existing solutions [1, 7, 16, 18, 19, 26, 28–30, 33, 34, 38–40] support emulation of part or all of the characteristics of a topology, but present a number of limitations. None allows researchers to deploy several network topologies *at the same time* and *on the same physical nodes* over a shared platform. Indeed, they enforce that a node of the testbed is used by one user, for one topology: this requires a large amount of physical resources, or imposes severe restrictions on the number of users and/or the size of their experiments. Furthermore, existing approaches require privileged or *root* access to the machines of the testbed, and often the use of dedicated machines or specialized operating systems to support network emulation. Finally, most of them require to completely reconfigure testbed nodes for every new emulated topology.

Contributions. The main contributions of this paper are the following:

- We propose a novel approach for supporting network emulation with user-space mechanisms and without support from the operating system. Our approach allows emulating complex topologies for which existing systems would require network queues implemented in the kernel space of dedicated emulation nodes.
- Our approach features configurable and modular network models. It supports complex topologies with inner routers and links, link sharing models, and overheads emulation.
- We introduce a fully decentralized monitoring algorithm for emulation of congestion, delays, and packet loss for inner nodes of the topology, without actually instantiating inner nodes nor requiring a centralized control point.

- We present support mechanisms for network emulation that enable simple selection and sharing of resources between multiple concurrent topologies and application deployments, without need for the user to directly access the physical nodes.
- We describe an implementation of our system, SPLAYNET, developed as an extension of the SPLAY [25], an open-source distributed framework that provides comprehensive facilities for the simple prototyping and deployment of networked applications and protocols.
- We evaluate our approach with several micro-benchmarks and networked applications deployed over various topologies. We compare our system to Model-Net [38] and Emulab [18, 40]. Results indicate that SPLAYNET achieves similar accuracy for network emulation but with lower resource requirements, and supports concurrent deployments without degradation of accuracy. Our approach scales well under heavy load and large topologies can be deployed with minimum management effort.

SPLAYNET is freely available as open-source software. It can be downloaded from `http://www.splay-project.org/splaynet` together with all data and source code for reproducing the experiments presented in this paper.

Outline. The paper is organized as follows. Section 2 reviews related work. Section 3 briefly introduces the open-source framework SPLAYNET builds upon. The design and internals of our system are described in Section 4. We present a detailed evaluation of SPLAYNET in Section 5 and conclude in Section 6.

2   Related Work

We classify work related to SPLAYNET along several perspectives, presented in Table 1. We distinguish solutions based on their operational mode (user or kernel), their need for specialized hardware or dedicated devices (switches, VLANs), and the type of orchestration for the emulation of the traffic at inner nodes/routers of the topology.[1] We also consider the support for *concurrent deployments*: multiple emulated topologies onto the same set of machines, for different users and different applications. We finally consider the ability to emulate traffic congestion along routing paths, as well as end-to-end bandwidth, delay, and packet loss. Although hardware-only emulation systems exist [21], in the remainder of this section we focus on solutions that operate partly or entirely in software. We do not consider emulators specializing in wireless networks [22, 43], nor do we focus on simulation tools [37].

ModelNet [38] uses a set of dedicated machines organized in a cluster, called *emulator nodes*. These nodes are in charge of shaping all the traffic emitted and received by the *edge nodes* supporting the application. ModelNet requires modifying the routing tables of the kernel at edge nodes to redirect all outgoing traffic toward emulator nodes. Traffic shaping rules (bandwidth and delay) are

---

[1] *Centralized* means that a single node is in charge of emulating the traffic for a given inner link, while different machines may be in charge of emulating different inner nodes. *Decentralized* on the other hand means that several nodes coordinate for emulating the same inner link.

Table 1. Classification of network emulation tools (B/D/P=bandwidth/delay/packet loss emulation)

Name	Mode	HW Sup.	Orchestr.	Concur. deploy.	Path congest.	Emul. B	D	P
ModelNet [38]	Kernel	×	Centralized	×	√	√	√	√
Emulab [18,40]	Kernel	√	Centralized	×	√	√	√	√
SliceTime [39]	Kernel	√	Centralized	×	√	√	√	×
Nist NET [7]	Kernel	×	Centralized	×	×	√	√	√
ACIM [33]	Kernel	×	Centralized	×	√	√	√	√
P2PLab [28]	Kernel	×	Centralized	×	×	√	√	√
IMUNES [30]	Kernel	√	Centralized	×	×	√	√	√
Netkit [29]	Kernel	×	Centralized	×	√	√	√	√
NetEm [16]	Kernel	×	*(N/A: single link emulation only)*			×	√	√
EmuSocket [1]	User	×	*(N/A: single link emulation only)*			√	√	×
MyP2P-World [34]	User	×	Centralized	×	×	√	√	√
WiDS [26]	User	×	Centralized	×	×	×	√	√
Mininet [24]	User	×	Centralized	×	×	√	√	√
SPLAYNET	User	×	Decentralized	√	√	√	√	√

applied to all packets by the means of DummyNet [6] pipes set up in the kernel of emulator nodes. It is possible to deploy only one emulated topology at a time. Every topology modification requires root access to the cluster for redeploying all emulator nodes and updating the kernel routing tables at edge nodes.

Emulab [18,40] is a shared platform that runs experiments on a dedicated emulation testbed. Although Emulab allows users to deploy several experiments under different network conditions, once a machine of the testbed is assigned to an experiment it cannot be used for any other. Emulab uses the same mechanisms as ModelNet [38] to shape traffic. To reduce the number of host machines required by each experiment, Emulab supports an *end-node-traffic-shaping* mode: the application's nodes shape the outgoing traffic themselves, relying on *tc* [16] or DummyNet [6] for, respectively, Linux- and BSD-based experiments.

Some network emulation tools are based on virtual machine deployment utilities. SliceTime [39] solves the time-drifting problem for large-scale experiments by providing a synchronization component to the deployed virtual machines. It relies on the Xen hypervisor [3]. SPLAYNET does not require the use of a hypervisor on the host machines, it only spawns new user-space processes to accommodate concurrent experiments.

P2PLab [28] relies on DummyNet mechanisms built in a BSD kernel. It organizes emulated networks in subnets. Each physical machine in a P2PLab cluster is responsible for a subnet and manages all the traffic within this subnet. Along the same lines, IMUNES [30] operates through a set of virtual machines interconnected via DummyNet pipes. Its originality resides in the management of the cluster hosting the virtual machines, which is driven by a peer-to-peer protocol. The protocol monitors the state of the machines and notifies the other nodes about failures and load conditions. This information is subsequently used when dispatching virtual machines. Network emulation itself operates similarly to other DummyNet-based emulators, and it requires the physical network hosting the experiments to provide programmable VLAN support.

Mininet [24] uses lightweight virtualization mechanisms to emulate software-defined networks on a *single host*. In contrast, SPLAYNET and the systems presented above target deployments onto a cluster of networked machines, allowing computationally intensive tasks and greater scalability. Other low-level tools aim at shaping the traffic originated by user-space processes. Trickle [12] is a user-space bandwidth shaper for unmodified Unix applications. DelayLine [19] requires the target program to statically link against traffic-shaping libraries. The authors of [1] and [34] both propose user-space emulation tools targeting P2P protocols implemented in Java: the latter provides bytecode-level compatibility with existing applications, whereas the former offers specialized APIs. These systems only support emulation of end-to-end links characteristics and not of complete topologies, thus categorizing them as traffic shapers rather than topology emulators.

In [31], the authors propose to deploy distributed rate limiters (DRL) for general purpose cloud services. Rate limiter nodes synchronize through a lightweight UDP protocol, which shares similarities with our decentralized congestion monitoring approach (Section 4.3). DRL does not provide any support for rate-limiting multiple services concurrently running on the same nodes. SPLAYNET provides a per-destination dedicated token bucket, while DRL mimics the behavior of a centralized token bucket algorithm at each rate limiter node.

The support of concurrent deployments requires appropriate resource selection mechanisms. Since physical network links will be shared by multiple emulated links, the resource selection must ensure that the capacity of the physical link is sufficient for all emulated links. No emulators feature such capabilities, and most require to deploy topologies on distinct sets of nodes, thus greatly impairing scalability. The few systems that support concurrent deployments on the same nodes leave to the user the responsibility of provisioning sufficient physical capacity for emulated links.

The present work represents the first attempt to propose user-space network emulation within an integrated distributed systems evaluation framework. It provides support for concurrent deployments while offering comparable performances to single-topology and kernel-space solutions, as will be shown in Section 5.

3   Background

We implement the contributions presented in this paper as an extension to the SPLAY [25] open-source distributed systems evaluation framework. We chose to build upon SPLAY as it allows to quickly prototype, deploy, and manage distributed experiments. We present in this section some background information about SPLAY. We note, however, that our contributions are not specific to SPLAY. User-level network emulation techniques presented in this paper are applicable to other systems and platforms.

SPLAY's goal is to ease rapid prototyping and development of distributed protocols. It features a concise and easy-to-learn language based on Lua (www.lua.org). The associated libraries support the functionalities that are typically required to

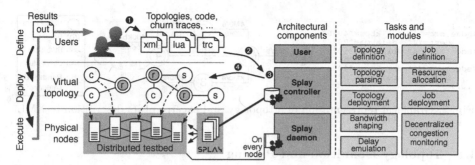

Fig. 1. The SPLAYNET architecture

implement distributed algorithms. The language and libraries allow implementations to be comparable in size (i.e., lines of code) to pseudo-code descriptions. This feature is on par with our objective of making network-emulated experiments and prototyping simple and fast. An example given in [25] is the Chord DHT [35]. A running implementation uses 58 lines of code, comparable in size with the pseudo-code in the original paper [35]. We use this implementation as an example application in our evaluation (Section 5). We note that the use of Lua also allows using existing code (e.g., C-based), by embedding it as a library, although we did not need to use this feature for our evaluation.

SPLAY also supports our objective of simplifying the usage of a testbed by providing simple multi-user resource management and deployment support. SPLAY runs a set of SPLAY *daemons* (`splayds`) on every node of the testbed. These daemons are deployed once, by the testbed administrator. They implement sandboxing by controlling and restricting usage to resources on the nodes. This is useful in a non-dedicated environment. A single access point, the SPLAY *controller* (`splayctl`), orchestrates the deployment of applications. It is the sole point of access to the system for users, who do not need to have administrative access or user accounts for the machines of the testbed. The `splayctl` allows users to select nodes for deploying an application according to various criteria, and dispatches the code to the corresponding `splayds`. The experiment is monitored and managed directly from the `splayctl`. The `splayctl` allows fine grain control of the experiments, for instance by replaying a *churn trace* that describe the dynamics of the system and is replayed by each of the `splayds` participating to the experiment, individually for each user and for each experiment. Our approach to topology emulation is inspired by this mechanism: a topology is provided by the user along with her code and is dispatched by the `splayctl` to all selected `splayds` part of the emulation. We describe these mechanisms and their integration in the next section.

4   The SPLAYNET Architecture

In this section we describe the various components necessary for supporting user-space network emulation and their integration in our SPLAYNET prototype. Figure 1 presents an overview of the implementation.

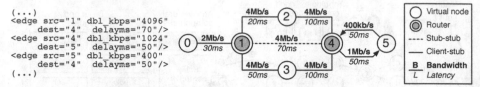

```
(...)
<edge src="1"  dbl_kbps="4096"
     dest="4"  delayms="70"/>
<edge src="4"  dbl_kbps="1024"
     dest="5"  delayms="50"/>
<edge src="5"  dbl_kbps="400"
     dest="4"  delayms="50"/>
(...)
```

Fig. 2. Graphical representation of a topology and excerpt of its description in XML

4.1   Topology Definition and Parsing

The first step is to define a network topology to emulate. Users write an abstract description that maps vertices and edges of an undirected cyclic graph to the physical connections of a network (Figure 1-❶). Users can specify the interconnections between nodes and routers, as well as the physical properties of the links (delays, bandwidth, and packet loss rate). Application nodes can be inner nodes in the topology (and not only end-nodes), in order to support relay-based applications such as coding [15] or in-network aggregation [11]. SPLAYNET supports two topology description formats: the ModelNet XML-based language [42] and the Emulab TCL-based language, itself based on the one used by the NS-2 network simulator [14]. A sample topology and an excerpt of its description in XML are given by Figure 2.

The second step is the deployment (Figure 1-❷). The user submits to the SPLAY controller the topology description, the code to execute, and any additional files required to drive the experiments. SPLAYNET's topology parser extracts the graph topology. Links in the topology description are uni-directional. Non-connected topologies are rejected. The user can however request implicit link symmetry: when there is no link between two elements but a corresponding reverse link exists, an implicit link can be created, with the same characteristics as the reverse one. This operation does not modify any of the links present in the original topology, thus supporting topologies where both symmetric and asymmetric links coexist. We then use an all-pairs-shortest-path algorithm based on links delays[2] and, for every shortest path, derives the maximum available bandwidth along the path (link with the lowest bandwidth), the overall delay (sum of the delays of individual links), and the packet loss probability (product of the packet loss of individual links).

4.2   Resource Allocation and Deployment

SPLAYNET allocates testbed resources for executing the user code on the emulated topology (Figure 1-❸). In the context of SPLAY, this problem corresponds to selecting a minimal set of splayds for executing the job. The allocation procedure ensures that the deployment of a topology does not impair on the accuracy of other deployed topologies, by avoiding saturating the bandwidth of

---

[2] Upon tie, we select a random link to balance the load but other strategies are possible, e.g., link with minimum latency or maximum bandwidth.

physical links beyond a safety margin. Finding a *minimal* set that satisfies all constraints on a shared infrastructure is a NP-hard problem [32]. Although efficient heuristics are known [10,32,41], they require knowing the start and duration of all experiments in advance, a requirement that is not met in our context. In SPLAYNET, we adopt a simple greedy approach to guide the selection of splayds. The objective is that all links in all emulated topologies are supported by physical links with enough available capacity. We do not consider delays as a selection criterion as we assume that SPLAYNET will be deployed in a cluster where the latencies observed on physical links are stable and much smaller than the latency requested for the emulated paths. The splayctl also keeps track of the current load of the machines, as part of the regular SPLAY operation. The administrator provides the maximal emulated bandwidth that can be emulated on a single physical link. This value depends on the cluster hardware and network. We use a value of 100 Mb/s in our experiments, as illustrated by the concurrent deployment experiment of Section 5.3. If several splayds are deployed on the same physical machine, the bandwidth available to each splayd is a fraction of the total available bandwidth and this value must be adjusted accordingly. For a new job, we select the least loaded nodes that satisfy the connectivity requirements, i.e., that have physical links to other nodes with sufficient available capacity taking into account the topology being deployed and those already running. If no such set of splayds is found, deployment is not allowed.

We only need to map *application nodes* to splayds. Routers are implicitly emulated by the communication links between the edge nodes. The advantages of this approach are twofold: first, it significantly reduces the amount of resources required to emulate large topologies; second, it frees the system from the need of powerful machines dedicated to shaping the traffic at routers. ModelNet [38] adopts a similar technique to reduce the amount of resources required for emulation in its *end-to-end* mode, but it does not emulate congestion at intermediary hops under this execution mode. We emulate traffic congestion at inner nodes with a distributed protocol and a link sharing model, described in Section 4.3.

The SPLAY controller finally dispatches the code to be executed to the selected splayds, along with the topology information required to initialize the network emulation layer (Figure 1-❹). This information is encoded with a compact marshaller that has negligible overhead on the traffic sent to the nodes. As an example, the information necessary to emulate the topology of Figure 2 adds only 430 bytes to the data sent to each splayd for the job deployment.

4.3   User-Space Network Emulation

SPLAYNET performs link and topology emulation only in user-space, and independently for the different deployed jobs on the same splayd. This brings a number of benefits. First, administrators do not need to have privileged access to the machines of the testbed nor to set up any hardware network infrastructure, since the emulated network layers are initialized at the application level. Second, it overcomes a common limitation of most other state-of-the-art systems by supporting the emulation of several topologies simultaneously.

Latency and Packet Loss Emulation. Links of the topology are first characterized by latency values and packet loss rates. To account for the associated delays, the `splayd` instantiates a *countdown queue* for each outgoing link of the node of the topology being emulated. Outgoing packets traverse this queue before they reach the network. A countdown timer is initialized to the link latency value when a packet enters the queue and, upon expiration, the packet is sent over the wire. Note that the actual latency of the physical topology is assumed to be orders of magnitude smaller than the emulated one, as all `splayds` are typically executed on a cluster. Otherwise, the value of the countdown timer should be adjusted to take into account delays observed at the physical level.

The reactivity to the timer expiration is crucial for accurate emulation, especially when emulating low-latency links, thus the choice of the underlying operating system plays an important role for achieving good performance in link delay emulation. We evaluated the scheduling accuracy on various operating systems, and reproduced results on par with those presented in [13]. Scheduling accuracy is around 0.1 ms for Linux 2.6, and in the order of a few milliseconds for Linux 2.4 and FreeBSD 7.3. This indicates that accurate latency emulation is achievable, with measurable errors in the order of milliseconds.

Packet loss is enforced by simply dropping random packets at the source according to the calculated loss rate on the path to their destination. Here again, we assume that the underlying physical network has a negligible packet loss rate that we do not need to compensate.

Bandwidth Shaping. In addition to latency, a topology specifies the maximal bandwidth for each of its links. The actual bandwidth available to the application will be smaller, and depends on the size of the messages sent through the socket. Our model takes into account emulation of overhead as follows.

For TPC/IP and UDP/IP, we use the default Ethernet MTU size of 1500 B (bytes). Ethernet overheads consist of 38 B for each message: 12 B of source and destination addresses, 8 B of preamble, 14 B of header, and 4 B of trailer. We then add the overhead of IPv4 (20 B), and TCP or UDP headers (20 and 28 B, respectively). The overhead factors in the number of packets for a given application-level message, and determines the bandwidth that is actually used on the emulated link. This overhead model, which can be easily modified to account for different network settings, allows us to precisely emulate the actual bandwidth available to an application sending messages of various sizes. It is also independent from the configuration of the supporting physical network (e.g., the use of jumbo frames).

We use a token bucket algorithm [36] to cap the throughput of outgoing traffic to the value specified in the emulated topology.[3] The algorithm operates by inserting a number of tokens at a fixed rate (determined according to the available bandwidth) into a virtual bucket. Each token represents a fixed amount of bytes that can be sent. Application-level packets are delivered over the wire

---

[3] The *tc* [16] tool integrated in the Linux kernel uses a similar approach to bandwidth shaping. However, SPLAYNET is cross-platform and does not rely on any kernel support as it integrates its own shaping mechanism.

only if the corresponding amount of tokens is available in the bucket. Otherwise, they are re-queued in the bucket. This simple strategy guarantees a consistent average throughput during emulation.

The bucket fill rates are initially configured to the minimum available bandwidth across all hops on the shortest path between the source and destination nodes. Afterwards, fill rates are dynamically adjusted by the decentralized congestion monitoring protocol based on the actual available bandwidth on the path, dynamically considering other flows taking place in the topology.

Decentralized Congestion Emulation. The delay emulation and bandwidth shaping mechanisms are the foundations of a decentralized network emulation platform, and are the first components of the emulated network model. They are, however, not sufficient for accurately emulating network congestion across multi-hop routing paths. This task is the responsibility of a decentralized congestion monitoring protocol, which constitutes the second part of our model. Note that the network model is modular: both parts can be modified independently of the emulation framework, and new models can be integrated, with different overheads, link sharing, or QoS policies.

In a centralized solution such as ModelNet [38], one or a small set of dedicated hosts are continuously keeping track of the network traffic on all possible paths of the topology, since all packets are routed through these hosts. This global view of the network allows throttling the data rates according to the limits imposed by the topology.

We advocate the use of a decentralized architecture that does not require specific nodes to handle all traffic passing across the topology. Instead, we rely on a distributed protocol to promptly distribute notifications about the start and end of data streams. These notifications are disseminated to all the nodes involved in the emulation of a given topology through fast and reliable UDP multicast channels (PGM).

View update. Whenever a node starts or stops sending data using TCP, it first updates its local view of ongoing network flows by incrementing the number of competing flows on every hop from itself to the destination node. Then, it disseminates this information to the other nodes by specifying the source, the destination, and the virtual routing hops involved in the stream. In the context of a large-scale topology deployment (Section 5.4) with 150 nodes, we observe average dissemination delays of 7.36 ms. Upon receiving this information, the other nodes adjust their local view accordingly by updating the number of competing streams on affected links and, if necessary, the token bucket's fill rates. In the case of UDP streams, it is not possible to determine the end of a communication as with TCP. Hence, we adopt a periodic report strategy: every 50 ms, the amount of data sent through the socket is propagated to other nodes, which update their state based on information from the previous period.

Each node needs to maintain an up-to-date view of ongoing data flows on the emulated network, whether originated by itself or by other nodes, and determine how internal links bandwidth is shared between competing flows. This view is efficiently modeled as a n-ary tree rooted at the local node.

The leaves of the tree represent the other virtual end-nodes, while inner nodes correspond to the routers. Edges of the tree are labeled with their maximum bandwidth capacity and latency, and they embed a counter that keeps track of the number of active data streams on the associated links. Each leaf is augmented with a token bucket that specifies the maximum data rate allowed to reach the corresponding node. The initial fill rate for each token bucket corresponds to the bandwidth allowed by the path from the local node to the leaf.

Link sharing model. Whenever multiple streams share a segment of the routing path, the token bucket fill rates are adjusted to split the bandwidth between the competing streams, for each of the internal links of the topology supporting multiple streams. The split depends on a bandwidth sharing models. The basic *Max-Min* sharing model introduced in [4] does not correctly reflect actual sharing behaviors [9]. Therefore, we use the *RTT-aware Max-Min* sharing model [20, 27], which is widely considered as accurate.

First, the allocation of bandwidth ρ_i for each flow f_i on a link is capped by the limitation of its bandwidth-delay product: the flow is capped by the ratio of the sending window size W_i and roundtrip RTT_i: $\rho_i \leq W_i/RTT_i$.[4] Second, the sum of ρ_i for all flows on the link must not exceed the capacity of the link F. The share ρ_i of the available bandwidth for each flow is then inversely proportional to the flow RTT_i, i.e., $\rho_i = F \times ((RTT_i)^{-1} \sum_{j=1..n} (RTT_j)^{-1})$ when the first capacity constraint does not apply to any flow. The allocation takes into account the fact that some hops in end-to-end paths are not able to use their full share of a given emulated link. In this case, the remaining bandwidth is redistributed to other existing communication flows under the model constraints until no further refinement is possible.[5]

Example. Figure 3 illustrates the tree maintained by node 0 in the topology of Figure 2 as communication flows are established between nodes. Initially, no communication takes place and the buckets are idle (first tree in the figure). Then, node 0 starts communicating with node 2. To that end, it sends to other nodes information about the path that has been estab-

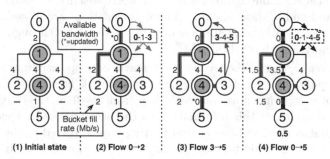

Fig. 3. Evolution of the tree maintained by node 0 for the topology of Figure 1 with the establishment of 3 communication flows

---

[4] We use a default value of 64 KB for the sending window size W_i, as found on most wired networked system.

[5] Note that the current model considers that the reverse-path bandwidth is sufficient to accommodate the traffic of ACKs. Refinement of the model may include these aspects, e.g., based on [17].

lished, and it updates its local view by adjusting the available bandwidth on links and the fill rate of the bucket at leaf 2 (second tree in the figure). After receiving a message from node 3 that starts sending data to node 5, node 1 simply updates the available bandwidth on the links but does not need to change the bucket fill rates as there is no competition with one of its communication flows (third tree in the figure). Finally, node 1 communicates with node 5. The new flow competes with the previous two as it shares a link with each of them: link 0→1 for the first flow, and link 4→5 for the second. The sharing of these links is determined according to the RTT-aware Min-Max sharing model and the bucket fill rate of leaves 2 and 5 are adjusted accordingly (fourth tree in the figure). From the topology description in Figure 2, we obtain the following RTTs: 0→2 is 100 ms, 3→5 is 300 ms and 0→5 is 300 ms. As a result, the 2 Mb/s of the link 0→1 are shared as 75% of 2 Mb/s = 1.5 Mb/s for 0→2, and 25% of 2 Mb/s = 0.5 Mb/s for 0→5. Note that the bandwidth allocated to flow 0→5 is the maximal allocatable, as link 4→5 is shared with flow 3→5 with the same RTT for both flows.

5   Evaluation

In this section we present an extensive evaluation of our contributions. We compare SPLAYNET with the *de facto* reference network emulators ModelNet [38] and Emulab [18,40]. Similarly to SPLAYNET, both systems provide complete emulation toolsets, from a topology description language to topology deployment facilities. We use the same application code over the three emulation systems, by using SPLAY and Lua stand-alone libraries on ModelNet and Emulab.

In Section 5.1 we first present a set of micro-benchmarks that measure the accuracy of the delay and bandwidth emulation on simple yet representative topologies. Our study then proceeds with a set of macro-benchmarks based on real-world applications (Section 5.2). We use the Chord DHT [35] as an example of delay-sensitive application and collaborative application-level multicast using parallel n-ary trees [5] as an example of a bandwidth-sensitive application.

One of the distinctive features of SPLAYNET is the support for concurrent deployments of multiple topologies on the same testbed. In Section 5.3, we investigate the scalability and accuracy of SPLAYNET when concurrently deploying several topologies. Finally, Section 5.4 concludes this evaluation by presenting the behavior of SPLAYNET when emulating large and complex topologies.

We set up a SPLAYNET cluster on top of a 1 Gb/s switched network with 60 machines, each with 8-Core Xeon CPUs and 8 GB of RAM. The ModelNet cluster is deployed on the same machines. We used the similarly powerful pc3000[6] machines for Emulab experiments.

The SPLAYNET modules executed by the splayds for network shaping are implemented in pure Lua. We use version 5.1.4 of the Lua virtual machine for all the experiments. The splayctl extensions are implemented in Ruby. Due to the small number of machines typically available on Emulab, we had to restrict our evaluations on this platform to a maximum of 20 nodes per experiment.

---

[6] emulab.net/shownodetype.php3?node_type=pc3000

5.1   Micro-Benchmarks

Latency. To evaluate the accuracy of link latency emulation, we deploy a simple client-server application using remote procedure calls (RPCs) at the edges of the topology, as shown in Figure 4.a (top). We measure the accuracy of the RPC's round-trip-time (RTT) for increasing emulated latencies. This experiment also includes results for Emulab configured in end-node-traffic-shaping (ENTS) mode to remove any latency overhead toward a third-party shaping node.

Figure 4.b presents the cumulative distribution function (CDF) of observed delays. The expected RTT is shown on the x-axis for each of the link latency values, with variations expressed as percentages. Performance over the 3 testbeds is very similar: emulated latencies never deviate more than 10% from the expected values, and never more than 5 milliseconds in absolute terms.

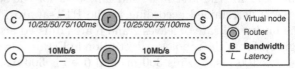

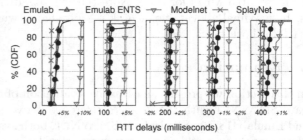

(a) Topologies: latency (top) and bandwidth (bottom).

(b) Link latency emulation.

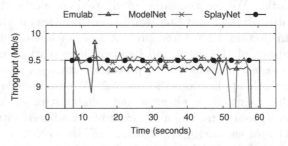

(c) Link bandwidth emulation.

Fig. 4. Link latency and bandwidth emulation for a client-server RPC benchmark

Bandwidth. Our second micro-benchmark evaluates the accuracy of the bandwidth emulation. We deploy the point-to-point topology of Figure 4.a (bottom) with two nodes connected by a single router. Link latencies are close to zero (bare latencies of the support cluster) to mitigate any bandwidth-delay-product effect [20,27] and to allow the maximum theoretical throughput. Emulab and ModelNet's link queue sizes are configured to the default size of 100 slots.

The client node continuously streams data to a server over a 10 Mb/s link via a pre-established TCP connection. Figure 4.c shows how the three systems let the application-level data stream, and emulated overhead, saturate the available link bandwidth up to the theoretical limits. ModelNet and Emulab present oscillations in the observed instantaneous throughput, while SPLAYNET provides a more steady download rate. This is a result of our choice of a decentralized, model-based network emulation that does not use kernel-level buffers at dedicated nodes. Oscillations are observed in real networks but to a much smaller

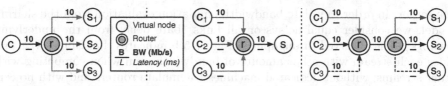

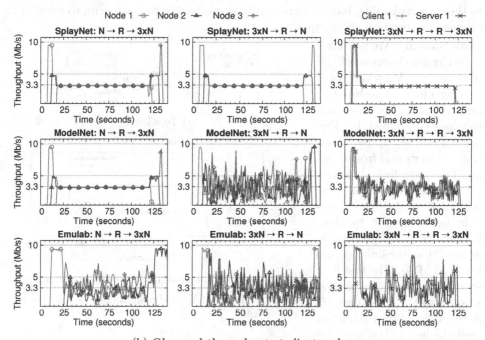

(a) Topologies for bandwidth emulation micro-benchmarks (N→R→3N, 3N→R→N, 3N→R→R→3N).

(b) Observed throughput at client nodes.

Fig. 5. Bandwidth shaping accuracy

extent than with ModelNet and Emulab. For the range of application of SPLAY-NET (evaluation of networked protocols), the current model allows reproducibility between runs and between applications. We emphasize that oscillatory bandwidth allocation or reverse ACK traffic [17] can be integrated in the model without re-engineering the other elements of SPLAYNET.

We deploy more complex scenarios in order to evaluate the accuracy of SPLAY-NET's bandwidth emulation when multiple clients concurrently stream data through common intermediate nodes. We use three topologies shown in Figure 5.a. Nodes are linked via 10 Mb/s links. Client nodes stream 50 MB of data to server nodes, competing for the bandwidth on the link that connects the client to the router (topology on the left, labeled N→R→3N), the link that connects the router to the server (topology on the center, labeled 3N→R→N), or the link between the two router nodes (topology on the right, labeled 3N→R→R→3N). Streams are started at intervals of 5 seconds. For the sake of clarity, in the case of 3N→R→R→3N, we only present the observed throughput at one client and one server. In order to isolate bandwidth emulation evaluation from the sharing model, we consider equal delays on all links (bare delay from the underlying network). The observed throughput in Figure 5.b indicates that SPLAYNET provides each stream with a fair amount of bandwidth even when competing with other streams, without dedicated machines to emulate routers and with no centralized traffic shaping orchestration. The results obtained with ModelNet and Emulab provide the applications an average throughput that is reasonably close to the expected value, but they are hardly reproducible from one run to another or over the duration of an experiment.

Link Sharing. We now evaluate the effectiveness of the RTT-aware Max-Min link sharing model introduced in Section 4.3. We use the topology described by Figure 6.a and set up two flows from c_1 to s_1 and from c_2 to s_2. The $r{\to}r$ link is shared by the two flows and the maximal bandwidth achievable by both due to their bandwidth-delay product is greater than the link's capacity of 10 Mb/s. The first flow starts at second 5 while the second starts at second 10. As expected, when the intermediate link is traversed by

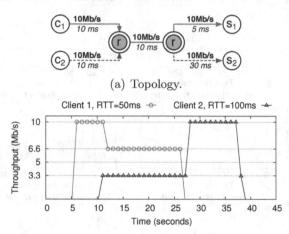

(a) Topology.

(b) Observed bandwidth at servers s_1 and s_2.

Fig. 6. RTT-aware Max-Min sharing of 10 Mb/s bottleneck link

both flows, its capacity is split according to the inverse of each flow's RTT: $\frac{50}{150} = \frac{2}{3}$ of 10 Mb/s for client 1 ($\sim$6.66 Mb/s), and the remaining $\frac{1}{3}$ of 10 Mb/s for client 2 ($\sim$3.33 Mb/s).

5.2   Macro-Benchmarks

For our set of macro-benchmarks, we deploy complete implementations of two representative distributed protocols, for which network emulation can be instrumental to evaluate the performance and behavior. For both experiments, using the Chord DHT [35] and a collaborative multicast application [5], nodes are deployed on an emulated star topology where all end-nodes are connected through a single central inner router. All links from the end-nodes to the router are emulated at 10 Mb/s (symmetric) with 30 ms latency.

Delay-sensitive: Chord DHT. Our first representative protocol is the Chord DHT [35]. After 20 nodes form a stabilized Chord ring, each node submits 50 queries for random keys. Note that the constructed rings do not perfectly overlap due to the nature of Chord node identifiers. In particular, node identifiers are initialized by hashing their IP and port, and Emulab does not allow choosing the network mask of the assigned machines.

Figure 7 presents the CDF of the delays for all queries (left) and the CDF of the number of *hops* required by the queries to reach the node in charge of the key (right). The results demonstrate similar behavior across all the testbeds in terms of latency emulation.

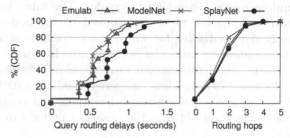

Fig. 7. Routing in a 20 nodes Chord ring

Bandwidth-sensitive: multicast. We now evaluate how SPLAYNET performs compared to ModelNet and Emulab for bandwidth-intensive protocols. We use a multicast protocol based on parallel n-ary trees [5]. We create $n=4$ distinct trees as done in SplitStream [8]. Each of the 20 nodes is an inner member in one tree and a leaf in the others. The data to transmit is split into 16 blocks of 2.5 MB each. Blocks are propagated in parallel along the 4 trees using a round-robin policy for tree selection.

Figure 8 presents the CDF of the download completion time for all 4 trees at all nodes. The results indicate that the three platforms offer comparable performance in terms of bandwidth emulation.

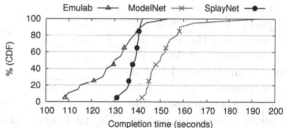

Fig. 8. Multicast diffusion on n-ary trees

5.3 Concurrent Deployments

We now evaluate the impact of concurrent deployments in the same testbed on the emulation accuracy for both delay- and bandwidth-sensitive protocols. In these experiments, we use only 10 physical nodes of our cluster to enforce a high level of concurrency. Each individual deployment consists of 20 nodes in a star-like topology with 30 ms latency and 10 Mb/s bandwidth links. In the most extreme case of 50 concurrent jobs, up to 1,000 application nodes run simultaneously on the testbed. We start with a delay-sensitive application.

Figure 9 presents the results of query routing delays when deploying up to 50 concurrent jobs, each running one instance of the Chord DHT. Each bar in a group of four presents a representative percentile (the first quartile, the median, the 90th and 99th percentile) of the routing delays for 50

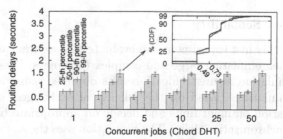

Fig. 9. Impact of concurrent deployments on delay-sensitive protocol Chord

random queries issued by the nodes. The inner graph shows the CDF of the routing delays for the queries issued by the nodes in the case of two concurrently deployed jobs, for which the percentiles give a compact representation. The standard deviation for each quantile is indicated on each bar.

For instance, the median routing delay for two concurrent experiments are 0.49 s and 0.73 s, yielding an average median of 0.61 s and a standard deviation of 0.17 s. The small standard deviations and consistent quantiles confirm the lack of variation between the observed performances of concurrently deployed jobs.

We continue by performing multiple concurrent deployments of a bandwidth-sensitive protocol, the parallel n-ary tree protocol previously described. Our objective is that concurrent experiments have little to no impact on one another, and in particular on the behavior of the protocol under test. The behavior of a set of protocols is represented by the CDF of the completion time for retrieving a file from the parallel trees. We use a star topology with low and high bandwidth requirements.

In low bandwidth settings, each link in the topology supports a bandwidth of 128 Kb/s and the transmitted file size is 2 MB. We observe in Figure 10 that the deployment of 1 to 50 concurrent instances of the protocol have no impact on their performance, allowing to safely rely on a shared emulation testbed. The emu-

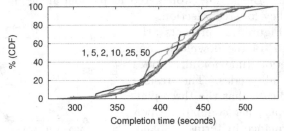

Fig. 10. Concurrent n-ary tree deployments: 2 MB of data with 128 Kb/s links (the number of concurrent deployments is indicated next to the respective lines)

lated traffic passing through each physical link of the cluster is below the threshold of 100 Mb/s we use in our experiments.

We also experimented in high bandwidth settings, with 10 Mb/s links in the emulated topology and a file size of 40 MB, and observed consistent behavior of the protocols and topologies from 1 to 5 concurrently deployed topologies. With more, as expected, concurrent deployments adversely impact one another due to the maximal emulated traffic of 100 Mb/s per physical link.

5.4   Scalability

In this last experiment, we evaluate the accuracy and scalability of SPLAYNET when emulating large and complex topologies. We compare the accuracy of the emulation against "ideal" results obtained using a centralized and omniscient simulation. Based on the full list of exchanges, we determine the exact congestion on inner links and decide on appropriate bandwidth allocation with no synchronization delay. The simulation uses the same mechanisms for deciding on bandwidth allocation (Section 4.3) but applies them to the full topology graph. We use a set of three topologies of size 50, 100, and 150 nodes, constructed using the *preferential attachment* method [2]. We start with a single node and add new nodes one by one, each with one outgoing link. We pick the destination of that link such that the selection probability is proportional to each node's actual in-degree. This method yields *scale-free* networks, representative of the characteristics of Internet topologies, with distribution of the degrees following a power-law. Nodes with no incoming link act as application nodes while other nodes are routers. Due to the scale-free nature of the graph, a large majority of paths between end-nodes share common inner links in the topology. This is a challenge for the distributed congestion evaluation mechanism. Each link has a random delay in the [10:30] ms range. Bandwidth between routers is 1 Mb/s, and 10 Mb/s from end-nodes to their respective routers, to prevent the last link be a bottleneck and to emphasize the effect of congestion on inner links.

We mimic a randomized bandwidth-sensitive communication workload. Some application nodes initiate a single communication of 10 MB of data over TCP to a randomly selected other node. This is similar to what would happen

Table 2. Accuracy versus centralized simulation, on large scale-free topologies, of a randomized high-bandwidth communication workload

nodes	routers	flows/s		accur. error (±%)			
		avg.	time	avg.	stdev.	min.	max.
30	20	4.54	398.92 s	1.02	0.92	0.04	2.61
		9.78	719.11 s	3.89	2.14	0.08	8.15
62	38	7.49	400.85 s	3.45	2.12	0.65	8.52
		15.34	959.56 s	5.63	3.38	1.46	17.12
98	52	9.79	566.56 s	4.00	1.80	1.83	7.68
		19.09	1201.38 s	11.94	4.75	0.23	24.48

for instance in a BitTorrent dissemination. For each topology, we use two workloads: a light and a heavy one (first and second line of Table 2, respectively), which differ in particular in the number of (concurrent) exchanges. The last four columns present the statistics for the accuracy, that is, the variation over the ideal simulation for the same exchanges. The average accuracy ranges from ±1.02% to ±11.94%, with only small variations across all flows and in all cases, i.e., a low standard deviation. Minimal and maximal inaccuracy is particularly low for the smallest graph and remains reasonable for the two others, well in the usability range for large-scale network emulation. We were not able to deploy the same experiment on Emulab due to the low number of available nodes on this platform.

6 Conclusion

Network emulation allows researchers to evaluate distributed applications by deploying them in a variety of network conditions. Previous solutions often relied on dedicated machines to shape the network traffic across the nodes involved in an experiment, and did not allow the concurrent deployment of different network topologies on the same nodes of a testbed.

This paper introduced SPLAYNET, an integrated user-space network emulation framework. SPLAYNET uses a distributed orchestration protocol to emulate congestion at inner nodes in a decentralized manner and without instantiating these inner nodes on physical machines. It allows the deployment of multiple experiments, each under different network emulation conditions, and running concurrently on the same set of machines. SPLAYNET offers equivalent performance to state-of-the-art systems, both in terms of latency emulation and bandwidth shaping accuracy. It has shown to scale well for concurrent deployments of real-world distributed protocols and large topologies. This work was partly supported by the Swiss National Foundation under agreement number 200021-127271/1.

References

1. Avvenuti, M., Vecchio, A.: Application-level network emulation: the EmuSocket toolkit. Journal of Network and Computer Applications 29(4) (2006)
2. Barabasi, A.-L., Albert, R.: Emergence of scaling in random networks. Science 286 (1999)
3. Barham, P., Dragovic, B., Fraser, K., Hand, S., Harris, T., Ho, A., Neugebauer, R., Pratt, I., Warfield, A.: Xen and the art of virtualization. In: SOSP (2003)
4. Bertsekas, D., Gallager, R.: Data Networks. Prentice-Hall (1992)
5. Biersack, E.W., Rodriguez, P., Felber, P.: Performance analysis of peer-to-peer networks for file distribution. In: Solé-Pareta, J., Smirnov, M., Van Mieghem, P., Domingo-Pascual, J., Monteiro, E., Reichl, P., Stiller, B., Gibbens, R.J. (eds.) QofIS 2004. LNCS, vol. 3266, pp. 1–10. Springer, Heidelberg (2004)
6. Carbone, M., Rizzo, L.: Dummynet revisited. SIGCOMM Comput. Commun. Rev. 40(2), 12–20 (2010)
7. Carson, M., Santay, D.: NIST Net-a linux-based network emulation tool. SIGCOMM Comput. Commun. Rev. 33(3), 111–126 (2003)
8. Castro, M., Druschel, P., Kermarrec, A.-M., Nandi, A., Rowstron, A., Singh, A.: Splitstream: high-bandwidth multicast in cooperative environments. In: SOSP (2003)
9. Chiu, D.M.: Some observations on fairness of bandwidth sharing. In: ISCC (2000)
10. Coffman Jr, E., Garey, M., Johnson, D.: Approximation algorithms for bin packing: A survey. In: Approximation algorithms for NP-hard problems, pp. 46–93. PWS Publishing Co. (1996)
11. Costa, P., Donnelly, A., Rowstron, A., O'Shea, G.: Camdoop: exploiting in-network aggregation for big data applications. In: NSDI (2012)
12. Eriksen, M. Trickle: A userland bandwidth shaper for unix-like systems. USENIX ATC (2005)
13. Etsion, Y., Tsafrir, D., Feitelson, D.: Effects of clock resolution on the scheduling of interactive and soft real-time processes. In: SIGMETRICS (2003)
14. Fall, K.: Network emulation in the Vint/NS simulator. In: ISCC (1999)
15. Gkantsidis, C., Rodriguez, P.: Network coding for large scale content distribution. In: INFOCOM (2005)
16. Hemminger, S.: Network emulation with NetEm. In: Linux Conference (2005)
17. Heusse, M., Merritt, S.A., Brown, T.X., Duda, A.: Two-way tcp connections: old problem, new insight. SIGCOMM Comput. Commun. Rev. 41(2), 5–15 (2011)
18. Hibler, M., Ricci, R., Stoller, L., Duerig, J., Guruprasad, S., Stack, T., Webb, K., Lepreau, J.: Large-scale virtualization in the emulab network testbed. USENIX ATC (2008)
19. Ingham, D.B., Parrington, G.D.: Delayline: a wide-area network emulation tool. Comput. Syst. 7(3), 313–332 (1994)
20. Kelly, F.P.: Charging and rate control for elastic traffic. European Trans. on Telecommunications 8, 33–37 (1997)

21. Kodama, Y., Kudoh, T., Takano, R., Sato, H., Tatebe, O., Sekiguchi, S.: GNET-1: Gigabit ethernet network testbed. In: CLUSTER (2004)
22. Kojo, M., Gurtov, A., Manner, J., Sarolahti, P., Alanko, T., Raatikainen, K.: Seawind: a wireless network emulator. In: MMB (2001)
23. Kristiansen, S., Plagemann, T., Goebel, V.: Towards scalable and realistic node models for network simulators. In: SIGCOMM (2011)
24. Lantz, B., Heller, B., McKeown, N.: A network in a laptop: rapid prototyping for software-defined networks. In: HotNets (2010)
25. Leonini, L., Rivière, E., Felber, P.: SPLAY: Distributed systems evaluation made simple. In: NSDI (2009)
26. Lin, S., Pan, A., Zhang, Z., Guo, R., Guo, Z.: WiDS: an integrated toolkit for distributed system development. In: HotOS (2005)
27. Massoulié, L., Roberts, J.: Bandwidth sharing: objectives and algorithms. IEEE/ACM Trans. Netw. 10(3), 320–328 (2002)
28. Nussbaum, L., Richard, O.: Lightweight emulation to study peer-to-peer systems. Concur. and Comput.: Practice and Experience 20(6), 735–749 (2008)
29. Pizzonia, M., Rimondini, M.: Netkit: easy emulation of complex networks on inexpensive hardware. In: TridentCom (2008)
30. Puljiz, Z., Penco, R., Mikuc, M.: Performance analysis of a decentralized network simulator based on IMUNES. In: SPECTS (2008)
31. Raghavan, B., Vishwanath, K., Ramabhadran, S., Yocum, K., Snoeren, A.: Cloud control with distributed rate limiting. SIGCOMM Comput. Commun. Rev. 37, 337–348 (2007)
32. Ricci, R., Alfeld, C., Lepreau, J.: A solver for the network testbed mapping problem. SIGCOMM Comput. Commun. Rev. 33(2), 65–81 (2003)
33. Ricci, R., Duerig, J., Sanaga, P., Gebhardt, D., Hibler, M., Atkinson, K., Zhang, J., Kasera, S., Lepreau, J.: The Flexlab approach to realistic evaluation of networked systems. In: NSDI (2007)
34. Roverso, R., Al-Aggan, M., Naiem, A., Dahlstrom, A., El-Ansary, S., El-Beltagy, M., Haridi, S.: MyP2PWorld: Highly reproducible application-level emulation of P2P systems. In: SASOW (2008)
35. Stoica, I., Morris, R., Liben-Nowell, D., Karger, D.R., Kaashoek, M.F., Dabek, F., Balakrishnan, H.: A scalable peer-to-peer lookup protocol for internet applications. IEEE/ACM Trans. Netw. 11(1), 17–32 (2003)
36. Tang, P., Tai, T.: Network traffic characterization using token bucket model. In: INFOCOM (2009)
37. Tazaki, H., Asaeda, H.: DNEmu: Design and implementation of distributed network emulation for smooth experimentation control. In: Korakis, T., Zink, M., Ott, M. (eds.) TridentCom 2012. LNICST, vol. 44, pp. 162–177. Springer, Heidelberg (2012)
38. Vahdat, A., Yocum, K., Walsh, K., Mahadevan, P., Kostic, D., Chase, J., Becker, D.: Scalability and accuracy in a large-scale network emulator. In: OSDI (2002)
39. Weingärtner, E., Schmidt, F., Lehn, H., Heer, T., Wehrle, K.: SliceTime: a platform for scalable and accurate network emulation. In: NSDI (2011)
40. White, B., Lepreau, J., Stoller, L., Ricci, R., Guruprasad, S., Newbold, M., Hibler, M., Barb, C., Joglekar, A.: An integrated experimental environment for distributed systems and networks. In: OSDI (2002)
41. Yin, Q., Roscoe, T.: VF2x: Fast, efficient virtual network mapping for real testbed workloads. In: Korakis, T., Zink, M., Ott, M. (eds.) TridentCom 2012. LNICST, vol. 44, pp. 271–286. Springer, Heidelberg (2012)
42. Zegura, E., Calvert, K., Bhattacharjee, S.: How to model an internetwork. In: INFOCOM (1996)
43. Zheng, P., Ni, L.: Empower: A network emulator for wireline and wireless networks. In: INFOCOM (2003)

Assured Cloud-Based Data Analysis
with ClusterBFT*

Julian James Stephen and Patrick Eugster

Purdue University

Abstract. The shift to cloud technologies is a paradigm change that offers considerable financial and administrative gains. However governmental and business institutions wanting to tap into these gains are concerned with security issues. The cloud presents new vulnerabilities and is dominated by new kinds of applications, which calls for new security solutions.

Intuitively, Byzantine fault tolerant (BFT) replication has many benefits to enforce integrity and availability in clouds. Existing BFT systems, however, are not suited for typical "data-flow processing" cloud applications which analyze large amounts of data in a parallelizable manner: indeed, existing BFT solutions focus on replicating single monolithic servers, whilst data-flow applications consist in several different stages, each of which may give rise to multiple components at runtime to exploit cheap hardware parallelism; similarly, BFT replication hinges on comparison of redundant outputs generated, which in the case of data-flow processing can represent huge amounts of data. In fact, current limits of data processing directly depend on the amount of data that can be processed per time unit.

In this paper we present ClusterBFT, a system that secures computations being run in the cloud by leveraging BFT replication coupled with fault isolation. In short, ClusterBFT leverages a combination of variable-degree clustering, approximated and offline output comparison, smart deployment, and separation of duty, to achieve a parameterized tradeoff between fault tolerance and overhead in practice. We demonstrate the low overhead achieved with ClusterBFT when securing data-flow computations expressed in Apache Pig, and Hadoop. Our solution allows assured computation with less than 10 percent latency overhead as shown by our evaluation.

Keywords: Cloud, Byzantine fault, replication, integrity, data analysis.

1 Introduction

The cloud as a computing platform is getting more popular and mature every day. Computational needs of industry, academia, and government are being increasingly met by processing data in the cloud. Recently announced government

---

* This work has been financially supported by DARPA grant # N11AP20014, Northrop Grumman Information Systems, Purdue Research Foundation grant # 204533, and Google Research Award "Geo-Distributed Big Data Processing".

D. Eyers and K. Schwan (Eds.): Middleware 2013, LNCS 8275, pp. 82–102, 2013.

policies [4] clearly show an urgent economic requirement for processing data in the cloud. Yet, a major roadblock to adopting cloud technologies is the lack of trust on the various facets of cloud computing. The fact that a potentially malicious entity can legally access computing resources in the same datacenter or even on the same machines as well-intended users increases the risk associated with moving computations into the cloud. Malicious programs, faulty hardware, and software bugs can lead to corrupt data or cause services to fail.

Model. In many scenarios, institutions can trust the cloud providers themselves, but not the users of the system. If we take the example of the US intelligence community, different agencies have their own *inhouse* clouds. They want to improve sharing of information with each other without exposing their own systems to potential weaknesses or infections in their peer systems [4]. Such a partial trust model also applies to many large corporations which include subdivisions hosting their own datacenters. Within this scenario, the present paper is concerned with ensuring (a) *integrity* and (b) *availability*, i.e., that computations indeed perform what they were supposed to (e.g., to avoid obfuscating terrorist activities), and that these computations can be performed in a timely manner (e.g., to be able to react to real threats on time). While our solution also includes mechanisms for *confidentiality* we focus on (a) and (b) in this paper.

State of the Art. Most approaches to cloud security focus by and large on either (a) *communication*, (b) *data*, or (c) *computation*. Communication-centric approaches (a) to security in public or inhouse clouds focus on setting up thick firewalls, which monitor in - and outbound traffic. Typically, ports that accept incoming data and specific protocols and services are allowed or disallowed based on the configuration of the firewall. Though required, such perimeter security is not sufficient to secure computations because, zero-day attacks may compromise one or many of the internal nodes. Once an internal node is compromised, it can alter computation output even without any communication across the perimeter. This can break the integrity of the system. In addition, as illustrated over and over again by the alleged organized attacks of chinese hacker groups on US installations, if there is a vulnerability in the perimeter defense system, it is very difficult to detect an ongoing attack. Data-centric approaches (b) protect data from malicious and benign failures but mainly focus on data at rest. In all functional systems, data is under constant churn. Computation adds, deletes and morphs data into new forms. Further, in many cloud storage systems data modification is replaced with data creation (append-only semantics) for performance and reliability reasons. Under such conditions, it is impossible to ensure integrity of data without assuring computations that work on data. Typical data-centric approaches focus on ensuring confidentiality when that data is accessed or computed on but do not verify computations themselves. Computation-centric approaches (c) to securing computation focus on fine-grained information-flow [17]. As with data-centric approaches, information-flow approaches aim at protecting (sensitive) data from leaking. However, they do not ensure that the computation is behaving according to specification, i.e., ensuring the computation is doing what it was intended to. In typical cloud data-flow processing applications, where new data-sets are generated as outcome of analysis and correlation of existing data-sets and stored for subsequent use, these outcomes must be trustworthy. In fact, since in the larger picture data-sets are derived from earlier data-sets, any false results computed violate integrity of the semantic information in the original data-sets.

BFT in Clouds. Intuitively, *Byzantine fault tolerant* (BFT) replication [23] is a powerful means of securing computation and thus achieving integrity and availability in cloud-based computing. BFT suggests the use of multiple replicas of a sensitive component, and hinges on the comparison of outcomes produced by these replicas to determine components with erratic behavior (assuming a correct "majority"). While several fundamental assumptions of BFT replication — e.g., determinism in replicas for comparisons, possibility of exploiting redundant hardware — are largely met by typical cloud-based data-flow applications, *existing* BFT *systems* are inapplicable to such applications: these focus on securing single monolithic servers, and only little work exists on applying BFT replication beyond such stand-alone servers. Cloud-based data-flow processing systems, inversely, leverage cheap hardware by breaking down applications into small components which are amenable to parallel execution. When applying BFT replication to any one of these components by running multiple replicas of each and comparing their respective outcomes overheads sum up very quickly.

ClusterBFT. This paper presents ClusterBFT for cloud-based assured data processing and analysis. ClusterBFT utilizes BFT techniques which impose less overhead than existing cryptographic primitives, but breaks away from the mold of individually replicating every client request. More precisely, ClusterBFT creates sub-graphs from acyclic data-flow graphs that are then replicated. This means, rather than enduring the overhead of BFT consensus at each component involved in the data-flow processing, we have a system with much less overhead that can dynamically adapt to changes in required responsiveness and perceived threat level as well as to dynamic deployment (elasticity). We use a combination of *variable-grain clustering* with *approximated* and *offline comparison, separation of duty*, and *smart deployment* to keep overheads of BFT repliation low while providing good fault isolation properties. In summary, the main contributions of the paper are (1) identification of challenges and solutions for achieving availability and integrity of cloud-based data-flow computations with BFT replication, (2) the architecture and implementation of a BFT solution for such computations, and (3) the evaluation of this solution. Our evaluation shows less than 10 percent latency overhead in most cases for even complex data analysis jobs.

Roadmap. The remainder of this paper is structured as follows. Section 2 provides background information. Section 3 lists design principles and challenges. Section 4 describes the ClusterBFT architecture in detail. Section 5 describes its implementation. Section 6 presents evaluation results. Section 7 presents related work. Section 8 draws conclusions.

2   Background and Preliminaries

This section presents information pertinent to the remainder of the paper.

2.1   BFT

Byzantine failures [23] model arbitrary faults that may occur in a process during execution, including malign and benign faults. In order to explain our system better, we further distinguish Byzantine failures by classifying them based on how they allow deviation from correct execution. We use the categorization of Kihlstrom et al. [20] which classifies Byzantine failures as follows:

- Omission (detectable): An omission failure occurs when a process does not send a message that it is expected to send. These can be detected by setting timeouts for messages. It is important to note here that in an asynchronous system, a timeout does not necessarily imply a faulty component.
- Commission (detectable): A commission failure occurs when a process sends a message it is not supposed to send. Such failures can be detected by checking if the message is in agreement with at least $f+1$ other replicas.
- Unobservable (non-detectable): Unobservable failures are those which other processes cannot detect based on the messages they receive.
- Undiagnosable (non-detectable): Undiagnosable failures are those that cannot be attributed to a specific process.

2.2   MapReduce and Pig

Big data analysis is one of the major use cases for moving towards cloud computing and most cloud-specific programming models reflect this. Corresponding runtime systems try to make use of large numbers of nodes available for data analysis to decrease latency. The popular MapReduce [16] framework partitions input data and assigns a mapper process to each input partition. These mapper processes produce "intermediate" key-value pairs as output which are grouped by key and fed by key to reducer processes which use these to generate final output. Hadoop [37] is a popular open source implementation of MapReduce.

Apache Pig [3] is a platform for data analysis that consists of the PigLatin [28] high-level language for expressing data analysis programs, and a runtime system. Pig Latin scripts are typically compiled to MapReduce jobs that are executed using a MapReduce engine such as Hadoop for Pig. To illustrate the benefits of our concepts, we focus in this paper on Pig data analysis jobs.

Throughout the paper, unless otherwise specified, we use the term *script* to refer to a Pig (Latin) script. We use the term *job* to refer to a MapReduce job and *task* to refer to map or reduce tasks within a MapReduce job. We use the term *job cluster* to refer to the group of nodes involved in executing a specific job.

2.3   System Model

We assume that the system is deployed on a cloud service that leases out virtual machines to users. We refer to one such virtual computation unit as a *node*. This means that there could be multiple nodes on the same physical machine. We assume that the number of nodes that are faulty at a given time is bounded. For the purpose of this paper we focus on computation and assume a trusted storage layer. We are aware that assuming correctness of a storage system prone to Byzantine faults is ambitious, but it is not unrealistic either. Systems like DepSky [8] show its feasibility. Further, the challenges that need to be solved even with the presence of a trusted storage are tough and warrant investigation. We present a system for two *adversary models*. For both models, we assume that the adversary cannot manipulate the cloud service provider or violate its specifications. This includes preventing communication between any two nodes, spawning new Byzantine nodes, and breaking computationally hard cryptographic primitives. A *strong adversary* can manipulate all internal aspects of a node and collude with other adversaries. This includes full control over the executing processes, physical memory and messages being sent out of the node. A *weak adversary* shares the same properties of a strong adversary, but may only cause omission or commission faults.

3   ClusterBFT Design

This section presents first our motivation for using BFT techniques in the cloud, before outlining challenges in such adoption and finally our solutions for overcoming these.

3.1   BFT and the Cloud

We decided to adopt BFT replication due to several intuitive benefits:

Attribution: Along with tolerating benign or malign failures, BFT techniques can also point to potentially faulty components which helps for attribution as well as auditing. Indeed, being able to shield computation from malicious entities is one thing, but in a sea of nodes such as a cloud datacenter it is also necessary to keep track of where such accesses were attempted, as these may hint to exploited leaks and intruders.

Portability and interoperability: BFT techniques can be applied at a higher level in the protocol stack — here typically at the level of data-flow program execution — which allows them to be deployed easily across different cloud platforms and infrastructures, thus supporting portability, cloud interoperability, and the cloud-of-clouds paradigm [38].

Determinism: Popularity of data-flow languages like PigLatin or DryadLINQ [40] shows the relevance of data analysis jobs that can be modeled as direct acyclic graphs (DAGs). These computations and their constituents are by-and-large deterministic, which simplifies the comparison of redundant

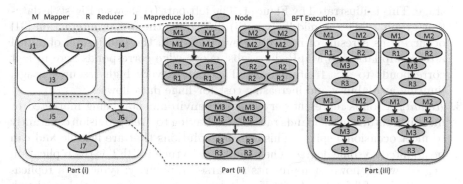

Fig. 1. Part (i) shows a data-flow graph with 7 phases. (ii) focuses on $n \times m$ replication of jobs J1, J2 and J3. (iii) shows clustered replication of J1, J2, J3 requiring only one round of BFT consensus. For simplicity we only show one map and one reduce task per MapReduce job.

results. Inversely, concurrent client accesses pose challenges when replicating large monolithic servers. Recent trends in cloud-based data processing include support for iterative and incremental jobs which contradict the straightforward DAG model [41] but do not hamper determinism.

Heterogeneity: BFT relies on heterogeneity of replicas to ensure that a majority of replicas are not compromised simultaneously by means of the same vulnerability. Cloud platforms do expose a uniform hypervisor layer on which operating systems are deployed, but cloud providers offer a variety of operating system images that can be deployed on these nodes. Within an operating system itself, adoption of address space layout randomization (ADSLR) introduces further heterogeneity. DARPA's Mission-Resilient Cloud program [25] funds several projects aiming at creating moving targets specifically to further narrow this gap [27].

3.2 Challenges in Adopting BFT in the Cloud

Though intuitively BFT seems like a good match in many ways for ensuring computation in the cloud, it has thus far not been adopted widely in such a context due to a variety of open challenges:

C1. *Scalability:* Datasets are typically many magnitudes higher in cloud-based programming than in previous scenarios. As BFT replication protocols hinge on comparison of redundant outcomes, this translates to large overheads.

C2. *Granularity:* Data analysis scripts also tend to have multiple *jobs* where output of one is fed to the second. This creates a *job-chain* in which a process that was a server for one job acts as a client for the second job. Ideally, every process is fine-grained and can be deployed dynamically. This means, naïve BFT replication of each job will result in $R = 3f+1$ replicas for each task, with $n \times m$ communication [31] and synchronization after every stage. This is illustrated by Figure 1. The left part (i) shows a Pig-style data-flow graph, while the middle part (ii) illustrates the $n \times m$ interaction [31] occurring as a result of replicating every node in the (sub)graph obtained after compilation to MapReduce jobs: every edge corresponds here in fact corresponds to 4×4 interactions. This causes very high resource usage, limiting availability and increasing cost for huge data-flows.

C3. *Rigidity:* Clouds represent very dynamic environments, being marketed to meet instantaneous demands rather than having to over-provision constantly to meet occasional spikes. This calls for solutions that are flexible and can be adapted to some degree. The main knob to turn in BFT is the replication degree, which however represents a coarse granularity: typically a replication degree of $3f + 1 = 4$ with $f = 1$ already leads to substantial overhead. The next larger step, $3f + 1 = 7$, to tolerate up to 2 failures already leads to prohibitively larger overhead.

There are are also non-technical factors deterring BFT adoption in the cloud. As explained by Birman et al. [9], many cloud middleware service providers have an inherent "fear of synchronization" irrespective of the existence of fast consensus protocols and success stories like Chubby [11].

3.3 ClusterBFT Principles and Architecture Overview

ClusterBFT addresses the challenges C1-C3 above as follows:

Variable Granularity: Observe that nothing forces us to replicate every individual node in the data-flow graph. We could in fact replicate the execution of an entire data-flow graph $3f + 1$-fold, and compare the outcomes at the very end. More generally speaking, we can choose any intermediate level for clustering nodes in the graph and replicate these subgraphs (addressing C2 above). This is illustrated by the right part (iii) of Figure 1, where the sub-graph of (ii) is replicated as a whole and comparison only occurs at the end of this sub-graph. The potential downside of such regrouping is that it may diminish the degree of fault tolerance and precision of fault attribution: a single deviant node in a group hampers the outcome of that replica, and identifying *which* node(s) in the group exhibit Byzantine behavior becomes harder. In addition, if we do not end up having sufficiently many identical replica responses, it takes longer to run additional replicas thus increasing job latency. This tradeoff leads to an additional knob for users to tweak (C3).

Variable Replication: The BFT replication model allows control over how resources are utilized. Based on the user's confidence in the cluster, different degrees of replication can be adopted with different guarantees. A user can specify an optimistic, $f+1$ replicas. In this case, the execution ensures safety, but may require repeated runs to get correct output. If the user specifies $2f + 1$ replicas, a correct result can be guaranteed if all replicas always reply (no omission failures). If $3f + 1$ replicas are specified, a correct result can be guaranteed under combination of any kind of Byzantine failure.

Approximate, Offline Redundancy: Instead of comparing the entire outputs of a replica set in one go upon sub-job completion, we can choose to (1) only compare *digests*, (2) start doing so *before sub-job completion*, and (3) allow the follow-up sub-job to proceed based on the complete output *before comparison completes*. This reduces the overhead of putting redundancy to work (addressing C1) in a way allowing further fine-tuning of tradeoffs between performance and security by control of the resilience of the digests (C3).

Separation of Duty: Rather than baking the entire data-flow handling logic into every node, we can separate architecturally the "front-end" of a data-flow processing system which accepts jobs from the actual cluster of worker nodes such as MapReduce nodes executing the jobs. This architectural division is illustrated in Figure 2 which outlines the architecture of our solution ClusterBFT detailed in the next section. Components in the *control* tier are command and control processes that provide direction and coordinate computations in the *computation* tier. The former tier is trusted, which is achievable by BFT replication or by implicitly trusting the nodes, i.e., by closely (even manually) monitoring nodes, or using nodes in the client network or private cloud. The benefit of this separation is that it limits certain strong assumptions and expensive mechanisms to the front-end, allowing the cluster to focus on work (cf. [39]) and to be handled more dynamically (C3). This in turns allows the worker node cluster to be adapted dynamically, by adding and removing nodes based on resource requirements, measured performance, and of course suspicions.

Fault Isolation: Another net advantage of the separation of duty is that the front-end can keep track of suspicions observed, and can use specific deployment policies to, for instance, narrow down the (set of) faulty node(s) in a replication group delivering a faulty response by intentionally partly overlaying the replication group of a different job on the same nodes. Similarly, dummy jobs can be used to further probe nodes in such a suspicious replication group. Thus the tradeoff with attribution precision introduced by variable granularity does not become a one-way path but becomes a tradeoff with the *time* it takes to recover precision (C3).

In the following section we describe the architecture of ClusterBFT and how we put these principles to work.

4 ClusterBFT Architecture and Components

In this section we look at the different components that make up ClusterBFT (see Figure 2). Table 1 presents a summary of the symbols used in the following.

4.1 Request Handler

The *request handler* component is in the control tier. It accepts scripts submitted by the client and submits the script for execution. It consists of three logical subcomponents outlined below.

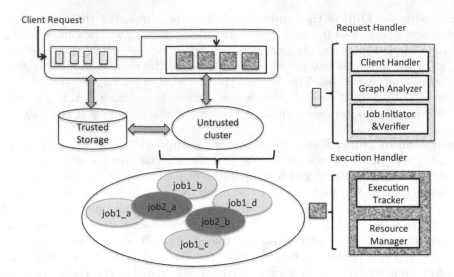

Fig. 2. Architecture

Client Handler. The client submits the script to the *client handler*. The client also specifies the number of expected failures f, a replication factor r and the total number of verification points n based on the perceived threat level. Verification points are vertices in the data-flow graph af-

Table 1. Symbols

Symbol	Meaning
r	Replication factor
n	Number of verification points
f	Number of expected failures
s	Suspicion level

ter which output from different replicas are matched. The client handler generates a logical plan from the script. This is given as input to the graph analyzer described below.

Graph Analyzer. In order to reduce overhead and improve utilization, we need to identify verification points in the data-flow graph that are most effective. Running verification after every operation will cause very high overhead and running verification scarcely will result in more re-computations (hence higher resource usage) when failures occur. The *graph analyzer* component, based on the adversary model, identifies points in the data-flow graph for performing verification. Under the strong adversary model, only points that correspond to data-flow between jobs are considered for verification. Under a weak adversary model, any point in the data flow graph can be considered for verification.

With n verification points requested by the user, we use the marker function defined in Figure 3 to identify the actual points. We explain the intuition behind the marker function using an example. Consider the data-flow graph in Figure 4 and assume the user specified one verification point. If we decide to perform verification right after the vertex *Load*1, then the probability of identifying a fault is very low. There is a much higher probability that at least one of the

Table 2. Notation

Notation	Meaning
$ir[v]$	Input ratio of v
$parents(v)$	All parents of vertex v
$level(v)$	$\begin{cases} 1 & \text{if } v = Load \\ \max\limits_{p \in parents(v)} 1 + level(p) & \text{else} \end{cases}$
$min(v, M)$	Number of edges between v and the vertex closest to v in M

V ▷ Vertex set
n ▷ Number of verification points
function MARK(V, n)
  $M \leftarrow \emptyset$ ▷ Set of marked vertices
  for 1.. n **do**
    $max \leftarrow 0$
    for all $v \in V$ **do**
      $score_v \leftarrow ir[v] + min(v, M)$
      if $score_v > max$ **then**
        $m \leftarrow v$
        $max \leftarrow score_v$
      end if
    end for
    $M \leftarrow M \cup \{m\}$
  end for
end function

Fig. 3. Marker function

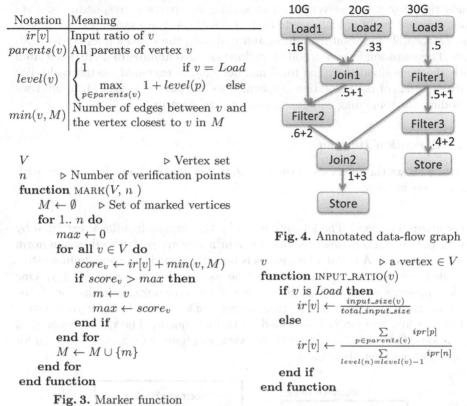

Fig. 4. Annotated data-flow graph

v ▷ a vertex $\in V$
function INPUT_RATIO(v)
  if v is $Load$ **then**
    $ir[v] \leftarrow \dfrac{input\_size(v)}{total\_input\_size}$
  else
    $ir[v] \leftarrow \dfrac{\sum\limits_{p \in parents(v)} ipr[p]}{\sum\limits_{level(n)=level(v)-1} ipr[n]}$
  end if
end function

Fig. 5. Computing input ratios

nodes that execute the vertices below *Load*1 is faulty simply because there are more of them. On the other end, if we run verification after *Join*2, then we most probably will know if result is going to be faulty, but the cost of re-computation, in case $f+1$ replicas do not agree becomes high; the entire sequence of operation needs to be recomputed. The marker function considers two main parameters to arrive at a verification point that is a good tradeoff between these two extremes. The ratio of input data that flows through a vertex and distance of a vertex from another verification point. Using these two values, the marker function arrives at a mid point suitable for verification. Once the verification point is identified, the logical plan is instrumented with a verification function and given to the *job initiator*. Details of what a verification function are described next.

Job Initiator and Verifier. The instrumented script gets compiled into one or more MapReduce jobs and the job initiator associates a sub graph identifier *sid* with each such job. The job initiator submits a total of r replicas of the job for execution to the execution handler. All replicas are configured to have the same number of reduce tasks. The verification function instrumented into the MapReduce job uses a cryptographic hash function (SHA-256 in our prototype) to compute a digest of the data streaming through the verification point and sends this digest to the verifier. The verifier compares corresponding digests from different replicas and asserts that at least $f + 1$ are same. The verifier is also responsible for isolating failures and updating the suspicion level s for each node. The suspicion level of a node is defined as total number of faults associated with the node divided by the total number of jobs executed on the node. For clarity, details of fault isolation is specified as a separate section (4.2), after we introduce the remaining components in our architecture.

4.2 Execution Handler

Figure 6 shows the internals of the *execution handler* and how it interacts with the request handler.

Execution Tracker. The job submitted by the request handler is executed by the execution tracker. Resources available in nodes are partitioned into uniform resource units ru. A list of all resources is initially loaded from an administrator-provided inclusion list into the *resource table* as a tuple $\langle nid, \#ru, \langle sid...\rangle, s \rangle$. One tuple represents a node id nid, the number of resource units ru in that node, the current allocation of $sids$ and suspicion level s of a node. When the job initiator submits a job, the job is first added to the job queue. The main sequence of operations that take place after this is shown in Figure 6 (others are omitted for simplicity), and detailed below:

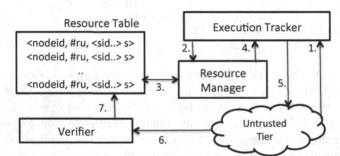

Fig. 6. Execution tracker & resource manager

1. A node in the untrusted domain with id nid sends a heartbeat message to the execution tracker.
2. The execution tracker checks with the *resource manager* to see if there is a task that can be scheduled on node nid.
3. The resource manager queries the resource allocation table to retrieve the $sids$ of tasks currently running on node nid. Using this, the resource manager looks at the list of running or submitted jobs to check if a there is a task from a job that does not already have a task running on node nid.
4. The resource manager provides a list of ready tasks corresponding to the number of free rus in node nid.

5. The execution tracker replies to the heartbeat message with the task that needs to be executed.
6. During task execution, the verification function creates a message digest of data streaming through the verification point and sends the digest to the verifier. The verifier checks for $f + 1$ matching message digests from different replicas. If the verifier times out without obtaining $f + 1$ matching message digests, the job is initiated again with a higher value for r.
7. Based on the number of non-matching digests, the verifier updates the suspicion levels of node $nid.$ in the resource table.

Resource Manager. We already outlined how the resource manager functions as part of the working of the execution tracker. There are two goals that we try to achieve by proper task selection: efficient execution and fast fault identification. Data local tasks enable faster execution. For fast fault identification job clusters can be overlapped in specific patterns. The scheduling strategy we use is to cause as many intersections as there are resource units in a node. That means if one node has three resource units, we try to pick tasks from three different jobs to execute. Other strategies can also be used to overlap clusters which we intend to explore in future work. The administrator can also configure a suspicion threshold such that if $s >$ threshold, then the resource manager will remove that node from its inclusion list and ignore further requests from that node. At this point administrators can intervene to re-initialize the node by taking the node off the grid, applying securing patches and reinserting the node.

4.3 Fault Identification and Isolation

As described in Section 4.2, the output verifier collects output digests and asserts that at least $f+1$ digests are the same. If the verifier receives an incorrect digest or

```
1:  D ← A set of disjoint sets.
2:  O ← A set of overlapping sets.
3:  function FAULT ANALYZER(S)          ▷
        S, the set of nodes in a cluster that just
        returned a commission fault.
4:      if ∀X | X ∈ D, S ∩ X = ∅ then
5:          D ← {S} ∪ D
6:      else if ∃Y | Y ∈ D and S ⊂ Y then
7:          D ← D \ {Y}
8:          O ← O ∪ {Y}
9:          D ← D ∪ {S}
10:     else
11:         O ← O ∪ {S}
12:     if |D| = f then
13:         for each X ∈ D do
14:             A ← A ∪ X
15:         for each X ∈ O do
16:             X ← X ∩ A
17:         for each X ∈ D do
18:             for each Y ∈ O do
19:                 if X ∩ Y ≠ ∅ then
20:                     I ← I ∪ (X ∩ Y)
21:                 if | I |= 1 then
22:                     D ← D \ {X}
23:                     D ← D ∪ {I}
24: end function
```

Fig. 7. Fault analyzer function

does not receive a digest from nodes executing the data-flow, the suspicion level of all involved nodes is updated. This means if there is a faulty node that is part of multiple job clusters, that faulty node is likely to have a higher suspicion level. Once the verifier identifies a job cluster as returning incorrect result, the *fault analyzer* function in Figure 7 is used to further narrow down the list of suspicious nodes. The fault analyzer works in two stages. In the first stage disjoint subsets of suspicious nodes are isolated. This set of subsets is denoted by D (line 1). This is done until the number of such subsets becomes equal to the highest value of f the system has seen so far (line 12). This allows us to identify subsets of nodes such that there is exactly one fault per subset. The second stage (lines 13-23) reduces the number of nodes in these subsets by creating the intersection of a subset with other sets of faulty nodes. The intuition for the second stage is that if there are f subsets in D and a new set of faulty nodes intersects with only one of those f subsets, then the nodes in the intersection must be faulty.

Byzantine behavior also means an infected node may be mostly producing correct output, and produce incorrect results occasionally. This means if nodes show malicious intent/fail frequently, fault isolation becomes faster.

5 Implementation

This section presents our prototype implementation of ClusterBFT. ClusterBFT is implemented in Java by modifying Hadoop 1.0.4 [19] and Pig 0.9.2. For instrumenting the Pig logical plan we modified the Penny [29] monitoring tool, distributed as part of Pig 0.9.2 source.

5.1 Hadoop

Hadoop uses a centralized *job tracker* and *task tracker*s on each computation node. The job tracker initiates a MapReduce job and task trackers spawn map or reduce tasks for the job, and send heartbeat messages and job status updates to the job tracker. It is relevant here to note that Hadoop allocates resources in a node as *task slots*. Each node may have multiple task slots depending on the number of CPU cores and physical memory available for processing. Typically 3-4 slots can be configured on a node with 4 CPU cores.

5.2 Request Handler

Penny consists of Penny agents that are inserted between Pig script states. These agents in turn are implemented as user defined functions that can exchange messages with other agents and a Penny coordinator. Our changes involve creating a verifying function as a Penny tool that creates a SHA-256 digest and sends the digest back to the coordinator in the trusted tier. We modified the Penny infrastructure to allow creation of multiple coordinators, so that different replicas can reply back to different coordinators.

5.3   Execution Handler

We implement the resource manager by creating a new task scheduler that extends the `TaskScheduler` class in Hadoop. Hadoop allows creation of multiple *job queues* to which jobs can be submitted. In ClusterBFT each replica of a job can be submitted to one queue. In order to tolerate faulty nodes, we also need to ensure that tasks from more than one replica of a job are not scheduled on a same node at any point of time. Such a collocation could result in one faulty node modifying the outcome of more than one replica and thus violating safety. Note that this does not prevent us from collocating tasks from different jobs on the same node. We added data structures to the `JobInProgress` class that will keep track of replica information to prevent this during task scheduling. We also added a new alphanumeric parameter `sub.graph.id` to the `JobConf` class. `sub.graph.id` corresponds to *sid* in Section 4.1 and is set during job initiation. All replicas of a single job must have the same `sub.graph.id`. `JobTracker` itself works without any modifications as our execution tracker.

5.4   Ensuring Determinism

The data parallelism leveraged by MapReduce may naturally lead to non-determinism, which can be observed through differing digest values across replicas even without faulty processes. For example in order to calculate an average, instead of finding the sum of all values of a key and dividing it by the number of values, users may decide to maintain a moving average, causing final outputs to differ (in the least few significant bits of precision). Our current prototype works around this issue by ensuring that the user programs deal with only integer values or truncate the last few decimal points before performing arithmetic operations. For a more general solution we intend to address this issue in future work by ordering the intermediate mapper output based on mapper ids.

6   Evaluation

To assess the benefits of our approach, we evaluate (a) overhead incurred by ClusterBFT, (b) gains of ClusterBFT under different replication degrees in the presence of failures (c) effectiveness of fault isolation algorithm and (d) system performance for higher approximation accuracy.

Setup. For evaluations in Section 6.1 and 6.2, we use planet-lab based Vicci [1] as our testbed. Machines are 12-core Intel Xeon servers with 48GB RAM virtualized using Linux containers. Our untrusted tier consists of 32 nodes and our trusted tier consists of 2 nodes. We use Amazon EC2 for the evaluation in Section 6.4 with 8 nodes in the untrusted tier and 4 nodes in the trusted tier.

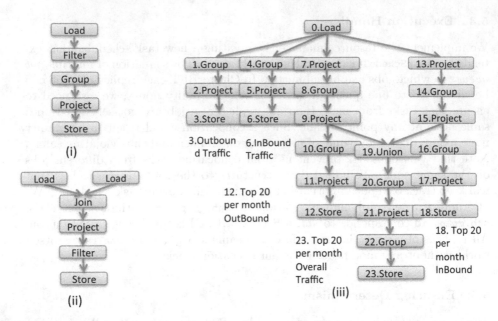

Fig. 8. Data-flow graph for (i) Twitter Follower Analysis (ii) Twitter Two Hop Analysis, (iii) Air Traffic Analysis

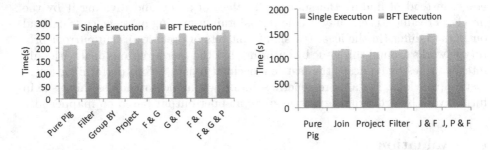

Fig. 9. Latency of running Twitter Follower Analysis

Fig. 10. Digest computation overhead for Twitter Two Hop Analysis

6.1   Verification Overhead: Twitter Data Analysis

First we measure the overhead involved in computing digests required for verification. For this we use the Twitter data-set from [22] and compute *SHA-256* digests at different points for two Pig scripts. The data-set consists of two columns, *user-id* and *follower-id* represented as numeric values. We run two Pig scripts outlined in [6]. The first script (Twitter Follower Analysis) counts the number of *followers* for each user. It loads the data, filters out empty records, groups the record by *user-id*, calculates the counts and saves the *user-id* and respective counts. The second script (Twitter Two Hop Analysis) lists pairs of users that are are two hops away from one another. This job does a self-join that matches

one user with all its *follower's followers*. The data-flow graphs for these two
scripts are presented in Figure 8 (i) and (ii) respectively. Figures 9 and 10 shows
the total time taken for job completion when digests are computed at different
points of the respective jobs. In both graphs, *Single Execution* shows the time
taken by a single replica of the script and *BFT Execution* shows the time taken
by 4 replicas of the script to execute. *BFT Execution* also includes the overhead
of matching $f + 1$ digests generated by the replicas. *Pure Pig* shows the baseline
run with no verification points or replication. When digests are computed at
multiple points in the data-flow graph, it is abbreviated using the first letter
of the verification point. When digests are computed at multiple points in the
data-flow graph, it is abbreviated using the first letter of the verification point.
Figure 9 show a minimal overhead of 8% and worst case of 9%, 14% and 19%
overhead with 1, 2 and 3 verification points respectively.

Table 3. ClusterBFT in the presence of Byzantine failures

Measure	$r = 2$ C	$r = 2$ P	$r = 3$, case 1 C	$r = 3$, case 1 P	$r = 3$, case 2 C	$r = 3$, case 2 P	$r = 4$ C	$r = 4$ P
Latency (s)	1.6×	2.1×	1.1×	1.1×	1.6×	2.1×	1.1×	1.1×
CPU time spent (ms)	3.5×	4.1×	3.1×	3.1×	4.5×	6.2×	4.2×	4.2×
File read (Bytes)	3.6×	4×	2.6×	3×	4.7×	6×	3.6×	4×
File write(Bytes)	3.4×	4×	2.4×	3×	4.7×	6×	3.4×	4×
HDFS write (Bytes)	2×	4×	2×	3×	2×	6×	3×	4×

6.2 Performance Under Failures: IRTA Airline Traffic Analysis

Next we look at ClusterBFT's performance in the presence of node failures. The
input data-set for this evaluation is a 1.3GB subset of airline data-set provided
by RITA [2]. We run a multi-store query outlined in [6] that finds the top 20
airports with respect to incoming flights, outgoing flights, and overall. The data-
flow graph for this script is shown in Figure 8 (iii). The evaluation is set up
for $f = 1$ and we show the benefits of ClusterBFT under various replication
degrees with 2 verification points. We compare ClusterBFT (C in Table 3) with
modified version of Pig which verifies digest of the final output only and not
anywhere else in the data-flow graph (P in Table 3). The results are shown in
terms of a multiplier over a single run of standard Pig without replication or
digest computation. For both executions (C and P), one node was set up to
always produce commission failures resulting in an incorrect digest. Also for
$r = 3$, we took two measurements. The first measurement (case 1) shows results
when all computations got done within the verifier timeout value. The second
measurement (case 2) shows one correct replica not responding within the verifier
timeout causing the script to be scheduled again with higher timeout value.
Results show that latency decreases by 23% ($r = 2, r = 3$ case 2) for test runs
that require rescheduling. For runs that do not require rescheduling, our latency
is on par with running multiple replicas, and show up to 14% reduced overhead.

6.3   Effectiveness of Fault Isolation: Simulation

Next we evaluate the fault analyzer algorithm outlined in Figure 7. We wrote a Java-based simulator that mimics resource allocation in a 250 node Hadoop cluster. Each node is given 3 slots on which tasks can be scheduled. We consider jobs as falling under three categories: *large* (requiring 20 to 30 slots), *medium* (10 to 15 slots) and *small* (3 to 5 slots). The exact number of slots is determined uniformly at random. Each job is also associated with a unit of time as length. We studied the algorithm under various ratios of *small, medium* and *large* jobs as well as various length for jobs. We present a subset of our results here. Figure 11 shows the average number of jobs that got completed when the number of disjoint faulty sets (D) becomes equal to f (Figure 7 line 12). This point is important because the number of suspicious nodes will not increase after this point. We show measurements for two ratios of job sizes and two values of f. Job size ratio $r1$ indicates $|large| : |medium| : |small| = 6 : 3 : 1$ and r2 indicates $2 : 2 : 1$. For $f = 1$, we used 4 replicas and $f = 2$, we used 7 replicas. The abscissa shows the probability with which a faulty node produces a commission failure. This result shows that if a node produces commission faults with very high probability, then by the time 10 jobs complete execution, we can isolate the fault to a much smaller subset. If a node produces commission faults with probability of .6 or more, less than 20 jobs are required to isolate the fault. The

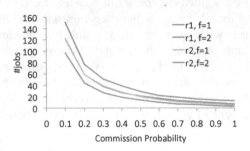

Fig. 11. Number of jobs required to identify disjoint set of faults

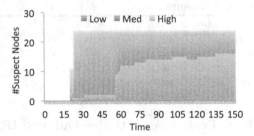

Fig. 12. Suspicion level changes over time

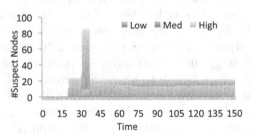

Fig. 13. Suspicion level spike as a result of multiple large clusters with faulty nodes

size of these subsets indicate the number of suspicious nodes, and this is explored in Figure 12 and Figure 13. In order to understand the number of nodes suspected by the algorithm and the suspicion level (s) of these nodes, we group suspicion level into four categories: no suspicion, *Low* (with $0 < s <= 0.33$), *Med* ($0.33 < s \leq 0.66$) and *High* ($0.66 < s \leq 1$). The goal of the algorithm is to narrow the suspicion down to fewer nodes, or in other words, we should have less nodes with high value for s. Figure 12 shows how s changes with time. The initial values $(Time < 15)$ indicates that no job has so far showed a commission fault. After this point we see that the number of nodes with $s > 0$ increases. It is also worthwhile to note that at around $Time = 25$, $|D|$ becomes equal to f and the number of nodes with $s > 0$ does not increase further. The graph clearly shows that nodes start with *High* and *Med* suspicion levels, but over time, the suspicion levels of faulty nodes remain *High*, and of others are reduced. In fact, in these trials, by $Time = 50$, only the real faulty nodes were left in the *High* suspicion category. In Figure 13, we show occasional spikes in the number of suspicious nodes that we observed in some of the runs. This happens before $|D|$ becomes equal to f. This is because it may so happen that two replicas of *large* jobs show commission fault and all nodes in them gets a non zero value for s. But within a few more runs the algorithm prunes the suspicion list and increasingly suspects the real faulty nodes as can be seen when $Time > 35$.

6.4   Approximation Accuracy: Weather Average Temperature

Here we test how ClusterBFT performs if we increase the approximation accuracy from the default, one digest at one verification point, to multiple digests at each verification points. For this experiment we move away from the assumption of implicit trust within the trusted tier and instantiate $3f + 1$ replicas of the request handler. We use the BFT-SMaRT [5] library for achieving Byzantine fault tolerance within these request handler replicas. Input data for this experiment is a 640MB subset of the Daily Surface Summary of Day weather data [26]. The script involves finding average temperate over multiple years for each weather station followed by counting the number of stations with the same average. We take measurements for different values of f and change the number of lines d for which a digest is created. Figure 14 shows the results. In the figure, *Full* refers to script execution with digest computed and verified only for the output. *ClusterBFT* refers to using ClusterBFT with 2 verification points and *Individual* refers to digest computed for each vertex of the data-flow graph. Results show that latency overhead of ClusterBFT is within 10-18% of full replication even with increasing approximation accuracy.

7   Related Work

BFT. Works like PBFT [12], Q/U protocol [7] and HQ Replication [15] show how to make BFT s in general practical. Libraries like UpRight [13], BFT-SMaRt [5] and EBAWA [35] make it practical for anyone to efficiently and quickly implement some of these systems. Recent work like Zyzzyva [21] (based on Fast Paxos [24,18]) further improve the performance and efficiency of some of these solutions. All these solutions focus on replicating monolithic servers and do not provide parameterizable tradeoffs between overhead and fault tolerance. Yin et al. [39] separate request ordering from request execution in BFT server

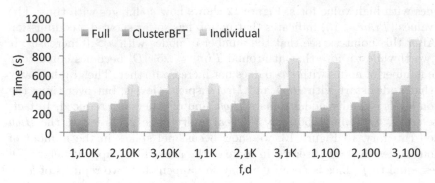

Fig. 14. Computing average weather temperatures

replication; we separate our architecture based on differences in the guarantees offered by nodes and not for consistency (no mutable shared state).

BFT in Cloud. With respect to cloud-based computations, Byzantine Fault Tolerant Mapreduce [14] explores executing Byzantine fault tolerant MapReduce jobs in the cloud and tries to reduce overhead by only starting $f + 1$ replicas of map and reduce tasks. Byzantine fault tolerance is achieved by restarting map and reduce tasks if $f + 1$ replicas do not agree on the output. This reduces the overhead when failures are not frequent but does not reduce the number of synchronization points required during job execution. BFTCloud [42] tries to secure generic computations run on voluntary resource clouds, but does not look at data-flow job specific optimizations. None of these solutions try to reduce the number of consensus instances required, or to actively identify faulty nodes by overlapping job clusters. ClusterBFT also provides parameterizeable tradeoffs between overhead and performance.

Verifiability. Works like Pepper [34] and Ginger [36] show that output verifiability is becoming more practical. These systems allows the computation initiator to encode the computation in such a way that it is possible to verify the result using the computation output and key. Pinocchio [30] further reduces the overhead involved and allows public verifiability. Even with these considerable improvements, these systems incur an overhead that is linearly proportional to the complexity of the computation. These systems are also limited with respected to computations involving dynamic looping constructs; requiring the programmer to inform the compiler how far the loop should be unrolled.

Confidentiality. We do not target to address confidentiality in this paper, but look at systems that preserve data privacy that can use ClusterBFT to secure computations. Airavat [33] adds operating system level mandatory access control to MapReduce to provide differential privacy. This allows untrusted mappers to work on sensitive data. It is possible to merge ClusterBFT with this system as they operate on mutually exclusive subsystems of Hadoop. sTile [10] distributes the input, output and intra-computation data across multiple nodes in the cloud, making it prohibitively costly for an attacker to piece together meaningful information. CryptDB [32] preserves privacy by executing queries directly over encrypted data in a *centralized* database.

8 Conclusion

We presented the design and evaluation of ClusterBFT, a system for assured data processing and analysis. ClusterBFT achieves its objectives with practical overheads by using variable-degree clustering, approximated output comparison, and separation of duty. We are working towards providing confidentiality by using ClusterBFT for analyzing data encrypted using partially homomorphic cryptosystems.

Acknowledgements. We are very grateful to Larry Peterson for making it possible for us to evaluate ClusterBFT on Vicci.

References

1. A programmable cloud-computing research testbed, http://www.vicci.org
2. Airline Data, http://stat-computing.org/dataexpo/2009/the-data.html
3. Apache Pig, http://pig.apache.org
4. Department of Defense Information Enterprise Strategic Plan (2011-2012), http://dodcio.defense.gov/docs/DodIESP-r16.pdf
5. High-performance Byzantine Fault-Tolerant State Machine Replication, https://code.google.com/p/bft-smart/
6. Pig Lab, https://github.com/michiard/CLOUDS-LAB/wiki/Hadoop-Pig-Laboratory
7. Abd-El-Malek, M., Ganger, G.R., Goodson, G.R., Reiter, M.K., Wylie, J.J.: Fault-scalable Byzantine Fault-tolerant Services. In: SIGOPS OSR, pp. 59–74 (2005)
8. Bessani, A., Correia, M., Quaresma, B., André, F., Sousa, P.: DepSky: Dependable and Secure Storage in a Cloud-of-Clouds. In: EuroSys 2011 (2011)
9. Birman, K., Chockler, G., van Renesse, R.: Toward a Cloud Computing Research Agenda. SIGACT News, 68–80 (2009)
10. Brun, Y., Medvidovic, N.: Keeping Data Private while Computing in the Cloud. In: CLOUD 2012 (2012)
11. Burrows, M.: The Chubby Lock Service for Loosely-coupled Distributed Systems. In: OSDI 2006 (2006)
12. Castro, M., Liskov, B.: Practical Byzantine Fault Tolerance. In: OSDI 1999 (1999)
13. Clement, A., Kapritsos, M., Lee, S., Wang, Y., Alvisi, L., Dahlin, M., Riche, T.: Upright Cluster Services. In: SOSP 2009 (2009)
14. Costa, P., Pasin, M., Bessani, A., Correia, M.: Byzantine Fault-Tolerant MapReduce: Faults are Not Just Crashes. In: CloudCom 2011 (2011)
15. Cowling, J., Myers, D., Liskov, B., Rodrigues, R., Shrira, L.: HQ Replication: A Hybrid Quorum Protocol for Byzantine Fault Tolerance. In: OSDI 2006 (2006)
16. Dean, J., Ghemawat, S.: MapReduce: Simplified Data Processing on Large Clusters. Commun. ACM, 107–113 (2008)
17. Denning, D.: A Lattice Model of Secure Information Flow. Commun. ACM 19(5) (1976)
18. Dutta, P., Guerraoui, R., Vukolic, M.: Best-Case Complexity of Asynchronous Byzantine Consensus. Tech. rep., EPFL (2005)
19. Hadoop: Hadoop, http://hadoop.apache.org/

20. Kihlstrom, K.P., Moser, L.E., Melliar-Smith, P.M.: Byzantine Fault Detectors for Solving Consensus. The Computer Journal, 16–35 (2003)
21. Kotla, R., Alvisi, L., Dahlin, M., Clement, A., Wong, E.: Zyzzyva: Speculative Byzantine Fault Tolerance. In: SOSP 2007 (2007)
22. Kwak, H., Lee, C., Park, H., Moon, S.: What is Twitter, a Social Network or a News Media? In: WWW 2010 (2010)
23. Lamport, L., Shostak, R., Pease, M.: The Byzantine Generals Problem. ACM Trans. Prog. Lang. and Sys., 382–401 (1982)
24. Lamport, L.: Lower bounds for asynchronous consensus. In: Schiper, A., Shvartsman, M.M.A.A., Weatherspoon, H., Zhao, B.Y. (eds.) Future Directions in Distributed Computing. LNCS, vol. 2584, pp. 22–23. Springer, Heidelberg (2003)
25. MRC: DARPA-BAA-11-55: I2O Mission-oriented Resilient Clouds (MRC), https://www.fbo.gov/spg/ODA/DARPA/CMO/DARPA-BAA-11-55/listing.html
26. NCDC: weatherdata snapshot, http://aws.amazon.com/datasets/2759
27. Newell, A., Obenshain, D., Tantillo, T., Nita-Rotaru, C., Amir, Y.: Increasing Network Resiliency by Optimally Assigning Diverse Variants to Routing Nodes. In: DSN 2013 (2013)
28. Olston, C., Reed, B., Srivastava, U., Kumar, R., Tomkins, A.: PigLatin: A Not-so-foreign Language for Data Processing. In: SIGMOD 2008 (2008)
29. Olston, C., Reed, B.: Inspector Gadget: A Framework for Custom Monitoring and Debugging of Distributed Dataflows. In: SIGMOD 2011 (2011)
30. Parno, B., Gentry, C., Howell, J., Raykova, M.: Pinocchio: Nearly Practical Verifiable Computation. Cryptology ePrint Archive, Report 2013/279 (2013)
31. Pleisch, S., Kupsys, A., Schiper, A.: Preventing Orphan Requests in the Context of Replicated Invocation. In: SRDS 2003 (2003)
32. Popa, R.A., Redfield, C.M.S., Zeldovich, N., Balakrishnan, H.: CryptDB: Protecting Confidentiality with Encrypted Query Processing. In: SOSP 2011 (2011)
33. Roy, I., Setty, S., Kilzer, A., Shmatikov, V., Witchel, E.: Airavat: Security and Privacy for MapReduce. In: NSDI 2010 (2010)
34. Setty, S., McPherson, R., Walfish, A.J.B.: M.: Making Argument Systems for Outsourced Computation Practical (Sometimes). In: NDSS 2012 (2012)
35. Santos Veronese, G., Correia, M., Bessani, A., Lung, L.C.: Ebawa: Efficient byzantine agreement for wide-area networks. In: HASE 2010 (2010)
36. Setty, S., Vu, V., Panpalia, N., Braun, B., Blumberg, A.J., Walfish, M.: Taking Proof-based Verified Computation a Few Steps Closer to Practicality. In: Security 2012 (2010)
37. Shvachko, K., Hairong, K., Radia, S., Chansler, R.: The Hadoop Distributed File System. In: MSST 2010 (2010)
38. Verissimo, P., Bessani, A., Pasin, M.: The TClouds Architecture: Open and Resilient Cloud-of-Clouds Computing. In: DSN Workshops 2012 (2012)
39. Yin, J., Martin, J.P., Venkataramani, A., Alvisi, L., Dahlin, M.: Separating Agreement from Execution for Byzantine Fault Tolerant Services. SIGOPS OSR, 253–267 (2003)
40. Yu, Y., Isard, M., Fetterly, D., Budiu, M., Erlingsson, U., Gunda, P., Currey, J.: DryadLINQ: a System for General-purpose Distributed Data-parallel Computing using a High-level Language. In: OSDI 2008 (2008)
41. Zaharia, M., Chowdhury, M., Das, T., Dave, A., Ma, J., McCauley, M., Franklin, M.J., Shenker, S., Stoica, I.: Resilient Distributed Datasets: A Fault-Tolerant Abstraction for In-Memory Cluster Computing. In: NSDI 2012 (2012)
42. Zhang, Y., Zheng, Z., Lyu, M.R.: BFTCloud: A Byzantine Fault Tolerance Framework for Voluntary-Resource Cloud Computing. In: CloudCom 2012 (2012)

FlowFlex: Malleable Scheduling for Flows of MapReduce Jobs

Viswanath Nagarajan[1], Joel Wolf[1], Andrey Balmin[2,*], and Kirsten Hildrum[1]

[1] IBM T. J. Watson Research Center
{viswanath,jlwolf,hildrum}@us.ibm.com
[2] GraphSQL
andrey@graphsql.com

Abstract. We introduce *FlowFlex*, a highly generic and effective scheduler for flows of MapReduce jobs connected by precedence constraints. Such a flow can result, for example, from a single user-level Pig, Hive or Jaql query. Each flow is associated with an arbitrary function describing the cost incurred in completing the flow at a particular time. The overall objective is to minimize either the total cost (minisum) or the maximum cost (minimax) of the flows. Our contributions are both theoretical and practical. Theoretically, we advance the state of the art in malleable parallel scheduling with precedence constraints. We employ resource augmentation analysis to provide bicriteria approximation algorithms for both minisum and minimax objective functions. As corollaries, we obtain approximation algorithms for total weighted completion time (and thus average completion time and average stretch), and for maximum weighted completion time (and thus makespan and maximum stretch). Practically, the *average* case performance of the *FlowFlex* scheduler is excellent, significantly better than other approaches. Specifically, we demonstrate via extensive experiments the overall performance of *FlowFlex* relative to optimal and also relative to other, standard MapReduce scheduling schemes. All told, *FlowFlex* dramatically extends the capabilities of the earlier *Flex* scheduler for singleton MapReduce jobs while simultaneously providing a solid theoretical foundation for both.

1 Introduction

MapReduce [8] is a fundamentally important programming paradigm for processing big data. Accordingly, there has already been considerable work on the design of high quality MapReduce schedulers [26,27,25,1,24]. All of the schedulers to date have quite naturally focused on the scheduling of collections of *singleton* MapReduce jobs. Indeed, single MapReduce jobs were the appropriate atomic unit of work early on. Lately, however, we have witnessed the emergence of more elaborate MapReduce work, and today it is common to see the submission of *flows* of interconnected MapReduce jobs. Such a MapReduce flow can result, for example, from a single user-level Pig [11], Hive [20] or Jaql [4] query. Each flow can be represented by a directed acyclic graph (DAG) in which the nodes

---

* Work performed while at IBM Almaden Research Center.

D. Eyers and K. Schwan (Eds.): Middleware 2013, LNCS 8275, pp. 103–122, 2013.

are singleton Map or Reduce phases and the directed arcs represent precedence. Significantly, flows have become the basic unit of MapReduce work, and it is the completion times of these flows that determines the appropriate measure of goodness, not the completion times of the individual MapReduce jobs.

This paper introduces *FlowFlex*, a scheduling algorithm for flows of MapReduce jobs. *FlowFlex* can attempt to optimize an arbitrary metric based on the completion times of the flows. Common examples include makespan, average completion time, average and maximum *stretch*[1] and metrics involving one or more deadlines. Any given metric will be appropriate for a particular scenario, and the precise algorithmic variant *FlowFlex* applies will depend on that metric. For example, in a batch environment one might care about makespan, to ensure that the batch window is not elongated. In an interactive environment users would typically care about average or maximum completion time, or about average or maximum stretch. There are also a variety of metrics associated with hard or soft deadlines. To the best of our knowledge scheduling schemes for flows of MapReduce jobs have never been considered previously in the literature.

Our contributions are both theoretical and practical. We advance the theory of *malleable* parallel scheduling with precedence constraints. Specifically, we employ *resource augmentation* analysis to provide *bicriteria approximation algorithms* for both minisum and minimax objective functions. As corollaries, we obtain *approximation algorithms* for *total weighted completion time* (and thus average completion time and average stretch), and for *maximum weighted completion time* (and thus makespan and maximum stretch). We also produce a highly generic and practical MapReduce scheduler for flows of jobs, called *FlowFlex*, and demonstrate its excellent average case performance experimentally.

The closest previous scheduling work for MapReduce jobs appeared in [25]. The *Flex* scheduler presented there is now incorporated in IBM BigInsights [5]. (See also the *FlexSight* visualization tool [7].) *Flex* schedules to optimize a variety of metrics as well, but differs from the current work in that it only considers singleton MapReduce jobs, not flows. Architecturally, *Flex* sits on top of the *Fair* MapReduce scheduler [26,27], essentially overriding its decisions while simultaneously making use of its infrastructure. The *FlowFlex* scheduling problem is clearly a major generalization of the *Flex* problem. With modest caveats, it can also be said that the *FlowFlex* algorithms significantly generalize those of *Flex*. They are also much more theoretically grounded. See also the special purpose schedulers [1] and *CircumFlex* [24], built to amortize shared Map phase scans.

There are fundamental differences between *Fair* and the three schedulers in the *Flex* family: *Fair* makes its decisions based on the current moment in time, and thus considers only the resource (slot) dimension. *Fair* is indeed fair in the sense of instantaneous *progress*, but does not directly consider completion time. On the other hand, *Flex*, *CircumFlex* and *FlowFlex* think in two dimensions, both resource and time. And they optimize towards completion time metrics. It is our contention that completion time rather than instantaneous progress determines the true quality of a schedule.

---

[1] Stretch is a fairness metric in which each flow weight is the reciprocal of its size.

The rest of this paper is organized as follows. Section 2 gives preliminaries and describes the good fit between the theory of malleable scheduling and the MapReduce enviornment. Section 3 introduces the scheduling model and lists our formal theoretical results. The *FlowFlex* scheduling algorithms are described in Section 4, and the proofs of the performance guarantees are outlined there. Space limitations prevent us from detailing all of these proofs, but interested readers can find them in [2]. In Section 5 we compare *FlowFlex* experimentally with *Fair* and *FIFO*, both naturally extended in order to handle precedence constraints. We also explain the practical considerations associated with implementing *FlowFlex* as an epoch-based scheduler. Conclusions appear in Section 6.

2   Preliminaries

The theory of malleable scheduling fits the reality of the MapReduce environment well. To understand this we give a brief, somewhat historically oriented overview of theoretical parallel scheduling and its relation to MapReduce.

The first parallel scheduling implementations and theoretical results involved what are today called *rigid* jobs. These jobs run on a fixed number of processors and are presumed to complete their work simultaneously. One can thus think of a job as corresponding to a rectangle whose height corresponds to the number of processors p, whose width corresponds to the execution time t of the job, and whose area $s = p \cdot t$ corresponds to the work performed by the job. Early papers, such as [6], focused on the makespan metric, providing some of the very first *approximation* algorithms. (These are polynomial time schemes with guaranteed performance bounds.)

Subsequent parallel scheduling research took a variety of directions, again more or less mirroring real scenarios of the time. One such direction involved what has now become known as *moldable* scheduling: Each job can be run on an arbitrary number of processors, but with an execution time which is a monotone non-increasing function of the number of processors. Thus the height of a job is turned from an input parameter to a decision variable. The first approximation algorithm for moldable scheduling with a makespan metric appeared in [23]. Later, [22] found the first approximation algorithm for both rigid and moldable scheduling problems with a (weighted) average completion time metric.

The notion of *malleable* scheduling is more general than moldable. Here the number of processors allocated to a job is allowed to vary over time. However, each job must still perform its fixed amount of work. One can consider the most general problem variant in which the rate at which work is done is a function of the number of allocated processors, so that the total work completed at any time is the integral of these rates through that time. However, this problem is enormously difficult, and so the literature to date [9,16] has focused on the special case where the speedup function is linear through a given maximum number of processors, and constant thereafter. Clearly, malleable schedules can only improve objective function values relative to moldable schedules. On the other hand, malleable scheduling problems are even harder to solve well than moldable scheduling problems. We will concentrate on malleable scheduling problems with linear speedup up to some maximum, with flow precedence constraints and any of several different metrics on the completion times of the flows. See [9,16] for more details on both moldable and malleable scheduling. The literature on the latter is quite limited, and this paper is a contribution.

Why does MapReduce fit the theory of malleable scheduling with linear speedup and processor maxima so neatly? There are multiple reasons.

1. *MapReduce and malleable scheduling are about allocation:* There is a natural decoupling of MapReduce scheduling into an *Allocation Layer* followed by an *Assignment Layer*. In the Allocation Layer, quantity decisions are made, and that is where any mathematical complexity resides. The Assignment Layer then implements these allocation decisions (to the extent possible, given locality issues [27] and such) in the MapReduce cluster. *Fair, Flex, CircumFlex* and our new *FlowFlex* scheduler reside in the Allocation Layer. The malleable (as well as rigid and moldable) scheduling literature is also about allocation rather than assignment.[2]

2. *MapReduce work exhibit roughly linear speedup, and maximum constraints occur naturally:* Both the Map and Reduce phases are composed of *many small, independent* tasks. Because they are independent they do not need to start simultaneously and can be processed with any degree of parallelism without significant overhead. This, in turn, means that the jobs will have nearly linear speedup: Remember that linear speedup is a statement about the rate at which work is completed. Maximum constraints in either the Map or Reduce phase occur because they happen to be small (and thus have few tasks), or when only a few tasks remain to be allocated.

3. *MapReduce fits the malleable model well:* Assuming the tasks are many and small, the decisions of the scheduler can be approximated closely. To understand this, consider Figure 1, which depicts the Assignment Layer implementing the decisions of the Allocation Layer. The Allocation Layer output is a hypothetical malleable schedule for three jobs. The Assignment Layer works locally at each node in the cluster. Suppose a task on that node completes, freeing a slot. The Assignment Layer simply determines which job is the most relatively underallocated according to the Allocation Layer schedule. And then, within certain practical constraints, it acts greedily, assigning a new task from that job to the slot. Examining the figure, the tasks are represented as "bricks" in the Assignment Layer. The point is that the large number and small size of the tasks makes the right-hand side a close approximation to the left-hand side. That is, Assignment Layer reality will be an excellent approximation to Allocation Layer theory.

The model is not perfect, of course. For example, if the number of tasks in a MapReduce job is modest, the idealized scenario depicted in Figure 1 will be less than perfect. Furthermore, there is a somewhat delicately defined notion[3]

---

[2] In MapReduce, the atomic unit of allocation is called a *slot*, which can be used for either Map or Reduce tasks. So "processor" in the theoretical literature corresponds to "slot" in a MapReduce context.

[3] This will be clarified in Subsection 5.2.

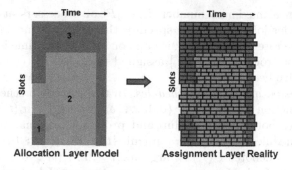

Fig. 1. MapReduce and Malleable Scheduling

of precedence between Map and Reduce tasks that is not cleanly modeled here. Recall that we model a single MapReduce job as a Map phase followed by a Reduce phase. In reality, some Reduce tasks can begin before all the Map tasks complete. But recall that *Flex* suffers from precisely the same issues, and has been used successfully in IBM BigInsights [5] for several years.

Practically speaking, *FlowFlex* and its predecessors are epoch-based. In each epoch *FlowFlex* wakes up, considers the current version of the scheduling problem, produces a hypothetical malleable schedule and outputs the *initial* allocations to be implemented by the assignment layer. Thus the size data as well as the flows and jobs themselves are each updated for each *FlowFlex* run, making the scheduler more robust.

Other Models for MapReduce. We briefly mention some other MapReduce models that have been considered in the literature. Moseley et al. [18] consider a "two-stage flexible flow shop" [21] model, and give approximation and online algorithms for total completion time of independent MapReduce jobs. Berlinska and Drozdowski [3] use "divisible load theory" to model a single MapReduce job and its communication details. Theoretical frameworks for MapReduce computation have been proposed in [14,15].

Compared to our setting, these models are at a finer level of granularity, that of individual Map and Reduce tasks. Our model, as described above, decouples the quantity decisions (allocation) from the actual assignment details in the cluster. We focus on obtaining algorithms for the allocation layer, which is abstracted as a precedence constrained malleable scheduling problem.

3   Formal Model and Results

As discussed, we model the MapReduce application as a parallel scheduling problem. There are P identical *processors* that correspond to resources (slots) in the MapReduce cluster. Each *flow* j is described by means of a directed acyclic graph. The nodes in each of these DAGs are *jobs*, and the directed arcs correspond to precedence relations. We use the standard notation $i_1 \prec i_2$ to indicate that job i_1 must be completed before job i_2 can begin. Each job i must perform a fixed amount of work s_i (also referred to as the job *size*), and can be performed on a maximum number $\delta_i \in [P]$ of processors at any point in time.[4] We consider jobs with linear speedup through their maximum numbers of processors: the rate at which work is done on job i at any time is proportional to the number of processors $p \in [\delta_i]$ assigned to it. Job i is complete when s_i units of work have been performed.

We are interested in *malleable schedules*. In this setting, a schedule for job i is given by a function $\tau_i : [0, \infty) \to \{0, 1, \ldots, \delta_i\}$ where $\int_{t=0}^{\infty} \tau_i(t)\, dt = s_i$. Note that this satisfies both linear speedup and processor maxima. We denote the *start time* of schedule τ_i by $S(\tau_i) := \arg\min\{t \geq 0 : \tau_i(t) > 0\}$; similarly the *completion time* is denoted $C(\tau_i) := \arg\max\{t \geq 0 : \tau_i(t) > 0\}$. A schedule for flow j (consisting of jobs I_j) is given by a set $\{\tau_i : i \in I_j\}$ of schedules for its jobs, where $C(\tau_{i_1}) \leq S(\tau_{i_2})$ for all $i_1 \prec i_2$. The completion time of flow j is $\max_{i \in I_j} C(\tau_i)$, the maximum completion time of its jobs. Our algorithms make use of the following two natural and standard lower bounds on the minimum possible completion time of a single flow j. (See, for example, [9].)

- Total load (or *squashed area*): $\frac{1}{P} \sum_{i \in I_j} s_i$.
- Critical path: maximum of $\sum_{r=1}^{\ell} \frac{s_{i_r}}{\delta_{i_r}}$ over all chains[5] $i_1 \prec \cdots \prec i_\ell$ in flow j.

Each flow j also specifies an arbitrary non-decreasing *cost function* $w_j : \mathbb{R}_+ \to \mathbb{R}_+$ where $w_j(t)$ is the cost incurred when job j is completed at time t. We consider both *minisum* and *minimax* objective functions. The minisum (resp. minimax) objective minimizes the sum (resp. maximum) of the cost functions over all flows. In the notation of [9,16] this scheduling environment is $P|var, p_i(k) = \frac{p_i(1)}{k}, \delta_i, prec|*$.[6] We refer to these problems collectively as *precedence constrained malleable scheduling with linear speedup*. Our highly general cost model can solve all the commonly used scheduling objectives: weighted average completion time, makespan (maximum completion time), average and maximum stretch, and deadline-based metrics associated with number of tardy jobs, service level agreements (SLAs) and so on. Figure 2 illustrates 4 basic types of cost functions.

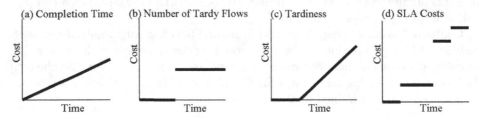

(a) Completion Time   (b) Number of Tardy Flows   (c) Tardiness   (d) SLA Costs

Fig. 2. Typical Cost Functions Types

The objective functions we consider are either *minisum* or *minimax*. Minisum scheduling problems involve the minimization of the (possibly weighted) sum of

---

[4] Throughout the paper, for any integer $\ell \geq 1$, we denote by $[\ell]$ the set $\{1, \ldots, \ell\}$.

[5] Chains are a special case of flows in which precedence is sequential.

[6] Here *var* stands for malleable scheduling, $p_i(k) = \frac{p_i(1)}{k}$ denotes linear speedup, δ_i is processor maxima, *prec* stands for precedence, and $*$ is for *any* objective function.

individual flow metrics, or, equivalently, their (weighted) average. On the other hand, minimax scheduling problems involve the minimization of the maximum of individual metrics, an indication of worst case flow performance.

Definition 1. *A polynomial time algorithm is said to be an α-approximation if it produces a schedule that has objective value at most $\alpha \geq 1$ times optimal.*

We would like to provide approximation algorithms for the above malleable scheduling problems. But as shown in [10], even under very special precedence constraints (chains of length three) the general minisum and minimax problems admit no finite approximation ratio unless P=NP. Hence we use resource augmentation [13] and focus on *bicriteria* approximation guarantees.

Definition 2. *A polynomial time algorithm is said to be an (α, β)-bicriteria approximation if it produces a schedule using $\beta \geq 1$ speed processors that has objective value at most $\alpha \geq 1$ times optimal (under unit speed processors).*

Our main result is that we can find approximation algorithms in some cases and bicriteria approximation algorithms in all others.

Theorem 1. *The precedence constrained malleable scheduling problem with linear speedup admits the following guarantees.*
- *$(2,3)$-bicriteria approximation algorithm for general minisum objectives.*
- *$(1,2)$-bicriteria approximation algorithm for general minimax objectives.*
- *6-approximation algorithm for total weighted completion time (including total stretch).*
- *2-approximation algorithm for maximum weighted completion time (including makespan and maximum stretch).*

The first two results on general minisum and minimax objectives imply the other two as corollaries. The main idea in our algorithms (for both minisum and minimax) is a reduction to strict *deadline metrics*, for which a simple greedy scheme is shown to achieve a good bicriteria approximation. The reduction from minisum objectives to deadline metrics is based on a *minimum cost flow* relaxation, and "rounding" the optimal flow solution. The reduction from minimax objectives to deadlines is much simpler and uses a bracket and bisection search.

4   The *FlowFlex* Scheduling Algorithm

Our scheduling algorithm has three sequential stages. See Figure 3 for an algorithmic overview. In a little more detail, the stages may be described as follows.
1. First we consider each flow j separately, and convert its (general) precedence constraint into a *chain* (total order) precedence constraint. We create a *pseudo-schedule* for each flow that assumes an infinite number of processors, but respects precedence constraints and the bounds δ_i on jobs i. Then we partition the pseudo-schedule into a chain of *pseudo-jobs*, where each pseudo-job k corresponds to an interval in the pseudo-schedule with uniform processor usage. Just like the original jobs, each pseudo-job k specifies a size

s_k and bound δ_k of the maximum number of processors it can be run on. We note that (unlike jobs) the bound δ_k of a pseudo-job may be larger than P. An important property here is that the squashed-area and critical-path lower bounds of each chain equal those of its original flow.

2. We now treat each flow as a chain of pseudo-jobs, and obtain a malleable schedule consisting of pseudo-jobs. This stage has two components:

   a. We first obtain a bicriteria approximation algorithm in the special case of metrics based on *strict* deadlines, employing a natural *greedy* scheme.

   b. We then obtain a bicriteria approximation algorithm for general cost metrics, by reduction to deadline metrics. For minsum cost functions we formulate a *minimum cost flow* subproblem based on the cost metric, which can be solved efficiently. The solution to this subproblem is then used to derive a deadline for each flow, which we can use in the greedy scheme. For minimax cost metrics we do not need to solve an minimun cost flow problem. We rely instead on a bracket and bisection scheme, each stage of which produces natural deadlines for each chain. We thus solve the greedy scheme multiple times.

   These performance guarantees are relative to the squashed-area and critical-path lower bounds of the chains, which, by Stage 1, equal those of the respective original flows. We now have a malleable schedule for the pseudo-jobs satisfying the chain precedence within each flow as well as the bounds δ_k.

3. The final stage combines Stages 1 and 2. We transform the malleable schedule of pseudo-jobs into a malleable schedule for the original jobs, while respecting the precedence constraints and bounds δ_i. We refer to this as *shape shifting*. Specifically, we convert the malleable schedule of each pseudo-job k into a malleable schedule for the (portions) of jobs i that comprise it. The full set of these transformations, over all pseudo-jobs k and flows j, produces the ultimate schedule.

```
1: for j = 1, ..., m do
2:    Run Stage 1 scheme on flow j, yielding pseudo-schedule for chain of pseudo-jobs.
3: Stage 2 scheme begins.
4: if minsum objective then
5:    Run algorithm in Figure 6.
6: else
7:    Run minimax algorithm in Figure 8.
8: Stage 2 scheme ends.
9: Run Stage 3 shape shifting algorithm using Stages 1 and 2 output.
```

Fig. 3. High Level Scheme *FlowFlex* Overview

4.1   Stage 1: General Precedence Constraints to Chains

We now describe a procedure to convert an arbitrary precedence constraint on jobs into a chain constraint on "pseudo-jobs". Consider any flow with n jobs where each job $i \in [n]$ has size s_i and processor bound δ_i. The precedence constraints are given by a directed acyclic graph on the jobs.

Construct a *pseudo-schedule* for the flow as follows. Allocate each job $i \in [n]$ its maximal number δ_i of processors, and assign job i the smallest *start time* $b_i \geq 0$ such that for all $i_1 \prec i_2$ we have $b_{i_2} \geq b_{i_1} + \frac{s_{i_1}}{\delta_{i_1}}$. The start times $\{b_i\}_{i=1}^n$ can be computed in $O(n^2)$ time using dynamic programming. The pseudo-schedule runs each job i on δ_i processors, between time b_i and $b_i + \frac{s_i}{\delta_i}$. Given an infinite number of processors the pseudo-schedule is a valid schedule satisfying precedence.

Next, we will construct *pseudo-jobs* corresponding to this flow. Let $T = \max_{i=1}^n (b_i + \frac{s_i}{\delta_i})$ denote the completion time of the pseudo-schedule; observe that T equals the critical path bound of the flow. Partition the time interval $[0, T]$ into maximal intervals $I_1, \ldots, I_h$ so that the set of jobs processed by the pseudo-schedule in each interval stays fixed. For each $k \in [h]$, if r_k denotes the total number of processors being used during I_k, define pseudo-job k to have processor bound $\delta(k) := r_k$ and size $s(k) := r_k \cdot |I_k|$ which is the total work done by the pseudo-schedule during I_k. (We employ this subtle change of notation to differentiate chains from more general precedence constraints.) Note that a pseudo-job consists of portions of work from multiple jobs; moreover, we may have $r_k > P$ since the pseudo-schedule is defined independent of P. Finally we enforce the chain precedence constraint $1 \prec 2 \prec \cdots h$ on pseudo-jobs. Notice that the squashed area and critical path lower bounds remain the *same* when computed in terms of pseudo-jobs instead of jobs.[7]

Figure 4(a) illustrates the directed acyclic graph of a particular flow. Figure 4(b) shows the resulting pseudo-schedule. Figures 4(c) and (d) show the decomposition into maximal intervals.

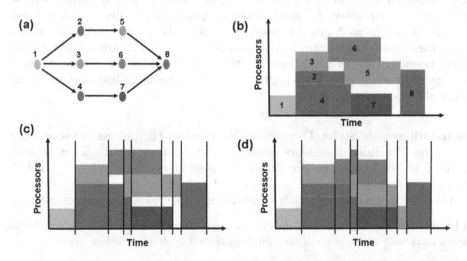

Fig. 4. *FlowFlex* Stage 1

---

[7] Clearly, the total size of pseudo-jobs $\sum_{k=1}^h s_k = \sum_{i=1}^n s_i$ the total size of jobs. Moreover, there is only one maximal chain of pseudo-jobs, which has critical path $\sum_{k=1}^h \frac{s_k}{\delta_k} = \sum_{k=1}^h |I_k| = T$, the original critical path bound.

4.2   Stage 2: Scheduling Flows with Chain Precedence Constraints

In this section, we consider the malleable scheduling problem on P parallel processors with *chain* precedence constraints and general cost functions. Each chain $j \in [m]$ is a sequence $k_1^j \prec k_2^j \prec \cdots k_{n(j)}^j$ of *pseudo-jobs*, where each pseudo-job k has a size $s(k)$ and specifies a maximum number $\delta(k)$ of processors that it can be run on. We note that the $\delta(k)$s may be larger than P. Each chain $j \in [m]$ also specifies a non-decreasing *cost function* $w_j : \mathbb{R}_+ \to \mathbb{R}_+$ where $w_j(t)$ is the cost incurred when chain j is completed at time t. The objective is to find a malleable schedule on P identical parallel processors that satisfies precedence constraints and minimizes the total cost.

Malleable schedules for pseudo-jobs (resp. chains of pseudo-jobs) are defined identically to jobs (resp. flows). To reduce notation, we denote a malleable schedule for *chain* j by a sequence $\tau^j = \langle \tau_1^j, \ldots, \tau_{n(j)}^j \rangle$ of schedules for its pseudo-jobs, where τ_r^j is a malleable schedule for pseudo-job k_r^j for each $r \in [n(j)]$. Note that chain precedence implies that for each $r \in \{1, \ldots, n(j) - 1\}$, the start time of k_{r+1}^j, $S(\tau_{r+1}^j) \geq C(\tau_r^j)$, the completion time of k_r^j. The completion time of this chain is $C(\tau^j) := C(\tau_{n(j)}^j)$.

Unfortunately, as shown in [10], this problem does not admit any finite approximation ratio unless P=NP. Given this hardness of approximation, we focus on bicriteria approximation guarantees. We first give a $(1, 2)$-approximation algorithm when the cost functions are based on strict deadlines. Then we obtain a $(2, 3)$-approximation algorithm for arbitrary minisum metrics and a $(1, 2)$-approximation algorithm for arbitrary minimax metrics. Importantly, all these performance guarantees are based on the squashed-area and critical-path lower bounds of the chains. Since the Stage 1 transformation (flows to chains) maintains these same lower bounds, the guarantees in Stage 2 are relative to the lower bounds of the original flows. So the objective value incurred in Stage 2 is a good approximation to the optimum of the scheduling instance under the original flows.

Scheduling with Strict Deadlines. We consider the problem of scheduling chains on P parallel processors under a strict deadline metric. That is, each chain $j \in [m]$ has a *deadline* d_j and its cost function is: $w_j(t) = 0$ if $t \leq d_j$ and ∞ otherwise.

We show that a natural greedy algorithm is a good bicriteria approximation.

Theorem 2. *There is a $(1, 2)$-bicriteria approximation algorithm for malleable scheduling with chain precedence constraints and a strict deadline metric.*

Proof Sketch. By renumbering chains, we assume that $d_1 \leq \cdots \leq d_m$. The algorithm schedules chains in increasing order of deadlines, and within each chain it schedules pseudo-jobs greedily by allocating the maximum possible number of processors. A formal description appears as Figure 5. The utilization function $\sigma : \mathbb{R}_+ \to \{0, 1, \ldots, P\}$ denotes the number of processors being used by the schedule at each point in time.

1: Initialize utilization function $\sigma : [0, \infty) \rightarrow \{0, 1, \ldots, P\}$ to zero.
2: **for** $j = 1, \ldots, m$ **do**
3:      **for** $i = 1, \ldots, n(j)$ **do**
4:          Set $S(\tau_i^j) \leftarrow 0$ if $i = 1$ and $S(\tau_i^j) \leftarrow C(\tau_{i-1}^j)$ otherwise.
5:          Initialize $\tau_i^j : [0, \infty) \rightarrow \{0, \ldots, P\}$ to zero.
6:          For each time $t \geq S(\tau_i^j)$ in increasing order, set

$$\tau_i^j(t) \;\leftarrow\; \min \left\{ P - \sigma(t), \, \delta(k_i^j) \right\}, \tag{1}$$

          until the area $\int_{t \geq S(\tau_i^j)} \tau_i^j(t)\, dt \;=\; s(k_i^j)$ the size of pseudo-job k_i^j.
7:          Set $C(\tau_i^j) \leftarrow \max\{z : \tau_i^j(z) > 0\}$.
8:          Update utilization function $\sigma \leftarrow \sigma - \tau_i^j$.
9:      Set $C(\tau^j) \leftarrow C(\tau_{n(j)}^j)$.
10:     **if** $C(\tau^j) > 2 \cdot d_j$ **then**
11:         Instance is *infeasible*.

Fig. 5. Algorithm for Scheduling Chains with Deadline Metric

Notice that this algorithm produces a valid malleable schedule that respects the chain precedence constraints and the maximum processor bounds. To prove the performance guarantee, we show that if there is any solution that meets all deadlines $\{d_\ell\}_{\ell=1}^m$ then the algorithm's schedule satisfies $C(\tau^j) \leq 2 \cdot d_j$ for all chains $j \in [m]$. The main idea is to divide the time $C(\tau^j)$ taken to complete any chain j into two types of events according to Equation (1), namely times where all P processors are fully utilized (i.e. $\tau_i^j(t) = P - \sigma(t)$) and times where a pseudo-job is fully run (i.e. $\tau_i^j(t) = \delta(k_i^j)$). The first event is bounded by the total area in the earliest j chains and the second by the critical path of chain j, each of which is at most d_j. So chain j's completion time $C(\tau^j) \leq 2 \cdot d_j$.

Minisum Scheduling. We now consider the problem of scheduling chains on P parallel processors under arbitrary minisum metrics. Recall that there are m chains, each having a non-decreasing cost function $w_j : \mathbb{R}_+ \rightarrow \mathbb{R}_+$, where $w_j(t)$ is the cost of completing chain j at time t. The goal in the minisum problem is to compute a schedule of minimum total cost. Let opt denote the optimal value of the given minisum scheduling instance.

Theorem 3. *There is a $(2, 3+o(1))$-bicriteria approximation algorithm for malleable scheduling with chain precedence constraints under minisum cost metrics.*

For each chain $j \in [m]$, define

$$Q_j \quad := \quad \max \left\{ \sum_{i=1}^{n(j)} \frac{s(k_i^j)}{\delta(k_i^j)} , \; \frac{1}{P} \sum_{i=1}^{n(j)} s(k_i^j) \right\}, \tag{2}$$

the maximum of the critical path and area lower bounds. Note that the completion time of each chain j (even if it is scheduled in isolation) is at least Q_j. So the optimal value opt $\geq \sum_{j=1}^m w_j(Q_j)$.

We may assume, without loss of generality, that every schedule for these chains completes by time $H := 2m \cdot \lceil \max_j Q_j \rceil$. In order to focus on the main ideas, we assume here that (i) each cost function $w_j(\cdot)$ has integer valued breakpoints (i.e. times where the cost changes) and (ii) provide an algorithm with runtime polynomial in H. In the full version, we show that both these assumptions can be removed. Before presenting the algorithm, we recall:

Definition 3 (Minimum cost flow). *The input is a network given by a directed graph (V, E) with designated source/sink nodes and demand ρ, where each arc $e \in E$ has a capacity α_e and cost (per unit of flow) of β_e . A flow satisfies arc capacities and node conservation (in-flow equals out-flow), and the goal is to find a flow of ρ units from source to sink having minimum cost.*

Our algorithm works in two phases. In the first phase, we treat each chain simply as a certain volume of work, and formulate a *minimum cost flow* subproblem using the cost functions w_js. The solution to this subproblem is used to determine candidate deadlines $\{d_j\}_{j=1}^m$ for the chains. Then in the second phase, we run our algorithm for deadline metrics using $\{d_j\}_{j=1}^m$ to obtain the final solution. The algorithm is described in Figure 6, followed by a high-level proof sketch (the details can be found in the full version).

1: Set volume $V_j \leftarrow \sum_{i=1}^{n(j)} s(k_i^j)$ for each chain $j \in [m]$.
2: Define network N on nodes $\{a_1, \ldots, a_m\} \cup \{b_1, \ldots, b_H\} \cup \{r, r'\}$, where r is the source and r' the sink.
3: Define arcs $E = E_1 \cup E_2 \cup E_3 \cup E_4$ of N as follows (see also Figure 7).

$$E_1 := \{(r, a_j) : j \in [m]\}, \text{ arc } (r, a_j) \text{ has cost 0, capacity } V_j,$$

$$E_2 := \{(a_j, b_t) \ : \ j \in [m], t \in [H], t \geq Q_j\}, \text{ arc } (a_j, b_t) \text{ has cost } \frac{w_j(t)}{V_j}, \text{ capacity } \infty,$$

$$E_3 := \{(b_t, r') : t \in [H]\}, \text{ arc } (b_t, r') \text{ has cost 0, capacity } P, \text{ and}$$

$$E_4 = \{(b_{t+1}, b_t) : t \in [H-1]\}, \text{ arc } (b_{t+1}, b_t) \text{ has cost 0, capacity } \infty.$$

4: Compute minimum-cost flow f in N of $\rho := \sum_{j=1}^m V_j$ demand from r to r'.
5: Set deadline $d_j \leftarrow \arg\min \{t : \sum_{s=1}^t f(a_j, b_s) \geq V_j/2\}$, for all $j \in [m]$.
6: Solve this deadline metric instance using Algorithm 5.

Fig. 6. Algorithm for Scheduling Chains with Minisum Metric

Proof Sketch of Theorem 3. In the first phase of our algorithm (Steps 1-4) we treat each chain $j \in [m]$ as work of volume V_j, which is the total size of pseudo-jobs in j. The key property of this phase is that the network flow instance on N is a *relaxation* of the original scheduling instance, i.e. the minimum cost flow f is at most opt. This property relies on the construction of N, where the nodes a_js correspond to chains and b_ts correspond to intervals $[t-1, t)$ in time. The arcs E_1 (together with the demand $\rho = \sum_{j=1}^m V_j$) enforce that V_j amount of flow is sent to each a_j, i.e. V_j work is done on each chain j. The arcs E_2 ensure that

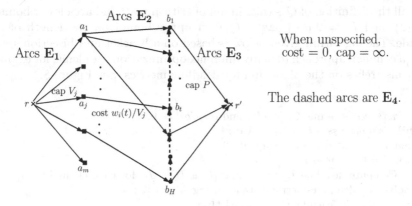

Fig. 7. The Minimum Cost Flow Network

flow from a_j can only go to nodes b_t with $t \geq Q_j$, i.e. chain j can complete only after Q_j. See (2). These arcs also model the minisum cost objective. Finally, arcs E_3 and E_4 correspond to using at most P processors at any time.

In the second phase of the algorithm (Steps 5-6) we use the min-cost flow solution f to obtain a feasible malleable schedule for the m chains. The candidate deadlines $\{d_j\}_{j=1}^m$ correspond to times when the chains are "half completed" in the solution f. Since the costs $w_j(\cdot)$ are non-decreasing, the cost $\sum_{j=1}^m w_j(d_j)$ of completing chains by their deadlines is at most $2 \cdot cost(f) \leq 2 \cdot \mathsf{opt}$. Then, using the definition of network N, we show that for each chain j, its critical path is at most d_j and the squashed area of earlier-deadline chains is at most $2 \cdot d_j$. These two bounds combined with the analysis of the deadline metric algorithm (Theorem 2) imply that each chain $j \in [m]$ is completed by time $3 \cdot d_j$.

In practice we could round the flow based on multiple values, not just the single halfway point described above. This would yield, in turn, multiple deadlines, and the best result could then be employed.

We note that in some cases the bicriteria guarantees can be combined.

Corollary 1. *There is a 6-approximation algorithm for minimizing weighted completion time in malleable scheduling with chain precedence constraints, including average stretch.*

Proof. This follows directly by observing that if a 3-speed schedule is executed at unit speed then each completion time scales up by a factor of three.

Minimax Scheduling Here we consider the problem of scheduling chains on P parallel processors under minimax metrics. Recall that there are m chains, each having a non-decreasing cost function $w_j : \mathbb{R}_+ \to \mathbb{R}_+$. The goal is to compute a schedule that minimizes the maximum cost of the m chains.

Theorem 4. *There is a $(1, 2+o(1))$-bicriteria approximation algorithm for malleable scheduling with chain precedence constraints under minimax cost metrics.*

Recall the definition of Q_js (maximum of critical path and area lower bounds) from (2); and $H = 2m \cdot \lceil \max_{j=1}^{m} Q_j \rceil$ an upper bound on the length of any schedule. The algorithm given below is based on a bracket and bisection search that is a common approach to many minimax optimization problems, for example [12]. It also relies on the algorithm for deadline metrics. See Figure 8.

1: Set $lastsuccess \leftarrow \max_{j=1}^{m} w_j(H)$ and $lastfail \leftarrow 0$.
2: **while** $lastsuccess - lastfail > 1$ **do**
3:     Set $L \leftarrow (lastsuccess + lastfail)/2$.
4:     **for** $j = 1, \ldots, m$ **do**
5:         Compute deadline $D_j := \arg\max\{t : w_j(t) \leq L\}$ for each chain $j \in [m]$.
6:     Solve this deadline-metric instance using Algorithm 5.
7:     **if** schedule is feasible with 2-speed **then**
8:         Set $lastsuccess \leftarrow L$.
9:     **else**
10:         Set $lastfail \leftarrow L$.
11: Output the schedule corresponding to $lastsuccess$.

Fig. 8. Algorithm for Scheduling Chains with Minimax Objective

Proof. Let opt denote the optimal minimax value of the given instance. Clearly, $0 \leq \mathsf{opt} \leq \max_j w_j(H)$. (We assume that the cost functions w_js are integer valued: this can always be ensured at the loss of a $1 + o(1)$ factor.)

Observe that for any value $L \geq \mathsf{opt}$, the deadline instance in Step 5: the optimal schedule itself must meet the deadlines $\{D_j\}$. Combined with the deadline-metric algorithm (Theorem 2), it follows that our algorithm's schedule for any value $L \geq \mathsf{opt}$ is feasible using 2-speed. Thus the final $lastsuccess$ value is at most opt, which is also an upper bound on the algorithm's minimax objective.

As in Corollary 1, the bicriteria guarantees can be combined for some metrics.

Corollary 2. *There is a 2-approximation algorithm for minimizing maximum completion time in malleable scheduling with chain precedence constraints, including makespan and maximum stretch.*

4.3   Stage 3: Converting Pseudo-Job Schedule into Valid Schedule

The final stage combines the output of Stages 1 and 2, converting any malleable schedule of pseudo-jobs and chains into a valid schedule of the original jobs and flows. We consider the schedule of each pseudo-job k separately. Using a generalization of McNaughton's Rule [17], we will construct a malleable schedule for the (portions of) jobs comprising pseudo-job k. The original precedence constraints are satisfied since the chain constraints are satisfied on pseudo-jobs, and the jobs participating in any single pseudo-job are independent.

Consider any pseudo-job k that corresponds to interval I_k in the pseudo-schedule (recall Stage 1), during which jobs $S \subseteq [n]$ are executed in parallel for a total of $r_k = \sum_{i \in S} \delta_i$ processors. Consider also any malleable schedule of pseudo-job k, that corresponds to a histogram σ (of processor usage) having area $s_k = |I_k| \cdot r_k$ and maximum number of processors at most r_k.

We now describe how to *shape shift* the pseudo-schedule for S in I_k into a valid schedule given by histogram σ. The idea is simple: Decompose the histogram σ into intervals $\mathcal{J}$ of constant numbers of processors. For each interval $J \in \mathcal{J}$, having height (number of processors) $\sigma(J)$, we will schedule the work from a time $\frac{|J| \cdot \sigma(J)}{r_k}$ sub-interval of I_k; observe that the respective areas in σ and I_k are equal. Since $\sum_{J \in \mathcal{J}} |J| \cdot \sigma(J) = s_k = |I_k| \cdot r_k$, taking such schedules over all $J \in \mathcal{J}$ gives a full schedule for I_k. For a particular interval J, we apply McNaughton's Rule to schedule the work from its I_k sub-interval. This rule was extended in [10] to cover a scenario more like ours. It has linear complexity. McNaughton's Rule is basically a wrap-around scheme: We order the jobs, and for the first job we fill the area *horizontally*, one processor at a time, until the total amount of work involving that job has been allotted. Then, starting where we left off, we fill the area needed for the second job, and so on. All appropriate constraints are easily seen to be satisfied.

Figure 9(a) shows a Stage 1 pseudo-schedule and highlights the *first* pseudo-job (interval I_1). The lowest histogram σ of Figure 9(b) illustrates the corresponding portion for this pseudo-job in the Stage 2 malleable greedy schedule; the constant histogram ranges are also shown. The equal area sub-intervals in I_1 are shown as vertical lines in Figure 9(a). Applying McNaughton's Rule to the first sub-interval of I_1 we get the schedule shown at the bottom-left of Figure 9(b). The scheme then proceeds with subsequent sub-intervals.

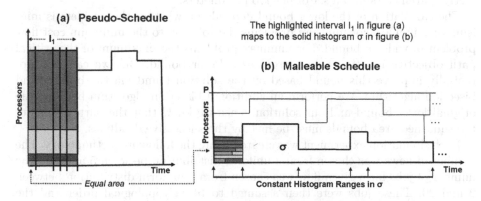

Fig. 9. *FlowFlex* Stage 3: Shape Shifting

5   Experimental Results

5.1   Simulation Experiments

In this section we describe the performance of our *FlowFlex* algorithm via a variety of simulation experiments. We consider two competitors, *Fair* [26] and

FIFO. We will compare the performance of each of these three in terms of the best lower bounds we can find for these NP-hard problems. (There is no real hope of finding the true optimal solutions in a reasonable amount of time, but these lower bounds will at least give pessimistic estimates of the quality of the *FlowFlex, Fair* and *FIFO* schedules.) We will consider nearly all combinatorial choices of scheduling metrics, from five basic types. They are based on either completion time, number of tardy jobs, tardiness and SLA step functions. (See Figure 2.) They can be either weighted or non-weighted, and the problem can be to minimize the sum (and hence average) or the maximum over all flows. So, for example, average and weighted average completion time are included for the minisum case. So is average stretch, which is simply completion time weighted by the reciprocal of the amount of work associated with the flow. Similarly, makespan (which is maximum completion time), maximum weighted completion time, and thus maximum stretch is included for the minimax case. Weighted or unweighted numbers of tardy jobs, total tardiness, total SLA costs are included in the minisum case. Maximum tardy job cost, maximum tardiness and maximum SLA cost are included in the minimax case. (A minimax problem involving unit weight tardy jobs would simply be 1 if tardy flows exist, and 0 otherwise, so we omit that metric.) We note that that these experiments are somewhat unfair to both *Fair* and *FIFO*, since both are completely agnostic with respect to the metrics we consider. But they do at least make sense, when implemented as ready-list algorithms. (In other words, they simply schedule all ready jobs by either *Fair* or *FIFO* rules, repeating as new jobs become ready.) We chose not to compare *FlowFlex* to *Flex*, because that algorithm *does* optimize to a particular metric, and it is not at all obvious how to "prorate" the flow-level metric parameters into a set of per job parameters.

The calculation of the lower bound depends on whether the problem is minisum or minimax. For minisum problems the solution to the minimum cost flow problem provides a bound. For minimax problems the maximum of the critical path objective function values provides a lower bound. But we can also potentially improve this bound based on the solution found via the bracket and bisection algorithm. We perform an additional bisection algorithm between the original lower bound and our solution, since we know that the partial sums of the squashed area bounds must be met by the successive deadlines.

Each simulation experiment was created using the following methodology. The number of flows was chosen from a uniform distribution between 5 and 20. The number of jobs for a given flow was chosen from a uniform distribution between 2 and 20. These jobs were then assumed to be in topological order and the precedence constraint between jobs j_1 and j_2 was chosen based on a probability of 0.5. Then all jobs without successors were assumed to precede the last job in the flow, to ensure connectivity. Sampling form a variety of parameters governed whether the flow itself was "big" in volume, and also whether the jobs in that flow were "tall" and/or "wide" (that is, having maximum height equal to the number of slots). Weights in the case of completion time, number of tardy jobs and tardiness were also chosen from a uniform distribution between 1 and 10.

The one exception was for stretch metrics, where the weights are predetermined by the size of the flow.) Similarly, in the case of SLA metrics, the number of steps and the incremental step heights were chosen from similar distributions with a maximum of 5 steps. Single deadlines for the tardy and tardiness cases was chosen so that it was possible to meet the deadline, with a uniform random choice of additional time given. Multiple successive deadlines for the SLA case were chosen similarly. The number of slots was set to 25.

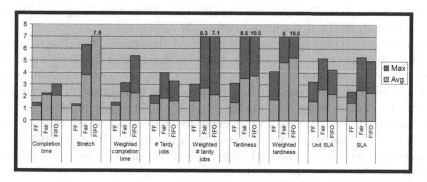

Fig. 10. Minisum Simulation Results: Average and Worst Case

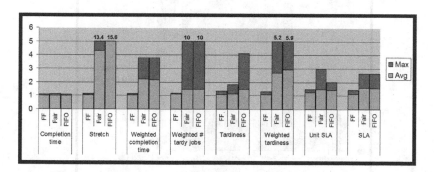

Fig. 11. Minimax Simulation Results: Average and Worst Case

Figure 10 illustrates both average and worst case performance (given 25 simulation experiments each) for 9 minisum metrics. Each column represents the ratio of the *FlowFlex, Fair* or *FIFO* algorithm to the best lower bound available.[8] Thus each ratio must be at least 1. Ratios close to 1 are by definition very good solutions, but, of course, solutions with poorer ratios may still be close to optimal. Note that *FlowFlex* performs significantly better than either *Fair* or *FIFO*, and often is close to optimal. *FIFO* performs particularly poorly on average stretch, because the weights can cause great volatility. *FlowFlex* also does dramatically better than either *Fair* or *FIFO* on the tardiness metrics. Similarly,

---

[8] To deal with lower bounds of 0, which is possible for some metrics, we added 1 to both the numerator and denominator. The effect is typically quite modest.

Figure 11 illustrates the comparable minimax experiments, for those 8 metrics which make sense. Here one sees that makespan is fine for all schemes, which is not particularly surprising. But *FlowFlex* does far better than either *Fair* or *FIFO* on all the others, and some of these are *very* difficult problems. Again, some of the *Fair* and *FIFO* ratios can be quite bad. In all 8 sets of experiments, *FlowFlex* is within 1.26 of "optimal" on average, and generally quite a lot better.

5.2   Cluster Experiments

We have prototyped *FlowFlex* on the IBM Platform Symphony MapReduce framework with IBM's BigInsights product [5].

We used a workload based on the standard Hadoop Gridmix2 benchmark. For each experiment we ran 10 flows, each consisting of 2 to 10 Gridmix jobs of random sizes, randomly wired into a dependency graph by the same basic procedure we used for simulation experiments. The experiment driver program submitted a job only when it was *ready*. That is, all of the jobs it depended upon were completed. We ran two sets of experiments: one where all flows arrived at once and another where flows arrived at random intervals chosen from an exponential distribution. For each type of experiment we ran three different random sets of arrival times and job sizes.

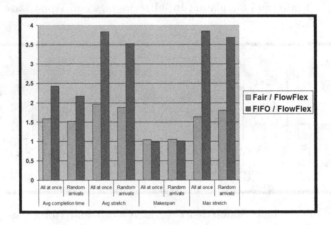

Fig. 12. Cluster Experiments, Gridmix2-based Live Benchmark

In these cluster experiments, the schedulers are running in something more like their natural environment. Specifically, they are epoch-based: Every epoch (roughly 2 seconds) they examine the newly revised problem instance. Thus the job sizes for *FlowFlex* change from epoch to epoch. And, of course, flows and jobs arrive and complete. *FlowFlex* then produces complete (theoretical) schedules for internal consumption, but also, more importantly, initial allocation suggestions. This is then implemented to the extent possible by the Assignment Layer.

A few comments should be mentioned here. First, we have not yet focused on integrating schemes for estimating the amount of work of each job in the various flows. We do know the number of tasks per job, however, and estimate work for unstarted jobs by using a default work prediction per task. For running jobs we continue to refine our work estimates by extrapolating based on data from the completed tasks. All of this can be improved in the future, for example by incorporating the techniques in [19]. Better estimates should improve the quality of our *FlowFlex* scheduler. The second comment is that we are using a slight variant of *FlowFlex* for minisum problems. This variant avoids the minimum cost flow problem. It is faster and approximately as effective. The third comment is that the Reduce phase is *ready* precisely when some fixed fraction of the Map phase tasks preceeding it have finished. *FlowFlex* simply coalesces all such ready tasks within a single MapReduce job and adjusts the maxima accordingly.

We compared *FlowFlex* to *Fair* and *FIFO* running for submitted jobs. (They were not aware of jobs that were not yet submitted.) Figure 12 reports the relative performance improvement of *FlowFlex* for average completion time, makespan, and average and maximum stretch for both sets of experiments. Essentially, we are evaluating the four most commonly used scheduling metrics.

6 Conclusion

In this paper we have introduced *FlowFlex*, a MapReduce scheduling algorithm of both theoretical and practical interest. Theoretically, we have extended the literature on malleable parallel scheduling with precedence constraints, linear speedup and processor maxima. We have provided a unified three-stage algorithm for any scheduling metric, and given worst-case performance bounds. These include approximation guarantees where possible, and bicriteria approximation guarantees where not. Practically, *FlowFlex* is the natural and ultimate extension of *Flex*, a MapReduce scheduler for singleton jobs already in use in IBM's BigInsights. We have evaluated *FlowFlex* experimentally, showing its excellent average case performance on all metrics. And we have shown the superiority of *FlowFlex* to natural extensions of both *Fair* and *FIFO*.

References

1. Agrawal, P., Kifer, D., Olston, C.: Scheduling Shared Scans of Large Data Files. In: Proceedings of VLDB (2008)
2. Balmin, A., Hildrum, K., Nagarajan, V., Wolf, J.: Malleable Scheduling for Flows of MapReduce Jobs, Research Report RC25364, IBM Research (2013)
3. Berlinska, J., Drozdowski, M.: Scheduling Divisible MapReduce Computations. Journal of Parallel and Distributed Computing 71, 450–459 (2011)
4. Beyer, K., Ercegovac, V., Gemulla, R., Balmin, A., Eltabakh, M., Kanne, C.-C., Ozcan, F., Shekita, E.: Jaql: A Scripting Language for Large Scale Semistructured Data Analysis. In: Proceedings of VLDB (2011)
5. BigInsights: http://www-01.ibm.com/software/data/infosphere/biginsights/
6. Coffman, E., Garey, M., Johnson, D., Tarjan, R.: Performance Bounds for Level-Oriented Two-Dimensional Packing Algorithms. SIAM Journal on Computing 9(4), 808–826 (1980)
7. De Pauw, W., Wolf, J., Balmin, A.: Visualizing Jobs with Shared Resources in Distributed Environments. In: IEEE Working Conference on Software Visualization, Eindhoven, Holland (2013)

8. Dean, J., Ghemawat, S.: Mapreduce: Simplified Data Processing on Large Clusters. ACM Transactions on Computer Systems 51(1), 107–113 (2008)
9. Drozdowski, M.: Scheduling for Parallel Processing. Springer (2009)
10. Drozdowski, M., Kubiak, W.: Scheduling Parallel Tasks With Sequential Heads and Tails. Annals of Operations Research 90, 221–246 (1999)
11. Gates, A., Natkovich, O., Chopra, S., Kamath, P., Narayanamurthy, S., Olston, C., Reed, B., Srinivasan, S., Srivastava, U.: Building a High-Level Dataflow System on Top of MapReduce: The Pig Experience. In: Proceedings of VLDB (2009)
12. Hochbaum, D.S., Shmoys, D.B.: A Unified Approach to Approximation Algorithms for Bottleneck Problems. J. ACM 33(3), 533–550 (1986)
13. Kalyanasundaram, B., Pruhs, K.: Speed is as Powerful as Clairvoyance. J. ACM 47(4), 617–643 (2000)
14. Karloff, H., Suri, S., Vassilvitskii, S.: A Model of Computation for MapReduce. In: SODA, pp. 938–948 (2010)
15. Koutris, P., Suciu, D.: Parallel evaluation of conjunctive queries. In: PODS, pp. 223–234 (2011)
16. Leung, J.: Handbook of Scheduling. Chapman and Hall/CRC (2004)
17. McNaughton, R.: Scheduling with Deadlines and Loss Functions. Management Science 6(1), 1–12 (1959)
18. Moseley, B., Dasgupta, A., Kumar, R., Sarlós, T.: On Scheduling in Map-Reduce and Flow-Shops. In: SPAA, pp. 289–298 (2011)
19. Popescu, A., Ercegovac, V., Balmin, A., Branco, M., Ailamaki, A.: Same Queries, Different Data: Can We Predict Runtime Performance? In: ICDE Workshops, pp. 275–280 (2012)
20. Thusoo, A., Sarma, J., Jain, N., Shao, Z., Chakka, P., Zhang, N., Anthony, S., Liu, H., Murthy, R.: Hive - a Petabyte Scale Data Warehouse using Hadoop. In: ICDE, pp. 996–1005 (2010)
21. Schuurman, P., Woeginger, G.J.: A Polynomial Time Approximation Scheme for the Two-Stage Multiprocessor Flow Shop Problem. Theor. Comput. Sci. 237(1-2), 105–122 (2000)
22. Schwiegelshohn, U., Ludwig, W., Wolf, J., Turek, J., Yu, P.: Smart SMART Bounds for Weighted Response Time Scheduling. SIAM Journal on Computing 28(1), 237–253 (1999)
23. Turek, J., Wolf, J., Yu, P.: Approximate Algorithms for Scheduling Parallelizable Tasks. In: SPAA (1992)
24. Wolf, J., Balmin, A., Rajan, D., Hildrum, K., Khandekar, R., Parekh, S., Wu, K.-L., Vernica, R.: On the Optimization of Schedules for MapReduce Workloads in the Presence of Shared Scans. VLDB Journal 21(5) (2012)
25. Wolf, J., Rajan, D., Hildrum, K., Khandekar, R., Kumar, V., Parekh, S., Wu, K.-L., Balmin, A.: FLEX: A Slot Allocation Scheduling Optimizer for MapReduce Workloads. In: Gupta, I., Mascolo, C. (eds.) Middleware 2010. LNCS, vol. 6452, pp. 1–20. Springer, Heidelberg (2010)
26. Zaharia, M., Borthakur, D., Sarma, J., Elmeleegy, K., Schenker, S., Stoica, I.: Job Scheduling for Multi-User MapReduce Clusters, UC Berkeley Technical Report EECS-2009-55 (2009)
27. Zaharia, M., Borthakur, D., Sarma, J., Elmeleegy, K., Shenker, S., Stoica, I.: Delay Scheduling: A Simple Technique for Achieving Locality and Fairness in Cluster Scheduling. In: EuroSys (2010)

DVFS Aware CPU Credit Enforcement
in a Virtualized System

Daniel Hagimont[1], Christine Mayap Kamga[1],
Laurent Broto[1], Alain Tchana[2], and Noel De Palma[2]

[1] University of Toulouse
first.last@enseeiht.fr
[2] Joseph Fourier University
first.last@imag.fr

Abstract. Nowadays, virtualization is present in almost all computing infrastructures. Thanks to VM migration and server consolidation, virtualization helps
reducing power consumption in distributed environments. On another side, Dynamic Voltage and Frequency Scaling (DVFS) allows servers to dynamically
modify the processor frequency (according to the CPU load) in order to achieve
less energy consumption. We observed that these two techniques have several incompatibilities. For instance, if two virtual machines VM1 and VM2 are running
on the same physical host (with their respective allocated credits), VM1 being
overloaded and VM2 being underloaded, the host may be globally underloaded
leading to a reduction of the processor frequency, which would penalize VM1
even if VM1's owner booked a given CPU capacity. In this paper, we analyze
the compatibility of available VM schedulers with DVFS management in virtualized environments, we identify key issues and finally propose a DVFS aware
VM scheduler which addresses these issues. We implemented and evaluated our
prototype in the Xen virtualized environment.

Keywords: DVFS, virtual machines, scheduling.

1 Introduction

Nowadays, many organizations tend to outsource the management of their physical
infrastructure to hosting centers. They subscribe for a quality of service (QoS) and
expect providers to fully meet it. By acting this way, companies aim at reducing their
costs by paying only for what they really need. The providers, instead, are interested in
saving resources while guaranteeing customers QoS requirements.

On the provider side, virtualization was introduced in order to facilitate resource
management. Virtualization is a software-based solution for building and running simultaneously several operating systems (called *guest OS* or *Virtual Machine*) on top of
an underlying OS (called *host OS* or *hypervisor*). In hosting centers, virtualization is
a means to implement server consolidation. Indeed, servers being underutilized most
of the time (below 30% of processor utilization [17]), VM (Virtual Machine) migration helps achieving better server utilization by migrating VMs on a minimal set of
machines, and switching unused machines off in order to save energy.

D. Eyers and K. Schwan (Eds.): Middleware 2013, LNCS 8275, pp. 123–142, 2013.

However, powerful computers with high processor frequency, multiple cores and multiple CPUs are an important factor contributing to the continuous increase of energy consumption in computing infrastructures. To reduce power consumption of such infrastructures, processor manufacturers have developed a hardware technology called *Dynamic Voltage and Frequency Scaling (DVFS)*. DVFS [12] allows dynamic processor frequency control, and hence, helps in reducing power consumption.

DVFS is largely used in non-virtualized systems, but its implementation in virtualized architectures reveals some incompatibilities with VM schedulers. In virtualized systems, VMs are generally created and configured with a fixed CPU share. DVFS, according to the host's global CPU load, dynamically scales the processor frequency regardless of the VM local loads. In a scenario with some overloaded VMs, but a globally underloaded host, DVFS will scale down processor frequency, which will penalize overloaded VMs.

The contributions of this paper are two folds. First, we analyze and highlight the incompatibility of available VM schedulers with DVFS management in virtualized systems. Second, we identify the key issues and propose a DVFS aware VM scheduler which addresses these issues. To demonstrate the effectiveness of our approach, we implemented and evaluated a prototype in the Xen [1] virtualized environment.

The rest of this paper is structured as follows. Section 2 presents the context of our work. Section 3 analyzes VM schedulers and DVFS principles and pinpoints their incompatibilities. In Section 4, we present our DVFS aware VM scheduler prototype. Section 5 presents our experiments and results. After a review of related works in section 6, we conclude the article in Section 7.

2　Context

In this section, we introduce the basic concepts of virtualization and DVFS.

2.1　Virtualization

Virtualization is a software and/or hardware-based solution for building and running simultaneously several *guest OS* on top of an underlying *host OS*. The key technique is to share hardware resources safely and efficiently between these guest OS. In the host OS, a *hypervisor* implements several execution environments also known as *Virtual Machines (VM)* in which guest OS can be executed. Thanks to the hypervisor, guest OS are isolated from each other, and have the illusion of being in the presence of several separate machines. The hypervisor is also the program that ensures good sharing of hardware resources among multiple guest OS. It emulates the underlying hardware for VMs[1] and enables communication between guest OS and real devices.

The hypervisor is responsible for scheduling VMs on the processor. Initially, VMs are created and configured in order to have, among other parameters, an execution priority and a CPU credit. The hypervisor scheduler chooses the VM to execute, according

---

[1] Each guest OS has the illusion of having host's processor, memory and other resources all to itself.

to its scheduling algorithm and the VM parameters. It ensures dynamic and fair allocation of CPU resources to VMs. However, in each VM, the execution of a guest OS implies the execution of processes scheduled by another process scheduler. Therefore, the execution of an application in a virtualized environment involves different levels of scheduler, but the hypervisor is not conscious of it. From its point of view, VMs are just processes which are scheduled in such a way that each VM receives its associated credit of the CPU [18] (a percentage of the CPU time).

In the rest of the article, we will use the term VM to refer to a guest OS running in a virtual machine.

2.2 Dynamic Voltage and Frequency Scaling (DVFS)

Today, all processors integrate dynamic frequency scaling (also known as CPU throttling) to adjust frequency at runtime. The system service which adapts frequency in the operating system is called a *governor*. Different governors can be implemented with different policies regarding frequency management.

In the Linux kernel, the *Ondemand* governor changes frequency depending on CPU utilization. It changes frequency between the lowest level (when CPU utilization is less than 20% [22]) and the highest level (when CPU load is higher). The *Performance* governor always keeps the frequency to the highest value while the *Powersave* governor keeps it at the lowest level. The *Conservative* governor decreases or increases frequency by one level through a range of values supported by the hardware, according to the CPU load. Finally, the *Userspace* governor allows user applications to manually set the processor frequency [13].

In order to control the CPU frequency, governors rely on an underlying subsystem inside the kernel called cpufreq [22]. Cpufreq provides a set of modularized interfaces to allow changing the CPU frequency.

As aforementioned, effective usage of DVFS brings the advantage of reducing power consumption by lowering the processor frequency. Moreover, almost all computing infrastructures rely on multi-core and high frequency processors. Therefore, the benefit from using DVFS has been experienced in many different systems.

2.3 Consolidation and DVFS

Virtualization allows VMs to be dynamically migrated between hosts, generally according to the CPU load on the different hosts, and to switch unused machines off. Ideally, a consolidation system should gather all the VMs on a reduced set of machines which should have a high CPU load, and DVFS would therefore be useless.

However, as argued in [16], an important bottleneck of such consolidation systems is memory. Any VM, even idle, needs physical memory, which limits the number of VMs that can be executed on a host. Therefore, even if consolidation can reduce the number of active machines in a hosting center, it cannot optimally guarantee full usage of CPU on active machines as it is memory bound. Consequently, DVFS is complementary to consolidation.

The next section analyzes the incompatibilities between virtualization and DVFS for energy saving.

3 Analysis

The overall goal of this paper is to show that combining virtualization and DVFS management may raise incompatibilities and that it is required a smart coordination between DVFS management and VM management (i.e., VM scheduling). In this section, we first review VM schedulers, especially those that are effectively used in virtualization solutions (such as Xen). We then analyze the issues that are raised when these schedulers are combined with DVFS management.

3.1 VM Schedulers

VM schedulers are in charge of allocating CPU to VMs. Commonly, schedulers are classified into three categories: *share*, *credit allocation* and *preemption* [6]. In our work, we focus on credit allocation schedulers as they aim at allocating a portion of processor to a VM. This portion of the processor corresponds to a SLA (service level agreement) negotiated between the provider and the customer, i.e. this portion of the CPU was bought by the client and has to be guarantee by the provider.

In the credit scheduler category, we distinguish: **fix credit** and **variable credit** schedulers.

With fix credit scheduler[2], the CPU credit of each VM is guaranteed, which means that the VM always obtains the time slices corresponding to this credit (a percentage of the processor). For instance, if two VMs are running on the same physical host with the same priority and CPU credit (50%), then each of them will receive at most 50% of the CPU time even if one of them becomes inactive.

With variable credit scheduler[3], the CPU credit of each VM is also guaranteed, but only if the VM has a computation load to effectively use it. In the case of unused CPU time slices, they are redistributed among active VMs. It means that the processor is idle only if there is no more runnable VM. For example, with two VMs with the same priority and CPU credit (50%), each of them will receive 50% of the CPU time slices if they are both fully using their time slices, but if one of them becomes inactive, the active VM may receive up to 100% of the CPU.

In this paper, we conducted our experiments with the Xen system (version 4.1.2). Xen has three schedulers called *Credit, Simple Earliest Deadline First (SEDF) and Credit2*. Credit2 scheduler is an updated version of Credit scheduler, with the intention of solving some of its weaknesses. This scheduler is currently available in a beta version. Credit is the default Xen scheduler and SEDF is about to be removed from Xen sources. In the following, we only consider credit and SEDF schedulers as they allow illustrating the incompatibilities (with DVFS) we aim at addressing.

Xen Credit scheduler is primarily a fix credit scheduler. A VM can be created with a given priority and a given credit, and the VM credit is always guaranteed. The only exception is when allocating a VM with a null credit. In this latter case, the VM will not have any credit limit and it can use any CPU time slices that are not used by other VMs (such a VM behaves as with a variable credit scheduler, except that it does not have any guaranteed credit).

---

[2] Also called *non-work conserving* scheduler
[3] Also called *work conserving* scheduler

With Xen SEDF scheduler, each VM is configured with a triplet (s,p,b), where s represents *the lowest slice* of time during each *period* of length p where the VM will use the CPU. The boolean flag b, indicate whether the VM is eligible or not to receive extra CPU time slices that are not used by other VMs. Therefore SEDF can be both used as a fix or variable credit scheduler (according to the b flag), and the credit allocated to a VM can be defined with the s and p parameters.

In our experiments, we create VMs with a given fraction of the CPU capacity (a credit corresponding to a SLA) and we illustrate the incompatibilities between DVFS and VM schedulers by using Xen Credit scheduler as fix credit scheduler and Xen SEDF scheduler as variable credit scheduler.

In the rest of the paper, we will not consider different VM priorities as we assume that the overall goal of a hosting center provider is to allocate portions of a processor (with VMs) to customers, without any priority between customers.

3.2 Combining DVFS and VM Scheduling

In version 4.1.2, Xen supports four governors (as described in Section 2.2): *ondemand, performance, powersave* and *userspace*.

The Ondemand governor is the most used for DVFS. Depending on the global host CPU load, the governor adjusts the processor frequency between the highest and the lowest level. However, the VM scheduler selects and executes VMs regardless of processor frequency, and therefore a processor frequency reduction influences VM performance.

Let us consider a Xen virtualized system with two VMs (V20 and V70) running on the same physical host. They are respectively configured with 20% and 70% of credit. The Ondemand governor will set the suitable processor frequency according to the load. We assume in the illustrative example used below that reducing the processor frequency slows down the processor by 50%.

Then, let us consider, the two following scenarios (with different schedulers).

Scenario 1 - Fix Credit Scheduler. We assume that the host is working with a fix credit scheduler. If V20 is overloaded (100% of its 20% CPU credits) and V70 is underloaded (0% of its 70% CPU credits), then the host is globally underloaded (the load is theoretically 20%). The Ondemand governor scales down the processor frequency. This reduction saves energy, but V20 is heavily penalized. Indeed, instead of receiving its percentage (20%) of the computing capacity, V20 receives less (50% of 20%) because of the frequency reduction. When a credit is allocated to a VM as a percentage of the total host CPU capacity, this percentage is a fraction of the processor capacity at the maximum frequency. If the processor frequency is decreased because V70 is not using its allocated credit (and the host is therefore globally underloaded), V20 does not obtain its initially allocated credit.

In summary in this scenario, scaling down frequency decreases V20's performance and therefore its applications QoS, because the fix credit scheduler is not aware of processor frequency scaling.

Scenario 2 - Variable Credit Scheduler. Now, consider that our host is working with a variable credit scheduler. With the same assumptions than in the previous section (V20 overloaded, V70 underloaded), V70's unused CPU time slices can be given to V20, because of variable credit allocation, which counterbalances the effects described with fix credit scheduler if we would have a frequency reduction. However, we will not have any frequency reduction. All the V70 unused time slices can be given to V20 (without any limit), which leads to a globally overloaded host, which in turn prevents the processor frequency be scaled down.

In this scenario, the problem with the variable credit scheduler is that by giving unused time slices to V20, it will prevent frequency scaling, thus wasting energy from the point of view of the provider.

Design Principles of Power Aware Scheduling. Because of the independence of VM schedulers and DVFS governors, either the provider cannot guarantee the QoS required by the customers (with the fix credit scheduler) or a VM will be allowed to use more CPU than its allocated credit, preventing DVFS scaling (with the variable credit scheduler). The previous scenarios reveal incompatibilities between schedulers and governors.

Our proposal is to take advantage of DVFS to lower power consumption while guaranteeing the credits allocated to VMs. Concretely, when the processor frequency is modified, we reconsider the credit associated with VMs in order to counterbalance the effect of the frequency modification. The consequence is that:

– the initially configured credit of a VM is a percentage of the computing capacity of the processor at the maximum frequency (20% for V20 and 70% for V70 in our scenario)
– a VM will see its credit increased (resp. decreased) whenever the processor frequency is decreased (resp. increased), this credit (at the new frequency) being equivalent to the initial credit (at the maximum frequency). In the previous scenario, when the processor frequency is decreased (slowing down the processor by 50%), V20 will be given 40% of credit to counterbalance the frequency reduction.
– a VM is never given more computing capacity than its allocated credit, enabling frequency reductions

The next section details this contribution.

4   Contributions

As previously argued, DVFS and VM schedulers have incompatibilities. DVFS was introduced for power reduction, but cannot directly be exploited for the same purpose in virtualized systems. Our contribution aims at managing DVFS in a virtualized environment while (i) benefiting from power reduction and (ii) guaranteeing allocated CPU credits.

We implemented our *Power Aware Scheduler* (*PAS* for short) in the Xen environment as an extension of the Xen Credit scheduler, which is the default and most achieved VM scheduler. The following subsections present our implementation choices and the implementation of the PAS scheduler.

4.1 Implementation Choices

We considered three possible implementations for our PAS scheduler:

- *user level - credit management*. In this design, we let the Ondemand governor manage the processor frequency. Then, a user level application monitors the processor frequency, and periodically computes and sets VM credits in order to guarantee initially allocated credits.
- *user level - credit and DVFS management*. In this design, a user level application monitors the VM loads. Periodically, it computes and sets the processor frequency which can accept the load, and it also computes and sets the updated VM credits. With this solution, the VM credits can be updated each time the processor frequency is modified.
- *in the Xen system - credit and DVFS management*: A user level implementation can be quite intrusive because of system calls and it may lack reactivity. Another possibility is to implement it as an extension of the VM scheduler. DVFS and VM credit computations and adaptations are then performed each time a scheduling decision is made.

We experimented with these three solutions. The results reported in this paper are based on the third implementation.

4.2 PAS Scheduler Implementation

In our implementation of the PAS scheduler, we rely on two main assumptions:

- proportionality of frequency and performance. This property means that if we modify the frequency of the processor, the impact on performance is proportional to the change of the frequency.
- proportionality of credit and performance. This property means that if we modify the credits allocated to a VM, the impact on performance is proportional to the change of the credits.

Proportionality of Frequency and Performance
This proportionality is defined by:

$$\frac{L_{max}}{L_i} = \frac{F_i}{F_{max}} \times cf_i \quad (cf_i \text{ is very close to 1}) \tag{1}$$

which means that if we decrease the frequency from F_{max} down to F_i, the load will proportionally increase from L_{max} to L_i. For instance, if F_{max} is 3000 and F_i is 1500, the frequency ratio is 0.5 which means that the processor is running 50% slower at F_i compared to F_{max}. So if we consider a load (L_{max}) of 10% at F_{max}, the load (L_i) should be $\frac{10\%}{0.5} = 20\%$ at F_i.

Even if cf_i is very close to 1, we kept this variable in our equations as we observed that it may vary according to the machine architecture and the considered frequency F_i.

A similar proportionality is defined for execution times. But we add here that execution times depend on the credit (j) allocated to the VM which hosts the computation (VM credits are considered below)[4].

$$\frac{T^j_{max}}{T^j_i} = \frac{F_i}{F_{max}} \times cf_i \tag{2}$$

We define the frequency ratio as $ratio_i = \frac{F_i}{F_{max}}$.

Proportionality of Credit and Performance

This proportionality is defined by:

$$\frac{T^{init}_i}{T^j_i} = \frac{C^j}{C^{init}} \tag{3}$$

which means that if we increase the credits of a VM from C^{init} up to C^j, the execution time will proportionally decrease from T^{init}_i to T^j_i. Here, the execution time also depends on the frequency (i) of the processor. For instance, if we increase the credits allocated to a VM from 10% to 20%, we double the computing capacity of the VM. Then the execution time should become half of the initial execution time.

These proportionality rules are validated at the beginning of the evaluation section (Section 5).

In our algorithms, the first equation (1) is used to estimate, for a given CPU load, what would be the load at a different processor frequency. Therefore, if we measure a load L_i at frequency F_i, we can compute the **absolute load**, i.e., the equivalent load at F_{max} which is $L_i * ratio_i * cf_i$. And if we want to check whether such an absolute load can be supported at a different frequency (i), we will check whether this absolute load is less than $100 * ratio_i * cf_i$.

The two other equations (2 and 3) are used to compute the modification of VM credits, which can compensate the performance penalty incurred by a frequency reduction. Assume that a VM is initially allocated credit C^{init} (which is a fraction of the processor at frequency F_{max}). Then assume that the frequency of the processor is reduced down to F_i. We are looking for the new credit C^j to assign to this VM, so that its execution time would be the same as with credit C^{init} and frequency F_{max}, i.e. so that $T^j_i = T^{init}_{max}$.

According to equation 3, $C^j = \frac{T^{init}_i * C^{init}}{T^j_i}$

According to equation 2, $T^j_i = \frac{T^j_{max}}{ratio_i * cf_i}$, so $T^{init}_i = \frac{T^{init}_{max}}{ratio_i * cf_i}$

Therefore, $C^j = \frac{T^{init}_{max} * C^{init}}{ratio_i * cf_i * T^j_i}$

and we want that $T^j_i = T^{init}_{max}$

So $C^j = \frac{T^{init}_{max} * C^{init}}{ratio_i * cf_i * T^{init}_{max}} = \frac{C^{init}}{ratio_i * cf_i}$

---

[4] in the following, frequencies are show as subscripts and credits as exponents

In summary:

$$C^j = \frac{C^{init}}{ratio_i * cf_i} \quad (4)$$

This means that with our assumptions, we can compensate the performance penalty incurred by a frequency reduction as follows:

- If we run a computation in a VM with 20% credit at the F_{max} frequency.
- If we reduce the processor frequency from F_{max} to F_i, for instance half the maximum frequency, so that $ratio_i$ is 0.5.
- we can change the credit to 20% ÷ 0.5 = 40% in order to have the same computing capacity, and we will have the same computation time or the same computation load under this new frequency (assuming that cf_i=1).

We now describe the implementation of the PAS scheduler.

The PAS scheduler relies on a set of variables that are used for the computation of the processor frequency to be used and the credits to be associated with VMs. We also define additional variables that are used to explain the behavior of our PAS scheduler in the evaluation section.

- *VM[]* is a table of the VMs managed by the scheduler and *nbVM* the number of VMs.
- *Credit[]* is a table of the credit associated with each VM.
- *Freq[]* is a table of the possible processor frequencies and *fmax* is the number of frequencies (so *Freq[fmax]* is the maximum frequency).
- *CF[]* is a table of the variables (cf_i) associated with the different frequencies.
- *CurrentFreq* is the current frequency of the processor.
- *VM_load* is the observed load of a VM (e.g., V20 has a VM_load of 100% in our previous scenario).
- *VM_global_load* is the contribution of a VM to the load of the processor (e.g., V20 which is allocated a credit of 20% and which has a *VM_load* of 100%, contributes to the processor load for 100% of 20%, that is 20%). If a VM is allocated a credit of *VM_credit*, then *VM_global_load = VM_load * VM_credit*.
- *Global_load* is the load of the processor. Therefore,
  $Global\_load = \sum VM\_global\_load.$ [5]
- *Absolute_load* is the processor load that we would have if processor was running at the maximum frequency. According to our previous assumption regarding frequencies, we have:
  $Absolute\_load = Global\_load * \frac{CurrentFreq}{Freq[max]} * cf_{CurrentFreq}.$

As mentioned in Section 4.1, the PAS scheduler has been implemented both at user level and at system level. In the following, we rely on the system implementation.

At each tick in the VM scheduler, we compute the appropriate processor frequency according to the *Absolute_load*, as depicted in the algorithm below (Listing 1.1). We

---

[5] Note that, each time we consider the *Global_load*, it represents an average of three successive processor utilization.

iterate on the processor frequencies (line 2). Following our assumption regarding frequencies, we compute for each frequency the frequency ratio (line 3) and check if the computing capacity of the processor at that frequency can absorb the current absolute load (line 4).

```
int computeNewFreq () {
  for (i=1; i<=fmax; i++) {
    int ratio = Freq[i]/Freq[fmax];
    if (ratio * 100 * CF[i] > Absolute_load)
      return Freq[i];
    }
  return Freq[fmax];
}
```

Listing 1.1. Algorithm for computing the next processor frequency

At each tick, we need to compute the new credits associated with VMs and to modify VM credits and the processor frequency. This is described in the algorithm below (Listing 1.2). For the new frequency of the processor, we compute the frequency ratio (line 3) and for each VM, we compute the new credit that has to be associated with each VM (line 5) and assign it (line 6). The credit of a VM increases when the frequency of the processor decreases. Finally, we modify the processor frequency (line 7).

An important remark is that with this algorithm, when the processor frequency is low, the sum of the VM credits may be more than 100%, because we computed the new credit limit for each VM.

```
void updateDvfsAndCredits () {
  int newFreq = computeNewFreq ();
  int ratio = newFreq/Freq[fmax];
  for (vm=1; i<=nbVM; vm++) {
    in newCredit = Credit[vm]/(ratio * CF[newFreq]);
    setCredit (VM[vm], newCredit);
  }
  setFrequency (newFreq);
}
```

Listing 1.2. Algorithm for computing VM credits, and setting VM credits and processor frequency

Some of these VM are active and some are lazy. For active VM, this new limit extends their computing capacities and compensate the frequency reduction. For lazy VM, this new limit is meaningless as it will not be reached (if the load of lazy VMs increases, the processor frequency will increase and VM credits will be decreased).

5   Evaluation

5.1   Environment

Our experiments were performed on a DELL Optiplex 755, with an Intel Core 2 Duo 2.66GHz with 4G RAM. We run a Linux Debian Squeeze (with the 2.6.32.27 kernel)

in a single processor mode. The Xen hypervisor (in his 4.1.2 version) is used as virtualization solution.

The evaluation described below were performed with two applications:

- when we aim at measuring an execution time, we use an application which computes an approximation of π. This application is called π-*app*.
- when we aim at measuring a CPU load, we use a web application (a Joomla CMS server) which receives a load generated by httperf [14]. This application is called *Web-app*. The Joomla server consists of Joomla 1.7, relying on Apache 2.2.16, PHP 5.3.3 installed into Apache with modphp5 and MySQL 5.1.49. This application is called *Web-app* in the following.

5.2 Verification of Our Assumptions

As said at the beginning of Section 4, the implementation of our PAS scheduler relies on two main assumptions: proportionality of frequency and performance (equation 1 & 2) and proportionality of credit and performance (equation 3).

In order to validate these two assumptions, we conducted the following experiments:

- Proportionality of frequency and performance. We ran different Web-app workloads at the different processor frequencies. For each workload, we measured the loads $L(freq)$ at the different $freq$ processor frequencies and we drew for each workload the ratios $\frac{L(freqmax)}{L(freq)}$ and $\frac{freq}{freqmax}$, in order to compute the cf_i values for each frequency and to verify that they were constant under various workloads (thus validating equation 1). We also ran different π-app workloads at different processor frequencies and measured the execution times, allowing us to verify the proportionality of frequency ratios and execution time ratios (equation 2).
- Proportionality of credit and performance. We ran different π-app workloads on VMs configured with different credits (with the Xen credit scheduler). For each workload and credit (index j), we measured the execution time and computed the credit ratio ($\frac{C^j}{C^{init}}$) and the execution time ratio ($\frac{T_i^{init}}{T_i^j}$), in order to verify equation 3.

These experiments allowed to validate these proportionality assumptions and to compute the cf_i values (more details are given in Section 5.8).

Finally, in order to verify the accuracy of equation 4 which is used to compensate (with a credit allocation) the performance penalty incurred by a frequency reduction, we executed π-app at the maximum frequency (2667 MHz) with different initial credits $(10, 20, 30 \ldots)$, then we ran the same experiment at frequency 2133 MHz, but computed with equation 4 what should be the associated credits which compensate this frequency reduction. Figure 1 shows our results. The X axis at the bottom gives the initial credits, the X axis at the top gives the computed credits, and the Y axis gives the execution times. This experiments shows that we can effectively compensate a frequency reduction with a credit allocation.

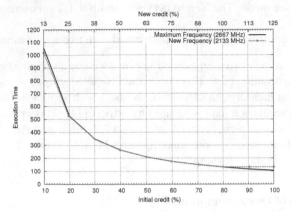

Fig. 1. Compensation of Frequency Reduction with Credit Allocation

5.3   Execution Profile

In the rest of this evaluation section, we rely on the Web-app application previously described and we consider 2 virtual machines called V20 and V70, with respectively 20% and 70% of initially allocated credit. The remaining 10% of credit are allocated for the hypervisor (the Dom0 in Xen) which is configured with the highest priority in the VM scheduler. The two VMs have the same priority.

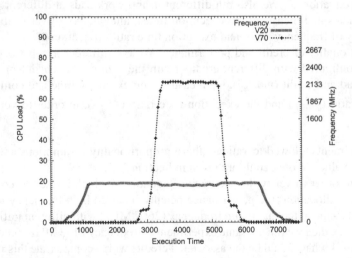

Fig. 2. Load profile (at the maximum frequency)

The objective of the execution profile we are considering is to reveal the scheduling problem we are addressing and to demonstrate the effectiveness of our solution (the PAS scheduler). Both VMs have a three-phase profile: inactive-active-inactive:

- inactive. During the inactive phase, the VM does not receive any load from the load injector (httperf).
- active. During the active phase, the VM may receive two types of load: either the injector is configured to generate a load which represents 100% of the VM capacity but not more (we call such a load an *exact load*), or it is configured to generate a load which exceeds the VM capacity (we call such a load a *thrashing load*).

Figure 2 shows the VM_global_load (as defined in Section 4, the contribution of the VM to the load of the processor) for both VMs when executing this profile with the credit scheduler, and with the processor frequency being kept at its maximum value (the frequency is shown on the Y axis on the right side). Notice here that the same performance figure is obtained with an exact load or a thrashing load, since the credit scheduler limits the amount of CPU that a VM may use (according to its initially allocated credit). This figure characterizes the execution profile we will use in the rest of the article.

5.4 Credit Scheduler in Default

We now run the same execution profile (with an exact load) with the credit scheduler, but with the Ondemand DVFS management governor.

As observed on Figure 3, the default Ondemand governor is quite aggressive and unstable. Therefore, we implemented our own (ondemand) governor, which is less aggressive and more stable, and consequently saves less energy. We performed the same experiments with both governors and observed the same overall behaviors (Figure 4), but without such oscillations with our governor (that we use in rest of this evaluation for readibility of figures).

In the two previous figures, when a VM is in the active phase, its VM_global_load is 70% for V70 and 20% for V20 (its contribution to the load of the processor).

While the previous Figures gave the observed VM_global_loads, Figure 5 shows the Absolute_load (defined in Section 4 as the processor load that it represents with a processor running at the maximum frequency, or more precisely Absolute_load = Global_load $* \frac{CurrentFreq}{Freq[max]} * cf_{CurrentFreq}$). We observe that in the first phase (when V20 is active and V70 inactive), the absolute load of V20 is close to 10%. This is due to the lowered processor frequency, since the global load of the processor is only 20%. However, as soon as V70 becomes active, the global load of the processor becomes high enough to scale up the processor frequency at the maximum level, and then the absolute load of V20 climbs to 20%. In summary, V20 is only granted its allocated (absolute) credit (20%) when the processor frequency is at the maximum level.

5.5 SEDF Scheduler Brings a Solution

We ran the same experiment with the SEDF scheduler. Remind that with SEDF, unused CPU time slices can be given to active VMs. Therefore, as observed on Figure 6, in

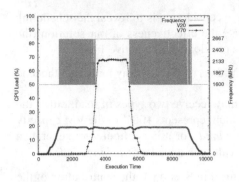

Fig. 3. Global loads with Ondemand governor / Credit scheduler / exact load

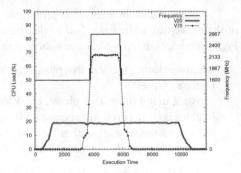

Fig. 4. Global loads with our governor / Credit scheduler / exact load

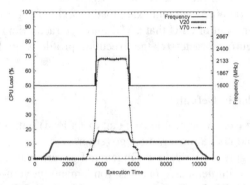

Fig. 5. Absolute loads with our governor / Credit scheduler / exact load

the first phase (when V20 is active and V70 inactive), V20 has a global load of 35%, because it is given time slices which are not used by V70. And when V70 becomes active, then the initially allocated credits are respected and V20 ends up with 20% of global load (at the maximum processor frequency).

And if we observe the absolute load in this experiment (Figure 7), we see that unused time slices that were given to V20 allowed to compensate the penalty of the lowered processor frequency. V20 has a 20% absolute load during the entire experiment. Therefore, SEDF brings a solution to our identified issue, i.e., the fact that an active VM can be victim of a frequency reduction (due to other VM laziness).

5.6 SEDF Scheduler in Default

However, the SEDF scheduler does not actually solve the problem. In the previous experiments, we used exact loads (which represents 100% of the VM capacity but not more). If we use thrashing loads (which exceed VM capacities), we observe (Figure 8) that in the first phase (when V20 is active and V70 inactive), the SEDF scheduler gives unused time slices to V20, which in turn brings the processor frequency at the highest level. In this first phase, V20 is allowed to consume 85% of the processor. This is not consistent from the point of view of the provider in a hosting infrastructure, since V20

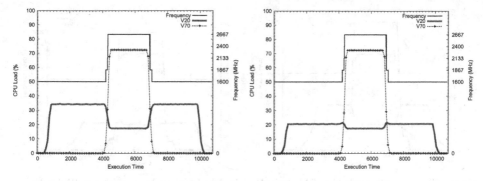

Fig. 6. Global loads with our ondemand governor / SEDF scheduler / exact load

Fig. 7. Absolute loads with our governor / SEDF scheduler / exact load

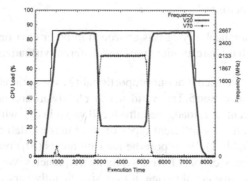

Fig. 8. Global or absolute loads with our governor / SEDF scheduler / thrashing load

was initially allocated 20% of credit and the provider does not benefit from a frequency reduction due to V70 inactivity.

In the second phase, when V70 becomes active, the SEDF scheduler guarantee the initially allocated credits and V20 cannot benefit from unused time slices anymore.

Notice here that in this experiment, the global and absolute load figures are the same (we only show a single figure) since the processor frequency is kept at the highest level during the whole experiment.

5.7 PAS Scheduler Solves the Problem

Our PAS scheduler recomputes credits allocated to VMs according to the frequency of the processor. Therefore, it provides the same benefits than the SEDF scheduler with the exact load, but also guarantees the respect of credits under thrashing loads. In Figure 9, the PAS scheduler computes that in the first phase, V20 should be granted 33% of credit in order to compensate the low processor frequency (1600 MHz). In the second phase, V20 is granted 20% of credit as the processor frequency reaches the maximum value. With this strategy, the absolute loads of each VM is consistent with credit allocations (Figure 10).

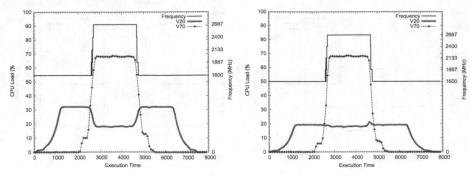

Fig. 9. Global loads with the PAS scheduler / thrashing load

Fig. 10. Absolute loads with the PAS scheduler / thrashing load

5.8 Other Environments

In order to study the applicability of this approach in other environments, we experimented with different hardware architectures and different virtualization systems.

Other Hardware. We verified that our proportionality assumptions, described in Section 4.2 and validated in Section 5.2 are valid on other hardware architectures. Therefore, we measured for different workloads the introduced variable cf_i, which may depend on the hardware architecture, for different types of machines available on Grid5000, the french national grid (Table 1). We report the measurements (cf_i) only for the minimal frequency, as many processors only have 2 available frequencies. We observed that even is cf_{min} is most of the time equal to one, it may significantly vary on particular architectures (e.g. Intel Xeon E5-2620).

Table 1. cf_{min} on different processors

	Intel Xeon X3440	Intel Xeon L5420	Intel Xeon E5-2620	AMD Opteron 6164 HE	Intel Core i7-3770
cf_{min}	0,94867	0,99903	0,80338	0,99508	0,86206

Other Virtualization Platforms. We verified that the issue we address is relevant in other virtualization platforms. Therefore, we ran the same scenario as in Section 5.3 on different virtualization environments and measured the execution time of the V20 virtual machine (Table 2). V20 can be penalized by a frequency reduction when V70 is lazy. These measurements were performed on the leading virtualization products (commercial or open-source) that we installed on the same hardware configuration, a HP compaq Elite 8300 (with an Intel Core i7-3770 3.4GHz with 8G RAM). This machine embeds hardware assisted virtualization technologies that were enabled in all our experiments. On the left part of the table, we compare solutions with a fix VM credit scheduler. The V20 virtual machine is significantly penalized on Hyper-V Server 2012, Vmware ESXi 5 and Xen (with its credit scheduler), and our PAS scheduler in Xen cancels this degradation by allocating additional credits to V20. On the right part of the table, solutions with variable credit schedulers have a much faster execution time, since the CPU capacity of V70 is given to V20 when V70 is lazy. However, V20 may consume any amount of unused CPU capacity, which prevents a reduction of the processor frequency, thus wasting energy.

Table 2. Execution Times on Different Virtualization Platforms

	Fix credit scheduler				Variable credit scheduler		
	Hyper-V	VMware	Xen/credit	Xen/PAS	Xen/SEDF	KVM	Vbox
Performance	1601	1550	1559	1559	616	599	625
OnDemand	3212	2132	2599	1560	616	599	625
Degradation(%)	50	27	40	0	0	0	0

6   Related Work

In recent years, we observed the rapid development of hosting infrastructures and their energy consumption became an important issue.

Energy saving in hosting centers
In order to better manage hosting center energy consumption, the *Green Grid* [2] association defined metrics, such as *Power Usage Effectiveness (PUE)*. *PUE* is a measure of how efficiently a hosting center uses its power; specifically, how much of the power is actually used for computing (in contrast to cooling and other overheads). It is computed as follows: PUE $= \frac{TotalFacilityPower}{ITEquipmentPower}$ where $TotalFacilityPower$ and $ITEquipmentPower$ represent respectively the global power consumption of the hosting center and the power associated with all the IT equipment (computers, storage, network equipments, etc.). The ideal value of PUE should be 1, meaning that all the power consumed by the hosting center is dedicated for computing. Such metrics allow the estimation of the energy efficiency of hosting centers, to compare the results against other hosting centers, and to determine if any energy management improvements can be made. For example, in [10], James Hamilton exploits the PUE metrics to determine the power distribution of his computing infrastructure in order to reduce high-scale data center costs.

Energy Saving for Computing Servers
Many research projects have focused on reducing the energy consumed by servers in hosting centers. The general orientation is to rely on dynamic resource allocation. In hosting centers, hardware resources are mutualized among multiples customers, which is a means to use less resources while fulfilling the requirements of customers. Customers subscribe for resources, but those resources are made available to customers only if effectively used. Therefore the amount of active resources can be reduced, thus leading to energy saving. Such energy management policies are generally implemented at the level of servers.

In 2001, Chase et al. [4] showed that hosting center servers used at least 60% of their peak power in idle state. Therefore, it is beneficial to gather computations on a reduced set of servers and to switch idle servers off. In this vein, servers Vary-On/Vary-Off (VOVO) [19] strategies have been proposed and adopted by many researchers. They consist in load-balancing a computing load on a set of servers, and according to the load, increasing or decreasing the number of active servers in that set [20]. Chen at al. [5] investigated the use of this strategy for power saving in a HPC system.

However, such VOVO approaches require applications to be structured following a master-slave model where a load-balancer balances the load between a number of slave servers, which can be adapted according to the received load. This is an important constraint on the design of applications.

Energy Saving in Virtualization Environments

If virtualization technologies were first introduced about 30 years ago [9], they are now increasingly used for resource management in hosting centers. In this context, the main advantage of virtualization is to relax the previous constraints on applications [21]. Application services can be deployed on separate virtual machines and a global resource manager is responsible for the allocation of resources to these VMs according to the load. This global manager can notably rely on VM migration [8] to gather VMs on fewer physical machines and to switch unused machines off. Such an approach is generally known as *server consolidation* [3,15]. Another important advantage of virtualization is isolation of applications, as consolidation may collocate VMs from different applications on the same physical host [1].

Energy Saving with Frequency Scaling

Beside the reduction of the number of active machines in a hosting center, another way to reduce energy consumption is to dynamically adapt the frequency of active machines according to the CPU load on these machines. Such techniques are known as Dynamic Voltage and Frequency Scaling (DVFS). Several studies showed that DVFS allows significant energy consumption reductions [7,11]. Moreover, recent works studied the impact of DVFS on applications performance and their Quality of Service. Chengjian Wen et al. [23] proposed to combine DVFS management and VM scheduling in a cluster in order to ensure fairness in the energy consumption of VMs, by accounting VMs power usage and prioritizing VMs accordingly. In the same vein, Laszewski et al. [12] investigated a similar approach while ensuring QoS in terms of execution times.

Positioning Our Contribution

Our contribution shares many objectives with the works mentioned in the previous paragraph. Similarly, our goal was to guarantee a QoS allocated to VMs while saving energy thanks to DVFS. However, these projects didn't consider that a VM is allocated a computing capacity (a credit) at creation time and that it has to be managed as a Service Level Agreement (SLA). Our Power-Aware Scheduler (PAS) allows DVFS management while guaranteeing that the computing capacity allocated to a VM (and bought by a customer) is available. We are not aware of any similar contribution to this issue.

7   Conclusion and Perspective

With the emergence of cloud computing environments, large scale hosting centers are being deployed and the energy consumption of such infrastructures has become a critical issue. In this context, two main orientations have been successfully followed for saving energy:

- Virtualization which allows to safely host several guest operating systems on the same physical machines and more importantly to migrate guest OS between machines, thus implementing server consolidation.
- DVFS which allows adaptation of the processor frequency according to the CPU load, thus reducing power usage.

We observed that these two techniques suffer from incompatibilities, as DVFS governors are implemented in the hypervisor and don't take into account the existence of different VMs with allocated credits and different loads. If a machine is globally underloaded but hosts a loaded VM (which consumes a significant part of its credit), then the frequency of the processor may be scaled down, thus affecting the computing capacity of the loaded VM.

In this paper, we proposed a Power-Aware Scheduler (PAS) which addresses this issue. A credit is associated with a VM at creation time and represents its allocated computing capacity. If the machine which hosts the VM is underloaded and its frequency is therefore scaled down, the credit associated with the VM is recomputed in order to maintain its computing capacity.

Our PAS scheduler was implemented in the Xen hypervisor and evaluated through different scenarios which demonstrate its advantage over the Credit and SEDF schedulers, the two schedulers available in Xen.

Our main perspective is to address the issue presented in Section 2.3. Memory is the main limitation factor for an efficient consolidation system. We are investigating energy aware resource management strategies which would coordinate VM scheduling, frequency scaling and memory management in a hosting center. Furthermore, we plan to extend our scheduler and take into account other technology factors such as hyper-threading, multi-core, per-socket DVFS, and per-core DVFS.

Acknowledgements. The work reported in this article benefited from the support of the French National Research Agency through projects Ctrl-Green (ANR-11-INFR-0012).

References

1. Barham, P., Dragovic, B., Fraser, K., Hand, S., Harris, T., Ho, A., Neugebauer, R., Pratt, I., Warfield, A.: Xen and the art of virtualization. In: Proceedings of the 9th ACM Symposium on Operating Systems Principles (2003)
2. Belady, C., Rawson, A., Pfleuger, J., Cader, T.: The green grid data center power efficiency metrics: PUE and DCiE. White paper (2007), http://www.thegreengrid.org/en/Global/Content/white-papers/The-Green-Grid-Data-Center-Power-Efficiency-Metrics-PUE-and-DCiE
3. Beloglazov, A., Buyya, R.: Energy efficient resource management in virtualized cloud data centers. In: Proceedings of the 10th IEEE/ACM International Conference on Cluster, Cloud and Grid Computing (2010)
4. Chase, J.S., Anderson, D.C., Thakar, P.N., Vahdat, A.M.: Managing energy and server resources in hosting centers. In: Proceedings of the Eighteenth ACM Symposium on Operating Systems Principles (2001)
5. Chen, W., Jiang, F., Zheng, W., Zhang, P.: A dynamic energy conservation scheme for clusters in computing centers. In: Yang, L.T., Zhou, X.-S., Zhao, W., Wu, Z., Zhu, Y., Lin, M. (eds.) ICESS 2005. LNCS, vol. 3820, pp. 244–255. Springer, Heidelberg (2005)

6. Cherkasova, L., Gupta, D., Vahdat, A.: Comparison of the three CPU schedulers in Xen. SIGMETRICS Performance Evaluation Review 35(2) (2007)
7. Chung-Hsing, H., Wu-Chun, F.: A Feasibility Analysis of Power Awareness in Commodity-Based High-Performance Clusters. In: Proceedings of the 7th IEEE International Conference on Cluster Computing (2005)
8. Clark, C., Fraser, K., Hand, S., Hansen, J.G., Jul, E., Limpach, C., Pratt, I., Warfield, A.: Live migration of virtual machines. In: Proceedings of the 2nd Conference on Symposium on Networked Systems Design & Implementation (2005)
9. Gum, P.H.: System/370 extended architecture: facilities for virtual machines. IBM Journal of Research and Development 27(6) (1983)
10. Hamilton, J.: Cooperative Expendable Micro-Slice Servers (CEMS): Low Cost, Low Power Servers for Internet-Scale Services. In: Proceedings of the Fourth Biennial Conference on Innovative Data Systems Research (2009)
11. Hsu, C., Feng, W.: A Power-Aware Run-Time System for High-Performance Computing. In: Proceedings of the ACM/IEEE Conference on Supercomputing (2005)
12. Laszewski, G.V., Wang, L., Younge, A.J., He, X.: Power-aware scheduling of virtual machines in DVFS-enabled clusters. In: Proceedings of the IEEE International Conference on Cluster Computing and Workshops (2009)
13. Miyakawa, D., Ishikawa, Y.: Process Oriented Power Management. In: Proceedings of the 2nd International Symposium on Industrial Embedded Systems (2007)
14. Mosberger, D., Jin, T.: httperf - A tool for measuring web server performance. SIGMETRICS Performance Evaluation Review 26(3) (1998)
15. Nathuji, R., Schwan, K.: VirtualPower: coordinated power management in virtualized enterprise systems. In: Proceedings of the 21st ACM SIGOPS Symposium on Operating Systems Principles (2007)
16. Norris, C., Cohen, H.M., Cohen, B.: Leveraging IBM eX5 Systems for Breakthrough Cost and Density Improvements in Virtualized x86 Environments. White paper (2011), ftp://public.dhe.ibm.com/common/ssi/ecm/en/xsw03099usen
17. Padala, P., Zhu, X., Wang, Z., Singhal, S., Shin, K.G.: Performance evaluation of virtualization technologies for server consolidation. HP Laboratories Palo Alto (2007), http://www.hpl.hp.com/techreports/2007/HPL-2007-59.pdf
18. Padhy, R.P., Patra, M.R., Sarapathy, S.C.: Virtualization Techniques & Technologies: State of the Art. Journal of Global Research in Computer Science 2(12) (2011)
19. Pinheiro, E., Bianchini, R., Carrera, E.V., Heath, T.: Compilers and operating systems for low power. In: The Book Dynamic Cluster Reconfiguration for Power and Performance. Kluwer Academic Publishers
20. Rajamanin, K., Lefurgy, C.: On evaluating request-distribution schemes for saving energy in server clusters. In: Proceedings of the IEEE International Symposium on Performance Analysis of Systems and Software (2003)
21. Soltesz, S., Potzl, H., Fiuczynski, M.E., Bavier, A., Peterson, L.: Container-based operating system virtualization: a scalable, high-performance alternative to hypervisors. In: Proceedings of the 2nd ACM SIGOPS/EuroSys European Conference on Computer Systems (2007)
22. Pallipadi, V., Starikovskiy, A.: The ondemand governor: past, present and future. In: Proceedings of Linux Symposium (2006)
23. Wen, C., He, J., Zhang, J., Long, X.: PCFS: Power Credit Based Fair Scheduler Under DVFS for Muliticore Virtualization Platform. In: Proceedings of the IEEE/ACM International Conference on Green Computing and Communications (2010)
24. Motahari-Nezhad, Hamid, R., Stephenson, B., Singhal, S.: Outsourcing business to cloud computing services: Opportunities and challenges. In: IEEE Internet Computing, Palo Alto (2009)

Elastic Remote Methods

K.R. Jayaram*

HP Labs, Palo Alto, CA
jayaramkr@hp.com

Abstract. For distributed applications to take full advantage of cloud computing systems, we need middleware systems that allow developers to build elasticity management components right into the applications.

This paper describes the design and implementation of ElasticRMI, a middleware system that (1) enables application developers to dynamically change the number of (server) objects available to handle remote method invocations with respect to the application's workload, without requiring major changes to clients (invokers) of remote methods, (2) enables flexible elastic scaling by allowing developers to use a combination of resource utilization metrics and fine-grained application-specific information like the properties of internal data structures to drive scaling decisions, (3) provides a high-level programming framework that handles elasticity at the level of classes and objects, masking low-level platform specific tasks (like provisioning VM images) from the developer, and (4) increases the portability of ElasticRMI applications across different private data centers/IaaS clouds through Apache Mesos [5].

Keywords: programmable elasticity, scalability, distributed objects.

1 Introduction

Elasticity, the key driver of cloud computing, is the ability of a distributed application to dynamically increase or decrease its use of computing resources, to preserve its performance in response to varying workloads. Elasticity can either be *explicit* or *implicit*.

Implicit vs. Explicit Elasticity. Implicit elasticity is typically associated with a specific programming framework or a Platform-as-a-Service (PaaS) cloud. Examples of frameworks providing implicit elasticity in the domain of "big data analytics" are map-reduce (Hadoop [13] and its PaaS counterpart Amazon Elastic Map Reduce [10]), Apache Pig [2], Giraph [12], etc. Implicit elasticity is handled by the PaaS implementation and is not the responsibility of the programmer. Despite being unable to support a wide variety of applications and computations, each of these systems simplifies application development and deployment, and employs distributed algorithms for elastic scaling that are optimized for its programming framework and application domain.

---

* Thanks to Patrick Eugster and Hans Boehm for helpful feedback.

D. Eyers and K. Schwan (Eds.): Middleware 2013, LNCS 8275, pp. 143–162, 2013.

Explicit Elasticity, on the other hand, is typically associated with Infrastructure-as-a-Service (IaaS) clouds and/or private data centers, which typically provide elasticity at the granularity of virtualized compute nodes (e.g., Amazon EC2) or virtualized storage (e.g., Amazon Elastic Block Store (EBS)) in a way that is agnostic of the application using these resources. It is the application developer's or the system administrator's responsibility to implement robust mechanisms to monitor the application's performance at runtime, request the addition or removal of resources, and perform *load-balancing*, i.e., redistribute the application's workload among the new set of resources.

Programmable Elasticity. To *optimize* the performance of *new or existing* distributed applications while *deploying or moving* them to the cloud, engineering robust elasticity management components is essential. This is especially vital for applications that do not fit the programming model of (implicit) elastic frameworks like Hadoop, Pig, etc., but require high performance (high throughput and low latency), scalability and elasticity – the best example is the class of *datacenter infrastructure applications* like key-value stores (e.g., memcached [22], Hyperdex [23]), consensus protocols (e.g., Paxos [15]), distributed lock managers (e.g., Chubby [7]) and message queues. Elasticity frameworks which rely on externally observable resource utilization metrics (CPU, RAM, etc.) are insufficient for such applications (as we demonstrate empirically in Section 5). A distributed key value store, for example, may have high CPU utilization when there is high contention to update a certain set of "hot keys". Relying on CPU utilization to simply add additional compute nodes will only degrade its performance further. Hence, there is an emerging need for a elasticity framework that bridges the gap between implicit and explicit elasticity, allowing the use *fine grained* application specific metrics (e.g., size of a queue/heap, number of aborted transactions or average number of attempts to acquire certain locks) to build an elasticity management component right into the application without compromising (1) security, by revealing application-level information to the cloud service provider, and (2) portability across different cloud vendors.

Why RMI?. Despite being criticized for introducing direct dependencies across nodes through remote object references, Remote Method Invocation (RMI) and Remote Procedure Call (RPC) remain a popular paradigm [3] for distributed programming, because of their simplicity. Their popularity has led to the development of Apache Thrift [3] with support for RPC across *different* languages, and the design of cloud computing paradigms like RAMCloud [16] with support for low-latency RPC. However, high-level support for elasticity is limited in existing RPC-like frameworks; and such support is vital to engineering efficient distributed applications and migrating existing applications to the cloud.

Contributions. This paper makes the following technical contributions:

1. ELASTICRMI – A framework for elastic distributed objects in Java:
   (a) with the same simplicity and ease of use of the Java RMI, handling elasticity at the level of classes and objects, while supporting implicit and explicit elasticity. (Section 2)

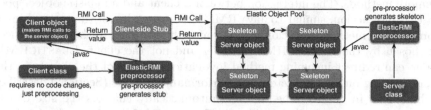

Fig. 1. ELASTICRMI – Overview

(b) that enables application developers to dynamically change the number of (server) objects available to handle remote method invocations with respect to the application's workload, without requiring any change to clients (invokers) of remote methods. (Section 3)

(c) enables flexible elastic scaling by allowing developers to use a combination of resource utilization metrics and fine-grained application-specific information to drive scaling decisions. (Section 3)

2. A runtime system that handles all the low-level mechanics of instantiating elastic objects, monitoring their workload, adding/removing additional objects as necessary and load balancing among them. (Section 4)

3. Performance evaluation of ELASTICRMI using elasticity metrics defined by SPEC [24] and using four *existing* real world applications – Marketcetera financial order processing, Paxos consensus protocol, Hedwig publish/subscribe system and a distributed coordination service. (Section 5)

2   ElasticRMI – Overview

Figure 1 illustrates the architecture of ELASTICRMI. In designing ELASTICRMI, our goals are (1) to retain the simple programming model of Java RMI, and mask the low level details of implementing elasticity like workload monitoring, load balancing, and adding/removing objects from the application developer. (2) require minimal changes, if any, to the clients of an object (3) make ELASTICRMI applications as portable as possible across different IaaS cloud implementations.

2.1   Elastic Classes and Object Pools

An ELASTICRMI application consists of multiple components (implemented as classes) interacting with each other. The basic elasticity abstraction in ELASTICRMI is an elastic class. An elastic class is also a remote class, and (some) of its methods may be invoked remotely from another JVM. The key difference between an elastic and a regular remote class is that an elastic class is instantiated into a pool of objects (referred to as elastic object pool), with each object executing on a separate JVM. But, the presence of multiple objects in an elastic object pool is transparent to its clients, because the pool behaves as a single remote object. Clients can only interact with the entire object pool, by invoking its remote methods. The interaction between a client and an elastic object pool is *unicast* interaction, similar to Java RMI. The processing of the method invocation, i.e., the method execution happens at a single object in the elastic object pool chosen by the ELASTICRMI runtime, and not the client. ELASTICRMIs runtime can redirect incoming method invocations to one of the objects in the pool, depending on various factors and performance metrics (Section 4 describes load balancing in detail). The runtime automatically changes the size of the pool depending on the pool's "workload". ELASTICRMI is different from certain frameworks where the same method invocation is multicast and consequently executes on multiple (replicated) objects for fault-tolerance.

2.2 Shared State and Consistency

In Java RMI, the *state* of a remote (server) object is a simple concept, because it resides on a single JVM and there is exactly one copy of all its fields. Clients of the remote object can set the value of instance fields by calling a remote method, and access the values in subsequent method calls. In ELASTICRMI, on the other hand, the entire object pool should appear to the client as a single remote object – thereby necessitating coordination between the objects in the pool to consistently update the values of instance fields. For consistency, we employ an *external* in-memory key-value store (HyperDex [23] in our implementation) to store the state (i.e., `public`, `private`, `protected` and `static` fields) of the elastic remote object pool. The key-value store is *not* used to store local variables in methods/blocks of code and parameters in method declarations. Local variables are instantiated on the JVM in which the object resides. The key-value store is shared between the objects in the pool, and executes on separate JVMs.

2.3 Stubs and Skeletons

ELASTICRMI modifies the standard mechanisms used to implement RPCs and Java RMI, as illustrated by Figure 1. The ELASTICRMI *pre-processor* analyzes elastic classes to generate *stubs* and *skeletons* for client-server communication. As in Java RMI, a stub for a remote object acts as a client's local representative or proxy for the remote object. The caller invokes a method on ELASTICRMI's local stub which (1) initiates a connection with the remote JVM, serializes and marshals parameters, waits for the result of the method invocation and unmarshals the return value/exception before returning it to the sender, and (2) performs load balancing among the objects in the elastic pool as necessary. The stub is generated by the ELASTICRMI preprocessor and is different from the client application, to which the entire object pool appears as a single object, i.e., the existence of a pool of objects is known to the stub but not to the client application. In the remote JVM, each object in the pool has a corresponding skeleton, which in addition to the duties performed in regular Java RMI, can also perform dynamic load balancing based on the CPU utilization of the object and redirect all further method invocations to other objects in the pool after ELASTICRMI decides to shut it down in response to decreasing workload.

2.4 Instantiation of Object Pools in a Cluster

An elastic class can only be instantiated by providing a minimum and maximum number of objects that constitute its elastic object pool. Obviously, instantiating all objects in the pool on separate JVMs on the *same* physical machine may degrade performance. Hence, ELASTICRMI attempts to instantiate each object in a virtual node in a compute cluster. Virtual nodes can be obtained either (1) from IaaS clouds by provisioning and instantiating virtual machines, or (2) from a cluster management/resource sharing system like Apache Mesos [5]. Our implementation of ELASTICRMI uses Apache Mesos [5] because it supports both clusters of physical nodes (in private data centers) or virtual nodes (from IaaS clouds). Mesos can also be viewed as a thin resource-sharing layer that manages a cluster of physical nodes/virtual machines. It divides these nodes into "slices" (called *resource offers* or slave nodes [5]), with each resource offer containing a configurable reservation of CPU power (e.g., 2 CPUs at 2GHz), memory (e.g., 2GB RAM), etc. on one of the nodes being managed. Mesos implements the "slice" abstraction by using Linux Containers (http://lxc.sourceforge.net) to implement lightweight virtualization, process isolation and resource guarantees (e.g., 2CPUs at 2GHz) [5]. While instantiating an elastic class, the ELASTICRMI runtime requests Mesos for a specified number of slave nodes, instantiating an object on each slave node.

Mesos aids in portability of ELASTICRMI applications, just like the JVM aids the portability of Java applications. Mesos can be installed on private data centers and many public cloud offerings (like Google Compute Engine, Amazon EC2, etc.). As long as Mesos is available, ELASTICRMI applications can be executed, making them portable across different cloud vendors.

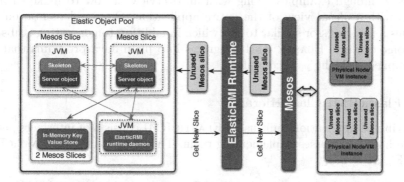

Fig. 2. ELASTICRMI – Server Side

2.5 Automatic Elastic Scaling

The key objective of ELASTICRMI is to change the number of objects in the elastic pool based on its workload. The "workload" of an elastic object can have several application-specific definitions, and consequently, ELASTICRMI allows programmers to define the workload of an elastic class and specify the conditions under which objects should be added or removed from the elastic pool. This can be done by overriding select methods in the ELASTICRMI framework, as discussed in detail in (the next) Section 3.1. During the lifetime of the elastic object, the ELASTICRMI runtime monitors a elastic object pool's workload and decides whether to change its size either based on default heuristics or by applying the programmer's logic by invoking the overridden methods discussed above.

If a decision has been made to increase the size of the pool, the ELASTICRMI runtime interacts with the Mesos master node to request additional compute resources. If the request is granted, ELASTICRMI runtime instantiates the additional object, and adds it to the pool (See Figure 2 for an illustration). If the decision is to remove an object, ELASTICRMI communicates with its skeleton to redirect subsequent remote method calls to other objects in the pool. Once redirection starts, ELASTICRMI sends a SHUTDOWN message to the object. The object acknowledges the message, and waits for all pending remote method invocations to finish execution or throw exceptions indicating abnormal termination. Then the object notifies the ELASTICRMI runtime that it is ready to be shutdown. ELASTICRMI terminates the object and relinquishes its slice to Mesos. This slice is then available to other elastic objects in the cluster, or for subsequent use by the same elastic object if a decision is made in the future to increase the size of its pool.

3   Programming with ElasticRMI

This section illustrates the use of ELASTICRMI for both implicit and explicit elasticity through examples, along with an overview of how to make such decisions with a *global* view of the entire application. Our implementation also includes a preprocessor similar to rmic which in addition to generating stubs and skeletons, converts ELASTICRMI programs into plain Java programs that can be compiled with the javac compiler.

3.1   ElasticRMI Class Hierarchy

A distributed application built using ELASTICRMI consists of interfaces declaring methods and classes implementing them. The key features of ELASTICRMI API (Figure 3) are:

- java.elasticrmi is the top-level package for programming ELASTICRMI server classes.
- An elastic interface is one that declares the set of methods that can be invoked from a remote JVM (client). All elastic interfaces must extend ELASTICRMI's marker interface - java.elasticrmi.Elastic, either directly or indirectly.
- The ElasticObject class implements all the basic functionalities of ELASTICRMI. An application-defined class becomes elastic by implementing one or more elastic interfaces and by extending ElasticObject.

```
interface Elastic extends Remote { } //marker interface used by preprocessor
//Optionally implemented by the application
abstract class Decider extends UnicastRemoteObject implements Elastic {
  abstract int getDesiredPoolSize(ElasticObject o);
}
abstract class ElasticObject extends UnicastRemoteObject {
  ElasticObject() //Default constructor
  ElasticObject(Decider d) //Consult d for scaling decisions

  void setMinPoolSize(int s) //Set min pool size
  void setMaxPoolSize(int s) //Set max pool size
  void setBurstInterval(float ival) //Make scaling decisions every 'ival' ms
  void setCPUIncrThreshold(float t) //Add objects when CPU util > t
  void setCPUDecrThreshold(float t) //Remove objects when CPU until < t
  void setRAMIncrThreshold(float t) //Add objects when RAM util > t
  void setRAMDecrThreshold(float t) //Remove objects when RAM until < t

  float getAvgCPUUsage() //Get CPU util averaged over burst interval
  public float getAvgRAMUsage() //Get RAM util averaged over burst interval
  int getPoolSize() //Get pool size
  //Returns average # of calls to each remote method over the burst interval
  HashMap<String,float> getMethodCallStats() {...}

  //Called by the runtime to poll each object about changes to the size of
  //the pool. Can return positive or negative integers
  abstract int changePoolSize();
}
```

Fig. 3. A snapshot of the ELASTICRMI server-side API.

```
class CacheImplicit          class CacheExplicit1 extends ElasticObject {
  extends ElasticObject        CacheExplicit1() {
  CacheImplicit() {              setMinPoolSize(5); setMaxPoolSize(50);
    setMinPoolSize(5);           setBurstInterval(5*60*1000); //5mins
    setMaxPoolSize(50);          setCPUIncrThreshold(85); setRAMIncrThreshold(70);
  }                              setCPUDecrThreshold(50); setRAMDecrThreshold(40);
  ...                          } ...
}                            }
```

   (a) Implicit elasticity   (b) Explicit elasticity using coarse-grained metrics.

Fig. 4. Example of two distributed cache classes implemented in ELASTICRMI

3.2 Programming with Implicit Elasticity

ELASTICRMI supports implicit elastic scaling, using average CPU utilization across the objects in an elastic pool as the default coarse-grained metric. A time interval, referred to as the *burst interval* (default 60s) is used to decide whether to change the size of elastic object pool. ELASTICRMI measures the average CPU utilization of each object in the elastic pool every 60s – objects are added (in increments of 1 object) when the average utilization exceeds 90% and removed when average utilization falls below 60%. Figure 4a shows an example of a distributed cache class (e.g., a web cache, content/object cache) that relies on ELASTICRMI's implicit elasticity mechanisms. The programmer simply implements a cache store based on some well-known algorithm and specifying the minimum and maximum size of the pool, without worrying about adapting to new resources and load balancing.

3.3   Programming with Explicit Elasticity

ELASTICRMI also allows programmers to *explicitly* define the workload of an elastic class and specify the conditions under which objects should be added or removed from the elastic pool. Workload definitions can either be coarse-grained or fine-grained.

Coarse-Grained Metrics. A programmer can override the default burst interval, and the average CPU utilization thresholds used for changing the number of objects in the pool by calling the appropriate methods (`setBurstInterval(...)`, `setCPUIncrThreshold(...)` and `setCPUDecrThreshold(...)`) in `java.elasticrmi.ElasticObject` which is available in all elastic classes since they extend `ElasticObject` (see Figure 3).

Figure 4b shows an example of a cache class that changes the CPU and memory (RAM) utilization thresholds that trigger elastic scaling. The core ELASTICRMI API includes specific methods to set CPU and memory thresholds because they are commonly used for elastic scaling – if both CPU and RAM thresholds are set, the runtime interprets them using a logical OR, i.e., in the example shown in Figure 4b, the ELASTICRMI runtime increases the size of the pool by in increments of 1 object every five minutes, either if average CPU utilization exceeds 85% or if average memory utilization exceeds 70% across the JVMs in the elastic object pool.

Fine-grained Metrics. ELASTICRMI provides additional support, through the `changePoolSize` method (see Figure 3) which can be overridden by any elastic class. The runtime periodically (every "burst interval") invokes `changePoolSize` to poll each object in the elastic object pool, about desired changes to the size of the pool. The method returns an integer – positive or negative corresponding to increasing or decreasing the pool's size. The values returned by the various objects in the pool are averaged to determine the number of objects that have to be added/removed. The logic used to decide on elastic scaling is left to the developer, and it may be based on (1) parameters of the JVM on which each object resides, (2) properties of shared instance fields of the elastic object, or of data structures used by the object, e.g., number of pending client operations stored in a queue, and (3) metrics computed by the object like average response time, throughput, etc. ELASTICRMI allows classes to use only a single decision mechanism for elastic scaling, i.e., if `changePoolSize` is overridden, then scaling based on CPU/Memory utilization is disabled.

Figure 5 illustrates the use of `changePoolSize` to make scaling decisions. The `CacheExplicit2` class is implemented to use metrics specific to distributed object caches, e.g., `avgLockAcqFailure` (which measures the failure rate of acquiring write locks to ensure consistency during a `put` operation on the cache) and `avgLockAcqLatency` (which measures the average latency to acquire write locks) to make decisions about changing the size of the elastic object pool. In Figure 5, the `CacheExplicit2` class does not add new objects to the pool when there is a lot of contention. When the failure rate for acquiring write locks (`avgLockAcqFailure` is greater than 50%) or

```
public class CacheExplicit2 extends ElasticObject {
  float avgLockAcqFailure, avgLockAcqLatency
  public int changePoolSize() {
    HashMap<String, float> sMap;
    sMap = getMethodCallStats();

    float putLatency = sMap.get("put").getLatency();
    float getLatency = sMap.get("get").getLatency();
    if(putLatency > 100 || putLatency > 3*getLatency) {
      if(avgLockAcqFailure > 50) return 0;
      if(avgLockAcqLatency >= 0.8*putLatency) return 0; else return 2;
    }
  }
}
```

Fig. 5. A distributed cache class which relies on ELASTICRMI's explicit elasticity support using fine-grained application-specific metrics.

when the predominant component of `putLatency` is `avgLockAcqLatency`, no additional objects are added to the pool because there is already high contention among objects serving client requests to acquire write locks. When these conditions are `false`, the size of the pool is increased by two – controlling the number of objects added is another feature of `changePoolSize`.

Making Application-Level Scaling Decisions. The mechanisms described above involve makes scaling decisions *local to an elastic class*, and may not be optimal for applications using multiple elastic classes (where the application contains *tiers* of elastic pools). ELASTICRMI also supports decision making at the level of the application using the `Decider` class. It is the developer's responsibility to ensure that elastic objects being monitored communicate with the monitoring components, either by using remote method invocations or through message passing. The ELASTICRMI runtime assumes responsibility for calling `changePoolSize` method of the monitoring class to get the desired size of each elastic object pool, and determines whether objects have to be added or removed. Due to space limitations, we refer the reader to our tech report for additional details [20].

4   The ElasticRMI Runtime

The runtime (1) handles shared state among the objects in an elastic object pool, (2) instantiates each object of a pool, (3) performs load balancing, and (4) is responsible for fault-tolerance.

4.1   Shared State and Consistency

The objects in the elastic object pool coordinate to update the state of its instance fields (`public`, `private`, `protected`) and `static` fields. For consistency, we use HyperDex [23], a distributed in-memory key-value store (with strong consistency). Using an in-memory store provides the same data durability guarantees as Java RMI which stores the state of instance fields in RAM in a single Java virtual machine heap. HyperDex is different from the distributed cache in the examples of Section 3, which is used for illustration purposes only. The ELASTI-CRMI preprocessor translates reads and writes of instance and static fields into get(...) and put(...) method calls of HyperDex.

Figure 6 shows a simple elastic class C1 and how it is transformed by the ELASTICRMI preprocessor to insert calls to HyperDex (abstracted by Store) and ELASTICRMI's runtime (abstracted by ERMI). For variable x, C1$x is used as the key in Store.

```
class C1                      |class C1Processed {
  extends ElasticObject {     |  void foo() {
    int x, z;                 |    int x=Store.get("C1$x");
                              |    if(x==5)
  void foo() {                |      Store.put("C1$z", 10);
    if(x = 5) z = 10;         |  }
  }                           |  void bar() {
  synchronized                |    while(!ERMI.lock("C1")) ;
    void bar() {              |    ...
    ...                       |    ERMI.unlock("C1");
  }                           |  }
}                             |}
```

Fig. 6. Handling shared state through an in-memory store (HyperDex [23] here)

For synchronized methods, ELASTICRMI uses a lock per class named after the class – the example in Figure 6 uses a lock called "C1".

If an elastic class has an instance or static field f, a method call on f is handled as follows:

- If f is a remote or elastic object, the method invocation is simply serialized and dispatched to the remote object or pool as the case may be.
- *Else*, if m is synchronized. the method call is handled as in Figure 6, but the runtime acquires a lock on f through HyperDex. In this case, ELASTICRMI guarantees mutual exclusion for the execution of $f.m(...)$ with respect to other methods of f.
- *Else*, (i.e., m is neither remote, elastic nor synchronized), $f.m(...)$ involves retrieving f from HyperDex and executing $m(...)$ locally on an object in the elastic object pool, and storing f back into HyperDex after $m(...)$ has completed executing.

ELASTICRMI aims to increase parallelism and hence the number of remote method executions per second when there is limited or no shared state. Increasing shared state increases latency due to the network delays involved in accessing HyperDex. Having shared state and mutual exclusion through locks or synchronized methods further decreases parallelism. However, we note that this is not a consequence of ELASTICRMI, but rather dependent on the needs of the distributed application. If the developer manually implements all aspects of elasticity by using plan Java RMI and an existing tool like Amazon Cloud-Watch+Autoscaling, he still has to use something like a key-value store to handle shared state. ELASTICRMI cannot and does not attempt to eliminate this problem – it is up to the programmer to reduce shared state.

Note that ELASTICRMI does not guarantee a transactional (ACID) execution of $m(...)$ with respect to other objects in the pool, and using synchronized does not provide ACID guarantees *either in RMI or in* ELASTICRMI.

4.2   Instantiation of Elastic Objects

An elastic class can only be instantiated by providing a minimum (≥ 2) and maximum number of objects that constitute its elastic object pool (see Figure 3). During instantiation, if the minimum number of objects is k, ElasticRMI's runtime creates k objects on k new JVM instances on k virtual nodes (Mesos slices), if k virtual nodes are available from Mesos [5]. If only $l < k$ are available, then only l objects are created. Under no circumstance does ELASTICRMI create two or more JVM instances on the same slice obtained from Mesos. Then, ELASTI-CRMI instantiates the HyperDex on one additional Mesos slice, and continues to monitor the performance of the HyperDex over the lifetime of the elastic object. ELASTICRMI may add additional nodes to HyperDex as necessary. ELASTI-CRMI also enables administrators to be notified if the utilization of the Mesos cluster exceeds or falls below (configurable) thresholds, enabling the proactive addition of computing resources before the cluster runs out of slices.

4.3   Load Balancing

Unlike websites or web services, where load balancing *has to be performed* on the server-side, ELASTICRMI has the advantage that both client and server programs are pre-processed to generate stubs and skeletons respectively. Hence, we employ a *hybrid* load balancing model involving both stubs and skeletons – note that *all* load balancing code is generated by the pre-processor, and the programmer *does not have to handle any aspect of it explicitly*. Please also note that this section describes the simple load balancing techniques used in ELASTICRMI, but we do not claim to have invented a new load balancing algorithm.

On the server side, the runtime, while instantiating skeletons in an elastic object pool, assigns monotonically increasing unique identifiers (*uid*) to each skeleton, and stores this information in HyperDex. The skeleton with the lowest *uid* is chosen by the runtime to be the leader of the elastic object pool, called the *sentinel*. This is similar to leader election algorithms that use a so-called "royal hierarchy" among processes in a distributed system. The sentinel, in addition to performing all the regular functions (forwarding remote method invocations) to *its* object in the pool, also helps in load balancing. The client stub created by the ELASTICRMI preprocessor (see Section 2.4) has the ability to communicate with the sentinel to invoke remote methods. While contacting the sentinel for the first time, the stub on the client JVM requests the identities (IP address and port number) of the other skeletons in the pool from the sentinel.

For load-balancing on the client-side, the stub then re-directs subsequent method invocations to other objects in the object pool either randomly or in a round-robin fashion. If an object has been removed from the pool after its identity is sent to a stub, i.e., if the sending itself fails, the remote method invocation throws an exception which is intercepted by the client stub. The stub then retries the invocation on other objects including the sentinel. If all attempts to communicate with the elastic object pool fail, the exception is propagated to the client application.

For load-balancing on the server side, the sentinel is also responsible for collecting and periodically broadcasting the state of the pool – number of objects, their identities and the number of pending invocations – to the skeletons of all its members. We use the JGroups group communication system for broadcasts. If the sentinel notices that any skeleton is overloaded with respect to others, it instructs the skeleton to redirect a portion of invocations to a set of other skeletons. To decide the number of invocations that have to be redirected from each overloaded skeleton, our implementation of the sentinel uses the first-fit greedy bin-packing approximation algorithm (See `http://en.wikipedia.org/wiki/Bin_packing_problem`). As mentioned in the previous paragraph, client-side load balancing occurs at the stub while server-side load balancing involves skeletons and the sentinel which monitor the state of the JVM and that of the elastic object pool to redirect incoming method invocations.

4.4   Fault Tolerance

Existing RMI applications implement fault tolerance protocols on top of Java RMI's fault- and fault tolerance model, where objects typically reside in main memory, and can crash in the middle of a remote method invocation. !e want to preserve it to make adoption of ELASTICRMI easier. In short, ELASTICRMI *does not hide/attempt to recover* from failures of client objects, key-value store (HyperDex) or the server-side runtime processes and propagates corresponding exceptions to the application. However, ELASTICRMI *attempts to recover* from failures of the sentinel and from Mesos-related failures. Sentinel failure triggers the leader election algorithm described in 4.3 to elect a new sentinel, and mesos-related failures affect the addition/removal of new objects until Mesos recovers.

5   Evaluation

In this section, we evaluate the performance of ELASTICRMI, using metrics relevant to elasticity. Due to space limitations, we refer the reader to our tech report for additional details [20].

5.1   Elasticity Metrics

Measuring elasticity is different from measuring scalability. (Recall that) Scalability is the ability of a distributed application to increase its "performance" proportionally (ideally linearly) with respect to the number of available resources, while elasticity is the ability of the application to adapt to increasing or decreasing workload; adding or removing resources to *maintain* a specific level of "performance" or "quality of service (QoS)" [24]. Performance/QoS is specific to the application – typically a combination of throughput and latency. A highly elastic system can scale to include newer compute nodes, as well as quickly provision those nodes. There are no standard *benchmarks* for elasticity, but the Standard Performance Evaluation Corporation (SPEC) has recommended elasticity *metrics* for IaaS and PaaS clouds [24].

Agility. This metric characterizes the ability of a system provisioned to be as close to the needs of the workload as possible [24]. Assuming a time interval $[t, t']$, which is divided into N sub-intervals, Agility maintained over $[t, t']$ can be defined as:

$$\frac{1}{N} (\sum_{i=0}^{N} Excess(i) + \sum_{i=0}^{N} Shortage(i))$$

where $(1) Excess(i)$ is the excess capacity for interval i as determined by $Cap\_prov(i) - Req\_min(i)$, when $Cap\_prov(i) > Req\_min(i)$ and zero otherwise. (2) $Shortage(i)$ is the shortage capacity for interval i as determined by $Req\_min(i) - Cap\_prov(i)$, when $Cap\_prov(i) < Req\_min(i)$ and zero otherwise. (3) $Req\_min(i)$ is the minimum capacity needed to meet an application's quality of service (QoS) at a given workload level for an interval i. (4) $Cap\_prov(i)$ is the recorded capacity provisioned for interval i, and (5) N is the total number of data samples collected over a measurement period $[t, t']$, i.e., one sample of both $Excess(i)$ and $Shortage(i)$ is collected per sub-interval of $[t, t']$.

Elasticity measures the shortage *and* excess of computing resources over a time period. For example, a value of elasticity of 2 over $[t, t']$ when there is no excess means that there is a mean shortage of 2 "compute nodes" over $[t, t']$. For an ideal system, agility should be as close to zero as possible – meaning that there is neither a shortage nor excess. Agility is a measurement of the ability to scale up and down while maintaining a specified QoS. The above definition of agility will not be valid in a context where the QoS is not met. It should be noted that there is ongoing debate over whether *Shortage* and *Excess* should be given equal weightage[24] in the Agility metric, but there are disagreements over what the weights should be otherwise.

Provisioning Interval. Provisioning Interval is defined as the time needed to bring up or drop a resource. This is the time between initiating the request to bring up a new resource, and when the resource serves the first request.

5.2   ElasticRMI Applications for Evaluation and Workloads

We have re-implemented four *existing* applications using ELASTICRMI to add elasticity management components to them. This does not involve altering the percentage of shared state or the frequency of accesses (reads or writes) to said state.

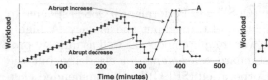
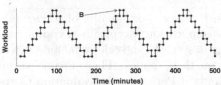
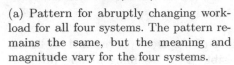

(a) Pattern for abruptly changing workload for all four systems. The pattern remains the same, but the meaning and magnitude vary for the four systems.

(b) Cyclical workload example for all four systems. As in Figure 7a, the pattern remains the same for all four systems but the meaning and magnitude are different.

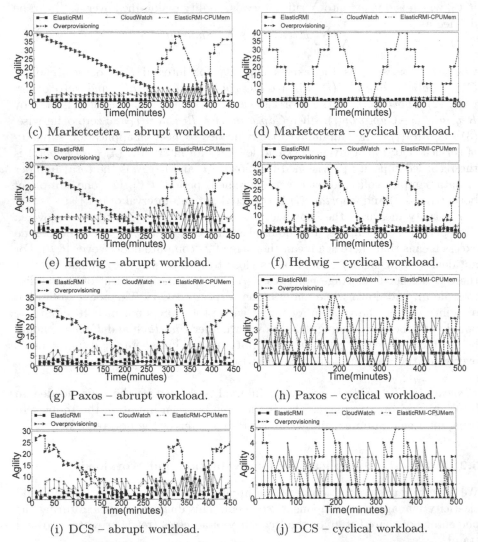

(c) Marketcetera – abrupt workload.

(d) Marketcetera – cyclical workload.

(e) Hedwig – abrupt workload.

(f) Hedwig – cyclical workload.

(g) Paxos – abrupt workload.

(h) Paxos – cyclical workload.

(i) DCS – abrupt workload.

(j) DCS – cyclical workload.

Fig. 7. Elasticity Benchmarking of Marketcetera order routing, Hedwig, Paxos and DCS. We compare the ELASTICRMI implementation of these applications with two other systems described in Section 5.4.

Marketcetera [11] Order Routing. Marketcetera is an NYSE-recommended algorithmic trading platform. The order routing system is the component that accepts orders from traders/automated strategy engines and routes them to various markets (stock/commodity), brokers and other financial intermediaries. For fault-tolerance, the order is persisted (stored) on two nodes. The workload for this system is a set of trading orders generated by the simulator included in the community edition of Marketcetera [11].

Apache Hedwig [14]. Hedwig is a topic-based publish-subscribe system designed for reliable and guaranteed at-most once delivery of messages from publishers to subscribers. Clients are associated with (publish to and subscribe from) a Hedwig instance (also referred to as a region), which consists of a number of servers called hubs. The hubs partition the topic ownership among themselves, and all publishes and subscribes to a topic must be done to its owning hub. The workload for this system is a set of messages generated by the default Hedwig benchmark included in the implementation.

Paxos [15]. Paxos is a family of protocols for solving consensus in a distributed system of unreliable processes. Consensus protocols are the basis for the state machine approach to distributed computing, and for our experiments we implement Paxos using a widely-used specification by Kirsch and Amir [15]. The workload for this system is the default benchmark included in libPaxos [21].

DCS. DCS is a distributed co-ordination service for datacenter applications, similar to Chubby [7] and Apache Zookeeper [25]. DCS has a hierarchical name space which can be used for distributed configuration and synchronization. Updates are totally ordered. The workload for this system is the default benchmark included in Apache Zookeeper [25].

5.3 Workload Pattern

To measure how well the system adapts to the changing workload, we use two patterns shown in Figures 7a and 7b. These two patterns capture all common scenarios in elastic scaling which we have observed by analyzing real world applications. The abrupt pattern shown in Figure 7a has all possible scenarios regarding abrupt changes in workload – gradual non-cyclic increase, gradual decrease, rapid increases and rapid decrease in workload. A cyclic change in workload is shown by the second pattern in Figure 7b. So, together the patterns in Figures 7a and 7b exhaustively cover all elastic scaling scenarios we observed. Note however, that although the pattern remains the same for varying the workload while evaluating all the four systems, the magnitude differs depending on the benchmark used, i.e., the values of points A and B in Figures 7a and 7b are different for the four systems depending on the benchmark. Point A, for example, is 50,000 orders/s for Marketcetera, 75,000 updates/s for DCS, 24,000 consensus rounds/s for Paxos and 30,000 messages/s for Hedwig. We set Point B at 20% above Point A – note that the specific values of Points A and B are immaterial because we are only measuring adaptability and not peak performance.

5.4   Overprovisioning and CloudWatch

We compare the ELASTICRMI implementation of the applications in Section 5.2 with the *existing* implementations of the same applications in two deployment scenarios – (1) Overprovisioning and (2) Amazon AutoScaling + CloudWatch [4][1]. The overprovisioning deployment scenario is similar to an "oracle" – the *peak* workload arrival rate i.e., point A for the abruptly changing workload and point B for the cyclic workload are known a priori to the oracle; and the number of nodes required to meet a desired QoS (throughput, latency) at A and B respectively is determined by the oracle through experimental evaluation. The oracle then provisions the application on a fixed set of nodes – the size of which is enough to maintain the desired QoS even at the peak workload arrival rate (A and B respectively). In a nutshell, the over provisioning scenario can be described as "knowing future workload patterns and provisioning enough resources to meet its demands". Overprovisioning is the alternative to elastic scaling – there are going to be excess provisioned resources when the workload is below the peak (A and B), but provisioning latency is zero because all necessary resources are always provisioned. In the CloudWatch scenario, we use a monitoring service – Amazon CloudWatch to collect utilization metrics (CPU/Memory) from the nodes in the cluster and use conditions on these metrics to decide whether to increase or decrease the number of nodes. The ELASTICRMI implementation of the above applications, however, uses a combination of resource utilization and application-level properties specific to Marketcetera, DCS, Paxos and Hedwig respectively to decide on elastic scaling. Since ELASTICRMI and CloudWatch are two different systems, we also compare the ELASTICRMI implementation of the four applications with another version, referred to as ElasticRMI-CPUMem in Figure 7, where no application-level properties are used but only the the conditions based on CPU/Memory utilization in CloudWatch are used.

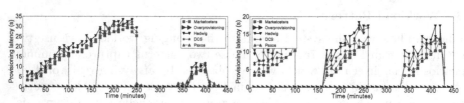

(a) Provisioning latency – Abrupt Work-(b) Provisioning latency – Cyclic Workload
load

Fig. 8. Provisioning latency in seconds for ElasticRMI and Overprovisioning (which is always 0). Provisioning latency for Amazon CloudWatch is not plotted because it is in several minutes and hence well above that of both ElasticRMI and Overprovisioning. You can see repeating patterns corresponding to the cyclic workload.

5.5   Agility Results

In this section, we compare the Agility of the ElasticRMI implementation of all four systems against Overprovisioning, CloudWatch and ElasticRMI-CPUMem.

Marketcetera Order Routing. The relevant QoS metrics for the order routing subsystem are order routing throughput, which is the number of orders routed from traders to brokers/exchanges per second and order propagation latency, which is the time taken for an order to propagate from the sender to the receiver. We compare the elasticity of the three deployments of the order routing system described in Section 5.4. The results are illustrated in Figure 7. Figures 7c and 7d plot the agility over the same time period as in Figures 7a and 7b for all the four deployments. From Figures 7c and 7d, we observe that the agility of ELASTICRMI is better than CloudWatch, ElasticRMI-CPUMem and overprovisioning. Ideally, agility must be zero, because agility is essentially a combination of resource wastage or resource under-provisioning. We observe that for abruptly changing workloads, agility of ELASTICRMI is close to 1 most of the time, and increases to 5 during abrupt changes in workload. We also observe that the the agility of ELASTICRMI oscillates between 0 and a positive value frequently. This proves that the elastic scaling mechanisms of ELASTICRMI perform well in trying to achieve optimal resource utilization, i.e., react aggressively by trying to push agility to zero. In summary, the average agility of ELASTICRMI for abruptly changing workload is 1.37. As expected, the agility of overprovisioning is the worst, up to 24× that of ELASTICRMI. This is not surprising, because its agility does reach zero at peak workload, when the agility of ELASTICRMI is 5, thus illustrating that overprovisioning optimizes for peak workloads. The average agility of overprovisioning is 17.2 for the cyclical workload and 24.1 for abruptly changing workload. CloudWatch performs much better than overprovisioning, but it is less agile than ELASTICRMI. Its agility is approximately 3.4× that of ELASTICRMI on average for abruptly changing workloads, and it does not oscillate to zero frequently like ELASTICRMI. The agility of ElasticRMI-CPUMem is approximately equal to CloudWatch and is 3.02× that of ELASTICRMI on average – this is in spite of ElasticRMI-CPUMem and CloudWatch being different systems. having different provisioning latencies. This is because the same conditions are used to decide on elastic scaling and because the provisioning latency of CloudWatch is well within the sampling interval of 10 minutes used in Figure 7.

Figure 7d shows that the agility of ELASTICRMI is again better than that of CloudWatch and overprovisioning for cyclic workloads. We also observe that as in the case of abrupt workloads, the agility of ELASTICRMI tends to decrease to zero more frequently than the other two deployments. Figure 7d also demonstrates the oscillating pattern in the agility of overprovisioning – the initial agility is high (and comes from *Excess*), and as the workload increases, *Excess* decreases, thereby decreasing Agility and bringing it to zero corresponding to Point B. Then *Excess* increases again as the workload decreases thereby increasing Agility. This repeats three times. As expected, the agility of ElasticRMI-CPUMem is similar to that of CloudWatch.

Hedwig. The relevant QoS metrics for Hedwig are also throughput and latency – the number of messages published per second and time taken for the message to propagate from the publisher to the subscriber. Figures 7e and 7f illustrate the agility corresponding to our experiments with Hedwig. From Figures 7e and 7f, we observe similar trends as in the case of Marketcetera order processing. ELASTICRMI has lower agility values than the other two deployments, and the agility of ELASTICRMI tends to oscillate between zero and a positive value. The agility values of CloudWatch are more than 4.5× that of ELASTICRMI, on average for abrupt workloads and 3× that of ELASTICRMI for cyclic workloads. As expected, the agility of over provisioning is the highest, and is worse than the values observed for Marketcetera in the case of cyclic workloads. We also observe a similar oscillating trend in the agility values of the overprovisioning deployment as in Marketcetera, but the agility values oscillate more frequently because $Req\_min(i)$ – the minimum capacity needed to maintain QoS under a certain workload changes more erratically than Marketcetera due to the replication and at-most once guarantees provided by Hedwig for delivered messages.

Paxos. The relevant QoS metrics for Paxos are the number of consensus rounds executed successfully per second, and the time taken to execute a consensus round. Figures 7g and 7h illustrate the agility corresponding to our experiments with Paxos. From Figures 7g and 7h, we observe similar trends to Hedwig and Marketcetera. The agility of CloudWatch in this case is 6.6× than of ELASTICRMI, on average for abrupt workloads and 2.2× that of ELASTICRMI for cyclic workloads. We also observe that the agility of ELASTICRMI returns to zero (the ideal agility) most frequently among the three deployments.

DCS The relevant QoS metrics for DCS are the number of updates to the hierarchical name-space per second and the end-to-end latency to perform an update as measured from the client. Figures 7i and 7j illustrate the agility corresponding to our experiments with DCS. From Figures 7i and 7j, we observe that the agility of CloudWatch in this case is 7.2× than of ELASTICRMI, on average for abrupt workloads and 3.2× that of ELASTICRMI for cyclic workloads.

5.6   Provisioning Latency

Figures 8a and 8b plot the provisioning latency of ELASTICRMIfor both abrupt and cyclic workloads. We observe that the provisioning latency of ELASTICRMI is less than 30 seconds in all cases, which compares very favorably to the time needed to provision new VM instances in Amazon CloudWatch (which is in the order of several minutes, and hence omitted from Figure 8). Provisioning latency is zero for the overprovisioning scenario, and that is the main purpose of overprovisioning – to have resources always ready and available. Also, we observe that as the workload increases, provisioning interval also increases, due to the overhead in determining the remote method calls that have to be redirected and also due to increasing demands on the resources of the sentinel object in ELASTICRMI's object pools.

6   Related Work

J-Orchestra [8,9] automatically partitions Java applications and makes them into distributed applications running on distinct JVMs, by using byte code transformations to change local method calls into distributed method calls as necessary. The key distinctions between J-Orchestra and ELASTICRMI are that (1) J-Orchestra tackles the complex problem of automatic distribution of Java programs while ELASTICRMI aims to add elasticity to already distributed programs and (2) ELASTICRMI partitions different invocations of a single remote method.

Self-Replicating Objects (SROs) [17] is a new elastic concurrent programming abstraction. An SRO is similar to an ordinary .NET object exposing an arbitrary API but exploits multicore CPUs by automatically partitioning its state into a set of replicas that can handle method calls (local and remote) in parallel, and merging replicas before processing calls that cannot execute in replicated state. SRO also does not require developers to explicitly protect access to shared data; the runtime makes all the decisions on synchronization, scheduling and splitting/merging state. Live Distributed Objects (LDO) [19] is a new programming paradigm and a platform, in which instances of distributed protocols are modeled as live distributed objects. Live objects can be used to represent distributed multi-party protocols and application components. Shared-state and synchronization between the objects is maintained using Quicksilver [18], a group communication system. Automatic scaling is not supported and must be explicitly implemented by the programmer using the abstractions provided by LDO.

Quality Objects (QuO) [6] is a seminal framework for providing quality of service (QoS) in network-centric distributed applications. When the requirements are not being met, QuO provides the ability to adapt at many levels in the system, including the middleware layer responsible for message transmission. In contrast to QuO, ELASTICRMI attempts to increase quality of service by changing the size of the remote object pool, and does not change the protocols used to transmit remote method invocations.

7   Conclusions

We have described the design and implementation of ELASTICRMI and have demonstrated through empirical evaluation using real-world applications that it is effective in engineering elastic distributed applications. Our empirical evaluation also demonstrates that relying solely on externally observable metrics like CPU/RAM/network utilization decreases elasticity, as demonstrated by the high agility values of CloudWatch. We have shown that our implementation of ELASTICRMI reduces resource wastage, and is sufficiently agile to meet the demands of applications with dynamically varying workloads. Through an implementation using Apache Mesos, we ensure portability of ELASTICRMI applications across Mesos installations, whether it is a private datacenter or a public cloud or a hybrid deployment between private data centers and public clouds.

We have demonstrated that ELASTICRMI applications can use fine-grained application specific metrics without revealing those metrics to the cloud infrastructure provider, unlike CloudWatch.

References

1. Amazon Web Services (AWS) Inc. Amazon CloudWatch (2012), http://aws.amazon.com/cloudwatch/
2. Apache Pig (2013), http://pig.apache.org
3. Apache Thrift (2012), http://thrift.apache.org/
4. AWS Inc. Amazon Auto Scaling (2012), http://aws.amazon.com/autoscaling/
5. Hindman, B., Konwinski, A., Zaharia, M., Ghodsi, A., Joseph, A., Katz, R., Shenker, S., Stoica, I.: Mesos: A Platform for Fine-grained Resource Sharing in the Data Center. In: NSDI 2011 (2011), http://incubator.apache.org/mesos/
6. BBN Technologies. Quality Objects (QuO) (2006), http://quo.bbn.com/
7. Burrows, M.: The Chubby Lock Service for Loosely-coupled Distributed Systems. In: OSDI 2006 (2006)
8. Tilevich, E., Smaragdakis, Y.: J-Orchestra: Automatic Java Application Partitioning. In: Magnusson, B. (ed.) ECOOP 2002. LNCS, vol. 2374, pp. 178–204. Springer, Heidelberg (2002)
9. Tilevich, E., Smaragdakis, Y.: Portable and Efficient Distributed Threads for Java. In: Jacobsen, H.-A. (ed.) Middleware 2004. LNCS, vol. 3231, pp. 478–492. Springer, Heidelberg (2004)
10. Elastic Map Reduce (2013), http://aws.amazon.com/elasticmapreduce/
11. Miller, G., Kuznets, T., Agostino, R.: Marketcetera Automated Trading Platform (2012), http://www.marketcetera.com/site/
12. Giraph (2013), http://incubator.apache.org/giraph/
13. Hadoop (2013), http://hadoop.apache.org
14. Hedwig (2013), https://cwiki.apache.org/ZOOKEEPER/hedwig.html
15. Kirsch, J., Amir, Y.: Paxos for Systems Builders (2008), http://www.cnds.jhu.edu/pub/papers/cnds-2008-2.pdf
16. Ousterhout, J., et al.: The Case for RAMCloud. In: CACM (2011)
17. Ostrowski, K., Sakoda, C., Birman, K.: Self-replicating Objects for Multicore Platforms. In: D'Hondt, T. (ed.) ECOOP 2010. LNCS, vol. 6183, pp. 452–477. Springer, Heidelberg (2010)
18. Ostrowski, K., Birman, K., Dolev, D.: Quicksilver Scalable Multicast (QSM). In: NCA 2008 (2008)
19. Ostrowski, K., Birman, K., Dolev, D., Ahnn, J.H.: Programming with Live Distributed Objects. In: Vitek, J. (ed.) ECOOP 2008. LNCS, vol. 5142, pp. 463–489. Springer, Heidelberg (2008)
20. Jayaram, K.R.: Elastic Remote Methods. Technical Report (2013), http://www.jayaramkr.com/elasticrmi
21. LibPaxos (2013), http://libpaxos.sourceforge.net/
22. Memcached (2013), http://www.memcached.org
23. Escriva, R., Wong, B., Sirer, E.: HyperDex: a Distributed, Searchable Key-Value Store. In: SIGCOMM 2012 (2012)
24. SPEC Open Systems Group (OSG). Report on Cloud Computing to the OSG Steering Committee (2012), http://www.spec.org/osgcloud/docs/osgcloudwgreport20120410.pdf
25. Zookeeper (2013), http://zookeeper.apache.org/

Atmosphere: A Universal Cross-Cloud Communication Infrastructure*

Chamikara Jayalath, Julian James Stephen, and Patrick Eugster

Purdue University, Department of Computer Science,
305 N. University Street, West Lafayette, IN 47907
{cjayalat,stephe22,peugster}@cs.purdue.edu

Abstract. As demonstrated by the emergence of paradigms like *fog computing* [1] or *cloud-of-clouds* [2], the landscape of third-party computation is moving beyond straightforward single datacenter-based cloud computing. However, building applications that execute efficiently across data-centers and clouds is tedious due to the variety of communication abstractions provided, and variations in latencies within and between datacenters.

The *publish/subscribe* paradigm seems like an adequate abstraction for supporting "cross-cloud" communication as it abstracts low-level communication and addressing and supports many-to-many communication between publishers and subscribers, of which one-to-one or one-to-many addressing can be viewed as special cases. In particular, *content-based publish/subscribe* (CPS) provides an expressive abstraction that matches well with the key-value pair model of many established cloud storage and computing systems, and decentralized overlay-based CPS implementations scale up well. On the flip side, such CPS systems perform poorly at small scale. This holds especially for multi-send scenarios which we refer to as entourages that range from a channel between a publisher and a single subscriber to a broadcast between a publisher and a handful of subscribers. These scenarios are common in datacenter computing, where cheap hardware is exploited for parallelism (efficiency) and redundancy (fault-tolerance).

In this paper, we present Atmosphere, a CPS system for cross-cloud communication that can dynamically identify entourages of publishers and corresponding subscribers, taking geographical constraints into account. Atmosphere connects publishers with their entourages through *überlays*, enabling low latency communication. We describe three case studies of systems that employ Atmosphere as communication framework, illustrating that Atmosphere can be utilized to considerably improve cross-cloud communication efficiency.

Keywords: cloud, publish/subscribe, unicast, multicast, multi-send.

1 Introduction

Consider recent paradigm shifts such as the advent of *cloud brokers* [3] for mediating between different cloud providers, the *cloud-of-clouds* [2] paradigm denoting the integration of different clouds, or *fog computing* [1] which similarly signals a departure

* Supported by DARPA grant # N11AP20014, PRF grant # 204533, Google Research Award "Geo-Distributed Big Data Processing", Cisco Research Award "A Fog Architecture".

D. Eyers and K. Schwan (Eds.): Middleware 2013, LNCS 8275, pp. 163–182, 2013.

from straightforward third-party computing in a single datacenter. However, building *cross-cloud* applications — applications that execute across datacenters and clouds — is tedious due to the variety of abstractions provided (e.g., Infrastructure as a Service vs. Platform as a Service).

Cross-Cloud Communication. One particularly tedious aspect of cross-cloud integration, addressed herein, is communication. Providing a communication middleware solution which supports efficient cross-cloud deployment goes through addressing a number of challenges. A candidate solution should namely

R1. support a variety of *communication patterns* (e.g., communication rate, number of interacting entities) effectively. Given the variety of target applications (e.g., social networking, web servers), the system must be able to cope with one-to-one communication as well as different forms of multicast (one-to-many, many-to-many). In particular, the system must be able to scale up as well as down ("elasticity") based on current needs [4] such as number of communicating endpoints.

R2. run on standard "low-level" network layers and abstractions without relying on any specific protocols such as IP Multicast [5] that may be deployed in certain clouds but not supported in others or across them [6].

R3. provide an interface which hides cloud-specific hardware addresses and integrates well with abstractions of widespread cloud storage and computing systems in order to support a wide variety of applications.

R4. operate efficiently despite varying network latencies within/across datacenters.

Publish/Subscribe for the Cloud. One candidate abstraction is *publish/subscribe*. Components act as *publishers* of messages, and dually as *subscribers* by delineating messages of interest. Examples of publish/subscribe services designed for and/or deployed in the cloud include Amazon's Simple Notification Service (SNS) [7], Apache Hedwig [8], LinkedIn's Kafka [9], or Blue Dove [4]. Intuitively, publish/subscribe is an adequate abstraction because it supports generic many-to-many interaction, shields applications from specific lower-level communication — in particular hardware addresses — thus supporting application interoperability and portability. In particular, *content-based publish/subscribe* (CPS) [10,11,12,13,14] promotes an addressing model based on message *properties* and corresponding values (subscribers delineate values of interest for relevant properties) which matches well the key-value pair abstractions used by many cloud storage (e.g., [15,16]) and computing (e.g., [17]) systems.

Limitations. However, existing publish/subscribe systems for the cloud are not designed to operate beyond single datacenters, and CPS systems focus on scaling *up* to large numbers of subscribers: to "mediate" between published messages and subscriptions, CPS systems typically employ an overlay network of brokers, with filtering happening downstream from publishers to subscribers based on upstream aggregation of subscriptions. When messages from a publisher are only of interest to one or few subscribers, such overlay-based multi-hop routing (and filtering) will impose increased latency compared to a direct *multi-send* via UDP or TCP from the publisher to its subscribers. Yet such scenarios are particularly wide-spread in third-party computing models, where many cheap resources are exploited for parallelism (efficiency) or redundancy (fault-tolerance). A particular example are distributed file-systems, which store data in a redundant manner to deal with crash failures [18], thus leading to frequent communication between an updating component and (typically 3) replicas. Another example for multi-sends are (group) chat sessions in social networks.

Existing approaches to adapting interaction and communication between participants based on *actual* communication patterns (e.g., [19,4,20]) are agnostic to deployment constraints such as network topology. *Topic-based publish/subscribe* (TPS) [21,22] — where messages are published to *topics* and delivered to consumers based on topics they subscribed to — is typically implemented by assigning topics to nodes. This limits the communication hops in multi-send scenarios, but also the number of subscribers.

In short, CPS is an appealing, generic, communication abstraction (R2, R3), but existing implementations are not efficient at small scale (R1), or, when adapting to application characteristics, do not consider deployment constraints in the network (R4); inversely, TPS is less expressive than CPS, and existing systems do not scale up as well.

Atmosphere. This paper describes Atmosphere, a middleware solution that aims at supporting the expressive CPS abstraction across datacenters and clouds in a way which is effective for a wide range of communication patterns. Specifically, our goal is to support the extreme cases of communication between individual pairs of publishers and subscribers (unicast) and large scale CPS, and to elastically scale both up *and* down between these cases, whilst providing performance which is comparable to more specialized solutions for individual communication patterns. This allows applications to focus on the logical content of communication rather than on peer addresses even in the unicast case: application components need not contain hardcoded addresses or use corresponding deployment parameters as the middleware automatically determines associations between publishers and subscribers based on advertisements and subscriptions.

Our approach relies on a CPS-like peer-based overlay network which is used primarily for "membership" purposes, i.e., to keep participants in an application connected, and as a fallback for content-based message routing. The system dynamically identifies clusters of publishers and their corresponding subscribers, termed *entourages* while taking network topology into account. Members of such entourages are connected directly via individual "over-overlays" termed *überlays*, so that they can communicate with low latency. The überlay may only involve publishers and subscribers or may involve one or many brokers depending on entourage characteristics and resource availabilities of involved publishers, subscribers, brokers, and network links. In any case, these *direct connections* which are gradually established based on resource availabilities, will effectively reduce the latency of message transfers from publishers to subscribers.

Contributions. Atmosphere adopts several concepts proposed in earlier CPS systems. In the present paper, we focus on the following novel contributions of Atmosphere:

1. a technique to dynamically identify topic-like entourages of publishers in a CPS system. Our technique hinges on precise advertisements. To not compromise on flexibility, advertisements can be updated at runtime;
2. a technique to efficiently and dynamically construct überlays interconnecting members of entourages with low latency based on resource availabilities;

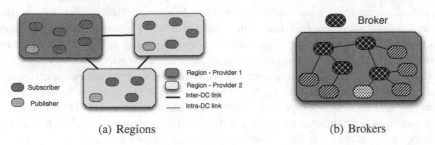

(a) Regions   (b) Brokers

Fig. 1. Bird's-eye View

3. the implementation of a scalable fault tolerant CPS system for geo-distributed deployments named Atmosphere that utilizes our entourage identification and überlay
   construction techniques;
4. an evaluation of Atmosphere using real-life applications, including social networking, news feeds, and the ZooKeeper [23] distributed lock service, demonstrating the
   efficiency and versatility of Atmosphere through performance improvements over
   more straightforward approaches.

Roadmap. Section 2 provides background information and related work. Section 3
presents our protocols. Section 4 introduces Atmosphere. Section 5 evaluates our solution. Section 6 draws conclusions.

2   Background and Related Work

This section presents background information and work related to our research.

2.1   System Model

We assume a system of processes communicating via unicast channels spanning g cloud
datacenters or more generally *regions*. Regions may be operated by different cloud
providers. Each region contains a number of components that produce messages and/or
that are interested in consuming messages produced. Figure 1(a) shows an example system with three regions from two different providers where each region hosts a single
producing and multiple consuming components.

2.2   CPS Communication

With *content-based publish/subscribe* (CPS), a message produced by a publisher contains a set of *property-value* pairs; inversely, components engage into consumption of
messages by issuing subscriptions which consist in ranges of values – typically defined
indirectly through operators such as $\leq$ or $\geq$ and corresponding threshold values.

A *broker overlay network* typically mediates the message distribution between publishers and subscribers. A broker, when receiving a message, analyzes the set of property-value pairs, and forwards the message to its neighbors accordingly. (For alignment with the terminology used in clouds we may refer to properties henceforth as *keys*.) Siena [24] is a seminal CPS framework for distributed wide-area networks that spearheaded the above-mentioned CPS overlay model. Siena's routing layer consists of broker nodes that maintain the interests of sub-brokers and end hosts connected to them in a *partially ordered set* (poset) structure. The root of the poset is sent to the *parent broker* to which the given broker is subscribed to. CPS systems like Siena employ *subscription summarization* [10,25] for brokers to construct a summary of the interests of the subscribers and brokers connected to it. This summary is sent to neighboring brokers. A broker that receives a published message determines the set of neighbors to which the message has to be forwarded by analyzing the corresponding subscription summaries. Summaries are continuously updated to reflect the changes to the routing network, occurring for instance through joins, leaves, and failures of subscribers or brokers.

2.3   Existing CPS System Limitations

When deployed naïvely, i.e., without considering topology, in the considered multi-region model (see Figure 1(a)) CPS overlays will perform poorly especially if following a DAG as is commonly the case, due to the differences in latencies between intra- and inter-region links. To cater for such differences, a broker network deployed *across regions* could be set up such that (1) brokers in *individual regions* are *hierarchically* arranged and each subscriber/publisher is connected to exactly one broker (see Figure 1(b)), and (2) root brokers of individual regions are connected (no DAG). The techniques that we propose shortly are tailored to this setup.

However, the problem with such a deployment is still that — no matter how well the broker graph matches the network topology — routing will happen in most cases over multiple hops which is ineffective for multi-send scenarios where few subscribers only are interested in messages of a given publisher. In the extreme case where messages produced by a publisher are consumed by a single subscriber there will be a huge overhead from application-level routing and filtering over multiple hops compared to a direct use of UDP or TCP. The same holds with multiple subscribers as long as the publisher has ample local resources to serve all subscribers over respective direct channels.

While several authors have proposed ways to identify and more effectively interconnect matching subscribers and publishers, these approaches are deployment-agnostic in that they do not consider network topology (or resource availabilities). Thus they trade *logical proximity* (in the message space) for *topological proximity*.

Majumder et al. [26] for instance show that using a single minimum spanning or a Steiner tree will not be optimal for subscriptions with differing interests. They propose a multiple tree-based approach and introduce an approximation algorithm for finding the optimum tree for a given type of publications. But unlike in our approach these trees are location agnostic hence when applied to our model a given tree may contain brokers/subscribers from multiple regions and a given message may get transmitted across region boundaries multiple times unnecessarily increasing the transmission latency. Sub-2-Sub [19] uses gossip-based protocols to identify subscribers with similar subscriptions and interconnect them in an effective manner along with their publishers. In this process, network topology is not taken into account, which is paramount in a multi-region setup with varying latencies. Similarly, Tariq et al. [20] employ spectral graph theory to efficiently regroup and connect components with matching interests, but do not take network topology or latencies into account. Thus these systems can not be readily deployed across regions. Publiy+ [27] introduces a publish/subscribe framework optimized for bulk data dissemination. Similar to our approach, brokers of Publiy+ identify publishers and their interested subscribers and instruct them to directly communicate for disseminating large bulk data. Publiy+ uses a secondary content-based publish/subscribe network only to connect publishers and interested subscribers in different regions. Publiy+ is not designed for dissemination of large amounts of small messages since the data dissemination between publishers and subscribers is always direct and the publish/subscribe network is only used to form these direct connections.

2.4 Other Solutions for Cloud Communication

Cloud service providers such as Microsoft and Amazon have introduced *content delivery networks* (CDNs) for communication between their datacenters. Microsoft Azure CDN caches Azure blob content at strategic locations to make them available around the globe. Amazon's CloudFront is a CDN service that can be used to transfer data across Amazon's datacenters. CloudFront can be used to transfer both static and streamed content using a global network of *edge locations*. CDNs focus on stored large multimedia data rather than on live communication. Also, both above-mentioned CDN networks can be used only within their respective service provider boundaries and regions.

Volley [28] strategically partitions geo-distributed *stored* data so that the individual data items are placed close to the global "centroid" of the past accesses.

Use of IP Multicast has been restricted in some regions and across the Internet due to difficulties arising with multicast storms or multicast DOS attacks. Dr. Multicast [6] is a protocol that can be implemented to mitigate these issues. The idea is to introduce a new logical group addressing layer on top of IP Multicast so that access to physical multicast groups and data rates can be controlled with a acceptable user policy. This way system administrators can place caps on the amount of data exchanged in groups and the members that can participate on a group. Dr. Multicast specializes on intra-datacenter communication and does not consider inter-datacenter communication.

3   Entourage Communication

In this section, we introduce our solution for efficient communication between publishers and "small" sets of subscribers on a two-level geo-distributed CPS network of brokers with hierarchical deployments within individual regions as outlined in Figure 2 for two regions. This solution can be adapted to existing overlay-based CPS systems characterized in Section 2.2.

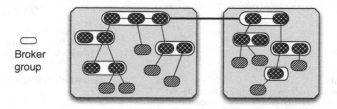

Fig. 2. Broker Hierarchies

3.1 Definition of Entourages

The range of messages published by a publisher p are identified by advertisements τ_p, which, as is customary in CPS, include the keys and the value ranges for each key. Analogously, the interest range of each subscriber or broker n is denoted by τ_n. $\tau_p \cap \tau_n$ denotes the common interest between a publisher p and a subscriber or broker n.

We define the interest match between a publisher p and a subscriber/broker n as a numerical value that represents the fraction of the publisher's messages that the subscriber/broker is interested in assuming the publisher to have an equal probability of publishing a message with any given value within its range. If the range τ_p of p is denoted by $\langle key_1, range_1 \rangle, \langle key_2, range_2 \rangle, ..., \langle key_x, range_x \rangle$ and $\langle key_1, range'_1 \rangle, \langle key_2, range'_2 \rangle, ..., \langle key_x, range'_x \rangle$ denotes the range τ_n of n, then the interest match is given by:

$$\Pi_{i=1}^{x} \frac{|range_i \cap range'_i|}{|range_i|}$$

So, the interest match is defined to be the product of the intersection of the value ranges that corresponds to the same key. If ranges that correspond to a given key have an empty intersection, then n is not interested in messages with the publishers value range for that key, hence there is zero interest match.

A publisher p and a set Φ_p of subscribers/brokers form a ψ-*close entourage* if each member of Φ_p has at least a ψ interest match with p where $0 \leq \psi \leq 1$. ψ is a parameter that defines how close the cluster is to a topic. If $\psi = 1$, each member of the cluster is interested in every message published by p, hence the cluster can be viewed as a topic.

3.2 Solution Overview

Next we describe our solution to efficient cross-cloud communication in entourages. The solution consists of three main parts which we describe in turn.

1. A decentralized protocol that can be used to identify entourages in a CPS system.
2. A mechanism to determine the maximum number K_p of direct connections a given publisher p can maintain without adversely affecting message transmission.
3. A mechanism to efficiently establish auxiliary networks termed *überlay* between publishers and their respective subscribers using information from above two.

```
1:  id                                                        {ID of the broker}
2:  super                                                     {ID of the parent broker}
3:  subbrokers                                                {Sub-brokers}
4:  subscribers                               {Subscribers directly connected to the broker}
5:  wait ← 0                                  {# of records to be received by sub-brokers}
6:  results ← ∅                                    {Results to be sent to the parent broker}

7:  when RECEIVE(COUNT, p, τ_p) from id'
8:      end ← false                              {Whether will be forwarding COUNT}
9:      for all node ∈ subbrokers ∪ subscribers do
10:         if interestMatch(τ_node, τ_p) ≥ ψ then                {Sufficient interest}
11:             if node ∈ subbrokers then
12:                 SEND(COUNT, p, τ_p) to subbroker                  {Forward COUNT}
13:                 wait ← wait + 1                           {# of results to wait for}
14:             else
15:                 results ← results ∪ {⟨node, 1⟩}                       {Add node}
16:         else
17:             end ← true
18:     if |wait| + |results| = 0 then                       {No matching nodes found}
19:         end ← true
20:     if end = true then
21:         results ← ∅                   {Resetting records; any responses discarded}
22:     reply ← false
23:     if end = true or (|results| > 1 and wait = 0) then
24:         reply ← true                       {Send the COUNTREPLY to parent broker}
25:     if reply = true or |results| + wait > 1 then
26:         results ← results ∪ {⟨id, 0⟩}               {Adding current broker}
27:     if reply = true then
28:         SEND(COUNTREPLY, p, results) to super              {Sending COUNTREPLY}

29: when RECEIVE(COUNTREPLY, p, results') from id'
30:     for all ⟨id'', depth⟩ ∈ results' do
31:         results ← results ∪ {⟨id'', depth + 1⟩}                     {Depth + 1}
32:     wait ← wait − 1                         {Have to wait for 1 less record}
33:     if wait = 0 then
34:         SEND(COUNTREPLY, p, results) to super             {Got all responses}
```

Fig. 3. DCI Protocol

3.3 Entourage Identification

We describe the *DCI (dynamic entourage identification) protocol* that can be used to identify entourages in a CPS-based application. The protocol assumes the brokers in region i to form a hierarchy, starting from one or more root brokers. An abstract version of the protocol is given in the Figure 3.

The protocol works by disseminating a message named COUNT along the message dissemination path of publishers. A message initiated by a publisher p contains τ_p and ψ values. Once the message reaches a root node of the publishers region, it is forwarded to each of the remote regions.

The brokers implement two main event handlers, (1) to handle COUNT messages (line 7) and (2) to handle replies to COUNT messages – COUNTREPLY messages (line 29.)

COUNT messages are embedded into advertisements and carry the keys and value ranges of the publisher. When a broker receives a COUNT message via event handler (1), it first determines the subscribers/brokers directly attached to it that have an interest match of at least ψ with the publisher p. If there is at least one subscriber/broker with a non-zero interest match that is smaller than ψ then the count message is not forwarded to any child. Otherwise the COUNT message is forwarded to all interested children. This is because children with less than ψ interest match are not considered to be direct members of the p's entourage and yet messages published by p have to be transmitted to all interested subscribers including those with less than ψ interest match. In such a situation, instead of creating direct connections with an ancestor node and some of the descendants, we choose to only establish direct connections with the ancestor node since establishing direct connections with both an ancestor and a descendent will result in duplicate message delivery and unfair latency advantages to a portion of subscribers. A subscriber or a broker that does not forward a COUNT message immediately creates a COUNTREPLY message with its own information and sends it back to the parent.

A broker does not add its own information to the reply sent to the parent broker if the broker forwarded the COUNT message to exactly one child. This is because a broker that is only used to transfer traffic between two other brokers or a broker and a subscriber has a child that has the same interest match with p but is hop-wise closer to the subscribers. This child is a better match when establishing an entourage.

In the latter event handler (2), a broker aggregates COUNTREPLY messages from its children that have at least a ψ interest match with p, and send this information to its respective parent broker through a new COUNTREPLY message. Aggregated COUNTREPLY messages are ultimately sent to p. To stop the COUNTREPLY messages from growing indefinitely, a broker may truncate COUNTREPLY messages that are larger than a predefined size M. When truncating, entries from the lowest levels of the hierarchy are removed first. When removing an entry, entries of all its siblings (i.e., entries that have the same parent) are also removed. This is because as mentioned before, our entourage establishment protocol does not create direct connections with both a ancestor node and one of its descendents.

A subscriber or a broker may decide to respond to its parent with a COUNTREJECT message instead of a COUNTREPLY, either due to policy decisions or local resource limitations. A broker that receives a COUNTREJECT from at least one of its children will discard COUNTREPLY messages for the same publisher from the rest of its children.

As a publisher's range of values in published messages evolves, it will have to send new advertisements with COUNT messages to keep its entourage up to date. This is supported in our system Atmosphere presented in the next section by exposing an advertisement update feature in the client API.

3.4   Entourage Size

We devise a heuristic to determine the maximum number of direct connections a given publisher can maintain to its entourage without adversely affecting the performance of transmission of messages.

Factors and Challenges. Capabilities of any node connected to a broker network are limited by a number of factors. A node obviously has to spend processor and memory resources to process and publish a stream of messages. The bandwidth between the node and the rest of the network could also become a bottleneck if messages are significantly large, or transmitted at a significantly high rate. This is particularly valid in a multi-tenant cloud environment. The transport protocols used by the publisher and latencies between it and the receivers could limit the rate at which the messages are transmitted.

If the implementation is done in a smart enough way, the increase in memory foot-print and the increase in latency due to transport deficiencies can be minimized. The additional memory required for creating data-structures for new connections is much smaller compared to the RAM available in todays computers (note that we do not consider embedded agents with significantly low memory footprints). The latencies could become a significant factor if the transport protocol is implemented in a naïve manner, e.g., with a single thread that sends messages via TCP directly to many nodes, one by one. The effect could be minimized by using smarter implementation techniques, e.g., by using features such as multi-threaded transport layers, custom built asynchronous transport protocols, and message aggregation.

Conversely, the processor and bandwidth consumption could significantly increase with the number of unicast channels maintained by a publisher as every message has to be repeatedly transmitted over each connection and every transmission requires CPU cycles and network bandwidth.

Number of Connections. First we determine the increase in processor usage of a given publisher due to establishing direct connections with subscribers or brokers. With each new direct connection, a publisher has to repeatedly send its messages along a new transport channel. So a safe worst case assumption is to assume that the amount of processing power needs to be proportional to the number of connections over which messages are transmitted.

Additionally, as mentioned previously, a given publisher p will have a bandwidth quota of W_p when communicating with *remote* regions. Considering both these factors, the number of direct connections K_p which publisher p can establish can be approximated by the expression $min(\frac{1}{U_p}, \frac{W_p}{r_p \times s_p})$.

This requires the publishers to keep track of their processor utilization; in most of the operating systems, processor utilization can be determined by using system services (e.g., the `top` command in Unix). The above bound on the number of directly connected nodes is not an absolute bound, but rather a initial measure used by any publisher to prevent itself from creating an unbounded number of connections. A publisher that establishes K_p connections and needs more connections will reevaluate its processor and bandwidth usage and will create further direct connections using the same heuristic, i.e., assuming the required processor and bandwidth usage to be proportional to the number of connections established.

3.5 Überlay Establishment

We use information obtained through the techniques described above to dynamically form "over-overlays" termed *überlays* between members of identified entourages so that they can communicate efficiently and with low latency.

Graph Construction. A publisher first constructs a graph data structure with the information received from the DCI protocol. This graph gives the publisher an abstract view of how its subscribers are connected to the brokers. There are three important differences between the graph constructed by the publisher ($G1$) and a graph constructed by globally observing the way subscribers are actually networked with the brokers ($G2$).

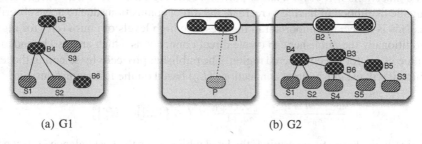

(a) G1   (b) G2

Fig. 4. Graph vs Overlay

a. $G1$ only shows brokers that distribute the publisher's traffic to two or more sub-brokers while $G2$ will also show any broker that simply forwards traffic between two other brokers or a broker and a subscriber.

b. $G1$ may have been truncated to show only a number of levels starting from the first broker that distribute the publisher's traffic into two children while $G2$ will show all the brokers and subscribers that receive the publisher's traffic.

c. $G1$ will only show brokers/subscribers that have at least a ψ interest match with the publisher while $G2$ will show all brokers/subscribers that show interest in some of the publisher's messages.

Figures 4(a) and 4(b) show an example graph constructed by a publisher and an actual network of brokers and subscribers that will result in the graph respectively. The broker $B5$ was not included in the former due to a. above and subscribers $S4$ and $S5$ may not have been included either due to b. or c. (i.e., either because the graph was truncated after three levels or because subscriber $S4$ or $S5$ did not have at least ψ interest match with the publisher p) or simply because $S4$ or $S5$ decided to reject the COUNT message from its parent due to one of many reasons given previously.

Connection Establishment. Once the graphs are established for each remote region publisher can go ahead and establish überlays. The publisher determine the number of direct connections it can establish with each remote region r (K_p^r) by dividing K_p among regions proportional to the sizes (number of nodes) of respective $G1$ graphs.

For each region r the publisher tries to decide if it should create direct connections with brokers/subscribers in one of the levels of the graph, and if so with which level. The former question is answered based on the existence of a non-empty graph. If the graph is empty, this means that none of the brokers/subscribers had at least ψ interest match with the publisher and hence forming an entourage for distributing messages of p is not viable. To answer the latter question, i.e., the level with which direct connections should be created, we compare two properties of the graph.

ad – the average distance to the subscribers.
cv – the portion of the total overlay of the region that will be covered by the selection.

By creating direct connections closer to the subscribers, the entourage will be able to deliver messages with low latency. By creating direct connections at higher levels, the direct connections will cover a larger portion of the region's broker network, hence reducing the likelihood of having to recreate the direct connections due to new subscriber joins. This is especially important in the presence high levels of churn (ch^r for region r). Additionally the publisher can create direct connections which are also bounded by the value of K_p^r for the considered region. The publisher proceeds by selecting the level to which it will establish direct connections (L_p) based on the following heuristic.

$$\frac{cv_{L_p} \times ch^r + 1}{ad_{L_p} + 1} \geq \frac{cv_l \times ch^r + 1}{ad_l + 1} \ \forall \ l \in \{1 \ldots \lfloor \log K_p^r \rfloor\}$$

Basically the heuristic determines the level which gives the best balance between the coverage and the average distance to subscribers. The importance of coverage depends on the churn of the system. Each factor of the heuristic is incremented by one so that the heuristic gives a non-zero and deterministic value when either churn or distance is zero. To measure the churn, each broker keeps track of the rate at which subscribers join/leave it. This information is aggregated and sent upwards towards the roots where the total churn of the region is determined.

If there are more than K_p^r nodes at the selected level then the publisher will first establish connections with K_p^r randomly selected nodes there. The publisher will keep sending messages through its parent so that the rest of the nodes receive the published messages. Any node that already establishes direct connections with the publisher will discard any message from the publisher received through the node's parent. Once these connections are established the publisher as mentioned previously reevaluates its resource usage and creates further direct connections as necessary.

If a new subscriber that is interested in messages from the publisher joins the system, initially it will get messages routed via the CPS overlay. The new subscriber will be identified, and a direct connection may be established in the next execution of the DCI protocol. If a node that is directly connected to the publisher needs to discard the connection, it can do so by sending a COUNTREJECT message directly to the publisher. A publisher upon seeing such a message will discard the direct connection established with the corresponding node.

4 Atmosphere

In this section, we describe Atmosphere, our CPS framework for multi-region deployments which employs the DCI protocol introduced previously. The core implementation of Atmosphere in Java has approximately 3200 lines of code.

4.1 Overlay Structure

Atmosphere uses a two-level overlay structure based on *broker* nodes. Every application node that wishes to communicate with other nodes has to initially connect to one of the brokers which will be identified as the node's *parent*. A set of peer brokers form a *broker group*. Each broker in a group is aware of other brokers in that group. Broker-groups are arranged to form *broker-hierarchies*. Broker-hierarchies are illustrated in Figure 2. As the figure depicts, a broker-hierarchy is established in each considered region. A region

can typically represent a LAN, a datacenter, or a zone within a datacenter. At the top
(root) level broker-groups of hierarchies are connected to each other. The administrator
has to decide on the number of broker-groups to be formed in each region and the
placement of broker-groups.

Atmosphere employs subscription summarization to route messages. Each broker
summarizes the interests of its subordinates and sends the summaries to its parent broker. Root-level brokers of a broker-hierarchy share their subscription summaries with
each other. At initiation, the administrator has to provide each root-level group the identifier of at least one root-level broker from each of the remote regions.

4.2 Fault Tolerance and Scalability

Atmosphere employs common mechanisms for fault tolerance and scalability. Each broker group maintains a strongly consistent membership, so that each broker is aware of
the live brokers within its group. A node that needs to connect to a broker-group has
to be initially aware of at least one live broker (which will become the node's parent).
Once connected, the parent broker provides the node with a list of live brokers within
its broker-group and keeps the node updated about membership changes. Each broker,
from time to time, sends heartbeat messages to its *children*.

If a node does not receive a heartbeat from its parent for a predefined amount of time,
the parent is presumed to have failed, and the node connects to a different broker of the
same group according to the last membership update from the failed parent. A node
that wishes to leave, sends an *unsubscription* message to its parent broker. The parent
removes the node from its records and updates the peer brokers as necessary.

Atmosphere can be scaled both horizontally and vertically. Horizontal scaling can
be performed by adding more brokers to groups. Additionally, Atmosphere can be vertically scaled by increasing the number of levels of the broker-hierarchy. Nodes may
subscribe to a broker in any level.

4.3 Flexible Communication

Atmosphere implements the DCI protocol of Section 3. To this end, each publisher
sends COUNT messages to its broker. These messages are propagated up the hierarchy
and once the root brokers are reached, distributed to the remote regions to identify
entourages. Once suitable entourages are identified, überlays are established which are
used to disseminate messages to interested subscribers with low latency.

When changes in subscriptions (e.g., joining/leaving of subscribers) arrive at brokers these may propagate corresponding notifications upstream even if subscriptions
are covered by existing summaries; when arriving at brokers involved in direct connections these can notify publishers directly of changes, prompting these to re-trigger
counts.

4.4 Advertisements

By wrapping it with the client library of Atmosphere the DCI protocol for publishers/-
subscribers is transparent to application components, at the exception of *advertisements*
which publishers can optionally issue to make effective use of direct connections.

Advertisements are supported in many overlay-based CPS systems, albeit not strictly required. Similarly, publishers in Atmosphere are not forced to issue such advertisements as Atmosphere, although effective direct connection establishment hinges on accurate knowledge of publication spaces. Atmosphere can employ runtime monitoring of published messages if necessary. For such inference, the client library of Atmosphere compares messages published by a given publisher against the currently stored advertisement and adapts the advertisement if required. When witnessing significant changes, the new advertisement is stored and the DCI protocol is re-triggered.

Note that messages beyond the scope of a current advertisement are nonetheless propagated over the direct connections in addition to the overlay. The latter is necessary to deal with joining subscribers in general as mentioned, while the former is done for performance reasons – the directly connected nodes might be interested in the message since the publisher's range of publications announced earlier can be a subset of the ranges covered by any subscriptions.

The obvious downside of obtaining advertisements only by inference is that überlay creation is delayed and thus latency is increased until the ideal connections are established. To avoid constraining publishers indefinitely to previously issued advertisements, the Atmosphere client library offers API calls to issue explicit advertisement updates. Such updates can be viewed as the publisher-side counterpart of *parametric subscriptions* [29] whose native support in a CPS overlay network have been shown to not only have benefits in the presence of changing subscriptions, but also to improve upstream propagation of changes in subscription summaries engendered via unsubscriptions and new subscriptions.

5 Evaluation

We demonstrate the efficiency and versatility of Atmosphere via several microbenchmarks and real-life applications.

5.1 Setup

We use two datacenters for our experiments, both from Amazon EC2. The datacenters are located in US east coast and US west coast respectively. From each of these datacenters we lease 10 *small* EC2 instances with 1.7GB of memory and 1 virtual core and 10 *medium* EC2 instances with 3.7GB of memory and 2 virtual cores each.

Our experiments are conducted using three publish/subscribe systems: (1) Atmosphere with DCI protocol disabled, representing a pure CPS system (referred to as CPS in the following); (2) Atmosphere with DCI protocol enabled (Atmosphere); (3) Apache ActiveMQ topic-based messaging system [21] (TPS). ActiveMQ is configured for fair comparison to use TCP just like Atmosphere and to not persist messages. All code is implemented in Java.

5.2 Microbenchmarks

We first assess the performance benefits of Atmosphere via micro-benchmarks.

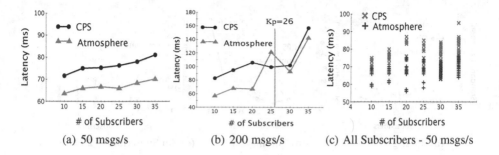

(a) 50 msgs/s   (b) 200 msgs/s   (c) All Subscribers - 50 msgs/s

Fig. 5. Latency and all Subscribers for 50 msgs/s

Latency. We conduct experiments to observe the message transmission latency of Atmosphere with and without DCI protocol enabled. The experiment is conducted across two datacenters and use *small* EC2 instances. A single publisher is deployed in the first datacenter, while between 10 and 35 subscribers are deployed in the second datacenter. Each datacenter maintain three root brokers.

Figures 5(a) and 5(b) show the latency for message rates 50 msgs/s and 200 msgs/s while Figures 6(a) and 6(b) show the standard latency deviations for the same rates. We separate latency from its standard deviation for clarity. Figures 5(c) and 6(c) show the average message transmission latency to individual subscribers for message rates 50 msgs/s and 200 msgs/s respectively.

As the graphs clearly show, when the number of interested subscribers is small, maintaining unicast channels between the publisher and the subscribers pays off, even considering that the relatively slow connection to the remote datacenter is always involved, and only local hops are avoided. This helps to dramatically reduce both the average message transmission latency and the variance of latency across subscribers. For message rates 50 and 200, when the number of subscribers is 10, maintaining direct connections reduce the latency by 11% and 31% respectively.

For message rates 50 and 200, the value of K_p is determined to be 50 and 26 respectively. The Figure 5(b) and 6(b) show that both the message transmission latency and the variation of it considerably increase when the publisher reaches this limit. Also the figures show the benefit of not using the überlay after the number of subscribers exceed K_p. For example, as shown in Figure 5(b) when publisher move from maintaining a überlay with its entourage to communicating using CPS (25 to 30 subscribers) the average message transmission latency reduce by 24%. The increase in latency at 35 subscribers is due to brokers being overloaded, which can be avoided in practical systems by adding more brokers to the overlay and distributing the subscribers among them. Also note that the broker overlay used for this experiment consist of only two levels which is the case where entourage überlays exhibit least benefits.

Number of Subscribers in an Entourage. We conduct experiments using three publisher setups: (1) a publisher uses a *small* EC2 instance (1 core) and sends messages of size 4KB (p_1); (2) a publisher uses a *medium* EC2 instance (2 cores) and sends messages of size 4KB (p_2); (3) a publisher uses a *small* EC2 instance and sends messages of size 8KB (p_3). Subscribers and publishers are placed in two different datacenters as

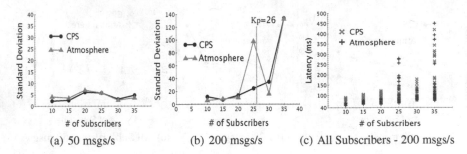

(a) 50 msgs/s   (b) 200 msgs/s   (c) All Subscribers - 200 msgs/s

Fig. 6. Standard Deviation of Latency and all Subscribers for 200 msgs/s

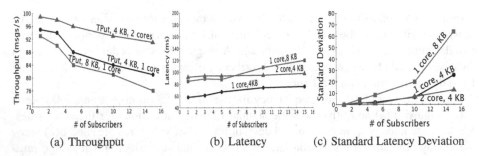

(a) Throughput   (b) Latency   (c) Standard Latency Deviation

Fig. 7. Effects of Resource Usage

previously. Publishers produce at the *highest possible rate* here. Figures 7(a), 7(b), and 7(c) show how message latency, throughput, and standard latency deviation, respectively, vary for these setups as the number of subscribers changes.

The throughput of p_2 is significantly higher than that of p_1. This is expected since the rate at which messages can be transmitted increases with the processing power within the relevant confines. Interestingly though, the average message transmission latency for p_2 is higher than the average transmission latency of messages published by p_1. This suggests that the latency depends on the throughput and not directly on the processing power; the throughput itself of course depends on processing power.

The size of the transmitted messages has a substantial effect on both throughput and latency. The latter effect becomes significant as the number of subscribers increases. Additionally, Figure 7(c) shows that the variation in transmission latency can be significantly reduced by increasing the processing power of the publisher or by decreasing the size of the transmitted messages (e.g., by using techniques such as compression).

Effect of ψ. To study the effects of the clustering factor (ψ) on latency, we deploy a system of one publisher and multiple subscribers. We generated subscribers with interest ranges (of size 20) starting randomly from a fixed set of 200 interests. The publisher publishes a message to one random interest at specific intervals. Brokers are organized into a fully complete binary tree with 3 levels and 40 subscribers are connected to leaf level brokers. On this setup, latency measurements are taken with different ψ values. Figure 8(a) shows the results. When ψ is high, entourages are not created because no broker has an interest match as high as ψ. This means messages get delivered to

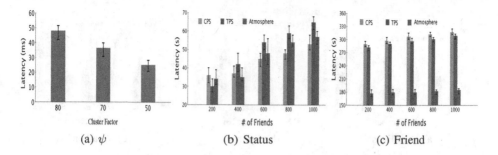

(a) ψ (b) Status   (c) Friend

Fig. 8. Effect of ψ and Evaluation of our Social Network App

root-level brokers which causes higher delays as the messages need to travel through all the levels in the broker network. For a lower value of ψ, an entourage is established, reducing latency.

5.3 Case Studies

We developed three test applications to show how Atmosphere can be used to make real world applications operate efficiently.

Social Network. Typical IM clients attached to social networking sites support the following two operations: (1) *status* updates, in which the current status (Busy/Active/Idle or a custom message) of a user is propagated to all users in his/her friend list; (2) the ability to start a conversation with another user in the friend list. Even when explicit status updates are infrequent, IM clients automatically update user status to Idle/Active generating a high number of status updates. We developed an instant messaging service that implements this functionality either on top of Atmosphere or ActiveMQ.

Figure 8(b) shows latency measurements for status updates. Figures 8(c) shows latency measurements for a randomly selected friend. For conversations, we use actual conversation logs posted by users of Cleverbot [30]. We evaluate this type of communication on Atmosphere, pure CPS with Atmosphere, and ActiveMQ. The results show that our system is 40% faster than pure CPS and 39% faster than ActiveMQ in delivering instant messages. For delivering status messages, in the worst case, Atmosphere is on par with both systems because our system distinguishes between the communication types required for status updates and instant message exchange and dynamically forms entourage überlays for delivering instant messages only.

News Service. We developed an Atmosphere-based news feed application that delivers news to subscribed clients. Our news service generates two types of messages: (1) messages containing news headlines categorized according to the type of news (e.g., sports, politics, weather); (2) messages containing detailed news items of a given category. This service can also operate on top of either Atmosphere or ActiveMQ.

In Figures 9(a), 9(b), and 9(c) we explore latency of the news application for three different communication patterns. The total number of subscribers varies from 200 to 1000 with a subset of 30 subscribers interested in sports-based news and a subset of 20

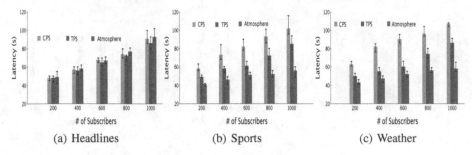

| (a) Headlines | (b) Sports | (c) Weather |

Fig. 9. News App Evaluation

subscribers interested in weather reports. We measure the average latency for delivering sports news and weather reports to these 30 and 20 subscribers. Other subscribers receive all news. Here again our system delivers sports and weather reports 35% faster than a pure CPS system and around 25% faster than ActiveMQ. This is because Atmosphere automatically creates entourages for delivering these posts.

Geo-distributed Lock Service. We implemented a geo-distributed lock service that can be used to store system configuration information in a consistently replicated manner for fault tolerance. The service is based on Apache ZooKeeper [23], a system for maintaining distributed configuration and lock services. ZooKeeper guarantees scalability and strong consistency by replicating data across a set of nodes called an *ensemble* and by executing consensus protocols among these nodes.

We maintain a ZooKeeper ensemble per datacenter and interconnect the ensembles (i.e., handle the application requests over the ensembles) using Atmosphere. We compare the Atmosphere-based lock service with a naïve distributed deployment of ZooKeeper (*Distributed*) where all ZooKeeper nodes participated in a single geo-distributed ensemble. This experiment uses three datacenters. For each run, a constant number of ZooKeeper servers are started at each datacenter. Our system provides the same guarantees as naïve ZooKeeper except the rare scenario of datacenter failure (in this case *Atmosphere* deployment may loose a part of the stored data).

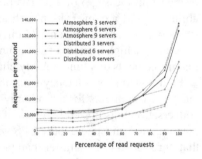

Fig. 10. Lock Service

We vary the percentage of read requests and observed the maximum load the systems could handle with 3, 6, and 9 total nodes forming ensembles. Figure 10 shows the results of the experiment for Atmosphere-based (*Atmosphere*) deployment and a distributed deployment of ZooKeeper where all ZooKeeper nodes participated in a single geo-distributed ensemble (*Distributed*). The figure shows that by establishing überlays, *Atmosphere* deployment can handle a larger load.

These case studies illustrate the general applicability of Atmosphere.

6 Conclusions

Developing and composing applications executing in the cloud-of-clouds requires generic communication mechanisms. Existing CPS frameworks — though providing generic communication abstractions — do not operate efficiently across communication patterns and regions, exhibiting large performance gaps to more specific solutions. In contrast, existing simpler TPS solutions cover fewer communication patterns but more effectively – in particular scenarios with few publishers and many subscribers which are wide-spread in cloud-based computing.

We introduced the DCI protocol, a mechanism that can be used to adapt existing solutions to efficiently support different patterns, and presented its implementation in Atmosphere, a scalable and fault-tolerant CPS framework suitable for multi-region-based deployments such as cross-cloud scenarios. We illustrated the benefits of our approach through different experiments evaluating multi-region deployments of Atmosphere.

We are currently working on complementary techniques that will further broaden the range of efficiently supported communication patterns, for example the migration of subscribers between brokers guided by resource usage on these brokers. Additionally we are exploring the use of Atmosphere as the communication backbone for other systems including our Rout [31] framework for efficiently executing Pig/PigLatin workflows in geo-distributed cloud setups and our G-MR [32] system for efficiently executing sequences of MapReduce jobs on geo-distributed datasets. More information about Atmosphere can be found at http://atmosphere.cs.purdue.edu.

References

1. Bonomi, F., Milito, R., Zhu, J., Addepalli, S.: Fog Computing and its Role in the Internet of Things. In: MCC (2012)
2. Bessani, A., Correia, M., Quaresma, B., André, F., Sousa, P.: DepSky: Dependable and Secure Storage in a Cloud-of-Clouds. In: EuroSys (2011)
3. Grivas, S., Uttam, K., Wache, H.: Cloud Broker: Bringing Intelligence into the Cloud. In: CLOUD (2010)
4. Li, M., Ye, F., Kim, M., Chen, H., Lei, H.: A Scalable and Elastic Publish/Subscribe Service. In: IPDPS (2011)
5. Deering, S., Cheriton, D.: Multicast Routing in Datagram Internetworks and Extended LANs. ACM TOCS 8(2), 85–110 (1990)
6. Vigfusson, Y., Abu-Libdeh, H., Balakrishnan, M., Birman, K., Burgess, R., Chockler, G., Li, H., Tock, Y.: Dr. Multicast: Rx for Data Center Communication Scalability. In: EuroSys (2010)
7. Amazon Inc.: Amazon SNS (2012), http://aws.amazon.com/sns/
8. Apache Software Foundation: Apache BookKeeper: Hedwig, http://zookeeper.apache.org/bookkeeper/
9. Kreps, J., Narkhede, N., Rao, J.: Kafka: a Distributed Messaging System for Log Processing. In: NetDB (2011)
10. Carzaniga, A., Rosenblum, D.S., Wolf, A.L.: Achieving Scalability and Expressiveness in an Internet-scale Event Notification Service. In: PODC (2000)
11. Pietzuch, P., Bacon, J.: Hermes: A Distributed Event-Based Middleware Architecture. In: ICDCSW (2002)

12. Fiege, L., Gärtner, F.C., Kasten, O., Zeidler, A.: Supporting Mobility in Content-Based Publish/Subscribe Middleware. In: Endler, M., Schmidt, D. (eds.) Middleware 2003. LNCS, vol. 2672, pp. 103–122. Springer, Heidelberg (2003)
13. Aguilera, M.K., Strom, R.E., Sturman, D.C., Astley, M., Chandra, T.D.: Matching Events in a Content-based Subscription System. In: PODC (1999)
14. Li, G., Hou, S., Jacobsen, H.A.: A Unified Approach to Routing, Covering and Merging in Publish/Subscribe Systems Based on Modified Binary Decision Diagrams. In: ICDCS (2005)
15. DeCandia, G., Hastorun, D., Jampani, M., Kakulapati, G., Lakshman, A., Pilchin, A., Sivasubramanian, S., Vosshall, P., Vogels, W.: Dynamo: Amazon's Highly Available Key-Value Store. In: SOSP (2007)
16. Das, S., Agrawal, D., Abbadi, A.E.: G-Store: A Scalable Data Store for Transactional Multi Key Access in the Cloud. In: SOCC (2010)
17. Dean, J., Ghemawat, S.: MapReduce: Simplified Data Processing on Large Clusters. CACM 51(1), 107–113 (2008)
18. Apache Software Foundation: Apache HDFS, http://hadoop.apache.org
19. Voulgaris, S., Riviere, E., Kermarrec, A.M., van Steen, M.: Sub-2-Sub: Self-Organizing Content-Based Publish Subscribe for Dynamic Large Scale Collaborative Networks. In: IPTPS (2006)
20. Tariq, M., Koldehofe, B., Koch, G., Rothermel, K.: Distributed Spectral Cluster Management: A Method for Building Dynamic Publish/Subscribe Systems. In: DEBS (2012)
21. Apache Software Foundation: Active MQ, http://activemq.apache.org/
22. IBM Inc.: Websphere MQ, http://www-01.ibm.com/software/integration/wmq/
23. Apache Software Foundation: Apache ZooKeeper, http://hadoop.apache.org/zookeeper/
24. Carzaniga, A., Rosenblum, D., Wolf, A.: Design and Evaluation of a Wide-Area Event Notification Service. ACM TOCS 19(3), 332–383 (2001)
25. Triantafillou, P., Economides, A.A.: Subscription Summarization: A New Paradigm for Efficient Publish/Subscribe Systems. In: ICDCS (2004)
26. Majumder, A., Shrivastava, N., Rastogi, R., Srinivasan, A.: Scalable Content-Based Routing in Pub/Sub Systems. In: INFOCOM (2009)
27. Kazemzadeh, R.S., Jacobsen, H.A.: Publiy+: A Peer-Assisted Publish/Subscribe Service for Timely Dissemination of Bulk Content. In: ICDCS (2012)
28. Agarwal, S., Dunagan, J., Jain, N., Saroiu, S., Wolman, A., Bhogan, H.: Volley: Automated Data Placement for Geo-Distributed Cloud Services. In: NSDI (2010)
29. Jayaram, K.R., Eugster, P., Jayalath, C.: Parametric Content-Based Publish/Subscribe. ACM TOCS 31(2), 4:1–4:52 (2013)
30. Carpenter, R.: Cleverbot, http://cleverbot.com/
31. Jayalath, C., Eugster, P.: Efficient Geo-Distributed Data Processing with Rout. In: ICDCS (2013)
32. Jayalath, C., Stephen, J., Eugster, P.: From the Cloud to the Atmosphere: Running MapReduce across Datacenters. IEEE TC - Special Issue on Cloud of Clouds (to appear)

VMAR: Optimizing I/O Performance and Resource Utilization in the Cloud

Zhiming Shen[1,*], Zhe Zhang[2], Andrzej Kochut[2], Alexei Karve[2], Han Chen[2], Minkyong Kim[2], Hui Lei[2], and Nicholas Fuller[2]

[1] Cornell University
zshen@cs.cornell.edu
[2] IBM T. J. Watson Research Center
{zhezhang,akochut,karve,chenhan,minkyong,hlei,nfuller}@us.ibm.com

Abstract. A key enabler for standardized cloud services is the encapsulation of software and data into VM images. With the rapid evolution of the cloud ecosystem, the number of VM images is growing at high speed. These images, each containing gigabytes or tens of gigabytes of data, create heavy disk and network I/O workloads in cloud data centers. Because these images contain identical or similar OS, middleware, and applications, there are plenty of data blocks with duplicate content among the VM images. However, current deduplication techniques cannot efficiently capitalize on this content similarity due to their warmup delay, resource overhead and algorithmic complexity.

We propose an instant, non-intrusive, and lightweight I/O optimization layer tailored for the cloud: *V*irtual *M*achine I/O *A*ccess *R*edirection (VMAR). VMAR generates a block translation map at VM image creation / capture time, and uses it to redirect accesses for identical blocks to the same filesystem address before they reach the OS. This greatly enhances the cache hit ratio of VM I/O requests and leads to up to 55% performance gains in instantiating VM operating systems (48% on average), and up to 45% gain in loading application stacks (38% on average). It also reduces the I/O resource consumption by as much as 70%.

1 Introduction

The economies of scale of cloud computing, which differentiates it from transitional IT services, comes from the capability to elastically multiplex different workloads on a shared pool of physical computing resources. This elasticity is driven by the standardization of workloads into moveable and shareable components. To date, virtual machine images are the *de facto* form of standard templates for cloud workloads. Typically, a cloud environment provides a set of "golden master" images containing the operating system and popular middleware and application software components. Cloud administrators and users start with these images and

---

* This work was conducted when Zhiming Shen was an intern at IBM and a Ph.D. student at North Carolina State University.

D. Eyers and K. Schwan (Eds.): Middleware 2013, LNCS 8275, pp. 183–203, 2013.
© IFIP International Federation for Information Processing 2013

create their own images by installing additional components. Through this process, a hierarchy of deviations of VM images emerges. For example, in [24], Peng *et al.* have studied a library of 355 VM images and constructed a hierarchical structure of images based on OS and applications, where the majority of images contain Linux with variation only on minor versions (i.e., v5.X).

Today's production cloud environments are facing an explosion of VM images, each containing gigabytes or tens of gigabytes of data. As of August 2011 Amazon Elastic Compute Cloud (EC2) has 6521 *public* VM images [4] (data on *private* EC2 VM images is unavailable). Storing and transferring these images introduces heavy disk and network I/O workloads on storage and compute/hypervisor servers. On the other hand, the evolutionary nature of the VM "ecosystem" determines that different VM images are likely to contain identical chunks of data. It has been reported that a VM repository from a production cloud environment contains around 70% redundant data chunks [15]. This has indicated rich opportunities to deduplicate the storage and I/O of VM images.

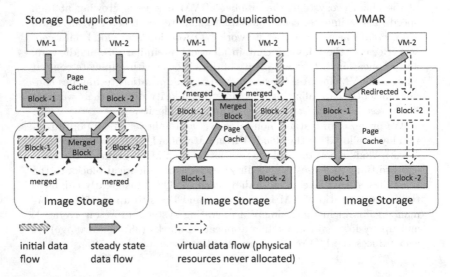

Fig. 1. Comparison of storage deduplication, memory deduplication, and VMAR.

To exploit this content redundancy, storage deduplication techniques have been actively studied and widely used [10,11,12,13,21,26,31]. As illustrated in Figure 1, storage deduplication mostly works on the block device layer and merges data blocks with identical content. The scope of storage deduplication is mainly to save storage capacity rather than to optimize the performance and resource consumption of I/O operations. As a matter of fact, most of them cause various degrees of overhead to both write and read operations.

On the other hand, memory deduplication techniques [5,7,16,18,28,29] save memory space by scanning the memory space and compressing identical pages. They also reduce the I/O bandwidth consumption by improving cache hit ratio. However, existing memory deduplication methods suffer from 2 fundamental drawbacks when applied to VM I/O optimization. First, savings can only be achieved after a "warm-up" period where similar data chunks are brought in the memory and become eligible for merging. Second, the merging process, including content identification, page table modification, as well as the copy-on-write logic (triggered when a shared page is updated), requires complex programs and competes with primary applications for computing resources.

As an alternative, this paper proposes **VMAR**, an *instant, non-intrusive*, and *lightweight* I/O optimization method tailored for cloud environments. **VMAR** is based on the idea of *Virtual Machine I/O Access Redirection*. It is a lightweight extension to the virtualization layer that can be easily deployed into the cloud incrementally, and does not need any modification to the guest OS or application stack. Compared to existing deduplication and I/O optimization methods, **VMAR** has two key distinctions.

1. *Ahead* of I/O requests: **VMAR** detects identical data blocks *when VM images are captured* and generates a block translation map. This way, even before a VM starts running, **VMAR** has rich knowledge on its future I/O accesses and is capable of linking them to other VMs' data blocks. The data hashing and comparison can be done lazily because a VM image is typically captured when the VM using it has just been terminated. By batching these operations at image capture time, **VMAR** also avoids keeping large amount of hash values as deduplication metadata at compute nodes.
2. *Upstream* in the I/O architecture: Using the block translation map, **VMAR** redirects VM read accesses for identical blocks to the same filesystem address *above the hypervisor Virtual Filesystem (VFS) layer*, which is the entry point for all file I/O requests into the OS. Since I/O operations are merged from the upstream instead of on the storage layer, each VM has a much higher chance to hit the file system page cache, which is already "warmed up" by its peers. The reduction of warmup phase is critical to cloud user experience, especially in development and test environments where VMs are short-lived.

We have implemented **VMAR** as a QEMU image driver. Our evaluation shows that in I/O-intensive settings **VMAR** reduces VM boot time by 39 ∼ 55% (48% on average) and application loading time by 24 ∼ 45% (38% on average). It also saves up to 70% of I/O traffic and memory cache usage.

The reminder of this article is organized as follows. Section 2 provides a background of VM image I/O. Section 3 details the design and implementation of **VMAR**. Section 4 presents the evaluation results. Section 5 surveys related work in storage and memory deduplication. Finally, section 6 concludes the paper.

2   Background

Most virtualization technologies present to VMs a *virtual disk* interface to emulate real hard disks (also known as *VM image*). Virtual disks typically appear as regular files on the hypervisor host (i.e., image files). I/O requests received at virtual disks are translated by the virtualization driver to regular file I/O requests to the image files.

Due to the large amount and size of VM images, it is impossible to store all image files on every hypervisor host. A typical cloud environment has a shared image storage system, which has a unified name space and is accessible by each hypervisor host. One commonly used architecture is to set up the shared storage system on a separate cluster from the hypervisor hosts, and connect the storage and hypervisor clusters via a storage area network. Another emerging scheme is to form a distributed storage system by aggregating the locally attached disks of hypervisor hosts [14]. In either scenario, when a VM is to be started on a hypervisor host, the majority of its image data is likely to be located remotely.

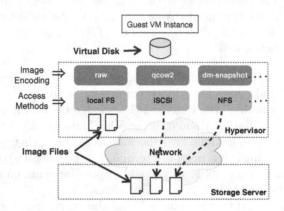

Fig. 2. Different configurations of virtual disks

Figure 2 illustrates different combinations of virtual disk configurations. First, VM images can be stored in different formats. The most straightforward option is the *raw* format, where I/O requests to the virtual disk are served via a simple block-to-block address mapping. In order to support multiple VMs running on the same base image, copy-on-write techniques have been widely used, where a local snapshot is created for each VM to store all modified data blocks. The underlying image files remain unchanged until new images are captured. As shown in Figure 2, there are different copy-on-write schemes, including Qcow2 [1], dm-snapshot, FVD [27], VirtualBox VDI [3], VMware VMDK [2], and so forth.

The second dimension of virtual disk configuration is how VM images are accessed. One way is to *pre-copy* the entire image from the image storage to the local file system of the target hypervisor before starting up a VM instance. Since a typical VM image file contains multiple gigabytes, or even tens of gigabytes of data, it may take a long time to start up a VM instance under this scheme. To overcome this problem, an alternative method is to fetch parts of a VM image from the storage system *on-demand*. Under the *on-demand* configuration, image data may need to be fetched from the remote storage during runtime, causing extra delay. However, as shown in [8], the runtime performance degradation is very limited. Therefore, in the rest of the paper, we have focused on applying **VMAR** on top of the *on-demand* configuration.

3   Design and Implementation

Figure 3 illustrates how VMAR interacts with a VM during its lifetime. First, when a new VM image is inserted into the image repository, either copied from external sources or captured from the disk of a VM, VMAR compares it against the existing images in the repository. It then generates the meta-data of the new image, including a block map that identifies common blocks between this image and other images in the repository. Section 3.1 discusses details of the block map generation process. When a new VM is created from the base image, the meta-data is forwarded to the compute node, and an image in VMAR format is created. With the VMAR images serving as the backing files for the Qcow2 images, I/O accesses to VM images are redirected and consolidated. Section 3.2 describes the access redirection mechanism. Finally, Section 3.3 presents techniques to optimize block map size and lookup performance.

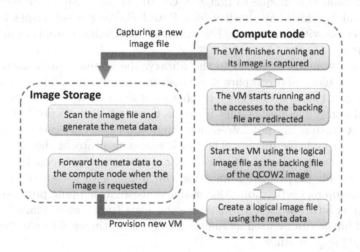

Fig. 3. Flow of VMAR

3.1   Hash-Based Block Map Generation

The block map generator of VMAR uses 4 KB blocks as the base unit. Each data block is identified by its hash value as the fingerprint. In capturing the content similarities among VM images, we leverage the concept of metadata *clusters* proposed in [17]. Each cluster represents the set of blocks that are common across a subset of images. The main benefit of using clusters in VMAR is that they greatly facilitate the search of all VM images having content overlaps with a given image. Therefore, when an image is modified or deleted from the image repository, it is easy to identify entries in the block map that should be updated.

For completeness we first briefly describe the concept of metadata clusters. Consider a simple example of three images: Image-0, Image-1 and Image-2 as shown in Fig. 4. In this illustration, CL-001, CL-010, CL-100 are singleton clusters, containing the blocks only from Image-0, 1 and 2, respectively. For example,

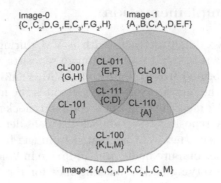

Fig. 4. Illustration of clusters for three example images

block with hash G is unique to Image-0. CL-011 is the cluster with blocks from Image-0 and 1, which have hash values E and F. We use subscripts to denote identical blocks within an image. For example, hash value C appears in Image-0 3 times, as C_1, C_2 and C_3.

When a new image is added to the library, the system computes the SHA1 hash for each block and compare it against existing clusters. Then each cluster is divided into two new clusters: one that contains the new block and another one that doesn't. The hash values in the new images that do not belong to the any current clusters are put into a new singleton cluster. A certain hash value can appear in multiple images. The block mapping protocol should be consistent and and ensure all requests for identical blocks are redirected to the same address. For this purpose we always use the image with the smallest sequence ID as the mapping destination. Alternative consistent mapping protocols can be considered as future work – for instance, the least fragmented image [20] or the most used image can be used as the target. These optimizations can potentially improve I/O sequentiality.

Hash	Contained images	Block list
	Image-0	0,1,5
C	Image-1	2
	Image-2	1,4,6
	Image-0	2
D	Image-1	4
	Image-2	2

Block number	Hash	Cluster	Target image	Target block number
0	A	CL-110	Image-1	0
1	B	CL-010	Image-1	1
2	C	CL-111	Image-0	0
3	A	CL-110	Image-1	0
4	D	CL-111	Image-0	2
5	E	CL-011	Image-0	4
6	F	CL-011	Image-0	6

Fig. 5. Meta-data of cluster CL-111   **Fig. 6.** Block map for Image-1

Fig. 5 illustrates the meta-data of cluster CL-111. Cluster CL-111 contains two hash values that are shared by all three images, so the accesses to any block belonging to CL-111 should be redirected to Image-0, which has the smallest ID. It is possible that there are multiple blocks having the same hash value in

```
function update_block(s, block)
  hash_prev: previous hash value of the block;
  hash_new: new hash value of the block;
  add s to update_list;
  let c = find_cluster_from_hash(hash_prev);
  remove block in the block list of hash_prev for image s in c;
  if the updated block list becomes empty:
    move the entry of hash_prev in c to the corresponding cluster;
  if the minimal image ID containing hash_prev is changed:
    for each image t that contains hash_prev do:
      add t to update_list;
    end for;
  let c' = find_cluster_from_hash(hash_new);
  if c' = None:
    add block into singleton of s;
  else:
    add block to c';
    if s does not contain c':
      move the entry of hash_new in c' to the corresponding cluster;
    if the minimal image ID containing hash_new is changed:
      for each image t that contains hash_new do:
        add t to update_list;
      end for;
  for each image t in update_list do:
    re-construct the block map for image t;
  end for;
end function;
```

Fig. 7. Pseudo-code of updating an image

Image-0, such as the blocks with hash value C. In this case, we always map them to the block with the smallest block number. For example, in the illustrated case, any block with hash value C will be mapped to block 0 in Image-0. Given the hash value of a block, we can quickly identify the target image and block we should map by looking up the hash table in each cluster. Fig. 6 shows the map for Image-1 and the cluster meta-data we use to construct the map.

The method update_map in Fig. 7 is executed when a VM image is updated. It search for all other images having blocks pointing to this image with the cluster data structure, and consequently update the map entries. A hash value can also be moved to another cluster if the ownership is changed due to the update.

Finally, to illustrate the offline computational overhead for creation of clusters and map, that is a one time cost to prepare the image library for redirection, we have run an experiment on a VM with 2.2 GHz cpu and 16 GB memory. We have used an image library with 84 images with total size of 1.5 TB. The images were a mix of Windows and Linux images of varying sizes ranging between 4 GB and 100 GB (used in a production Cloud). This image library resulted in creation of 453 clusters. The total time to create the clusters and mappings for all images was 15 minutes.

3.2 I/O Deduplication through Access Redirection

Figure 8 illustrates the overall architecture of VMAR's access redirection mechanism. The VMAR image serves as the backing file of the Qcow2 image. When a read request R is received by the QEMU virtual I/O driver, the copy-on-write

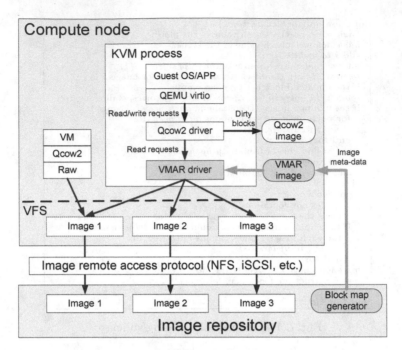

Fig. 8. Architecture of VMAR

logic in Qcow2 first checks whether it is for base image data or VM private/dirty data. If R is for VM private/dirty data, Qcow2 forwards the request to a local copy-on-write file. If R is for base image data, the Qcow2 driver forwards the request to the backing image. In both cases, R is translated as a regular file request which is handled by the VFS layer of the host OS. Unless the file is opened in direct I/O mode, R will be checked against the host page cache before being sent to the host hard disk drive.

The VMAR image driver implements address translation and access redirection. When a read request R is received, VMAR looks up the block map introduced in Section 3.1 to find the destination addresses of the requested blocks. If the requested blocks belong to different base images, or are noncontinuous in the same base image, then R is broken down into multiple smaller "descendant" requests. The descendant requests are sent to the corresponding base images. Upon the completion of all descendant requests, the VMAR driver returns the whole buffer back to the Qcow2 driver.

The descendant requests are issued concurrently to maximize throughput. We leverage the asynchronous I/O threadpool in the KVM hypervisor to issue concurrent requests. To serve a request R, the application's buffer is divided into multiple regions and a set of I/O vectors are created. Each I/O vector represents a region of the buffer and fills the region with the fetched data. A counter for the application buffer keeps track of the number of issued and completed descendant requests. The last callback of the descendant request will return the buffer back to the application.

VMAR updates the *inode* numbers of the descendant requests of R to the destination / redirected base image files before sending them to the host OS VFS layer and checked against the page cache. If the corresponding blocks in the destination files have been read into the page cache by other VMs, the new requests will hit the cache as "free riders". As discussed in Section 3.1, if a block appears in multiple images, the block map entry always points the image with the smallest ID. Therefore, all requests for the same content are always redirected to the same destination address, which increases the chance of "free riding".

VMAR redirects accesses to VM images, but not to private/dirty data. The reason is twofold. First, the data generated during runtime has a much smaller chance to be shared than that of the data in the base images, which contain operating systems, libraries and application binaries. Second, deduplication of private/dirty data incurs significant overhead because the content of each newly generated block has to be hashed and compared to existing blocks during runtime.

3.3   Block Map Optimizations

Block Map Size Reduction. A straightforward method to support redirection lookup is to create a block-to-block map. Based on the offset of the requested block in the source image, we can calculate the position of its entry in the block map directly. Each map entry has two attributes: {ID$_{target}$, Block$_{target}$}. The lookup of block-to-block map is fast. However, the map size will grow linearly with the image size. For example, Figure 9 shows that the map size for a 32 GB image can grow up to 64 MB before optimization.

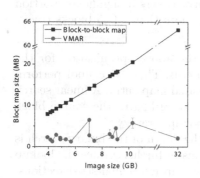

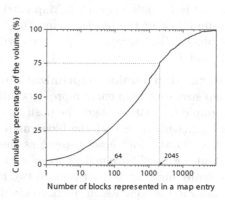

Fig. 9. Block map size optimization.

Fig. 10. CDF of the volume in the clusters with different sizes.

To reduce the map size and increase the scalability, we merge the map entries for the blocks that are continuous in the source image, and are also mapped continuously into the same target image. Since they are mapped continuously, we can use a single entry with four attributes to represent all of them: {offset$_{source}$, length, ID$_{target}$, offset$_{target}$}. Note that the length that each entry represents may be different. Thus, the lookup of the map requires checking whether a given block number falls into the range represented by an entry.

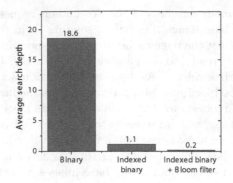

Fig. 11. Average binary search depth for each search scheme

To further reduce the map size, we also eliminate map entries for zero blocks. If a block cannot find a corresponding entry in the map, it is a zero block. In this case, the VMAR driver simply uses *memset* to create a zero-filled memory buffer. This saves the time and bandwidth overheads of a full memory copy.

Figure 9 shows that after optimization, the map size for VMAR is reduced significantly (mostly under 5 MB). In the VM images we have worked on, many continuous clusters have been detected. This is because the common sharing granularity between pairs of VM images is the files stored on their virtual disks. For example, the ram-disk file of the kernel, application binaries and libraries. Figure 10 presents the cumulative percentage of the the number of blocks represented in a single map entry. Map entries containing more than 64 blocks cover around 75% of the blocks. Some "big" map entry covers a significant portion of blocks. For example, map entries with a size more than 2,045 blocks covers around 25% of blocks.

Block Map Lookup Optimization. After the above optimization for the map size, each map entry represents different lengths. Thus, we cannot perform a simple calculation to get the position of the desired map entry. A linear search is inefficient. Note that the block map is sorted according to the source block offset. So we adopt *binary search* as the basic lookup strategy.

Since we still have many entries in the map, the depth of the binary search is typically high. So we have applied two mechanisms to further reduce the lookup time. First, we create an index to divide a large map into equal-sized sections. Each index entry has two pointers pointing the first and the last entry in the map that covers the corresponding section. Since the sections are equal-sized, given a block offset we can directly calculate the corresponding index entry. From the index entry, we can get the range within which we should perform binary search. This mechanism reduces search depth significantly. Second, to avoid searching to the maximum depth for zero blocks, we use a bloom filter to quickly identify them. Figure 11 shows the average search depth during the VM instantiation and application loading stage. We can see that our optimization mechanisms reduce the average search depth from 18.6 to 0.2.

4 Evaluation

4.1 Experiment Setup

We have implemented VMAR based on QEMU-KVM 0.14.0, and conducted the experiments using two physical hosts. Each host has two Intel Xeon E5649 processors (12 MB L3 Cache, 2.53 GHz) with 12 hyper-threading physical cores (24 logical cores in total), 64 GB memory, and gigabit network connection. The hosts run Red Hat Enterprise Linux Server (RHEL) release 6.1 with kernel 2.6.32 and libvirt 0.8.7. One host serves as the image repository and the other one is the compute node on which the VMs will be created. The compute node accesses the images repository using the iSCSI protocol.

To drive the experiments, we have obtained a random subset of 40 images from a production enterprise cloud. The size of the images ranges from 4 GB to over 100 GB. The VMs are instantiated using libvirt. Each VM is configured with two CPU cores, 2 GB memory, bridged network and disk access through virtio in the Qcow2 format. 23 of the images run RHEL 5.5, and 17 of them run SUSE Linux Enterprise Server 11.

The impact of VMAR on the VM instantiation performance is assessed by starting VMs from the images and measuring the time it takes before the VMs can be accessed from the network. This emulates the service response time that a customer perceives for provisioning new VMs in an Infrastructure as a Service (IaaS) cloud. In each image, we have added a simple script to send a special network packet right after the network is initialized. Most time is spent on booting up the OS and startup services. A daemon on the compute node waits for the packet sent by our script and records the timing.

After VM instantiation, another time-consuming step in cloud workload deployment is to load the application software stack into the VM memory space. This can take even longer in complex enterprise workloads, where a software installation (e.g., database management system) contains hundreds of megabytes or gigabytes of data. Due to the lack of semantic information on the production images, we added four additional images into the repository. On each image, we installed IBM DB2 database software version X and WebSphere Application Server (WAS) version Y, where $X \in \{9.0, 9.1\}$ and $Y \in \{7.0.0.17, 7.0.0.19\}$ [1]. These images run RHEL 6.0 and use the same VM configuration as other images. We have measured the application software loading time in the four images, while instantiating other images as a background workload.

As discussed in section 2, our evaluation uses the *on-demand* policy as the *baseline* configuration, where VM images stay in the storage server and the compute node obtains required blocks through the iSCSI protocol. Besides VMAR we have also included *lessfs* [19] and *KSM* [5] in the evaluation, which are widely used storage and memory deduplication mechanisms for Linux. Therefore, the rest of this section compares 4 configurations to the *baseline*: 1) VMAR used to start VMs on compute node; 2) *lessfs* used on storage server to store VM images; 3) *KSM* used on compute node to merge memory pages (*KSM* is triggered

---

[1] DB2+WAS is commonly used in online transaction processing (OLTP) workloads.

only when the system is under memory pressure, therefore only evaluated in such settings); 4) *lessfs* (on storage server) +VMAR (on compute node). The first 3 configurations represent the typical usage of the individual optimization techniques. The fourth configuration explores using VMAR on top of storage deduplication to save both storage and I/O resources.

In our experiments, the arrival of VM instantiation commands follows a Poisson distribution. Different Poisson arrival rates have been used to emulate various levels of I/O workload. Each experiment is repeated three times and average values are reported with the standard deviation as error bars.

4.2   Experiment Results

This section shows the experiment results, including an analysis of content similarity in the VM image repository we use, the results for VM instantiation and application loading, and the overhead of VMAR.

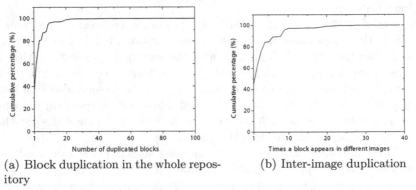

(a) Block duplication in the whole repository   (b) Inter-image duplication

Fig. 12. Image blocks similarity statistics

Similarity in the Image Repository.   We first analyze the content similarity among our 40 images. In this analysis, we only consider non-zero data blocks. Figure 12(a) shows the CDF of the number of duplicated blocks in the entire repository of 40 images. More than 60% of the blocks are duplicated at least twice, and 10% of the blocks are duplicated more than eight times. This verifies the intuition that duplicated blocks are common in the VM image repositories of production clouds. A block can be duplicated within the same image, or across different images. Figure 12(b) shows the CDF of of the number of times that a block appears in different images. More than 50% of the blocks are shared by at least two images. Around 25% of the blocks are shared by more than three images. Therefore, opportunities are rich for VMAR to deduplicate accesses to identical blocks.

VM Instantiation   Figure 13 shows the performance and resource consumption of VM instantiation when different numbers of VMs are booted. In this experiment, a new VM is provisioned every five seconds on average. During the

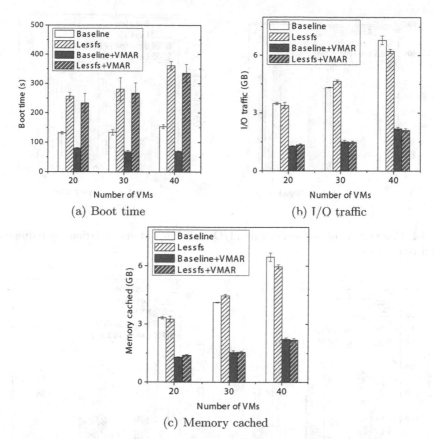

(a) Boot time

(b) I/O traffic

(c) Memory cached

Fig. 13. Comparison of performance and resource utilization in VM instantiation, with different number of VMs

VM instantiation phase, the majority of the I/O workload is to load the OS into the VM's memory, causing few data re-accesses *within a single VM*. Therefore, under the *baseline* configuration, almost every read request goes through the network and the disk, and the data block eventually enters the memory cache of the compute node. As shown in Figures 13(b) and 13(c), the amount of I/O traffic and memory cache space usage are roughly the same, both increasing almost linearly with the number of VMs. Consequently, as shown in Figure 13(a), the average time it takes for a VM to boot up is over 100 seconds. The boot time increases when more VMs are booted, causing the disk and the network to be more congested.

With VMAR, each VM benefits from the data blocks brought into the hypervisor's memory page cache by other VMs that are booted earlier. Therefore, the average boot time is significantly reduced (by $39 \sim 55\%$). Moreover, the average boot time with VMAR decreases when more VMs are booted and the cache is "warmer". VMAR also reduces I/O traffic and memory consumption by $63 \sim 68\%$, by trimming unnecessary disk and network accesses up in the memory cache.

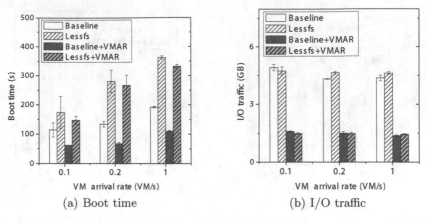

Fig. 14. Comparison of performance and I/O traffic in VM instantiation, with different VM arrival rates

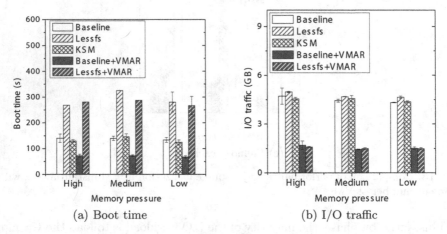

Fig. 15. Comparison of VM boot time and I/O traffic in VM instantiation, with different available memory sizes

More importantly, the I/O traffic grows at a much slower rate than the *baseline* because the amount of "unique" content in every incoming VM image drops quickly as the hypervisor hosts more images. This is a critical benefit in resource overcommitted cloud environments.

With *lessfs*, the I/O traffic and memory cache usage are about the same as the *baseline*. This is because *lessfs* compresses data on the block storage layer, which is below VFS and thus doesn't change cache hit/miss events or the number of disk I/O requests. The VM boot time is worse than the *baseline*, mainly because it runs in the user space (based on *FUSE*), and incurs high context switch overhead. Deduplication techniques implemented in the kernel could have smaller overhead, but similar to *lessfs*, they will not improve filesystem cache performance and utilization. When *lessfs*+VMAR is used, the majority of I/O

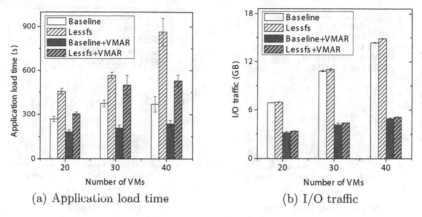

Fig. 16. Comparison of performance and I/O traffic in application loading, with different number of VMs

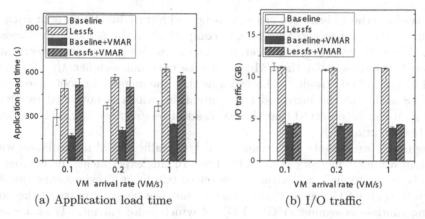

Fig. 17. Comparison of performance and I/O traffic in application loading, with different VM arrival rates

requests hit the page cache of the compute node without reaching to *lessfs* at all. This improves the boot time results. However, the degree of performance improvement (7% on average) is much lower than the saving in I/O traffic (66.6% on average). This is because both **VMAR** and *lessfs* break sequential I/O patterns, thereby exaggerating the context switch and disk seek overhead. To mitigate this issue, replica selection optimizations similar to [18] can be investigated as interesting future work.

Figure 14 presents the performance and resource consumption of VM instantiation under different VM arrival rates, while the total number of instantiated VMs is fixed at 30. Figure 14(a) shows the average boot time when a new VM is provisioned every $\{10 - 5 - 1\}$ seconds on average. Since higher VM arrival rates lead to more severe I/O contentions, the average boot time with the *baseline* scheme increases quickly. In contrast, with the help of **VMAR**, a lot of disk

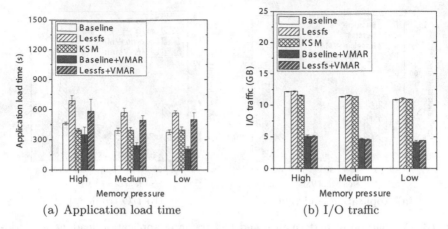

(a) Application load time   (b) I/O traffic

Fig. 18. Comparison of performance and I/O traffic in application loading, with different available memory sizes

accesses from the VMs hit the memory cache and return directly without triggering any real device access. Therefore, in comparison to the *baseline*, the average boot time with VMAR is much lower, and increases slowly with the arrival rate. Figure 14(b) shows that the VM arrival rate does not significantly affect the total amount of I/O traffic [2]. This confirms that the increase in boot time under *baseline* is due to the increased I/O contention, which is mitigated by VMAR. Finally, it can be observed that the overhead of *lessfs* grows fast with the level of I/O contention.

Figure 15 presents the performance and I/O traffic of VM instantiation with different available memory sizes on the host. In this experiment, the number of VMs is set to 30 and the arrival rate is set to 0.2. From previous experiments, which uses all 64 GB memory, we observe that the memory usage of the host during runtime is around 11 GB, 4 GB of which is for caching. Thus, we test the scenarios where the available memory size is 9 GB and 11 GB respectively. Under all configurations, the instantiation time is insensitive to memory pressure, and the reason is twofold. First, VMAR has consolidated the I/O traffic and only requires very small amount of memory (∼1.5 GB) to cache all I/O requests, which can be satisfied even under high memory pressure. Second, without VMAR, data re-access rate is very low, which diminishes the benefit of abundant memory. The *page_sharing* counter of *KSM* indicates that it saves ∼ 3.5 GB of memory by compressing similar pages. However, because the saving is achieved after the data blocks are loaded into memory, it incurs almost the same amount of I/O traffic as *baseline*, and therefore does not lead to notable performance improvement.

Application Loading. Figures 16, 17, and 18 show the results of application loading performance and I/O traffic. Again, in Figure 16, {20 − 30 − 40} VMs are booted with a fixed arrival rate of 0.2; in Figure 17, the number of VMs is set

---

[2] In the rest of this section, memory usage results will be omitted because they are similar to the amount of I/O traffic.

to 30, and $\{10 - 5 - 1\}$ VMs are booted every second; in Figure 18, 30 VMs are booted at a rate of 0.2, under different memory pressures. As discussed above, we replace 4 of the production images with 4 new images installed with different versions of IBM DB2 and WAS, and only measure the application loading time of the 4 images. Other VMs serve as the background workload.

Loading enterprise applications is an I/O intensive workload, where a large number of application binaries and libraries are read into the memory. The 4 images we measure contain different versions of the same application stack, and thus share a lot of data blocks. Therefore, the results demonstrate a similar trend as that of the VM instantiation experiments. With the help of VMAR, the average load time and I/O traffic are much lower, and increase at a much slower pace with resource contention than the *baseline*. The *lessfs* scheme still causes significant overhead to I/O performance. When the system is under memory pressure, *KSM* is not able to reduce I/O traffic or improve performance.

Compared to *lessfs*, the *lessfs*+VMAR configuration improves application loading time by 15% on average, which is more than twice the improvement in VM instantiation time (7%). This is because in the application loading workload, data sharing among images is in large sequential chunks, which enables VMAR to redirect large I/O requests without creating too many descendants.

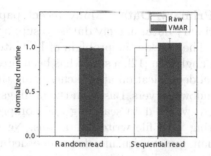

Fig. 19. Comparison of runtime for running random/sequential reading benchmark

Runtime Overhead.   VMAR intercepts each read request to the VM image and incurs additional processing (address translation and redirection). We test this overhead with both random and sequential I/O by issuing dd commands within a VM, with 1 MB block size and direct I/O mode. For random I/O, 3,000 non-zero blocks are read on random locations of the virtual disk. For sequential I/O, a 350 MB non-zero file is read. To eliminate the impact of other factors, the benchmarks run twice when the VM is idle. After the first run, all the data has been brought into the host page cache. We measure the runtime of the second run, which only copies the data from the host memory. Figure 19 shows the runtime normalized to using a raw image. The result shows that the overhead of VMAR is within 5% for sequential I/O and negligible for random I/O.

5   Related Work

This section surveys existing efforts on I/O resource optimization by leveraging data content similarities in various workload scenarios.

5.1   Deduplicated Storage and File Systems

Deduplication for Backup Data.   Due to the explosive generation of digital data, deduplication techniques have been widely used to reduce the storage capacity in backup and archival systems. In general, storage deduplication techniques break each dataset (file or object) into smaller chunks, compare the content of each chunk, and merge chunks with the same content. Much research effort has been made to enhance the effectiveness and efficiency of these operations [10,11,13,21,31]. For instance, Zhu et al. [31] have proposed three techniques to improve the deduplication throughput, which improve the content identification performance, deduplicated storage layout, and metadata cache management respectively. Meyer et al. [21] have provided the insight that deduplication on the whole-file level can achieve about $\frac{3}{4}$ of the space savings of block-level deduplication, while significantly reducing disk fragmentations.

Deduplication for Primary Data.   Many recent papers have focused on the deduplication of primary data, namely datasets supporting runtime I/O requests [12,18,19,23,26]. They tackle the problem of I/O latency caused by deduplication from different angles. In [12], a study has been presented to analyze the file-level and chunk-level deduplication approaches using the dataset of primary data collected from Windows servers. Based on the findings, a deduplication system has been developed, where data scanning and compression are performed offline without interfering with file write operations. Ng et. al have proposed optimized metadata management schemes for inline deduplication of VM images [23]. iDedup [26] has used a minimum sequence threshold to determine whether to deduplicate a group of blocks, and thereby preserving the spatial locality in the disk layout. DEDE [9] focuses on distributing the workload of duplicate detection to the cluster of compute notes. It also demonstrates that the VM instantiation time can be significantly improved by improving the storage array cache hit rate.

5.2   Memory Deduplication

Many techniques have been proposed to leverage the similarities among processes or VMs running on a physical server and reduce their memory usage. Back in 1997, Disco [7] has introduced page sharing in NUMA multiprocessors. More recently, VMware ESX Server [28] has proposed *content-based page sharing*, in which pages with identical content can be shared by modifying the page table supporting the VMs. When a shared page is modified, the copy-on-write logic is triggered and a private copy of the page is created. Many optimizations have been proposed to reduce the memory scanning overhead and increase sharing opportunities [16,18,22,25,29].

Among the above techniques, Satori [22] and I/O Deduplication [18] are the most relevant to VMAR. The sharing-aware block device in Satori and the content-based cache in I/O Deduplication both capture short-lived sharing opportunities by detecting similar pages at *page loading time*. However, Satori consolidates pages belonging to different VMs by modifying the guest OS, while VMAR works entirely on the host level and stays transparent to VM guests. I/O Deduplication introduces a secondary content-based cache under the VFS page cache, making it difficult to avoid duplicates across the two caching levels. As a matter of fact, VMAR may complement both by providing the block maps as hints for identical pages, which they need at page loading time.

6   Conclusion

In this paper we propose VMAR, which is a thin I/O optimization layer that improves VM instantiation and runtime performance by redirecting data accesses between pairs of VM images. By creating a content-based block map during image capture time and always directing accesses of identical blocks to the same destination address, VMAR enables VMs to give each other "free rides" when bringing their image data to the memory page cache. Compared to existing memory and I/O deduplication techniques, VMAR operates *ahead* of VM I/O requests and *upstream* in the I/O architecture. As a result, VMAR incurs small overhead and optimizes the entire I/O stack. Moreover, implemented as a new image format, VMAR is a configurable option for each VM. This enables cloud administrators to "test drive" it before complete deployment.

On top of the main access redirection mechanism, VMAR also includes two optimizations of the block map. The first one is to reduce block map size by merging contiguous map entries. The second one is to reduce the number of block map lookup operations by using an index to quickly guide a request into the correct region of the map. Experiments have demonstrated that in I/O-intensive settings VMAR reduces VM boot time by as much as 55% and reduces application loading time up to 45%.

VMAR is a disk image driver and does not rely on any specific CPU/memory virtualization technology. Thus, it is straightforward to make it work with other virtualization platforms such as Xen [6]. Currently VMAR works entirely on the host level. As future work, we plan to integrate VMAR with our previous work on VM exclusive caching [30] to achieve further savings on the VM level. We also plan to evaluate VMAR in an image pool with a larger scale and more types of operating systems, and explore adding a second level of redirection on the block storage layer to enhance sequential I/O pattern.

References

1. The QCOW2 Image Format, http://www.linux-kvm.org/page/Qcow2
2. Virtual machine disk format (VMDK),
   http://www.vmware.com/technical-resources/interfaces/vmdk.html

3. Virtualbox vdi image storage, http://www.virtualbox.org/manual/ch05.html
4. Amazon Web Services (AWS). Elastic Compute Cloud (EC2),
   http://aws.amazon.com (VM image data retrieved from AWS console on July 08,
   2011)
5. Arcangeli, A., Eidus, I., Wright, C.: Increasing memory density by using KSM. In:
   Linux Symposium 2009 (2009)
6. Barham, P., Dragovic, B., Fraser, K., Hand, S., Harris, T., Ho, A., Neugebauer,
   R., Pratt, I., Warfield, A.: Xen and the art of virtualization. In: SOSP 2003 (2003)
7. Bugnion, E., Devine, S., Govil, K., Rosenblum, M.: Disco: running commodity
   operating systems on scalable multiprocessors. ACM Trans. Comput. Syst. 15(4)
   (November 1997)
8. Chen, H., Kim, M., Zhang, Z., Lei, H.: Empirical study of application runtime
   performance using on-demand streaming virtual disks in the cloud. In: Middleware
   2012 (2012)
9. Clements, A.T., Ahmad, I., Vilayannur, M., Li, J.: Decentralized deduplication in
   SAN cluster file systems. In: USENIX ATC 2009 (2009)
10. Dong, W., Douglis, F., Li, K., Patterson, H., Reddy, S., Shilane, P.: Tradeoffs in
    scalable data routing for deduplication clusters. In: FAST 2011 (2011)
11. Dubnicki, C., Gryz, L., Heldt, L., Kaczmarczyk, M., Kilian, W., Strzelczak, P.,
    Szczepkowski, J., Ungureanu, C., Welnicki, M.: HYDRAstor: a Scalable Secondary
    Storage. In: FAST 2009 (2009)
12. El-Shimi, A., Kalach, R., Kumar, A., Oltean, A., Li, J., Sengupta, S.: Primary
    Data Deduplication Large Scale Study and System Design. In: USENIX ATC 2012
    (2012)
13. Guo, F., Efstathopoulos, P.: Building a high-performance deduplication system.
    In: USENIX ATC 2011 (2011)
14. Gupta, K., Jain, R., Koltsidas, I., Pucha, H., Sarkar, P., Seaman, M., Subhraveti,
    D.: GPFS-SNC: An enterprise storage framework for virtual-machine clouds. IBM
    Journal of Research and Development 55(6) (November-December 2011)
15. Jayaram, K. R., Peng, C., Zhang, Z., Kim, M., Chen, H., Lei, H.: An empirical
    analysis of similarity in virtual machine images. In: Middleware 2011 (2011)
16. Kim, H., Jo, H., Lee, J.: XHive: Efficient Cooperative Caching for Virtual Machines.
    IEEE Trans. Comput. 60 (January 2011)
17. Kochut, A., Karve, A.: Leveraging Local Image Redundancy for Efficient Virtual
    Machine Provisioning. In: NOMS 2012 (2012)
18. Koller, R., Rangaswami, R.: I/O Deduplication: Utilizing content similarity to
    improve I/O performance. Trans. Storage 6(3) (September 2010)
19. Koutoupis, P.: Data deduplication with Linux. Linux Journal 207 (2011)
20. Liang, S., Jiang, S., Zhang, X.: STEP: Sequentiality and Thrashing Detection
    Based Prefetching to Improve Performance of Networked Storage Servers. In:
    ICDCS 2007 (2007)
21. Meyer, D.T., Bolosky, W.J.: A study of practical deduplication. In: FAST 2011
    (2011)
22. Miłós, G., Murray, D.G., Hand, S., Fetterman, M.A.: Satori: enlightened page shar-
    ing. In: USENIX ATC 2009 (2009)
23. Ng, C.-H., Ma, M., Wong, T.-Y., Lee, P.P.C., Lui, J.C.S.: Live deduplication storage
    of virtual machine images in an open-source cloud. In: Kon, F., Kermarrec, A.-M.
    (eds.) Middleware 2011. LNCS, vol. 7049, pp. 81–100. Springer, Heidelberg (2011)
24. Peng, C., Kim, M., Zhang, Z., Lei, H.: VDN: Virtual machine image distribution
    network for cloud data centers. In: INFOCOM 2012 (2012)

25. Sharma, P., Kulkarni, P.: Singleton: system-wide page deduplication in virtual environments. In: HPDC 2012 (2012)
26. Srinivasan, K., Bisson, T., Goodson, G., Voruganti, K.: iDedup: Latency-aware, Inline Data Deduplication for Primary Storage. In: FAST 2012 (2012)
27. Tang, C.: FVD: a high-performance virtual machine image format for cloud. In: USENIXATC 2011 (2011)
28. Waldspurger, C.A.: Memory Resource Management in VMware ESX Server. In: OSDI 2002 (2002)
29. Wood, T., Tarasuk-Levin, G., Shenoy, P., Desnoyers, P., Cecchet, E., Corner, M.D.: Memory buddies: exploiting page sharing for smart colocation in virtualized data centers. In: VEE 2009 (2009)
30. Zhang, Z., Chen, H., Lei, H.: Small is big: functionally partitioned file caching in virtualized environments. In: HotCloud 2012 (2012)
31. Zhu, B., Li, K., Patterson, H.: Avoiding the disk bottleneck in the data domain deduplication file system. In: FAST 2008 (2008)

I2Map: Cloud Disaster Recovery
Based on Image-Instance Mapping

Shripad Nadgowda, Praveen Jayachandran, and Akshat Verma

IBM Research, India
{shnadgow,praveen.j,akshatverma}@in.ibm.com

Abstract. Virtual machines (VMs) in a cloud use standardized 'golden master' images, standard software catalog and management tools. This facilitates quick provisioning of VMs and helps reduce the cost of managing the cloud by reducing the need for specialized software skills. However, knowledge of this similarity is lost post-provisioning, as VMs could experience different changes and may drift away from one another. In this work, we propose the I2Map system, which maintains a mapping between each instance and the golden master image from which it was created, consisting of a record of all changes to the instance since provisioning. We motivate that this mapping can aid several cloud management activities such as disaster recovery, system administration, and troubleshooting. We build a host-based disaster recovery solution based on *I2Map*, which is ideally suited for low cost cloud VMs that do not have access to dedicated block-based storage recovery solutions. Our solution deduplicates changes across VMs and needs to replicate only the unique changes, significantly reducing replication traffic on end hosts. We demonstrate that *I2Map* is able to deliver on tight recovery time and recovery point objectives of the order of minutes with low overhead. Compared to state-of-the-art host-based recovery solutions, *I2Map* is able to save 50-87% network bandwidth on the primary data center.

1 Introduction

Enterprises are moving their IT infrastructure to cloud in order to gain greater flexibility in acquiring and relinquishing resources on demand, focus on core capabilities, reduce costs and avoid capital lock-in. Despite the obvious advantages of the cloud delivery model, CIOs remain skeptical about its potential with concerns primarily regarding availability. A survey [7] attributes increasing customer reluctance to move to the cloud to the problem of poor performance. For instance, outages in Amazon's EC2 and AWS [2] have costed companies millions of dollars. While most cloud providers offer high availability services [3,11,22,8], these come at a premium that is unaffordable for many enterprises. Block-based storage replication solutions such as [15,13] require expensive specialized storage controllers, storage area networks, or other hardware. Network-based replication is performed by a separate component from SAN/NAS or the hosts and can work between multi-vendor products. However, these solutions require intelligent switches which are expensive. Highly available cloud services at an affordable cost remains a distant dream. There is a need for solutions that can work with commodity hardware, is cheap, and yet provides good recovery performance.

D. Eyers and K. Schwan (Eds.): Middleware 2013, LNCS 8275, pp. 204–225, 2013.

Host-based solutions [4,16] are cheaper and less complex than storage-based or network-based solutions as they can be implemented completely in software. They do not require any specialized hardware. They are usually file-based and asynchronous, and work by trapping and forwarding write changes to the replication target. Their overheads and performance are also typically worse than the other two approaches.

The core idea of this work is to leverage the similarity of virtual machines (VMs) in a data center to provide a low-cost host-based disaster recovery solution. A few standardized 'golden master' images are used to provision VMs in a cloud, to ensure quick provisioning and to reduce management costs. Hence, VMs which are provisioned from the same golden master tend to be similar to one another. However, knowledge of this similarity is lost post-provisioning as instances could be used for different purposes and may drift away from one another. We build *I2Map*, which maintains a record of all changes to an instance, as a mapping between the instance and the golden master image from which it was provisioned. A light-weight agent running on each VM records all changes and transmits them to a set of aggregators. The aggregators deduplicate these changes across VMs, store only the unique changes, and maintain the mapping for each VM. A snapshot-mirroring technique can then be applied to backup the aggregators on to a remote site. This recovery process allows us to trade-off recovery performance for cost. We evaluate *I2Map* on representative activities such as installing new software, patching the operating system, and running hadoop-based applications. We demonstrate that individual VMs can receive good recovery performance of a few minutes without having to invest in dedicated and specialized hardware. We conduct a 24-hour high-load case study experiment where we recover a failed VM within a recovery time of 20 minutes and having a recovery point of less than 4 minutes. We show that *I2Map* uses 50-87% lesser network bandwidth on the primary data center compared to the state-of-the-art host-based recovery solutions.

The image-instance mapping can potentially be used for other applications such as system administration or troubleshooting failures. We discuss these as part of future work in Section 7. For the rest of this paper, we focus on the disaster recovery solution.

The rest of this paper is organized as follows. We provide some background and motivate our problem and solution in Section 2. We present the design of *I2Map* in Section 3. Section 4 describes our implementation of *I2Map* and certain optimizations we performed. We evaluate *I2Map* and report the results in Section 5. Section 6 discusses related work, and Section 7 highlights the limitations and other potential applications of *I2Map*. We finally conclude this paper in Section 8.

2   Background and Motivation

The motivation for our work stems from two important trends in cloud computing.

The first trend is increased standardization and automation of IT services delivery in clouds. Virtual servers are created automatically from virtual image templates and managed via standard tools and processes [21]. Applications are deployed from standard software catalog, which contain standardized version of popular middleware and application software. Cloud computing providers use standardization to drive automation of IT delivery as well as to keep the costs down. It has been widely reported that standardization allows system management costs to be significantly reduced [1]. Standardization of virtual image templates, software catalog and management tools lead to high similarity in cloud managed servers. Servers in a data center are already known to exhibit high similarity [5,14] and standardization increases content similarity in virtual machines even further.

The second trend that drives our work is the increasing use of commodity servers and storage in infrastructure clouds. This helps cloud present a low-cost IT model by achieving significant cost-savings. While there are several block-based disaster recovery solutions [3,13,11,8,15] that provide replication across different availability zones, they all require high-end servers and storage technologies like SAN. By contrast, clouds often use commodity servers with attached storage. Commodity hardware does not contain enterprise features like high-availability, block-level replication, fault tolerance and these features need to be implemented at cluster management layer. Disaster recovery is a popular system management functionality, which is impacted by use of commodity hardware. Disaster recovery is often characterized by the Recovery Time Objective (RTO) or the time taken to recover a protected server, the Recovery Point Objective (RPO) or the maximum period of data loss, and the impact of replication on application performance. In a low-cost cloud, disaster recovery depends on host-based replication, which leads to high network traffic and impacts application performance.

In this work, we conjecture that standardization-induced similarity in cloud managed servers can significantly improve system management. Virtual servers instantiated from common image templates and with software deployed from a common catalog, share common content. However, current system management technologies work within virtual server boundaries and are unable to leverage this similarity. If we can create a succinct representation of instances as they evolve from a common image template and software catalog, this representation captures the similarity between instances in an instantly usable format. We call this representation an image-instance mapping called *I2Map* and capture it as a tree, where the master image is the root and each leaf node is a virtual server instance.

We use the *I2Map* tree to implement improved disaster recovery in low cost clouds. Replicating the *I2Map* tree to a secondary site is enough to recreate all the virtual servers on the secondary site. Hence, disaster recovery is trivially supported using the *I2Map* tree. The *I2Map* tree keeps only one copy of an update even if the update is made across a large number of cloud instances. Hence, the tree automatically eliminates redundancy and reduces network traffic, while replicating the tree on a secondary site. We also design techniques to ensure that the tree can be created without propagating updates from end hosts, leading to low traffic overhead even within the primary site.

3   Design

In this work, we design and build *I2Map*, a host-based disaster recovery solution that leverages redundancy in operations across VMs in a data center. We first outline the challenges we faced, describe the *I2Map* architecture, and then highlight the key design ideas that helped overcome the challenges.

3.1   Design Challenges

Identify Duplicates Across VMs without Transferring Data: Every write operation incurs an overhead with storage-based deduplication. Network-based techniques deduplicate only across data centers after bytes have been transmitted over the internal network. Host-based replication techniques deduplicate changes only on the backup server. Can we exclude duplicates across VMs without transferring the actual data?

Control Overhead: Although, host-based techniques have a low cost and complexity of implementation, they have the disadvantage of having an agent running on each of the VMs. The agent uses network, CPU and memory resources leading to application impact. It is critical to control the overhead incurred by this agent and ensure that running applications are not affected.

Handle Large Files with Small Changes: Large files (e.g., log files) could undergo few minor changes or additions. How do we avoid transmitting the entire file each time they are modified?

Handle High Load: When the load is high, the agent should not consume more resources. The overhead needs to be bounded.

Handle Rapid Updates to the Same File: Rapid updates are typically correlated with high load. How can we handle rapid updates within the bounded resources?

Scaling Deduplication: Deduplication often requires centralization. How do we scale deduplication in a cloud with thousands of servers?

3.2   *I2Map* Architecture

In this section, we present the architecture and main components of our *I2Map* disaster recovery solution. A light-weight agent runs on each VM that continuously monitors and reports meta-information regarding any changes on the VM. Dedicated aggregator machines collect reports from all the VMs, identify duplicates, request for and retrieve unique data from the agents running on the VMs. The aggregators also maintain information regarding which files are contained in each VM. Snapshots of the aggregators are backed up on to a remote site periodically. As copies of the aggregators are available

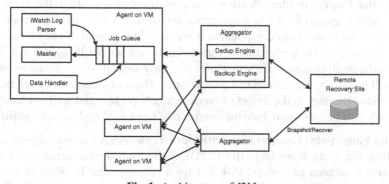

Fig. 1. Architecture of *I2Map*

on the remote site, any VM can be easily retrieved using its golden master image and the catalog of changes to the file system for the VM.

The *I2Map* agent comprises of three components. A file system monitor such as iWatch in Linux, monitors all changes to the file system. A `Parser` identifies files with changes to their meta-information (such as permissions and ownership) or to their content. A report of these changes (without file content) is sent to the aggregators. Files with changes in content are added to a job queue. The `Master` module picks up files from the job queue and computes Rabin fingerprints [18]. Rabin fingerprinting creates cryptographic hashes for variable size shift-resistant blocks. The hashes for each block are then transmitted to the aggregators. The `Dedup Engine` on the aggregator identifies blocks that are unique and requests one of the VMs holding each block to transmit the contents. The `Data Handler` on the agent receives these requests and transmits all blocks requested from it. The `Backup engine` on the aggregator maintains the *I2Map* tree and records the changes to the file system for each VM. Periodically, snapshots of the aggregator are transmitted to a remote recovery site. Recovery for any VM can then be performed on-demand on the remote site. We describe the functioning of each of these modules in detail in Section 4.

3.3 Key Design Ideas

We next highlight and discuss certain key design ideas that enabled us overcome the challenges identified in Section 3.1.

Two-Round Data Transfer: In order to ensure that duplicate data is not transferred from a protected host, we transfer data from agent to aggregator in a two round scheme. In the first round, fingerprints of file segments are sent to the aggregator. The aggregator maintains a hash index of fingerprints for all data that it has aggregated and requests data only for segments that are not already present in its hash index.

Separating Deduplication and Replication: We separate duplicate identification from data replication. Duplicate identification and aggregation of unique data is handled using a two round protocol between agent and aggregator. Data replication to secondary site is performed independently by the aggregators. This allows duplicate elimination to work at LAN speed, while replication can be performed at WAN speed.

Variable Size Duplicate Identification: For each file that is written, the agent computes a Rabin fingerprint. Rabin fingerprints are shift-resistant, as the division into variable-size blocks and hash computation is based on the content of each block rather than any fixed offset. The hashes for the various blocks are sent to the aggregator. Therefore, even if a small change is made to a large file, only a small block of data around the change will need to be transmitted to the aggregator. The remaining blocks will be identified by the aggregator as duplicates of blocks already present and will not have to be transmitted. This helps us to reduce the overhead of file-based replication significantly.

Pipelining Fingerprint Computation with Data Transfer: A two-round protocol can lead to high Recovery Point Objective (RPO), if the rounds were serialized. Further, both rounds may need to perform disk I/O for a file segment. In order to speed up the process of identifying duplicates and aggregating unique data, we pipeline the different operations performed on the agent. The Parser, Master, and Data Handler are implemented as separate threads in order to allow them to progress parallelly acting on different data elements. Further, Master and Data Handler use a producer-consumer cache to minimize disk I/O. Master populates the cache with file segments, when it computes the fingerprints in the first round. In the second round, when Data Handler needs to send data, it reads the file segment from the cache, instead of reading it again from the disk.

Change Coalescing: The agent's parser module looks ahead and identifies multiple successive writes to a file within a short duration and transmits information only once to the aggregator. This change coalescing helps *I2Map* deal with rapid updates to a file even during periods of high load.

Agent Throttling: We allow the agent to be configured with a throttling parameter, in order to ensure that it does not consume too much of the CPU and memory resources of the VM. This further reduces the overhead and ensures that applications that generate high I/O load operate smoothly.

Stable Aggregator Mapping: In order to scale to large data centers, we allow multiple aggregators to be created in *I2Map*. If multiple agents find common content, duplicate elimination requires all (or at least most) agents to send this content to the same aggregator. Clearly, this requires aggregator mapping to be defined based on content. Further, if a part of the file changes, we would like to send only the changed content to the aggregator. This places a restriction that the aggregator mapping should not change due to a small change in content. In order to deal with these conflicting requirements, we use hash of the first $4KB$ of a file to map its aggregator. Changes in other parts of the file do not lead to change in aggregator. Also, files across VMs with the same content, map to the same aggregator most of the time, meeting both our requirements.

4 Implementation

In this section, we describe the implementation of *I2Map* and highlight important optimizations that helped us keep overhead in check.

4.1 *I2Map* Agent

The agent comprises of three modules as depicted in Figure 1, implemented in Python.

iWatch and Parser. The agent, at its core uses iWatch, a real-time file monitoring utility written in perl, based on iNotify, a file change notification system in the linux kernel. We monitor the entire file system excluding device files and temporary files in folders such as /dev. Whenever a file's contents or metadata (including permissions and ownership) is modified, iWatch generates a log. The Parser module thread checkpoints the log, processes all entries up to the checkpoint, and then zeroes all lines up to the checkpoint. This ensures that the iWatch log file is never too large, and *I2Map* does not incur the overhead of opening a large file to read.

The Parser computes a hash of the first $4KB$ of each file that is written. This hash is used to decide which aggregator is in charge of holding the file (we choose the first

$4KB$ only, to ensure content-based stable mapping). The vector space of all the hash values is evenly split among all the aggregators and each aggregator is responsible for managing files with hash values in its vector space. The `Parser` creates reports, one for each aggregator, with meta-information regarding all changes to files managed by that aggregator. Information regarding files that are deleted are sent to all aggregators, and the aggregator to which the file is relevant can then delete the file. Files that are modified are treated as a delete followed by a create.

The `Parser` also adds any files that are newly created or have changed in content on to a job queue. The job queue contains the ID of the aggregator responsible for the file along with certain file meta-data. However, before adding the file entry, the `Parser` takes a peek at the job queue. If an entry already exists for the file, then the `Parser` skips entering the file again into the job queue. This allows the agent to optimize during periods of rapid writes, when a file is written multiple times in quick succession.

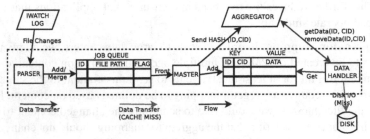

Fig. 2. Detailed Design of *I2Map* Agent

Master. The `Parser` and the `Master` share a producer-consumer relationship with respect to the elements in the job queue (Figure 2). The job queue is controlled by a lock and both the `Parser` and the `Master` need to acquire the lock before writing to it. The `Master` picks up each file entry written by the `Parser`, and computes a Rabin fingerprint for the file, implemented in C. The Rabin fingerprint divides each file into variable-sized blocks based on the content rather than any fixed offset. This makes these blocks shift-resistant, that is, for example changes to the start of a file will not affect all the blocks. The fingerprint consists of cryptographic hash values for each of the blocks. The `Master` sends the hash values for blocks of each file to the corresponding aggregator, as identified in the job queue. In our implementation, we did not limit the size of the job queue, as we observed that the size never grew beyond 700 entries, with each entry being less than 30 bytes.

In order to ensure that even under high I/O load the agent does not consume too much of the VM's resources, *I2Map* can be configured with a throttling parameter. For instance, a throttling parameter of 67% would run the agent for $5s$ and then sleep for the next $10s$. In our implementation, we kept the awake time to be constant at $5s$, and alter the sleep time based on the throttling parameter. We observed that the Rabin fingerprinting and the actual data transfer were the costliest operations, while the parser was extremely light-weight. A crucial design choice was to selectively throttle the `Master` and the `Data Handler`, but not the `Parser`. Apart from throttling the most time-consuming tasks of the agent, this had the added advantage that any duplicate file writes within the VM would be safely omitted by the parser, as the file has not yet been read by the `Master`. Separating these modules into parallel threads and having the job queue as a shared resource between them was important to achieve this.

Data Handler. The `Data Handler` responds to requests from each aggregator, with the content of the specific blocks of files requested by that aggregator. We noticed that we were reading the file twice, once for computing the Rabin fingerprint and a second time for the block transfer. This was adversely affecting performance. To alleviate this problem, we introduced a key-value store cache (Figure 2). When computing the Rabin fingerprint, the `Master` would write the blocks onto this cache. The `Data Handler` will look into the cache first for each block, and will read the file system only if it is unable to find the block in the cache. If found, the `Data Handler` would remove the entry from cache, after use. The `Data Handler` also removes those entries from the cache, which the aggregator already has and does not require. This ensures that only file segments not yet processed by the `Data Handler` stay in cache.

This considerably helped improve performance. From our experiments, we observed that typically the cache had about 400-500 entries (even for data-intensive hadoop experiments), with each entry holding a Rabin fingerprint for a block. The lag between computing the Rabin fingerprint and the data transfer was always small enough to keep the cache small. We limited the cache to 1000 entries and Rabin fingerprint blocks were restricted to a maximum size of $64KB$, ensuring that the cache had a maximum size of $64MB$. Since the workload is scan-based, we never replace unprocessed entries from the cache. Instead, the `Master` waits till a cache block is made available by the `Data Handler`. We also conducted a few overload experiments where the cache was fully utilized and tested a few replacement algorithms. We observed that not replacing entries in the cache, if the cache was full performed the best.

When transmitting blocks of requested files to an aggregator, the `Data Handler` sends at most 500 blocks at a time, to ensure that packet sizes aren't too big. We used a base64 encoding for file transfer as some files, especially those written by hadoop, had certain special characters.

4.2 Aggregator

The aggregator consists of two main modules. The `Dedup Engine` communicates with the agents and identifies blocks that are unique. For each unique block, it requests the contents of the block from one of the VMs holding it. The `Backup Engine` maintains a record of all the files and blocks (among those managed by this aggregator) contained in each VM. An *I2Map* tree is constructed for each golden-master image, where the master image is the root, and each leaf node is a virtual machine instance. Edges in the tree represent changes to files. If a set of VMs experience the same changes to files (e.g., a patch is applied), the `Dedup Engine` would ensure that only one copy of the change is stored. Replicating this tree on a remote site is sufficient for disaster recovery, as any VM can now be recreated by starting with its golden master image.

Interestingly, for the disaster recovery use case, *I2Map* does not even need to create the entire tree. Instead, what we maintain is a list of instances that are relevant for each update to the tree. For example, if a file got overwritten in 5 instances, we store the change along with the 5 instances, whose I2Map tree contain the change. The I2Map tree is thus stored as a set of nodes (one node for the golden master and one node for each instance). The intermediate nodes, which capture the transition from a golden master to an instance are not stored. Instead, a list of all changes are stored along with the impacted instances. Multiple updates to the same file segment are merged leading to a compact I2Map tree, whose size is proportional to the minimum set of changes needed to convert a golden master to any required instance.

4.3   Remote Recovery

The remote recovery site maintains periodic incremental snapshots of all aggregators. Snapshots are taken at 5 minute intervals (a configurable parameter) for each aggregator. We use Linux rsync [20] to transmit the snapshots to the recovery site. Prior to taking a snapshot, the aggregator waits for any packets sent on the wire, freezes all operations for an instant, and takes a filesystem dump of the database and tree. This operation, including taking the snapshot, takes less than a second. In the event of a site failure, the aggregators are recreated and the *I2Map* tree with record of changes to files is used to recreate VMs. We perform incremental recovery by merging updates for each VM periodically (default is 24 hours). This does not require a live VM at the recovery site as only the updates are gathered and stored in an offline VM image. When recovery is triggered, the latest updates are merged and an instance is provisioned from this image.

The Recovery Point Objective (RPO), or the worst-case duration for which recovery cannot be guaranteed, that *I2Map* can support depends on two factors - the maximum time lag of all agents to send data to the aggregators, and the snapshot interval. The RPO for host failure is the lag between agents and aggregator, whereas the RPO for site failure is the sum of the two lags. We show in our evaluation that *I2Map* can guarantee an RPO of less than 4 minutes for host failures and an RPO of less than 9 minutes for site failure, sufficient for most non-critical applications (assuming 70 MBps within the primary site, 700-3300 KBps over WAN, and 1 GB data generated per minute).

Aggregators maintain a heartbeat among one another. In the event of an aggregator failure, one of the live aggregators (e.g., a chosen leader) takes up the responsibility of storing content on behalf of the failed aggregator. Agents are intimated accordingly. Recovery is initiated for the aggregator using snapshots on the remote site. Until recovery for the aggregator is complete, the acting aggregator may not be able to perform efficient deduplication. This, however, does not compromise safety of the system.

5   Evaluation

We evaluate *I2Map* on a heterogeneous set of 6 VMs running Ubuntu 10.04.2 64-bit. The VMs were hosted on 2 IBM BladeCenter servers, one with 4 cores $2.33GHz$ and $8GB$ memory, and the other with 8 cores $3GHz$ and $16GB$ memory. The memory and CPU specifications of the VMs are shown in Table 1. We did not set an upper limit to the CPU available for a VM, and it was bounded only by the availability of resources on the server hosting it. The aggregator was run on a physical server with an 8-core $2.27GHz$ Xeon processor and $16GB$ memory. Recovery is performed on a server with 24-core

3.07*GHz* Xeon(R) processor and 64*GB* memory. The primary site was located in New Delhi and the remote recovery site was located in Bangalore, over 2000*kms* away. We observed speeds of about 70*MBps* within the primary site (between the agents and the aggregators). The WAN bandwidth between New Delhi and Bangalore varied with time of the day and was between 700*KBps* to 3.3*MBps*. With better network speeds, our recovery performance will only improve.

Table 1. Virtual Machine Specifications

VM-ID	Memory (MB)	vCPUs	CPU Reservation
vm-1	1024	4	0
vm-2	2048	2	684
vm-3	2048	2	684
vm-4	2048	2	1500
vm-5	3072	4	2300
vm-6	3072	2	0

We evaluate *I2Map* based on several metrics. We define *dedup* as the ratio of the total bytes written on a VM to the bytes transferred from the VM to the aggregators. $1 - 1/dedup$ captures the reduction in network traffic for each VM by *I2Map* over state-of-the-art host-based replication solutions. We also define *dedup_aggr*, which is the aggregated measure of the total bytes written across all VMs to the total bytes transferred from all VMs to the aggregator. This is a measure of savings in storage and network transfer within the data center due to *I2Map* over state-of-the-art techniques. We measure the (*time lag*) between when a file is written and when it is transmitted to the aggregator (if requested by the aggregator). This measure captures the RPO for host failure and together with the time taken to transfer from the aggregators to the remote recovery node, represents the RPO for site failure. We also measure the CPU and memory utilization (*CPU_Util* and *Mem_Util*) of our agent running on each VM to quantify the overhead of our approach. Finally, in the event of an actual failure of a VM, we measure the recovery time objective (RTO) achieved by *I2Map*.

5.1 Micro Experiments

In this section, we describe micro experiments that we conducted to analyze the performance of *I2Map*. We chose three common activities in a cloud - namely, software installation from a software catalog, patching VMs in a change window, and running clustered applications, for these experiments.

Software Installation. For this experiment we downloaded and installed two software along with all their dependencies, with a 150*s* sleep time between the two. This process was repeated in sequence on 6 VMs. We chose freecad, an open source autocad software, and avgscan, an anti-virus scanning software, for their relatively large size and the number of dependencies with other software and libraries. It is possible that some VMs already had the dependent software and didn't need them to be installed. Freecad had a download size of 60.6*MB* and an install size of 197*MB*. Avgscan had a download size of about 100*MB* and a similar install size. The software installation scenario is one where a large number of files are written within a very short duration of time.

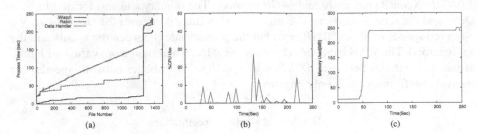

Fig. 3. (a)Time plot showing the split between iWatch, Rabin, and data transfer on vm-1 (b) CPU Utilization (c) Memory Usage

For each file modified or added on a VM, we monitored the time at which the `Parser` (iWatch), `Master` (Rabin), and `Data Handler` handled the file. We plot this in Figure 3(a) for one of the VMs (other VMs were similar). The difference between the successive operations shows the time lag in executing these steps. Observe that the Freecad installation wrote about 1250 files in about 20s (the iWatch curve), and the data handler was able to catch up with this load at around 170s. The figure also shows that the Rabin fingerprinting and the data transfer took nearly equal amount of time. Avgscan, on the other hand, writes only about 150 files (has bigger files than Freecad). *I2Map* is able to handle this load better and has a lag of only about 30s, with most of the delay being due to the data transfer. Hence, *I2Map* is able to achieve an RPO for host failure of less than 3 mins.

Figures 3(b) and (c) show the CPU and memory usage of *I2Map* during this experiment for one VM. We notice that CPU utilization is below 10% except for a couple of brief spikes and the memory usage is less than 250MB, which for servers today is less than 10% of total available memory. Note that this experiment was run without throttling and the resource consumption can be made even lower with throttling.

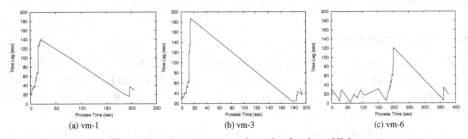

(a) vm-1   (b) vm-3   (c) vm-6

Fig. 4. Time lag vs process time plot for three VMs

We next take a closer look at the time lag of *I2Map* over the course of the experiment. At any given time instant, the time lag is measured as the amount of time required by *I2Map* to process and transmit files written up to that time instant, and plotted in Figure 4 for three VMs. The lag increases in spurts when files are written, but then tapers down as *I2Map* catches up. Unlike vm-1 and vm-3, vm-6 does not have a large spike at the start of the experiment as files were quickly identified as duplicates. However, it has a sharp increase in time lag for the avgscan installation (it was the first to perform it), where it had several files to transmit to the aggregators. These files were identified as duplicates for the other VMs and the experiment concluded earlier for them. Overall, the time lag never increased beyond 160*s*, which is sufficiently low compared to the aggregator snapshot period and the recovery point objective.

Table 2. Average time lag and overhead for each VM

VM-ID	Avg Lag (sec)	Avg %CPU	Avg Mem (MB)
vm-1	78	4.97	170
vm-2	52	1.30	33
vm-3	100	2.81	148
vm-4	88	3.80	114
vm-5	82	1.65	67
vm-6	64	2.41	170

We summarize the average lag and the average CPU and memory usage for each of the six VMs in Table 2. The average lag is less than 100*s*, and the average CPU and memory utilization is less than 5% and 170*MB* respectively. Note that the installation was performed on vm-1 first before the other VMs, and so vm-1 was responsible for transferring most of the data to the aggregators. This was the reason why vm-1 consumed more CPU and memory compared to the other VMs. This is also corroborated in Table 3, which shows for each VM the number of file system change notifications, the number of notifications processed after the Parser eliminated intra-VM duplicates, the number of bytes written to disk and the number of bytes transferred to aggregators.

Table 3. Comparison of dedup values with and without removing duplicate writes for each VM

VM-ID	Total FS Notifications	Processed Notifications	Total Data Change(MB)	Transferred Data (MB)	Dedup
vm-1	21893	2357	447	276	1.62
vm-2	14643	847	337	0.11	3063.6
vm-3	30811	2350	450	1.2	375
vm-4	20041	2802	438	0.54	811.1
vm-5	33320	2335	437	0.09	4855.6
vm-6	49668	1526	551	80.32	6.86
Total			2660	358.26	7.42

We make several interesting observations. First, while around 1400 unique files were written during the experiment (from Figure 3), 20000-40000 file writes were generated on each VM. However, *I2Map* only processed less than 3000 notifications for each VM. This justifies our design choice of *pipelining* and *change coalescing* for multiple changes to the same file. Any storage-based deduplication technique such as [15,8] incurs an overhead for each of the 20000-40000 file writes. In terms of the number of bytes, observe that vm-1 transmitted only 276*MB*, compared to the 447*MB* written to disk. This is primarily due to the division into blocks performed by Rabin fingerprinting and any blocks that did not change would not be transmitted to the aggregators, justifying the use of *variable size* blocks. The other VMs transfer negligible amounts of data to the aggregator as they were similar to vm-1 and our *two-round data transfer* protocol helped them eliminate transfer of duplicate data. vm-6 was an exception as it was the first to have avgscan installed. It therefore transmitted an additional 80*MB*. If every write were to be captured and replicated, like in other host-based solutions, without the 'deduplication before data transfer' feature of *I2Map*, a total of 2660*MB* of data would need to be transferred. In comparison, *I2Map* transfers only 358.6*MB* of data between the agents and the aggregators, a reduction by a factor of over 7 (*dedup_aggr*).

Patching. In our next micro experiment, we apply a set of 55 security patches for Ubuntu on 6 VMs. For one of the VMs, vm-6, 19 of these patches were relevant, while for the other VMs, 49-52 patches were relevant (10 patches were not relevant for at least one VM excluding vm-6). The total download size of the 55 patches was about 480*MB*, with 4 patches each about 100*MB*, and 30 patches each less than 500*KB*. We used Tivoli Endpoint Manager [12], an endpoint management tool, to apply the patches in an automated fashion. The experiment took between 130 and 170 minutes to complete on each of the VMs.

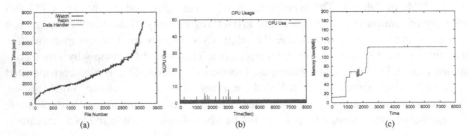

(a)   (b)   (c)

Fig. 5. (a) Time plot showing the split between iWatch, Rabin, and data transfer on vm-2 (b) CPU utilization (c) Memory usage

In Figure 5(a) we present the split between when Parser (iWatch), Master (Rabin), and Data Handler process each file for one sample VM, vm-2. Over 3000 files are modified in about 140 minutes. We observe that the time lag is less than 100*s* most of the time. The CPU utilization is less than 10%, except for a couple of spikes, and the memory usage is less than 120*MB* as shown in Figures 5(b) and (c).

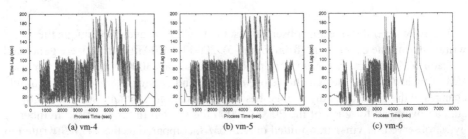

(a) vm-4   (b) vm-5   (c) vm-6

Fig. 6. Time lag vs process time plot for 3 VMs

Table 4. Average time lag, and overhead for each VM

VM-ID	Avg Lag (sec)	Avg %CPU	Avg Mem (MB)
vm-1	58	1.14	106
vm-2	69	1.24	148
vm-3	75	0.98	94
vm-4	65	1.19	143
vm-5	46	1.80	207
vm-6	72	1.05	112

Similar to the software install experiment, Figure 6 depicts the time lag of *I2Map* over the course of the experiment. As most patches are small in size, we see many small spikes in the time lag. The larger patches take longer to download and are processed in the second half of the experiment with fewer spikes.

A summary of the average lag and the average CPU and memory usage for each VM is presented in Table 4. The average time lag is less than $80s$ for all the VMs. Unlike the software installation experiment, where the first VM transferred all the data to the aggregators, the patches were applied in different orders on the VMs. Hence, the overhead is more or less uniform across all the VMs.

Table 5. Comparison of dedup values with and without removing duplicate writes for each VM

VM-ID	Total FS Notifications	Processed Notifications	Unique Data (MB)	Dedup Data (MB)	Transferred Data (MD)	Dedup
vm-1	63017	16990	10	212	38	5.84
vm-2	32877	10038	10	124	62	2.16
vm-3	62533	16789	13	209	101	2.20
vm-4	63064	16916	10	199	36	5.81
vm-5	55000	15112	10	184	74	2.62
vm-6	58323	3890	106	353	397	1.16
Total			159	1281	708	2.03

Table 5 summarizes the deduplication information for the patch experiment similar to Table 3. The intra-VM deduplication and change coalescing of *I2Map* reduces the number of writes that need to be processed to about 16000 from about 60000 total writes. This is not as significant a reduction as in the software install case, as the same files are not rewritten multiple times and the time between file writes is longer reducing the amount of intra-VM deduplication possible. The deduplication achieved is mainly due to multiple patches writing the same files. The total data change is split into unique data and dedup data in Table 5. Unique data represents the amount of data that is unique to that VM, and dedup data represents the amount of data that is found in at least one other VM. Observe that a large fraction of the data written on each VM has duplicates. vm-6 is an exception with a larger fraction of unique data. Since, it had only 19 patches relevant, TEM got to apply patches on vm-6 ahead of the other VMs (patches on all 6 VMs were started simultaneously). Hence, a bulk of the data got transferred from vm-6 on to the aggregators, serendipitously achieving load-balancing. The total amount of data transferred to the aggregators was $708MB$, only a half of the $1440MB$ ($1281MB + 159MB$) of total data written across all the VMs (*dedup_aggr* = 2.03).

Hadoop Sort. Our third and final micro experiment is with running the Hadoop Teragen-Terasort application on a cluster of 5 VMs. Terasort is a distributed sort algorithm on 1*GB* data, that is created by Teragen. The sorted data is written separately from the input data. Hadoop uses a distributed file system that is append-only. This creates a challenge for *I2Map* as it creates and appends data on to large files. It waits until a block reaches 64*MB* and then writes the block to disk. Further, we employ triple replication of data within Hadoop's file system, so the experiment wrote 6*GB* of data in all by the end of the experiment. Identifying and leveraging this replication is critically dependent on the shift-resistant blocks created by the fingerprint. The triple replication also means that a tremendous amount of data is written within a very short amount of time, stress testing both the disk as well as *I2Map*. If ineffective, we may end up transferring a lot of duplicate data. Unless specified otherwise, we use a default value of 67% throttling for this experiment, where the agent is awake for 5*s* and then sleeps for 10*s*.

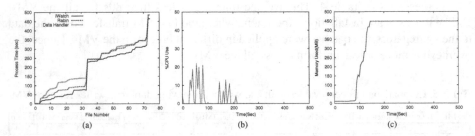

(a)   (b)   (c)

Fig. 7. (a) Time plot showing the split between iWatch, Rabin, and data transfer on vm-2 (b) CPU Utilization (c) Memory Utilization

We observe from Figure 7(a) that the time lag never exceeds 100*s*. This is better compared to the install and patch experiments as data writes are more or less uniform and don't happen in a burst. However, CPU and memory usage are higher as observed in Figures 7(b) and (c). This can be attributed to the larger file sizes, the append-only behavior of hadoop, and the triple replication (the total amount of data written during this experiment is 6*GB* in about 450*s*).

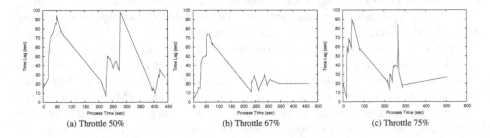

(a) Throttle 50%   (b) Throttle 67%   (c) Throttle 75%

Fig. 8. Time lag vs process time plot for different values of throttling agent process

Figure 8 shows the time lag as a function of the process time for one VM for different values of the throttling parameter. The lag uniformly increases till about 80*s*. Then, we observe a pause in file writes till about 225*s*, as hadoop gathers data till it can write 64*MB* blocks. This is followed by another set of writes. More strikingly, increasing the throttling does not discernably increase the time lag, suggesting that much of the lag is due to the network transfer between the agent and the aggregators. This is encouraging as a better network would help reduce the overhead of *I2Map*.

Table 6. Overhead for each VM and on aggregator

VM-ID	Avg Lag (sec)	Avg %CPU	Avg Mem (MB)
vm-1	41	2.46	360
vm-2	33	1.33	257
vm-3	38	2.02	363
vm-4	59	8.91	361
vm-5	50	2.86	257

Avg %CPU	Avg Mem (MB)
36.86	103

Table 6 shows the average lag and overhead for each of the VMs and the aggregator for the above experiment. The average lag is more or less uniform and less than 60*s* for all the VMs. vm-4 handled the maximum data transfer (as we show in Table 8), which explains the higher lag and overhead seen. The aggregator doesn't perform any file based computations, and only needs to dedup file blocks and receive data from the agents, leaving it with a relatively low memory footprint, but a higher CPU consumption. Even at such a high load, one aggregator can handle 17 agents without throttling and up to 25 agents with throttling, which is an acceptable management overhead (the system can easily scale by adding more aggregators as needed).

Table 7. Average time lag for different values of throttling agent process

	Throttle 50%		Throttle 75%	
VM-ID	Avg Lag (sec)	%CPU	Avg Lag (sec)	%CPU
vm-1	35	2.64	43	1.43
vm-2	37	1.91	39	1.80
vm-3	46	5.95	64	7.78
vm-4	51	3.36	62	1.67
vm-5	53	3.30	61	2.03

The above experiment was conducted with the default throttling value of 67%. We ran the experiment with 50% (5*s* wake and 5*s* sleep) and 75% (5*s* wake and 15*s* sleep) throttling, the results of which are presented in Table 7. The average overhead values typically decrease as we increase throttling, but is not strictly the case. This aberration is an artifact of how hadoop assigns jobs to nodes and is not something we can explicitly control. While the overall CPU and memory utilization can be reduced using throttling, we observe that the time lag increases only marginally for increasing throttling values.

We summarize the deduplication information for the 5 VMs in Table 8. As noted earlier, this experiment has significantly fewer file writes, but each write is for a large chunk of data. This would mean that we will need to process most of the file writes as

Table 8. Comparison of dedup values with and without removing duplicate file writes on VM

VM-ID	Total FS Notifications	Processed Notifications	Unique Data (MB)	Dedup Data (MB)	Transferred Data (MB)	Dedup
vm-1	93	67	0.66	910	90	10.11
vm-2	135	79	0.02	1136	270	4.20
vm-3	132	85	0.02	1617	67	24.13
vm-4	90	69	0.03	1174	669	1.75
vm-5	188	139	0.02	3326	1007	3.30
Total			0.7	8163	2103	3.88

they are sufficiently separated in time from one another. The effectiveness of *I2Map* is demonstrated by the high volume of data in each VM identified as duplicate with at least one other VM. Further, compared to the total amount of data generated, 8163.7*MB*, the amount of data actually transferred is only 2103*MB* across all VMs, which is a reduction by a factor of 3.88 (*dedup_aggr*).

Summary. Our micro-benchmark experiments establish the effectiveness of *I2Map*. We are able to ensure an RPO of less than 3 minutes for VM and host failure, reduce the replication traffic by a factor of 2 to 7.5 (*dedup_aggr*), while using less than 5% CPU and 400*MB* memory during periods of intense I/O loads. The reduction in replication traffic translates into network bandwidth savings of $50 - 87\%$ $(1 - 1/dedup\_aggr)$ in the primary data center, compared to state-of-the-art host-based recovery solutions. We are able to reduce the number of file changes we process by a factor of 2 to 10 due to change coalescing and need only 1 aggregator per 25 managed VMs. While our experiments were conducted with 6 VMs, having a larger pool of VMs using *I2Map* will only increase the deduplication possible. Under normal operation, we believe we can achieve even better performance at lower resource overheads.

5.2 Case Study

We conducted a 24 hour case study where we mimicked a real-world scenario where an application is running continuously at high load, is then brought down, the operating system is patched, rebooted, and the application is restored once again. At the end of the 24 hours we artificially failed one VM, which triggered recovery. In this section, we report results from this experiment, including *I2Map*'s recovery performance.

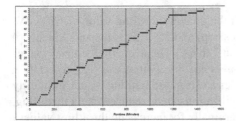

VM-ID	Avg Lag	Max Lag	Avg %CPU	Avg Mem
vm-1	49s	210s	0.50	115 MB
vm-2	62s	196s	0.65	138 MB
vm-3	52s	243s	0.65	57 MB
vm-4	76s	189s	0.71	113 MB
vm-5	58s	227s	0.69	113 MB
vm-6	75s	192s	1.01	112 MB

Fig. 9. Gannt chart showing duration of each hadoop run during the case study experiment **Fig. 10.** Average time lag, and overhead for each VM

We successively ran Teragen-Terasort on hadoop on the 6 VMs. Between every two runs of Teragen-Terasort we added a think time derived from a lognormal distribution with a mean of $120s$. About 19 hours into the experiment, we brought down the hadoop application and started patching the VMs. This patch experiment was similar to the micro-experiment that we conducted, and lasted about 3 hours. Once patching of all VMs completed, we rebooted the VMs and restored the hadoop application. A Gannt chart showing the duration of each hadoop run and the think time between them is plotted in Figure 5.2. Overall, the hadoop-based application was running for 87.6% of the time. This is a very high load (as most enterprise systems run at a load of about 25%), created to stress-test *I2Map*. Notice the long sleep time between about 1150 and 1330 minutes, which was when the patching experiment was conducted.

Figure 10 shows the average and maximum time lag for agents to transfer files to the aggregator, as well as the average CPU and memory usage for each VM. We observe that the average lag is less than 1.5 minutes and the maximum lag at any instant is about 4 minutes. Thus, *I2Map* is able to achieve an RPO for host failures of approximately 4 minutes, even during periods of high write load. Including the time to transmit snapshots to the recovery site, the RPO for site failures is less than 9 minutes. This is very competitive compared to a best guarantee of 15 minutes provided by many commercial disaster recovery solutions [22,8]. The average CPU usage was under 1% for all the VMs, and the memory usage was less than $140MB$. Despite heavy load from the hadoop application, *I2Map* was able to operate with minimal overhead on the agents.

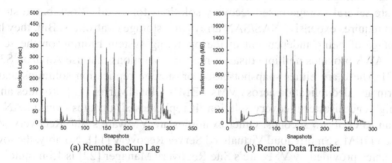

(a) Remote Backup Lag   (b) Remote Data Transfer

Fig. 11. Snapshot Backup Lag and Data Transfer

Snapshots of the aggregator were taken every 5 minutes and transmitted to the remote recovery site using Linux rsync [20]. Figure 11(a) shows the snapshot lag, the duration of time between when a snapshot was taken and when it was fully saved on the remote site, for each snapshot. This is primarily the delay over the network between the primary site and the remote backup site. Observe that the maximum lag is about 7.5 minutes, which happens whenever a new run of hadoop is started and Teragen generates new data. For most snapshots the lag is negligible. Figure 11(b) shows the amount of data transferred for each incremental snapshot, which is about $1 - 1.7$ GB for the large spikes. Most snapshots transmit only about $100MB$ of data. The total data transferred across the Delhi-Bangalore WAN during the course of the experiment was about $26GB$. In comparison, the total data written on all the 5 VMs taken together was about $70GB$. The total aggregated deduplication $dedup\_aggr$ can be calculated as $70/26 = 2.69$.

At the end of 24 hours, we artificially failed a VM, which triggered recovery on the remote site. We mounted a copy of the golden master image corresponding to the VM, identified files belonging to the VM, and wrote their current version on to the mounted copy. This recovered the VM to its last known state. This process involved writing 14.88GB of data and took 719s, at 21.19$MBps$. If a snapshot was being transferred to the remote site when the VM failed, then recovery may be delayed until completion of the transfer, adding up to 8 minutes to the recovery time. Hence, the total recovery time achieved by *I2Map* for this experiment can be estimated as 12 − 20 minutes for a VM with plenty of writes, which is highly competitive with commercial DR solutions.

6   Related Work

Disaster recovery, as a concept, has existed for over three decades. Today, it forms the cornerstone of business continuity and every major IT service provider has a disaster recovery solution. These solutions require NAS/SAN arrays, storage controllers, smart network switches, or other specialized hardware. With the gaining popularity of the cloud, enterprises are looking to reduce their IT-spend and disinvest in hardware. In a bid to meet the expectations of their clients, cloud service providers are building low-cost clouds using commodity off-the-shelf hardware. In this section, we discuss the pros and cons of various replication and disaster recovery technologies. They can be broadly classified into storage-based, network-based, and host-based solutions.

There are several storage-based recovery solutions for cloud. Block-based storage replication requires expensive NAS/SAN arrays and storage controllers. But, they have the advantage of being independent of the operating system running on the server. Amazon's AWS provides multiple disaster recovery solutions that use Amazon S3 for backup [3]. These are either snapshot-based or storage replication solutions and do not perform any deduplication across VMs. IBM's GlobalMirror [13] provides an extremely high-end disaster recovery solution. It replicates all updates over a SAN and provides an RPO of 3-5 seconds. Other examples are VMware's Site Recovery Manager [22] and IBM's SmartCloud Virtualized Server Recovery [11]. Notably, the lowest RPO guarantee provided by VMware's Site Recovery Manager [22] is 15 minutes. We have demonstrated that *I2Map*'s host-based solution can provide a comparable RPO, perform deduplication, and work using commodity hardware.

There are several disaster recovery solutions that do perform different kinds of deduplication. Dell's AppAssure [8] deduplicates and compresses data on the WAN while replicating storage disks. We argue that deduplicating data on the WAN is still too late as costly storage and network resources are consumed within the primary data center to support disaster recovery. NetApp's storage solutions [15] are specialized storage devices that perform deduplication using the Data ONTAP operating environment and the WAFL file system. They report that each write operation incurs a 7% additional overhead, in return for considerable savings in storage, which also translates into lower network bandwidth consumed when replicating the data across a WAN, using their SnapMirror solution [17]. However, deduplication can only be performed across VMs stored on the same storage device and comes with the cost burden of additional specialized hardware.

Network-based disaster recovery solutions perform deduplication on the bytes transmitted over the network. While useful, they do not leverage deduplication within the primary data center. Individuals VMs or servers are still required to transmit all their data across the local network. Some examples include Riverbed [19] and EMC's RecoverPoint [9]. Citrix cloud solution for disaster recovery [6] uses a combination of storage-based and network-based optimizations.

Host-based solutions have the advantage of not requiring specialized hardware and not locking the user into using a specific kind of storage device. Disadvantages include solution being dependent on the operating system used and having an agent running on the host and using its computing resources. Examples of existing solutions include CA's ARCserve [4] and Neverfail [16]. Neither of them perform deduplication on the primary data center. While ARCserve performs deduplication of data on the backup server (after the individual VMs have transmitted all their data), Neverfail uses what they call WANsmart in-line data deduplication, a form of network-based deduplication.

The concept of transmitting only the incremental changes relative to a base VM and dynamically synthesizing them at the time of provisioning has been used in the context of Cloudlets [10]. VM-based cloudlets have been proposed as offload sites for resource intensive or latency sensitive computations for mobile multimedia applications. The technique in [10] works by creating a binary difference between VM images, which is computed only on-demand when required. This is not a disaster recovery solution where continuous monitoring and data replication is desired.

In summary, there are a wide range of disaster recovery solutions that use a variety of technologies, have different requirements, and support different RTO and RPO guarantees. However, these solutions do not cater to the express need of low-cost clouds to support an efficient disaster recovery solution that can perform effective and early deduplication within and across VMs without transferring data, and work with commodity hardware. The *I2Map* disaster recovery solution presented in this paper addresses this concern, and its various optimizations ensure a competitive RPO and RTO guarantee along with low overhead on the VMs.

7 Limitations and Future Work

The disaster recovery solution presented in this paper caters to a specific need for having a low-cost, low-overhead solution that can work with commodity hardware. However, it does have its limitations. As with other host-based solutions, it requires an agent to be running on each VM, using up its computing resources. While we have demonstrated that the overhead can be contained to less than 5%, for many security-critical applications it may be inadmissible to have an agent (trusted as it might be) running on the VM. *I2Map* is not suitable for such applications. A majority of system management tools require agents (e.g., for monitoring, patching, backup) and we believe that having a well-tested agent with minimal performance impact may be acceptable to a large fraction of customers. Also, if the data is encrypted in the file system, *I2Map* will be unable to perform deduplication across VMs effectively. Security over the network is another issue faced by all DR solutions. This can be overcome by adding a layer of encryption before transmitting over network. Further, our current implementation of *I2Map* works only for linux-based VMs and new agents need to be developed for supporting any other operating systems.

Another issue that we have not investigated in this paper is the requirement and load on aggregators. If we were to scale up our disaster recovery solution to several hundred VMs, we may need more aggregators. This is an additional cost burden and we need ways to reduce the number of aggregators needed. The two round data transfer using aggregators does have its advantages, as it ensures that duplicate data is not transferred from protected hosts. Further, the aggregators separate the protected hosts from any WAN overheads, in case the transfer over the WAN were to be slow. As part of future work, we intend to study the costs and benefits of aggregators, especially at scale.

A limitation of all DR solutions (including *I2Map*) is that they only recover the state of the disk and not the memory. The state of memory is far more dynamic and one would have to quiesce any running applications in order to get a snapshot of memory. This is done in certain scenarios (e.g., live migration of a VM), but would be prohibitively expensive to perform on a regular basis and is not required by *I2Map*.

The notion of similarity captured by the *I2Map* tree can be used for performing other data center management tasks as well. The first is in troubleshooting software failures. For instance, system administrators routinely apply software upgrades and patches on a large set of VMs in the data center. If some of these upgrades fail, they have no clue to the cause of the failure. Analyzing the *I2Map* tree for similarities and differences between VMs could provide crucial insight into why the upgrade might have failed, and could even provide clues to how the situation can be remedied. Second, similarity between VMs as captured by the *I2Map* tree can also be used in assigning admins to VMs in a data center. Each admin could manage their VMs better, if they were all similar and had the same software. We intend to explore these applications of *I2Map* in our future work.

8 Conclusion

In this paper, we present *I2Map*, a host-based disaster recovery solution. *I2Map* leverages similarity across VMs in a data center and performs intra- and inter-VM deduplication to reduce the overhead of the solution. It maintains a mapping between instances and the golden master image from which it was created as an *I2Map* tree, which captures all the changes to the instance with respect to the master image. Unlike existing disaster recovery solutions, *I2Map* does not require any expensive specialized storage devices or hardware. It separates deduplication and replication, allowing deduplication to be performed even before any data is transferred from a protected host. Extensive evaluation demonstrates that *I2Map* provides competitive recovery point and recovery time objective of the order of minutes, with low overhead.

References

1. IDC Linux Standardization White Paper: Executive Summary (2011),
   http://www.redhat.com/f/pdf/IDC_Standard-ize_RHEL_1118_Exec_summary.pdf
2. Amazon: Summary of the AWS Service Event in the US East Region (2012),
   http://aws.amazon.com/message/67457/

3. Amazon: Using Amazon Web Services for Disaster Recovery. White paper (2012)
4. Associates, C.: ARCServe, http://www.arcserve.com
5. Campello, D., Crespo, C., Verma, A., Rangaswami, R., Jayachandran, P.: Coriolis: Scalable VM Clustering in Clouds. In: USENIX ICAC (2013)
6. Citrix: Citrix Cloud Solution for Disaster Recovery. White paper (2010)
7. Compuware: Performance in the cloud. White paper (2011)
8. Dell: AppAssure (2012),
   http://www.appassure.com/downloads/Dell_AppAssure_Specsheet.pdf
9. EMC, C.: EMC RecoverPoint Support for Cisco MDS 9000 SANTap Service: Intelligent Fabric-based Data Replication. White paper (2007)
10. Ha, K., Pillai, P., Richter, W., Abe, Y., Satyanarayanan, M.: Just-in-time provisioning for cyber foraging. In: ACM Mobisys, pp. 153–166 (2013)
11. IBM: SmartCloud Virtualized Server Recovery,
    http://www-935.ibm.com/services/in/en/it-services/
    smartcloud-virtualized-server-recovery-service.html
12. IBM: Tivoli Endpoint Manager,
    http://www-01.ibm.com/software/tivoli/solutions/endpoint/
13. IBM: Global Mirror Whitepaper. White paper (2008)
14. Jayaram, K.R., Peng, C., Zhang, Z., Kim, M., Chen, H., Lei, H.: An Empirical Analysis of Similarity in Virtual Machine Images. In: ACM Middleware (Industrial Track) (2011)
15. NetApp: Back to Basics: Deduplication (2012),
    https://communities.netapp.com/docs/DOC-9949
16. NeverFail: Continuous Availability Suite: Neverfail Solution Architecture. White paper (2012)
17. Patterson, H., Manley, S., Federwisch, M., Hitz, D., Kleiman, S., Owara, S.: Snapmirror: File system based asynchronous mirroring for disaster recovery. In: USENIX FAST (2002)
18. Rabin, M.O.: Fingerprinting by random polynomials. Tech. Rep. TR-15-81, Center for Research in Computing Technology, Harvard University (1981)
19. Riverbed Technologies: Riverbed Whitewater WAN Optimization and Steelhead Cloud Storage, http://www.riverbed.com
20. Tridgell, A., Mackerras, P.: The rsync algorithm. Tech. Rep. TR-CS-96-05, Australian National University (1996)
21. Viswanathan, B., Verma, A., Krishnamurthy, B., Jayachandran, P., Bhattacharya, K., Ananthanarayanan, R.: Rapid adjustment and adoption to MIaaS clouds. In: ACM Middleware, Industry Track (2012)
22. VMware: vSphere Site Recovery Manager (2012), http://www.vmware.com/files/pdf/products/SRM/VMware-vCenter-SRM-Datasheet.pdf

Cross-Tier Application and Data Partitioning of Web Applications for Hybrid Cloud Deployment

Nima Kaviani, Eric Wohlstadter, and Rodger Lea

{nkaviani,wohlstad}@cs.ubc.ca, rlea@magic.ubc.ca
University of British Columbia, Vancouver, Canada

Abstract. Hybrid cloud deployment offers flexibility in trade-offs between the cost-savings/scalability of the public cloud and control over data resources provided at a private premise. However, this flexibility comes at the expense of complexity in distributing a system over these two locations. For multi-tier web applications, this challenge manifests itself primarily in the partitioning of application- and database-tiers. While there is existing research that focuses on either application-tier or data-tier partitioning, we show that optimized partitioning of web applications benefits from both tiers being considered simultaneously. We present our research on a new cross-tier partitioning approach to help developers make effective trade-offs between performance and cost in a hybrid cloud deployment. In two case studies the approach results in up to 54% reduction in monetary costs compared to a premise only deployment and 56% improvement in execution time compared to a naïve partitioning where application-tier is deployed in the cloud and data-tier is on private infrastructure.

1   Introduction

While there are advantages to deploying Web applications on public cloud infrastructure, many companies wish to retain control over specific resources [8] by keeping them at a private premise. As a result, *hybrid cloud computing*, has become a popular architecture where systems are built to take advantage of both public and private infrastructure to meet different requirements. However, architecting an efficient distributed system across these locations requires significant effort. An effective partitioning should not only guarantee that privacy constraints and performance objectives are met, but also should deliver on one of the primary reasons for using the public cloud, a cheaper deployment.

In this paper we focus on partitioning of Online Transaction Processing (OLTP) style web applications. Such applications are an important target for hybrid architecture due to their popularity. Web applications follow the well known multi-tier architecture, generally consisting of tiers such as: client-tier, application-tier[1] (serving dynamic web content), and back-end data-tier. Since the hybrid architecture is motivated by the management of sensitive data resources, our research focuses on combined partitioning of the data-tier (which hosts data resources) and

---

[1] In the rest of the paper we use the terms code and application-tier interchangeably.

D. Eyers and K. Schwan (Eds.): Middleware 2013, LNCS 8275, pp. 226–246, 2013.
© IFIP International Federation for Information Processing 2013

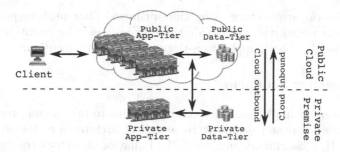

Fig. 1. High-level hybrid architecture with cross-tier partitioning of code and data

the application-tier (which directly uses data resources). Figure 1 shows a high-level diagram of these tiers being jointly partitioned across a hybrid architecture, which we refer to as *cross-tier partitioning*.

Existing research only applies partitioning to one of the application- or data tiers and does not address cross-tier partitioning. Systems such as CloneCloud [11], Cloudward Bound [14], Leymann et al.'s [20], and our own work on MANTICORE [17] partition only software but not data. Other work in the area provides for partitioning of relational databases [18] or Map-Reduce job/data components [6,19,29]. Unfortunately, one cannot "cobble together" a cross-tier solution by using independent results from such approaches. A new approach is needed that integrates application and data partitioning natively. Thus we argue that research into cross-tier partitioning is both *important* and *challenging*.

First, cross-tier partitioning is important because the data-flow between these tiers is tightly coupled. The application-tier can make several queries during its execution, passing information to and from different queries; an example is discussed in Section 2. Even though developers follow best practices to ensure the source code for the business logic and the data access layer are loosely coupled, this loose coupling does not apply to the data-flow. The data-flow crosscuts application- and data-tiers requiring an optimization that considers the two simultaneously. Any optimization must avoid, whenever possible, the latency and bandwidth requirements imposed by distributing such data-flow.

Second, cross-tier partitioning is challenging because it requires an analysis that simultaneously reasons about the execution of application-tier code and data-tier queries. On the one hand, previous work on partitioning of code is not applicable to database queries because it does not account for modeling of query execution plans. On the other hand, existing work on data partitioning does not account for the data-flow or execution footprint of the application-tier [18]. To capture a representation for cross-tier optimization, our contribution in this paper includes a new approach for modeling dependencies across both tiers as a combined *binary integer program* (BIP) [25].

We provide a tool which collects performance profiles of web application execution on a single host and converts it to the BIP format. The BIP is fed to an off-the-shelf optimizer whose output yields suggestions for placement of application- and data-tier components to either public cloud or private premise. Using proper tooling and middleware, a new system can now be distributed across the hybrid architecture using the optimized placement suggestions. To the best of our knowledge, we provide the first approach for partitioning which integrates models of both application-tier and data-tier execution.

2   Motivating Scenario

As a motivating example, assume a company plans to take its on-premise trading software system and deploy it to a hybrid architecture. We use Apache DayTrader [1], a benchmark emulating the behavior of a stock trading system, to express this scenario. DayTrader implements business logic in the application-tier as different request types, for example, allowing users to login (doLogin), view/update their account information (doAccount & doAccountUpdate), etc. At the data-tier it consists of tables storing data for account, accountprofile, holding, quote, etc. Let us further assume that, as part of company regulations, user information (account & accountprofile) must remain on-premise.

Figure 2 shows the output of our cross-tier partitioning for doLogin. The figure shows the call-tree of function execution in the application-tier as well as data-tier query plans at the leaves. In the figure, we see four categories of components: (i) data on premise shown as black nodes, (ii) data in the cloud as square nodes, (iii) functions on premise as gray nodes, and (iv) functions in the cloud as white nodes. Here we use each of these four categories to motivate cross-tier partitioning.

First, some data is not suitable for deployment in the cloud due to privacy concerns or regulations [14]. Thus, many enterprises avoid committing deployment of certain data in the public cloud, instead hosting it on private infrastructure (e.g., account & accountprofile in Figure 2). Our primary usecase here is to support cases with restrictions on where data is stored not where it flows.

Second, function execution requires CPU resources which are generally cheaper and easier to scale in the public cloud (some reports claim a typical 80% savings using public cloud versus on-premise private systems [21]). Thus placing function execution in the public cloud is useful to limit the amount of on-premise infrastructure. On the other hand, sunk cost of existing hardware encourages some private deployments. So without regard to other factors, we would want to execute application-tier functions in the cloud and yet utilize existing hardware.

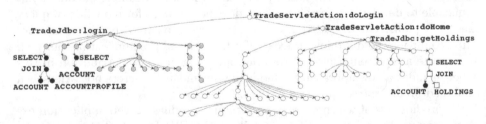

Fig. 2. A cross-tier partitioning suggested by our tool for the doLogin request from DayTrader showing a partitioned application- and data-tier: data on premise (black nodes), data in the cloud (square nodes), functions on premise (gray nodes), and functions in the cloud (white nodes)

Third, since we would like to deploy functions to the cloud, the associated data bound to those functions should be deployed to the cloud, otherwise we will incur additional latency and bandwidth usage. So there is motivation to move non-sensitive data to the cloud. However, such non-sensitive data may be bound to sensitive data through queries which operate over both. For this reason, moving non-sensitive data to the public cloud is not always a winning proposition. We will need an analysis which can reason about the benefit of moving data closer to functions executing in the public cloud versus the drawback of pulling it away from the sensitive data on premise.

Finally, executing all functions in the public cloud is also not always a winning proposition. Some functions are written as transactions over several data resources. Such functions may incur too much communication overhead if they execute in the public cloud but operate on private premise data. So the benefit of executing them in the cloud needs to be balanced with this overhead.

These four cases help to illustrate the inter-dependencies between the application-tier and data-tier. In the case of doLogin, a developer may manually arrive at a similar partitioning with only minor inconvenience. However, to cover an entire application, developers need to simultaneously reason about the effects of component placements across all request types. This motivates the need for research on automation for cross-tier partitioning.

3   Background: Application-Tier Partitioning

Binary Integer Programming [25] has been utilized previously for partitioning of applications (although not for cross-tier partitioning) [10,17,22,30]. A binary integer program (BIP) consists of the following:

- Binary variables: A set of binary variables $x_1, x_2, ..., x_n \in \{0, 1\}$.
- Constraints: A set of linear constraints between variables where each constraint has the form: $c_0 x_0 + c_1 x_1 + ... + c_n x_n \{\leq, =, \geq\} c_m$ and c_i is a constant.
- Objective: A linear expression to minimize or maximize: $cost_1 x_1 + cost_2 x_2 + ... + cost_n x_n$, with $cost_i$ being the cost charged to the model when $x_i = 1$. The job of a BIP optimizer is to choose the set of values for the binary variables which minimize/maximize this expression.

Formulating a cross-tier BIP for partitioning will require combining one BIP for the application-tier and another for the data-tier. Creating each BIP consists of the same high-level steps (although the specific details vary): (i) profiling, (ii) analysis, (iii) generating the BIP constraints and (iv) generating the BIP objective function. The overall process of applying cross-tier partitioning is shown in Figure 3. In the top left we see an application before partitioning. Notice that the profiling results are split in two branches. Here we focus on the flow following from the Profiling Logs branch, discussing the Explain Plan flow in Section 4. Our approach for generating a BIP for the application-tier follows from our previous work on MANTICORE [17] and is summarized as background here.

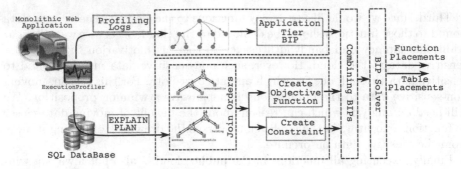

Fig. 3. The overall process of applying cross-tier partitioning to a monolithic web application (process flows from left to right)

Profiling: The typical profiling process for application partitioning starts by taking existing software and applying instrumentation of its binaries. The software is then exercised on representative workloads, using the instrumentation to collect data on measured CPU usage of software functions and data exchange between them. This log of profiling information will be converted to the relevant variables and costs of a BIP.

Analysis: The log of profile data is converted to a graph model before being converted to a BIP, as shown in the top flow of Figure 3. Let $App(V, E)$ represent a model of the application, where $\forall v \in V$, v corresponds to a function execution in the application. Similarly $\forall u, v \in V$, $e_{(u,v)} \in E$ implies that there is data exchange between functions in the application corresponding to u and v in *App*. $\forall e_{(u,v)} \in E$, we define $d_{u \leftrightarrow v}$ as the amount of data exchanged between u to v.

BIP Constraints: The graph model is then used to formulate a BIP. For every node u in the model we consider a variable $x_u \in \{0, 1\}$. Using input from a developer some nodes can be constrained to a particular location by fixing their value, e.g., (0: private premise, 1: public cloud). Unconstrained variables are free for an optimizer to choose their values so as to minimize the objective function. These values are then translated to placement decisions for function executions.

BIP Objective: For each $v \in V$ we define $cost_{exec_v}$ to represent the cost of executing v on-premise and $cost'_{exec_v}$ to represent cost of executing v in the cloud. We also define $latency_{(u,v)}$ to represent the latency cost on edge $e_{(u,v)}$ and calculate the communication cost ($cost_{comm_{u,v}}$) for edge $e_{(u,v)}$ as follows:

$$cost_{comm_{u,v}} = latency_{(u,v)} + \frac{d_{u \leftrightarrow v}}{D_{unit}} \times cost_{comm_{unit}} \qquad (1)$$

where D_{unit} would be the unit of data to which cloud data charges are applied and $cost_{comm_{unit}}$ would be the cloud charges for D_{unit} of data transfer, and $d_{u \leftrightarrow v}$ represents data exchange between vertices u and v. As demonstrated by work such as Cloudward Bound [14], in a cloud computing setting such raw performance costs such as measured CPU usage and data transfer can be converted to monetary costs using the advertised infrastructure costs of vendors such as Amazon EC2. This allows developers to optimize for trade-offs in performance cost and monetary cost objectives.

Using such costs we can define an objective expression (The non-linear expression in the objective function can be relaxed by making the expansion in [22]):

$$\min \sum_{i \in V} x_i cost_{exec_i} + \sum_{(i,j) \in E} (x_i - x_j)^2 cost_{comm_{i,j}} \qquad (2)$$

Finally, the BIP is fed to a solver which determines an assignment of functions to locations. By choosing the location for each function execution, the optimizer chooses an efficient partitioning by placing functions in the cloud when possible if it does not introduce too much additional latency or bandwidth requirements.

Different from previous work, our cross-tier partitioning incorporates a new BIP model of query plan execution into this overall process. In the next section, we describe these details which follow the bottom flow of Figure 3.

4   BIP for Data-Tier Partitioning

The technical details of extending application-tier partitioning to integrate the data-tier are motivated by four requirements: (i) weighing the benefits of distributing queries, (ii) comparing the trade-offs between join orders, (iii) taking into account intra-request data-dependencies and (iv) providing a query execution model comparable to application-tier function execution. In this section, we first further motivate cross-tier partitioning by describing each of these points, then we cover the technical details for the steps of partitioning as they relate to the data-tier. We focus on a data-tier implemented with a traditional SQL database. While some web application workloads can benefit from the use of alternative NoSQL techniques, we chose to focus initially on SQL due to its generality and widespread adoption.

First, as described in Section 2, placing more of the less-sensitive data in the cloud will allow for the corresponding code from the application-tier to also be placed in the cloud, thus increasing the overall efficiency of the deployment and reducing data transfer. However, this can result in splitting the set of tables used in a query across public and private locations. For our DayTrader example, each user can have many stocks in her holdings which makes the HOLDING table quite large. As shown in Figure 2, splitting the *join* operation can push the HOLDINGS table to the cloud (square nodes) and eliminate the traffic of moving its data to the cloud. This splitting also maintains our constraint to have the privacy sensitive ACCOUNT table on the private premise. An effective modeling of the data-tier needs to help the BIP optimizer reason about the trade-offs of distributing such queries across the hybrid architecture.

Second, the order that tables are joined can have an effect not only on traditional processing time but also on round-trip latency. We use a running example throughout this section of the query shown in Figure 4, with two different join orders, left and right. If the query results are processed in the public cloud

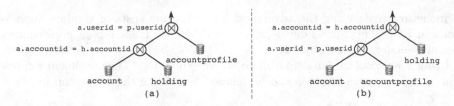

Fig. 4. Two possible query plans from one of the queries in DayTrader:
SELECT p.*, h.* FROM holding h, accountprofile p, account a WHERE
h.accountid = a.accountid AND a.userid = p.userid AND h.quote_symbol = ?
AND a.accountid = ?

where the HOLDING table is in the cloud and ACCOUNT and ACCOUNTPROFILE
are stored on the private premise, then the plan on the left will incur two-round
trips from the public to private locations for distributed processing. On the other
hand, the query on the right only requires one round-trip. Modeling the data-
tier should help the BIP optimizer reason about the cost of execution plans for
different placements of tables.

Third, some application requests execute more than one query. In these cases,
it may be beneficial to partition functions to group execution with data at a
single location. Such grouping helps to eliminate latency overhead otherwise
needed to move data to the location where the application-tier code executes.
An example of this is shown in Figure 2, where a sub-tree of function executions
for TradeJdbc:login are labeled as "private" (gray nodes). By pushing this sub-
tree to the private premise, the computation needed for working over ACCOUNT
and ACCOUNTPROFILE data in the two queries under TradeJdbc:login can be
completed at the premise without multiple round-trips between locations.

Fourth, since the trade-offs on function placement depend on the placement
of data and vice-versa, we need a model that can reason simultaneously about
both application-tier function execution and query plan execution. Thus the
model for the data-tier should be compatible for integration with an approach
to application partitioning such as the one described in Section 3.

Having motivated the need for a model of query execution to incorporate
the data-tier in a cross-tier partitioning, we now explore the details, following
the bottom flow of Figure 3. The overall process is as follows. We first, profile
query execution using EXPLAIN PLAN (Section 4.1). This information is used
to collect statistics for query plan operators by interrogating the database for
different join orders (Section 4.2). The statistics are then used to generate both
BIP constraints (Section 4.3) and a BIP objective function (Section 4.4). Finally,
these constraints and objective are combined with that from the application-tier
to encode a cross-tier partitioning model for a BIP solver.

4.1   Database Profiling with EXPLAIN PLAN

Profiling information is available for query execution through the EXPLAIN
PLAN SQL command. Given a particular query, this command provides a tree-
structured result set detailing the execution of the query. We use a custom JDBC

driver wrapper to collect information on the execution of queries. During application profiling (cf. Section 3) whenever a query is issued by the application-tier, our JDBC wrapper intercepts the query and collects the plan for its execution. The plan returned by the database contains the following information:

1. type(*op*): Each node in the query plan is an operator such as a join, table access, selection (i.e. filter), sort, etc. To simplify presentation of the technical details, we assume that each operator is either a join or a table access. Other operators are handled by our implementation but they don't add extra complexity compared to a join operator. For example, in Figure 4, the selection (i.e. filter) operators are elided. We leverage the database's own cost model directly by recording from the provided plan how much each operator costs. Hence, we don't need to evaluate different operator implementations to evaluate their costs. On the other hand, we do need to handle joins specially because table placement is greatly affected by their ordering.
2. cpu(*op*): This statistic gives the expected time of execution for a specific operator. In general, we assume that the execution of a request in a hybrid web application will be dominated by the CPU processing of the application-tier and the network latency. So in many cases, this statistic is negligible. However, we include it to detect the odd case of expensive query operations which can benefit from executing on the public cloud.
3. size(*op*): This statistic captures the expected number of bytes output by an operator which is equal to the expected number of rows times the size of each retrieved row. From the perspective of the plan tree-structure, this is the data which flows from a child operator to its parent.
4. predicates(*joinOp*): Each join operator combines two inputs based on a set of predicates which relate those inputs. We use these predicates to determine if alternative join orders are possible for a query.

When profiling the application, the profiler observes and collects execution statistics only for plans that get executed but not for alternative join orders. However, the optimal plan executed by the database engine in a distributed hybrid deployment can be different from the one observed during profiling. In order to make the BIP partitioner aware of alternative orders, we have extended our JDBC wrapper to consult the database engine and examine the alternatives by utilizing a combination of EXPLAIN PLAN and join order hints. Our motivation is to leverage the already existing cost model from a production database for cost estimation of local operator processing, while still covering the space of all query plans. The profiler also captures which sets of tables are accessed together as part of an atomic transaction. This information is used to model additional costs of applying a two-phase commit protocol, should the tables get partitioned.

4.2   Join Order Enumeration

We need to encode enough information in the BIP so it can reason over all possible plans. Otherwise, the BIP optimizer would mistakenly assume that the plan executed during our initial profiling is the only one possible. For example, during initial profiling on a single host, we may only observe the left plan from Figure 4. However, in the example scenario, we saw that the right plan introduces fewer round-trips across a hybrid architecture. We need to make sure the right plan is accounted for when deciding about table placement. Our strategy to collect the necessary information for all plans consists of two steps: (i) gather statistics for all operators in all plans irrespective of how they are joined, and (ii) encode BIP constraints about how the operators from step (i) can be joined. Here we describe step 1 and then describe step 2 in the next subsection. The novelty of our approach is that instead of optimizing to a specific join order in isolation of the structure of application-tier execution, we encode the possible orders together with the BIP of the application-tier as a combined BIP.

As is commonly the case in production databases, we assume a query plan to be left-deep. In a left-deep query plan, a join takes two inputs: one from a single base relation (i.e. table) providing immediate input (referred to as the "inner relation"); and another one potentially derived as an intermediate result from a different set of relations (the "outer relation"). The identity of the inner relation and the set of tables comprising the outer relation uniquely determine the estimated best cost for an individual join operator. This is true regardless of the join order in which the outer relation was derived [26]. For convenience in our presentation, we call this information the operator's *id*, because we use it to represent an operator in the BIP. For example, the root operator in Figure 4a takes ACCOUNTPROFILE as an inner input and {HOLDING, ACCOUNT} as an outer input. The operator's id is then {(HOLDING, ACCOUNT), ACCOUNTPROFILE}. We will refer to the union of these two inputs as a *join set* (the set of tables joined by that operator). For example, the join set of the aforementioned operator is {HOLDING, ACCOUNT, ACCOUNTPROFILE}. Notably, while the join sets for the roots of Figures 4a & 4b are the same, Figures 4b's root node has the operator id {(ACCOUNTPROFILE, ACCOUNT), HOLDING} allowing us to differentiate the operators in our BIP formulation. Our task in this section is to collect statistics for the possible join operators with unique ids.

Most databases provide the capability for developers to provide hints to the query optimizer in order to force certain joins. For example in Oracle, a developer can use the hint LEADING(X, Y, Z, ...). This tells the optimizer to create a plan where X and Y are joined first, then their intermediate result is joined with Z, etc. We use this capability to extract statistics for all join orders.

```
1  Function collectOperatorStats(Q)
2      tables ← getTables(Q);
3      for i ← 1 to |tables| do
4          foreach t ∈ tables do
5              foreach S ∈ P_i(tables − {t}) do
6                  if isJoinable(S, t) then
7                      explainPlanWithLeadingRelations(S, t);
```

Algorithm 1. Function to collect statistics for alternative query plan operators for the input query Q. $\mathcal{P}_i$ is the powerset operator over sets of size i.

Algorithm 1 takes as input a query observed during profiling. In line 2, we extract the set of all tables referenced in the query. Next, we start collecting operator statistics for joins over two tables and progressively expand the size through each iteration of the loop on line 3. The table t, selected for each iteration of line 4 can be considered as the inner input of a join. Then, on line 5 we loop through all sets of tables of size i which don't contain t. On line 6, we verify if t is joinable with the set S by making sure that at least one table in the set S shares a join (access) predicate with t. This set forms the outer input to a join. Finally, on line 7, we collect statistics for this join operator by forcing the database to explain a plan in which the join order is prefixed by the outer input set, followed by the inner input relation. We record the information for each operator by associating it with its id. For example, consider Figure 4 as the input Q to Algorithm 1. In a particular iteration of line 5, i might be chosen as 2 and t as ACCOUNTPROFILE. Since ACCOUNTPROFILE has a predicate shared with ACCOUNT, S could be chosen as the set of size 2: {ACCOUNT, HOLDINGS}. Now on line 6, `explainPlanWithLeadingTables`({ACCOUNT, HOLDINGS}, AC-COUNTPROFILE) will get called and the statistics for the join operator with the corresponding id will get recorded.

The bottom-up structure of the algorithm follows similarly to the classic dynamic programming algorithm for query optimization [26]. However, in our case we make calls into the database to extract costs by leveraging EXPLAIN PLAN and the `LEADING` hint. The complexity of Algorithm 1 is $O(2^n)$ (where n is the number of tables in each single query); i.e., same as the classic algorithm for query optimization [26], so our approach scales in a similar fashion. Even though Algorithm 1's complexity is exponential, queries typically operate on an order of tens of tables.

4.3   BIP Constraints

Now that we know the statistics for all operators with a unique id, we need to instruct the BIP how they can be composed. Our general strategy is to model each query plan operator, op, as a binary variable in a BIP. The variable will take on the value 1 if the operator is part of the query plan which minimizes the objective of the BIP and 0 otherwise. Each possible join set is also modeled as a variable. Constraints are used to create a connection between operators

Table 1. Constraint generation functions

Function	`genChoice`($joinSet$, $\{op_1 \ldots op_n\}$)
Generated constraint	$op_1 + \ldots + op_n = joinSet$
Description	a $joinSet$ is produced by one and only one of the operators $op_1 \ldots op_n$
Function	`genInputConstraint`(op, $\{in_{left}, in_{right}\}$)
Generated constraint	$-2 \times op + in_{left} + in_{right} \geq 0$
Description	If op is 1, then variables representing its left and right inputs (in_{left} and in_{right}) must both be 1

```
1  Function createConstraints(joinSet)
2  |   ops ← getOperatorsForJoinSet(joinSet);
3  |   genChoice(joinSet, ops);
4  |   foreach op ∈ ops do
5  |   |   inputs ← getInputs(op);
6  |   |   genInputConstraint(op, inputs);
7  |   |   if sizeof(left(inputs)) > 0 then
8  |   |   |   createConstraints(left(inputs));
```

Algorithm 2. Constraint generation, using functions from Table 1. The details for the functions getOperatorsForJoinSet, getInputs, sizeof, and left are not shown but their uses are described in the text.

that create a join set and operators that consume a join set (cf. Table 1). The optimizer will choose a plan having the least cost given both the optimizers choice of table placement and function execution placement (for the application-tier). Each operator also has associated variables op_{cloud} and $op_{premise}$ which indicate the placement of the operator. Table placement is controlled by each table's associated table access operators. The values of these variables for operators in the same query plan will allow us to model the communication costs associated with distributed queries.

Our algorithm to formulate these composition constraints makes use of two helper functions as shown in Table 1, namely genChoice and genInputConstraint. When these functions are called by our algorithms, they append the generated constraint to the BIP that was already built for the application-tier. The first function, genChoice, encodes that a particular join set may be derived by multiple possible join operators (e.g., {HOLDING, ACCOUNT, ACCOUNTPROFILE} could be derived by either of the root nodes in Figure 4). The second function, genInputConstraint, encodes that a particular join operator takes as inputs the join sets of its two children. It ensures that if op is selected, both its children's join sets (in_{left} and in_{right}) are selected as well, constraining which subtrees of the execution plan can appear under this operator. The "$\geq$" inequality in Table 1 helps to encode the boolean logic $op \rightarrow in_{left} \wedge in_{right}$.

Starting with the final output join set of a query, Algorithm 2 recursively generates these constraints encoding choices between join operators and how parent operators are connected to their children. It starts on line 2 by calling a function to retrieve all operator ids which could produce that join set (these operators were all collected during the execution of Algorithm 1). It passes this information to genChoice on line 3. On line 4, we loop over all these operator ids, decomposing each into its two inputs on line 5. This information is then passed to genInputConstraint. Finally on line 7, we test for the base case of a table access operator. If we have not hit the base case, then the left input becomes the join set for recursion on line 8.

4.4   BIP Objective

Creating the optimization objective function consists of two parts: (i) determining the costs associated with the execution of individual operators, and (ii) creating a mathematical formulation of those costs. The magnitude of the execution cost for each operator and the communication cost between operators that are split across the network are computed using a similar cost model to previous work [31]. This accounts for the variation between local execution and distributed execution in that the latter will make use of a semi-join optimization to reduce costs (i.e. input data to a distributed join operator will transmit only the columns needed to collect matching rows). We extend the previous cost model to account for possible transaction delays. We assume that if the tables involved in an atomic transaction are split across the cloud and the private premise, by default the transaction will be resolved using the two-phase commit protocol.

Performance overhead from atomic two-phase distributed transactions comes primarily from two sources: protocol overhead and lock contention. Protocol overhead is caused by the latency of prepare and commit messages in a database's two-phase commit protocol. Lock contention is caused by queuing delay which increases as transactions over common table rows become blocked. We provide two alternatives to account for such overhead:

- For some transactions, lock contention is negligible. This is because the application semantics don't induce sharing of table rows between multiple user sessions. For example, in DayTrader, although ACCOUNT and HOLDINGS tables are involved in an atomic transaction, specific rows of these tables are only ever accessed by a single user concurrently. In such cases we charge the cost of two extra round-trips between the cloud and the private premise to the objective function, one to prepare the remote site for the transaction and another to commit it.
- For cases where lock contention is expected to be considerable, developers can request that certain tables be co-located in any partitioning suggested by our tool. This prevents locking for transactions over those tables to be delayed by network latency. Since such decisions require knowledge of appli-

Table 2. Functions for generating objective helper constraints

Function	genAtMostOneLocation(op)
Generated constraint	$op_{cloud} + op_{premise} = op$
Description	If the variable representing op is 1, then either the variable representing it being placed in the cloud is 1 or the variable representing it being place in the premise is 1
Function	genSeparated(op_1, op_2)
Generated constraint	$op_{1cloud} + op_{2premise} - cut_{op_1,op_2} \leq 1$ $op_{1premise} + op_{2cloud} - cut_{op_1,op_2} \leq 1$
Description	If the variables representing the locations of two operators are different, then the variable cut_{op_1,op_2} is 1

cation semantics that are difficult to infer automatically, our tool provides an interactive visualization of partitioning results, as shown in Figure 2. This allows developers to work through different "what-if" scenarios of table co-location constraints and the resulting suggested partitioning. We plan to further assist developers in making their decisions by profiling the frequency for concurrent transactions to update rows.

Next, we need to encode information on CPU and data transmission costs into the objective function. In addition to generating a BIP objective, we will need some additional constraints that ensure the calculated objective is actually feasible. Table 2 shows functions to generate these constraints. The first constraint specifies that if an operator is included as part of a chosen query plan (its associated id variable is set to 1), then either the auxiliary variable op_{cloud} or $op_{premise}$ will have to be 1 but not both. This enforces a single placement location for op. The second builds on the first and toggles the auxiliary variable cut_{op_1,op_2} when op_{1cloud} and $op_{2premise}$ are 1, or when $op_{1premise}$ and op_{2cloud} are 1.

The objective function itself is generated using two functions in Table 3. The first possibly charges to the objective function either the execution cost of the operator on the cloud infrastructure or on the premise infrastructure. Note that it will never charge both due to the constraints of Table 2. The second function

Table 3. Functions for generating objective function

Function	genExecutionCost(op)
Generated objective component	$op_{cloud} \times$ **execCost**$_{cloud}(op)$ + $op_{premise} \times$ **execCost**$_{premise}(op)$
Description	If the variable representing op deployed in the cloud/premise is 1, then charge the associated cost of executing it in the cloud/premise respectively
Function	genCommCost(op_1, op_2)
Generated objective component	$cut_{op_1,op_2} \times$ **commCost**(op_1, op_2)
Description	If cut_{op_1,op_2} for two operators op_1 and op_2 was set to 1, then charge their cost of communication

```
1  Function createObjFunction(joinSet)
2      ops ← getOperatorsForJoinSet(joinSet);
3      foreach op ∈ ops do
4          genAtMostOneLocation(op);
5          genExecutionCost(op);
6          inputs ← getInputs(op);
7          foreach input ∈ inputs do
8              foreach childOp ∈ getOperatorsForJoinSet(input) do
9                  genSeparated(op, childOp);
10                 genCommCost(op, childOp);
11         if sizeof(left(inputs)) > 0 then
12             createObjFunction(left(inputs));
```

Algorithm 3. Objective generation

charges the communication cost between two operators if the associated *cut* variable was set to 1. In the case that there is no communication between two operators this cost is simply 0.

Algorithm 3 takes a join set as input and follows a similar structure to Algorithm 2. The outer loop on line 3, iterates over each operator that could produce the particular join set. It generates the location constraints on line 4 and the execution cost component to the objective function on line 5. Next, on line 7, it iterates over the two inputs to the operator. For each, it extracts the operators that could produce that input (line 8) and generates the communication constraint and objective function component. Finally, if the left input is not a base relation (line 11), it recurses using the left input now as the next join set.

Having appended the constraints and objective components associated with query execution to the application-tier BIP, we make a connection between the two by encoding the dependency between each function that executes a query and the possible root operators for the associated query plan.

5   Implementation

We have implemented our cross-tier partitioning as a framework. It conducts profiling, partitioning, and distribution of web applications which have their business logic implemented in Java. Besides the profiling data, the analyzer also accepts a declarative XML policy and cost parameters. The cost parameters encode the monetary costs charged by a chosen cloud infrastructure provider and expected environmental parameters such as available bandwidth and network latency. The declarative policy allows for specification of database table placement and co-location constraints. In general we consider the placement of privacy sensitive data to be the primary consideration for partitioning decisions. However, developers may wish to monitor and constrain the placement of function executions that operate over this sensitive data. For this purpose we rely on existing work using taint tracking [9] which we have integrated into our profiler.

For partitioning, we use the off-the-shelf integer programming solver lp_solve [2] to solve the discussed BIP optimization problem. The results lead to generating a *distribution plan* describing which entities need to be separated from one another (*cut-points*). A cut-point may separate functions from one another, functions from data, and data from one another. Separation of code and data is achievable by accessing the database engine through the database driver. Separating inter-code or inter-data dependencies requires extra middleware.

For functions, we have developed a bytecode rewriting engine as well as an HTTP remoting library that takes the partitioning plan generated by the analyzer, injects remoting code at each *cut-point*, and serializes data between the two locations. This remoting instrumentation is essentially a simplified version of J-Orchestra [28] implemented over HTTP (but is not yet as complete as the original J-Orchestra work). In order to allow for distribution of data entities, we have taken advantage of Oracle's distributed database management system (DDBMS). This allows for tables remote to a local Oracle DBMS, to be identified and queried for data through the local Oracle DBMS. This is possible by providing a database link (@dblink) between the local and the remote DBMS systems. Once a bidirectional dblink is established, the two databases can execute SQL statements targeting tables from one another. This allows us to use the distribution plan from our analyzer system to perform vertical sharding at the level of database tables. Note that the distributed query engine acts on the deployment of a system after a decision about the placement of tables has been made by our partitioning algorithm. We have provided an Eclipse plugin implementation of the analyzer framework available online [3].

6   Evaluation

We evaluate our work using two different applications: *DayTrader* [1] and *RU-BiS* [4]. DayTrader (cf. Section 2) is a Java benchmark of a stock trading system. RUBiS implements the functionality of an auctioning Web site. Both applications have already been used in evaluating previous cloud computing research [16,27].

We can have 9 possible deployment variations with each of the data-tier and the application tier being (i) on the private premise, (ii) on the public cloud, or (iii) partitioned for hybrid deployment. Out of all the placements we eliminate the 3 that place all data in the cloud as it contradicts the constraints to have privacy sensitive information on-premise. Also, we consider deployments with only data partitioned as a subset of deployments with both code and data partitioned, and thus do not provide separate deployments for them. The remaining four models deployed for evaluations were as follows: (i) both code and data are deployed to the premise (*Private-Premise*); (ii) data is on-premise and code is in the cloud (*Naïve-Hybrid*); (iii) data is on-premise and code is partitioned (*Split-Code*); and (iv) both data and code are partitioned (*Cross-Tier*).

For both DayTrader and RUBiS, we consider privacy incentives to be the reason behind constraining placement for some database tables. As such, when partitioning data, we constrain tables storing user information (account and accountprofile for DayTrader and users for RUBiS) to be placed on-premise. The remaining tables are allowed to be flexibly placed on-premise or in the cloud.

We used the following setup for the evaluation: for the premise machines, we used two 3.5 GHz dual core machines with 8.0 GB of memory, one as the application server and another as our database server. Both machines were located at our lab in Vancouver, and were connected through a 100 Mb/sec data link. For the cloud machines, we used an extra large EC2 instance with 8 EC2 Compute Units and 7.0 GB of memory as our application server and another extra large instance as our database server. Both machines were leased from Amazon's US West region (Oregon) and were connected by a 1 Gb/sec data link. We use Jetty as the Web server and Oracle 11g Express Edition as the database servers. We measured the round-trip latency between the cloud and our lab to be 15 milliseconds. Our intentions for choosing these setups is to create an environment where the cloud offers the faster and more scalable environment. To generate load for the deployments, we launched simulated clients from a 3.0 GHz quad core machine with 8 GB of memory located in our lab in Vancouver. DayTrader comes with a random client workload generator with uniform distribution on all requests. For RUBiS, we used its embedded client simulator in its *buy mode*, with an 80-20 ratio of browse-to-buy request distribution. In the rest of this section we provide the following evaluation results for the four deployments described above: execution times (Section 6.1), expected monetary deployment costs (Section 6.2), and scalability under varying load (Section 6.3).

6.1   Evaluation of Performance

We measured the execution time across all business logic functionality in Day-Trader and RUBiS under a load of 100 requests per second, for ten minutes. By execution time we mean the elapsed wall clock time from the beginning to the end of each servlet execution. Figure 5 shows those with largest average execution times. We model a situation where CPU resources are not under significant load. As shown in Figure 5, execution time in cross-tier partitioning is significantly better than any other model of hybrid deployment and is closely comparable to a non-distributed private premise deployment. As an example, response time for DayTrader's `doLogin` under *Cross-Tier* is 50% faster than *Naïve-Hybrid* while `doLogin`'s response time for *Cross-Tier* is only 5% slower compared to *Private-Premise* (i.e., the lowest bar in the graph). It can also be seen that, for `doLogin`, *Cross-Tier* has 25% better response time compared to *Split-Code*, showing its effectiveness compared to partitioning only at the application-tier.

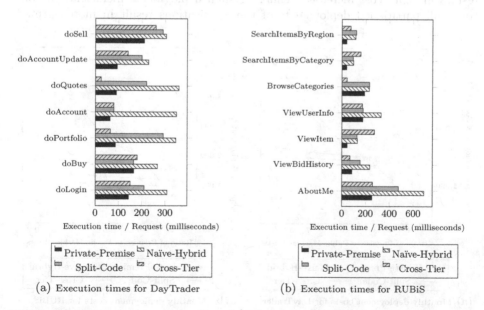

(a) Execution times for DayTrader   (b) Execution times for RUBiS

Fig. 5. Measured execution times for selected request types in the four deployments of DayTrader and RUBiS

Similarly for other business logic functionality, we note that cross-tier partitioning achieves considerable performance improvements when compared to other distributed deployment models. It results in performance measures broadly similar to a full premise deployment. For the case of DayTrader - across all business logic functionality of Figure 5a - *Cross-Tier* results in an overall performance improvement of 56% compared to *Naïve-Hybrid* and a performance improvement of around 45% compared to *Split-Code*.

We observed similar performance improvements for RUBiS. *Cross-Tier* RUBiS performs 28.3% better - across all business logic functionality of Figure 5b - compared to its *Naïve-Hybrid*, and 15.2% better compared to *Split-Code*. Based on the results, cross-tier partitioning provides more flexibility for moving function execution to the cloud and can significantly increase performance for a hybrid deployment of an application.

6.2   Evaluation of Deployment Costs

For computing monetary costs of deployments, we use parameters taken from the advertised Amazon EC2 service where the cost of an extra large EC2 instance is $0.48/hour and the cost of data transfer is $0.12/GB. To evaluate deployment costs, we apply these machine and data transfer costs to the performance results from Section 6.1, scale the ten minute deployment times to one month, and gradually change the ratio of premise-to-cloud deployment costs to assess the effects of varying cost of private premise on the overall deployment costs.

As shown in both graphs, a *Private-Premise* deployment of web applications results in rapid cost increases, rendering such deployments inefficient. In contrast, all partitioned deployments of the applications result in more optimal

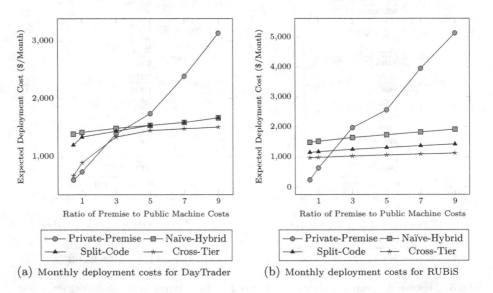

(a) Monthly deployment costs for DayTrader   (b) Monthly deployment costs for RUBiS

Fig. 6. Monthly cost comparison for different deployments of DayTrader and RUBiS

deployments with *Cross-Tier* being the most efficient. For a cloud cost 80% cheaper than the private-premise cost (5 times ratio), DayTrader's *Cross-Tier* is 20.4% cheaper than *Private-Premise* and 11.8% cheaper than *Naïve-Hybrid* and *Split-Code* deployments. RUBiS achieves even better cost savings with *Cross-Tier* being 54% cheaper than *Private-Premise*, 29% cheaper than *Naïve-Hybrid*, and 12% cheaper than *Split-Code*. As shown in Figure 6a, in cases where only code is partitioned, a gradual increase in costs for machines on-premise eventually results in the algorithm pushing more code to the cloud to the point where all code is in the cloud and all data is on-premise. In such a situation *Split-Code* eventually converges to *Naïve-Hybrid*; i.e., pushing all the code to the cloud. Similarly, *Cross-Tier* will finally stabilize. However since in *Cross-Tier* part of the data is also moved to the cloud, the overall cost is lower than *Naïve-Hybrid* and *Split-Code*.

6.3   Evaluation of Scalability

We also performed scalability analyses for both DayTrader and RUBiS to see how different placement choices affect application throughput. For both Day-Trader and RUBiS we used a range of 10 to 1000 client threads to send requests to the applications in 5 minute intervals with 1 minute ramp-up. Results are shown in Figure 7. As the figure shows, for both applications, after the number of requests reaches a certain threshold, *Private-Premise* becomes overloaded. For *Naïve-Hybrid* and *Split-Code*, the applications progressively provide better throughput. However, due to the significant bottleneck when accessing the data, both deployments maintain a consistent but rather low throughput during their executions. Finally, *Cross-Tier* achieved the best scalability. With a big portion

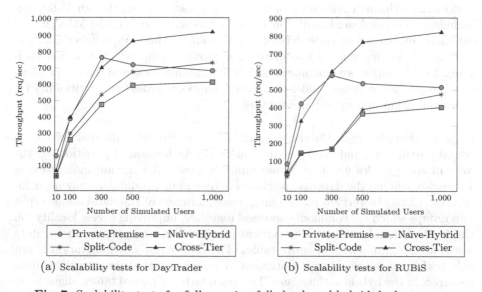

(a) Scalability tests for DayTrader   (b) Scalability tests for RUBiS

Fig. 7. Scalability tests for full premise, full cloud, and hybrid deployments

of the data in the cloud, the underlying resources for both code and data can scale to reach a much better overall throughput for the applications. Despite having part of the data on the private premise, due to its small size the database machine on premise gets congested at a slower rate and the deployment can keep a high throughput.

7   Related Work

Our research bridges the two areas of application and database partitioning but differs from previous work in that it uses a new BIP formulation that considers both areas. Our focus is not on providing all of the many features provided by every previous project either on application partitioning or database partitioning. Instead, we have focused on providing a new interface between the two using our combined BIP. We describe the differences in more detail by first describing some related work in application partitioning and then database partitioning.

Application Partitioning: Coign [15] is an example of classic application partitioning research which provides partitioning of Microsoft COM components. Other work focuses specifically on partitioning of web/mobile applications such as Swift [10], Hilda [30], and AlfredO [24]. However that work is focused on partitioning the application-tier in order to off-load computation from the server-side to a client. That work does not handle partitioning of the data-tier.

Minimizing cost and improving performance for deployment of software services has also been the focus of cloud computing research [19]. While approaches like Volley [6] reduce network traffic by relocating data, others like CloneCloud [11], Cloudward Bound[14], and our own MANTICORE [17] improve performance through relocation of server components. Even though Volley examines data dependencies and CloneCloud, Cloudward Bound, and MANTICORE examine component or code dependencies, none of these approaches combine code and data dependencies to drive their partitioning and distribution decisions. In this paper, we demonstrated how combining code and data dependencies can provide a richer model that better supports cross-tier partitioning for web application in a hybrid architecture.

Database Partitioning: Database partitioning is generally divided into horizontal partitioning and vertical partitioning [7]. In horizontal partitioning, the rows of some tables are split across multiple hosts. A common motivation is for load-balancing the database workload across multiple database manager instances [12,23]. In vertical partitioning, some columns of the database are split into groups which are commonly accessed together, improving access locality [5]. Unlike traditional horizontal or vertical partitioning, our partitioning of data works at the granularity of entire tables. This is because our motivation is not only performance based but is motivated by policies on the management of data resources in the hybrid architecture. The granularity of logical tables aligns more naturally than columns with common business policies and access controls. That being said, we believe if motivated by the right use-case, our technical approach could likely be extended for column-level partitioning as well.

8 Limitations, Future Work, and Conclusion

While our approach simplifies manual reasoning for hybrid cloud partitioning, it requires some input from a developer. First, we require a representative workload for profiling. Second, a developer may need to provide input about the impact that atomic transactions have on partitioning. After partitioning, a developer may also want to consider changes to the implementation to handle some transactions in an alternative fashion, e.g. providing forward compensation [13]. Also as noted, our current implementation and experience is limited to Java-based web applications and SQL-based databases.

In future work we plan to support a more loosely coupled service-oriented architecture for partitioning applications. Our current implementation of data-tier partitioning relies on leveraging the distributed query engine from a production database. In some environments, relying on a homogeneous integration of data by the underlying platform may not be realistic. We are currently working to automatically generate REST interfaces to integrate data between the public cloud and private premise rather than relying on a SQL layer.

In this paper we have demonstrated that combining code and data dependency models can lead to cheaper and better performing hybrid deployment of Web applications. In particular, we showed that for our evaluated applications, combined code and data partitioning can achieve up to 56% performance improvement compared to a naïve partitioning of code and data between the cloud and the premise and a more than 40% performance improvement compared to when only code is partitioned (see Section 6.1). Similarly, for deployment costs, we showed that combining code and data can provide up to 54% expected cost savings compared to a fully premise deployment and almost 30% expected savings compared to a naïvely partitioned deployment of code and data or a deployment where only code is partitioned (cf. Section 6.2).

References

1. Apache DayTrader, https://cwiki.apache.org/GMOxDOC20/daytrader.html
2. lp_solve Linear Programming solver, http://lpsolve.sourceforge.net/
3. Manticore Homepage, http://nima.magic.ubc.ca/manticore
4. RUBiS: Rice University Bidding System, http://rubis.ow2.org/
5. Abadi, D.J., Marcus, A., Madden, S.R., Hollenbach, K.: Sw-store: a vertically partitioned dbms for semantic web data management. VLDB Jour. 18(2) (2009)
6. Agarwal, S., Dunagan, J., Jain, N., Saroiu, S., Wolman, A.: Volley: Automated data placement for geo-distributed cloud services. In: Proc. of NSDI (2010)
7. Agrawal, S., Narasayya, V., Yang, B.: Integrating vertical and horizontal partitioning into automated physical database design. In: Proc. of SIGMOD (2004)
8. Armbrust, M., Fox, A., Griffith, R., et al.: Above the Clouds: A Berkeley View of Cloud Computing. Technical Report UCB/EECS-2009-28, UC Berkeley (2009)

9. Chin, E., Wagner, D.: Efficient character-level taint tracking for Java. In: Proc. of Wsh. on Secure Web Services (2009)
10. Chong, S., Liu, J., Myers, A., Qi, X., Vikram, K., Zheng, L., Zheng, X.: Building secure web applications with automatic partitioning. In: Proc. of SOSP (2009)
11. Chun, B.-G., Ihm, S., Maniatis, P., Naik, M., Patti, A.: Clonecloud: elastic execution between mobile device and cloud. In: Proc. of EuroSys (2011)
12. Curino, C., Jones, E., Zhang, Y., Madden, S.: Schism: a workload-driven approach to database replication and partitioning. Proc. VLDB Endow. 3(1-2) (2010)
13. Garcia-Molina, H., Salem, K.: Sagas. In: Proc. of SIGMOD (1987)
14. Hajjat, M., Sun, X., Sung, Y.-W.E., Maltz, D., Rao, S., Sripanidkulchai, K., Tawarmalani, M.: Cloudward bound: planning for beneficial migration of enterprise applications to the cloud. In: Proc. of SIGCOMM (2010)
15. Hunt, G., Scott, M.: The Coign automatic distributed partitioning system. In: Proc. of Symp. on Operating Systems Design and Implementation, OSDI (1999)
16. Iqbal, W., Dailey, M.N., Carrera, D.: SLA-driven dynamic resource management for multi-tier web applications in a cloud. In: CCGRID (2010)
17. Kaviani, N., Wohlstadter, E., Lea, R.: Manticore: A Framework for Partitioning of Software Services for Hybrid Cloud. In: Proc. of IEEE CloudCom (2012)
18. Khadilkar, V., Kantarcioglu, M., Thuraisingham, B.: Risk-Aware Data Processing in Hybrid Clouds. Technical report, University of Texas at Dallas (2011)
19. Ko, S.Y., Jeon, K., Morales, R.: The HybrEx model for confidentiality and privacy in cloud computing. In: Proc. of HotCloud (2011)
20. Leymann, F., Fehling, C., Mietzner, R., Nowak, A., Dustdar, S.: Moving applications to the cloud: an approach based on application model enrichment. Int. J. Cooperative Inf. Syst. 20(3), 307–356 (2011)
21. Microsoft. The Economics of the Cloud, USA (November 2010)
22. Newton, R., Toledo, S., Girod, L., Balakrishnan, H., Madden, S.: Wishbone: Profile-based Partitioning for Sensornet Applications. In: Proc. of NSDI (2009)
23. Pavlo, A., Curino, C., Zdonik, S.: Skew-aware automatic database partitioning in shared-nothing, parallel oltp systems. In: Proc. of SIGMOD (2012)
24. Rellermeyer, J.S., Riva, O., Alonso, G.: AlfredO: An architecture for flexible interaction with electronic devices. In: Issarny, V., Schantz, R. (eds.) Middleware 2008. LNCS, vol. 5346, pp. 22–41. Springer, Heidelberg (2008)
25. Schrijver, A.: Theory of Linear and Integer Programming. Wiley & Sons (1998)
26. Selinger, G., Astrahan, M., Chamberlin, D., Lorie, R., Price, T.: Access path selection in a relational database management system. In: SIGMOD (1979)
27. Stewart, C., Leventi, M., Shen, K.: Empirical examination of a collaborative web application. In: IISWC 2008 (2008)
28. Tilevich, E., Smaragdakis, Y.: J-Orchestra: Automatic Java Application Partitioning. In: Magnusson, B. (ed.) ECOOP 2002. LNCS, vol. 2374, pp. 178–204. Springer, Heidelberg (2002)
29. Wieder, A., Bhatotia, P., Post, A., Rodrigues, R.: Orchestrating the deployment of computations in the cloud conductor. In: Proc. of NSDI (2012)
30. Yang, F., Shanmugasundaram, J., Riedewald, M., Gehrke, J.: Hilda: A high-level language for data-driven web applications. In: WWW (2006)
31. Yu, C.T., Chang, C.C.: Distributed Query Processing. Comp. Surv. (1984)

Sprinkler — Reliable Broadcast for Geographically Dispersed Datacenters

Haoyan Geng and Robbert van Renesse

Cornell University, Ithaca, New York, USA

Abstract. This paper describes and evaluates Sprinkler, a reliable high-throughput broadcast facility for geographically dispersed datacenters. For scaling cloud services, datacenters use caching throughout their infrastructure. Sprinkler can be used to broadcast update events that invalidate cache entries. The number of recipients can scale to many thousands in such scenarios. The Sprinkler infrastructure consists of two layers: one layer to disseminate events among datacenters, and a second layer to disseminate events among machines within a datacenter. A novel garbage collection interface is introduced to save storage space and network bandwidth. The first layer is evaluated using an implementation deployed on Emulab. For the second layer, involving thousands of nodes, we use a discrete event simulation. The effect of garbage collection is analyzed using simulation. The evaluation shows that Sprinkler can disseminate millions of events per second throughout a large cloud infrastructure, and garbage collection is effective in workloads like cache invalidation.

Keywords: Broadcast, performance, fault tolerance, garbage collection.

1 Introduction

Today's large scale web applications such as Facebook, Amazon, eBay, Google+, and so on, rely heavily on caching for providing low latency responses to client queries. Enterprise data is stored in reliable but slow back-end databases. In order to be able to keep up with load and provide low latency responses, client query results are computed and opportunistically cached in memory on many thousands of machines throughout the organization's various datacenters [21]. But when a database is updated, all affected cache entries have to be invalidated. Until this is completed, inconsistent data can be exposed to clients. Since the databases cannot keep track of where these cache entries are, it is necessary to multicast an invalidation notification to all machines that may have cached query results. The rate of such invalidations can reach hundreds of thousands per second. If any invalidation gets lost, inconsistencies exposed to clients may be long-term. Other important uses of reliable high-throughput broadcast throughout a geoplex of datacenters include disseminating events in multi-player games and stock updates in financial trading.

Much work has been done on publish-subscribe and broadcast mechanisms (see Section 6). Pub-sub services focus on support for high throughput in the face of many topics or even content-based filtering, but reliability is often a secondary issue and slow subscribers may not see all updates. Some recent systems [4,20]

D. Eyers and K. Schwan (Eds.): Middleware 2013, LNCS 8275, pp. 247–266, 2013.

do provide high reliability and many topics, but the number of subscribers per topic is assumed to be small (such as a collection of logging servers). Group communication systems focus on high reliability, but such systems may stall in the face of slow group members and, partly for that reason, assume that group membership is small.

This paper describes Sprinkler, a high-throughput broadcast facility that is scalable in the number of recipients while providing reliable delivery. Sprinkler achieves its objectives through a novel broadcast API that includes support for garbage collection and through a careful implementation that is cognizant of the physical networking infrastructure.

Garbage collection both reduces load and makes it easier for clients or datacenters to recover from an outage. For example, if there are two updates or invalidations to the same key, then the first update is obsolete and it is no longer necessary to try and deliver it to clients. Similarly, if a temporary key is deleted, all outstanding updates can be garbage collected. As we show in Section 5, in applications where there are many updates to a small set of popular keys, and where there is significant use of temporary keys, such garbage collection can significantly reduce the demands on the broadcast service.

Sprinkler is designed for a system consisting of a small and mostly static number of datacenters each containing a large and dynamic set of machines. Consequently, Sprinkler uses two protocols: reliable multi-hop broadcast between datacenters, followed by reliable broadcast within a datacenter. Each datacenter deploys a replicated *proxy* to participate in the first protocol. While the details are different, both protocols depend on each peer periodically notifying its neighbors about its state (*i.e.*, gossip [13]).

To evaluate Sprinkler and find suitable values for certain configuration parameters, we conducted throughput, latency, and fault tolerance experiments. We first evaluated an incomplete prototype implementation of Sprinkler. Using Emulab [1] we were able to emulate realistic deployment scenarios and see what broadcast throughput is possible through a small number of datacenters. As a datacenter may contain thousands or tens of thousands of clients, we evaluated a complete implementation of the protocol through simulation, calibrated using measurements from experiments on the prototype implementation. We also quantified the effectiveness of garbage collection by conducting a simulation study on savings in storage space and network bandwidth using a workload mimicking cache invalidation in Facebook [21]. As a result of these experiments, we believe that Sprinkler is capable of disseminating millions of events per second throughout a large cloud infrastructure even in the face of failures.

The scientific contributions of this paper can be summarized as follows:

- the design and implementation of Sprinkler, a reliable high-throughput broadcast facility that scales in the number of recipients;
- a novel garbage collection interface that allows publishers to specify which messages are obsolete and do not need to be delivered;
- an evaluation of the throughput, latency, fault tolerance, and garbage collection of Sprinkler.

This paper is organized as follows. We start by giving an overview of the Sprinkler interface, as well as of the environment in which Sprinkler is intended to be deployed, in Section 2. Section 3 provides details of the various protocols that make up Sprinkler. Section 4 briefly describes the current implementation of Sprinkler. Evaluation of Sprinkler is presented in Section 5. Section 6 describes background and related work in the area of publish-subscribe and broadcast facilities. Section 7 concludes and presents areas for future work.

2 System Overview

2.1 Sprinkler Interface

Sprinkler has the following simple interface:

- `client.getEvent()` $\rightarrow$ *event*   - `client.publish(event)`

Each event e belongs to a *stream*, *e.stream*. There are three types of events: *data events*, *garbage collection events*, and *tombstone events*. Data events are simple byte arrays. A garbage collection event is like a data event, but also contains a predicate $P(e)$ on events e—if $P(e)$ holds, then the application considers e obsolete. A tombstone event is a placeholder for a sequence of events all of which are garbage collected. An event is considered *published* once the corresponding `client.publish(event)` interface returns. We consider each event that is published unique. An event e is considered *delivered* to a particular client when `client.getEvent()` $\rightarrow e'$ returns and either $e' = e$ or e' is a tombstone event for e.

The interfaces satisfy the following: Sprinkler only delivers data and garbage collection events that are published, or tombstone events for events that were published and garbage collected. Published events for the same stream s are ordered by a relation $\prec_s$, and events for s are delivered to each client in that order. If the same client publishes e and e' for stream s in that order, then $e \prec_s e'$.

For each event e that is published for stream s, each client is either delivered e or tombstone event for e followed by a matching garbage collection event g. A garbage collection event g containing predicate $g.P$ matches e if $g.P(e) \wedge e \prec_s g$ holds—that is, a garbage collection event cannot match a future event. A garbage collection event g can match another garbage collection event g'. In that case we require (of the application programmer) that $\forall e : e \prec_s g' \Rightarrow (g'.P(e) \Rightarrow g.P(e))$. For example, if g' matches all events (prior to g') that are red, then g also matches all events (prior to g') that are red. The intention is to ensure that garbage collection is final and cannot be undone.

A tombstone event matches a sequence of events that have been garbage collected. For each event being garbage collected, at least one tombstone event matching it is generated. A tombstone event t can also be garbage collected by another tombstone event t' that contains all events in t. For example, two consecutive tombstone events as well as two overlapping tombstone events can be replaced by a single tombstone event. However, tombstone events cannot contain "holes" (missing events in a consecutive sequences of events).

These properties hold even in the case of client crashes, except that events are no longer delivered to clients that have crashed. Sprinkler is not designed to deal with Byzantine failures. Note that the Sprinkler interface requires that all events are delivered to each correct client, and events can only be garbage collected if matched by a garbage collection event. Trivial implementations that deliver no events or garbage collect all events are thereby prevented.

2.2 Implementation Overview

Sprinkler is intended for an environment consisting of a relatively small and static number of datacenters, which we call *regions*, each containing a large and dynamic number of clients. A stream belongs to a region—we support only a small number of streams per region. A typical stream is "key invalidation" and a corresponding event contains the (hash of the) key that is being invalidated. The key's master copy is stored in the stream's region, as only the key's master copy broadcasts invalidation messages.

The rate at which events get published may be high, so high throughput is required. Low latency is desirable as well, although the environment is asynchronous and thus we cannot guarantee bounds on delivery latencies.

Each region runs a service, called a *proxy*, each in charge of a small number of streams. The proxy may be replicated for fault-tolerance. Sprinkler clients connect to the local proxy. When a client publishes an event, it connects to the proxy that manages the stream for the event. (Typically a client only publishes events to streams that are local to the client's region.) The proxy assigns a per-stream sequence number to the event and disseminates the event among the other proxies through the *proxy-level protocol* (PLP). Each proxy that receives the event stores the event locally and disseminates the event among the local clients through the *region-level protocol* (RLP). The details of the two protocols are described in the next section, and more on the implementation follows in Section 4.

3   Details of the Protocols

3.1 Proxy-Level Protocol (PLP)

Figure 1 contains a state-transition specification for proxies. The state of a proxy p is contained in the following variables:

- $pxID_p$ contains a unique immutable identifier for p;
- $streams_p$ contains the set of streams that p is responsible for;
- $Hist_p$ contains the events received by p and that are not yet garbage collected. $Hist_p$ is empty initially;
- cnt_p^s: an event counter for each stream s, initially 0;
- $expects_p^s$: for each stream s, a tuple consisting of a proxy identifier, a counter, and a timestamp.

Events are uniquely identified by the tuple ($e.type, e.stream, e.seq, e.range$). Here $e.type$ is one of DATA, GC, or TOMBSTONE; $e.stream$ is the stream of the event,

---

specification Proxy-Level-Protocol:
   state:
      $pxID_p$: **unique id of proxy** p
      $streams_p$: **set of stream ids managed by** p
      $Hist_p$: **set of events that proxy** p **stores**
      cnt_p^s: **counters for each stream** s
      $expects_p^s$: **(proxy, counter, time)**

   initially:
      $\forall p$:
         $Hist_p := \emptyset$
         $\forall p' : p' \neq p \Rightarrow$
               $pxID_p \neq pxID_{p'}$
               $streams_p \cap streams_{p'} = \emptyset$
      $\forall s$:
         $cnt_p^s = 0$
         $expects_p^s = (\bot, 0, 0)$

   transition addLocalEvent(p, e):
      precondition:
         $e.stream \in streams_p \wedge e.seq = \bot$
      action:
         $cnt_p^{e.stream} := cnt_p^{e.stream} + 1;$
         $e.seq := cnt_p^{e.stream};$
         $Hist_p := filter(Hist_p \cup \{e\});$

   transition addRemoteEvent(p, e):
      precondition:
         $e.stream \notin streams_p \wedge e.seq > cnt_p^{e.stream}$
      action:
         $cnt_p^{e.stream} := e.seq;$
         $Hist_p := filter(Hist_p \cup \{e\});$

   transition rcvAdvertisement(p, p', cnt, T):
      precondition:
         TRUE
      action:
         $\forall s \notin streams_p$:
             if $cnt^s > expects_p^s.seq +$
                  $C/(T - expects_p^s.time)$ then
               if $expects_p^s.source \neq p'.pxID$ then
                  if $expects_p^s.source \neq \bot$ then
                     Unsubscribe$(expects_p^s.source, T')$
                  Subscribe$(p'.pxID, s, cnt^s)$
                  $expects_p^s = (p'.pxID, cnt^s, T)$

Fig. 1. Specification of a proxy. $filter(H)$ is a function on histories that replaced all events from H that are matched by a garbage collection event in H with a tombstone event.

and $e.seq$ is the sequence number of the event. For tombstone events, $e.range$ is the number of garbage-collected events represented by the tombstone—and $e.seq$ is the sequence number of the last such event. For non-tombstone events, $e.range = 1$.

Transition $\mathtt{addLocalEvent}(p, e)$ is performed when proxy p receives an event from a client that is trying to publish the event. The proxy only accepts the event if it manages the stream of the event, and in that case assigns a sequence number to the event. Finally, e is added to the history and a filter is applied to replace garbage collected events by tombstone events and to aggregate consecutive and overlapping tombstone events into single tombstone events.

Events for a stream s are ordered by their sequence number, that is, $e \prec_s e'$ iff $e.stream = e'.stream = s \wedge e.seq < e'.seq$.

Proxies forward events to one another over FIFO channels. Performing transition $\mathtt{addRemoteEvent}(p, e)$ adds an event to p's history for a stream that is not managed by p but by some other proxy. The transition applies the same filter to replace events that are garbage collected by tombstone events, and also updates $cnt_p^{e.stream}$ to keep track of the maximum sequence number seen for $e.stream$.

It is an invariant that $Hist_p$ does not contain any events e for which $e.seq > cnt_p^{e.stream}$, as is clear from the specification. We note without proof that it is also invariant that $Hist_p$ contains all published events with $e.seq \leq cnt_p^{e.stream}$, or matching tombstone event and garbage collection events.

A simple way for events to propagate between proxies would be to have each proxy broadcast its events to the other proxies. However, such an approach may not work if certain datacenters can no longer communicate directly. To address this, the way a proxy receives events from another proxy is through a subscription mechanism. For each non-local stream, a proxy subscribes to events from at most one other proxy, which does not have to be the owner of that stream. Periodically, each proxy p' broadcasts *advertisements* containing $cnt_{p'}$ to the other proxies, notifying them of its progress on each stream.

Proxy p maintains for each stream s a variable $expects_p^s$, containing a tuple consisting of a proxy identifier, a sequence number, and a timestamp. If p is not subscribed for the stream as is initially the case, then the tuple is $(\bot, 0, 0)$. If p is subscribed to receiving events from p', then $expects_p^s$ contains the proxy identifier of p', and the sequence number and time that p received in the latest advertisement from p'.

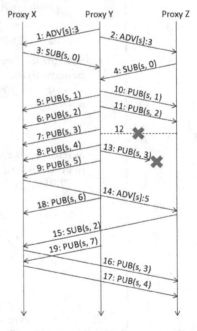

Fig. 2.   Space-time diagram for subscription change when the link between two datacenters goes down

Transition rcvAdvertisement($p, p', cnt_{p'}, T$) shows what happens when proxy p receives an advertisement from p' at time T. For each non-local stream, p checks to see if the advertisement is further advanced than the last advertisement that it got for the same stream and by how much. C is a configuration variable. If set to 0, proxies tend to switch between subscriptions too aggressively. We divide C by the time expired since the last advertisement so that a proxy does not indefinitely wait for a proxy that may have crashed. When switching from one proxy to another p', p specifies to p' how far it got so that p' knows which event to send to p first.

Figure 2 illustrates how the subscription pattern changes adaptively in the presence of network outage. The figure shows three proxies X, Y, and Z, and messages flowing between them. For convenient reference, all messages are numbered. Initially, proxies can communicate with each other directly. Proxy Y is in charge of stream s, and events up to 3 have already been published. Proxies X and Z do not yet store any events for s, and are not subscribed to any source.

Messages 1 and 2 are advertisement messages for s, in which the count for s is 3. (Actual advertisement messages also include counters for other streams, but only s is shown for brevity.) Proxies X and Z send messages 3 and 4 to subscribe to stream s from proxy Y. In response, proxy Y starts sending events for s to proxies X and Z, shown as messages 5 through 11. The network between proxies Y and Z goes down at the broken line that is labeled 12, and subsequent events published by proxy Y cannot get through to Z (message 13). Message 14 is an advertisement message sent from proxy X to proxy Z for stream s, which contains a larger sequence number for stream s than the most recent advertisement message that proxy Z received from Y. So proxy Z changes its subscription to proxy X using message 15, and consequently starts receiving events from proxy X (messages 16 and 17). Meanwhile, proxy X continues to receive events for s directly from proxy Y, as illustrated by messages 18 and 19.

3.2   Region-Level Protocol (RLP)

The Region-Level Protocol delivers events from a proxy to all the clients within the region of the proxy. Reliability and throughput are key requirements: all events should be delivered to each correct client at high rate as long as it does not crash. Compared to the Proxy-Level Protocol, there are the following important differences: First, there are only a few number of proxies and the set of proxies is more or less static, while there are many clients in a region (on the order of thousands typically) and clients come and go as a function of reconfigurations for a variety of reasons. Second, proxies are dedicated, high-end, and homogeneous machines with resources chosen for the task they are designed for, while clients have other tasks and only limited resources for event dissemination. Third, proxies may be replicated for fault tolerance of event dissemination, but clients cannot be.

The Region-Level Protocol (RLP) consists of two sub-protocols: a gossip-based membership protocol based on [5], combined with a peer-to-peer event dissemination protocol loosely based on Chainsaw [23]. The membership protocol provides each client with a *view* that consists of a small random subset of the other clients in the same region. The views are updated frequently through gossip. At any particular time, the clients and their views induce a directed graph over which clients notify their progress to their neighbors and request missing events, similar to the Proxy-Level Protocol. However, unlike proxies, clients do not keep track of old events for long because they have only limited capacity. But clients that cannot retrieve events from their neighbors can always fall back onto their local proxy, a luxury proxies do not possess.

We describe the two protocols in more detail below.

Membership Protocol. In the membership protocol, each client maintains a *local view*, which is a subset of other clients that has to grow logarithmically with the total number of clients. In the current implementation, the maximum view size V is configured and should be chosen large enough to prevent partitioning [5]: selecting a large view size increases overhead but makes partitions in the graph less likely and reduces the diameter of the graph and consequently event dissemination latency. Typically, V is on the order of 10 to 20 clients.

We call the members of the view the client's *neighbors*. A client periodically updates its local view by periodically gossiping with its neighbors. When a client c receives a view from its neighbor c', c computes the union of its own view and the view of c', and then randomly removes members from the new view until it has the required size. However, it makes sure that c' is in the new view. This last constraint, called *reinforcement* [5], is subtle but turns out to be important— without it the induced graph is likely to become star-like rather than to converge to a random graph. [5] shows that with reinforcement the protocol maintains a well-connected graph of clients with $O(\log N)$ diameter, where N is the total number of clients. Clients that have crashed or have been configured to no longer participate in the protocol automatically disappear from views of other clients because they do not reinforce themselves.

The Sprinkler membership protocol deviates from [5] in only minor ways. The local proxy is one of the clients that is gossiping. While partitioning in this graph is rare, it can happen. For this reason, each client occasionally gossips with its local proxy even if the proxy is not in its view. This causes partitions to fix themselves automatically. As shown in [5], partitions tend to be small in size: on the order of two to three clients. Therefore, if the view of a Sprinkler client is smaller than V, the client adds the local proxy to its view automatically. Such small partitions thus join the larger graph immediately. New clients start with a view consisting of only the local proxy.

Data Dissemination Protocol. Figure 3 presents a state-transition diagram for the data dissemination protocol. The state of a client c is contained in the following variables:

- $Recv_c$ contains the events delivered to c and that are not yet discarded. $Recv_c$ is empty initially. If c is a proxy, then $Recv_c = Hist_c$;
- cnt_c^s: is the sequence number for the last event that c received for stream s, initially -1;

specification Region-Level-Protocol:
  state:
    $Recv_c$: **set of events that node** c **stores**
    cnt_c^s: **counters for delivered events for stream** s
    $next_c^s$: **counters for requests for stream** s
  initially:
    $Recv_c := \emptyset$
    $\forall t$:
      $cnt_c^s = -1$
      $next_c^s = 0$

  transition deliverEvent(c, e):
    precondition:
      $e.seq - e.range \leq cnt_c^{e.stream} < e.seq$
    action:
      $Recv_c := filter(Recv_c \cup \{e\})$
      $cnt_c^{e.stream} := e.seq$
      $\text{sendNotify}(e.stream, cnt_c^{e.stream})$

  transition receiveNotify(c, c', s, cnt):
    precondition:
      $next_c^s \leq cnt$
    action:
      $\text{sendRequest}(c', s, next_c^s, cnt)$
      $next_c^s := cnt + 1$

  transition receiveRequest(c, c', s, nxt, cnt):
    precondition:
      TRUE
    action:
      $E := \{e \in Recv_c \mid e.stream = s \;\wedge$
           $\exists s \in (e.seq - e.range, e.seq] : nxt \leq s \leq cnt\}$
      $\text{sendEvents}(c', cnt_c^s, E)$

  transition discardEvent(c, e):
    precondition:
      $e \in Recv_c$
    action:
      $Recv_c := Recv_c - \{e\}$

  transition requestFromProxy(c, p, s):
    precondition:
      $cnt_c^s < next_c^s - 1$
      $s \in p.streams$
    action:
      $\text{sendRequest}(p, s, cnt_c^s + 1, next_c^s - 1)$

Fig. 3. Specification of a client for data dissemination

- $next_c^s$: is the sequence number of the next event that c wants to request for stream s, initially 0.

Performing transition deliverEvent(c, e) delivers an event to client c. If c is a proxy, this corresponds to c receiving the event in an addLocalEvent(c, e) or addRemoteEvent(c, e) transition. Otherwise c is an ordinary client that received the event either from the proxy or from a peer client in its region. Event e is delivered only if its sequence number is directly after the maximum sequence number delivered to c. When delivered, e is added to $Recv_c$ and $cnt_c^{e.stream}$ is updated. Finally, client c broadcasts a NOTIFY message its current neighbors (determined by the membership protocol), notifying them of its progress with respect to $e.stream$.

Transition receiveNotify(c, c', s, cnt) shows what happens when client c receives a NOTIFY message from client c' for stream s. If the sequence number in the NOTIFY message exceeds the events that client c has already requested, then c sends a REQUEST message to c' for the missing events.

Transition receiveRequest(c, c', s, nxt, cnt) is performed when client c receives a request from client c' for stream s. The client responds with an EVENTS message containing all events between nxt and cnt (possibly a sequence with holes, or even an empty sequence). The message also contains cnt_c^s so the recipient can detect what events exactly are missing from $Recv_c$.

Non-proxy clients may have limited space to store events. The Sprinkler specification gives clients the option of not keeping all events. In our implementation each client c has only limited capacity in $Recv_c$ and replace the oldest events with the newest events. Transition discardEvent(c, e) happens when client c removes event e from $Recv_c$.

Because clients do not keep all events, clients sometimes need to request missing events from the local proxy. In transition requestFromProxy(c, p, e), client c sends a REQUEST to the client's local proxy p. The client only sends requests for events that it previously requested from other clients.

Shuffling. In the protocol described above, a client c broadcasts a NOTIFY message to all its neighbors, each neighbor immediately sends REQUEST message to c, and c immediately responds with the requested events. Depending on the view size of c (bounded by V), this could create a large load on c.

In order to deal with this imbalance, each client only broadcasts the NOTIFY message to a subset of its neighbors of size F (for Fanout). This subset is of configurable size, and is changed periodically, something we call a *shuffle*. In the limit $F = 1$, but as we shall see in evaluation studies, a slightly larger subset has benefits for performance. We provide a simulation-based analysis on the effect of choosing different values for F and the *shuffle time*.

3.3 Fault Tolerance of a Proxy

So far we have described a proxy as if it were a single process, and as such it would be a single point of failure, depriving clients in its region from receiving events.

The Sprinkler proxy is replicated using Chain Replication [27]. To tolerate f failures in a region, there are $f + 1$ proxy replicas configured in a chain. Clients submit events by sending them to the head of the chain. The events are forwarded along the replicas in the chain, each replica storing the events in its copy of *Hist*. The tail of the chain communicates with the head replicas of its peer proxies, and also participates in the local RLP.

The chain is under the management of a local configuration service. In case a replica fails, it is removed from the chain. If the removed replica is not the tail, the impact is minimal—the predecessor of the replica may have to retransmit missing events to its new successor. It the head is removed, peer proxies and clients that try to publish events have to be notified. If it is the tail that is removed, a new tail ensues that has to set up new connections with the head nodes of its peer proxies. Both endpoints on each new connection exchange advertisements to allow the proxies to recover. A beneficial feature of Chain Replication is that the new tail is guaranteed to have all events that the old tail stored, and thus no events can get lost until all replicas in the chain fail and lose their state.

Sprinkler allows recovery of a crashed replica, as well as adding a replica with no initial state. The replica to the end of the chain, beyond the current tail, and will start receiving the events that it missed. Once the new tail is caught up, the old tail gives up its function and passes a token to the new replica. The replica then sets up new connections as described above.

3.4   Garbage Collection

In typical settings, Sprinkler broadcasts each event to thousands of hosts. All the events that are not garbage collected are stored at each of the proxies. In an environment with high load, the amount of data needs to be stored and transferred is huge. Efficient garbage collection would save critical storage space and network bandwidth. In this section, we give two examples of garbage collection policy.

One possible approach for garbage collection is to keep only the most recent events, and discard old events once they meet certain "age" criteria. An example is to keep only the most recent N events. In this case, each data event is also a garbage collection event: an event at index i collects all events with indices less that $i - N$. Another example is to discard all the events that are older than a certain period of time, say, k days. If this policy is enforced in a daily basis, the system generates one garbage collection event each day that collects all the events that are more than k days old. Such approach is useful if there is time bound on the usefulness of the data. LinkedIn uses such approach in processing log data with Kafka [20].

Another class of policy is key-based. In applications like cache invalidation, each data event states that the cache entry for a specific key is no longer valid. For any two events invalidates the same key, the later event implies the earlier one. From a client's perspective, if the later event is delivered, there is no need for the earlier one. So in this case, each data event is also a garbage collection event that collects all previous events on the same key.

The effectiveness of the key-based policy depends on actual workload. We show in section 5 that it is effective under our synthesized workload that shares similar properties to that of a popular, real web service.

4 Implementation

We have implemented a limited prototype of Sprinkler in the C programming language. We also have implemented a discrete event simulator of the full Sprinkler protocol described in this paper.

Nodes in the Sprinkler prototype communicate by exchanging messages across TCP connections. Each message starts with a header followed by an optional payload that contains the application data if needed. Batching of multiple events within a message is extensively used to optimize throughput.

We also have an initial implementation of the client library, except that we do not yet provide a comprehensive evaluation of it. Instead, in our evaluation, each client is configured to just receive events from proxies. Each proxy process also acts as client and is running both the Proxy-Level Protocol and the Region-Level Protocol. Proxy replication has only been implemented in the simulator.

5 Evaluation

In this section we evaluate the throughput and latency provided by Sprinkler for various scenarios, determine good values for parameters such as the fanout F, and investigate the efficacy of fault tolerance mechanisms within Sprinkler.

The performance of Sprinkler depends on both the Proxy-Level Protocol and the Region-Level Protocol. Given the small number of regions in a typical cloud infrastructure, we can use a prototype implementation of proxies to evaluate the Proxy-Level Protocol. However, since each region may have many thousands of clients, we evaluate the Region-Level Protocol using discrete event simulation. We use experimental measurements of the prototype implementation to calibrate the simulation of a large number of clients. For these measurements, each proxy is configured with a static view of clients.

5.1 Throughput of Proxy-Level Protocol

We tested the Proxy-Level protocol on an Emulab cluster[1]. Each node in the cluster is equipped with an AMD 1.6 GHz Opteron 242 processor and 16 GB of RAM. Nodes are connected to a single gigabit Ethernet switch.

We set up experiments with one, two, or three proxies. In these experiments, each proxy can communicate directly with each other proxy. The maximum view size V and the *fanout* F are both set to 3, and as described above, the local view of proxies do not change over time. Consequently there is no shuffling present in these experiments.

---

[1] We used the Marmot cluster of the PRObE project [3].

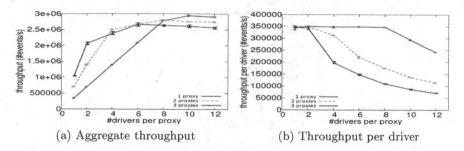

(a) Aggregate throughput   (b) Throughput per driver

Fig. 4. Throughput as a function of the number of drivers per proxy

Some clients are used to publish events, and we call those clients *drivers*. Drivers do not receive any events—they just send events to proxies. Consequently, drivers do not run the Region-Level Protocol. Each driver invokes `publish()` in a closed loop with no wait time between invocations. The size of each event is fixed at 10 bytes, large enough to contain the hash of a key to be invalidated, say. Each published event is a garbage collection event: an event at index i specifies that all events with indices less than $i - 100,000,000$ can be garbage collected. We control the load on Sprinkler by varying the number of drivers attached to a proxy. In our experiments, each process, whether proxy, client, or driver, runs on a separate machine.

Figure 4(a) shows the throughput as a function of the number of drivers per proxy. Each data point shows an average over five experiments, as well as minima and maxima. The graph has three lines, one for each scenario. As the number of drivers increases, the throughput increases until the traffic load saturates the system. Peak throughput decreases slightly as the number of proxies increases because of the overhead of forwarding events between proxies. Figure 4(b) shows the throughput per driver for the same experiment.

5.2 Simulation Study

In the next experiment, we evaluate the performance of the complete Sprinkler protocol using discrete time simulation. The basic settings are as follows: There are three regions connected by 10 Gbps links (the bandwidth that is provided by the National Lambda Rail, a transcontinental fiber-optic network). Figure 5(a) shows the latencies between the three regions, chosen to reflect typical latencies for datacenters located on the west coast and the east coast of the United States.

Within a region, processes communicate over 1 Gbps networks and one-way latencies are 1ms. Each region has 1000 clients and a proxy that has three replicas. Each client (as well as the tail server of the proxy) maintains a maximum view size of 20 peers.

In the 3-region prototype experiment of the previous section, the throughput peaks between 2.6-2.7 million events per second. We send 864k events per second to each proxy at a fixed rate, for a total of 2.592 million events per second, approximately matching the maximum throughput of the prototype.

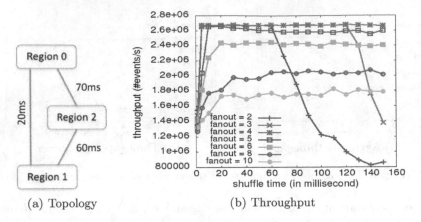

(a) Topology   (b) Throughput

Fig. 5. (a) The experimental topology used to simulate throughput and latency. (b) Average throughput as a function of shuffle time.

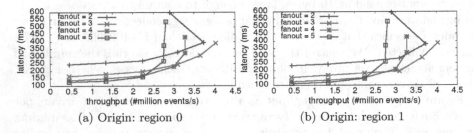

(a) Origin: region 0   (b) Origin: region 1

Fig. 6. Average latency and throughput observed as load is increased. The figures shows events added by clients in two different regions. The third region is similar.

Figure 5(b) shows the average throughput the simulator achieves varying the fanout F and the shuffle time. We do not show variance for clarity—it is small in our simulations. Each data point is the average throughput. To remove bias, measurements do not start until 300ms into an experiment, at which point the subscriptions are established and the throughput has stabilized. As can be seen, a consequence of this is that the throughput is slightly higher than the load added to the system, as the proxies catch up to deliver old events. Eventually, the throughput matches the load imposed on the system. The best throughput is achieved for a fanout of 4. For larger fanouts, the outbound bandwidth of a client gets exhausted for a relatively small number of events. Such clients cannot forward other events and start dropping events from their *Recv* buffer. This in turn results in an increase of requests made for missing events to the proxy, competing with bandwidth for normal traffic.

A similar effect happens when the fanout is small, but the shuffle time is long. Decreasing the shuffle time allows a client to forward events to more neighbors, effectively reducing the diameter of the forwarding graph, in turn reducing event loss in clients and the load on proxies.

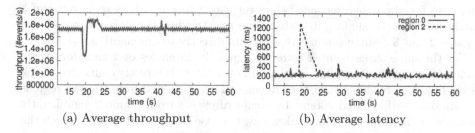

(a) Average throughput   (b) Average latency

Fig. 7. Performance over time with inter-region link failure

Figure 6 shows latency and throughput as load is increased, for various values for the fanout F. The latency of an event is the time from the event arriving at the local proxy until it is delivered to all clients. The shuffle time in these experiments is fixed at 30ms. In each line there are 6 data points, corresponding to increasing the load. At the first (leftmost) data point, 1/6 of the maximum throughput of the prototype implementation is introduced, that is, 1/6th of 2.592 million events per second. At the next data points we add 1/3rd of the load successively. Consequently, at the last data point we introduce $1/6 + 5 \times 1/3 = 11/6$ of the maximum load achieved on the prototype implementation. The halfway point on the line corresponds to the maximum load. Note that in some experiments the system becomes overloaded and cannot keep up with the load. We show results for events originating from different regions separately.

As shown in the figure, throughput gradually goes up until the system saturates. Before saturation, latency of events disseminated to 3000 clients is generally below 300ms.

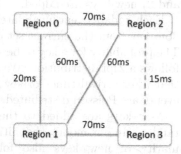

5.3   Impact of Inter-Region Link Failure

Inter-region link failure blocks one region from communicating directly with another. The Proxy-Level Protocol supports indirect routing through other regions, and thus as long as there is transitive connectivity events should continue flowing to all clients. To evaluate this, we set up a four-region network, with inter-region latencies as shown in Figure 8. Latencies are chosen based on typical numbers for cross-country datacenter deployment.

Fig. 8. The experimental topology used to simulate the impact of inter-region link failure, with the failed link (15ms) on the right side

At the start of the experiment, all regions can directly communicate. After time $t = 19$, the link between regions 2 and 3 is taken out, and restored at time $t = 41$.

Figure 7a shows throughput as a function of time. The network outage results in the brief drop in throughput at time $t = 19$, caused by the interruption of events flowing between regions 2 and 3. The throughput recovers shortly after time $t = 20$, after the new advertisement messages from regions 0 and 1 arrive and regions 2 and 3 update their subscriptions accordingly. The throughput increases for about five seconds before returning to normal, as regions 2 and 3 catch up. Note the slight glitch after time $t = 41$ when the link is restored and regions 2 and 3 resume sending their events directly to one another.

For the same experiment, Figure 7b shows the latencies over time for events added from regions 0 and 2. Note that only the latter is directly connected to the failed link. Before the outage, the latencies of events added from the two regions are similar, both around 200ms. Latencies of events from region 2 significantly increase at the time the link is taken out, because those events cannot reach the proxy in region 3 until the subscription changes. The latencies of events from region 2 recover after the new subscription. Latencies are slightly higher than before because the path to region 3 has greater latency. After the link is restored, latencies drop to the original level after a short period of adjustment.

5.4 Effectiveness of Garbage Collection

In this section, we first describe the workload we use to evaluate the efficacy of garbage collection and show the workload is realistic. Next we show simulation results of the effectiveness of garbage collection.

Workload Description. In our model, there are two kinds of updates: 1) keys are updated with new values, and 2) new keys are added.

Each update event invalidates a random key from the current set of keys. The probability for a key to be selected follows a Zipf distribution. We assume that inter-arrival times of key update events are Poisson distributed.

New keys are added to the set at random. In our model, the initial popularity of new keys also follows a heavy-tailed distribution. We choose a

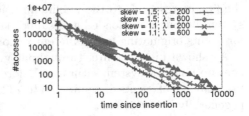

Fig. 9. Number of invalidations to keys with varying time since their addition. *skew* is the parameter for the Zeta distribution, while λ is the parameter for the Poisson distribution of inter-arrival times of invalidation events.

Zeta distribution (Zipf distribution over an infinite set) because for simulation purposes it is easy to scale up to a large number of keys. A single parameter, *skew*, determines the shape of a Zeta distribution. For simplicity, we assume that the Zeta distribution has the same skew as the Zipfian popularity distribution of keys. We also assume that inter-arrival times for new key events are Poisson distributed—we fix the parameter λ at 10 for these experiments.

Figure 9 shows the aggregated number of invalidation events on keys as a function of age. A data point at coordinates (x, y) shows that during the experiment, y invalidations are made to any object that have been inserted x ticks ago when such an invalidation was generated. The figure shows that new objects tend to attract more updates than old objects, because over time new objects come in, making old ones gradually less popular. popularity decrease also roughly follows

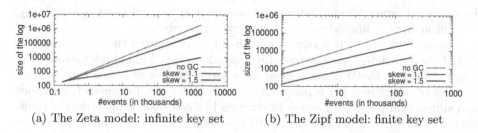

(a) The Zeta model: infinite key set   (b) The Zipf model: finite key set

Fig. 10. Number of events stored at each proxy as a function of total number of events generated on log-log scale

a Zipf-like distribution. The slope of the line is steeper with larger *skew*, since the most popular objects get invalidated with higher probability. For the same skew, the plotted line is higher for larger λ as more invalidation events are generated.

In private communication with an engineer at a popular social network based web service provider, we confirmed that our workload, in particular the line with $skew = 1.1, \lambda = 200$, exhibits properties similar to their real workload.

Evaluation Results. We evaluated the performance of garbage collection with the workload described above. The metric is the amount of storage needed at each proxy. Note that since events of the same stream arrive in FIFO order at each proxy, there is no need to store tombstone events explicitly. A tombstone event is always followed by a corresponding data event.

Figure 10a shows the number of events to be stored at each proxy as new events are generated. Garbage collection saves roughly three-fourths of the space needed to store events. The effect becomes more significant if the workload is more heavily skewed.

In a real-world application, the number of keys are generally bounded. Figure 10b shows the same experiment on a slight variant of the above model: the set of possible keys is finite, and a Zipf distribution over the finite set is used to model the popularity. In this experiment, there are 100,000 keys in the set initially. For each chosen skew value, we study two cases: a) the set of keys is fixed over time; and b) new keys are inserted into the system with a 1 : 10 insertion/invalidation ratio. The result shows that garbage collection saves roughly 85% of the space with a skew of 1.1, and more with a higher skew. Only the results for the case of fixed set of keys are shown in the figure, since the addition of new keys makes little difference to the results.

6 Related Work

Sprinkler provides roughly similar functionality to topic-based publish-subscribe systems such as Information Bus [22] (TIBCO), iBus [6], JMS Queue [12], WebSphere MQ [2], and so on. The main focus of such systems is to support high throughput, but, unlike Sprinkler, slow subscribers or subscribers that join late may not receive all updates. Topic-based pub-sub systems are closely related to group communication systems [24], as topics can be viewed as groups [14].

Examples of group communication systems such as ISIS [8] focus on reliability, but throughput is limited by the slowest group member.

Apache HedWig [4] is a recent publish-subscribe system that is designed to distribute data across the Internet. Like Sprinkler, HedWig provides reliable delivery. However, HedWig is intended for a large number of topics with a small number of subscribers per topic (no more than about 10). In contract, Sprinkler can support only a small number of streams but can scale to hundreds of thousands of subscribers per stream. HedWig uses a separate coordination service (ZooKeeper [17]) to keep its metadata. To provide high throughput in the face of slow subscribers, HedWig logs all events to disk before delivery.

LinkedIn's Kafka [20] is another recent publish-subscribe system that provides high throughput and persistent on-disk storage of large amounts of data. Messages are guaranteed to be delivered and in order within a so-called partition (a sharding unit within a topic). Like HedWig, Kafka relies on ZooKeeper to maintain group membership and subscription relationships, but unlike Sprinkler does not deal with deployments in geographically dispersed locations.

Sprinkler is strongly inspired by gossip protocols. Proxies as well as clients gossip their state to their peers, and Sprinkler's per-region membership protocol is gossip-based as well. First introduced in [13], gossip has received considerable research. The first gossip protocols assumed all participants to gossip all their state with all other participants, providing strong reliability properties but limiting scalability drastically. Bimodal multicast [7] is an IP-multicast protocol that provides reliability with high probability through such a gossip mechanism. However, both IP multicast and uniform gossip limits its scalability. To obtain good scalability it is necessary to gossip in a more restricted manner.

Another gossip-based option is to provide each member with a small and dynamic view consisting of a random subset of peers, inducing a random graph that is connected with high probability [15,16,25,5]. SelectCast [9] (based on Astrolabe [26]) is a publish-subscribe protocol that builds a tree-structured overlay on participants using gossip. The overlay is then used to disseminate events. Sprinkler's membership protocol is entirely based upon [5]. Our Region-Level Protocol is influenced by the Chainsaw protocol [23]. While Chainsaw is intended for streaming video and can afford to lose video frames, RLP provides provides reliable delivery of (usually) small events.

Early large scale multicast protocols such as [18] build network overlays, but only provide best effort service. Multicast protocols such as SCRIBE [10], SplitStream [11] and Bullet [19] use Distributed Hash Tables to build tree-based overlays. Such protocols, besides providing only best effort service, tend to suffer from relatively high "stretch" as messages are forwarded pseudo-randomly through the overlay.

7 Conclusion and Future Work

We have described the design, implementation, and initial evaluation of Sprinkler, a high-throughput reliable broadcast facility that scales in the number of recipients. Prior approaches either assume a small number of recipients per topic or drop events to slow recipients or temporarily disconnected recipients. In order to reach our objectives, we have added a garbage collection facility that replaces application-specified obsolete events with tombstone events. Such tombstone events can be readily aggregated. Garbage collection is particularly effective in the face of updates to keys that are skewed by popularity, or in the face of keys that are used temporarily for intermediate results. Combined with a careful design that separates inter-datacenter forwarding from intra-datacenter forwarding and specializes each case, we have shown that Sprinkler can provide high throughput in the face of millions of recipients.

At the time of this writing, we only have an initial implementation and evaluation of Sprinkler. Garbage collection events currently support predicates that remove events prior to a certain sequence number, or all previous events for the same key. We want to support a richer language for predicates, but have to ensure that Sprinkler proxy CPUs do not get overloaded by evaluation of predicates. We are working on a design of a predicate evaluation language as well as an index for events that allow fast identification of events that match a predicate.

Proxies have the option to maintain all events in memory, or to sync events onto disk to make them persistent. For this paper, we only implemented and evaluated the first option. While keeping everything in memory works well if garbage collection is sufficiently effective and replication prevents data loss, we want to evaluate the performance of storing events on disk. Most access will be sequential writing, and modern disks spin at an impressive 15,000rpm. As disks are cheap, we can deploy multiple disks in parallel to further increase bandwidth. Also SSDs are becoming increasingly cost effective. Cache controllers with battery-backed caches mask the latency of disks—they can complete writes even as the main CPU has crashed. We thus do not expect massive slowdown in the face of disk logging of events.

Acknowledgements. We are grateful for the anonymous reviews and the partial funding by grants from DARPA, AFOSR, NSF, ARPAe, iAd, Amazon.com and Microsoft Corporation.

References

1. Emulab, http://www.emulab.net
2. IBM WebSphere MQ, http://www.ibm.com/WebSphere-MQ
3. PRObE: Parallel Reconf. Observational Env.,
   http://newmexicoconsortium.org/probe
4. Apache HedWig (2010), https://cwiki.apache.org/ZOOKEEPER/hedwig.html
5. Allavena, A., Demers, A., Hopcroft, J.E.: Correctness of a gossip based membership protocol. In: Proc. of the 24th ACM Symp. on Principles of Distributed Computing, pp. 292–301 (2005)
6. Altherr, M., Erzberger, M., Maffeis, S.: iBus - a software bus middleware for the Java platform. In: Proceedings of the Workshop on Reliable Middleware Systems, pp. 43–53 (1999)
7. Birman, K., Hayden, M., Ozkasap, O., Xiao, Z., Budiu, M., Minsky, Y.: Bimodal Multicast. ACM Transactions on Computer Systems 17(2), 41–88 (1999)
8. Birman, K.P., Joseph, T.A.: Exploiting virtual synchrony in distributed systems. In: Proc. of the 11th ACM Symp. on Operating Systems Principles (1987)

9. Bozdog, A., van Renesse, R., Dumitriu, D.: SelectCast – a scalable and self-repairing multicast overlay routing facility. In: First ACM Workshop on Survivable and Self-Regenerative Systems, Fairfax, VA (October 2003)
10. Castro, M., Druschel, P., Kermarrec, A., Rowstron, A.: SCRIBE: A large-scale and decentralized application-level multicast infrastructure. IEEE Journal on Selected Areas in Communications (JSAC) 20(8) (2002)
11. Castro, M., Druschel, P., Kermarrec, A.-M., Nandi, A., Rowstron, A., Singh, A.: SplitStream: high-bandwidth multicast in cooperative environments. In: Proc. of the 19th ACM Symp. on Operating Systems Principles, pp. 298–313 (2003)
12. Curry, E.: Message-Oriented Middleware. In: Mahmoud, Q.H. (ed.) Middleware for Communications, Chichester, UK. John Wiley and Sons, Ltd. (2005)
13. Demers, A., Greene, D., Hauser, C., Irish, W., Larson, J., Shenker, S., Sturgis, H., Swinehart, D., Terry, D.: Epidemic algorithms for replicated database maintenance. In: Proc. of the 6th ACM Symp. on Principles of Distributed Computing, pp. 1–12 (1987)
14. Eugster, P.T., Felber, P.A., Guerraoui, R., Kermarrec, A.-M.: The many faces of publish/subscribe. ACM Comput. Surv. 35(2), 114–131 (2003)
15. Eugster, P.T., Guerraoui, R., Handurukande, S.B., Kouznetsov, P., Kermarrec, A.-M.: Lightweight probabilistic broadcast. ACM Trans. Comput. Syst. 21(4), 341–374 (2003)
16. Ganesh, A.J., Kermarrec, A.-M., Massoulié, L.: Peer-to-peer membership management for gossip-based protocols. IEEE Trans. Comput. 52(2), 139–149 (2003)
17. Hunt, P., Konar, M., Junqueira, F.P., Reed, B.: Zookeeper: wait-free coordination for internet-scale systems. In: Proceedings of the 2010 USENIX Annual Technical Conference, pp. 145–158 (2010)
18. Jannotti, J., Gifford, D., Johnson, K., Kaashoek, M., O'Toole, J.W.: Overcast: Reliable multicasting with an overlay network. In: Proc. of the 4th Symp. on Operating Systems Design and Implementation (October 2000)
19. Kostić, D., Rodriguez, A., Albrecht, J., Vahdat, A.: Bullet: high bandwidth data dissemination using an overlay mesh. In: Proc. of the 19th ACM Symp. on Operating Systems Principles, pp. 282–297 (2003)
20. Kreps, J., Narkhede, N., Rao, J.: Kafka: a distributed messaging system for log processing. In: 6th International Workshop on Networking Meets Databases, NetDB 2011 (2011)
21. Nishtala, R., Fugal, H., Grimm, S., Kwiatkowski, M., Lee, H., Li, H.C., McElroy, R., Paleczny, M., Peek, D., Saab, P., Stafford, D., Tung, T., Venkataramani, V.: Scaling Memcache at Facebook. In: Proc. of the 10th Symp. on Networked Systems Design and Implementation, Lombard, IL (April 2013)
22. Oki, B.M., Pfluegl, M., Siegel, A., Skeen, D.: The Information Bus—an architecture for extensible distributed systems. In: Proc. of the 14th ACM Symp. on Operating Systems Principles, Asheville, NC, pp. 58–68 (December 1993)
23. Pai, V., Kumar, K., Tamilmani, K., Sambamurthy, V., Mohr, A.E.: Chainsaw: Eliminating trees from overlay multicast. In: van Renesse, R. (ed.) IPTPS 2005. LNCS, vol. 3640, pp. 127–140. Springer, Heidelberg (2005)
24. Powell, D.: Group communication. Commun. ACM 39(4), 50–53 (1996)
25. Shen, K.: Structure management for scalable overlay service construction. In: Proc. of the 1st Symp. on Networked Systems Design and Impl., pp. 281–294 (2004)
26. Van Renesse, R., Birman, K.P., Vogels, W.: Astrolabe: A robust and scalable technology for distributed system monitoring, management, and data mining. ACM Trans. Comput. Syst. 21(2), 164–206 (2003)
27. van Renesse, R., Schneider, F.B.: Chain Replication for supporting high throughput and availability. In: Proc. of the 6th Symp. on Operating Systems Design and Implementation (December 2004)

Transactional Failure Recovery
for a Distributed Key-Value Store

Muhammad Yousuf Ahmad[1], Bettina Kemme[1],
Ivan Brondino[2], Marta Patiño-Martínez[2] and Ricardo Jiménez-Peris[2]

[1] McGill University
[2] Universidad Politécnica de Madrid

Abstract. With the advent of cloud computing, many applications have embraced the ensuing paradigm shift towards modern distributed key-value data stores, like HBase, in order to benefit from the elastic scalability on offer. However, many applications still hesitate to make the leap from the traditional relational database model simply because they cannot compromise on the standard transactional guarantees of atomicity, isolation, and durability. To get the best of both worlds, one option is to integrate an independent transaction management component with a distributed key-value store. In this paper, we discuss the implications of this approach for durability. In particular, if the transaction manager provides durability (e.g., through logging), then we can relax durability constraints in the key-value store. However, if a component fails (e.g., a client or a key-value server), then we need a coordinated recovery procedure to ensure that commits are persisted correctly. In our research, we integrate an independent transaction manager with HBase. Our main contribution is a failure recovery middleware for the integrated system, which tracks the progress of each commit as it is flushed down by the client and persisted within HBase, so that we can recover reliably from failures. During recovery, commits that were interrupted by the failure are replayed from the transaction management log. Importantly, the recovery process does not interrupt transaction processing on the available servers. Using a benchmark, we evaluate the impact of component failure, and subsequent recovery, on application performance.

Keywords: Cloud computing, key-value store, transaction processing, OLTP, fault tolerance, failure recovery.

1 Introduction

Traditional online transaction processing (OLTP) applications generally cannot compromise on the basic transactional guarantees of atomicity, consistency, isolation, and durability. On the other hand, modern distributed key-value data stores do not provide transactional semantics out of the box. One way to bridge this gap is through the integration of an independent transaction management component with a distributed key-value store. This approach can allow a traditional OLTP application to benefit from the elastic scalability of cloud computing infrastructure without sacrificing on transactional semantics. Providing

D. Eyers and K. Schwan (Eds.): Middleware 2013, LNCS 8275, pp. 267–286, 2013.

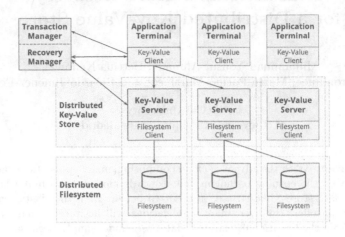

Fig. 1. System Architecture

transactional properties for key-value stores has been proposed in several contexts [7,8,17,19,20]. Figure 1 shows the principle architecture of our approach. The interface of the key-value store is enhanced to provide the transactional primitives *begin*, *commit*, and *abort*, and all read and write accesses to the key-value store are encapsulated in a transactional context. Existing solutions vary in how they implement the various transactional properties as well as how tightly or loosely coupled transaction management is with the data store. We believe that transaction management is ideally as much separated from the data storage as possible, i.e., it should mainly be the transaction management component, rather than the key-value store, that provides the transactional properties.

While the tasks of isolation and atomicity have been the main topic for most of the work so far, relatively little attention has been given to durability. In general, current key-value stores provide durability as they typically persist each update they receive, i.e., they provide durability on a per-object basis. This can be exploited by the transaction manager, since all updates are automatically durable at the time of commit. However, this per-object durability is very costly, in particular as many key-value stores use a reliable file system for persistence that leads to further distribution and replication. Thus, end-to-end latency suffers significantly.

In fact, the cost of writing all changes individually to stable storage before commit is already considered unacceptable in traditional monolithic database systems. Instead, they provide durability with the help of a recovery log [10]. All the changes a transaction performs are recorded in an append-only recovery log that is made persistent just before the transaction commits with a single I/O operation. In contrast, the updates on the actual data pages are not written to stable storage before commit, since this is expensive in terms of I/O. In case of a failure, the updates in the recovery log are replayed to put the stable storage back into a consistent state. As it would be extremely costly as well as unnecessary to replay the entire recovery log since system startup (as most updates are likely to be already persisted), checkpoints are used to accelerate the recovery process.

In this paper, we propose to use a similar mechanism within the transaction manager of our transactional cloud data store: the transaction manager takes responsibility for the durability of a committed transaction by means of a recovery log, while the key-value store does not need to persist its updates immediately upon receiving them. Rather, it can almost instantly store the updates in, and serve them out of its main memory, thereby reducing end-to-end latency. In fact, when durability is achieved through the recovery log maintained by the transaction manager, it might not even be necessary to send updates to the key-value store before the commit, further increasing the performance during standard processing. However, given the more complex architecture of the multi-layered system, both checkpointing as well as recovery become more complicated, since a transaction crosses several layers and might perform updates on several data store servers. As a result, figuring out the set of transactions that are actually affected by a failure becomes more complicated. Furthermore, both client and server failures have to be considered. In the event that a key-value server fails, updates that were still in the server's memory (and not yet persisted to the underlying reliable filesystem) must be replayed. In case a client fails, we must replay the updates of transactions that were already committed but whose writes were not yet fully flushed to the data store.

In summary, this paper presents a comprehensive solution to recovery in a multi-tier transactional key-value store where most of the transaction management tasks are performed by a middleware-based transaction manager. In particular we make the following contributions.

- We rely on efficient transaction logging for persistence in order to provide fast execution for OLTP workloads. As such, there are no forced flushes to stable storage at the key-value store. Updates can even be sent to the key-value store after commit.
- We handle failures of key-value clients and servers. Upon failure, we determine exactly which updates were not persisted at the server-side, and replay those updates before resuming normal processing. For this, we perform lightweight observations at clients and servers during normal processing, somewhat similar to checkpointing in a traditional database system.
- Our approach attempts to separate transaction management as much as possible from data processing. Our extensions to the key-value store to provide a transactional interface and failure recovery are kept to a minimum.
- We have implemented and evaluated our approach using HBase[1], a distributed key-value store that uses HDFS[2] for persistence. Our analysis shows that recovery-related tasks during normal processing incur little overhead and recovery is smooth and efficient.

---

[1] http://hbase.apache.org/
[2] http://hadoop.apache.org/

2 System Model

In this section, we discuss the main components of both the distributed key-value store and an independent transaction manager that are relevant for durability and atomicity. Note that, while we assume that the system also implements some form of concurrency control in order to achieve isolation, isolation and concurrency control are outside the scope of this paper.

2.1 HBase

HBase is a modern distributed key-value data store based on Google BigTable [5]. We believe that it is a representative candidate since many other key-value stores have similar features. HBase offers the abstraction of a table. Each row in a table represents a key-value pair – it is uniquely identified by a key and can have an arbitrary number of secondary columns. Each table is partitioned into one or more chunks called regions. A region is a contiguous set of rows sorted by key. Every region is assigned to one of the multiple region servers in the HBase cluster. A master server coordinates region assignment. Through well-balanced region placement, the application workload can be evenly distributed across the cluster. Moreover, when the existing region servers become overloaded, new region servers can be added dynamically, thus allowing for elastic scalability.

HBase persists its data in the Hadoop Distributed File System (HDFS), which is a reliable and scalable filesystem based on the Google File System [9]. In the HDFS layer, a region is physically stored as one or more immutable files.

An HBase region server serves read requests by fetching the requested data from the underlying filesystem. Typically, it has a large main-memory cache to reduce interactions with HDFS. Additionally, it also maintains, per region, an in-memory store (memstore) that stores the latest updates performed on that region. The contents of each memstore are flushed to HDFS in a batch.

When a server fails, its regions are re-assigned to other servers. Although the persisted data of a region can be read back from HDFS, any in-memory updates that had not yet been persisted to the filesystem are lost. To provide durability against this data loss, HBase first persists each incoming update to its write-ahead log (also stored in HDFS) before applying it to the in-memory store. In this way, after a server failure, the HBase recovery procedure is able to recover lost in-memory updates by replaying them from its log, thus bringing the data store back to a consistent state. As soon as a region has been re-assigned to an available server and recovered to a consistent state, it is made available once again. Each region server maintains a single write-ahead log, to which all updates, whichever region they belong to, are appended. Therefore, the recovery procedure first needs to split the log file and group the updates by region. Once this is done, any region server attempting to recover a region's data can simply read the group of updates associated with that region and apply them to a freshly initialized memstore. Note that, for performance reasons, HBase allows the deactivation of a synchronous flush of the write-ahead log to HDFS. In this case, the server may return from an update operation before the update is persisted to HDFS. In this case, HBase's own recovery cannot guarantee that all updates executed before a server's failure will be recovered.

Applications interact with HBase through an embedded HBase client, a library that provides an advanced interface with get/put operations to access individual key-value pairs and filtered scans for fetching larger result sets.

2.2 Transaction Management

Applications interact with the system through one or more client processes. The task of the independent transaction management is to provide transactional properties (isolation, durability and atomicity) to the application. The application must be provided with an appropriate interface so that it can start, commit, and abort transactions. Also, the system must be able to associate read and write operations to the data store with a unique transaction context. We assume each transaction is executed by a single client and it may touch one or more key-value servers. A client can execute multiple transactions concurrently.

Transaction Execution. The HBase client is the interface between the application and the HBase servers. Thus, the HBase client must be extended to offer a transactional interface to the client. It is also the key player that interacts with the transaction manager, while the modifications to the HBase server have been kept to a minimum. The extended client interface needs to provide the transactional primitives *begin*, *commit*, and *abort*. When the application calls *begin*, a transactional context is created, and all subsequent read/write calls, as well as a final commit/abort, can be associated with this context. The creation and management of the transactional context is the responsibility of the transaction management component and therefore is outside the scope this paper.

In our current approach, we assume that transaction execution follows a deferred-update approach, i.e., updates are not propagated to the HBase servers before commit. This approach is beneficial since it greatly reduces the communication between remote components. For our solution, it is not relevant where the updates are buffered (they could be buffered at the application, the HBase client, or the transaction manager). In our concrete implementation, we keep the write-set of a transaction (i.e., the set of values that a transaction inserts, updates, or deletes), at the HBase client. We assume that updates are idempotent, i.e., applying the write-set at the key-value store multiple times produces the same result every time. This is possible since HBase allows us to specify a version number for each update, and we stamp each transaction's write-set (i.e., each of its updates) with a unique version number, i.e., the commit timestamp of that transaction.

When the application calls *commit*, the transaction termination phase starts. If the transaction manager decides that the transaction can commit, the transaction receives a commit timestamp and its write-set, together with the commit timestamp and a client identifier, is flushed to the recovery log to make it persistent. At this point, the transaction is considered committed. The write-set is flushed to the HBase servers only after the commit. Note that a transaction might have updates for several servers and many updates for a single server. Thus, the flush is usually a non-atomic operation. Once the entire write-set has been flushed, transaction termination is completed. Depending on the concurrency control mechanism implemented in the transaction manager, there could be several transactions terminating concurrently and they could flush their write-sets in any order. The transaction manager would have to ensure that serializability guarantees are not violated (basically, these transactions should not conflict). Focusing on durability and recovery, we assume that commit timestamps are monotonically increasing and that the commit timestamp determines the serialization order for transactions. In other words, if the recovery procedure applies write-sets in commit timestamp order, then this produces a correct execution.

If the application submits an abort request or the transaction manager decides to abort a transaction, the buffered write-set can simply be discarded. It is not stored in the recovery log nor flushed to the HBase servers.

As the transaction manager guarantees the immediate durability of committed write-sets, we deactivate the synchronous flushing of the HBase write-ahead log. Thus, upon receiving an update, the HBase server first appends it to its (in-memory) write-ahead log buffer, then applies it to the memstore, and then immediately returns to the client. Shortly thereafter, (i.e., asynchronously), we sync the write-ahead log buffer to HDFS. At some point later, the actual updates in the memstore are eventually persisted to HDFS.

Transaction Phases. In summary, an update transaction can be in one of the following states at any given time.

- *executing* – the transaction has been started but not yet committed or aborted by the transaction manager
- *aborted* – the transaction manager has aborted the transaction
- *committed* – the transaction manager has declared the transaction as committed, having persisted the write-set to its log
- *flushed* – the committed write-set has been received by all participating HBase servers and applied to their in-memory stores
- *persisted* – the flushed write-set has been persisted by all participating servers (at least the HBase write-ahead log was persisted to HDFS)

3 Recovery Management

In this section, we present our implementation of a failure detection and recovery service for the integrated system. The primary aim is to detect client and server failures and recover from them reliably so that we do not violate the atomicity and durability of committed transactions. The HBase client and server components have been enhanced to provide the necessary support for recovery purposes. Furthermore, we implement a recovery manager, which is a middleware service associated with the transaction manager, that coordinates failure detection and recovery actions across clients and servers.

When an HBase client fails, the recovery manager's recovery procedure replays from the transaction manager's recovery log any of the client's write-sets that were committed but not yet completely flushed to their participating servers. This is necessary because our client holds the write-set until commit time, so we may lose the committed write-set if a client failure occurs before or during the flush phase. Note that write-sets that were not yet committed to the transaction manager's recovery log are permanently lost when the client fails. These transactions are considered aborted. This is not a problem because only the durability of committed transactions must be guaranteed. Uncommitted transaction can be restarted on another client by the application.

When an HBase server fails, the recovery procedure has to replay all committed write-sets that this server participated in that were flushed by the client but not persisted before the server failure occurred. This is necessary because our server persists received write-sets asynchronously, so we may lose a write-set if a server failure occurs before or during the persist phase. Once a write-set has been fully persisted by its participating servers, we can then rely on the key-value store to guarantee the durability of the write-set.

In principle, it would be correct if the recovery manager simply replays all write-sets that exist in the recovery log, as replaying write-sets is idempotent. That is, if a write-set is already reflected in the data store, replaying it will not lead to a different state. However, replaying all write-sets would be extremely inefficient. In a traditional database system, relevant checkpointing information is added to the recovery log during normal processing to determine during recovery the subset of transactions that actually have to be replayed. In a distributed environment, obtaining such checkpointing information is, however, more complex. In our solution, the recovery manager relies on the HBase client and server components to provide the relevant information. On a regular basis, both send the information of what they have flushed and persisted, respectively. This information can be sent asynchronously, or even periodically, as it will serve as a lower bound on which write-sets have to be replayed in case of recovery.

In the following, we first show how the HBase client and recovery manager collaborate in order to: (1) be able to detect client failures, (2) keep track of the transactions that the client has already flushed to the servers, and (3) recover after a client failure. Then we show the corresponding steps for the HBase server.

3.1   Handling Client Failures

Algorithm 1 describes what is done within the HBase client. Algorithm 2 describes the actions performed by the recovery manager to handle client failures.

Client Failure Detection. To detect client failures, we implement a simple heartbeat mechanism. When a client initializes, it registers its heartbeat with the recovery manager, which then starts to monitor the heartbeat. The client regularly sends heartbeat messages to the recovery manager with a configurable frequency. When the client completes execution correctly, it unregisters from

---

Algorithm 1. At client c

1: **On startup:**
2:    register(c)   ▷ register with recovery manager
3:    $T_F \leftarrow T_F^*$ ▷ local ts threshold
4:    $FQ \leftarrow$ synchronized priority queue   ▷ committed txns in commit order
5:    $FQ' \leftarrow$ synchronized priority queue   ▷ flushed txns in commit order
6: **On shutdown:**   ▷ clean shutdown
7:    heartbeat()   ▷ pre-shutdown heartbeat
8:    unregister(c)   ▷ unregister with recovery manager
9: **On heartbeat:**   ▷ called periodically
10:    **while** $|FQ| > 0$ AND $|FQ'| > 0$ **do**
11:        **if** $FQ.head = FQ'.head$ **then**   ▷ earliest tracked flush completed?
12:            $T_F \leftarrow FQ'.head$ ▷ make local progress
13:            FQ.dequeue()   ▷ remove its trackers
14:            FQ'.dequeue()
15:        **else**
16:            break   ▷ respect local commit ordering
17:    send_heartbeat(c, T_F)   ▷ to recovery manager
18: **On receiving commit timestamp T:**   ▷ received commit ts
19:    FQ.enqueue(T)   ▷ add commit tracker
20: **On post-flush of transaction T:**   ▷ called by commit protocol after flush
21:    FQ'.enqueue(T)   ▷ add post-flush tracker

---

the recovery manager cleanly. However, if the recovery manager detects that the client has missed successive heartbeats, it declares the client dead and immediately initiates a recovery procedure. Since we treat a network partition as a crash failure, if any further messages are received from a dead client, they are ignored until the recovery procedure is completed. If a network partition is the cause, the client heartbeat will not be able to contact the recovery manager, which will result in it terminating itself.

Client Tracking. The recovery manager relies on the HBase clients to keep track of when write-sets are flushed to the server. Each client piggybacks the relevant information on its heartbeat messages. In a simple approach, the client could simply send to the recovery manager the commit timestamps of all transactions for which it has completely flushed the write-set to all participating servers. However, that can incur considerable overhead in terms of message size. Instead, each client c maintains a threshold timestamp $T_F(c)$ and sends this timestamp with its heartbeat messages. $T_F(c)$ obeys the following local invariant: the write-set of every local transaction, executing at this client c, with commit timestamp T smaller than or equal to $T_F(c)$ (i.e., where $T \leq T_F(c)$) has been fully flushed to its participant servers. Periodically, we advance $T_F(c)$ as local transactions are committed and flushed. $T_F(c)$ increases monotonically, in increments that correspond to the local commit sequence. In other words, for any two local

Algorithm 2. At recovery manager (client related)

1: **On register(c):**   ▷ register client
2:    C.add(c)
3:    $T_F^r(c) \leftarrow T_F^*$
4: **On unregister(c):**   ▷ unregister client
5:    C.remove(c)
6:    T_F^r.remove(c)
7: **On receive_heartbeat(c, T_F):**
8:    $T_F^r(c) \leftarrow T_F$ ▷ keep track of threshold
9:    $T_F^* \leftarrow \forall i \in C : min(T_F^r(i))$ ▷ update global flushed ts threshold
10: **On failure(c):**   ▷ client failure detected (missed heartbeats)
11:    $L \leftarrow$ fetch_logs(c, $T_F^r(c)$)   ▷ fetch from log txns committed by c after $T_F^r(c)$
12:    **for each** $(T, WS(T))$ **in** L **do**
13:        c_R.flush(T, $WS(T)$)   ▷ replay write-set using recovery client c_R

transactions with commit timestamps $T_i < T_j$, $T_F(c)$ will always advance from T_i to T_j, even if the flush of T_j is completed before that of T_i.

Maintaining $T_F(c)$ is not trivial, since c may flush its transactions in any order. However, the transaction manager ensures that c's transactions receive commit timestamps that are monotonically increasing, i.e., if T receives its timestamp before T', then $T < T'$. In our implementation, a client keeps track of $T_F(c)$ with the help of two queues: FQ keeps track of all transactions in the commit phase, and FQ' keeps track of all transactions that have been successfully flushed. When the timestamps at the heads of both queues match up, we can dequeue that timestamp and advance $T_F(c)$ accordingly. Thus, by adding transactions to FQ in commit timestamp order, we guarantee that $T_F(c)$ is advanced in the proper order.

For each client c, the recovery manager keeps track of the threshold timestamp $T_F^r(c)$ it has received through the last heartbeat message received from c. Due to the periodic delay in heartbeat messages, $T_F^r(c)$ is a conservative threshold representing the flushing process at client c. In order words, while c might have progressed further than $T_F^r(c)$ since its last heartbeat was received, the recovery manager uses $T_F^r(c)$ to represent the current state of c's progress. No transactions with timestamp $T < T_F^r(c)$ have to replayed in case c fails.

Furthermore, the recovery manager maintains a global client threshold $T_F^* = \forall c : min(T_F^r(c))$, which is the lowest $T_F^r(c)$ among all clients. It represents a system-wide threshold that upholds the following global invariant: all transactions that were committed up until time T_F^* have been flushed to and received in full by their participant servers.

Note that maintaining a conservative threshold means that some write-sets might be replayed unnecessarily during recovery. However, this overhead only presents itself during the recovery process and does not affect performance during normal operation. Moreover, the number of write-sets that need to be recovered upon failure is bound by the client's throughput and heartbeat interval.

Finally, in order to ensure that T_F^* advances, clients that shut down properly have to unregister cleanly so that the recovery manager does not take them into consideration anymore for maintaining T_F^*.

Client Recovery. When the recovery manager detects that a client c has failed, it will fetch and replay from the transaction management log those write-sets that were committed by c *after* time $T_F^r(c)$, which is the $T_F(c)$ received by the recovery manager with the most recent heartbeat from c (before it failed). The recovery manager replays these updates via its local client c_R, which differs from a regular client in that it replays the recovered updates using the commit timestamp of the original transaction, rather than obtaining a new one.

3.2   Handling Server Failures

Algorithm 3 describes what is done within the HBase server. Algorithm 4 describes the actions performed by the recovery manager to handle server failures.

Server Failure. For server failure, we depend on HBase to notify us whenever one of its servers dies. Internally, HBase, too, uses heartbeats to monitor server health. When HBase detects that one of its servers has died (due to a crash failure or network partition), the master server initiates a recovery procedure that reassigns the regions of the failed server to other live servers. We added a hook in the master server that notifies our recovery manager whenever a server fails. Each affected region, upon being reassigned to some live server, undergoes HBase's internal recovery procedure during initialization as outlined in Section 2.1. Note that different regions can be assigned to different servers leading to parallel recovery. Recovery replays any un-persisted updates that are associated with this region from the HBase write-ahead log of the failed server. We add another hook in the region initialization process that notifies our recovery manager once this internal recovery procedure is completed, and then waits for a response from our recovery manager before proceeding to actually declare the region online. When the recovery manager receives the notification from the hook, it initiates our transactional recovery procedure for the region. Once our recovery procedure is completed, we notify the region waiting on us that it may proceed to declare itself online. Delaying transaction execution until our recovery procedure is completed, ensures that transactional atomicity is not violated, since, if a region affected by a server failure is brought online before our recovery manager has supplemented the internal region recovery process, clients can potentially end up reading partially recovered write-sets.

Server Tracking. Similar to the client case, each server keeps track of up to which transaction the received write-sets have been persisted to HDFS (i.e., to the HBase write-ahead log). It also sends this information to the recovery manager via regular heartbeat messages. Persisted transactions do not need

---

Algorithm 3. At server s

1: **On startup:**
2:     register(s)   ▷ register with recovery manager
3:     $T_P \leftarrow T_F^*$ ▷ local ts threshold
4:     $PQ \leftarrow$ synchronized priority queue   ▷ received write-sets in commit order
5: **On shutdown:**   ▷ clean shutdown
6:     heartbeat()   ▷ pre-shutdown heartbeat
7:     unregister(s)   ▷ unregister with recovery manager
8: **On heartbeat:**
9:     $T_P' \leftarrow T_F^*$ ▷ read latest T_F^* from recovery manager
10:     **while** $|PQ| > 0$ **do**
11:         $(T, WS(T)) \leftarrow PQ.\text{dequeue}()$
12:         persist($WS(T)$)   ▷ persist write-set
13:     $T_P \leftarrow T_P'$ ▷ make local progress
14:     send_heartbeat(s, T_P)   ▷ to recovery manager
15: **On receive(T, $WS(T)$):**   ▷ received write-set from client
16:     apply($WS(T)$)   ▷ apply updates to in-memory store
17:     $PQ.\text{queue}((T, WS(T)))$ ▷ add tracker
18: **On receive(T, $WS(T)$, $T_P(s')$):**   ▷ received write-set from recovery client
19:     receive(T, $WS(T)$)   ▷ process as usual
20:     **if** $T_P(s') < T_P$ **then**
21:         $T_P \leftarrow T_P(s')$ ▷ inherit responsibility for replayed updates
22:         heartbeat()   ▷ persist and inform recovery manager
23: **On opening_region(r):**   ▷ hook after internal recovery completed...
24:                               ▷ but before declaring r online
25:     **wait**   ▷ until transactional recovery completed...
26:     **until** is_recovered(r)   ▷ by recovery manager

---

to be replayed during recovery in case the server fails. To keep track of these transactions in a compact form, each server s maintains a threshold timestamp $T_p(s)$ that obeys the following local invariant: the write-set of every transaction with commit timestamp T smaller than or equal to $T_P(s)$ (i.e., where $T \leq T_p(s)$), and where the server is a participant, has been received in full by the server and fully persisted (that is, the part of the write-ahead log containing these write-sets has been written to HDFS).

However, it is not that simple for a server to deduce that this invariant holds. While clients know exactly which transactions are currently active, and thus, know which transactions with lower timestamps have been completely flushed, things are not as simple at the server. For instance, assume a server has received and persisted write-sets of transactions with timestamps 20, 22, and 23, but misses 21. Then, it could be that the server is not a participant in transaction 21, in which case, its $T_p(s)$ should be set to 23; but it could also be that the client executing transaction 21 has simply not yet flushed this write-set (but will do so in the future), in which case, $T_p(s)$ should be held at 20.

Algorithm 4. At recovery manager (server related)

1: **On register(s):**   ▷ register server
2:     S.add(s)
3:     $T_P^r(s) \leftarrow T_P^*$

4: **On unregister(s):**   ▷ unregister server
5:     S.remove(s)
6:     T_P^r.remove(s)

7: **On receive_heartbeat(s, T_P):**
8:     $T_P^r(s) \leftarrow T_P$ ▷ update threshold ts
9:     $T_P^* \leftarrow \forall i \in S : min(T_P^r(i))$ ▷ update global persisted ts threshold

10: **On failure(s):**   ▷ notified of server failure (by key-value store)
11:     $L \leftarrow$ fetch_logs($T_P^r(s)$)   ▷ fetch from log txns committed after $T_P^r(s)$
12:     $R \leftarrow$ affected_regions(s)   ▷ fetch from master server
13:     **for each** $r \in R$ **do**   ▷ recover each affected region one-by-one
14:         **for each** $(T, WS(T))$ **in** L **do**
15:             replay($T, WS(T), s, r$)
16:         notify_region(r)   ▷ notify region so it can go online

17: **On replay($T, WS(T), s, r$):**   ▷ replay write-set using recovery client c_R
18:     $T' \leftarrow T$ ▷ new txn with same commit timestamp
19:     **for each** u **in** $WS(T)$ **do**   ▷ for each update in recovered write-set
20:         **if** u.region $= r$ **then**   ▷ if the update u falls in region r
21:             $WS(T')$.add(u)   ▷ else skip other updates
22:     **if** $|WS(T')| > 0$ **then**   ▷ if any updates were selected
23:         c_R.flush($T', WS(T'), T_P^r(s)$)   ▷ replay recovered updates

Therefore, we use a conservative value for $T_p(s)$ by ensuring that $T_P(s) \leq T_F^*$. For any committed transaction with timestamp $T \leq T_F^*$, we know that its write-sets have been successfully flushed to all participating servers. That is, if a server s has received and persisted a transaction $T \leq T_F^*$, then s knows that it also has received all transactions with timestamp $T' < T$. Therefore, periodically, we can persist all write-sets received up until T_F^* and then advance $T_P(s)$ to T_F^*. For that purpose, each server has to receive the latest value of T_F^* from the recovery manager on a regular basis.

For each server s, the recovery manager keeps track of the threshold timestamp $T_P^r(s)$ it has received through the last heartbeat message received from s. $T_P^r(s)$ is a conservative threshold of what s has persisted so far. No transactions with timestamp $T < T_P^r(s)$ have to be replayed in case s fails.

Furthermore, we saw earlier that $T_P^r(s) < T_F^*$. Based on this information, the recovery manager can declare that $T_P^* = \forall s : min(T_P^r(s))$, i.e., the lowest $T_P^r(s)$ among all servers, is a system-wide threshold that upholds the following global invariant: all transactions that were committed up until time T_P^* have been flushed to, received in full, and safely persisted by their participant servers. Therefore, T_P^* also represents a global checkpoint for the purposes of commit logging and failure recovery. That is, transactions with timestamp $T < T_P^*$ may be truncated from the recovery log since they have been safely persisted.

Server Recovery. In the event of a server failure, we lose the state of the in-memory store on that server. Since we persist these updates and the HBase write-ahead log asynchronously, lost updates must be recovered from the transaction management log to ensure their durability.

When the recovery manager detects that a server s has failed, it will first wait for the key-value store to perform its standard recovery process to recover, one-by-one, the set $R(s)$ of regions affected by this failure. For each affected region r, once its in-memory store has been reconstructed by HBase, our recovery manager will take over. It will replay from the transaction manager's recovery log those write-sets that were committed *after* time $T_P^r(s)$, which is the piggybacked value received by the recovery manager with the most recent heartbeat from server s (before it failed). These are the write-sets that have potentially not yet been persisted. The recovery manager replays them via its local client c_R. Once our recovery process for a region r has completed, the region is brought back online. Server recovery is complete once all affected regions have been recovered.

There are three important ways in which the recovery client c_R differs from a regular client. First, it replays the recovered updates using the commit timestamp of the original (recovered) transaction, rather than requesting a fresh commit timestamp from the transaction manager. This applies also to client recovery. The other two modifications apply only to server recovery. During server recovery, when replaying a write-set to an affected region r, the recovery client checks each update in the write-set to see if it falls within r, replaying it if it does, and skipping it otherwise. This means that we only replay those updates that were left un-persisted due to this specific server failure. Secondly, the recovery client piggybacks $T_P^r(s)$ on every replayed update when performing the recovery procedure for a failed server s. To understand why this is necessary, consider the following scenario. During recovery, we replay an update u, which belongs to the write-set of some transaction T, where $T_P^r(s) < T$, and which falls under region r, one of the affected regions in $R(s)$. A live server s', which now hosts r, receives u, applies it to its in-memory store, queues it for persistence, and then returns to the client. At this point, if s' fails, we can end up losing u under the following condition: $T_P^r(s) < T \le T_P^r(s')$, since the recovery procedure for s' will only recover write-sets of transactions committed later than $T_P^r(s')$. In order to avoid this situation, once we add u to the in-memory store of s', we modify $T_P(s')$ to $T_P^r(s)$, before returning to the client. This ensures that s' correctly inherits the responsibility for the recovered updates of s.

One scenario that we must also consider is that a server failure will interrupt any incoming client flushes. A client c in this situation will retry, multiple times, to flush the remaining part of the write-set to the target regions. As soon as the affected regions are recovered and brought back online, the client will be able to proceed again normally and complete any interrupted flushes. However, if a client flush eventually runs out of retries or times out, $T_F(c)$ can be permanently blocked from advancing, even after the affected regions comes back online a little later. Even though other concurrent flushes of the same client c may have been unaffected by the failure, we cannot advance $T_F(c)$, since it must advance in step with the local commit order at c. This will then block the progress of our global timestamp thresholds, since T_F^* is bound to the lowest $T_F(c)$ among all clients, and T_P^* is bound to T_F^*. Therefore, we work around this by removing the retry and timeout limits so that the client keeps retrying until it succeeds. During this time, the client can at least continue to execute read-only transactions on older snapshots of the data. Alternatively, we could terminate the client to induce the recovery manager to attempt a recovery of the interrupted write-set.

If a region remains unavailable forever (i.e., it cannot be recovered for some reason), then a system administrator must intervene and manually recover the region. In order to detect such incidents, each client/server monitors the size of its flush/persist queue (which reflects the transactions flushed/persisted, but not yet reflected in the corresponding threshold timestamps) and alerts the recovery manager if the size exceeds a configurable threshold. Once the problematic region is recovered, the blocked timestamp thresholds are able to advance until they become current again.

3.3   Recovery Manager Failure

As a final note, the failure of the recovery manager also has to be considered. The only data the recovery manager maintains are the threshold timestamps. These timestamps can also be written to the recovery log periodically or stored in a highly reliable service such as ZooKeeper[3]. Our implementation uses ZooKeeper for coordination between the recovery manager and clients/servers (i.e., heartbeat messages are exchanged via ZooKeeper). Upon failure, the recovery manager is restarted and contacts ZooKeeper to catch up with the system's progress. Transaction processing can continue while the recovery manager is down.

4   Performance Evaluation

In this section, we present a preliminary performance evaluation of our integrated implementation. We first look at the performance benefits of asynchronous versus synchronous persistence. Next, we show that the overhead for providing a reliable transaction processing framework for HBase, using our failure recovery scheme, is small. Finally, we look at the effects of a server failure on runtime performance. Our experiments measure transaction throughput and response time.

4.1   Benchmark and Setup

We use YCSB[4] to evaluate our implementation. We extended YCSB to support true transactional workloads and implemented a simple type of update

---

[3] http://zookeeper.apache.org/
[4] http://github.com/brianfrankcooper/YCSB

transaction that executes 10 random row operations, with a 50/50 ratio of reads/updates. We loaded our test table with half a million rows.

We ran our experiments on virtual machines hosted on a cluster of Dell R310 quad-core servers. Each VM was allocated two processor cores and 2 GB of main memory. The machines were connected over a 100 Mbps Ethernet switch. We ran our experiments using one client node and two server nodes. On each server node, we ran an HBase region server co-located with an HDFS datanode. We allocated two thirds of the region server's available memory for the block cache (for reads) and the remaining one third for the memstore (for updates). The size of our test dataset was chosen such that it could fit completely into the cumulative block cache of a single region server, so that we could compensate for the failure of one of the servers. We used a data replication factor of two (instead of the default of three) in HDFS. We populated a fresh dataset and warmed up the block cache before the start of each experiment.

The transaction management and recovery management components were co-hosted on one VM. The transaction management component provides an efficient concurrency control mechanism based on snapshot isolation. Its internal structure is highly scalable and fully reliable. The overall architecture of the transaction management component will soon be submitted for publication in an independent manuscript, and thus, is not further detailed here. The logging sub-component supports group commit, has access to its own high performance stable storage, and can be distributed across several nodes should one logging node not be sufficient. It offers the interface methods for the recovery manager to retrieve the necessary logs at the time of recovery.

4.2   Benefits of Asynchronous Persistence

We evaluated the advantages of persisting updates asynchronously to the key-value store. We used two region servers. Figure 2(a) shows a performance comparison between synchronous and asynchronous persistence. The graph shows response time (in milliseconds) against throughput (in transactions per second (tps)). We achieve lower response times with asynchronous persistence. These results reflect our original premise that asynchronous persistence offers a performance advantage because it eliminates the latency associated with flushing and persisting updates to the key-value store from end-to-end response times.

Note that our transactions are quite short, in which case, transaction management related tasks make up a considerable part of the execution time (timestamp management, logging, etc.). With longer transactions that perform more read and write operations one can expect a larger performance gain. Also, we can expect the gap between the two curves to be greater if the HDFS data nodes are not physically co-located with the HBase servers, as that worsens end-to-end latency under synchronous persistence.

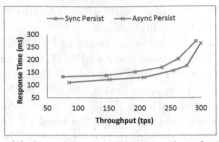
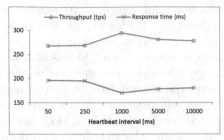

(a) Asynchronous persistence benefits   (b) Transaction tracking overheads

Fig. 2. Performance improvements and overheads

4.3 Overhead of Providing Reliability

We evaluated the overhead associated with providing reliability under the asynchronous persistence approach. Each client and server component performs some light-weight tracking of their local transaction progress. This tracking involves the use of synchronized data structures. Periodically, just before sending its heartbeat, each component updates its local tracking information, which the recovery manager then uses to update its global trackers. The system throughput and the length of the heartbeat interval together determine the amount of processing performed with each heartbeat. The shorter the interval, the more frequently we update the tracking information and the less the information processed per heartbeat. On the other hand, our tracking data structures need to be synchronized, since they are accessed concurrently by multiple threads. Thus, updating the tracking information too frequently can potentially reduce performance due to added contention. We use trial-and-error to determine a good heartbeat interval. In our experiments, we varied this interval from 50 ms to 10 seconds for 50 client threads and two region servers. As Figure 2(b) shows, both throughput and response time vary as a function of the heartbeat interval, and we are able to find a good interval value for our setup.

4.4 Evaluating Failure Recovery

We evaluated the effects of a component failure on transaction processing. We measured the runtime performance of 50 client threads with two region servers. We simulated a workload of 250 tps, which in our setup is near the peak capacity for a single region server serving 50 client threads. We set the heartbeat intervals to one second. In Figure 3, runtime throughput and response time readings are plotted on the vertical axis against wall-clock time on the horizontal axis. We manually induced a server failure during the experiment. The server crash causes a sharp drop in throughput and a corresponding peak in response time. The performance returns to nearly pre-failure readings over the next 30 seconds. In our tests, we observed that the actual recovery process takes only a few seconds, whereas the longer delay in returning to pre-failure performance levels is due

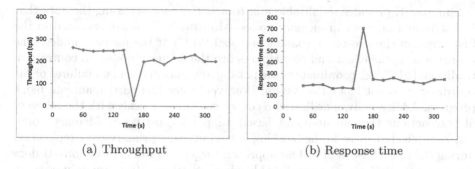

(a) Throughput   (b) Response time

Fig. 3. Failure detection and recovery

to the region server cache taking a while to warm up to the recovered regions' data. Note that transaction processing is not interrupted (i.e., transactions are not lost) by the failure.

5   Related Work

There has been considerable work in adding transaction functionality to key-value stores [7,8,17,19,20], some of which discusses logging and recovery to some extend. CloudTPS [20] supports scalable transactions by distributing the transaction management among a set of local transaction managers and partitioning the data using the key-value store for persistence. Similar to our model, the updates are not written to the storage during commit but buffered in-memory for performance reasons and only sent to the key-value store periodically. Updates are replicated across several local transaction managers (LTMs) to guarantee availability in the advent of failures. This requires coordination among the replicas. If there is a failure, data is recovered from a LTM replica. Since some data items in the replica may have been written to storage, to avoid repeating writes, they keep track and replicate in some LTMs the latest checkpointed timestamp for each data item. Again timestamps are replicated in batches. Compared to our approach, the checkpointing overhead is considerably larger as it is on a per-item basis vs. per-transaction basis. Furthermore, their approach assumes that once data is written to the data store it is persistent, while we also handle asynchronous writes at the data store.

Calvin [19] is a fault-tolerant replicated transactional system that provides transactions across multiple data partitions. In contrast to our approach, their transaction management and data store are tightly coupled and build a holistic system, while our approach keeps the data store backend nearly unchanged. Calvin logs the history of transactional input (that is, logical logging instead of physical logging). If there is a failure, the input can be replayed during recovery. Different checkpointing techniques are implemented to limit the number of transactions that are re-executed. Checkpointing, however, has considerable performance implications during normal processing.

Sinfonia [1] provides serializable *minitransactions* for accessing the data that is distributed on a set of memory nodes. Minitransactions are executed in the first phase of the two-phase commit protocol (2PC) at the memory nodes. The coordinator is the client and participants are the memory nodes. In contrast to traditional 2PC, the coordinator does not log any information and failures of the coordinator do not block the system. However, a crashed participant can block progress. Additionally, a dedicated recovery coordinator deals with the recovery of transactions that are in-doubt based on participant votes. Memory nodes can be replicated to avoid the blocking behavior, using primary-copy replication during the first phase of 2PC. Our approach targets regular transactions. It does not resort to 2PC, thereby avoiding blocking situations. Recovery only uses the information in the log and does not contact data nodes to decide on the outcome of transactions. Data is kept in HBase/HDFS, which eventually provides data durability without adding extra latency to transaction execution.

Omid is similar to our system in that it implements transactions on top of HBase [11,21]. According to [11], Omid updates the data in HBase as part of the transaction execution, whereas our proposal is based on the deferred-update model (changes are only applied to HBase after the transaction commits). Omid uses a distributed logging service, BookKeeper[5], for write-ahead logging. Recovery is not described.

G-Store [8] provides transactions over partitioned groups of keys on top of a key-value store. Groups are dynamically created. One of the keys in a group is the leader, which grants read/write access to the group's keys. G-Store uses write-ahead logging and flushes changes asynchronously to the data store. All the information related to groups is also logged, and recovery deals also with in-progress creation and deletion of groups at the time the failure occurred. However, recovery itself is not discussed. No checkpointing mechanism is described that would show how to limit recovery costs.

ElasTraS [7] provides an elastic key-value data store where transactions execute within a single data partition (static partitions), and partitions can be migrated online from one server to another. ElasTraS uses write-ahead logging for durability and stores the log in HDFS. Once data is persisted in the key-value store, the log is updated in order to enable truncation. However, no further analysis is provided regarding the logging and recovery processes.

In [4], a database is built on top of Amazon S3, analyzing how various Amazon services can be used for database purposes. The approach presents a global solution where transaction management is tightly integrated with the other components. Amazon's Simple Queuing System is used to store log records. However, failure and recovery are not described or analyzed in detail.

Deuteronomy [14] supports transactions over arbitrary data. It decouples transaction processing from data storage, as already done in [15,16]. Just as in our approach logging is done at the transaction manager, which has to coordinate with the data stores. In the case of Deuteronomy, the transaction manager tells the data store when to persist data items. In contrast, we let the clients

---

[5] http://zookeeper.apache.org/bookkeeper/

and servers tell the recovery manager what has been flushed and persisted, respectively. In Deuteronomy, if the transaction manager fails, a new transaction manager is initialized and performs recovery using the log. Recovery may also need to undo updates, which is not necessary in our approach since we only flush after commit.

In recent years, geo-replicated transactions have received attention in order to achieve consistency across geographically distributed data stores [6,12,18]. The idea is to remain available through wide-area replication even if individual data centers go down. The main focus is coordination through 2PC and Paxos [13]. In such a context, recovery costs are less important because availability is maintained through replication, and the costs of persistence play a lesser role as wide-area coordination is the main factor.

Hyder [2] is a log-structured multi-version key-value database shared by many servers where the log not only guarantees durability but also is used to update the actual server state. The idea is that server caches are a (partial) copy of the database. Transactions write their changes to the log, and servers run a meld algorithm [3] that traverses the log to keep the cache copy up-to-date while at the same time performing concurrency control.

6 Conclusion

In this paper, we present a logging and recovery infrastructure where a modular transaction manager is combined with a distributed key-value store. Transaction write-sets are persisted to the transaction manager's recovery log at commit time and then flushed asynchronously to the key-value store and then eventually persisted to the distributed filesystem. Transaction progress is tracked at the key-value clients and servers. Light-weight checkpointing is performed in order to limit the amount of recovery that has to be performed at recovery time.

Acknowledgments. This research has been partially funded by the Ministère de l'Enseignement supérieur, de la Recherche, de la Science et de la Technologie of Quebec and by the European Commission under project CumuloNimbo (FP7-257993), the Madrid Regional Council (CAM), FSE and FEDER under project CLOUDS (S2009TIC-1692), and the Spanish Research Agency MICINN under project CloudStorm (TIN2010-19077).

References

1. Aguilera, M.K., Merchant, A., Shah, M.A., Veitch, A.C., Karamanolis, C.T.: Sinfonia: A new paradigm for building scalable distributed systems. ACM Trans. Comput. Syst. 27(3) (2009)
2. Bernstein, P.A., Reid, C.W., Das, S.: Hyder - a transactional record manager for shared flash. In: CIDR, pp. 9–20 (2011)
3. Bernstein, P.A., Reid, C.W., Wu, M., Yuan, X.: Optimistic concurrency control by melding trees. PVLDB 4(11), 944–955 (2011)

4. Brantner, M., Florescu, D., Graf, D.A., Kossmann, D., Kraska, T.: Building a database on s3. In: SIGMOD Conference, pp. 251–264 (2008)
5. Chang, F., et al.: Bigtable: a distributed storage system for structured data. In: Proceedings of the 7th USENIX Symposium on Operating Systems Design and Implementation, OSDI 2006, vol. 7, p. 15. USENIX Association, Berkeley (2006)
6. Corbett, J.C., et al.: Spanner: Google's globally-distributed database. In: Proceedings of the 10th USENIX Conference on Operating Systems Design and Implementation, OSDI 2012, pp. 251–264. USENIX Association, Berkeley (2012)
7. Das, S., Agrawal, D., El Abbadi, A.: Elastras: an elastic transactional data store in the cloud. In: Proceedings of the 2009 Conference on Hot Topics in Cloud Computing, HotCloud 2009. USENIX Association, Berkeley (2009)
8. Das, S., Agrawal, D., El Abbadi, A.: G-store: a scalable data store for transactional multi key access in the cloud. In: Proceedings of the 1st ACM Symposium on Cloud Computing, SoCC 2010, pp. 163–174. ACM, New York (2010)
9. Ghemawat, S., Gobioff, H., Leung, S.T.: The google file system. In: SOSP, pp. 29–43 (2003)
10. Gray, J., Reuter, A.: Transaction Processing: Concepts and Techniques, 1st edn. Morgan Kaufmann Publishers Inc., San Francisco (1992)
11. Junqueira, F., Reed, B., Yabandeh, M.: Lock-free transactional support for large-scale storage systems. In: DSN Workshops, pp. 176–181 (2011)
12. Kraska, T., Pang, G., Franklin, M.J., Madden, S., Fekete, A.: Mdcc: multi-data center consistency. In: EuroSys, pp. 113–126 (2013)
13. Lamport, L.: The part-time parliament. ACM Trans. Comput. Syst. 16(2), 133–169 (1998)
14. Levandoski, J.J., Lomet, D.B., Mokbel, M.F., Zhao, K.: Deuteronomy: Transaction support for cloud data. In: CIDR, pp. 123–133 (2011)
15. Lomet, D.B., Fekete, A., Weikum, G., Zwilling, M.J.: Unbundling transaction services in the cloud. In: CIDR (2009)
16. Lomet, D.B., Mokbel, M.F.: Locking key ranges with unbundled transaction services. PVLDB 2(1), 265–276 (2009)
17. Peng, D., Dabek, F.: Large-scale incremental processing using distributed transactions and notifications. In: OSDI, pp. 251–264 (2010)
18. Sovran, Y., Power, R., Aguilera, M.K., Li, J.: Transactional storage for geo-replicated systems. In: SOSP, pp. 385–400 (2011)
19. Thomson, A., Diamond, T., Weng, S.C., Ren, K., Shao, P., Abadi, D.J.: Calvin: fast distributed transactions for partitioned database systems. In: SIGMOD Conference, pp. 1–12 (2012)
20. Wei, Z., Pierre, G., Chi, C.H.: Cloudtps: Scalable transactions for web applications in the cloud. IEEE T. Services Computing 5(4), 525–539 (2012)
21. Yabandeh, M., Gómez Ferro, D.: A critique of snapshot isolation. In: Proceedings of the 7th ACM European Conference on Computer Systems, EuroSys 2012, pp. 155–168. ACM, New York (2012)

Views and Transactional Storage
for Large Graphs

Michael M. Lee[1], Indrajit Roy[2], Alvin AuYoung[2], Vanish Talwar[2],
K. R. Jayaram[2], and Yuanyuan Zhou[1]

[1] University of California, San Diego
{mmlee,yyzhou}@cs.ucsd.edu
[2] HP Labs
{indrajitr,alvina,vanish.talwar,jayaramkr}@hp.com

Abstract. A growing number of applications store and analyze graph-structured data. These applications impose challenging infrastructure demands due to a need for scalable, high-throughput, and low-latency graph processing. Existing state-of-the-art storage systems and data processing systems are limited in at least one of these dimensions, and simply layering these technologies is inadequate.

We present Concerto, a graph store based on distributed, in-memory data structures. In addition to enabling efficient graph traversals by co-locating graph nodes and associated edges where possible, Concerto provides transactional updates while scaling to hundreds of nodes. Concerto introduces graph *views* to denote sub-graphs on which user-defined functions can be invoked. Using graph views, programmers can perform event-driven analysis and dynamically optimize application performance. Our results show that Concerto is significantly faster than in-memory MySQL, in-memory Neo4j, and GemFire for graph insertions as well as graph queries. We demonstrate the utility of Concerto's features in the design of two real-world applications: real-time incident impact analysis on a road network and targeted advertising in a social network.

Keywords: Graphs, transactions, views, event-driven analysis.

1 Introduction

Graph-processing applications are quickly emerging as a critical component in domains like social networks, road traffic, and biological networks where data exhibit natural graph structure. Building large-scale graph applications requires middleware support for storing data and for accelerating graph queries. Many of today's graph applications exhibit a need for high volume storage, low-latency updates, and interactive responsiveness. Individually, these requirements do not present a unique challenge, but taken together, they pose a significant challenge to both state-of-the-art storage and data-processing systems. We detail two of these emerging requirements, and how they translate into challenges for the supporting system infrastructure:

- **Scalability and consistency.** Because many of today's graph applications run on the critical path of an on-line workflow, a graph store needs to provide

D. Eyers and K. Schwan (Eds.): Middleware 2013, LNCS 8275, pp. 287–306, 2013.
© IFIP International Federation for Information Processing 2013

a combination of adequate query throughput and data ingestion rate. For example, Facebook receives more than 200,000 events per second [1] while Twitter ingests approximately 80 TB/day of new data [2]. However, without meaningful consistency semantics, such as transactional guarantees, writing distributed graph applications will be difficult and error prone.

- **Event-driven processing.** Some graph applications, such as those used by emergency technicians to respond to incidents, must be real-time to be useful [3]. For example, the California highway road sensors requires ingestion of new data every 30 seconds for over 26,000 sensors [4]. Such an application is largely event-driven based upon incidents (i.e., accidents, slowdowns) occurring on the road graph, and triggers computation to predict the spread and duration of the incidents. Supporting an API with flexible event processing on the graph store eases the development of these graph applications. Multiple applications monitoring similar events can avoid redundant client-side computation on event detection. Moreover, events can be used to monitor and dynamically optimize the store itself (such as graph layout) to further improve query performance.

1.1   Limitations of Current Systems

State-of-the-art solutions are not designed to address these challenges simultaneously. Traditional storage systems such as relational databases and NoSQL stores do not inherently retain the structure of the graph, and are unsuitable for computing graph algorithms [5]. As shown in Table 1, using a fast caching layer such as Memcached on top of a relational database can scale the performance of resolving graph queries. However, this approach relies on pre-computing the set of queries, and thus requires the workload to be known in advance, or returning a computation based upon stale data.

Distributed in-memory stores (GemFire [6]) provide dynamic scalability and high performance while also supporting transactions. However, similar to traditional relational databases, they do not provide native support for graph objects and hence are slow for graph queries.

Contemporary data-processing frameworks such as MapReduce [7], Pregel [5], Spark [8], or GraphLab [9] optimize for batch analysis by assuming data is largely read-only, and hence are ill-suited for concurrent read and write queries. Since many of these systems are designed for long running distributed graph analyses, the overhead from additional communication and setup costs may exceed the actual computation time for small graph queries [10].

In contrast, specialized graph databases perform complex graph queries quickly, and concurrently with graph updates [11,12,13,14,15,16]. These systems are, however, limited to a single machine (or a set of replicated images) and therefore do not scale with either the query rate, storage capacity, or data ingestion rate. Trinity [17], a distributed graph engine, lacks support for transactional storage of graph objects. Additionally, none of these graph databases support event-driven processing.

Table 1. Comparison with competitive approaches. Concerto has multiple advantages over each system.

Technology	Graph queries	Transactions	Event processing	Scalable
RDBMS (MySQL, etc.)	Slow due to table joins	Yes	Yes, using triggers	No
RDBMS + memcached [18]	Fast but stale results	No	No	Yes
Distributed in-memory stores [6]	Slow	Yes	Yes, using triggers	Yes
Batch graph frameworks [5]	Fast but offline	No	No	Yes
Graph DBs (Neo4j [12], DEX [15])	Fast, online	Yes	No	No
Trinity [17]	Fast, online	No, explicit locks	No	Yes
Concerto Design choice →	**Fast, online** In-memory data structures	**Yes** Distributed transactions	**Yes** Graph views, notifications	**Yes** Distributed processing

1.2   Contributions

We have designed Concerto, a graph store that preserves the functionality of specialized graph databases without sacrificing the ability to scale or build event-driven applications. As shown in Table 1, Concerto differs from existing work in its combination of two fundamental design principles.

First, Concerto provides distributed, *in-memory, transactional storage* of graph elements. Unlike traditional databases, Concerto embeds the graph structure within the aggregate memory of the cluster. While this layout incurs more storage than a traditional table-based layout, it enables otherwise expensive graph traversals to be performed quickly. Unlike existing graph databases, Concerto is designed to maintain data consistency across *multiple* servers using distributed transactions. The costs of the distributed transaction protocol are compensated by several performance optimizations: in-memory representation, fewer network roundtrips, and parallel computation.

Second, Concerto introduces the notion of *graph views*, which allows an application to denote subgraphs of interest. Applications can compose different views to form meaningful groups and run graph analysis on them. Applications can also register user-defined event handlers on a view. As we discuss in Section 6, some graph applications are naturally expressed as event-driven programs, and in our experience, the extensibility provided by Concerto improves performance and simplifies application programming. Moreover, views act as hints about which graph entities are related, thereby providing a means to enhance data migration, or partitioning policies [19,20,21] and reduce communication overhead.

We empirically compare Concerto against in-memory executions of MySQL, a standard relational database; Neo4j, an open-source graph database; and Gem-Fire, a commercial in-memory distributed store. Concerto is 10× faster in bulk insertion throughput than Neo4j while consuming 3× less memory. Similarly, Concerto is more than 7× faster than MySQL for interactive k-hop query performance. Scaling results on 64 instances shows that Concerto can complete a 3-core computation of a 90-million node graph in only 12 minutes, compared to nearly 6 hours on 64 instances of GemFire. We also demonstrate Concerto's features through two real-world inspired applications: real-time incident impact analysis on a road network, and targeted advertising in a social network.

2   Graph Storage

Concerto stores graph objects in memory and across distributed commodity servers in data centers (Figure 1a). A distributed shared memory implementation provides a global address space on which graph objects are allocated. Graph traversals take place on the distributed graph representation using server-side RPC calls batched for performance. Concerto's key contributions are in the *in-memory graph representation* and the use of *efficient, distributed transactions* to provide concurrent access and online data migration.

2.1   Graph Representation

Concerto has three basic data types to store the application graph data: `vertex`, `edge`, and `property`. A `property` element contains attributes and can be attached to a vertex or edge. Vertices and edges can have multiple properties. Concerto exposes APIs to graph applications to create and update the above graph elements. New graph objects are allocated on a global address space provided by Sinfonia [22], a distributed shared memory system. Sinfonia exposes a flat memory region per-server called memnode which are combined to create a single global address space.

Concerto stores the logical graph using a layout optimized for in-memory reads and inserts. As shown in Figure 1b, vertices, edges, and properties are represented as records with pointers. A vertex has a pointer to a list of its outgoing edges. An edge has pointers to its source and destination vertices and to the next edge of the source vertex. Thus, all outgoing edges of a vertex can be accessed consecutively starting from the first edge. Co-locating vertices and edges in contiguous blocks of memory, and storing pointers to related graph objects allow graph traversals to be performed quickly at the cost of additional storage. Similar to edges, properties are chained together as a list. Both vertex and edge records point to the head of their property lists.

In Concerto, each vertex and edge is a fixed-size record while properties can be of variable size. Using an appropriate fixed size, a vertex or edge can be retrieved in one read transaction (one network roundtrip between a client and a Concerto server) as both the address and size of the data are known in advance. However, accessing properties of a vertex or edge may require more than one transaction. First, the vertex has to be read to determine the address of the property and then the property is read in the next transaction. In some applications, certain properties are accessed often. To retrieve these frequently accessed objects in one read transaction, properties can optionally be *embedded* in the vertex or edge records. Figure 1b depicts embedded properties attached to vertices and edges.

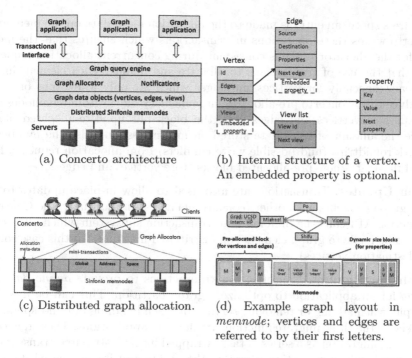

(a) Concerto architecture

(b) Internal structure of a vertex. An embedded property is optional.

(c) Distributed graph allocation.

(d) Example graph layout in *memnode*; vertices and edges are referred to by their first letters.

Fig. 1. Overview of Concerto

2.2   Use of Transactions

Concerto uses distributed transactions to provide consistency and concurrency for graph allocation, access, and updates. Unlike simple key-value data, graph data can seldom be partitioned into shared nothing regions, and hence we need to support transactions that occur *across* machines. To balance consistency with efficiency, Concerto leverages a distributed compare-and-swap primitive called a *mini-transaction* provided by Sinfonia to support such distributed transactions. Mini-transactions are a performance-optimized implementation of the two-phase commit protocol. Concerto also provides other optimizations to minimize the number of transactions used. These include batching graph operations during traversals and reducing the number of indirections for graph object access. Using these optimizations, Concerto can, in the common case, perform reads of vertices, edges or attributes in a single network roundtrip, and finish writes in two network roundtrips. By comparison, transactionally updating even a single value in GemFire requires at least three network roundtrips. Below, we discuss examples of how transactions are used in Concerto.

Graph Allocation. During allocation of new graph elements (e.g., `vertex`, `edge`) it is important to ensure a unique address is assigned to the graph element even if two concurrent users request memory. Concerto uses transactions to achieve this. As shown in Figure 1c, whenever an allocation request is received, the Concerto graph allocator contacts the Sinfonia memnode. Upon allocation of an address space, an entry is made to the allocation meta-data on the memnode. Concerto wraps these operations in transactions which ensures that the meta-data for the allocator remains consistent during concurrent allocation requests. Note that the use of transactions to allocate and manage each element incurs overhead, especially for vertices and edges which are only a few tens of bytes. To reduce this, Concerto pre-allocates large memory blocks from memnodes and appends new vertices and edges until the block fills up. Pre-allocated blocks reduce the amount of meta-data stored on memnodes, and also the number of network roundtrips (and possible write conflicts) from allocation requests. Figure 1d illustrates how pre-allocated blocks store vertices and edges.

Graph Updates. Transactions are also used to allow in-place updates to existing graph elements with other (concurrent) accesses. Internally, the Concerto transaction API calls the Sinfonia mini-transaction subsystem which allows updates to be made to graph elements on distributed machines (in this case source and destination vertices).

Graph Partitioning. Concerto uses transactions to provide *online data migration* for an application to optimize a graph partition. This can be used, for example, when adding or removing servers, or when handling data hotspots. Table 2 shows the three migrate functions available to applications. These functions implement migration as a series of tasks wrapped inside distributed transactions. For example, when migrating a vertex, the vertex and its associated data are copied to the new server, the original copy is deleted, and all incoming pointers to the vertex are updated. These tasks happen inside a transaction during which time other non-conflicting operations can continue concurrently.

Table 2. Functions to migrate data

Function	Description
migrateVertex(V, s)	Move V and its data to server s
migrateView(View, s)	Move view elements to server s
migrateGraph(View, map)	Move elements based on map

3   Graph Views

The primary programming innovation of Concerto is the notion of application-specific event processing using *graph views*. The concept of views is well-studied in the database literature. Concerto extends this concept to distributed graph stores. In Concerto, a view is a subgraph of interest on which applications can run graph algorithms and also register generic event handlers. By using event handlers, an application is easily expressed as an event-driven program.

3.1   Programming Model

Concerto provides a `View` class to create and manage graph views. Views are subgraphs and comprise of a list of vertices, edges, and properties. Views are

Table 3. View API for event-driven processing

Function	Description
onReadVertex(V) onReadEdge(E) onReadProperty(P)	Invoked on read operation. Passes element where read occurred.
onUpdateVertex(V) onUpdateEdge(E) onUpdateProperty(P, val)	Invoked on write operation. Passes element where write occurred. Old value of property also passed.

primarily created to isolate regions of interest and can constrain a query to execute only on a subgraph. For example, Concerto applications use the BSP programming model to implement distributed graph algorithms by specifying code that runs on each vertex [5,23]. Graph views provide application-specific semantics to these algorithms: applications can compose multiple views and then execute a distributed algorithm on the complex view. Consider the example mentioned in the introduction where the graph G represents a road traffic network and the graph application performs real-time accident impact analysis [3] on G. The application developer might create a view P and M corresponding to the cities of Palo Alto and Mountain View, respectively. If an accident occurs in Palo Alto, then the application can localize the execution of its impact analysis algorithm on P and demarcate the affected region I=impactAnalysis(P). Now, the application can be easily extended to provide useful functionality; to find the best path from a location in Mountain View to Palo Alto, while avoiding the impacted region, a user would simply run a shortest path algorithm on the composed view:(P - I)∪M. Concerto supports basic set operations, such as union, intersection, and subtraction, on views. For example, two views can be merged or their common elements subtracted.

Views simplify the support for event-driven processing. Applications can define a view upon which to register event handlers. The View API (Table 3) can be invoked when read or write events occur in the subgraph. For example, onreadVertex function can be invoked when a read event occurs on a vertex in the view, and onUpdateProperty function is invoked on a write event to a property element in the view. To implement function invocation, the view pointers are stored in graph elements (Figure 1b). Specifically, whenever a read or an write occurs on a graph element, the view pointer(s) associated with the graph element are traversed and the corresponding function is invoked.

Applications can invoke custom code using the View API. In our experience, read functions are broadly useful for gathering statistics and for monitoring the store. For example, the onReadVertex function can be overwritten to determine whether too many clients are reading the view members. By monitoring read throughput, data may be migrated proactively to reduce hotspots. Handlers for write events may benefit from more customization. For example, in our road traffic application, write events might specify the location of an accident, which would trigger execution of the traffic impact analysis in that region.

3.2   Data Structures

Supporting graph views requires a trade-off between compact storage and fast subgraph traversal. For fast graph traversals, the ideal approach makes a copy of the subgraph corresponding to a view, enabling traversals to occur directly on the subgraph. However, this approach has serious shortcomings. For large graphs, applications may create hundreds or thousands of views. Some of these views may overlap and store (possibly) large, redundant portions of the original graph. Therefore, this approach may lead to unnecessary space explosion from duplicate copies of nodes and edges. Additionally, when updates occur, preserving the structural consistency across the views and the original graph will result in significant overhead.

To overcome these problems, the View class only stores the identifiers of its members (vertices and edges), and a scratch space to store properties about the view itself. Therefore, views store only membership information and not structural information. This storage format has the singular advantage of low space overhead. However the compact representation has the unfortunate side-effect that by looking at only the internal representation of a view, it is not possible to traverse the subgraph. For example, the view may not contain enough information to determine the neighbors of a certain vertex. Instead, the view's stored information has to be combined with the actual graph to traverse the subgraph contained in the view.

Concerto uses hash maps to speed up traversals on a view's subgraph. Vertex and edge identifiers are hashed for fast lookups. To execute a graph algorithm on a view, the application specifies the code that runs at each vertex, but Concerto ensures that the algorithm will be constrained to only the view members.

3.3   Event-Driven Processing

Supporting event processing in a graph store raises several questions. Since events on a graph can span different servers, how should the graph store aggregate such information? Intercepting each event may introduce undesirable processing overhead. If so, how do we prevent event processing from unduly impacting the query throughput of the graph store?

Views store the functions to be invoked when specified events occur. For example, views map the six function names in Table 3, such as `onUpdateVertex`, to the programmer-specified functions. Whenever events occur in a view, the runtime invokes the corresponding functions. Applications register functions to a view by calling `register()` on the the view. For example, `V.register(`

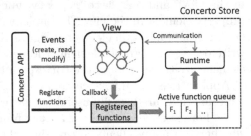

Fig. 2. Control flow of event processing

`onUpdateVertex, myFunc)` will register the function `myFunc`. Concerto will invoke this function whenever any vertex is updated in the view `V`. Internally, the function is stored as an executable.

When the events of interest, e.g., vertex updates, occur on a graph element, the Concerto runtime needs to determine which function registered with the view should be invoked. As explained in Section 2, view members, such as vertices, have a reverse pointer to their view object. This pointer is used to reach the functions that need to be executed after the event occurs at the graph element. Figure 2 illustrates the control flow during event-driven processing. The invoked functions are first appended to a queue. These queued functions are executed by a dedicated thread pool (separate from those handling queries) and, hence, provide coarse-grain performance isolation between queries and event processing. During execution, these functions can use the Concerto runtime for read access to elements of the view. For example, after a traffic accident the impact analysis function may traverse the vertices in the view to determine the affected region. The invoked functions can also store persistent data in the property fields of the view for subsequent processing. For example, a monitoring function may store statistics about reads and writes as a property of the view.

Concerto can leverage off-the-shelf publish-subscribe systems for large-scale event propagation. We believe our work to be complementary to these systems.

4   Fault Tolerance and Security

Concerto simplifies the graph store architecture by delegating most of the fault recovery mechanisms to Sinfonia. Sinfonia provides atomicity, consistency, isolation, durability (ACID), and availability if replication is enabled. These guarantees are independent of client-failures and the size of the graph. This design choice ensures that the graph store can easily be ported to other platforms such as distributed key-value stores. The Concerto prototype uses Sinfonia's disk-logging mechanisms to recover from memnode failures.

Sinfonia's fault tolerant global address space implies that data stored in Concerto is recoverable. However, we need mechanisms in Concerto to regain consistency (upon recovery) of the graph allocators. Graph allocators store all their meta-data in the memnodes. However, if a graph allocator fails then some of the memory may be leaked (e.g., pre-allocated blocks may be left dangling). The recovery process in Concerto goes through the allocator meta-data in each memnode and entrusts any dangling memory block to an active graph allocator.

Unlike data operations, event processing in Concerto's current prototype is not completely fault-tolerant. The difference in guarantees occurs because events are processed asynchronously to isolate query performance from event processing. As a result, an untimely fault can result in lost events. For example, when an update occurs, the write operation may return results to the client even though the triggered event processing code may still be executing a computation. If there is a fault before the update operation returns, then Concerto's recovery process will ensure that both the write operation and the event-processing code is correctly re-executed (or the client is notified of the failure and can retry). However, if a fault occurs after the update operation completes but before the event processing code completes, then the event may be lost. One can make event-processing fault tolerant by using a fault-tolerant message queue which we plan as future work.

Concerto assumes that functions registered with views are written by trusted applications. Malicious code can impact both the graph store and the stored data. The current prototype does not provide additional security features to constrain malicious functions. In the future, standard security techniques, such as sandboxes, may be used to limit the power of these functions [24]. Also, eventual consistency will let Concerto scale to more servers, improve its performance via asynchronous updates, and may decrease the latency of graph operations. However, eventual consistency is difficult to reason about and program.

5   Evaluation

Concerto consists of approximately 4,500 lines of C++ code for distributed data allocation, query API, distributed graph traversals, and event processing. These lines of code do not include the Sinfonia codebase.

We compare Concerto against MySQL, a well known relational database; against Neo4j, a commercial graph database; and GemFire [6], a commercial, in-memory distributed data management platform. GemFire uses hashing to store data in memory regions distributed over multiple nodes and provides a SQL-like interface. All experiments are performed using a cluster of 100 HP SL390 servers running Ubuntu 11.04. Each server has two Intel Xeon X5650 processors (total of twelve 2.67GHz cores), 96GB of DRAM, 120GB SSD drives, and 10 Gbps NIC. In some cases, where the 96 GB memory limit was exceeded, we ran Neo4j on a separate 1 TB memory server, however 96 GB was never approached for a single Concerto memnode in these graphs.

In our experiments, all systems run *in-memory*: Neo4j is run on a `ramfs` partition, MySQL uses its memory engine, and Concerto is run without replication. GemFire is run with one logical data region, distributed over multiple nodes (the number of nodes is specified in each experiment). In MySQL and GemFire, the graph is stored as a table of edges. We optimize MySQL query performance by using B-tree and hash indexes (GemFire uses hash maps). Workload generators are located on different servers from those hosting the store.

From our evaluation, we find that:

- Concerto is *fast*. It can ingest millions of vertices and edges per second and is more than 25× faster than other systems for k-core on large graphs and uses 3× less memory than Neo4j.
- Concerto's performance *scales* with the additional servers. It can calculate the 3-core on a 90 million vertex graph in less than 12 minutes on 64 instances compared to 45 minutes on a single memnode. The same computation takes more than 6 hours by GemFire.
- Concerto's graph views provide *extensibility*. Due to views and event-processing, Concerto's implementation of a road traffic application is 10× faster than a poll based system.

Table 4 describes the graphs used in our experiments. For example, *Twitter-L* represents 51 million users with 2 billion follower relationships that was collected

Table 4. Graphs used in different experiments

Graph	Vertices	Edges	File size	Experiments
Twitter-S	33M	282M	6.5GB	Insert, k-hop,
Twitter-L	51M	2B	38GB	monitoring
Social-S	3M	13M	197MB	Insert, k-core
Social-L	90M	405M	7.5GB	
Road-CA [26]	2M	5M	84MB	Traffic analysis

Table 5. Comparison of insertion throughput. Concerto/GemFire-1,10 represent running with 1 and 10 instances, respectively

Inserts/sec	Vertex	Edge	Vertex(bulk)	Edge(bulk)
Neo4j	282	337	6,120	6,467
MySQL	21,898	15,457	504,209	324,352
GemFire-1	5,234	6,001	153,245	165,324
Concerto-1	6,584	7,089	1.1 million	0.9 million
GemFire-10	27,512	23,092	1.3 million	1.0 million
Concerto-10	29,695	27,122	2.6 million	1.8 million

from the Twitter Web site. The *Social-S/L* graphs represent synthetic social network graphs generated using the model proposed by Newman [25].

5.1 Performance Results

We first compare the insertion throughput and query latency of Concerto, Neo4j, GemFire, and MySQL.

Insertion throughput. Table 5 compares how many vertex and edge elements can be inserted per second by the different stores for the Twitter-S graph. We also compare bulk loading all the vertices and edges of the Twitter-S graph for the different stores. Bulk loading avoids overhead from multiple memory allocations by inserting vertices and edges in one request. Insertion requests are issued from multiple clients to maximize the throughput. Our results show that a single instance Concerto is more than 21× faster than Neo4j. For example, Concerto can insert more than 6,500 vertices/second compared to only 282 vertices/second for Neo4j. Inserting single data items into MySQL is faster than a single-server instance of Concerto and GemFire because MySQL is highly tuned and stores the graph in a simple table format. However, as we discuss in the next section, this table representation considerably limits graph query performance in MySQL. GemFire and Concerto exhibit similar performance with single-item insertions, but Concerto is 1.8 − 7× faster than GemFire with bulk insertions. Similar to single-insertion, GemFire still needs to hash every element in the bulk insertion case resulting in lower performance. Concerto can parallelize ingestion to increase throughput. With 10 instances, Concerto inserts approximately 2.6 million vertices/second and 1.8 million edges/second. Scaling ingestion throughput is particularly useful for applications that must load very large graphs.

Graph query: k-hop. A common query in many graph applications is to retrieve a vertex and its neighbors that are k-hop distance away. Figure 3 compares the

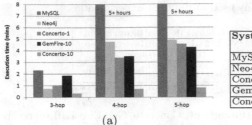

System	1-hop (ms)	2-hop (ms)
MySQL (in-memory)	9	303
Neo4j (in-memory)	42	1,320
Concerto-1	2	340
GemFire-10	10	295
Concerto-10	2	265

(a)   (b)

Fig. 3. K-hop latency. For clarity, 1 and 2 hop results are in the table

latency of retrieving upto 5-hop neighbors of a vertex in the different systems. For a 1-hop distance, MySQL and Concerto have similar performance, while Neo4j is noticeably slower. Neo4j's Java implementation is the main reason for the slowdown. However, for queries requiring more than 2-hops, MySQL is the slowest. This result is not surprising because for each hop, it has to perform a join operation, which is known to be an expensive operation for a database. For fewer than 3-hops, the overhead from two table join operations is insignificant due to use of the MySQL index. On the other hand, graph databases are optimized for such larger traversals. For greater than 2-hops, both Neo4j and Concerto-1 are at least 2-100× faster than MySQL, with the speedup increasing with the number of hops in the query. GemFire-1 performs worse than MySQL and hence we show only the GemFire-10 numbers. While Neo4j exhibits similar or better performance than the single-server instantiation of Concerto, Concerto-10 is 2-6× faster than Neo4j and and 5× faster than GemFire-10.

Graph algorithm: k-core. The k-core of a graph determines the subgraph where each vertex has at least k neighbors on the induced subgraph. Vertices with a larger "coreness" value (i.e. k) correspond to nodes with a more central position in the network structure [27]. The k-core of a graph is obtained by recur-

System	Social-S	Social-L
Neo4j	6 min	64 hrs
GemFire-1	5 min	25 hrs
MySQL	4 min	22 hrs
Concerto-1	1 min	45 min

Fig. 4. 3-core execution time

sively deleting vertices with degree less than k, until the degrees of remaining vertices is larger than or equal to k.

For Concerto, we implement the parallel k-core decomposition algorithm [27]. Table 4 shows the time taken by different systems to calculate the 3-core of two social graphs. For the 3 million vertex Social-S graph, MySQL, GemFire and Neo4j perform similarly, computing the 3-core of the graph in 4, 5 and 6 minutes respectively. Concerto, however, computes the 3-core much faster, requiring only 1 minute. For the 90 million vertex Social-L graph, Neo4j requires over two days to compute the 3-core, whereas MySQL and GemFire complete the same computation in 22 and 25 hours, respectively. Concerto completes the computation in only 45 minutes.

To understand these numbers, we observe that each round of the k-core decomposition consists primarily of two phases: a graph scan to find the vertices

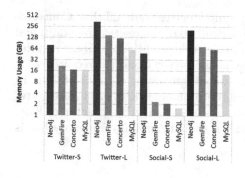

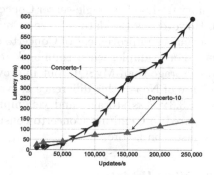

Fig. 5. Comparison of memory usage   **Fig. 6.** View update latency

that need to be deleted, and a short traversal of each vertex to find their degree in the induced subgraph. The bottleneck in Neo4j is the part of the algorithm that must perform a scan of all the data; such scans are known to be slow in Neo4j for large graphs. MySQL's and GemFire's advantage in scans and predicate evaluation (using indexes) is the primary reason for the speedup relative to Neo4j for large datasets. We note that for the Social-L graph we used a hash index since MySQL could not create such a large B-Tree index due to a known unresolved bug in its implementation [1]. In contrast, the design of Concerto allows it to perform both graph scans and traversals quickly. It calculates the 3-core in approximately 45 minutes, which is 29× faster than MySQL, 33× faster than GemFire, and 85× faster than Neo4j.

5.2   Memory Footprint

In Figure 5, we compare the storage footprint of each system, which, in this case, is entirely in memory. For MySQL we quote the numbers when only a hash index is created, which is much more memory efficient than creating a B-Tree index. Over all data-sets, MySQL has the smallest storage footprint as it stores only the edge information in the form of a table. Concerto requires 1.3 − 4.7× more storage than MySQL, and requires similar storage as GemFire but is 2.8 − 22.7× more space efficient compared to Neo4j. GemFire consumes less memory than Neo4j due to optimizations in object serialization and deserialization – only cached objects exist in deserialized forms, while remaining objects exist in smaller, serialized form. Apart from the overhead of Java, Neo4j also stores extra metadata and hence consumes more memory than Concerto. For example, in Neo4j the outgoing edges of a vertex are stored in a doubly linked list which incurs the additional cost of a back pointer per edge.

Revisiting the performance numbers from k-hop and k-core in the context of memory footprint reveals that for simple queries (e.g., 1-hop or 3-core) over small data sets, running in-memory MySQL offers roughly the same performance-vs-

---

[1] http://bugs.mysql.com/bug.php?id=44138

memory trade-off as single-server Concerto and a better trade-off than Concerto-10. However, as the data set size or query complexity increases, the additional performance improvement of Concerto outweighs the additional storage requirement. For example, when running k-core, single-server Concerto requires $4.7\times$ more storage than MySQL, but improves k-core latency by a factor of $29\times$. In the case of Neo4j, this difference is even more pronounced, where Concerto requires $3.3\times$ *less* storage, and yet improves k-core latency by a factor of $85\times$. Compared to GemFire, Concerto consumes a similar amount of memory but is $33\times$ faster on k-core.

5.3 View Updates

Figure 6 is a microbenchmark to measure the latency in processing view updates. We created a view on the Twitter-S graph such that 20% of the vertices are part of the view (around 7M). We use a client to send randomly generated updates to vertices both within and outside the view . Whenever a vertex is updated in the view, we use event-processing to increment the count of writes occurring on the view. The Y-axis in the plot shows the time interval between a vertex update and the completion of the event handler. In Concerto-1, the latency increases substantially as the update rate becomes more than 50K/s. The increased latency is because the single server reaches full capacity utilization and incurs queuing delay. In Concerto-10, the view update latency is higher than Concerto-1 initially, due to the network communication to update the view statistic that resides at one server. However, since the graph is distributed across multiple nodes, Concerto-10 can handle a higher update rate. The average delay is under 150ms for Concerto-10 even when the update rate is 250K updates/s. As a reference point for update rates, Twitter and Facebook receive 100K-200K update events per second [1,2].

5.4 Scalability Results

Unlike Neo4j, Concerto can leverage distributed parallelism to improve performance. Figure 7 shows the effect of scaling on the execution time of 3-core on the Social-L graph. As we increase the number of Concerto instances to 64, the execution time drops from 45 minutes to 12 minutes. At four Concerto instances the execution time is higher than the single server case because of the extra communication required. Similarly, beyond 80 instances the communication overhead for this dataset overshadows the benefit of increasing parallelism. The table in Figure 7 shows that GemFire's performance improves with more instances. However, even at 64 instances it still requires 6 hours to complete.

6   Case Studies with Views

In this section, we consider how views and event-processing in Concerto can ease development and improve performance of real-world inspired applications.

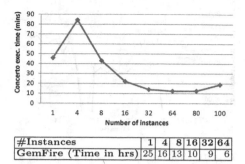

#Instances	1	4	8	16	32	64
GemFire (Time in hrs)	25	16	13	10	9	6

Fig. 7. Distributed k-core: Concerto, GemFire execution time (Social-L)

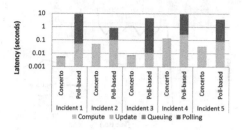

Fig. 8. End-to-end latency in finding incident impact region: Comparison between Concerto and a polling based system. Lower is better.

6.1 Real-Time Traffic Impact Analysis

The California Performance Measurement System (PeMS) is a network of road sensors spanning the major metropolitan freeways in California; these 26,000 sensors collect data every 30 seconds, generating over 2 GB of data each day [4]. The primary challenge isn't the scale of the data, but the *real-time* nature of the application. We revisit the example described in sub-section 3.1 and implement an application considered by both Kwon et al., and Miller et al: a statistical technique to estimate the time and spatial impact of a road incident (e.g., an accident, obstruction) on surrounding traffic [3,28]. When any such incident occurs, the application needs to react by analyzing the road network graph to predict the impact region of this incident, and possible re-calculated the shortest path between two endpoints of an impacted commute. Low latency is of the essence in order to notify the appropriate authorities to respond [3].

The application leverages Concerto in three ways. First, road sensors are stored as vertices, and connecting road segments are stored as associated edges in a graph. Each vertex contains information collected by its associated sensor (i.e., traffic flow, velocity, external incidents, which are uploaded from external sources). Second, a specific region of interest – for example, a municipality – forms a graph view such that the relevant client can run analysis when events occur. Finally, a function is registered with each view to run the impact analysis algorithm upon occurrence of an incident. The analysis function can use the information contained in the sensors that span the view.

We construct a graph based on the California road network [26], and generate 10 independent views (non-overlapping subgraphs) of size 2000 to approximate independent municipalities. We drive the experiment using synthetic traffic and incident data over a 25-minute window; this data is drawn from a distribution sampled by historical PeMS data, and approximately matches the findings of Miller, et al [3]. Therefore, at every 30-second interval, a traffic update invokes an `updateProperty(sensorID,sensorData)` in Concerto, and when an incident occurs (also associated with a specific sensor), `updateProperty(sensorID, incident)` is invoked. Upon completing the incident impact analysis, a shortest

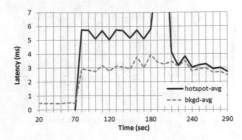
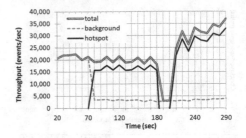

Fig. 9. Request latency observed during a hotspot and migration (clipped points represent downtime)

Fig. 10. Throughput observed during a hotspot and migration

path between a fixed source and destination municipality is recalculated, with any impacted subgraph removed from the calculation.

Figure 8 shows the end-to-end latency of determining the impact region for the first five incidents. To measure the performance benefit of using Concerto, we compare the latency of implementing this application in Concerto without event-driven processing, thus requiring polling and client side processing (*poll-based* in Figure 8). We show a breakdown of the time it takes to compute the impacted region, update the incident sensor, and from queueing delay, and polling overhead. We use a 10-second polling interval, which is close to the time taken to scan all the vertices in the ten views and read whether an incident has occurred. In Figure 8 we see that Concerto can find the impacted region in less than 100 milliseconds, largely due to server-side processing in both the event handling and code execution. The polling-based system takes from 1 to 10 seconds, and thus is slower by upto two orders of magnitude from Concerto. Even discounting the polling overhead, the poll-based system takes one second to complete because of the costly client-side graph traversal.

6.2 Hotspot Migration

Large social networks such as Facebook expose their infrastructure to third-party advertisers wishing to target particular users (e.g, through Facebook Ads API [29]). An increase in targeted advertising usually coincides with increases in traffic from trending topics or external events that impact the social graph (e.g., the Super Bowl). This rapid increase in traffic can cause a workload hotspot, especially if members of the view are co-located on the same set of physical servers. Concerto can dynamically load balance data corresponding to a view to mitigate such workload hotspots. To demonstrate these features, we replay a synthetic trace of read and write traffic on the Twitter-S graph stored across three Concerto instances. To simulate peak load, we create a view (called *hotspot*) by randomly selecting 1,000 Twitter users (these correspond to vertices in the Twitter-S graph) stored in the same Concerto sever. We assign a designated set of clients to this view to simulate heavy-hitters and continuously send requests to those vertices. Concerto handles the heavy hitters by using a migration policy such that the view members are evenly distributed across the three Concerto servers. This policy is implemented by gathering statistics of the number of requests hitting the view and when it exceeds a threshold (i.e hotspot occurs), the data migration policy is invoked. All of this is done using the View event-driven processing API described in Section 3.1. Figure 9 shows the timeline for the above scenario. The hotspot occurs at time 70 seconds, at that time the average request latency seen by the heavy hitters ($hotspot\text{-}avg$) increases to 6ms compared to less than a millisecond initially. The average latency of other clients in the store also increases ($bkgd\text{-}avg$) as some of their queries are on the view data. At time 180 seconds, the migration starts and moves approximately one-third of the view members to the remaining servers. During migration 683 vertices have to be moved which requires updating $10,916$ edges. The total migration time takes approximately 19.3 seconds, representing a downtime window during which the heavy hitters cannot access the store. Note that our migration implementation isn't well optimized and the migration time of 19.3 seconds is on the higher side which can be reduced. At the end of the migration, the average latency for both the heavy hitters and the other users becomes the same. Also, as shown in Figure 10, after the migration, the store can handle more traffic from the heavy hitters as the data is now spread across more servers. The effect of this migration is reflected by the increase in the total throughput beyond time 200 seconds. Online data migration can also be used to optimize query performance in other cases. For example, in another experiment, we observe that executing 3-core on the 3M vertex graph (Social-S) is 1.6× better running on 10 Concerto servers than executing it on 32 instances. Due to the communication overhead, it takes 24 seconds to calculate 3-core on 32 instances compared to less than 15 seconds with only 10 instances. Therefore, in this case, the social media application can move the data of a view to span fewer machines before running the k-core query. Note that Concerto does not automatically partition the graph for optimal performance. But applications can use known partitioning schemes and register the partitioning logic with Concerto for dynamic data partitioning.

7   Related Work

Relational Databases. Common graph queries such as shortest-path and k-hop are both difficult to express and inefficient to implement in a relational model. Because these queries cannot be completed quickly enough to support interactive or real-time responses. Web 2.0 sites such as Facebook, Flickr, and Wikipedia complement their SQL-based backing store with an in-memory cache such as Memcached [18] to provide low-latency response. Unfortunately the need to use a caching layer to achieve performance scalability comes at the cost of relaxed transactional semantics, a severely restricted set of supported graph queries, and lack of extensibility using application defined functions.

Distributed Datastores. GemFire [6] is the most closely related system to Concerto in that it is a scalable datastore that supports parallel query processing, event-driven processing and transactions. It exports an SQL-like query interface on top of a distributed key-value storage layer. It is capable of performing dynamic load balancing, event-processing over data, and in-memory caching of data objects across servers. Like relational databases and key-value stores, however, it does not provide explicit support for graph objects, thereby making graph queries inefficient.

Batch Analysis. Existing approaches to large graph analysis focus on optimizing offline computation. Systems like Pregel [5], GraphLab [9], Horton [30] and algorithmic methodologies in the high-performance community [31,32] primarily address the challenge of scaling computation with the size of graph data, generally on the order of billions of nodes and edges. As a result, these domains restrict themselves to immutable, read-only data. On the other hand, Concerto is designed to address the challenge of providing low-latency computation with transactional semantics for complex graph problems where data is continuously ingested and modified.

Graph Databases. Many specialized graph databases provide transactional guarantees and are optimized for typical graph operations, but largely do not scale storage [12,14,15] or storage or computation [11,16] to multiple servers. Kineograph [33] and Trinity [17] are the most closely related graph projects to Concerto, but do not provide semantics for user-defined functions or event-based, active computation. Kineograph is designed to provide transactional support for real-time graph updates in a distributed graph storage system; however, it does not explicitly support fast graph computations and instead stores graph elements using hash-based partitioning across graph storage nodes. Trinity does not provide transactional storage, and makes a different trade-off with how edges are named and represented in the graph. In the case of InfiniteGraph, no detailed technical documentation is available to provide a more informed comparison.

Graph Views. Gutierrez et. al. [34] proposed database graph views as an abstraction mechanism on relational and object oriented databases. Their work includes derivation operators such as union, intersection, difference to define new graph views. However, their work is in the context of traditional databases and they do not provide a specific implementation. Concerto's view mechanisms build upon this prior work and provide a specific implementation in a distributed environment for non-relational, in-memory graph stores.

8   Conclusion

Many emerging applications require both scalable, transactional data storage, and interactive, low-latency graph analysis. Concerto is a distributed graph store that fills the gap between tiered database systems that scale, but perform poorly on graph queries, and recent graph frameworks which can efficiently compute graph algorithms but are offline and don't provide transactional storage semantics. Concerto's abstraction of graph views simplifies how graph applications are expressed, and provides mechanisms that can sustain update rates reported by Twitter and Facebook.

Acknowledgments. We thank the anonymous reviewers for their valuable feedback. Part of this research was sponsored by the DARPA GRAPHS program (BAA-12-01).

References

1. Facebook's new realtime analytics system: Hbase to process 20 billion events per day, `http://highscalability.com/blog/2011/3/22/facebooks-new-realtime-analytics-system-hbase-to-process-20.html`
2. Twitter by the numbers, `http://mehack.com/twitter-by-the-numbers`
3. Miller, M., Gupta, C., Wang, Y.: An empirical analysis of the impact of incidents on freeway traffic. Research paper HPL-2011-134, Hewlett Packard, Palo Alto, CA, USA (2011)
4. Caltrans performance measurement system (pems), `http://pems.dot.ca.gov/`
5. Malewicz, G., Austern, M.H., Bik, A.J., Dehnert, J.C., Horn, I., Leiser, N., Czajkowski, G.: Pregel: A system for large-scale graph processing. In: Proceedings of SIGMOD, pp. 135–146 (2010)
6. GemFire: Technical white paper, copyright 2005 by gemstone systems (2005), `http://community.gemstone.com/display/gemfire60/EDF+Technical+White+Paper`
7. Dean, J., Ghemawat, S.: MapReduce: Simplified data processing on large clusters. In: Proceedings of OSDI 2004, pp. 137–150 (December 2004)
8. Zaharia, M., Chowdhury, M., Das, T., Dave, A., Ma, J., McCauley, M., Franklin, M.J., Shenker, S., Stoica, I.: Resilient distributed datasets: a fault-tolerant abstraction for in-memory cluster computing. In: Proceedings of NSDI, San Jose, CA, pp. 1–14 (2012)
9. Gonzalez, J.E., Low, Y., Gu, H., Bickson, D., Guestrin, C.: Powergraph: Distributed graph-parallel computation on natural graphs. In: Proceedings of OSDI, Hollywood, pp. 1–14 (October 2012)
10. Lattanzi, S., Moseley, B., Suri, S., Vassilvitskii, S.: Filtering: a method for solving graph problems in mapreduce. In: Proceedings of SPAA, 85–94 (2011)
11. Infinitegraph: The distributed graph database, `http://www.infinitegraph.com/`
12. Neo4j: Nosql for the enterprise, `http://neo4j.org/`
13. Twitter flockdb, `http://engineering.twitter.com/2010/05/introducing-flockdb.html`
14. Iordanov, B.: HyperGraphDB: A generalized graph database. In: Shen, H.T., Pei, J., Özsu, M.T., Zou, L., Lu, J., Ling, T.-W., Yu, G., Zhuang, Y., Shao, J. (eds.) WAIM 2010. LNCS, vol. 6185, pp. 25–36. Springer, Heidelberg (2010)
15. Martínez-Bazan, N., Gómez-Villamor, S., Escale-Claveras, F.: Dex: A high-performance graph database management system. In: Proceedings of IEEE ICDE Workshop on Graph Data Management, pp. 124–127. IEEE (2011)
16. Prabhakaran, V., Wu, M., Weng, X., McSherry, F., Zhou, L., Haridasan, M.: Managing large graphs on multi-cores with graph awareness. In: Proceedings of USENIX ATC, Berkeley, CA, USA, pp. 1–12 (2012)
17. Shao, B., Wang, H., Li, Y.: Trinity: A distributed graph engine on a memory cloud. In: Proceedings of SIGMOD (2013)
18. Fitzpatrick, B.: Distributed caching with memcached. Linux Journal 2004(124), 5
19. Huang, J., Abadi, D.J., Ren, K.: Scalable sparql querying of large rdf graphs, 1123–1134 (August 2011)

20. Karypis, G., Kumar, V.: Metis - unstructured graph partitioning and sparse matrix ordering system. Technical report, University of Minnesota (1995)
21. Mondal, J., Deshpande, A.: Managing Large Dynamic Graphs Efficiently. In: Proceedings of SIGMOD, pp. 145–156 (2012)
22. Aguilera, M.K., Merchant, A., Shah, M.A., Veitch, A.C., Karamanolis, C.T.: Sinfonia: A new paradigm for building scalable distributed systems. ACM Trans. Comput. Syst. 27(3), 1–5 (2009)
23. Valiant, L.G.: A bridging model for parallel computation. Commun. ACM 33, 103–111 (1990)
24. Geambasu, R., Levy, A.A., Kohno, T., Krishnamurthy, A., Levy, H.M.: Comet: An active distributed key-value store. In: Proceedings of OSDI, pp. 1–13 (2010)
25. Newman, M.E.J., Watts, D.J., Strogatz, S.H.: Random graph models of social networks. Proceedings of the National Academy of Sciences of the United States of America 99, 2566–2572 (2002)
26. Stanford large network dataset collection, http://snap.stanford.edu/data/index.html
27. Montresor, A., De Pellegrini, F., Miorandi, D.: Distributed k-core decomposition. In: Proceedings of PODC, pp. 207–208 (2011)
28. Kwon, J., Mauch, M., Varaiya, P.: The components of congestion: delay from incidents, special events, lane closures, weather, potential ramp metering gain, and demand. In: Proceedings of the TRB 85th Annual Meeting (2006)
29. Facebook developers: custom audience targeting, https://developers.facebook.com/docs/reference/ads-api/custom-audience-targeting/
30. Sarwat, M., Elnikety, S., He, Y., Kliot, G.: Horton: Online query execution engine for large distributed graphs. In: Proceedings of ICDE. Demonstration (2012)
31. Agarwal, V., Petrini, F., Pasetto, D., Bader, D.A.: Scalable graph exploration on multicore processors. In: Proceedings of ACM/IEEE Supercomputing, pp. 1–11. IEEE Computer Society, Washington, DC (2010)
32. Pearce, R., Gokhale, M., Amato, N.M.: Multithreaded asynchronous graph traversal for in-memory and semi-external memory. In: Proceedings of ACM/IEEE Supercomputing, pp. 1–11. IEEE Computer Society, Washington, DC (2010)
33. Cheng, R., Hong, J., Kyrola, A., Miao, Y., Weng, X., Wu, M., Yang, F., Zhou, L., Zhao, F., Chen, E.: Kineograph: taking the pulse of a fast-changing and connected world. In: Proceedings of EuroSys, pp. 85–98. ACM, New York (2012)
34. Gutiérrez, A., Pucheral, P., Steffen, H., Thévenin, J.M.: Database graph views: A practical model to manage persistent graphs. In: Proceedings of the 20th International Conference on Very Large Data Bases, VLDB (1994)

Efficient Batched Synchronization
in Dropbox-Like Cloud Storage Services

Zhenhua Li[1,2], Christo Wilson[3], Zhefu Jiang[4], Yao Liu[5],
Ben Y. Zhao[6], Cheng Jin[7], Zhi-Li Zhang[7], and Yafei Dai[1]

[1] Peking University
[2] Tsinghua University
[3] Northeastern University
[4] Cornell University
[5] Binghamton University
[6] UCSB
[7] University of Minnesota
{lizhenhua1983,guokeno0,jincheng117}@gmail.com,
cbw@ccs.neu.edu, yaoliu@cs.binghamton.edu, ravenben@cs.ucsb.edu,
zhzhang@cs.umn.edu, dyf@pku.edu.cn

Abstract. As tools for personal storage, file synchronization and data sharing, cloud storage services such as Dropbox have quickly gained popularity. These services provide users with ubiquitous, reliable data storage that can be automatically synced across multiple devices, and also shared among a group of users. To minimize the network overhead, cloud storage services employ binary diff, data compression, and other mechanisms when transferring updates among users. However, despite these optimizations, we observe that in the presence of *frequent, short updates* to user data, the network traffic generated by cloud storage services often exhibits pathological inefficiencies. Through comprehensive measurements and detailed analysis, we demonstrate that many cloud storage applications generate session maintenance traffic that *far exceeds* the useful update traffic. We refer to this behavior as the *traffic overuse problem*. To address this problem, we propose the *update-batched delayed synchronization* (UDS) mechanism. Acting as a middleware between the user's file storage system and a cloud storage application, UDS batches updates from clients to significantly reduce the overhead caused by session maintenance traffic, while preserving the rapid file synchronization that users expect from cloud storage services. Furthermore, we extend UDS with a backwards compatible Linux kernel modification that further improves the performance of cloud storage applications by reducing the CPU usage.

Keywords: Cloud storage service, Dropbox, Data synchronization, Traffic overuse.

1 Introduction

As tools for personal storage, file synchronization and data sharing, cloud storage services such as Dropbox, Google Drive, and SkyDrive have become extremely popular. These services provide users with ubiquitous, reliable data storage that can be synchronized ("sync'ed") across multiple devices, and also shared among a group of users.

D. Eyers and K. Schwan (Eds.): Middleware 2013, LNCS 8275, pp. 307–327, 2013.

Dropbox is arguably the most popular cloud storage service, reportedly hitting more than 100 million users who store or update one billion files per day [4].

Cloud storage services are characterized by two key components: a (front-end) client application that runs on user devices, and a (back-end) storage service that resides within the "cloud," hosting users' files in huge data centers. A user can "drop" files into or directly modify files in a special "sync folder" that is then automatically synchronized with cloud storage by the client application.

Cloud storage applications typically use two algorithms to minimize the amount of network traffic that they generate. First, the client application computes the binary diff of modified files and only sends the altered bits to the cloud. Second, all updates are compressed before they are sent to the cloud. As a simple example, if we append 100 MB of identical characters (*e.g.* "a") to an existing file in the Dropbox sync folder (thus the binary diff size is 100 MB), the resulting network traffic is merely 40 KB. This amount of traffic is just slightly more than the traffic incurred by appending a single byte "a" (*i.e.* around 38 KB, including meta-data overhead).

The Traffic Overuse Problem. However, despite these performance optimizations, we observe that the network traffic generated by cloud storage applications exhibits pathological inefficiencies in the presence of *frequent, short updates* to user data. Each time a synced file is modified, the cloud storage application's *update-triggered real-time synchronization* (URS) mechanism is activated. URS computes and compresses the binary diff of the new data, and sends the update to the cloud along with some *session maintenance data*. Unfortunately, when there are frequent, short updates to synced files, the amount of session maintenance traffic *far exceeds* the amount of useful update traffic sent by the client over time. We call this behavior the *traffic overuse problem*. In essence, the traffic overuse problem originates from the *update sensitivity* of URS.

Our investigation into the traffic overuse problem reveals that this issue is pervasive among users. By analyzing data released from a large-scale measurement of Dropbox [17], we discover that for around 8.5% of users, $\geq 10\%$ of their traffic is generated in response to frequent, short updates (refer to § 4.1). In addition to Dropbox, we examine seven other popular cloud storage applications across three different operating systems, and discover that their software also exhibits the traffic overuse problem.

As we show in § 4, the traffic overuse problem is exacerbated by "power users" who leverage cloud storage in situations it was not designed for. Specifically, cloud storage applications were originally designed for simple use cases like storing music and sharing photos. However, cloud storage applications are now used in place of traditional source control systems (Dropbox markets their Teams service specifically for this purpose [6]). The problem is especially acute in situations where files are shared between multiple users, since frequent, short updates by one user force all users to download updates. Similarly, users now employ cloud storage for even more advanced use cases like setting up databases [1].

Deep Understanding of the Problem. To better understand the traffic overuse problem, we conduct extensive, carefully controlled experiments with the Dropbox application (§ 3). In our tests, we artificially generate streams of updates to synced files, while varying the size and frequency of updates. Although Dropbox is a closed-source

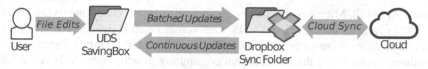

Fig. 1. High-level design of the UDS middleware

application and its data packets are SSL encrypted, we are able to conduct black-box measurements of its network traffic by capturing packets with Wireshark [10].

By examining the time series of Dropbox's packets, coupled with some analysis of the Dropbox binary, we quantitatively explore the reasons why the ratio of session maintenance traffic to update traffic is poor during frequent, short file updates. In particular, we identify the operating system features that trigger Dropbox's URS mechanism, and isolate the series of steps that the application goes through before it uploads data to the cloud. This knowledge enables us to identify the precise update-frequency intervals and update sizes that lead to the generation of pathological session maintenance traffic. We reinforce these findings by examining traces from real Dropbox users in § 4.

UDS: Addressing the Traffic Overuse Problem. Guided by our measurement findings, we develop a solution to the traffic overuse problem called *update-batched delayed synchronization* (UDS) (§ 5). As depicted in Fig. 1, UDS acts as a middleware between the user's file storage system and a cloud storage client application (*e.g.* Dropbox). UDS is independent of any specific cloud storage service and requires no modifications to proprietary software, which makes UDS simple to deploy. Specifically, UDS instantiates a "SavingBox" folder that replaces the sync folder used by the cloud storage application. UDS detects and batches frequent, short data updates to files in the SavingBox and delays the release of updated files to the cloud storage application. In effect, UDS forces the cloud storage application to batch file updates that would otherwise trigger pathological behavior. In practice, the additional delay caused by batching file updates is very small (around several seconds), meaning that users are unlikely to notice, and the integrity of cloud-replicated files will not be adversely affected.

To evaluate the performance of UDS, we implement a version for Linux. Our prototype uses the inotify kernel API [8] to track changes to files in the SavingBox folder, while using rsync [9] to generate compressed diffs of modified files. Results from our prototype demonstrate that it reduces the overhead of session maintenance traffic to less than 30%, compared to 620% overhead in the worst case for Dropbox.

UDS+: Reducing CPU Overhead. Both URS and UDS have a drawback: in the case of frequent data updates, they generate considerable CPU overhead from constantly *re-indexing* the updated file (*i.e.* splitting the file into chunks, checksumming each chunk, and calculating diffs from previous versions of each chunk). This re-indexing occurs because the inotify kernel API reports *what* file/directory has been modified on disk, but not *how* it has been modified. Thus, rsync (or an equivalent algorithm) must be run over the entire modified file to determine how it has changed.

To address this problem, we modify the Linux inotify API to return the *size* and *location* of file updates. This information is readily available inside the kernel; our modified API simply exposes this information to applications in a backwards compatible manner. We implement an improved version of our system, called UDS+, that leverages the new API (§ 6). Microbenchmark results demonstrate that UDS+ incurs significantly less CPU overhead than URS and UDS. Our kernel patch is available at https://www.dropbox.com/s/oor7vo9z49urgrp/inotify-patch.html.

Although convincing the Linux kernel community to adopt new APIs is a difficult task, we believe that our extension to inotify is a worthwhile addition to the operating system. Using the strace command, we tracked the system calls made by many commercial cloud storage applications (e.g. Dropbox, UbuntuOne, TeamDrive, SpiderOak, etc.) and confirmed that they all use the inotify API. Thus, there is a large class of applications that would benefit from merging our modified API into the Linux kernel.

2   Related Work

As the popularity of cloud storage services has quickly grown, so too have the number of research papers related to these services. Hu *et al.* performed the first measurement study on cloud storage services, focusing on Dropbox, Mozy, CrashPlan, and Carbonite [21]. Their aim was to gauge the relative upload/download performance of different services, and they find that Dropbox performs best while Mozy performs worst.

Several studies have focused specifically on Dropbox. Drago *et al.* study the detailed architecture of the Dropbox service and conduct measurements based on ISP-level traces of Dropbox network traffic [17]. The data from this paper is open-source, and we leverage it in § 4 to conduct trace-driven simulations of Dropbox behavior. Drago *et al.* further compare the system capabilities of Dropbox, Google Drive, SkyDrive, Wuala, and Amazon Cloud Drive, and find that each service has its limitations and advantages [16]. A study by Wang *et al.* reveals that the scalability of Dropbox is limited by their use of Amazon's EC2 hosting service, and they propose novel mechanisms for overcoming these bottlenecks [31]. Dropbox cloud storage deduplication is studied in [20] [18], and some security/privacy issues of Dropbox are discussed in [25] [21].

Amazon's cloud storage infrastructure has also been quantitatively analyzed. Burgen *et al.* measure the performance of Amazon S3 from a client's perspective [11]. They point out that the perceived performance at the client is primarily dependent on the transfer bandwidth between the client and Amazon S3, rather than the upload bandwidth of the cloud. Consequently, the designers of cloud storage services must pay special attention to the client-side, perceived quality of service.

Li *et al.* develop a tool called "CloudCmp" [23] to comprehensively compare the performances of four major cloud providers: Amazon AWS [22], Microsoft Azure [14], Google AppEngine and Rackspace CloudServers. They find that the performance of cloud storage can vary significantly across providers. Specifically, Amazon S3 is observed to be more suitable for handling large data objects rather than small data objects, which is consistent with our observation in this paper.

Based on two large-scale network-attached storage file system traces from a real-world enterprise datacenter, Chen *et al.* conduct a multi-dimensional analysis of data access patterns at the user, application, file, and directory levels [15]. Based on this analysis, they derive 12 design implications for how storage systems can be specialized for specific data access patterns. Wallace *et al.* also present a comprehensive characterization of backup workloads in a large production backup system [30]. Our work follows a similar methodology: study the data access patterns of cloud storage users and then leverage the knowledge to optimize these systems for improved performance.

Finally, there are more works related to Dropbox-like cloud storage services, such as the cloud-backed file systems [28] [29], delta compression [27], real-time compression [19], dependable cloud storage design [24] [12], and economic issues like the market-oriented paradigm [13] and the Storage Exchange model [26].

3 Understanding Cloud Storage Services

In this section, we present a brief overview of the data synchronization mechanism of cloud storage services, and perform fine-grained measurements of network usage by cloud storage applications. Although we focus on Dropbox as the most popular service, we demonstrate that our findings generalize to other services as well.

3.1 Data Synchronization Mechanism of Cloud Storage Services

Fig. 2 depicts a high-level outline of Dropbox's data sync mechanism. Each instance of the Dropbox client application sends three different types of traffic. *First*, each client maintains a connection to an *index server*. The index server authenticates each user, and stores meta-data about the user's files, including: the list of the user's files, their sizes and attributes, and pointers to where the files can be found on Amazon's S3 storage service. *Second*, file data

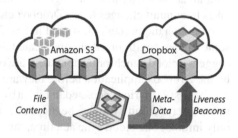

Fig. 2. Dropbox data sync mechanism

is stored on Amazon's S3 storage service. The Dropbox client compresses files before storing them in S3, and modifications to synced files are uploaded to S3 as compressed, binary diffs. *Third*, each client maintains a connection to a *beacon server*. Periodically, the Dropbox client sends a message to the user's beacon server to report its online status, as well as receives notifications from the cloud (*e.g.* a shared file has been modified by another user and should be re-synced).

Relationship between the Disk and the Network. In addition to understanding the network connections made by Dropbox, we also seek to understand what activity on the local file system triggers updates to the Dropbox cloud. To measure the fine-grained behavior of the Dropbox application, we leverage the Dropbox command-line interface (CLI) [2], which is a Python script that enables low-level monitoring of the Dropbox application. Using Dropbox CLI, we can programmatically query the status of the Dropbox application after adding files to or modifying files in the Dropbox Sync folder.

By repeatedly observing the behavior of the Dropbox application in response to file system changes, we are able to discern the inner workings of Dropbox's *update-triggered real-time synchronization* (URS) system. Fig. 3(a) depicts the basic operation of URS. First, a change is made on disk within the Dropbox Sync folder, *e.g.* a new file is created or an existing file is modified. The Dropbox application uses OS-specific

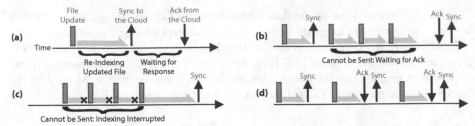

Fig. 3. Diagrams showing the low-level behavior of the Dropbox application following a file update. (a) shows the fundamental operations, while (b) and (c) show situations where file updates are batched together. (d) shows the worst-case scenario where no file updates are batched together.

APIs to monitor for changes to files and directories of interest. After receiving a change notification, the Dropbox application indexes or re-indexes the affected file(s). Next, the compressed file or binary diff is sent to Amazon S3, and the file meta-data is sent to the Dropbox cloud. This process is labeled as "Sync to the Cloud" in Fig. 3(a). After these changes have been committed in the cloud, the Dropbox cloud responds to the client with an acknowledgment message. In § 3.2, we investigate the actual length of time it takes to commit changes to the Dropbox cloud.

Although the process illustrated in Fig. 3(a) appears to be straightforward, there are some hidden conditions that complicate the process. Specifically, not every file update triggers a cloud synchronization: there are two situations where file updates are batched by the Dropbox application before they are sent to the cloud.

The first scenario is depicted in Fig. 3(b). In this situation, a file is modified numerous times after a cloud sync has begun, but before the acknowledgment is received. URS only initiates one cloud sync at a time, thus file modifications made during the network wait interval get batched until the current sync is complete. After the acknowledgment is received, the batched file changes are immediately synced to the cloud.

The second scenario is shown in Fig. 3(c). In this situation, a file is modified several times in such rapid succession that URS does not have time to finish indexing the file. Dropbox cannot begin syncing changes to the cloud until after the file is completely indexed, thus these rapid edits prevent the client from sending any network traffic.

The two cases in Fig. 3(b) and 3(c) reveal that there are complicated interactions between on-disk activity and the network traffic sent by Dropbox. On one hand, a carefully timed series of file edits can generate only a single network transfer if they occur fast enough to repeatedly interrupt file indexing. On the other hand, a poorly timed series of edits can initiate an enormous number of network transfers if the Dropbox software is not able to batch them. Fig. 3(d) depicts this worst-case situation: each file edit (regardless of how trivially small) results in a cloud synchronization. In § 4, we demonstrate that this worst-case scenario actually occurs under real-world usage conditions.

3.2   Controlled Measurements

Our investigation of the low-level behavior of the Dropbox application reveal complex interactions between file writes on disk and Dropbox's network traffic to the cloud. In this section, we delve deeper into this relationship by performing carefully controlled

Table 1. Network traffic generated by adding new files to the Dropbox Sync folder

New File Size	Index Server Traffic	Amazon S3 Traffic	α	Sync Delay (s)
1 B	29.8 KB	6.5 KB	38200	4.0
1 KB	31.3 KB	6.8 KB	40.1	4.0
10 KB	31.8 KB	13.9 KB	4.63	4.1
100 KB	32.3 KB	118.7 KB	1.528	4.8
1 MB	35.3 KB	1.2 MB	1.22	9.2
10 MB	35.1 KB	11.5 MB	1.149	54.7
100 MB	38.5 KB	112.6 MB	1.1266	496.3

microbenchmarks of cloud storage applications. In particular, our goal is to quantify the relationship between frequency and size of file updates with the amount of traffic generated by cloud storage applications. As before we focus on Dropbox, however we also demonstrate that our results generalize to other cloud storage systems as well.

All of our benchmarks are conducted on two test systems located in the United States in 2012. The first is a laptop with a dual-core Intel processor @2.26 GHz, 2 GB of RAM, and a 5400 RPM, 250 GB hard drive disk (HDD). The second is a desktop with a dual-core Intel processor @3.0 GHz, 4 GB of RAM, and a 7200 RPM, 1 TB HDD. We conduct tests on machines with different hard drive rotational speeds because this impacts the time it takes for cloud storage software to index files. Both machines run Ubuntu Linux 12.04, the Linux Dropbox application version 0.7.1 [3], and the Dropbox CLI extension [2]. Both machines are connected to a 4 Mbps Internet connection, which gives Dropbox ample resources for syncing files to the cloud.

File Creation. First, we examine the amount of network traffic generated by Dropbox when new files are created in the Sync folder. Table 1 shows the amount of traffic sent to the index server and to Amazon S3 when files of different sizes are placed in the Sync folder on the 5400 RPM machine. We use JPEG files for our tests (except the 1 byte test) because JPEGs are a compressed file format. This prevents the Dropbox application from being able to further compress data updates to the cloud.

Table 1 reveals several interesting facets about Dropbox traffic. First, regardless of the size of the created file, the size of the meta-data sent to the index server remains almost constant. Conversely, the amount of data sent to Amazon S3 closely tracks the size of the created file. This result makes sense, since the actual file data (plus some checksumming and HTTP overhead) are stored on S3.

The α column in Table 1 reports the ratio of total Dropbox traffic to the size of new file. α close to 1 is ideal, since that indicates that Dropbox has very little overhead beyond the size of the user's file. For small files, α is large because the fixed size of the index server meta-data dwarfs the actual size of the file. For larger files α is more reasonable, since Dropbox's overhead is amortized over the file size.

The last column of Table 1 reports the average time taken to complete the cloud synchronization. These tests reveal that, regardless of file size, all cloud synchronizations take at least 4 seconds on average. This minimum time interval is dictated by Dropbox's cloud infrastructure, and is not a function of hard drive speed, Internet connection speed or RTT. For larger files, the sync delay grows commensurately larger. In these cases, the delay is dominated by the time it takes to upload the file to Amazon S3.

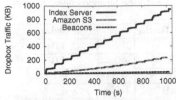
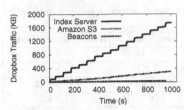

Fig. 4. Dropbox traffic corresponding to rapid, 1 byte appends to a file (5400 RPM HDD)

Fig. 5. Dropbox traffic corresponding to rapid, 1 byte appends to a file (7200 RPM HDD).

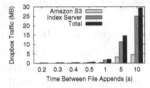
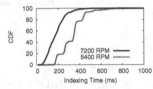

Fig. 6. Dropbox traffic as the time between 1 byte appends is varied (5400 RPM HDD)

Fig. 7. Dropbox traffic as the time between 1 byte appends is varied (7200 RPM HDD)

Fig. 8. Distribution of Dropbox file indexing time. Total file size is 1 KB

Short File Updates. The next set of experiments examine the behavior of Dropbox in the presence of short updates to an existing file. Each test starts with an empty file in the Dropbox Sync folder, and then periodically we append one random byte to the file until its size reaches 1 KB. Appending random bytes ensures that it is difficult for Dropbox to compress the binary diff of the file.

Fig. 4 and 5 show the network traffic generated by Dropbox when 1 byte per second is appended on the 5400 RPM and 7200 RPM machines. Although each append is only 1 byte long, and the total file size never exceeds 1 KB, the total traffic sent by Dropbox reaches 1.2 MB on the 5400 RPM machine, and 2 MB on the 7200 RPM machine. The majority of Dropbox's traffic is due to meta-data updates to the index server. As shown in Table 1, each index server update is roughly 30 KB in size, which dwarfs the size of our file and each individual update. The traffic sent to Amazon S3 is also significant, despite the small size of our file, while Beacon traffic is negligible. Overall, Fig. 4 and 5 clearly demonstrate that under certain conditions, the amount of traffic generated by Dropbox can be several orders of magnitude larger than the amount of underlying user data. The faster, 7200 RPM hard drive actually makes the situation worse.

Timing of File Updates. As depicted in Fig. 3(b) and 3(c), the timing of file updates can impact Dropbox's network utilization. To examine the relationship between up-date timing and network traffic, we now conduct experiments where the time interval between 1 byte file appends in varied from 100 ms to 10 seconds.

Fig. 6 and 7 display the amount of network traffic generated by Dropbox during each experiment on the 5400 and 7200 RPM machines. The results show a clear trend: faster file updates result in less network traffic. This is due to the mechanisms highlighted in Fig. 3(b) and 3(c), *i.e.* Dropbox is able to batch updates that occur very quickly. This batching reduces the total number of meta-data updates that are sent to the index sever, and allows multiple appended bytes in the file to be aggregated into a single binary diff for Amazon S3. Unfortunately, Dropbox is able to perform less batching as the time

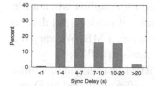
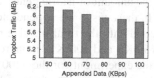
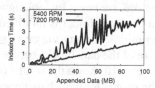

Fig. 9. Distribution of sync delays. Total file size is 1 KB

Fig. 10. Network traffic as the
speed of file appends is varied

Fig. 11. File indexing time as
the total file size is varied

interval between appends grows. This is particularly evident for the 5 and 10 second
tests in Fig. 6 and 7. This case represents the extreme scenario shown in Fig. 3(d),
where almost every 1 byte update triggers a full synchronization with the cloud.

Indexing Time of Files. The results in Fig. 6 and 7 reveal that the timing of file updates impacts Dropbox's network traffic. However, at this point we do not know which
factor is responsible for lowering network usage: is it the network waiting interval as in
Fig. 3(b), the interrupted file indexing as in Fig. 3(c), or some combination of the two?

To answer this question, we perform microbenchmarks to examine how long it takes
Dropbox to index files. As before, we begin with an empty file and periodically append
one random byte until the file size reaches 1 KB. In these tests, we wait 5 seconds in-
between appends, since this time is long enough that the indexing operation is never
interrupted. We measure the time Dropbox spends indexing the modified file by monitoring the Dropbox process using Dropbox CLI.

Fig. 8 shows the indexing time distribution for Dropbox. The median indexing time
for the 5400 and 7200 RPM drives are ≈400 ms and ≈200 ms, respectively. The longest
indexing time we observed was 960 ms. These results indicates that file updates that occur within ≈200-400 ms of each other (depending on hard drive speed) should interrupt
Dropbox's indexing process, causing it to restart and batch the updates together.

Comparing the results from Fig. 6 and 7 to Fig. 8 reveals that indexing interrupts play
a role in reducing Dropbox's network traffic. The amount of traffic generated by Dropbox steadily rises as the time between file appends increases from 200 to 500 ms. This
corresponds to the likelihood of file appends interrupting the indexing process shown
in Fig. 8. When the time between appends is 1 second, it is highly unlikely that sequential appends will interrupt the indexing process (the longest index we observed took 960
ms). Consequently, the amount of network traffic generated during the 1 second interval
test is more than double the amount generated during the 500 ms test.

Although indexing interrupts are responsible for Dropbox's network traffic patterns
at short time scales, they cannot explain the sharp increase in network traffic that occurs
when the time between appends rises from 1 to 5 seconds. Instead, in these situations the
delimiting factor is the network synchronization delay depicted in Fig. 3(b). As shown
in Fig. 9, one third of Dropbox synchronizations complete in 1-4 seconds, while another
third complete in 4-7 seconds. Thus, increasing the time between file appends from 1
to 10 seconds causes the number of file updates that trigger network synchronization to
rise (*i.e.* there is little batching of updates).

Long File Updates. So far, all of our results have focused on very short, 1 byte updates
to files. We now seek to measure the behavior of Dropbox when updates are longer. As

before, we begin by looking at the amount of traffic generated by Dropbox when a file in the Sync folder is modified. In these tests, we append blocks of randomized data to an initially empty file every second until the total file size reaches 5 MB. We vary the size of the data blocks between 50 KB and 100 KB, in increments of 10KB.

Fig. 10 shows the results of the experiment for the 5400 RPM test machine. Unlike the results for the 1 byte append tests, the amount of network traffic generated by Dropbox in these experiments is comparable to the total file size (5 MB). As the number of kilobytes per second appended to the file increases, the ratio of network traffic to total file size falls. These results reiterate the point that the Dropbox application uses network resources more effectively when dealing with larger files.

Fig. 11 explores the relationship between the size of appended data and the file indexing time for Dropbox. There is a clear linear relationship between these two variables: as the size of the appended data increases, so does the indexing time of the file. This makes intuitive sense, since it takes more time to load larger files from disk.

Fig. 11 indicates that interrupted indexing will be a more common occurrence with larger files, since they take longer to index, especially on devices with slower hard drives. Therefore, Dropbox will use network resources more efficiently when dealing with files on the order of megabytes in size. Similarly, the fixed overhead of updating the index server is easier to amortize over large files.

3.3 Other Cloud Storage Services and Operating Systems

We now survey seven additional cloud storage services to see if they also exhibit the traffic overuse problem. For this experiment, we re-run our 1 byte per second append test on each cloud storage application. As before, the maximum size of the file is 1 KB. All of our measurements are conducted on the following two test machines: a desktop with a dual-core Intel processor @3.0 GHz, 4 GB of RAM, and a 7200 RPM, 1 TB hard drive, and a MacBook Pro laptop with a dual-core Intel processor @2.5 GHz, 4 GB of RAM, and a 7200 RPM, 512 GB hard drive. The desktop dual boots Ubuntu 12.04 and Windows 7 SP1, while the laptop runs OS X Lion 10.7. We test each cloud storage application on all OSes it supports. Because 360 CloudDisk, Everbox, Kanbox, Kuaipan, and VDisk are Chinese services, we executed these tests in China. Dropbox, UbuntuOne, and IDriveSync were tested in the US.

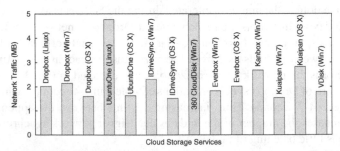

Fig. 12. Total network traffic for various cloud storage applications running on three OSes after appending 1 byte to a file 1024 times

Fig. 12 displays the results of our experiments, from which there are two important takeaways. First, we observe that the traffic overuse problem is pervasive across different cloud storage applications. All of the tested applications generate megabytes of traffic when faced with frequent, short file updates, even though the actual size of the file in only 1 KB. All applications perform equal to or worse than Dropbox. Secondly, we see that the traffic overuse problem exists whether the client is run on Windows, Linux, or OS X.

3.4   Summary

Below we briefly summarize our observations and insights got from the experimental results in this section.

- The Dropbox client only synchronizes data to the cloud after the local data has been indexed, and any prior synchronizations have been resolved. File updates that occur within 200-400 ms intervals are likely to be batched due to file indexing. Similarly, file updates that occur within a 4 second interval may be batched due to waiting for a previous cloud synchronization to finish.
- The traffic overuse problem occurs when there are numerous, small updates to files that occur at intervals on the order of several seconds. Under these conditions, cloud storage applications are unable to batch updates together, causing the amount of sync traffic to be several orders of magnitude larger than the actual size of the file.
- Our tests reveal that the traffic overuse problem is pervasive across cloud storage applications. The traffic overuse problem occurs on different OSes, and is actually made worse by faster hard drive speeds.

4   The Traffic Overuse Problem in Practice

The results in the previous section demonstrate that under controlled conditions, cloud storage applications generate large amounts of network traffic that far exceed the size of users' actual data. In this section, we address a new question: are users actually affected by the traffic overuse problem? To answer this question, we measure the characteristics of Dropbox network traffic in real-world scenarios. First, we analyze data from a large-scale trace of Dropbox traffic to illustrate the pervasiveness of the traffic overuse problem in the real world. To confirm these findings, we use data from the trace to drive a simulation on our test machines. Second, we experiment with two practical Dropbox usage scenarios that may trigger the traffic overuse problem. The results of these tests reveal that the amount of network traffic generated by Dropbox is anywhere from 11 to 130 times the size of data on disk. This confirms that the traffic overuse problem can arise under real-world use cases.

4.1   Analysis of Real-World Dropbox Network Traces

To understand the pervasiveness of the traffic overuse problem, we analyze network-level traces from a recent, large-scale measurement study of Dropbox [5]. This trace is collected at the ISP level, and involves over 10,000 unique IP addresses and millions of data updates to/from Dropbox. To analyze the behavior of each Dropbox user, we assume all traffic generated from a given IP address corresponds to a single Dropbox user (unfortunately, we are unable to disambiguate multiple users behind a NAT). For each user, we calculate the percentage of Dropbox requests and traffic that can be attributed to frequent, short file updates *in a coarse-grained and conservative manner*.

As mentioned in § 3.4, the exact parameters for frequent, short updates that trigger the traffic overuse problem vary from system to system. Thus, we adopt the following *conservative* metrics to locate a frequent, short update (U_i): 1) the inter-update time between updates U_i and U_{i-1} is <1 second, and 2) the size of (compressed) data associated with U_i is <1 KB.

Figures 13 and 14 plot the percentage of requests and network traffic caused by frequent, short updates, respectively. In both figures, users are sorted in descending order by percentage of short, frequent requests/traffic. Fig. 13 reveals that for 11% of users, ≥10% of their Dropbox requests are caused by frequent, short updates. Fig. 14 shows that for 8.5% of users, ≥10% of their traffic is due to frequent, short updates. These results demonstrate that a significant portion of the network traffic from a particular population of Dropbox users is due to the traffic overuse problem.

Log Appending Experiment. To confirm that frequent, short updates are the cause of the traffic patterns observed in Figures 13 and 14, we chose one trace from an active user and recreated her/his traffic on our test machine (*i.e.* the same Ubuntu laptop used in § 3). Specifically, we play back the user's trace by writing the events to an empty log in the Dropbox Sync folder. We use the event timestamps from the trace to ensure that updates are written to the log at precisely the same rate that they actually occurred. The user chosen for this experiment uses Dropbox for four hours, with an average inter-update time of 2.6 seconds. Fig. 15 shows the amount of network traffic generated by Dropbox as well as the true size of the log file over time. By the end of the test, Dropbox generates 21 times as much traffic as the size of data on disk. This result confirms that an active real-world Dropbox user can trigger the traffic overuse problem.

4.2 Examining Practical Dropbox Usage Scenarios

In the previous section, we showed that real-world users are impacted by the traffic overuse problem. However, the traces do not tell us what high-level user behavior generates the observed frequent, short updates. In this section, we analyze two practical use cases for Dropbox that involve frequent, short updates.

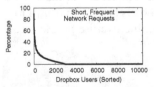 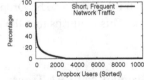 

Fig. 13. Each user's percentage of frequent, short network requests, in descending order

Fig. 14. Each user's percentage of frequent, short network traffic, in descending order

Fig. 15. Dropbox network traffic and log size corresponding to an active user's trace

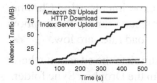 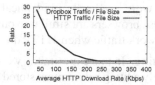 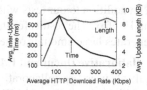

Fig. 16. Dropbox upload traffic as a 5MB file is downloaded into the Sync folder via HTTP.

Fig. 17. Ratio of network traffic to real file size for the Dropbox upload and HTTP download.

Fig. 18. Average inter-update time and data update length as HTTP download rate varies.

HTTP File Download. One of the primary use cases for Dropbox is sharing files with friends and colleagues. In some cases, it may be expedient for users to download files from the Web directly into the Dropbox Sync folder to share them with others. In this case, the browser writes chunks of the file to disk as pieces arrive via HTTP from the web. This manifests as repeated appends to the file at the disk-level. How does the Dropbox application react to this file writing pattern?

To answer this question, we used wget to download a compressed, 5 MB file into the Dropbox Sync folder. All network traffic was captured using Wireshark. As before, we use a compressed file for the test because this prevents Dropbox from being able to perform any additional compression while uploading data to the cloud.

Fig. 16 plots the amount of traffic from the incoming HTTP download and the outgoing Dropbox upload. For this test, we fixed the download rate of wget at 80 Kbps. The 75 MB of traffic generated by Dropbox is far greater than the 5.5 MB of traffic generated by the HTTP download (5 MB file plus HTTP header overhead). Fig. 16 and Fig. 4 demonstrate very similar results: in both cases, Dropbox transmits at least one order of magnitude more data to the cloud than the data in the actual file.

We now examine the behavior of the Dropbox software as the HTTP download rate is varied. Fig. 17 examines the ratio of network traffic to actual file size for Dropbox and HTTP as the HTTP download rate is varied. For the HTTP download, the ratio between the amount of incoming network traffic and the actual file size (5 MB) is constantly 1.1. The slight amount of overhead comes from the HTTP headers. For Dropbox, the ratio between outgoing traffic and file size varies between 30 and 1.1. The best case occurs when the HTTP download rate is high.

To explain why the network overhead for Dropbox is lowest when the HTTP download rate is high, we examine the interactions between wget and the hard drive. Fig. 18 shows the time between hard drive writes by wget, as well as the size of writes, as the HTTP download rate is varied. The left hand axis and solid line correspond to the inter-update time, while the right hand axis and dashed line depict the size of writes. The network overhead for Dropbox is lowest when the HTTP download rate is ≥ 200 Kbps. This corresponds to the scenario where file updates are written to disk every 300 ms, and the sizes of the updates are maximal (≈ 9 KB per update). Under these conditions, the Dropbox software is able to batch many updates together. Conversely, when the HTTP download rate is low, the inter-update time between hard disk writes is longer, and the size per write is smaller. Thus, Dropbox has fewer opportunities to batch updates, which triggers the traffic overuse problem.

In addition to our tests with wget, we have run identical experiments using Chrome and Firefox. The results for these browsers are similar to our results for wget: Dropbox generates large amounts of network traffic when HTTP download rates are low.

Collaborative Document Editing. In this experiment, we simulate the situation where multiple users are collaboratively editing a document stored in the Dropbox Sync folder. Specifically, we place a 1 MB file full of random ASCII characters in the Dropbox Sync folder and share the file with a second Dropbox user. Each user edits the document by modifying or appending l random bytes at location x every t seconds, where l is a random integer between 1 and 10, and t is a random float between 0 and 10. Each user performs modifying and appending operations with the same probability (=0.5). If a user appends to the file, x is set to the end of the file.

We ran the collaborative document editing experiment for a single hour. During this period of time, we measured the amount of network traffic generated by Dropbox. By the end of the experiment, Dropbox had generated close to 130 MB of network traffic: two orders of magnitude more data than the size of the file (1 MB).

5 The UDS Middleware

In § 3, we demonstrate that the design of cloud storage applications gives rise to situations where they can send orders-of-magnitude more traffic than would be reasonably expected. We follow this up in § 4 by showing that this pathological application behavior can actually be triggered in real-world situations.

To overcome the traffic overuse problem, we implement an application-level mechanism that dramatically reduces the network utilization of cloud storage applications. We call this mechanism *update-batched delayed synchronization* (UDS). The high-level operation of UDS is shown in Fig. 1. Intuitively, UDS is implemented as a replacement for the normal cloud sync folder (*e.g.* the Dropbox Sync folder). UDS proactively detects and batches frequent, short updates to files in its "SavingBox" folder. These batched updates are then merged into the true cloud-sync folder, so they can be transferred to the cloud. Thus, UDS acts as a middleware that protects the cloud storage application from file update patterns that would otherwise trigger the traffic overuse problem.

In this section, we discuss the implementation details of UDS, and present benchmarks of the system. In keeping with the methodology in previous sections, we pair UDS with Dropbox when conducting experiments. Our benchmarks reveal that UDS effectively eliminates the traffic overuse problem, while only adding a few seconds of additional delay to Dropbox's cloud synchronization.

5.1 UDS Implementation

At a high level the design of UDS is driven by two goals. First, the mechanism should fix the traffic overuse problem by forcing the cloud storage application to batch file updates. Second, the mechanism should be compatible with multiple cloud storage services. This second goal rules out directly modifying an existing application (*e.g.* the Dropbox application) or writing a custom client for a specific cloud storage service.

To satisfy these goals, we implement UDS as a middleware layer that sits between the user and an existing cloud storage application. From the user's perspective, UDS acts just like any existing cloud storage service. UDS creates a "SavingBox" folder on the user's hard drive, and monitors the files and folders placed in the SavingBox. When the user adds new files to the SavingBox, UDS automatically computes a compressed version of the data. Similarly, when a file in the SavingBox folder is modified, UDS calculates a compressed, binary diff of the file versus the original. If a time period t elapses after the last file update, or the total size of file updates surpasses a threshold c, then UDS pushes the updates over to the true cloud sync folder (*e.g.* the Dropbox Sync folder). At this point, the user's cloud storage application (*e.g.* Dropbox) syncs the new/modified files to the cloud normally. In the event that files in the true cloud sync folder are modified (*e.g.* by a remote user acting on a shared file), UDS will copy the updated files to the SavingBox. Thus, the contents of the SavingBox are always consistent with content in the true cloud-synchronization folder.

As a proof of concept, we implement a version of UDS for Linux. We tested our implementation by pairing it with the Linux Dropbox client. However, we stress that it would be trivial to reconfigure UDS to work with other cloud storage software as well (*e.g.* Google Drive, SkyDrive, and UbuntuOne). Similarly, there is nothing fundamental about our implementation that prevents it from being ported to Windows, OS X, or Linux derivatives such as Android.

Implementation Details. Our UDS implementation uses the Linux inotify APIs to monitor changes to the SavingBox folder. Specifically, UDS calls inotify_add_watch() to set up a callback that is invoked by the kernel whenever files or folders of interest are modified by the user. Once the callback is invoked, UDS writes information such as the type of event (*e.g.* file created, file modified, *etc.*) and the file path to an event log. If the target file is new, UDS computes the compressed size of the file using gzip. However, if the target file has been modified then UDS uses the standard rsync tool to compute a binary diff between the updated file and the original version in the cloud-synchronization folder. UDS then computes the compressed size of the binary diff.

Periodically, UDS pushes new/modified files from the SavingBox to the true cloud sync folder. In the case of new files, UDS copies them entirely to the cloud sync folder. Alternatively, in the case of modified files, the binary diff previously computed by UDS is applied to the copy of the file in the cloud sync folder.

Internally, UDS maintains two variables that determine how often new/modified files are pushed to the true cloud sync folder. Intuitively, these two variables control the frequency of batched updates to the cloud. The first variable is a timer: whenever a file is created/modified, the timer gets reset to zero. If the timer reaches a threshold value t, then all new/modified files in the SavingBox are pushed to the true cloud sync folder.

The second variable is a byte counter that ensures frequent, small updates to files are batched together into chunks of at least some minimum size before they get pushed to the cloud. Specifically, UDS records the total size of all compressed data that has not been pushed to cloud storage. If this counter exceeds a threshold c, then all new/modified files in the SavingBox are pushed to the true cloud-synchronization folder. Note that all cloud storage software may not use gzip for file compression: thus, UDS's byte counter is an estimate of the amount of data the cloud storage software will send on the network.

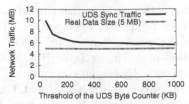
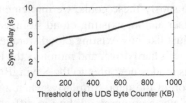

Fig. 19. Network traffic corresponding to various thresholds of the UDS byte counter c

Fig. 20. Sync delay corresponding to various thresholds of the UDS byte counter c

Although UDS's estimate may not perfectly reflect the behavior of the cloud storage application, we show in the next section that this does not impact UDS's performance.

As a fail-safe mechanism, UDS includes a second timer that pushes updates to the cloud on a coarse timeframe. This fail-safe is necessary because pathological file update patterns could otherwise block UDS's synchronization mechanisms. For example, consider the case where bytes are appended to a file. If c is large, then it may take some time before the threshold is breached. Similarly, if the appends occur at intervals $< t$, the first timer will always be reset before the threshold is reached. In this practically unlikely but possible scenario, the fail-safe timer ensures that the append operations cannot perpetually block cloud synchronization. In our UDS implementation, the fail-safe timer automatically causes UDS to push updates to the cloud every 30 seconds.

5.2   Configuring and Benchmarking UDS

In this section we investigate two aspects of UDS. First, we establish values for the UDS variables c and t that offer a good tradeoff between reduced network traffic and low synchronization delay. Second, we compare the performance of UDS to the stock Dropbox application by re-running our earlier benchmarks. In this section, all experiments are conducted on a laptop with a dual-core Intel processor 2.26GHz, 2 GB of RAM, and a 5400 RPM, 250 GB hard drive. Our results show that when properly configured, UDS eliminates the traffic overuse problem.

Choosing Threshold Values. Before we can benchmark the performance of UDS, the values of the time threshold t and byte counter threshold c must be established. Intuitively, these variables represent a tradeoff between network traffic and timeliness of updates to the cloud. On one hand, a short time interval and a small byte counter would cause UDS to push updates to the cloud very quickly. This reduces the delay between file modifications on disk and syncing those updates to the cloud, at the expense of increased traffic. Conversely, a long timer and large byte counter causes many file updates to be batched together, reducing traffic at the expense of increased sync delay.

What we want is to locate a good tradeoff between network traffic and delay. To locate this point, we conduct an experiment: we append random bytes to an empty file in the SavingBox folder until its size reaches 5 MB while recording how much network traffic is generated by UDS (by forwarding updates to Dropbox) and the resulting sync delay. We run this experiment several times, varying the size of the byte counter threshold c to observe its impact on network traffic and sync delay.

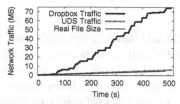
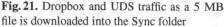
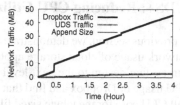

Fig. 21. Dropbox and UDS traffic as a 5 MB file is downloaded into the Sync folder

Fig. 22. Dropbox and UDS traffic corresponding to an active user's log file backup process

Fig. 19 and 20 show the results of this experiment. As expected, UDS generates a greater amount of network traffic but incurs shorter sync delay when c is small because there is less batching of file updates. The interesting feature of Fig. 19 is that the amount of network traffic quickly declines and then levels off. The ideal tradeoff between network traffic and delay occurs when $c = 250$ KB; any smaller and network traffic quickly rises, any larger and there are diminishing returns in terms of enhanced network performance. On the other hand, Fig. 20 illustrates an approximately linear relationship between UDS's batching threshold and the resulting sync delay, so there is no especially "good" threshold c in terms of the sync delay. Therefore, we use $c = 250$ KB for the remainder of our experiments.

We configure the timer threshold t to be 5 seconds. This value is chosen as a qualitative tradeoff between network performance and user perception. Longer times allow for more batching of updates, however long delays also negatively impact the perceived performance of cloud storage systems (*i.e.* the time between file updates and availability of that data in the cloud). We manually evaluated our UDS prototype, and determined that a 5 second delay does not negatively impact the end-user experience of cloud storage systems, but is long enough to mitigate the traffic overuse problem.

Although the values for c and t presented here were calculated on a specific machine configuration, we have conducted the same battery of tests on other, faster machines as well. Even when the speed of the hard drive is increased, $c = 250$ KB and $t = 5$ seconds are adequate to prevent the traffic overuse problem.

UDS's Performance vs. Dropbox. Having configured UDS's threshold values, we can now compare its performance to a stock instance of Dropbox. To this end, we re-run 1) the wget experiment and 2) the active user's log file experiment from § 4. Fig. 21 plots the total traffic generated by a stock instance of Dropbox, UDS (which batches updates before pushing them to Dropbox), and the amount of real data downloaded over time by wget. The results for Dropbox are identical to those presented in Fig. 16, and the traffic overuse problem is clearly visible. In contrast, the amount of traffic generated by UDS is only slightly more than the real data traffic. By the end of the HTTP download, UDS has generated 6.2 MB of traffic, compared to the true file size of 5 MB.

Fig. 22 plots the results of the log file append test. As in the previous experiment, the network traffic of UDS is only slightly more than the true size of the log file, and much less than that of Dropbox. These results clearly demonstrate that UDS's batching mechanism is able to eliminate the traffic overuse problem.

6   UDS+: Reducing CPU Utilization

In the previous section, we demonstrate how our UDS middleware successfully reduces the network usage of cloud storage applications. In this section, we take our evaluation and our system design to the next level by analyzing its CPU usage. First, we analyze the CPU usage of Dropbox and find that it uses significant resources to index files (up to one full CPU core for megabyte sized files). In contrast, our UDS software significantly reduces the CPU overhead of cloud storage. Next, we extend the kernel level APIs of Linux in order to further improve the CPU performance of UDS. We call this modified system UDS+. We show that by extending Linux's existing APIs, the CPU overhead of UDS (and by extension, all cloud storage software) can be further reduced.

6.1   CPU Usage of Dropbox and UDS

We begin by evaluating the CPU usage characteristics of the Dropbox cloud storage application by itself (*i.e.* without the use of UDS). As in § 3, our test setup is a generic laptop with a dual-core Intel processor @2.26 GHz, 2 GB of RAM, and a 5400 RPM, 250 GB hard drive. On this platform, we conduct a benchmark where 2K random bytes are appended to an initially empty file in the Dropbox Sync folder every 200 ms for 1000 seconds. Thus, the final size of the file is 10 MB. During this process, we record the CPU utilization of the Dropbox process.

Fig. 23 shows the percentage of CPU resources being used by the Dropbox application over the course of the benchmark. The Dropbox application is single threaded, thus it only uses resources on one of the laptop's two CPUs. There are two main findings visible in Fig. 23. First, the Dropbox application exhibits two large jumps in CPU utilization that occur around 400 seconds (4 MB file size) and 800 seconds (8 MB). These jumps occur because the Dropbox application segments files into 4 MB chunks [25]. Second, the average CPU utilization of Dropbox is 54% during the benchmark, which is quite high. There are even periods when Dropbox uses 100% of the CPU.

CPU usage of UDS. Next, we evaluate the CPU usage of our UDS middleware when paired with Dropbox. We conduct the same benchmark as before, except in this case the target file is placed in UDS's SavingBox folder. Fig. 24 shows the results of the benchmark (note that the scale of the y-axis has changed from Fig. 23). Immediately, it is clear that the combination of UDS and Dropbox uses much less CPU than Dropbox alone: on average, CPU utilization is just 12% during the UDS/Dropbox benchmark. Between 6% and 20% of CPU resources are used by UDS (specifically, by rsync), while the Dropbox application averages 2% CPU utilization. The large reduction in overall CPU utilization is due to UDS's batching of file updates, which reduces the frequency and amount of work done by the Dropbox application. The CPU usage of UDS does increase over time as the size of the target file grows.

6.2   Reducing the CPU Utilization of UDS

Although UDS significantly reduces the CPU overhead of using cloud storage software, we pose the question: can the system still be further improved? In particular, while

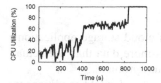

Fig. 23. Original CPU utilization of Dropbox

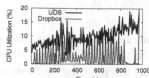

Fig. 24. CPU utilization of UDS and Dropbox

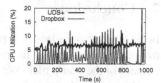

Fig. 25. CPU utilization of UDS+ and Dropbox

developing UDS, we noticed a shortcoming in the Linux inotify API: the callback that reports file modification events includes parameters stating which file was changed, but not *where* the modification occurred within the file or *how much* data was written. These two pieces of information are very important to all cloud storage applications, since they capture the byte range of the diff from the previous version of the file. Currently, cloud storage applications must calculate this information independently, *e.g.* using rsync.

Our key insight is that these two pieces of meta-information are available inside the kernel; they just are not exposed by the existing Linux inotify API. Thus, having the kernel report where and how much a file is modified imposes no additional overhead on the kernel, but it would save cloud storage applications the trouble of calculating this information independently.

To implement this idea, we changed the inotify API of the Linux kernel to report: 1) the byte offset of file modifications, and 2) the number of bytes that were modified. Making these changes requires altering the inotify and fsnotify [7] functions listed in Table 2 (fsnotify is the subsystem that inotify is built on). Two integer variables are added to the fsnotify_event and inotify_event structures to store the additional file meta-data. We also updated ker-

Table 2. Modified kernel functions.

fsnotify_create_event()
fsnotify_modify()
fsnotify_access()
inotify_add_watch()
copy_event_to_user()
vfs_write()
nfsd_vfs_write()
compat_do_readv_writev()

nel functions that rely directly on the inotify and fsnotify APIs. In total, we changed around 160 lines of code in the kernel, spread over eight functions.

UDS+. Having updated the kernel inotify API, we created an updated version of UDS, called UDS+, that leverages the new API. The implementation of UDS+ is significantly simpler than that of UDS, since it no longer needs to use rsync to compute binary diffs. Instead, UDS+ simply leverages the "where" and "how much" information provided by the new inotify APIs. Based on this information, UDS+ can read the fresh data from the disk, compress it using gzip, and update the byte counter.

To evaluate the performance improvement of UDS+, we re-run the earlier benchmark scenario using UDS+ paired with Dropbox, and present the results in Fig. 25. UDS+ performs even better than UDS: the average CPU utilization during the UDS+ test is only 7%, compared to 12% for UDS. UDS+ exhibits more even and predictable CPU utilization than UDS. Furthermore, the CPU usage of UDS+ increases much more slowly over time, since it no longer relies on rsync.

7 Conclusion

In this paper, we identify a pathological issue that causes cloud storage applications to upload large amount of traffic to the cloud: many times more data than the actual content of the user's files. We call this issue the traffic overuse problem.

We measure the traffic overuse problem under synthetic and real-world conditions to understand the underlying causes that trigger this problem. Guided by this knowledge, we develop UDS: a middleware layer that sits between the user and the cloud storage application, to batch file updates in the background before handing them off to the true cloud storage software. UDS significantly reduces the traffic overhead of cloud storage applications, while only adding several seconds of delay to file transfers to the cloud. Importantly, UDS is compatible with any cloud storage application, and can easily be ported to different OSes.

Finally, by making proof-of-concept modifications to the Linux kernel that can be leveraged by cloud storage services to increase their performance, we implement an enhanced version of our middleware, called UDS+. UDS+ leverages these kernel enhancements to further reduce the CPU usage of cloud storage applications.

Acknowledgements. This work is supported in part by the National Basic Research Program of China (973) Grant. 2011CB302305, the NSFC Grant. 61073015, 61190110 (China Major Program), and 61232004. Prof. Ben Y. Zhao is supported in part by the US NSF Grant. IIS-1321083 and CNS-1224100. Prof. Zhi-Li Zhang is supported in part by the US NSF Grant. CNS-1017647 and CNS-1117536, the DTRA Grant. HDTRA1-09-1-0050, and the DoD ARO MURI Award W911NF-12-1-0385.

We appreciate the instructive comments made by the reviewers, and the helpful advice offered by Prof. Baochun Li (University of Toronto), Prof. Yunhao Liu (Tsinghua University), Dr. Tianyin Xu (UCSD), and the 360 CloudDisk development team.

References

1. Dropbox-as-a-Database, the tutorial, http://blog.opalang.org/2012/11/dropbox-as-database-tutorial.html
2. Dropbox CLI (Command Line Interface), http://www.dropboxwiki.com/Using_Dropbox_CLI
3. Dropbox client (Ubuntu Linux version), http://linux.dropbox.com/packages/ubuntu/nautilus-dropbox_0.7.1_i386.deb
4. Dropbox is now the data fabric tying together devices for 100M registered users who save 1B files a day, http://techcrunch.com/2012/11/13/dropbox-100-million
5. Dropbox traces, http://traces.simpleweb.org/wiki/Dropbox_Traces
6. DropboxTeams, http://dropbox.com/teams
7. fsnotify git hub, https://github.com/howeyc/fsnotify
8. inotify man page, http://linux.die.net/man/7/inotify
9. rsync web site, http://www.samba.org/rsync
10. Wireshark web site, http://www.wireshark.org
11. Bergen, A., Coady, Y., McGeer, R.: Client Bandwidth: The Forgotten Metric of Online Storage Providers. In: Proc. of PacRim (2011)

12. Bessani, A., Correia, M., Quaresma, B., André, F., Sousa, P.: DepSky: Dependable and Secure Storage in a Cloud-of-clouds. In: Proc. of EuroSys (2011)
13. Buyya, R., Yeo, C., Venugopal, S.: Market-oriented Cloud Computing: Vision, Hype, and Reality for Delivering IT Services as Computing Utilities. In: Proc. of HPCC (2008)
14. Calder, B., et al.: Windows Azure Storage: A Highly Available Cloud Storage Service with Strong Consistency. In: Proc. of SOSP (2011)
15. Chen, Y., Srinivasan, K., Goodson, G., Katz, R.: Implications for Enterprise Storage Systems via Multi-dimensional Trace Analysis. In: Proc. of SOSP (2011)
16. Drago, I., Bocchi, E., Mellia, M., Slatman, H., Pras, A.: Benchmarking Personal Cloud Storage. In: Proc. of IMC (2013)
17. Drago, I., Mellia, M., Munafò, M.M., Sperotto, A., Sadre, R., Pras, A.: Inside Dropbox: Understanding Personal Cloud Storage Services. In: Proc. of IMC (2012)
18. Halevi, S., Harnik, D., Pinkas, B., Shulman-Peleg, A.: Proofs of Pwnership in Remote Storage Systems. In: Proc. of CCS (2011)
19. Harnik, D., Kat, R., Sotnikov, D., Traeger, A., Margalit, O.: To Zip or Not to Zip: Effective Resource Usage for Real-Time Compression. In: Proc. of FAST (2013)
20. Harnik, D., Pinkas, B., Shulman-Peleg, A.: Side Channels in Cloud Services: Deduplication in Cloud Storage. IEEE Security & Privacy 8(6), 40–47 (2010)
21. Hu, W., Yang, T., Matthews, J.: The Good, the Bad and the Ugly of Consumer Cloud Storage. ACM SIGOPS Operating Systems Review 44(3), 110–115 (2010)
22. Jackson, K., et al.: Performance Analysis of High Performance Computing Applications on the Amazon Web Services Cloud. In: Proc. of CloudCom (2010)
23. Li, A., Yang, X., Kandula, S., Zhang, M.: CloudCmp: Comparing Public Cloud Providers. In: Proc. of IMC (2010)
24. Mahajan, P., et al.: Depot: Cloud Storage with Minimal Trust. ACM Transactions on Computer Systems (TOCS) 29(4), 12 (2011)
25. Mulazzani, M., Schrittwieser, S., et al.: Dark Clouds on the Horizon: Using Cloud Storage as Attack Vector and Online Slack Space. In: Proc. of USENIX Security (2011)
26. Placek, M., Buyya, R.: Storage Exchange: A Global Trading Platform for Storage Services. In: Proc. of EuroPar (2006)
27. Shilane, P., Huang, M., Wallace, G., Hsu, W.: WAN Optimized Replication of Backup Datasets Using Stream-informed Delta Compression. In: Proc. of FAST (2012)
28. Vrable, M., Savage, S., Voelker, G.M.: Cumulus: Filesystem Backup to the Cloud. ACM Transactions on Storage (TOS) 5(4), 14 (2009)
29. Vrable, M., Savage, S., Voelker, G.: Bluesky: A Cloud-backed File System for the Enterprise. In: Proc. of FAST (2012)
30. Wallace, G., Douglis, F., Qian, H., Shilane, P., Smaldone, S., et al.: Characteristics of Backup Workloads in Production Systems. In: Proc. of FAST (2012)
31. Wang, H., Shea, R., Wang, F., Liu, J.: On the Impact of Virtualization on Dropbox-like Cloud File Storage/Synchronization Services. In: Proc. of IWQoS (2012)

Back to the Future: Using Magnetic Tapes in Cloud Based Storage Infrastructures

Varun S. Prakash, Xi Zhao, Yuanfeng Wen, and Weidong Shi

Department of Computer Science, University of Houston
4800 Calhoun Road, Houston, TX 77004, U.S.A
vsprakash@uh.edu, xzhao21@central.uh.edu, {wyf,larryshi}@cs.uh.edu

Abstract. Data backup and archiving is an important aspect of business processes to avoid loss due to system failures and natural calamities. As the amount of data and applications grow in number, concerns regarding cost efficient data preservation force organizations to scout for inexpensive storage options. Addressing these concerns, we present Tape Cloud, a novel, highly cost effective, unified storage solution. We leverage the notably economic nature of Magnetic Tapes and design a cloud storage infrastructure-as-a-service that provides a centralized storage platform for unstructured data generated by many diverse applications. We propose and evaluate a proficient middleware that manages data and IO requests, overcomes latencies and improves the overall response time of the storage system. We analyze traces obtained by live archiving applications to obtain workload characteristics. Based on this analysis, we synthesize archiving workloads and design suitable algorithms to evaluate the performance of the middleware and storage tiers. From the results, we see that the use of the middleware provides close to 100% improvement in task distribution efficiency within the system leading to a 70% reduction in overall response time of data retrieval from storage. Due to its easy adaptability with the state of the art storage practices, the middleware contributes in providing the much needed boost in reducing storage costs for data archiving in cloud and colocated infrastructures.

Keywords: Data Storage, Backup, Archiving, Cloud, Data Centers, Cost Efficiency, Magnetic Tapes, Middleware, Read Probability Weight, Priority Queue.

1 Introduction

The last decade has witnessed an explosion of data generated by individuals and organizations. For instance, the amount of video data captured by a single HD surveillance camera at 30fps in 14 days requires 1TB storage space [1]. The number of CCTV cameras in UK alone is estimated to be 1.85 million [2]. One of the major concerns that is correlated with managing such data is its storage and backup[3]. In cloud based storage services, there are usually more than one players involved, such as service providers and users. From the service user's perspective, the motives for choice of storage would be reduced costs per unit

D. Eyers and K. Schwan (Eds.): Middleware 2013, LNCS 8275, pp. 328–347, 2013.
© IFIP International Federation for Information Processing 2013

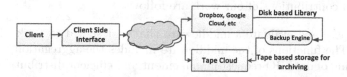

Fig. 1. Tape Cloud is a cloud storage service that uses magnetic tapes as the main storage media to store unstructured and big data unlike most of the commercial cloud storage solution available today

data stored, efficient retrieval, data criticality dependent support benefits and a secure, long term data storage. But, a service provider's considerations span operating cost efficiency, labor, scalability, support for different types of data, varied policies from multiple clients and managing workload uncertainty among others. A closer observation shows that the cost factor favors either players but rarely both. The likelihood of recovery of data after back up, also firmly influences both players. Varying archiving rates and backup needs of multiple clients is an eminently common feature leading to the need for multiple storage configuration. Thus, a sensible inclusion in the storage tiers to archive low-read/write-only data would be a low cost, low maintenance yet durable media [4].

Magnetic tapes, which started of as a primary storage media decades ago, have been preferred for archiving data generated by organizations for a long time now. Despite the advantages of tapes, there has not been a steady increase in its usage due to high initial investment needed for the operating hardware and its inability to promise high data rate transactions[5]. By addressing these key issues, it is possible to tap into the economic advantages that the tape media provides.

Tape Cloud (figure 1) is a venture that seeks to find suitable solutions to these issues. Tape Cloud is a cloud based, nearline storage Infrastructure-as-a-Service which makes use of magnetic tapes as the main backend storage media. The cloud model exempts users from the large initial investments needed for in-house backup infrastructure, external tiers for archiving legacy data and its maintenance. From the service providers perspective, using tapes allows hassle free scaling of systems and reduces the total cost of ownership due to its characteristic low power usage, durability and form factor per unit data.

Our principle intention is to **1.** Reduce the average response times for read requests issued by applications; **2.** Conjointly, ensure efficient data writes to the tapes tier of storage; and **3.** Strengthen the infrastructure's support for a large and diverse client base[6]. However, overcoming the latency offered by tapes is a complex problem to be solved. Even with the latest in tape technology, high performance in terms of fast data read and efficient data write cannot be achieved as delays caused due to seeking and winding of tapes is still persistent. There is also a delay induced by the stock robots and other ambulatory mechanics within the tape library which physically handle and move the tape cartridges.

The main contributions of our work are follows,

- We propose and evaluate a middleware that is designed to work with Tape Cloud. The functions of the middleware includes the aggregation and batch processing of data, IO request management and efficient distribution of data over available resources.
- The middleware, which is constituted by a FUSE based filesystem, implementation of priority based queuing of IO tasks and a latency preemptive, probabilistic data distribution scheme, acts between the backup application tier and proprietary filesystems that is commonly used with tapes.
- We observe and record the common delays incurred in the operation of commercially available tape libraries. Some of the latencies of tape drives and tape filesystem are analysed using typical benchmarking tools. This data, along with delay is used to model the performance characteristics of unit hardware, which is later used to simulate large scale data centers.
- Backup and archiving application traces are analysed to obtain typical workload characteristics. We employ methods to trace the operations at different stages in the infrastructure and aggregate them into meaningful statistics. This not only provides information about backend storage media activity, but also provides data at the application server and filesystem levels.
- We use synthetic workloads which emphasise prominent features of backup applications to evaluate the impact of using the proposed middleware in a simulation of a large scale deployment of Tape Cloud. In keeping with our goals, we demonstrate the improved data distribution ability, improved response time for read requests originating from each of the applications and regulation of write requests that the middleware provides.
- The proposed tape cloud framework points to a new direction for creating service oriented, cost effective, massive scale infrastructure to meet the growing storage challenge in the coming era of big data enabled industries and research.

2   Analyzing and Modeling Tape Associated Latencies

2.1   The Tape, Library and the Drive

In order to design an infrastructure around a particular storage media, it is important to understand the characteristics, related costs, advantages and weaknesses that are associated with it. A clear understanding of the media and devices can lead to its large scale deployment in data centers.

We evaluate the state of the art in tape technology with the use of a commercially available Tandberg T24 LTO5 tape library. The tape library has an HP tape drive and slots that can hold 12 LTO5 Ultrium tapes each of 2.5TB capacity and can be extended to 24 tapes. At full capacity, the library can hold 60TB of uncompressed data. The tape library depends on robotic carriers that grab tapes from the slots, carries them to the tape drive at the end of the library and loads the tape for IO operations. The robots instills a greater delay into the

Table 1. Tandgerg T24 Robot, Load and Unload Delays

Type	From (slot)	To	Motion (sec)	Load (sec)	Type	From	To (slot)	Motion (sec)	Load (sec)
LOAD	1	Drive	52.4	23.3	UNLOAD	Drive	1	51.6	20.1
LOAD	2	Drive	52.9	21.9	UNLOAD	Drive	2	52.3	20.6
LOAD	3	Drive	54.06	22.6	UNLOAD	Drive	3	52.26	20.3
LOAD	4	Drive	55.2	24.6	UNLOAD	Drive	4	54.0	20.3
LOAD	5	Drive	52.42	24.0	UNLOAD	Drive	5	51.3	20.9
LOAD	6	Drive	53.3	23.6	UNLOAD	Drive	6	51.76	21.01
LOAD	7	Drive	54.2	21.3	UNLOAD	Drive	7	52.22	20.1
LOAD	8	Drive	55.45	23.9	UNLOAD	Drive	8	53.8	19.62
LOAD	9	Drive	51.8	24.0	UNLOAD	Drive	9	50.7	20.3
LOAD	10	Drive	52.3	21.6	UNLOAD	Drive	10	51.4	20.34
LOAD	11	Drive	53.7	22.23	UNLOAD	Drive	11	51.97	23.9
LOAD	12	Drive	54.02	23.8	UNLOAD	Drive	12	53.6	22.59
Average	–	–	**53.52**	**23.1**	**Average**	–	–	**52.24**	**21.21**

system in addition to the one caused by tape drives. The averages from multi trail recordings of the traverse time of the robots and loading time is provided in table 1.

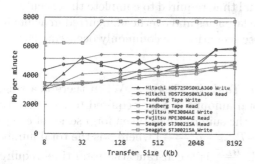

Fig. 2. Sequential read and write performance of an LTO5 tape drive in comparison with commercial hard disks

The results of a study performed for various block sizes show that tape drives have a uniform data transfer rate compared to three other hard disks shown in figure 2. However, a difference in performance can be seen when random reads and writes are performed. The time spent in changing tapes, loading and seeking to the correct point on the tape creates delays that are out of proportion as compared to the sequential performance of tapes. An important takeaway from the results is to assure the tape drive and the infrastructure spends most of the time either writing or reading to tapes and less time performing seek operations. This helps us in deciding important parameters such as rate of batch processing of data.

2.2 Generic Models for Tape Based Latency

Based on the facts obtained about the hardware and delays, we try to model the latency for generic cases[7]. For the models, the following are some of the constants that need to be considered.

- $T_{search}(i)$ is the time taken by the robot to locate and move to the tape to execute the ith request in the task queue.
- T_{load} is the time taken to load the tape into the drive.
- T_{unload} is the time taken to unload the tape from the drive.

- T_{seek} (average) is the time to wind the tape to seek to the position of the first byte to execute the new task. We consider the average time for LTO5 tapes in this case.
- γ_{read} is the data transfer rate for read operations of the tape. Similarly γ_{write} is the data transfer rate for write operations of the tape.
- The smallest unit of a data that is considered in this case is a block. A single read or write might involve transaction of a varying number of blocks. We represent a unit block as BLK.

We aim to employ able techniques to reduce the average response time T_{read} for read tasks and furthermore, ensure that these read-friendly techniques, cause minimal distortion to the throughput and total time T_{write} required to collect data and write it onto tapes. Thus, for a workload Θ,

$$T_{opt}(\Theta) = min(T_{read}(\Theta) + \Delta T_{write}(\Theta)) \tag{1}$$

Where $T_{opt}(\Theta)$ is the minimal optimal time required to complete the execution of workload Θ. We analyse some of the latencies and overhead incurred in achieving this goal in different scenarios. These scenarios are commonly occurring cases in storage systems.

Scenario 1: Single Read/Write Task in Queue: When there is a single read task in the task queue, the total amount of time required to complete the task and obtain the data is given as the sum of times taken for a series of events. Thus $T_{singleRead} = T_{search} + T_{load} + T_{seek} + n(\frac{BLK}{\gamma_{read}})$ where n is the total number of unit blocks that need to be read. $\frac{BLK}{\gamma_{read}}$ is a constant, the total time required to read a single block and can be substituted by Γ_{read} to get

$$T_{singleRead} = T_{search} + T_{load} + T_{seek} + n\Gamma_{read} \tag{2}$$

Similarly, a single write operation in a queue undergoes similar delays as read operations, the only difference being the rate at which data is written to tapes. The delay for a single write operation is given by

$$T_{singleWrite} = T_{search} + T_{load} + T_{seek} + n\Gamma_{write} \tag{3}$$

Scenario 2: Write task(s) before Read task in Queue: In scenarios where there are one or more write tasks in the queue before a read task, the total time required to obtain the data will include the time required to complete the write task too. For a single write task before the read task, the total time required to complete the task will be equal to $T_{total} = T_{search} + T_{load} + T_{seek} + n\Gamma_{write} + T_{unload} + T_{search} + T_{load} + T_{seek} + n\Gamma_{read}$. This can simply be written as $T_{total} = T_{singleWrite} + T_{unload} + T_{singleRead}$. Generalizing this, when we have N write tasks before a read task, we have

$$T_{total} = N(T_{singleWrite}) + \xi(T_{unload}) + T_{singleRead} \tag{4}$$

where $0 \leq \xi \leq (N - 1)$. ξ is called the tape switch rational which determines the probable number of tape changes that need to be made and is based on BLK and n. Thus BLK is an important value that influences the efficiency of write operations and helps in deciding the maximum size of data that can be written as a continuous process on to a single tape.

Scenario 3: Other Read Task(s) before Read Task in Queue: The total time required for a particular read task to complete when there are one or more read task ahead of it differs from the previous scenarios in that, read requests are usually not localized to a single tape mostly due to replication and data striping. Continuous read requests mean more number of search, load and seek operations, thus increasing the overall time taken. In the worst case, the total time taken can be given by

$$T_{total} = (N + 1)(T_{singleRead}) + (N)(T_{unload}) \tag{5}$$

where there are N read requests ahead of the read task in question. This not only causes excessive delays in retrieving data but also leads to the pile up of write tasks at the queue in scenarios where there is an equal ratio of read to write requests.

3   Proposed System's Approach to Overcome Latency

3.1   Prioritizing Read Tasks over Write Tasks

From equation 4, we can see that a major share of the delay occurs due to the tasks ahead of the read task in the queue. In order to reduce the over all time taken for retrieving data, an approach that can be opted is biasing between read and write tasks. The read tasks can be given a higher preference over write tasks. For this, we create a Priority Queue for read tasks for each tape drive. When a read task arrives at a tape drive, the subsequent write task is blocked and the tape drive immediately caters to the read task after finishing the current execution. Thus we have

$$T(Pri)_{total} = T_{total} - (N(T_{singleWrite}) + \xi(T_{unload})) + (T_{unload} + T_{singleRead}) \tag{6}$$

$$T(Pri)_{total} = \rho + T_{unload} + T_{singleRead} \tag{7}$$

where $T(Pri)_{total}$ is the total time taken when priority queueing is applied. ρ is the time spent for completion of current task and $\lceil \rho \rceil = T_{singleWrite}$ and $0 \leq \xi \leq (N - 1)$. By implementing the priority queuing, read tasks can be accelerated to be completed much faster.

3.2   Read Probability Weight (RPW) Based Data Distribution

Under the circumstances of scenario 3, applying priority queueing would not significantly reduce the total response time as subsequent read operations that need to be performed on different tapes still induce delay associated with the search and seeking processes. We propose a method to overcome this by considering the Balls into Bins problem [8][9][10].

Every block of data that needs to be written to tapes have a certain probability of being read again. This probability or "weight" is based on the type of application and its historic transactions with the storage system. Intuitively we can see that blocks of data with a higher weight causes higher delay when written to tapes by the same tape drive as compared to data with lower weight (because the read requests that come in eventually still have to be queued at the same tape drive). So the motive to reduce this delay has to be to distribute the data blocks of higher weight equally among the available tape drives such that a single tape drive need not take the entire burden of heavy weighted objects. This is similar to a Balls into Bins problem except that in our case, balls are of different weights. Assume that there are n types of data blocks, where $W_n = \{P_r^1, P_r^2...P_r^n\}$ are its respective weights. Given m tape drives $T_{drive} = \{t_1, t_2...t_m\}$, the RPW data distribution makes sure that

$$\forall t\epsilon(T_{drive}), (\sum_{i=0}^{k} P_r^i)/k \approx \varphi(W_n) \tag{8}$$

where $\varphi(W_n)$ is the arithmetic mean of all the elements in the set (W_n) and

$$\sum_{j=0}^{p/2}((\sum_{i=0}^{k} P_r^i)/k) - \sum_{j=p/2}^{m}((\sum_{i=0}^{k} P_r^i)/k) \approx 0 \tag{9}$$

Where k is the total number of write tasks in a particular queue t. If data originating from an application q is assigned a weight P_q at any point of time, then each queue will have a weight S_q equivalent to $P_q/\sum_{n=1}^{N} P_n$ of data pertaining to application q where N is the total number of weighted tasks in the queue. No single application can have all its data written to a single location. RPW based data distribution coupled with priority queueing not only improves average response time efficiency, but also contributes towards maintaining write throughput as it reduces the overall delay caused due to continuous blocking of write tasks by a series of read tasks. An evaluation of RPW usage has been shown in figure 12.

4   System and Middleware Design

Figure 3 shows a bird/s eye view of the Tape Cloud architecture. We propose a hybrid middleware that performs efficient hard disk caching, data block management, data distribution and IO task scheduling. This middleware functions as an agent arbitrating various components in order to reduce the overhead caused by using the slower backend media. Figure 4 provides the logical representation of the middleware and some of its functionalities. The data that needs to be written to tapes is collected and channelled suitably before it reaches its destination. Data is processed in batches. This helps in easy retrieval of data from collection servers and fixed set of parameters for efficient distribution.

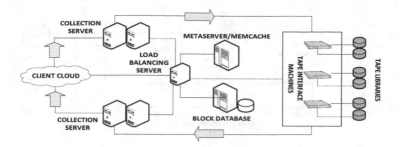

Fig. 3. Implementation Architecture of Tape Cloud. The arrows represent the direction of flow of data. The infrastructure is a hybrid structure which makes use of hard disk caches and databases.

4.1   Data Source or Clients

The focus of Tape Cloud is consistent with most cloud based services and provides an efficient storage service for a variety of data. Clients who wish to archive data on Tape Cloud, run a service to deliver data to the storage collection servers(see figure 3). One of the features of Tape Cloud is that it allows clients to deliver data in more than one ways. Large data sets(which is an unavoidable attribute of archive data) can also be delivered by mailing the media itself. From the storage system's perspective, each client is tagged and labelled based on the physical attributes of the data, relative storage activity over time, space requirements and the frequency of requests for data IO that is derived from the clients. This information serves as policies which is used by the middleware to make decisions on the location of data, level of security, distribution of data blocks and also provides the recipe to cook the read probability weight (RPW) information of data pertaining to particular clients. The data manager, with access to the central block database, updates and maintains mapping of blocks of data to its physical location on tapes, in libraries and section of the data center.

4.2   Data and Resource Manager

The Data Manager is the point of interaction between the clients and the storage infrastructure. More importantly, it is the interaction point between the client application and the middleware as no data is directly written to tapes without the data manager's consent. The data manager module runs on the load balancing server and manages the other parts of the middleware such as the filesystem, task queues and data distribution modules. To perform efficient management, the data manager relies on informative references to the actual client data. These references or metadata contains details about the blocks of data such as its location in the filesystem, size, type and RPW along with other client specific information. The metadata is used as representatives of data blocks in the queuing and the distribution modules of the middleware. This prevents the overhead of moving around large amounts of data within the system.

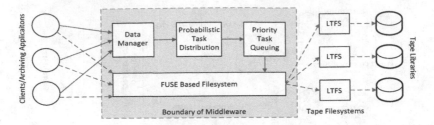

Fig. 4. The placement and interfacing of the functional blocks of the Middleware. The solid lines show the path taken by control statements and meta data while dotted lines show the path of the actual data blocks to be stored on tapes.

An important task the data manager undertakes is the grouping of data stored in the middleware's filesystem to be processed in batches. The data manager employs a specific technique to pick metadata pertaining to blocks of data which are most probable to be retrieved as a single unit from the filesystem, packages them and passes them to the data distribution module. Other responsibilities include the attestation of data deposition requests from and client and allocating suitable resources.

4.3   Multi Tier File System

FUSE [11] is a framework to help develop customized file system. FUSE module has been officially merged into the Linux kernel tree since kernel version 2.6.14. FUSE provides 35 interfaces to fully comply with POSIX file operations. We design a file system using FUSE to operate in the middleware of the architecture. The implementation presents a monolithic image of the filesystem, but internal divisions exist based on functionalities. Figure 5 shows the pathway taken by data to be written to tapes and the various operations that act upon it. The filesystem depends on external databases to maintain records of the locations of blocks of data. In order to prevent loss of data due to server failure, the filesystem performs a replication of similar data in multiple location similar to HDFS.

The filesystem manages data and chunks based on a hierarchical partitioning technique of the data set. Tape Cloud follows an application centric approach to group data chunks to be written to tapes and a method called hierarchical partitioning that is used, contributes to this cause. Every file that needs to be written to or read from tapes is encrypted, optionally segmented(to avoid singular large files) and replicated to result in a unit entity or chunk. The chunks of data are grouped and bagged in structures called containers. Based on the load, these containers are then distributed to the tape interface machines to be written to tapes.

4.4   Probabilistic Data Distribution

The analysis of latencies that is performed leads to induction of a technique where some of the delays are preempted before data is written to tapes. As

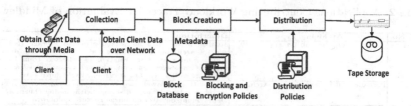

Fig. 5. Stages and functions of each stage of the filesystem for Tape Cloud. Although distributed by functionality, the filesystem is monolithic across the storage system.

discussed in section 3, this is to ensure that a small group of task queues do not take the burden of a large number of discontinuous read tasks. The probabilistic data distribution module is an important part of the middleware that distributes blocks of data to the tape interface machines based on a particular weight associated with the data. The weight or the read probability weight (RPW) is the probability of the block of data being read once written onto tape. The probabilistic data distribution module is designed to obtain the RPW by two ways. It can be enclosed in the metadata that is handed down by the data manager. The other avenue that can be taken to deduce the RPW is over time, when the middleware notices that there are some blocks of data that have undergone access in a manner inconsistent with its knowledge about the RPW. In this scenario, the middleware updates the RPW of data incoming from the client and adapts to the workloads of different clients over time. After the references have been assigned specific tapes or drives, the references of data blocks are handed over to the task queuing module of the middleware.

4.5 Task Queueing

The large scale operation of the storage system involves the use of multiple tape drives. The entire tape storage facility is divided into sections, each of which can be serviced by a tape drive. Each of these tape drives have an exclusive queue assigned to it which holds the IO task to be performed on tapes which are in its logical vicinity. These tasks queues are maintained and used by the middleware and should not be confused with the ones that are used by the storage media or drivers. One of the approaches to decrease the delay in retrieving data is to prioritize between the read and write requests as discussed in section 3. The task queueing module caters to this need by assigning each tape drive with two virtual queues, one each for write and read requests. Read requests having higher priority over write requests are granted resources immediately after the completion of the current task regardless of the depth of the write queue. After completion of the read task, the system continues with the execution of other tasks in the write queues. Assuming an efficient distribution of data, the task queueing module ensures that read tasks are performed under strict time constraints while maintaining acceptable standards of throughput for write tasks. The task queues provide periodic feedbacks to the data manager about the overall time taken in

Table 2. Applications Contributing Workload Traces for Evaluation of Middleware

Sl. No.	Archiving Type	Description
1	Periodic Full Backup	10 disk array on 3 networked attached storage (NAS) servers archiving surveillance video and security data. Videos and related information is collected from local systems once every 24 hours through a customized asynchronous pull server based system. High churn rate.
2	Periodic Full Backup + LRU Archiving	Application archived least recently used support files on larger disk based backend storage with smaller churn rate. Deployment details and infrastructure unknown.
3	Incremental+Full Backup	Incremental backup of hard disks and virtual disks at the end of every login session and periodic full backup of 22 computers on hard disk based NAS storage running CryptoNAS software.
4	Non Periodic Mirroring Backup	Document archiving of unknown number of computers. Simple FreeNAS storage with a duplication based archiving client running on individual computers.

performing tasks associated with a specific batch. This feedback is used by the data manager to assess the overall performance of the data distribution module and the distribution parameters in the system.

5   Synthesis of Workload for Middleware Evaluation

5.1   Characterizing Archive Workload from Traces

The accepted method to evaluate a storage infrastructure is by testing its performance with benchmark workloads. While a number of articles provide benchmarks and suggest methods to evaluate various aspects of storage such as the media, queues, IO charecterization[12] and filesystem [13][14], there has been a comparatively limited literature about performance of archival storage systems. Kavalanekar et. al.[15] provide elaborate results on storage workloads from production windows servers. But the variation in workload type between non archival and archival storage varies as suggested by Lee et. al. in [16], who make an attempt to create benchmarks. But their work is limited to providing a better understanding of the type of files and sizes rather than provide a complete set of results. Another important contribution has been provided by Wallace et. al.[17] for EMC production servers. Although a large number of aspects have been covered, the impact of different types of archiving and application level transactions with the storage have not been projected.

In order to perform a bias free evaluation of the middleware, we subject it to a workload that has been characterized by traces obtained from live archiving applications. The traces are collected from the archiving infrastructure of IVigil, a company that provides video surveillance services to a local client base. The backed up data usually includes surveillance videos, security related data, virtual disks and documents that are wielded by the company on a daily bases. Aspects which are important to the working of the middleware such as rate of requests with respect time, inter arrival time of requests and a comparison of the rate of read to write request are recorded and analysed. Table 2 provides some information about the characteristics of the infrastructure.

The applications show characteristics that prove common beliefs about archival data wrong[16]. The application level traces help in understanding the frequency with which IO requests are generated. This serves as a clear indicator of how backup

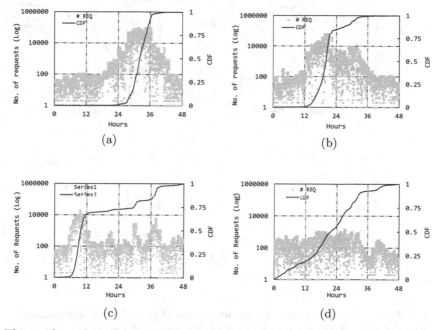

Fig. 6. The total number of requests generated by archiving applications 1(a), 2(b), 3(c) and 4(d). The number of requests are collected at the application level for discrete read or write requests to the underlying filesystems.

types differ from each other. The filesystem level traces provide a defined understanding of what each IO request generated by the application demands. Each of the applications vary in infrastructure so it is important to co-relate traces obtained to reflect a common operation at each stage. The following are the results of the characteristic extraction from the traces.

Figure 6 is the total number of IO requests generated by the archiving applications and figure 7, the interarrival time of these requests. These have been recorded at the application level or at the first level of the storage infrastructure. The number of storage requests generated is an important feature to be considering as it provides valuable insight into the nature of application and guidelines on the capacity that the middleware needs to cope. Interarrival time helps in setting parameters such as the queue lengths, batch processing rate etc.

As discussed earlier, random IO is responsible for the major share of the delay in a tape infrastructure. Figure 8 and figure 9 provides a better understanding of the number of read requests obtained as a ratio of write requests and how frequently 200 individual "hot" files are accessed within the storage system.

5.2   Workload Modeling and Generation

There have been many projects in developing synthetic workload to test storage systems such as [18][7] which depend on models created by Markov chains of

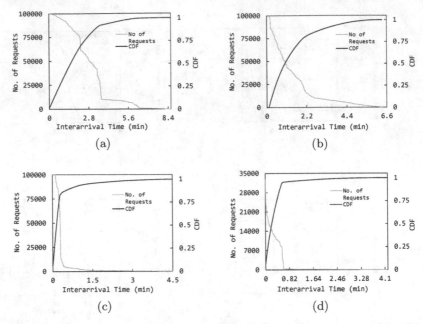

Fig. 7. Interarrival(IA) time of requests generated by archiving applications 1(a), 2(b), 3(c) and 4(d). Application, type of data, file sizes and temporal locality are some of the factors influencing interarrival time. The asynchronous nature of some applications and storage system softwares also affect IA time.

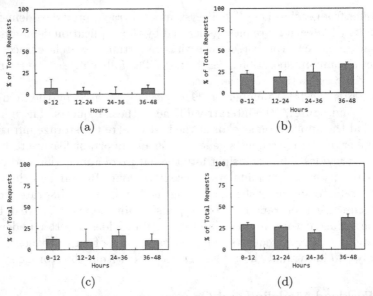

Fig. 8. Average number of read requests as a percentage of the total IO requests in 12 hour buckets by archiving applications 1(a), 2(b), 3(c) and 4(d). The whiskers show the maximum percent of read requests received during the particular 12 hour interval.

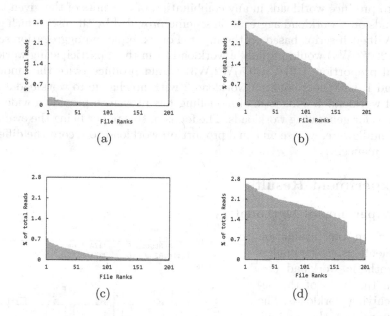

Fig. 9. Total number of read requests for the 200 most frequently accessed files as a percentage of the total read requests received by archiving applications 1(a), 2(b), 3(c) and 4(d).

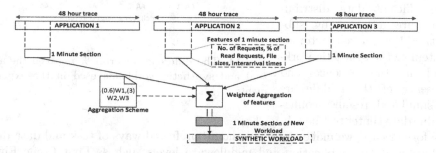

Fig. 10. The process of synthesizing a workload based on previously analysed application traces. The traces are divided based on a user defined time interval, features extracted and an aggregation performed to create a block of the new artificial workload

states and virtualized environments. The commendable results focus on workloads that vary from archiving workloads. We synthesize a workload using Vdbench[19] in order to test the middleware's performance. The workload generator is carefully designed by performing a sectional analysis of the results obtained in the real archive workload traces. The real time workloads are spliced on the basis of a user defined time interval and the features of each division such as number of requests, types of requests, file sizes and interarrival times are extracted. The newly created workload is essentially a time based, weighted aggregation hybrid of the workloads. The weighted aggregation provides the flexibility to produce workloads in any combination of amounts of the given traces. It depends on a workload aggregation scheme provided by the user which generates a Vdbench script based on the input. For example, an aggregation scheme (W1,W2,W3,W4) would produce a workload from the 4 participating workloads in equal proportion, ((2)W1,(0.5)W2,W3) would produce twice the amount of workload 1, half the amount of workload 2 with no change to workload 3 an no trace of workload 4. This type of modelling has proven to provide a wide range of options for generating workloads. The focus of this paper being the evaluation of the middleware, we use an equal proportion workload to record the difference in performance.

6   Experiment Results

6.1   Experimental Methodology

We perform our evaluation experiments using the models and synthetic workload created on the basis of the actual archiving workloads. The performance of the middleware and its contribution in achieving the goals to minimize average response time and efficient data distribution, are assessed by subjecting the backend storage system to the synthetic workload in the absence and presence of the middleware on simulated, resource configurable data center test bed. In

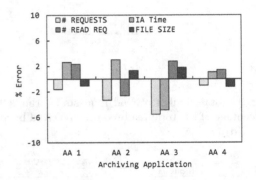

Fig. 11. The difference or error % between the actual and synthetic workloads used in the experiments.

the former case, we make use of commonly preferred ways of task and data distribution at the application and middleware levels such as First Come First Serve (FCFS)+Round Robin and Application specific task queuing techniques. To evaluate the middleware, we consider the Priority Queuing and evaluate its performance. As mentioned in section 2, the priority queueing technique has a few drawbacks which is then overcome with RPW Data distribution method. All tests are conducted along with the middleware filesystem. First of all, it is important to check for inconsistencies in the synthetic workloads as compared to the real time workloads obtained from traces. Figure 11 gives the error percentage of the synthetic workloads.

6.2   Read Probability Weight based Data Distribution

The novel idea of preempting delay caused due to large number of read requests especially in a system like Tape Cloud calls for preliminary evaluation of the

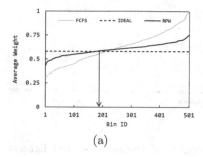
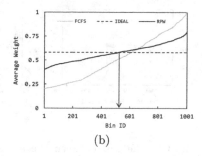

(a)   (b)

Fig. 12. Verifying the correctness of the RPW approach. Compared to FCFS, RPW offers a higher convergence to the ideal case. Here Fig(a) is with 500 bins and Fig(b) is with 1000 bins. The arrow points to the queue ID which serves as the point of distribution balance.

technique. RPW considers the probability of a block of data being read once written to tapes and distributes blocks based on this probability. To verify the correctness of our assumption, we consider 10000 randomly weighted objects and distribute them into bins. Two tests are performed, where each has 500 and 1000 bins. This emulates blocks with different probabilities that need to be assigned to different tape drives. Figure 12 shows that RPW offers a distribution that is closer to the ideal case than other approaches like FCFS in both cases.

In evaluating the RPW using the synthetic workload, we consider two cases where we have 500 tape drives (figure 13) and 1000 tape drives (figure 14). We compare RPW with FCFS and Application Specific Queueing which distributes data blocks generated by specific applications to specific queues. The application specific approach has clear boundaries between queues for each application in the system. When we vary the number of total requests generated by the synthetic workload, we see that RPW provides a more efficient distribution where the gap between the queue with the largest average weight and the queue with smallest average weight is much lesser than that of the other approaches. The whiskers show the largest and smallest average weights of queues.

6.3   Average Response Time for Read Requests

The use of RPW based data distribution helps in avoiding long stretches of read operations that is localized to a small set of task queues. This in turn reduces the average delay caused at each of the queues. When we test Tape Cloud with the synthetic workload, the absence of the middleware leads us to use conventional data distribution and queueing techniques such as FCFS, Round Robin and application specific queueing of tasks. But with the middleware and enhanced task management, there is an overall reduction in the response time for read tasks generated by every application as shown in figure 15. The graphs have Log values in X axis which show the rate of change of average response time when number of requests are varied and the RPW have negligible rate of change of response time even for large number of requests.

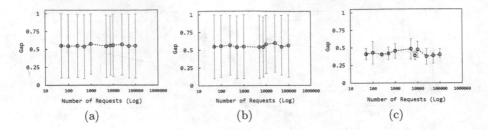

Fig. 13. The gap between the average weights of the heaviest and lightest queues for different number of requests for 500 queues. FCFS (a) and Application Specific Queueing (b) show inefficient weight distribution as compared to RPW (c).

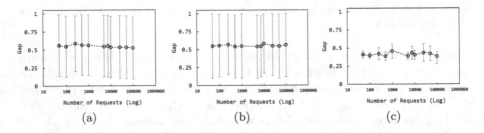

Fig. 14. The gap between the average weights of the heaviest and lightest queues for different number of requests for 1000 queues. FCFS (a) and Application Specific Queueing (b) show inefficient weight distribution as compared to RPW (c).

One of the notable differences that can be seen in the traces of the four application is the variation in number of requests over time. Theoretically, the induction of RPW based data distribution along with priority queueing must make the average response time immune to the number of total number of requests. We perform an hourly analysis of average response time for read requests from application 1 and application 2 because application 1 has the highest write requests and application 2 has the highest read requests. We see from figure 16 that, along with having the smallest response time, the combination of priority queueing and RPW distribution provides a nearly constant response time over the entire period of the test, making it independent of other requests.

6.4   Preserving Rate of Write Task Execution

In keeping with our goals, we test if the middleware brings about a negative impact on the write task completion rate of the workload. Figure 17 provides a comparison of the write performance before and after the deployment of the middleware. We test cases that present extreme scenarios such as application 1 which has the highest write requests and application 2 which has the highest read requests for the aggregation scheme in use and it is very clear that, along with dutifully improving data retrieval efficiency, the middleware also maintains that similar justice be done to write tasks as well. There is only a negligible reduction

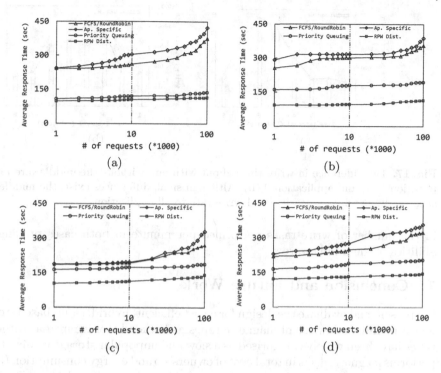

Fig. 15. The average response time of read requests under the synthetic workload for application 1 (a), application 2 (b), application 3 (c) and application 4 (d). Note the clear difference and reduction of the average response time for each of the applications. Also, RPW based data distribution offers very small rate of increase of response time even over larger variations of the number of requests

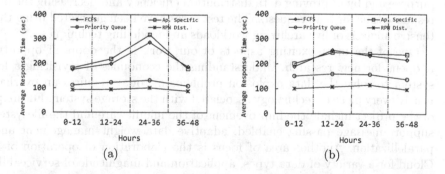

Fig. 16. Time based average response time for application 1 (a) and application 2 (b). Applications 1 and 2 are considered because application 1 has the highest write requests and application 2 has highest read requests. Compared to the other methods such as FCFS and Application specific Queuing, RPW based data distribution maintains a stable average response time regardless of the density of the workload

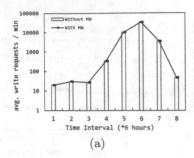 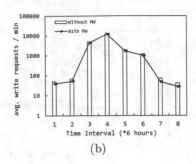

(a)   (b)

Fig. 17. The difference in write throughput with and without the middleware for application 1 (a) and application 2 (b). Although small differences exist, the middleware successfully provides a nearly equal write rate to all applications.

in the number of write tasks performed per minute in both cases proving the abilities of the middleware.

7   Conclusion and Future Work

We present and evaluate the design for a cost efficient, hybrid, cloud based storage which mainly makes use of magnetic tapes as backend storage media. Although tapes have been widely categorised as a slow and unpopular storage media, it outperforms magnetic disks in total cost of ownership and energy consumption (tapes don't consume power when stored in a tape library), which makes tape technology an ideal choice for cloud based archiving services. We explore the benefits of the state of the art in tape storage technology. The need for a managerial middleware, which is a combination of algorithms and data distribution policies, that contributes in overcoming the latency offered by tapes in order to improve performance of IO processes is proposed and evaluated. The middleware serves its purpose and by improving data distribution efficiency and decreasing the overall response time for read requests. The test cases have been generated using the extensive analysis of live archiving workloads and modelling techniques.

One of the most exciting aspects of our work is the doors of opportunity it opens for new research. Understanding the economics of revisiting a legacy system to solve the data explosion problems of today requires an overhaul of nearly every piece of technology associated with the storage system. Future plans of the project include the improvement of the middleware and the filesystem to support message passing enabled, adaptive data weight management and IO paralellization. Another area of focus is the elaboration of operation of Tape Cloud for a variety of data types, application and magnitude of serviceability.

References

1. Seagate, Video surveillance storage: How much is enough?
2. County of cameras: Cheshire constabulary aims to count every private camera in the county, CCTV Image Online

3. Chamness, M.: Capacity forecasting in a backup storage environment. In: Usenix LISA 2011 (2011)
4. Jackson, J.: Most network data sits untouched. Government Computer News (July 2008), http://gcn.com/Articles/2008/07/01/Most-network-data-sits-untouched.aspx
5. Sandstå, O., Olav, S., St, A., Midtstraum, R.: Improving the access time performance of serpentine tape drives (1999)
6. Giurgiu, I., Castillo, C., Tantawi, A., Steinder, M.: Enabling efficient placement of virtual infrastructures in the cloud. In: Narasimhan, P., Triantafillou, P. (eds.) Middleware 2012. LNCS, vol. 7662, pp. 332–353. Springer, Heidelberg (2012)
7. Gulati, A., Kumar, C., Ahmad, I.: Modeling workloads and devices for io load balancing in virtualized environments. SIGMETRICS Perform. Eval. Rev.
8. Raab, M., Steger, A.: "Balls into bins" - A simple and tight analysis. In: Rolim, J.D.P., Serna, M., Luby, M. (eds.) RANDOM 1998. LNCS, vol. 1518, pp. 159–170. Springer, Heidelberg (1998)
9. Peres, Y., Talwar, K., Wieder, U.: The $(1 + \beta)$-choice process and weighted balls-into-bins
10. Berenbrink, P., Friedetzky, T., Hu, Z., Martin, R.: On weighted balls-into-bins games. Theor. Comput. Sci.
11. Fuse filesystem project, http://fuse.sourceforge.net/
12. Ahmad, I.: Easy and efficient disk i/o workload characterization in vmware esx server. In: Proceedings of the 2007 IEEE 10th International Symposium on Workload Characterization, IISWC 2007, IEEE Computer Society, Washington, DC (2007)
13. Agrawal, N., Bolosky, W.J., Douceur, J.R., Lorch, J.R.: A five-year study of file-system metadata. Trans. Storage
14. Douceur, J.R., Bolosky, W.J.: A large-scale study of file-system contents. In: Proceedings of the 1999 ACM SIGMETRICS International Conference on Measurement and Modeling of Computer Systems, SIGMETRICS 1999. ACM, New York (1999)
15. Kavalanekar, S., Worthington, B., Zhang, Q., Sharda, V.: Characterization of storage workload traces from production windows servers. In: IEEE International Symposium on Workload Characterization, IISWC 2008, pp. 119–128 (2008)
16. Lee, D., O'Sullivan, M., Walker, C.: Benchmarking and modeling disk-based storage tiers for practical storage design. SIGMETRICS Perform. Eval. Rev. 40(2), 113–118 (2012), http://doi.acm.org/10.1145/2381056.2381080
17. Wallace, G., Douglis, F., Qian, H., Shilane, P., Smaldone, S., Chamness, M., Hsu, W.: Characteristics of backup workloads in production systems
18. Delimitrou, C., Sankar, S., Vaid, K., Kozyrakis, C.: Decoupling datacenter studies from access to large-scale applications: A modeling approach for storage workloads. In: 2011 IEEE International Symposium on Workload Characterization, IISWC (2011)
19. Vdbench, http://vdbench.sourceforge.net/

Efficient Node Bootstrapping for Decentralised Shared-Nothing Key-Value Stores

Han Li and Srikumar Venugopal

The University of New South Wales
Sydney, Australia
{hli,srikumarv}@cse.unsw.edu.au

Abstract. Distributed key-value stores (KVSs) have become an important component for data management in cloud applications. Since resources can be provisioned on demand in the cloud, there is a need for efficient node bootstrapping and decommissioning, i.e. to incorporate or eliminate the provisioned resources as a members of the KVS. It requires the data be handed over and the load be shifted across the nodes quickly. However, the data partitioning schemes in the current-state shared nothing KVSs are not efficient in quick bootstrapping. In this paper, we have designed a middleware layer that provides a decentralised scheme of auto-sharding with a two-phase bootstrapping. We experimentally demonstrate that our scheme reduces bootstrap time and improves load-balancing thereby increasing scalability of the KVS.

Keywords: Cloud computing, Key-value Stores, Elasticity, Performance.

1 Introduction

Distributed key-value stores (KVSs) [3,5,10] have become a standard component for many web services and applications due to their inherent scalability, reliability and data availability, even in the face of hardware failures. While KVSs have been mostly used in data centres, many enterprises are now adopting them for use on servers leased from Infrastructure-as-a-Service (IaaS) cloud.

IaaS providers offer compute resources in the form of virtual machines (VMs), which can be provisioned or de-provisioned anytime on-demand. To deal with increasing workload, new VMs are acquired to improve the system's capacity (i.e. scale up). Since IaaS providers normally follow the "pay-as-you-go" pricing model, redundant VMs can be shut down in the face of declining demand (i.e. scale down) to save on economic costs . In this paper, the process of incorporating a new empty VM as a member of KVS is termed as node *bootstrapping*. In contrast, the process of eliminating an existing member with redundant data off the KVS is called node *decommissioning*.

The storage model of a KVS determines its performance of data movement during node bootstrapping and decommissioning. In shared storage KVSs, the persistent data is stored in the underlying networked attached storage or distributed file system (DFS). The data can be migrated between nodes without

D. Eyers and K. Schwan (Eds.): Middleware 2013, LNCS 8275, pp. 348–367, 2013.

actual data transfer, simply by exchanging the metadata (e.g., identifiers or ownership) of data blocks in the shared storage [9]. In contrast, shared-nothing KVSs consist of distributed nodes, each with their own separate storage, coordinated as a distributed hash table (DHT). When a new node joins the system, it has to obtain data from its peers. This process is slow in the case of KVS with large data volume. Thus, it is non-trivial to bootstrap or decommission a node *quickly* and *frictionlessly*, i.e. without affecting the online query processing.

The challenge of node bootstrapping in the shared-nothing KVSs lies in redistributing the data when a new node is added. Specifically, it requires a mechanism that *partitions* the key space of a database and then *re-allocates* the partition replicas during node bootstrapping. Moreover, most shared-nothing KVSs [10,15] are essentially DHTs, deployed in a completely decentralised architecture (i.e. peer-to-peer, or P2P). There is a need for decentralised coordination between the peers to execute data partitioning.

This paper aims at improving the efficiency of node bootstrapping for decentralised shared-nothing KVSs. The goal of efficiency is three-fold. First, the side-effect of data movement (against front-end query processing) should be minimised. Second, data consistency and availability should be maintained during bootstrapping. Third, the load in terms of both data volume and workload that each node undertakes, should be re-balanced after bootstrapping. Node decommissioning is also discussed, but it is applied with caution to avoid data loss.

In this paper, we describe the design of a middleware layer that provides a decentralised scheme of data partitioning and placement to improve the efficiency of node bootstrapping. The main contribution of this paper is a decentralised auto-sharding scheme, extending from the concept of "virtual node" [19], that consolidates each partition of data into single transferable replicas to eliminate the overhead of migrating individual key-value pairs. Through sharding, the data volume of each partition replica is confined into a bounded range.

We also discuss a related placement algorithm, that evenly re-allocates the partition replicas when a node is bootstrapped and decommissioned, with the objectives of: i) rebalancing the volume of data; ii) maintaining high data availability; and iii) minimising data movement at startup for quick bootstrapping. We have also implemented a token ownership mechanism to provide eventual consistency when a replica is migrated between nodes.

We have implemented these partitioning and placement mechanisms on top of Apache Cassandra, an open source KVS, to build *ElasCass*. We present experimental evaluations, carried out using public IaaS cloud, that demonstrate that our proposed scheme of data partitioning and placement reduces the time to bootstrap nodes, distributes data and workload more evenly among the nodes, and improves throughput of the KVS.

The rest of this paper is structured as follows. In the next section, we discuss the state-of-the-art in node bootstrapping and replica placement in distributed databases. The system design is presented in Section 3. The data consistency issue is discussed in Section 4. We present the experimental evaluations in Section 5. Finally, we conclude in Section 6.

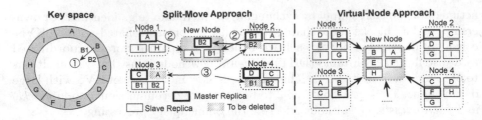

Fig. 1. A node joins the key-value store

2 Background and Related Work

The bootstrap process for a KVS executing on IaaS begins with provisioning a VM as a node and starting a KVS process. The next step is for the node to acquire a list of key ranges from existing nodes. Finally, the node acquires the data belonging to the key ranges. At this point, the node is ready to serve queries. We denote the time between the start of the KVS process and the point when the node is ready to serve queries as the *bootstrap time*. The efficiency of bootstrap is determined by the acquisition of the key ranges and the associated data. This is determined by the data management - partitioning and placement - strategies, the state-of-the-art in which is discussed in the following sections.

2.1 Partitioning in Key-Value Stores

Figure 1 illustrates several approaches for migrating the data during node bootstrapping, described as follows.

Split-Move **Approach**. This approach is commonly used in distributed hash tables (DHTs), and was adopted by Cassandra [15]. Typically, consistent hashing [13] is used, as it introduces minimal disruption when a hash table (e.g. a key range or a partition) is resized during node bootstrapping. The key space is split into a list of consecutive key ranges, each assigned to one node. Thereby, each node maintains one master replica for its own range, and also stores the slave replicas of several other key ranges for high availability. When a new node joins the KVS, the key space of the database is re-partitioned. One or several existing partitions are *split* into two sets of data (e.g. B1 and B2 as in Figure 1). One is retained in the existing nodes. The other set of data is *moved* pair-by-pair and reassembled at the new node.

There are multiple drawbacks to this approach. One is the overhead of moving individual key-value pairs. When a partition is split, the node contributing the subset has to scan its entire dataset to prepare a list of key-value pairs for the new node, which, on receiving the data, has to reassemble the key-value pairs into files. Both scanning and reassembling are heavyweight operations.

The other drawback is that, consistent hashing aims at remapping a minimised number of keys when the number of nodes changes. As a result, only a limited number of nodes can participate in bootstrapping, each undertaking relatively heavy workload. According to Amazon [10], this bootstrapping approach is highly resource intensive, and is only suitable to run at a lower priority. However, low priority results in significantly slow bootstrapping, which adapts less quickly to dynamic load.

Virtual-Node **Approach**. A virtual node is a consolidated data partition that is transferable as a single unit. The idea of "virtual node" was introduced in Chord [19] and other consistent hashing systems, upon which KVSs such as Dynamo [10], Voldemort [1] and Cassandra [15] are based. Other KVSs, such as BigTable [3] and PNUTS [5], use the term "tablet" instead.

This approach avoids the overhead of scanning and reassembling as in the **split-move** approach. In practice, the key space is over-partitioned, such that the number of virtual nodes is made much greater than the data nodes. Each data node is assigned many virtual nodes. Hence, a new node can be bootstrapped by multiple existing nodes, each offering one or several virtual nodes. Thereby, each participating node shares a relatively small amount of workload in bootstrapping.

However, there is a lack of efficient data partitioning schemes for completely decentralised KVSs. The current-state research efforts [10,15] use a *simplified* partitioning strategy, wherein the key space is split into static key ranges of equal length, or hashed into buckets with equal capacity. Although this strategy avoids complex coordination amongst the peer nodes, it leads to data skew for biased key distributions. Data skew results in some "giant" partitions that are difficult to migrate because of the large volume of data [5].

One refinement is to re-hash the inserted keys using uniform hash functions, most of which, however, are not order-preserving, making the support of range queries more difficult. For those uniform order-preserving hash functions, there is a fundamental limitation: the key space is discrete and cannot adapt to any arbitrary application key distributions [1]. Alternatively, PNUTS [5] proposed to shard the tablets (i.e. partitions) into bounded sizes. However, it relies on a centralised component that limits the efficiency of partitioning in the KVS.

Metadata-Only **Approach**. This approach is used by shared storage KVSs such as BigTable [3], Spanner [7] and HBase [2]. The persistent data is not stored in the nodes of KVSs, but in underlying distributed file systems such as GFS [11] or HDFS [18]. For this storage model, Das et al. [9] proposed that data can be migrated by exchanging only the **metadata** (i.e. *identifiers* or ownership) of data blocks between the nodes of database systems (or KVSs), while the persistent data remains unmoved in the shared storage. A centralised controller is also used for metadata management. Although this approach minimises the cost of data migration, it is not applicable to decentralised shared-nothing KVSs.

2.2 Data Placement

The data placement problem has been extensively studied in literature. The common approach in state-of-the-art KVSs to data placement is to manage the data through coarse grain structures such as buckets or virtual nodes rather than identifying an optimal placement strategy at the granularity of single data items [14].

---

[1] Voldemort: http://www.project-voldemort.com/voldemort
[2] Apache HBase: http://hbase.apache.org

Consistent hashing-based KVSs [10,15] have typically adopted a random placement strategy, in which a random hash function is used to assign groups of data items (i.e. buckets or virtual nodes) to nodes. This allows key lookups to be performed locally, in a very efficient manner [10]. Other KVSs [3,7,5] rely on dedicated directory services that provide flexible mapping from virtual nodes to physical nodes. Essentially, this approach also uses random placement strategy. The advantages of this strategy are simplicity and the effectiveness of load-balancing [10,3].

There is also extensive work of finding optimal data placement strategies. Ursa [21] and Schism [8] rely on centralised components to compute the placement and to maintain a location map, which is not applicable to our system. Others research efforts [16,22] have proposed distributed replica placement algorithms. However, these efforts only consider the placement of read-only replicas, while we discuss the ownership management of virtual nodes to support both read and write operations.

In this paper, we extend the **virtual-node** approach to confine each transferable partition into a bounded size, that is enforced by auto-sharding, to avoid data skew. The novelty lies in executing auto-sharding using decentralised coordination. We also describe a random placement scheme to compliment the auto-sharding mechanism, in order to achieve fast bootstrap time and load-balancing.

3   Design

Our system follows the typical decentralised shared-nothing architecture. The key space of a database is hashed into multiple partitions. Each partition, denoted as P_i, is replicated to multiple nodes for high availability. The data is stored in a separate persistent storage volume, each attached to an individual node. Each node (denoted as n_i) serves many partitions for load balancing purposes. The nodes are organised as peer-to-peer (P2P), similar to DHTs [17,19]. Each node maintains enough routing information locally so as to route a request to the appropriate node directly, i.e. in *0-hop* [12]. Thus, clients can connect to any node for query execution.

We have designed a middleware layer that sits between the key space of a database and the storage of nodes. This middleware was implemented on a KVS that already has gossip-based [20] membership protocol and failure detection, hinted handoff [10] to handle node failures, and timestamp based reconciliation to ensure eventual consistency. This section describes the synthesis of decentralised auto-sharding and replica placement algorithms in this layer that improves the efficiency of node bootstrapping.

3.1   Data Partitioning for Building Transferable Replicas

Our partitioning algorithm builds on consistent hashing [13], in which the largest hash value is wrapped around to the smallest to form a ring of key space.

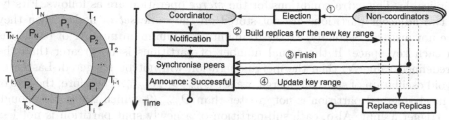

(a) Consistent hashing   (b) Auto-sharding with election-based coordination

Fig. 2. Data Partitioning

As shown in Figure 2(a), when a database is created, a number of tokens, $\{T_i : 0 < i \leq N\}$, are generated to segment the key space of the database into N consecutive equal-size key ranges, where N is configurable by the KVS administrators. Each key range defines one partition of data. Therefore, each partition P_i can be associated with the token T_i, which defines the upper bound of P_i. The lower bound is determined by the predecessor T_{i-1}.

Sharding Operations. The aim of auto-sharding is to confine the actual volume of data in each partition. Building on the **virtual-node** approach described in Section 2, we propose to shard the partitions online to address the problem of data skew. Let $Size(P_i)$ be the data volume of partition P_i. The maximum size Θ_{max} and the minimum size Θ_{min} are defined as in Equation 1 and Equation 2, respectively.

$$\forall i \in [1, N], Size(P_i) \leq \Theta_{max} \tag{1}$$
$$\forall i \in [1, N-1], Size(P_i) + Size(P_{i+1}) \geq \Theta_{min} \tag{2}$$

The partition P_i is *split* when $Size(P_i)$ exceeds Θ_{max}. A new token T_{new} is inserted between T_{i-1} and T_i, such that the resulting sub-ranges $(T_{i-1}, T_{new}]$ and $(T_{new}, T_i]$ contain roughly equal volumes of data. In contrast, two adjacent partitions (e.g. P_i and P_{i+1}) are *merged*, if their total size is below Θ_{min}. To merge P_i and P_{i+1}, the token T_i that sets the boundary of these two partitions is removed. Thus, the merged key range is $(T_{i-1}, T_{i+1}]$.

The challenge of sharding, either split or merge, lies in the consolidation of each partition replica as a single transferable unit for better performance of data migration. To consolidate a replica, key-value pairs belonging to different partitions, are stored in separated files. To execute a sharding, new replicas (i.e. data files) are created, to store *every* (and *only*) key-value pair belonging to sharded partition. Hence, *rebuilding replicas* of the affected partition is the key operation in sharding.

In addition, we discuss the need for merging partitions. In practice, there is less harm in retaining "sparse" partitions that contain small volume of data, rather than merging them aggressively, since a small-sized partition replica is easy to move. Nevertheless, in order to reduce the number of sparse partitions for better performance of query processing, we attempt to merge partitions when applicable. The extra conditions for the *merge* operation are as follows. Firstly, if two adjacent partitions are not stored on the same *set* of nodes, then they are not merged. Secondly, we try to maintain a minimum number of partitions in each key space. If the actual number of partitions is no greater than the predefined value N, then the merge operation will not be triggered. Lastly, to avoid oscillation of split and merge, we set $\Theta_{max} \geq 2\Theta_{min}$. Therefore, the size of a newly-merged partition is not greater than $\Theta_{max}/2$, which is not big enough to trigger a split. Also, each sub-partition of a newly split partition is not less than Θ_{min}, which is not small enough to trigger a merge.

Coordinating Sharding. The key operation of sharding is *rebuilding replicas*. However, since each partition is replicated to multiple nodes, the operation of rebuilding each local replica is executed by different nodes asynchronously. Thus, coordination is required to ensure the consistency of the key space and persistent data across the nodes that participate in sharding. As shown in Figure 2(b), sharding in a distributed KVS is coordinated in four steps:

Step 1: Election. When the data volume of a partition replica reaches the boundary (Θ_{max} or Θ_{min}), the node that serves the partition initiates the sharding. A coordinator is elected with a distributed consensus policy. In this paper, we have leveraged the Chubby implementation [2] for electing the coordinator. According to Chubby, the coordinator must obtain votes from a majority of the participating nodes, plus promises that those participating nodes will not elect a different coordinator for a time interval known as the *master lease*, which is periodically renewed. In our implementation, the node that initiates the sharding retrieves the complete list of nodes that store the partition. The list is sorted by certain criteria, and the node on top is voted as the *coordinator* (for this single operation only). The other participating nodes also vote for the node on top of the list. Since every node maintains the complete partition-node mapping locally, the sorted list is unique. The node on top wins a majority of the vote.

Step 2: Notification. There is a prerequisite before launching the sharding. In the case of split, the coordinator calculates the splitting token T_{new} that will be used by all the participating nodes. In the case of merge, the coordinator examines whether the extra conditions for merging are satisfied. Once the prerequisite is met, the coordinator notifies that a sharding should be launched. Then, all the participating nodes start to shard their own replica simultaneously.

Step 3: Synchronisation. The operation of *rebuilding replicas* is executed and completed asynchronously by different nodes. When a node finishes, it notifies the coordinator and then waits for further announcement. The coordinator synchronises this operation until all the participating nodes have finished.

Step 4: Announcement. Once the coordinator has received the notification of *Finish* from all the participating nodes, it announces globally that the key range of the affected partition should be updated to the new range. On receiving this final announcement, every node in the KVS updates the query routing information, and each participating node replaces the old replicas with the newly-built replicas asynchronously. In this way, a sharding operation is completed.

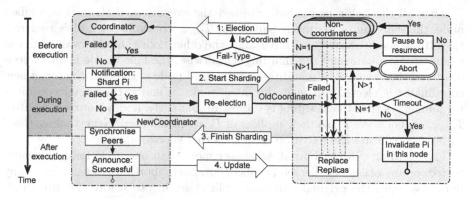

Fig. 3. Failure recovery in the election-based coordination

Failover During Sharding. Based on the four-step coordination as described, we discuss how to handle node failures during a sharding operation. Figure 3, extended from Figure 2(b), depicts the failure recovery.

The failure detection in our system is gossip-based [20]. We assume detection error exists, since a failure detector is not always completely accurate. A detection error, when caused by message loss, is *false-positive*, in which case a node is not dead, but detected as dead. In contrast, in a *false-negative* detection error, due to the delay in detection, a node is actually dead but considered as still alive. In our design, the communication between a coordinator and a non-coordinator follows the typical handshake policy. Hence, the false-negative error can be easily corrected. Therefore, we focus on addressing the false-positive detection error.

This failover scheme focuses on two scenarios: i) if only one participating node fails during the process, the sharding can succeed with or without the failed node's resurrection; ii) if more than one participating node fail, the sharding can be aborted and rolled back without data loss. We discuss the failover when a participating node is detected as failed (by gossip) *before*, *during*, or *after* the execution of rebuilding replicas of P_i. In the following, T_{pause} is defined as a time period that is longer than twice the end-to-end gossip broadcast delay.

Before the execution, if a participating node is detected as failed, the sharding procedure is paused for T_{pause}, to await whether the failed node can resurrect (e.g., due to false detection). If it is the coordinator node that fails, a different coordinator should be elected following the pause, even when the previous coordinator resurrects. After the pause, the sharding continues if at most one node fails, or is aborted (by any participating node) if there are more than one node failures. Nodes resurrecting after T_{pause} can no longer serve P_i.

During the execution, every participating node maintains the complete list of nodes that are sharding P_i. Whenever more than one participating nodes are detected as failed, and remain dead for a period of T_{pause}, any participating node that detects this event can abort the sharding via broadcast. Otherwise, if only one node (even the coordinator) fails, every other participating node continues the operation of rebuilding replicas regardlessly.

After all the living nodes have finished the execution, if there is one failed node, the sharding procedure is paused for T_{pause} to await the node's resurrection. If the node resurrects within T_{pause}, the other nodes should await until the resurrected node finishes the sharding. Otherwise, the failed node is announced dead and then removed. In addition, if the dead node is the coordinator, a new coordinator is elected amongst the living nodes. Finally, the (new) coordinator announces that the sharding is successful. Similarly, nodes resurrecting after T_{pause} cannot serve P_i, so their replicas of P_i are invalidated. Nevertheless, these nodes can replicate the partition from the other successful nodes.

The sharding can be aborted, whenever more than one node failures are detected, or any other unexpected events occur. Such abortion does not incur any data loss, since the original partition replicas are in use before the announcement of success. The details of maintaining data consistency are discussed in Section 4.1. The aborted sharding will be reinitiated after a long pause.

Thus, our partitioning algorithm consolidates partitions that are suitable for efficient data migration. Based on such consolidated replicas, we discuss the data placement strategy for node bootstrapping (and decommissioning).

3.2 Selecting Partition Replicas for Bootstrapping

The aim of replica placement is to achieve load balancing and quick node bootstrapping. When a new empty node is to be bootstrapped, it selects and pulls a list of partition replicas from the existing nodes based on a set of rules.

Rule 1: Complexity Reduction. Partition reallocation and sharding are mutually exclusive. That is, partitions that are being sharded will not be selected for replication, and partitions that are being reallocated will not be sharded. Hence, we reduce the complexity of coordinating data reallocation and sharding.

Rule 2: High Availability. Each partition P_i has ν_i replicas allocated in ν_i different nodes. We defined the replication number K, such that $\forall i \in [1, N], \nu_i \geq K$, wherein N is the number of partitions. If a partition has less than K replicas (e.g. due to node failure), a replica is duplicated to the new node.

Rule 3: Load Balancing. The nodes with higher workloads have higher priority to offer replicas. Hence, heavily loaded nodes have the priority to move out more replicas (thus shifting the workload) to the new node.

Rule 4: Data Balancing. Since each partition replica is confined into bounded sizes by sharding, balancing the number of partition replicas can result in balancing the volume of data stored in each node. Let $\overline{R}$ be the average number of replicas each node has. Before bootstrapping, the new node recalculates $\overline{R} = \sum_{i=1}^{N} \nu_i / (n + 1)$, in which n is the number of existing nodes. The new node can obtain no more than $\overline{R}$ replicas, while an existing node can offer (i.e. move out) replicas as long as it has more than $\overline{R}$ replicas.

To achieve quick bootstrapping, we propose a two-phase data migration strategy. In the *pre-bootstrapping* phase, the new node aims at maintaining high availability (referring to Rule 2) and alleviating the nodes that are under heavy workloads (Rule 3). Each heavily loaded node is requested to move out a small portion, e.g. 10%, of its replicas. Once the new node receives these replicas, it completes bootstrapping and starts serving queries as a member of the KVS immediately. In our implementation, we used the CPU usage to estimate the workload each node undertakes. The CPU usage is piggybacked on the heartbeat gossip message, sent by each living node periodically and cached by every other node. Therefore, a new node can download the complete workload information from any existing node. A node is marked (by the new node) as *heavily loaded*, if its CPU usage is over 50% and reasonably (e.g. 20%) greater than the average of all the nodes. The threshold for identifying a heavily-load node is configurable by the system administrators.

In the *post-bootstrapping* phase, as long as Rule 4 is satisfied, the newly joined node continues to pull in more replicas from a list of nodes sorted according to Rule 3. This process is run in a background thread, with data transfer rate throttled, such that the side-effects towards front-end query processing are minimised. In this two-phase procedure, the new node receives the majority of its replicas in the *post-bootstrapping* phase, since in the *pre-bootstrapping* phase there are limited number of *heavily loaded* nodes, each offering only a small number of replicas. Therefore, the new node completes the *pre-bootstrapping* phase in a timely manner, i.e. quick bootstrapping.

There are also considerations on how to select partition replicas when an existing node is requested (e.g. by the new node) to offer data. Each node maintains an exponential moving average (EMA) of the *local* hit count for each replica, which is updated periodically as in Equation 3. The moving average hit count of partition P_i at time t is denoted as $H_{i,t}$, and the actual hit count of P_i between time $t - 1$ and t is denoted as $h_{i,t-1}$. The coefficient α represents the degree of weighting decrease.

$$H_{i,t} = \alpha h_{i,t-1} + (1 - \alpha)H_{i,t-1} \tag{3}$$

To select a replica to move out, the node sorts its own replicas by the EMA of hit count. We avoid the greedy heuristic (i.e. move the hottest or coldest replica), since it may destabilise the system by causing more data movement. Instead, the node traverses the list starting from the middle, until it finds the first replica that does not exist in the destination node.

3.3   Node Decommissioning

We have also designed a replica placement scheme for node decommissioning. There are circumstances when node decommissioning is necessary: i) a living node is misbehaving, e.g. it is failing more often than it should or its performance is noticeably slow. ii) there are redundant compute resources, e.g. none of the living nodes is *heavily loaded* and there exists nodes that receive less queries than expected. In any case, the decision to decommission a node is made by the KVS administrators. In this paper we only discuss how to reallocate the replicas when node decommissioning is requested.

The node to be decommissioned moves out its replicas *one by one* to the other living nodes. It can safely leave the KVS when there is no more replica under its ownership. To choose a destination node for a replica (e.g. P_i), the node retrieves a list of living nodes that do not own P_i. Then it selects the least loaded node from the list as the destination. We prefer to balance the query workload (i.e. CPU usage) rather than the data volume, since storage is rarely the bottleneck in the cloud. Note that the workload information is gossiped periodically. Each time when the node attempts to move out a replica, it may choose a different node as the destination. In this way, the decommissioning node distributes its own replicas to the peers, and then leaves the KVS without data loss.

4   Data Recovery and Consistency

As our implementation builds on the Apache Cassandra project, we have leveraged hinted handoff [10] implemented in Cassandra to recover the data for node failure. When a replica node for the key is down, a hint is written to the coordinator node of the related partition. The coordinator node is chosen with the same election policy as in auto-sharding. However, unlike Cassandra, wherein users can define a consistency level for each individual query, we proposed to enforce each write to be saved in every replica of the targeted partition. Therefore, our consistency strategy caters for read-intensive workloads. The consistency issues during partition sharding and replica movement are discussed as follows.

4.1   Data Consistency During Sharding

While the replicas of a partition is being rebuilt during sharding, there are two sets of replicas (i.e. data files) coexisting in each participating node. One set belongs to the original partition, and the other set of data files belongs to the future partition (i.e. after sharding). Reads and writes of a key-value pair are treated differently to maintain data consistency.

Writes (i.e. update or delete) are saved in the data files of the future partition. If the sharding is completed successfully, the files of the original partition can be abandoned safely. Otherwise, if the operation fails, the key-value pairs written to the future partition are merged back to the original partition. In the extreme case where the sharding fails very often, writes are enforced in "dual play", i.e. saved in both the original and future partitions. Thereby, the data files of the future partition can be safely discarded whenever a sharding fails.

Reads are dealt with depending on how writes are processed. If writes are enforced in "dual play", the data value can be retrieved directly from the replicas of the original partition. Otherwise, if writes are saved to the replicas of the future partition only, the node retrieves the data value from both the original and future partitions. We have leveraged timestamp-based reconciliation in Dynamo [10] to allow multiple versions of an object to be present in the system. The timestamps of multiple collided values are compared, and the latest value "wins". Thereby, we maintain eventual consistency across different sets of replicas.

At the end of sharding, after the operation is announced successful, the file handlers of the partition replica is replaced in an atomic operation within each participating node, independently and asynchronously from other nodes. Thus, data files of the original partitions are deleted safely from all the nodes.

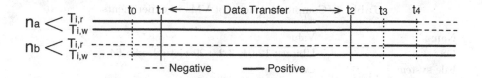

Fig. 4. Switching token values during replica migration for data consistency

4.2 Data Consistency When Moving Replicas

We have implemented a token ownership policy to ensure data consistency for partition replicas that are being moved or duplicated. As discussed, a list of tokens $\{T_i\}$ split the key space into consecutive key ranges. Each partition P_i is associated with one token T_i. For query-execution purpose, every node maintains two boolean values for each P_i: one readable token $T_{i,r}$, and one writable token $T_{i,w}$. The nodes that own the *positive* value of $T_{i,r}$ or $T_{i,w}$ are entitled to serve reads or writes from P_i, respectively.

Figure 4 depicts when and how to switch the values of $T_{i,r}$ and $T_{i,w}$, when a replica of the partition P_i is moved from n_a to n_b. The time intervals between (t_0, t_1), (t_2, t_3) and (t_3, t_4) are longer than the end-to-end gossip broadcast delay, so that every updated value is well propagated. Before and during data migration, the source node n_a, which is serving P_i, owns the *positive* $T_{i,r}$ and $T_{i,w}$. The destination n_b, which does not serve P_i initially, owns the *negative* tokens. Before the data is transferred, n_b switches its $T_{i,w}$ to *positive* at t_0, so that n_b is entitled to receive the latest updates destined for P_i. After the data is transferred, n_b switches its $T_{i,r}$ to *positive* at t_3, since n_b is now eligible to serve reads from P_i. After n_b has taken over P_i, n_a resets both its tokens to *negative* at t_4. In the end, the replica of P_i in n_a is discarded.

The operation of duplicating replicas (e.g. from n_a to n_b) is very similar to moving replicas. The only difference is that, in duplication, the source node n_a owns the positive $T_{i,r}$ and $T_{i,w}$ at all times. Thus, n_a neither resets tokens to *negative* at t_4, nor deletes replicas at the end of data transfer.

5 Evaluation

We have evaluated ElasCass against Apache Cassandra (version 1.0.5) that uses **split-move** as discussed in Section 2. Thus, this section evaluates the efficiency of the proposed approach against the split-move approach for node bootstrapping. Hence, the experimental results of Cassandra are labeled as **split-move**.

5.1 Experimental Setup

The experiments were conducted on Amazon EC2. Each VM runs as one node of the KVS. All of the VM instances are based off a common Linux image. The

Table 1. Compute capacity of VMs in experiments

Name	Value
OS	Ubuntu 12.04, 3.2.0-29-virtual, x86_64
File system	ext3
Instance Type	m1.large
Memory	7.5 GB
CPU	2 virtual cores with 2 EC2 Compute Units each
Storage	2 ephemeral storage with 420GB each
Disk I/O	High

Table 2. Parameters configured in YCSB

Name	Value
records	size = 1KB, count = 100 million
insert order	hashed with 64-bit FNV
read/update ratio	50/50 for write-intensive, 95/5 for read-intensive
request distribution	zipfian (constant = 0.99)
	hotspot (80% of requests targeting at 20% of data)
ConsistencyLevel	write: *ALL*; read: *ONE*

compute capacity is shown in Table 1. For performance reasons, the persistent data of the KVS was stored on the 400 GB ephemeral storage of the VM, rather than on an Elastic Block Storage (EBS) volume. This is consistent with known production deployments of Cassandra on EC2 [4]. The I/O performance of this ephemeral storage is categorised as "High". According to Amazon[3], *High* I/O instances can deliver in excess of 100,000 random read IOPS and as many as 80,000 random write IOPS.

The YCSB benchmark (version 0.1.4) [6] was used in this experiment with parameters configured as shown in Table 2. The dataset is generated by the YCSB client in the *loading* section. The total size is approximately 100GB. The inserted keys are hashed with the 64-bit FNV function[4], so the hotspot data is scattered onto many partitions. Both write-intensive and read-intensive workloads were generated using YCSB. Each workload was generated with two different request distributions, i.e. zipfian and hotspot. The consistency level[5] is set as *ALL* for write operations, and *ONE* for read operations. This parameter specifies how many replicas must respond before a result is returned to the client. It tunes response time versus data accuracy, but does not affect the eventual consistency in key-value stores.

To evaluate load balancing, an *imbalance* index I_L is defined to indicate the imbalance in load $\{L_i\}_{i=1}^{n}$ across a group of n nodes. Let $I_L = \sigma_L / \overline{L}$, where $\overline{L}$

---

[3] http://aws.amazon.com/ec2/instance-types/

[4] FowlerNollVo is a non-cryptographic hash function created by Glenn Fowler, Landon Curt Noll, and Phong Vo.

[5] http://www.datastax.com/docs/1.0/dml/data_consistency

is the average value of all the loads $\{L_i\}_{i=1}^n$, and σ_L is the standard deviation of $\{L_i\}_{i=1}^n$. This index shows the proportion of the variation (or dispersion) from the average. A smaller value of I_L indicates better load balancing. We have evaluated the balancing of both the data volume and the query workload.

In addition, the average CPU utilisation is used to quantify the workload per node. We monitored the CPU usage periodically using the linux command "sar $-u$ 5 2", which reports the average CPU usage every 10 seconds.

5.2 Node Bootstrapping

In this experiment, we demonstrate the effects of bootstrapping nodes one after another, in a relatively short time, in each KVS. Apart from the bootstrap time, we measure the volume of data acquired by a node at bootstrap (*bootstrap volume*). Ideally, the ith node should share $1/i$ of the total volume of data in the system (*Balance Volume*). However, this is affected by the partitioning and placement strategies employed. Therefore, we also measure the imbalance index of data distribution across the nodes.

Both ElasCass and the original Apache Cassandra were initialised with one node. The 100GB data was loaded on to the first node, with $\Theta_{max}=2$GB and $\Theta_{min}=1$GB in ElasCass. The replication level of both systems is configured as $K = 2$. Therefore, when the next node was added, the 100GB data was automatically replicated to the second node fully. From two nodes onwards, one empty node was added at each time. The data was reallocated according to different strategies in these two systems.

During the whole process of node bootstrapping, both systems were subjected to a read-intensive background workload that followed the hotspot distribution (Table 2). Each time before a new node was initiated, we made sure that every existing node had been serving queries for at least 15 minutes as a normal member of the KVS. Then, we tuned the number of threads in the YCSB client, such that the CPU usage of the most loaded node was less than 80%, while the average CPU usage of all the existing nodes fluctuated around 50%. Therefore, both systems were *moderately* loaded before a new node was added.

Figure 5(d) shows the bootstrap times for ElasCass and original Cassandra with increasing number of nodes. The bootstrap time for ElasCass is bounded while Cassandra, following the split-move approach, starts with a high bootstrap time (over 100 minutes) that reduces with the number of nodes. This can be explained by the bootstrap volume as shown in Figure 5(a). At all scales from three nodes onwards, ElasCass managed to transfer less than 10GB of data constantly at bootstrap, as the remaining replicas were migrated in the post-bootstrapping phase. In contrast, with the split-move approach, the volume of data migrated decreases from over 80GB to merely 1GB. Specifically, from seven nodes onwards, the split-move approach did not migrate enough data as ElasCass did, thus requiring less time for bootstrapping. The penalty is that split-move suffered from load imbalance issue, revealed in Figure 5(e).

Figure 5(b) depicts the volume of data transferred in ElasCass during and after bootstrap. As shown, the total volume of data transferred in both phases

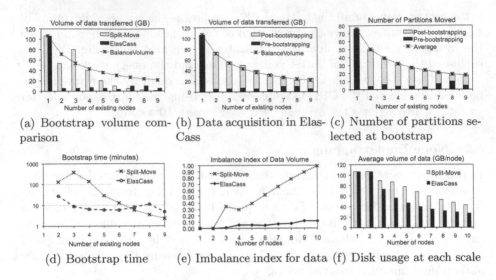

(a) Bootstrap volume comparison

(b) Data acquisition in ElasCass

(c) Number of partitions selected at bootstrap

(d) Bootstrap time

(e) Imbalance index for data

(f) Disk usage at each scale

Fig. 5. Performance of bootstrapping one node with different nodes

is roughly equal to *BalanceVolume* at each scale. Figure 5(c) demonstrates the same result in the form of numbers of partition replicas moved. The total number of replicas moved is exactly equal to the average number of replicas each node owns. This means that the data distribution in ElasCass is closer to the ideal than that produced by the split-move approach.

With the split-move approach, the data volume drops exponentially as the system scales up. The reason is that, when a key range of data is moved to the new node, the persistent data is retained in (but no longer served by) the source node, until the files are re-*compact*ed, so as to avoid the loss of data and the overhead of deleting large amounts of individual key-value pairs. However, since file *compaction* is a heavyweight operation, it is rarely triggered when serving read-intensive workloads. As a result, during the evaluation, all the new nodes chose the same node (i.e. the node with the most data on disk) as the data source. Even worse, each time the chosen node had to offer half of its remaining key range, which was reduced exponentially as new nodes were added.

Figure 5(e) backs this up by comparing the imbalance indices for both ElasCass and the split-move approach. The imbalance index of ElasCass is low, which indicates that the data is evenly distributed. In contrast, in the split-move approach, the data is less balanced when more new nodes are added. Figure 5(f) shows the average volume of data stored on disk in all the nodes. The split-move approach occupies more storage because the source node that offers data at bootstrap tends to retain the invalid data on disk.

Overall, this experiment demonstrates that, as the system scales, ElasCass is able to: i) bootstrap an empty node within a relatively short time (i.e. 10 minutes), by limiting the number of partition replicas transferred pre-bootstrapping; ii) distributes the data more evenly amongst the nodes in the post-bootstrapping phase; and iii) occupy less storage than the split-move approach.

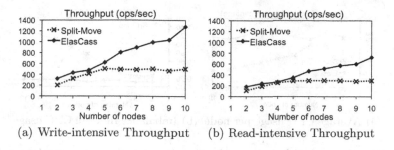

(a) Write-intensive Throughput   (b) Read-intensive Throughput

Fig. 6. The performance of query processing with zipfian distribution

5.3 Performance of Query Processing

We focussed on the improvement of workload throughput as the system scaled. In order to measure the steady-state throughput, we set an upper-bound for the average read latency as 100 milliseconds. Before each test, we tuned the number of threads in the YCSB client, such that the average read latency is one-step below this bound. Based on this latency, we tuned the operation count (i.e. number of requests), so that the test can last long enough (at least 1000 seconds). Therefore, in all the tests presented, the average read latency is slightly less than 100 ms, and each run lasts at least 1000 seconds.

Apart from workload throughput, we also measure the CPU utilisation to quantify the workload each node undertakes. We calculate the average CPU usage per node to indicate resource utilisation, and the imbalance index (defined in Subsection 5.1) of the CPU usage of all the nodes to evaluate load balancing in the system. The experimental results for the workload following the zipfian distribution are extremely similar to the results for the hotspot distribution. Due to space limits, we present the experimental results for the zipfian distribution only in this section.

Figure 6 depicts the throughputs of query processing in Cassandra (using split-move) and ElasCass against increasing number of nodes. As can be seen in Figure 6(a), when the system is subject to write-intensive workloads, the throughput of the KVS using split-move stops improving after adding the 5th node, while in ElasCass, the throughput increases linearly with the number of nodes. Figure 6(b) depicts a similar trend. ElasCass continues to demonstrate better scalability than split-move under read-intensive workloads.

Moreover, if we compare Figure 6(b) with 6(a), it can be seen that both systems have higher throughputs under write-intensive workloads than read-intensive. This is because write operations are buffered in memory and written in batch mode, while read operations require random disk I/Os, which are confined by the I/O performance.

The reason why ElasCass outperformed the KVS using split-move by such an extent is due to the imbalance in data distribution in the latter (Figure 5(e)). Due to the lack of data moved to the new nodes, the split-move approach was not able to scale properly. In practice, a *compaction* can be launched manually

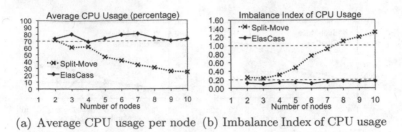

(a) Average CPU usage per node   (b) Imbalance Index of CPU usage

Fig. 7. How the workload is balanced across nodes under read-intensive workloads following the zipfian distribution

before bootstrapping a node. Compaction will update the information about the data volume on each node, so that a new node can choose source nodes more appropriately. However, this evaluation was designed to demonstrate how the system will behave without human intervention. The KVS using split-move was not able to complete a file *compaction* during the evaluation, which makes it unadaptable in the scenario where new nodes are added one after another in a relatively short time. In contrast, ElasCass is able to move a small portion of partitions from heavily loaded nodes during the pre-bootstrapping phase for quick bootstrapping, and then retrieves a large volume of data in the post-bootstrapping phase to achieve the balancing of workload and data volume.

Figure 7 shows the average CPU usage of all the nodes during the tests under the read-intensive workloads. The results for the write-intensive workloads show a similar trend, so they are not presented due to page limit. As seen, the average CPU usage of ElasCass remains above 70%. However, in the KVS using split-move, the CPU usage declines gradually as the system scales up. The results indicate that ElasCass is able to fully utilise the provisioned compute resources at different scales for serving queries, while in Cassandra the newly added nodes were not efficiently incorporated into query processing.

Figure 7(b) presents the imbalance index of the CPU usage. With the split-move approach, the imbalance index climbs up as the system scales. From the scale of eight nodes onwards, the index even goes beyond 1.0, which means that the standard deviation of the CPU usages is even greater than the average usage. The results indicate that some nodes are heavily loaded, while the others remain idle. The workload was not balanced with split-move. However, this index in ElasCass remains below 0.2 in all the tests. A small value of imbalance index indicates that the workload is well balanced in ElasCass.

Overall, this set of experiments demonstrates that, due to better balancing of data volume in ElasCass, it outperforms the KVS using split-move in query processing by a large extent in terms of scalability and load balancing.

5.4   Data Partitioning

In this experiment, we demonstrate how the maximum size Θ_{max} and the minimum size Θ_{min} (defined in Equation 1 and 2) can affect the partitioning results

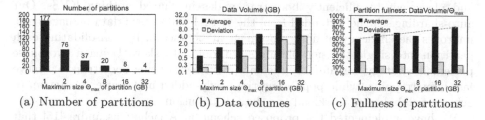

(a) Number of partitions   (b) Data volumes   (c) Fullness of partitions

Fig. 8. Partitioning 100GB of data under different sharding threshold

with our sharding strategy. We used the same setting for the YCSB client to generate the 100GB dataset (Table 2), but the dataset was loaded independently in each test with different values of Θ_{max} and Θ_{min}. There are six tests, in which the maximum size Θ_{max} increases from 1GB to 32GB exponentially. The minimum size is set as one half of the upper, i.e. $\Theta_{min} = \Theta_{max}/2$.

Given different values of Θ_{max}, Figure 8(a) shows the total number of partitions generated, while Figure 8(b) shows the volume of data stored in the partitions. As can be seen, as the value of Θ_{max} increases, the resulted number of partitions decreases inversely, whilst the average volume of data in each partition grows linearly with Θ_{max}.

Different settings of Θ_{max} can affect the system's performance. If Θ_{max} is too small, partitions are sharded very frequently, which increases the overhead of building replicas. In addition, small Θ_{max} results in a large number of partitions, which increases the complexity of partition reallocation. On the other hand, if Θ_{max} is too large, the resulted partitions will contain a large volume of data. Moving a large-size partition replica may end up in overwhelming the node that takes it over. Moreover, it takes substantially long time to reallocate a large-size replica, which is not efficient. Therefore, in the remaining evaluations, we set Θ_{max}=2GB and Θ_{min}=1GB.

In Figure 8(c), we use the term "fullness" to compare the data volume shown in Figure 8(b). The value of fullness is calculated as the data volume of the partition divided by Θ_{max}. In other words, the fullness indicates how full the partition is before it reaches the maximum capacity. Figure 8(c) shows that the average fullness of the partition ranges between 60% and 80%, and the standard deviation of fullness is consistently below 20% given different Θ_{max}. The results indicate that the dataset is effectively segmented into a list of partitions that are of roughly equal sizes, without sparse partitions (i.e. having little data) generated. In addition, there is a trend that larger values of Θ_{max} tend to result in greater fullness. This is because smaller upper bounds increase the frequency of partition splitting. Note that when a partition is split, the data volume of the resulting partitions is only half of Θ_{max}, i.e. the fullness is 50%.

6   Conclusion

Efficient node bootstrapping is an important feature for distributed KVSs running on IaaS. We have presented a decentralised scheme of data partitioning and placement to efficiently bootstrap nodes in shared nothing KVSs. Our auto-sharding scheme, extended from the virtual-node based data management, improves the efficiency of data movement at bootstrap, by consolidating each partition into single transferable units without data skew. Using a two-phase placement strategy, we minimise the data movement during bootstrap to achieve fast bootstrapping, while populating the newly-added nodes after bootstrap to achieve well balanced workload and data distribution.

We have implemented the proposed scheme in Apache Cassandra [15] that follows the split-move strategy, to present ElasCass. We evaluated our scheme against the split-move approach, by experimentally evaluating ElasCass against Cassandra using YCSB on public IaaS. We demonstrated that ElasCass was capable of incorporating new empty nodes consecutively in a relatively short time, with ideally balanced data distribution and much better balanced workload than Cassandra. As a result, ElasCass exhibited better resource utilisation in compute and storage, and outperformed Cassandra in scalability by a large extent under the biased workloads. We also demonstrated the capability of our auto-sharding scheme to confine each partition into a bounded size, without data skew or sparse partitions.

In the future, we plan to augment this scheme with the control logic that determines when and how many nodes should be bootstrapped or decommissioned. This control logic along with the ability to add and remove nodes efficiently, form the basis for autonomous elasticity in shared nothing KVSs on IaaS platforms.

Acknowledgments. The authors would like to thank Smart Services CRC Pty Ltd for the grant of Services Aggregation project that made this work possible.

References

1. Aberer, K.: Peer-to-peer data management. Synthesis Lectures on Data Management 3(2), 1–150 (2011)
2. Burrows, M.: The chubby lock service for loosely-coupled distributed systems. In: Proceedings of the 7th Symposium on Operating Systems Design and Implementation, pp. 335–350. USENIX Association (2006)
3. Chang, F., Dean, J., Ghemawat, S., Hsieh, W., Wallach, D., Burrows, M., Chandra, T., Fikes, A., Gruber, R.: Bigtable: A distributed storage system for structured data. ACM Transactions on Computer Systems (TOCS) 26(2), 1–26 (2008)
4. Cockroft, A.: Netflix goes global. In: Proc. 14th International Workshop on High Performance Transaction Systems (HPTS). USENIX (2011)
5. Cooper, B., Ramakrishnan, R., Srivastava, U., Silberstein, A., Bohannon, P., Jacobsen, H., Puz, N., Weaver, D., Yerneni, R.: Pnuts: Yahoo!'s hosted data serving platform. Proceedings of the VLDB Endowment 1(2), 1277–1288 (2008)
6. Cooper, B., Silberstein, A., Tam, E., Ramakrishnan, R., Sears, R.: Benchmarking cloud serving systems with ycsb. In: Proceedings of the 1st ACM Symposium on Cloud Computing, pp. 143–154. ACM (2010)
7. Corbett, J.C., Dean, J., Epstein, M., Fikes, A., Frost, C., Furman, J., Ghemawat, S., Gubarev, A., Heiser, C., Hochschild, P., et al.: Spanner: Googles globally-distributed database. In: Proceedings of OSDI, vol. 1 (2012)

8. Curino, C., Jones, E., Zhang, Y., Madden, S.: Schism: a workload-driven approach to database replication and partitioning. Proceedings of the VLDB Endowment 3(1-2), 48–57 (2010)

9. Das, S., Nishimura, S., Agrawal, D., El Abbadi, A.: Albatross: lightweight elasticity in shared storage databases for the cloud using live data migration. Proceedings of the VLDB Endowment 4(8), 494–505 (2011)

10. DeCandia, G., Hastorun, D., Jampani, M., Kakulapati, G., Lakshman, A., Pilchin, A., Sivasubramanian, S., Vosshall, P., Vogels, W.: Dynamo: amazon's highly available key-value store. In: SOSP, vol. 7, pp. 205–220 (2007)

11. Ghemawat, S., Gobioff, H., Leung, S.: The Google file system. In: ACM SIGOPS Operating Systems Review, vol. 37, pp. 29–43. ACM (2003)

12. Gupta, A., Liskov, B., Rodrigues, R.: One hop lookups for peer-to-peer overlays. In: HotOS, pp. 7–12 (2003)

13. Karger, D., Lehman, E., Leighton, T., Panigrahy, R., Levine, M., Lewin, D.: Consistent hashing and random trees: Distributed caching protocols for relieving hot spots on the world wide web. In: Proceedings of the Twenty-Ninth Annual ACM Symposium on Theory of Computing, pp. 654–663. ACM (1997)

14. Krishnan, P., Raz, D., Shavitt, Y.: The cache location problem. IEEE/ACM Transactions on Networking (TON) 8(5), 568–582 (2000)

15. Lakshman, A., Malik, P.: Cassandra: a decentralized structured storage system. ACM SIGOPS Operating Systems Review 44(2), 35–40 (2010)

16. Laoutaris, N., Telelis, O., Zissimopoulos, V., Stavrakakis, I.: Distributed selfish replication. IEEE Transactions on Parallel and Distributed Systems 17(12), 1401–1413 (2006)

17. Rowstron, A., Druschel, P.: Pastry: Scalable, decentralized object location, and routing for large-scale peer-to-peer systems. In: Guerraoui, R. (ed.) Middleware 2001. LNCS, vol. 2218, pp. 329–350. Springer, Heidelberg (2001)

18. Shvachko, K., Kuang, H., Radia, S., Chansler, R.: The hadoop distributed file system. In: 2010 IEEE 26th Symposium on Mass Storage Systems and Technologies (MSST), pp. 1–10. IEEE (2010)

19. Stoica, I., Morris, R., Karger, D., Kaashoek, M., Balakrishnan, H.: Chord: A scalable peer-to-peer lookup service for internet applications. ACM SIGCOMM Computer Communication Review 31(4), 149–160 (2001)

20. Van Renesse, R., Minsky, Y., Hayden, M.: A gossip-style failure detection service. In: Middleware 1998, pp. 55–70. Springer (1998)

21. You, G.-W., Hwang, S.-W., Jain, N.: Scalable Load Balancing in Cluster Storage Systems. In: Kon, F., Kermarrec, A.-M. (eds.) Middleware 2011. LNCS, vol. 7049, pp. 101–122. Springer, Heidelberg (2011)

22. Zaman, S., Grosu, D.: A distributed algorithm for the replica placement problem. IEEE Transactions on Parallel and Distributed Systems 22(9), 1455–1468 (2011)

Testing Idempotence for Infrastructure as Code

Waldemar Hummer[1], Florian Rosenberg[2], Fábio Oliveira[2], and Tamar Eilam[2]

[1] Distributed Systems Group, Vienna University of Technology, Austria
hummer@dsg.tuwien.ac.at
[2] IBM T.J. Watson Research Center, Yorktown Heights, NY, USA
{rosenberg,fabolive,eilamt}@us.ibm.com

Abstract. Due to the competitiveness of the computing industry, software developers are pressured to quickly deliver new code releases. At the same time, operators are expected to update and keep production systems stable at all times. To overcome the development–operations barrier, organizations have started to adopt *Infrastructure as Code* (IaC) tools to efficiently deploy middleware and applications using automation scripts. These automations comprise a series of steps that should be *idempotent* to guarantee repeatability and convergence. Rigorous testing is required to ensure that the system idempotently converges to a desired state, starting from arbitrary states. We propose and evaluate a model-based testing framework for IaC. An abstracted system model is utilized to derive state transition graphs, based on which we systematically generate test cases for the automation. The test cases are executed in light-weight virtual machine environments. Our prototype targets one popular IaC tool (Chef), but the approach is general. We apply our framework to a large base of public IaC scripts written by operators, showing that it correctly detects non-idempotent automations.

Keywords: Middleware Deployment, Software Automation, Idempotence, Convergence, Infrastructure as Code, Software Testing.

1 Introduction

The ever-increasing need for rapidly delivering code changes to satisfy new requirements has led many organizations to rethink their development practices. A common impediment to this demand for quick code delivery cycles is the well-known tension between software developers and operators: the former are constantly pressured to deliver new releases, whereas the latter must keep production systems stable at all times. Not surprisingly, operators are reluctant to accept changes and tend to consume new code slower than developers would like.

In order to repeatedly deploy middleware and applications to the production environment, operations teams typically rely on automation logic (e.g., scripts). As new application releases become available, this logic may need to be revisited to accommodate new requirements imposed on the production infrastructure. As automation logic is traditionally not developed following the same rigor of software engineering used by application developers (e.g., modularity, re-usability),

D. Eyers and K. Schwan (Eds.): Middleware 2013, LNCS 8275, pp. 368–388, 2013.
© IFIP International Federation for Information Processing 2013

automations tend to never achieve the same level of maturity and quality, incurring an increased risk of compromising the stability of the deployments.

This state-of-affairs has been fueling the adoption of *DevOps* [1,2,3] practices to bridge the gap between developers and operators. One of the pillars of DevOps is the notion of *Infrastructure as Code (IaC)* [1,4], which facilitates the development of automation logic for deploying, configuring, and upgrading inter-related middleware components following key principles in software engineering. IaC automations are expected to be repeatable by design, so they can bring the system to a *desired state* starting from any arbitrary state. To realize this model, state-of-the-art IaC tools, such as Chef [5] and Puppet [6], provide developers with several abstractions to express automation steps as *idempotent* units of work.

The notion of *idempotence* has been identified as the foundation for repeatable, robust automations [7,8]. Idempotent tasks can be executed multiple times always yielding the same result. Importantly, idempotence is a requirement for *convergence* [7], the ability to reach a certain desired state under different circumstances in potentially multiple iterations. The algebraic foundations of these concepts are well-studied; however, despite (1) their importance as key elements of DevOps automations and (2) the critical role of automations to enable frequent deployment of complex infrastructures, testing of idempotence in real systems has received little attention. To the best of our knowledge, no work to date has studied the practical implications of idempotence or sought to support developers ascertain that their automations idempotently make the system converge.

We tackle this problem and propose a framework for systematic testing of IaC automation scripts. Given a formal model of the problem domain and input coverage goals based on well-defined criteria, a State Transition Graph (STG) of the automation under test is constructed. The resulting STG is used to derive test cases. Although our prototype implementation is based on Chef, the approach is designed for general applicability. We rely on Aspect-Oriented Programming (AOP) to seamlessly hook the test execution harness into Chef, with practically no configuration effort required. Since efficient execution of test cases is a key issue, our prototype utilizes Linux containers (LXC) as light-weight virtual machine (VM) environments that can be instantiated within seconds. Our extensive evaluation covers testing of roughly 300 publicly available, real-life Chef scripts [9]. After executing 3671 test cases, our framework correctly identified 92 of those scripts as non-idempotent in our test environment.

Next, we provide some background on Chef and highlight typical threats to idempotence in automations (§ 2), present an overview of our approach (§ 3), detail the underlying formal model (§ 4), delve into STG-based test case generation and execution (§ 5), unveil our prototype implementation (§ 6), discuss evaluation results (§ 7), summarize related work (§ 8), and wrap up the paper (§ 9).

2   Background and Motivation

In this section we explain the principles behind modern IaC tools and the importance of testing IaC automations for idempotence. Although we couch our discussion in the context of Chef [5], the same principles apply to all such tools.

Chef Background. In Chef terminology, automation logic is written as *recipes*, and a *cookbook* packages related recipes. Following a declarative paradigm, recipes describe a series of *resources* that should be in a particular state. Listing 1.1 shows a sample recipe for the following desired state: directory "/tmp/my_dir" must exist with the specified permissions; package "tomcat6" must be installed; OS service "tomcat6" must run and be configured to start at boot time.

Each resource type (e.g., package) is implemented by platform-dependent providers that properly configure the associated resource instances. Chef ensures the implementation of resource providers is idempotent. Thus, even if our sample recipe is executed multiple times, it will not fail trying to create a directory that already exists. These declarative, idempotent abstractions provide a uniform mechanism for repeatable execution. This model of repeatability is important because recipes are meant to be run periodically to override out-of-band changes, i.e., prevent drifts from the desired state. In other words, a recipe is expected to continuously make the system converge to the desired state.

```
1   directory "tmp/my_dir" do
2       owner "root"
3       group "root"
4       mode 0755
5       action :create
6   end
7   package "tomcat6" do
8       action :install
9   end
10  service "tomcat6" do
11      action [:start, :enable]
12  end
```

Listing 1.1. Declarative Chef Recipe

```
1   bash "build php" do
2       cwd Config[:file_cache_path]
3       code <<-EOF
4
5   tar -zxvf php-#{version}.tar.gz
6   cd php-#{version}
7   ./configure #{options}
8   make && make install
9
10  EOF
11      not_if "which php"
12  end
```

Listing 1.2. Imperative Chef Recipe

Supporting the most common configuration tasks, Chef currently provides more than 20 declarative resource types whose underlying implementation guarantees idempotent and repeatable execution. However, given the complexity of certain tasks that operators need to automate, the available declarative resource types may not provide enough expressiveness. Hence, Chef also supports imperative scripting resources such as *bash* (shell scripts) or *ruby_block* (Ruby code).

Listing 1.2 illustrates an excerpt from a recipe that installs and configures PHP (taken from [9]). This excerpt shows the common scenario of installing software from source code—unpack, compile, install. The imperative shell statements are in the *code* block (lines 5–8). To encourage idempotence even for arbitrary scripts, Chef gives users statements such as not_if (line 11) and only_if to indicate conditional execution. In our sample, PHP is not compiled and installed if it is already present in the system. Blindly re-executing those steps could cause the script to fail; thus, checking if the steps are needed (line 11) is paramount to avoid errors upon multiple recipe runs triggered by Chef.

Threats to Overall Idempotence. Idempotence is critical to the correctness of recipes in light of Chef's model of continuous execution and desired-state convergence. Nonetheless, we identify several challenges when it comes to ensuring that a recipe as a whole is idempotent and can make the system converge to a desired state irrespective of the system's state at the start of execution. Because of these challenges, IaC automation developers need thorough testing support.

First, for imperative script resources, the user has the burden of implementing the script in an idempotent way. The user has to decide the appropriate granularity at which idempotence must be enforced so that desired-state convergence can always be achieved with no failures or undesirable side effects. This may not be trivial for recipes with long code blocks or multiple script resources.

Second, the need to use script resources, not surprisingly, occurs often. E.g., out of all 665 publicly available cookbooks in the Opscode community [9] (as of February 2013, only counting cookbooks with at least one resource), we found that 364 (more than 50%) use at least one script resource. What is more, out of 7077 resources from all cookbooks, almost 15% were script resources.

Third, although Chef guarantees that the declarative resource types (e.g., `directory`) are idempotent, there is no guarantee that a sequence of multiple instances as a whole is idempotent, as outlined in [7], specially in the face of script resources. Recall that a recipe typically contains a series of several resource instances of different types, and the entire recipe is re-executed periodically.

Finally, if recipes depend on an external component (e.g., a download server), writing the recipe to achieve overall idempotence may become harder due to unforeseen interactions with the external component (e.g., server may be down).

3   Approach Synopsis

Our work proposes an approach and framework for testing IaC automations for idempotence. We follow a model-based testing approach [10], according to the process outlined in Figure 1. The process contains five main steps with different input and output artifacts. Our test model consists of two main parts: 1) a system model of the automation under test and its environment, including the involved tasks, parameters, system states, and state changes; 2) a state transition graph (STG) model that can be directly derived from the system model.

The input to the first step in Figure 1 consists of the IaC scripts, and additional metadata. The scripts are parsed to obtain the basic system model. IaC frameworks like Chef allow for automatic extraction of most required data, and additional metadata can be provided to complete the model (e.g., value domains

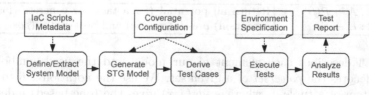

Fig. 1. Model-based testing process

for automation parameters). Given the sequence of tasks and their expected state transitions, an STG is constructed which models the possible state transitions that result from executing the automation in different configurations and starting from arbitrary states. Step three in the process derives test case specifications, taking into account user-defined coverage criteria. The test cases are materialized and executed in the real system in step four. During execution, the system is monitored for state changes by intercepting the automation tasks. Test analysis is applied to the collected data in step five, which identifies idempotence issues based on well-defined criteria, and generates a detailed test report.

4   System Model

This section introduces a model for the IaC domain and a formal definition of idempotence, as considered in this paper. The model and definitions provide the foundation for test generation and the semantics of our test execution engine.

Table 1. System Model

Symbol	Description
K, V	Set of possible **state property keys** (K) and **values** (V).
$d : K \to \mathcal{P}(V)$	**Domain** of possible values for a given state property key.
$P := K \times V$	Possible **property assignments**. $\forall \, (k, v) \in P \colon v \in d(k)$
$S \subseteq [K \to V]$	Set of possible **system states**. The state is defined by (a subset of) the state properties and their values.
$A = \{a_1, a_2, .., a_n\}$	Set of **tasks** (or activities) an automation consists of.
$p : A \to I$	Set of **input parameters** (denoted by set I) for a task.
$D \subseteq \mathcal{P}(A \times A)$	**Task dependency** relationship: task a_1 must be executed before task a_2 iff $(a_1, a_2) \in D$.
$R = \{r_1, r_2, .., r_m\}$	Set of all historical **automation runs**.
$E = \{e_1, e_2, .., e_l\}$	Set of all historical **task executions**.
$r : E \to R$	Maps task executions to automation runs.
$e : (A \cup R) \to E^{\mathbb{N}}$	**List of task executions** for a task or automation run.
$o : E \to \{success, error\}$	Whether a task execution yielded a **success output**.
$succ, pred : A \to A \cup \varnothing$	Task's **successor** or **predecessor** within an automation.
$st, ft : (E \cup R) \to \mathbb{N}$	Timestamp of the **start time** (st) and **finish time** (ft).
$t : (S \times A) \to S$	Expected **state transition** of each task. **Pre-state** maps to **post-state**.
$c : E^{\mathbb{N}} \to [S \to S]$	Actual **state changes** effected by a list of task executions. (state difference between first pre-state and last post-state)
$pre, post : A \to \mathcal{P}(S)$ $pre, post : E \to S$	Return all potential (for a task) or concrete (for a task execution) pre-states (pre) and post-states $(post)$.

Table 1 describes each element of our model and the used symbols. Note that $\mathcal{P}$ denotes the *powerset* of a given set. We use the notation $x[i]$ to refer to the ith item of a tuple x, whereas $idx(j, x)$ gives the (one-based) index of the first occurrence of item j in tuple x or $\varnothing$ if j does not exist in x. Moreover, $X^{\mathbb{N}} := \bigcup_{n \in \mathbb{N}} X^n$ denotes the set of all tuples (with any length) over the set X.

4.1 Automation and Automation Tasks

An automation (A) consists of multiple tasks with dependencies (D) between them. We assume a total ordering of tasks, i.e., $\forall a_1, a_2 \in A : (a_1 \neq a_2) \iff ((a_1, a_2) \in D) \oplus ((a_2, a_1) \in D)$. An automation is executed in one or multiple automation runs (R), which in turn consist of a multitude of task executions (E).

Table 2. Key Automation Tasks of the Sample Scenario

#	Task	Parameters
a_1	Install MySQL	-
a_2	Set MySQL password	$p2$ = root password
a_3	Install Apache & PHP	$p3$ = operating system distribution (e.g., 'debian')
a_4	Deploy Application	$p4$ = application context path (e.g., '/myapp')

For clarity, we relate the above concepts to a concrete Chef scenario. Consider a Chef recipe that installs and configures a *LAMP* stack (Linux-Apache-MySQL-PHP) to run a Web application. For simplicity, let us assume our recipe defines four resource instances corresponding to the tasks described in Table 2.

A Chef recipe corresponds to an *automation*, and each resource in the recipe is a *task*. Given our model and the recipe summarized in Table 2, we have $A = \{a_1, a_2, a_3, a_4\}$. Note that a_1 could be a package resource to install MySQL, similar to the package resource shown in the recipe of Listing 1.1, whereas a_3 could be implemented by a script resource similar to the one shown in Listing 1.2 (see Section 2). Table 2 also shows the input parameters consumed by each task.

As discussed in Section 2, an automation (Chef recipe) is supposed to make the system converge to a *desired state*. Each task leads to a certain state transition, converting the system from a pre-state to a post-state. A system state $s \in S$ consists of a number of system properties, defined as (key,value) pairs. For our scenario, let us assume we track the state of open ports and OS services installed, such that $K = \{$'open_ports', 'services'$\}$. Also, suppose that, prior to the automation run, the initial system state is given by $s_0 = \{($'open_ports', $\{22\})$, ('services', $\{$'ssh', 'acpid'$\})\}$, i.e., port 22 is open and two OS services (ssh and acpid) are running. After task a_1's execution, the system will transition to a new state $s_1 = \{($'open_ports', $\{22, 3306\})$, ('services', $\{$'ssh', 'acpid', 'mysql'$\})\}$, i.e., task a_1 installs the mysql service which will be started and open port 3306. Our prototype testing framework tracks the following pieces of state: network routes, OS services, open ports, mounted file systems, file contents and permissions, OS users and groups, cron jobs, installed packages, and consumed resources.

We distinguish the *expected state transition* (expressed via function t) and the *actual state change* (function c) that took place after executing a task. The expected state transitions are used to build a state transition graph (Section 4.2), whereas the actual state changes are monitored and used for test result analysis.

4.2 State Transition Graph

The system model established so far in this section can be directly translated into a *state transition graph* (STG) which we then use for test generation. The

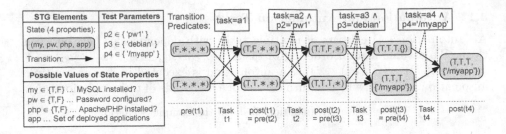

Fig. 2. Simple State Transition Graph Corresponding to Table 2

$STG = (V_G, T_G)$ is a directed graph, where V_G represents the possible system states, and T_G is the set of edges representing the expected state transitions.

Figure 2 depicts an STG which contains the pre-states and post-states of the four tasks used in our scenario. For illustration, a tuple of four properties is encoded in each state: my (MySQL installed?), pw (password configured?), php (Apache and PHP installed?), and app (set of applications deployed in the Apache Web server). For space limitations, branches (e.g., based on which operating system is used) are not included in the graph, and the wildcard symbol ($*$) is used as a placeholder for arbitrary values. The pre-states of each task should cover all possible values of the state properties that are (potentially) changed by this task. For instance, the automation should succeed regardless of whether MySQL is already installed or not. Hence, the pre-states of task $t1$ contain both values $my = F$ and $my = T$. Note that instead of the wildcard symbol we could also expand the graph and add one state for each possible value, which is not possible here for space reasons.

4.3   Idempotence of Automation Tasks

Following [7], a task $a \in A$ is *idempotent* with respect to an equivalence relation $\approx$ and a sequence operator $\circ$ if repeating a has the same effect as executing it once, $a \circ a \approx a$. Applied to our model, we define the conditions under which a task is considered idempotent based on the evidence provided by historical task executions (see Definition 3). As the basis for our definition, we introduce the notion of *non-conflicting system states* in Definition 1.

Definition 1. *A state property assignment* $(k, v_2) \in P$ *is* non-conflicting *with another assignment* $(k, v_1) \in P$, *denoted* $nonConf((k, v_1), (k, v_2))$, *if either 1)* $v_1 = v_2$ *or 2)* v_1 *indicates a state which eventually leads to state* v_2.

That is, non-conflicting state is used to express state properties in transition. For example, consider that k denotes the status of the MySQL server. Clearly, for two state values $v_1 = v_2 = $ '*started*', (k, v_2) is non-conflicting with (k, v_1). If v_1 indicates that the server is currently starting up ($v_1 = $ '*booting*'), then (k, v_2) is also non-conflicting with (k, v_1). The notion of non-conflicting state properties accounts for long-running automations which are repeatedly executed until the target state is eventually reached. In general, domain-specific knowledge is required to define concrete non-conflicting properties. By default, we consider state properties as non-conflicting if they are equal. Moreover, if we use a wildcard symbol ($*$) to denote that the value of k is unknown, then (k, v_x) is considered non-conflicting with $(k, *)$ for any $v_x \in V$.

Definition 2. *A state $s_2 \in S$ is* non-conflicting *with some other state $s_1 \in S$ if* $\forall (k_1, v_1) \in s_1, (k_2, v_2) \in s_2 : (k_1 = k_2) \implies nonConf((k_1, v_1), (k_2, v_2))$.

Put simply, non-conflicting states require that all state properties in one state be non-conflicting with corresponding state properties in the other state. Based on the notion of non-conflicting states, Definition 3 introduces idempotent tasks.

Definition 3. *An automation task $a \in A$ is considered* idempotent *with respect to its historical executions $e(a) = \langle e_1, e_2, \ldots, e_n \rangle$ iff for each two executions $e_x, e_y \in e(a)$ the following holds:*
$(ft(e_x) \leq st(e_y) \wedge o(e_x) = success) \Rightarrow$
$(o(e_y) = success \wedge (c(\langle e_y \rangle) = \emptyset \vee nonConf(post(e_y), pre(e_y))))$

In verbal terms, if a task execution $e_x \in e(a)$ succeeds at some point, then all following executions (e_y) must yield a successful result, and either (1) effect no state change, or (2) effect a state change where the post-state is non-conflicting with the pre-state. Equivalently, we define idempotence for task sequences.

Definition 4. *A task sequence $a_{seq} = \langle a_1, a_2, \ldots, a_n \rangle \in A^n$ is considered* idempotent *iff for each two sequences of subsequent task executions $e'_{seq}, e''_{seq} \in (e(a_1) \times e(a_2) \times \ldots \times e(a_n))$ the following holds:*
$ft(e'_{seq}[n]) \leq st(e''_{seq}[1]) \Rightarrow$
$((\forall i \in \{1, \ldots, n\} : o(e'_{seq}[i]) = success \Rightarrow o(e''_{seq}[i]) = success) \wedge$
$(c(e''_{seq}) = \emptyset \vee nonConf(post(e''_{seq}[i]), pre(e''_{seq}[i]))))$

Note that our notion of idempotence basically corresponds to the definition in [7], with two subtle differences: first, we not only consider the tasks' post-state, but also distinguish between successful/unsuccessful task executions; second, we do not require post-states to be strictly equal, but allow for non-conflicting states.

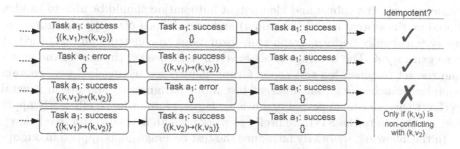

Fig. 3. Idempotence for Different Task Execution Patterns

Figure 3 illustrates idempotence of four distinct task execution sequences. Each execution is represented by a rounded rectangle which contains the result and the set of state changes. For simplicity, the figure is based on a single task a_1, but the same principle applies also to task sequences. Sequence 1 is clearly idempotent, since all executions are successful and the state change from pre-state (k, v_1) to post-state (k, v_2) only happens for the first execution. Sequence 2 is idempotent, even though it contains an unsuccessful execution in the beginning. This is an important case that accounts for repeatedly executed automations which initially fail until a certain requirement is fulfilled (e.g., Apache server waits until MySQL has been configured on another host). Sequence 3 is non-idempotent (even though no state changes take place after the first execution) because an execution with error follows a successful one. As a typical example, consider a script resource which moves a file using command "mv X Y". On second execution, the task returns an error code, because file X does not exist anymore. In sequence 4, idempotence depends on whether (k, v_3) represents a state property value that is non-conflicting with (k, v_2). For instance, assume $k = \text{'}service.mysql\text{'}$ denotes whether MySQL is started. If $v_2 = \text{'}booting\text{'}$ and $v_3 = \text{'}started\text{'}$, then a_1 is considered idempotent. Otherwise, if $v_2 = \text{'}booting\text{'}$ and $v_3 = \text{'}stopped\text{'}$, then v_3 is conflicting with v_2, and hence a_1 is not idempotent.

5   Test Design

This section details the approach for testing idempotence of IaC automations. In Section 5.1, we discuss how test cases are derived from a graph representation of the possible system states and transitions, thereby considering customizable test coverage goals. Section 5.2 covers details about the test execution in isolated virtualized environments, as well as test parallelization and distribution.

5.1   STG-Based Test Generation

We observe that the illustrative STG in Figure 2 represents a baseline vanilla case. Our aim is to transform and "perturb" this baseline execution sequence in various ways, simulating different starting states and repeated executions of task sequences, which a robust and idempotent automation should be able to handle. Based on the system model (Section 4) and user-defined coverage configuration, we systematically perform graph transformations to construct an STG for test case generation. The coverage goals have an influence on the size of the graph and the set of generated test cases. Graph models for testing IaC may contain complex branches (e.g., for different test input parameters) and are in general cyclic (to account for repeated execution). However, in order to efficiently apply test generation to the STG, we prefer to work with an acyclic graph (see below).

In the following, we briefly introduce the test coverage goals applied in our approach, discuss the procedure for applying the coverage configuration to concrete graph instances, and finally define the specification of test cases.

Test Coverage Goals. We define specific test coverage goals that are tailored to testing idempotence and convergence of IaC automations.

idemN: This coverage parameter specifies a set of task sequence lengths for which idempotence should be tested. The possible values range from $idemN = \{1\}$ (idempotence of single tasks) to $idemN = \{1, \ldots, |A|\}$ (maximum sequence length covering all automation tasks). Evidently, higher values produce more test cases, whereas lower values have the risk that problems related to dependencies between "distant" tasks are potentially not detected (see also Section 7.2).

repeatN: This parameter controls the number of times each task is (at most) repeated. If the automation is supposed to converge after a single run (most Chef recipes are designed that way, see our evaluation in Section 7), it is usually sufficient to have $repeatN = 1$, because many idempotence related problems are already detected after executing a task (sequence) twice. However, certain scenarios might require higher values for *repeatN*, in particular automations that are continuously repeated in order to eventually converge. The tester then has to use domain knowledge to set a reasonable upper bound of repetitions.

restart: The boolean parameter *restart* determines whether tasks are arbitrarily repeated in the middle of the automation ($restart = false$), or the whole automation always gets restarted from scratch ($restart = true$). Consider our scenario automation with task sequence $\langle a_1, a_2, a_3, a_4 \rangle$. If we require $idemN = 3$ with $restart = true$, then the test cases could for instance include the task sequences $\langle a_1, a_1, \ldots \rangle$, $\langle a_1, a_2, a_1, \ldots \rangle$, $\langle a_1, a_2, a_3, a_1, \ldots \rangle$. If $restart = false$, we have additional test cases, including $\langle a_1, a_2, a_3, a_2, a_3, \ldots \rangle$, $\langle a_1, a_2, a_3, a_4, a_2, a_3, \ldots \rangle$, etc.

forcePre: This parameter specifies whether different pre-states for each task are considered in the graph. If $forcePre = true$, then there needs to exist a graph node for each potential pre-state $s \in pre(a)$ of each task $a \in A$ (see, e.g., Figure 2). Note that the potential pre-state should also cover all post-states, because of repeated task execution. Contrary, $forcePre = false$ indicates that a wildcard can be used for each pre-state, which reduces the number of state nodes in Figure 2 from 9 to 5. The latter ($forcePre = false$) is a good baseline case if pre-states are unknown or hard to produce. In fact, enforcing a certain pre-state either involves executing the task (if the desired pre-state matches a corresponding post-state) or accessing the system state directly, which is in general not trivial.

graph: This parameter refers to the STG-based coverage goal that should be achieved. Offut et al. [11] define four testing goals (with increased level of coverage) to derive test cases from state-based specifications. *Transition coverage*, *full predicate coverage* (one test case for each clause on each transition predicate, cf. Figure 2), *transition-pair coverage* (for each state node, all combinations of incoming and outgoing transitions are tested), and *full sequence coverage* (each possible and relevant execution path is tested, usually constrained by applying domain knowledge to ensure a finite set of tests [11]). By default, we utilize transition coverage on a cycle-free graph. Details are discussed next.

Coverage-Specific STG Construction. In Figure 4, graph construction is illustrated by means of an STG which is gradually enriched and modified as new coverage parameters are defined. The STG is again based on our scenario (labels

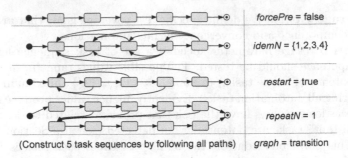

Fig. 4. Coverage-Specific STG Construction

of state properties and transition predicates are left out). First, $forcePre = false$ reduces the number of states as compared to Figure 2. Then, we require that task sequences of any length should be tested for idempotence ($idemN = \{1, 2, 3, 4\}$), which introduces new transitions and cycles into the graph. The configuration $restart = true$ removes part of the transitions, cycles still remain. After the fourth configuration step, $repeatN = 1$, we have determined the maximum number of iterations and construct an acyclic graph.

To satisfy the $graph = transition$ criterion in the last step, we perform a deep graph search to find any paths from the start node to the terminal node. The procedure is trivial, since the graph is already acyclic at this point. Each generated execution path corresponds to one test case, and the transition predicates along the path correspond to the inputs for each task (e.g., MySQL password parameter $p2$, cf. Figure 2). For brevity, our scenario does not illustrate the use of alternative task parameter inputs, but it is easy to see how input parameters can be mapped to transition predicates. As part of our future work, we consider combining our approach with combinatorial testing techniques [12] to cover different input parameters. It should be noted, though, that (user-defined) input parameters in the context of testing IaC are way less important than in traditional software testing, since the core "input" to automation scripts is typically defined by the characteristics of the environment they operate in.

Test Case Specification. The coverage-specific graph-based test model is used to generate executable tests. Table 3 summarizes the key information of a test case: 1) the input parameters consumed by the tasks (in), 2) the end-to-end sequence of tasks to be executed (seq), and 3) the automation run that resulted from executing the test case (res), which is used for result analysis. For 1), default parameters can be provided along with the system model (cf. Figure 1). Moreover, automation scripts in IaC frameworks like Chef often define reasonable default values suitable for most purposes. For 2), we traverse the cycle-free STG constructed earlier, and each path (task sequence) represents a separate test.

5.2   Test Execution

Since our tests rely on extraction of state information, it is vital that each test be executed in a clean and isolated environment. At the same time, tests should

Table 3. Simplified Model for Test Case Specification

Symbol	Description
$C; T \subseteq C$	Set of all possible **test cases** (C) for the automation under test; **test suite** (T) with the set of actual test cases to be executed.
$in : C \to [I \to V]$	**Parameter assignment** with concrete input values for a test case.
$seq : C \to A^{\mathbb{N}}$	Entire **task sequence** to be executed by a test case.
$res : C \to R$	**Automation run** that results from executing a test case.

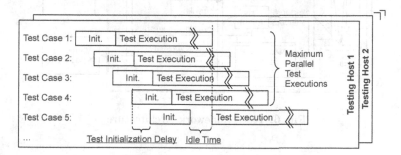

Fig. 5. Test Execution Pipeline

be parallelized for efficient usage of computing resources. Virtual machine (VM) containers provide the right level of abstraction for this purpose. A VM operates within a host operating system (OS) and encapsulates the filesystem, networking stack, process space, and other relevant system state. Details about VM containers in our implementation are given in Section 6.

The execution is managed in a testing pipeline, as illustrated in Figure 5. Prior to the actual execution, each container is provided with a short initialization time with exclusive resource access for booting the OS, initializing the automation environment and configuring all parameters. Test execution is then parallelized in two dimensions: the tests are distributed to multiple testing hosts, and a (limited) number of test containers can run in parallel on a single host.

6   Implementation

This section discusses the prototypical implementation of our distributed testing framework. Figure 6 illustrates the architecture from the perspective of a single testing host. A Web user interface guides the test execution. Each host runs a test manager which materializes tests and creates new containers for each test case.

Our framework parallelizes the execution in two dimensions: first, multiple testing hosts are started from a pre-configured VM image; second, each testing host contains several containers executing test cases in parallel. We utilize the highly efficient Linux containers[1] (LXC). Each container has a dedicated root directory within the host's file system. We use the notion of *prototype* container

---

[1] http://lxc.sourceforge.net/

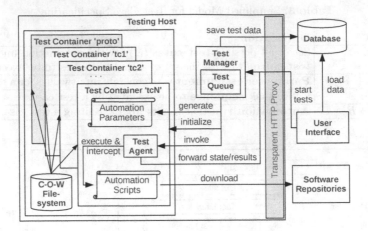

Fig. 6. Test Framework Architecture

templates (denoted 'proto' in Figure 6) to provide a clean environment for each test. Each prototype contains a base operating system (Ubuntu 12.04 and Fedora 16 in our case) and basic services such as a secure shell (SSH) daemon. Instead of duplicating the entire filesystem for each container, we use a *btrfs*[2] copy-on-write (C-O-W) filesystem, which allows to spawn new instances within a few seconds. To avoid unnecessary re-downloads of external resources (e.g., software packages), each host is equipped with a *Squid*[3] proxy server.

The test agent within each container is responsible for launching the automation scripts and reporting the results back to the test manager which stores them in a MongoDB database. Our framework uses *aquarium*[4], an AOP library for Ruby, to intercept the execution of Chef scripts and extract the relevant system state. Chef's execution model makes that task fairly easy: an aspect that we defined uses a method join point `run_action` in the class `Chef::Runner`. The aspect then records the state snapshots before and after each task. We created an extensible mechanism to define which Chef resources can lead to which state changes. For example, the `user` Chef resource may add a user. Whenever this resource is executed we record whether a user was actually added in the OS. As part of the interception, we leverage this mapping to determine the corresponding system state in the container via Chef's discovery tool *Ohai*. We extended *Ohai* with our own plugins to capture the level of detail required. In future work, we plan to additionally monitor the execution on system call level using *strace*, which will allow to capture additional state changes that we currently miss.

If an exception is raised during the test execution, the details are stored in the testing DB. Finally, after each task execution we check whether any task needs to be repeated at this time (based on the test case specification).

---

[2] https://btrfs.wiki.kernel.org/

[3] http://www.squid-cache.org/

[4] http://aquarium.rubyforge.org/

7 Evaluation

To assess the effectiveness of our approach and prototype implementation, we have performed a comprehensive evaluation, based on publicly available Chef cookbooks maintained by the Opscode community. Out of the 665 executable Opscode cookbooks (as of February 2013), we selected a representative sample of 161 cookbooks, some tested in different versions (see Section 7.4), resulting in a total of 298 tested cookbooks. Our selection criteria were based on 1) popularity in terms of number of downloads, 2) achieving a mix of recipes using imperative scripting (e.g., `bash`, `execute`) and declarative resources (e.g., `service`, `file`).

In Section 7.1 we present aggregated test results over the set of automation scripts used for evaluation, Section 7.2 discusses some interesting cases in more detail, in Section 7.3 we contrast the idempotence results for different task types, and Section 7.4 analyzes the evolution of different versions of popular cookbooks.

7.1 Aggregated Test Results

In this section we summarize the test results achieved from applying our testing approach to the selected Opscode Chef cookbooks. For space limitations, we can only highlight the core findings, but we provide a Web page[5] with accompanying material and detailed test results. Table 4 gives an overview of the overall evaluation results. The "min/max/total" values indicate the minimum/maximum value over all individual cookbooks, and the total number for all cookbooks.

Table 4. Aggregated Evaluation Test Results

Tested Cookbooks	298
Number of Test Cases	3671
Number of Tasks (min/max/total)	1 / 103 / 4112
Total Task Executions	187986
Captured State Changes	164117
Total Non-Idempotent Tasks	263
Cookbooks With Non-Idempotent Tasks	92
Overall Net Execution Time	25.7 CPU-days
Overall Gross Execution Time	44.07 CPU-days

We have tested a total of 298 cookbooks, selected by high popularity (download count) and number of imperative tasks (script resources). Cookbooks were tested in their most recent version, and for the 20 most popular cookbooks we tested (up to) 10 versions into the past, in order to assess their evolution with respect to idempotence (see Section 7.4). As part of the selection process, we manually filtered cookbooks that are not of interest or not suitable for testing: for instance, cookbook `application` defines only attributes and no tasks, or cookbook `pxe_install_server` downloads an entire 700MB Ubuntu image file.

---

[5] http://dsg.tuwien.ac.at/testIaC/

The 298 tested cookbooks contain 4112 tasks in total. In our experiments, task sequences of arbitrary length are tested ($\{1, .., |A|\}$), tasks are repeated at most once ($repeatN = 1$), and the automation is always restarted from the first task ($restart = true$). Based on this coverage, a total of 3671 test cases (i.e., individual instantiations with different configurations) were executed. 187986 task executions were registered in the database, and 164117 state changes were captured as a direct result. The test execution occupied our hardware for an overall gross time of 44.07 CPU-days. Extracting the overhead of our tool, which includes mostly capturing of system state and computation of state changes, the net time is 25.7 CPU-days. Due to parallelization (4 testing hosts, max. 5 containers each) the tests actually finished in much shorter time (roughly 5 days).

The tests have led to the identification of 263 non-idempotent tasks. Recall from Section 4 that a task is non-idempotent if any repeated executions lead to state changes or yield a different success status than the previous executions.

7.2   Selected Result Details

To provide a more detailed picture, we discuss interesting cases of non-idempotent recipes. We explain for each case how our approach detected the idempotence issue. We also discuss how we tracked down the actual problem, to verify the results and understand the underlying implementation bug. It should be noted, however, that our focus is on problem detection, not debugging or root cause analysis. However, using the comprehensive data gathered during testing, our framework has also significantly helped us find the root of these problems.

Chef Cookbook `timezone`. A short illustrative cookbook is `timezone` v0.0.1 which configures the time zone in `/etc/timezone`. Table 5 lists the three tasks: a_1 installs package `tzdata` and initializes the file with "Etc/UTC", a_2 writes "UTC" to the file, and a_3 reconfigures the package `tzdata`, resetting the file content. For our tests, "UTC" and "Etc/UTC" are treated as conflicting property values. Hence, tasks a_2 and a_3 are clearly non-idempotent, e.g., considering the execution sequence $\langle a_1, a_2, a_3, a_1, a_2, a_3 \rangle$: on second execution, a_1 has no effect (package is already installed), but a_2, a_3 are re-executed, effectively overwriting each other's state changes. Note that $\langle a_1, a_2 \rangle$ and $\langle a_1, a_2, a_3 \rangle$ are idempotent as a sequence; however, a perfectly idempotent automation would ensure that tasks do not alternatingly overwrite changes. Moreover, the overhead of re-executing tasks a_2, a_3 could be avoided, which is crucial for frequently repeated automations.

Table 5. Tasks in Chef Cookbook `timezone`

Task	Resource Type	Description
a_1	package	Installs package `tzdata`, writes "Etc/UTC" to `/etc/timezone`
a_2	template	Writes timezone value "UTC" to `/etc/timezone`
a_3	bash	Runs `dpkg-reconfigure tzdata`, again writes "Etc/UTC" to `/etc/timezone`

Chef Cookbook `tomcat6`. In the popular cookbook `tomcat6` v0.5.4 ($>$ 2000 downloads), we identified a non-trivial idempotence bug related to incorrect file permissions. The version number indicates that the cookbook has undergone a number of revisions and fixes, but this issue was apparently not detected.

Table 6. Tasks in Chef Cookbook `tomcat6`

Task	Resource Type	Description
...	...	...
a_9	directory	Creates directory `/etc/tomcat6/`
...	...	...
a_{16}	bash	Copies files to `/etc/tomcat6/` as user `tomcat`; **only** executed if `/etc/tomcat6/tomcat6.conf` does not exist.
...	...	...
a_{21}	file	Writes to `/etc/tomcat6/logging.properties` as user `root`.
a_{22}	service	Enables the service `tomcat` (i.e., automatic start at boot)
a_{23}	file	Creates file `/etc/tomcat6/tomcat6.conf`
...	...	...

The crucial tasks are outlined in Table 6 (the entire automation consists of 25 tasks). Applying the test coverage settings from Section 7.1, the test suite for this cookbook consists of 23 test cases, out of which two test cases (denoted $t1, t2$) failed. Test t_1 is configured to run task sequence $\langle a_1, ..., a_{21}, a_1, ..., a_{25} \rangle$ (simulating that the automation is terminated and repeated after task a_{21}), and test t_2 is configured with task sequence $\langle a_1, ..., a_{22}, a_1, ..., a_{25} \rangle$ (restarting after task a_{22}). Both test cases failed at the second execution of task a_{16}, denoted $e(a_{16})[2]$ in our model, which copies configuration files to a directory previously created by task a_9. In the following we clarify why and how this fault happens.

The reason why t_1 and t_2 failed when executing $e(a_{16})[2]$ is that at the time of execution the file `/etc/tomcat6/logging.properties` is owned by user `root`, and a_{16} attempts to write to the same file as user `tomcat` (resulting in "permission denied" from the operating system). We observe that task a_{21} also writes to the same file, but in contrast to task a_{16} not as user `tomcat`, but as user `root`. At execution $e(a_{21})[1]$, the content of the file gets updated and the file ownership is set to `root`. Hence, the cookbook developer has introduced an implicit dependency between tasks a_{16} and a_{21}, which leads to idempotence problems. Note that the other 21 test cases did not fail. Clearly, all test cases in which the automation is restarted *before* the execution of task a_{21} are not affected by the bug, since the ownership of the file does not get overwritten. The remaining test cases in which the automation was restarted after a_{21} (i.e., after a_{23}, a_{24}, and a_{25}) did not fail due to a conditional statement `not_if` which ensures that a_{16} is only executed if `/etc/tomcat6/tomcat6.conf` does not exist.

Chef Cookbook `mongodb-10gen`. The third interesting case we discuss is cookbook `mongodb-10gen` (installs *MongoDB*), for which our framework allowed us to detect an idempotence bug in the Chef implementation itself. The relevant tasks are illustrated in Table 7: a_{11} installs package mongodb-10gen, a_{12} creates a directory, and a_{13} creates another sub-directory and places configuration files in it. If installed properly, the package mongodb-10gen creates user and group mongodb on the system. However, since the cookbook does not configure the repository properly, this package cannot be installed, i.e., task a_{11} failed in our tests. Now, as task a_{12} is executed, it attempts to create a directory with user/group mongodb, which both do not exist at that time. Let us assume the test case with task sequence $\langle a_1, \ldots, a_{13}, a_1, \ldots, a_{13} \rangle$. As it turns out, the first execution of a_{13} creates /data/mongodb with user/group set to root/mongodb (even though group mongodb does not exist). On the second execution of a_{12}, however, Chef again tries to set the directory's ownership and reports an error that user mongodb does not exist. This behavior is clearly against Chef's notion of idempotence, because the error should have been reported on the first task execution already. In fact, if the cookbook was run only once, this configuration error would not be detected, but may lead to problems at runtime. We submitted a bug report (Opscode ticket CHEF-4236) which has been confirmed by Chef developers.

Table 7. Tasks in Chef Cookbook mongodb-10gen

Task	Resource Type	Description
...	...	...
a_{11}	package	Installs package mongodb-10gen
a_{12}	directory	Creates directory /data
a_{13}	remote_directory	Creates directory /data/mongodb as user/group mongodb

Lessons Learned. The key take-away message of these illustrative real-world examples is that automations may contain complex implicit dependencies, which IaC developers are often not aware of, but which can be efficiently tested by our approach. For instance, the conditional not_if in a_{16} of recipe tomcat6 was introduced to avoid that the config file gets overwritten, but the developer was apparently not aware that this change breaks the idempotence and convergence of the automation. This example demonstrates nicely that some idempotence and convergence problems (particularly those involving dependencies among multiple tasks) cannot be avoided solely by providing declarative and idempotent resource implementations (e.g., as provided in Chef) and hence require systematic testing.

7.3 Idempotence for Different Task Types

Table 8 shows the number of identified non-idempotent tasks (denoted #NI) for different task types. The task types correspond to the Chef resources used in the evaluated cookbooks. The set of scripting tasks (execute, bash, script, ruby_block) makes up for 90 of the total 263 non-idempotent tasks, which confirms our suspicion that these tasks are error-prone. Interestingly, the service task type also shows many non-idempotent occurrences. Looking further into this issue, we observed that service tasks often contain custom code commands to start/restart/enable services, which are prone to idempotence problems.

Table 8. Non-Idempotent Tasks By Task Type

Task Type	#NI	Task Type	#NI	Task Type	#NI
service	66	directory	10	link	3
execute	44	remote_file	10	bluepill_service	2
package	30	gem_package	7	cookbook_file	2
bash	27	file	5	git	2
template	19	python_pip	5	user	2
script	15	ruby_block	4	apt_package	1

7.4 Idempotence for Different Cookbook Versions

We analyzed the evolution of the 20 most popular Chef cookbooks. The results in Table 9 leave out cookbooks with empty default recipes (application, openssl, users) and cookbooks without any non-idempotent tasks: mysql, java, postgresql, build-essential, runit, nodejs, git, ntp, python, revealcloud, graylog2. For the cookbooks under test, new releases fixed idempotence issues, or at least did not introduce new issues. Our tool automatically determines these data, hence it can be used to test automations for regressions and new bugs.

Table 9. Evolution of Non-Idempotent Tasks By Increasing Version

Cookbook	i-9	i-8	i-7	i-6	i-5	i-4	i-3	i-2	i-1	i
apache2 (i=1.4.2)	1	1	1	0	0	0	0	0	0	0
nagios (i=3.1.0)	1	1	0	0	0	0	0	0	0	0
zabbix (i=0.0.40)	2	2	2	2	2	2	2	2	2	2
php (i=1.1.4)	1	1	0	0	0	0	0	0	0	0
tomcat6 (i=0.5.4)			3	3	3	3	3	3	2	1
riak (i=1.2.1)	1	1	1	1	1	1	0	0	0	0

8 Related Work

Existing work has identified the importance of idempotence for building reliable distributed systems [13] and database systems [14]. Over the last years, the importance of building testable system administration [8] based on convergent models [15,7] became more prevalent. *cfengine* [16] was among the first tools in this space. More recently, other IaC frameworks such as Chef [5] or Puppet [6] heavily rely on these concepts. However, automated and systematic testing of IaC for verifying idempotence and convergence has received little attention, despite the increasing trend of automating multi-node system deployments (i.e., continuous delivery [17]) and placement of virtual infrastructures in the Cloud [18].

Existing IaC test frameworks allow developers to manually write test code using common Behavior-Driven Development (BDD) techniques. ChefSpec [19] or Cucumber-puppet [20] allow to encode the desired behavior for verifying individual automation tasks (unit testing). Test Kitchen [21] goes one step further by enabling testing of multi-node system deployments. It provisions isolated test environments using VMs which execute the automation under test and verify the results using the provided test framework primitives. This kind of testing is a manual and labor intensive process. Our framework takes a different approach by systematically generating test cases for IaC and executing them in a scalable virtualized environment (LXC) to detect errors and idempotence issues.

Extensive research is conducted on automated software debugging and testing techniques, including model-based testing [22] or symbolic execution [23], as well as their application to specialized problem areas, for instance control flow based [24] or data flow based [25] testing approaches. Most existing work and tools, however, are not directly applicable to the domain of IaC, for two main reasons: (i) IaC exposes fairly different characteristics than traditional software systems, i.e., idempotence and convergence; (ii) IaC needs to be tested in real environments to ensure that system state changes triggered by automation scripts can be asserted accordingly. Such tests are hard to simulate, hence symbolic execution would have little practical value. Even though dry-run capabilities exist (e.g, Chef's *why-run* capability), they cannot replace systematic testing. The applicability of automated testing is a key requirement identified by other approaches [26,27,28], whether the test target is system software or IaC.

Existing approaches for middleware testing have largely focused on performance and efficiency. Casale et al. [29] use automatic stress testing for multi-tier systems. Their work places bursty service demands on system resources, in order to identify performance bottlenecks as well as latency and throughput degradations. Other work focuses on testing middleware for elasticity [30], which is becoming a key property for Cloud applications. Bucur et al. [26] propose an automated software testing approach that parallelizes symbolic executions for efficiency. The system under test can interact with the environment via a "symbolic system call" layer that implements a set of common POSIX primitives. Their approach could potentially enhance our work and may speed up the performance, but requires a complete implementation of the system call layer.

Other approaches deal with finding and fixing configuration errors [31,32]. Faults caused by configuration errors are often introduced during deployment and remain dormant until activated by a particular action. Detecting such errors is challenging, but tools like AutoBash [32] or Chronus [31] can effectively help. A natural extension would be to also take into account the IaC scripts to find the configuration parameter that potentially caused the problem. Burg et al. [28] propose automated system tests using declarative virtual machines. Declarative specifications describe external dependencies (e.g., access to external services) together with an imperative test script. Their tool then builds and instantiates the virtual machine necessary to run the script. Our approach leverages prebuilt containers in LXC; dynamically creating a declarative specification would be possible but building a VM is more costly than bringing up an LXC container.

9   Conclusion

We propose an approach for model-based testing of *Infrastructure as Code*, aiming to verify whether IaC automations, such as Chef recipes, can repeatedly make the target system converge to a desired state in an idempotent manner. Given the IaC model of periodic re-executions, idempotence is a critical property which ensures repeatability and allows automations to start executing from arbitrary initial or intermediate states. Our extensive evaluation with real-world IaC scripts from the OpsCode community revealed that the approach effectively detects non-idempotence. Out of roughly 300 tested Chef scripts, almost a third were identified as non-idempotent. In addition, we were able to detect and report a bug in the Chef implementation itself.

Our novel approach opens up exciting future research directions. First, we will extend our prototype to handle the execution of distributed automations with cross-node dependencies, which is often used to deploy multi-node systems. Second, we plan to apply the approach to other IaC frameworks like Puppet, whose execution model does not assume total task ordering. Third, we envision that systematic debugging/analysis can be pushed further to identify implicit dependencies introduced by IaC developers. Moreover, we are currently extending the state capturing mechanism to detect fine-grained changes on system call level. The hypothesis is that the improved mechanism can lead to detection of additional non-idempotence cases stemming from side effects we currently miss.

References

1. Hüttermann, M.: DevOps for Developers. Apress (2012)
2. Loukides, M.: What is DevOps? O'Reilly Media (2012)
3. Schaefer, A., Reichenbach, M., Fey, D.: Continuous Integration and Automation for Devops. IAENG Trans. on Engineering Technologies 170, 345–358 (2013)
4. Nelson-Smith, S.: Test-Driven Infrastructure with Chef. O'Reilly (2011)
5. Opscode: http://www.opscode.com/chef/
6. Puppet Labs: http://puppetlabs.com/
7. Couch, A.L., Sun, Y.: On the algebraic structure of convergence. In: Brunner, M., Keller, A. (eds.) DSOM 2003. LNCS, vol. 2867, pp. 28–40. Springer, Heidelberg (2003)
8. Burgess, M.: Testable system administration. Commun. ACM 54(3), 44–49 (2011)
9. Opscode Community: http://community.opscode.com/
10. Utting, M., Pretschner, A., Legeard, B.: A taxonomy of model-based testing approaches. Software Testing, Verification and Reliability 22(5), 297–312 (2012)
11. Offutt, J., Liu, S., Abdurazik, A., Ammann, P.: Generating test data from state-based specifications. Software Testing, Verification and Reliability 13, 25–53 (2003)
12. Nie, C., Leung, H.: A survey of combinatorial testing. ACM Comp. Surv. (2011)
13. Helland, P.: Idempotence is not a medical condition. ACM Queue 10(4) (2012)
14. Helland, P., Campbell, D.: Building on quicksand. In: Conference on Innovative Data Systems Research, CIDR (2009)
15. Traugott, S.: Why order matters: Turing equivalence in automated systems administration. In: 16th Conference on Systems Administration (LISA), pp. 99–120 (2002)
16. Zamboni, D.: Learning CFEngine 3: Automated system administration for sites of any size. O'Reilly Media, Inc. (2012)
17. Humble, J., Farley, D.: Continuous Delivery: Reliable Software Releases through Build, Test, and Deployment Automation. Addison-Wesley Professional (2010)

18. Giurgiu, I., Castillo, C., Tantawi, A., Steinder, M.: Enabling efficient placement of virtual infrastructures in the cloud. In: Narasimhan, P., Triantafillou, P. (eds.) Middleware 2012. LNCS, vol. 7662, pp. 332–353. Springer, Heidelberg (2012)
19. ChefSpec: https://github.com/acrmp/chefspec
20. Cucumber-puppet: http://projects.puppetlabs.com/projects/cucumber-puppet
21. Test Kitchen: https://github.com/opscode/test-kitchen
22. Pretschner, A.: Model-based testing. In: Proceedings of the 27th International Conference on Software Engineering, ICSE 2005, pp. 722–723 (2005)
23. Cadar, C., Godefroid, P., et al.: Symbolic execution for software testing in practice: preliminary assessment. In: 33rd Int. Conf. on Software Engineering, ICSE (2011)
24. Benavides Navarro, L.D., Douence, R., Südholt, M.: Debugging and testing middleware with aspect-based control-flow and causal patterns. In: Issarny, V., Schantz, R. (eds.) Middleware 2008. LNCS, vol. 5346, pp. 183–202. Springer, Heidelberg (2008)
25. Hummer, W., Raz, O., Shehory, O., Leitner, P., Dustdar, S.: Testing of data-centric and event-based dynamic service compositions. In: Softw. Test., Verif. & Reliab. (2013)
26. Bucur, S., Ureche, V., Zamfir, C., Candea, G.: Parallel symbolic execution for automated real-world software testing. In: ACM EuroSys. Conf., pp. 183–198 (2011)
27. Candea, G., Bucur, S., Zamfir, C.: Automated software testing as a service. In: 1st ACM Symposium on Cloud Computing (SoCC), pp. 155–160 (2010)
28. van der Burg, S., Dolstra, E.: Automating system tests using declarative virtual machines. In: 21st Int. Symposium on Software Reliability Engineering (2010)
29. Casale, G., Kalbasi, A., Krishnamurthy, D., Rolia, J.: Automatic stress testing of multi-tier systems by dynamic bottleneck switch generation. In: Bacon, J.M., Cooper, B.F. (eds.) Middleware 2009. LNCS, vol. 5896, pp. 393–413. Springer, Heidelberg (2009)
30. Gambi, A., Hummer, W., Truong, H.L., Dustdar, S.: Testing Elastic Computing Systems. IEEE Internet Computing (2013)
31. Whitaker, A., Cox, R., Gribble, S.: Configuration debugging as search: finding the needle in the haystack. In: Symp. on Op. Sys. Design & Impl (OSDI), p. 6 (2004)
32. Su, Y.Y., Attariyan, M., Flinn, J.: AutoBash: improving configuration management with operating system causality analysis. In: SOSP (2007)

Self-scalable Benchmarking as a Service
with Automatic Saturation Detection

Alain Tchana[1], Bruno Dillenseger[2], Noel De Palma[1], Xavier Etchevers[2],
Jean-Marc Vincent[1], Nabila Salmi[2], and Ahmed Harbaoui[2]

[1] Joseph Fourier University, LIG, Grenoble, France
`first.last@imag.fr`
[2] Orange Labs, Grenoble, France
`firstname.lastname@orange.com`

Abstract. Software applications providers have always been required
to perform load testing prior to launching new applications. This crucial
test phase is expensive in human and hardware terms, and the solutions
generally used would benefit from further development. In particular, designing an appropriate load profile to stress an application is difficult and
must be done carefully to avoid skewed testing. In addition, static testing platforms are exceedingly complex to set up. New opportunities to
ease load testing solutions are becoming available thanks to cloud computing. This paper describes a Benchmark-as-a-Service platform based
on: (i) intelligent generation of traffic to the benched application without inducing thrashing (avoiding predefined load profiles), (ii) a virtualized and self-scalable load injection system. This platform was found
to reduce the cost of testing by 50% compared to more commonly used
solutions. It was experimented on the reference JEE benchmark RUBiS.
This involved detecting bottleneck tiers.

Keywords: Benchmarking as a service, Saturation detection, Cloud.

1 Introduction

Software applications providers have always been required to perform load and
performance testing. This crucial activity is expensive in both human and resource terms. Traditionally, testing leverages a platform capable of generating
enough traffic to stress a System Under Test (SUT), and thus determine its limits. This stress aims to detect the maximal throughput for a distributed system
while ensuring an acceptable response time, to determine where bottlenecks lie
or how performance is affected by adjusting configuration parameters.

To generate an appropriate level of traffic, commonly used solutions are based
on load profiles designed by testers, using empirical expertise. Profiles should
be designed to stress the system without trashing it. As IT systems become
increasingly complex and distributed, the task of designing an appropriate load
profile has become increasingly difficult.

In addition to this increasing difficulty, static testing platforms are exceedingly
complex to set up, and are prohibitively costly in terms of human and hardware

D. Eyers and K. Schwan (Eds.): Middleware 2013, LNCS 8275, pp. 389–404, 2013.

resources. A typical test campaign requires several load injection machines to generate enough traffic to the SUT (see Fig. 1), but the number of necessary load injection machines is not known in advance.

To overcome this uncertainty, the injection machines are generally statically provisioned, with the risk of encountering resource shortage or waste. In summary, the tester must empirically cope with two risks:

- provisioning too few load injection machines, which may distort the benchmarking results;
- provisioning too many load injection machines, resulting in useless expenses.

Test system scalability may benefit greatly from the opportunities presented by cloud computing, through its capacity to deliver IT resources and services automatically on-demand, as part of a self-service system. Cloud computing allows IT resources to be provisioned in a matter of minutes, rather than days or weeks. This allows load testing solutions to be developed on-demand as a service on the cloud. This type of Benchmark-as-a-Service platform (BaaSP) provides significant benefits in terms of cost and resources as hardware, software and tools are charged for on a per-use basis. The platform setup for the tests is also greatly simplified, allowing testers to focus on analyzing test campaign results. This paper describes a BaaSP, Benchmark-as-a-Service platform, that:

- returns the maximum number of virtual users a system under test (SUT) can serve, while satisfying operational constraints (e.g. avoid CPU or memory saturation) as well as quality of service constraints (e.g. acceptable response time). This set of constraints is referred to as the *saturation policy*.
- automates load injection until saturation is reached. This eliminates the need for a predefined load profile.
- automates provisioning of load injection virtual machines when necessary, avoiding resource over-booking for BaaSP itself. For detecting when a new virtual machine is required for load injection, the platform uses the same mechanism as the one used to detect SUT saturation.

We tested our platform by stressing a JEE benchmark (RUBiS [1]) to determine the bottleneck tiers. Our solution halved the cost of the test (in terms of VMs uptime) compared to a statically provisioned testing platform. The results for this particular use case show that the data base tier is the bottleneck when receiving a browsing workload. These results are consistent with previous research [13].

Section 2 of this article presents the load injection framework our work is based on for traffic generation. Section 3 describes the BaaSP's architecture, while section 4 details its design. Section 5 presents the experiments performed as part of this study; section 6 related work; and section 7 concludes our study.

2   The CLIF Load Injection Framework

This work builds on previous work [4] based on the CLIF load injection framework [2]. The CLIF open source project provides Java software to define, deploy

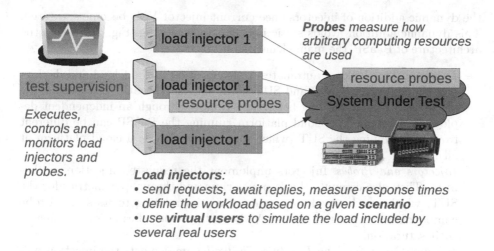

Fig. 1. Overview of the load testing infrastructure

and run performance tests on many kinds of SUT. A CLIF workload is specified through a scenario defining the traffic generated by each load injector. A scenario defines one or several virtual user (*vUser*) behaviors, and the number of active *vUsers* of each behavior over time. This is known as the *load profile*. A *behavior* is basically a sequence of requests separated by *think times* (i.e. pauses), but it can be enriched by adding conditional and loop statements, as well as probabilistic branches. Beyond this logical constructs, behaviors make use of plug-ins to support a variety of features, mainly injection protocols (HTTP, FTP, SIP...) and external data provisioning to enable variability in request parameters.

As shown by figure 1, a CLIF test consists of a number of distributed components: *load injectors*, to generate traffic, and *probes*, to monitor resources usage. Each injector contributes to the global workload by executing a scenario, and measures the response time of each generated request. Probes measure how given resources (CPU, memory, network adapter or equipment, database, middleware, etc.) are used. Injectors and probes are bound to a central test control and monitoring component, the *Supervisor*, and a central *Storage* component which gathers all measurements upon test completion. The next section describes how we adapted CLIF to design the BaaSP platform.

3   Architecture Overview

BaaSP is based on the CLIF load injection framework; it automatically and dynamically drives the number of active virtual users to test a system's capacity. Starting with a minimal load, i.e. a single virtual user, BaaSP increases the number of virtual users step-by-step until the saturation policy is violated. Step duration and increment levels are defined by an *injection policy*, which is computed from a live queuing model equivalent to the SUT. This protocol relies on the dynamic addition of injectors once current injector VMs become saturated. This dynamic addition avoids static injector dimensioning. Fig. 2 presents the architecture of BaaSP, the main elements of which are:

- *Deployer.* The deployer automates VM allocation in the Cloud and deploys and configures all BaaSP and SUT components. The SUT can also be deployed and configured long before the BaaSP, through an independent deployment system. The cloud platform running the BaaSP can be different from that running the SUT (which may not be run on a cloud platform at all).
- *Injectors and Probes.* Injectors implement the requested injection mechanism. They also compute the response time and throughput metrics for the SUT, which can be used to provide statistics relating to its state. Probe components monitor the injector VMs and provide information relating to their saturation.
- *InjectionController.* The *Injection Controller* implements the injection policy. The injection controller examines the state of the SUT, based on injector statistics, and decides how much and when to increase vUsers and to dispatch them to the injector VMs. A delicate balance must be maintained, with stress applied progressively to the application. The ideal level of stress is near the application's limit, but without causing application trashing.
- *InjectorsSaturationController.* The injector saturation controller monitors saturation of injector VMs (via their associated probes) and triggers the addition of new injector VMs in line with the saturation policies.
- *SutSaturationController.* The SUT saturation controller monitors SUT saturation using injector statistics and based on the SUT's saturation policies. When the SUT becomes saturated, the SUT saturation controller returns the number of vUsers causing saturation, the maximum throughput, the average response time and the resource consumption. The next section provides details on how our solution was designed.

4   Automated Load Injection Design

The self-regulated load injection approach we are using in this work comes from our earlier results [4] and has been extended with dynamic provisioning of injection virtual machines as described in this section.

4.1   Injection Policy

On start-up, BaaSP makes minimal assumptions about SUT performance, applying a single virtual user workload and observing requests response times and throughput. Then, as illustrated on Fig. 3, the virtual user population is increased step-by-step. Each step is characterized by:

- the number of virtual users to add (*injection step*);

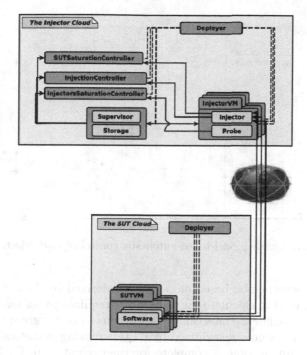

Fig. 2. The BaaSP Architecture

- the step duration, which can be subdivided into a *stabilization time* and a *sampling time*. The stabilization time begins with a fixed *ramp-up delay*, which allows these virtual users to be added progressively.

The ramp-up delay is used to avoid stressing the SUT and the load injectors. Excessive stress and trashing could be induced by a sudden increase in workload. BaaSP aims to determine the maximum number of virtual users possible in stable workload conditions. As part of this, response time measurements are discarded during the ramp-up to ignore transitional effects. Similarly, measurements are also discarded during stabilization. The initial stabilization time is given as a parameter, but subsequent stabilization times are computed for each step by estimating the convergence time for the Markov chain [5], [6] underlying the queue model representing the SUT.

The sampling time is the period for measuring response times. Because of networking and computing overload threats, it is not possible to get all response time measurements during test run-time. Instead, BaaSP relies on CLIF's ability to deliver moving statistics on load injectors and probes. Over a polling period, the injection controller obtains the continuous statistics from the injectors: mean and standard deviation for response times, and the total number of requests issued. Using these numbers, the injection controller periodically assesses the significance of the statistical sample by combining the following two criteria: (1) the minimal number of requests issued (given as a parameter), and (2) the

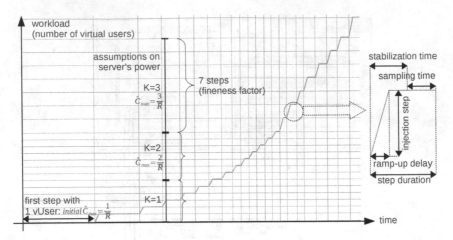

Fig. 3. Queue model-based automatic control of load injection

stability of measurements, based on a formula derived by Jain et al. [7]. This formula can be used to calculate the sample size required to achieve a given level of accuracy and confidence interval. We apply this formula, given the mean and standard deviation values determined by CLIF's moving statistics.

When the sampling time is complete for the current step, BaaSP estimates the queue model parameters, as explained in the next section.

4.2   Estimation of Maximal Load

The Kendall notation [5] of an elementary queuing system, denoted by $T/X/K$, was used in our estimation of the maximal load permissible for a SUT. In this notation, T indicates the distribution of the inter-arrival times, X the service times distribution, and K the number of servers ($K \geq 1$). The number of servers is representative of the parallel processing capability, which is bound to, but not predefined by, the number of physical processing cores. To simplify calculations, K is generally considered to be an integer number, although in reality it is more likely to be a decimal number.

The maximal supported load, $\hat{C}_{max}$, is first estimated from an initial load injection phase assuming a minimal value of 1 for K. During this phase, the SUT is loaded with markovian interarrival requests from a single virtual user, and statistics on response times R are polled from the load injectors. When a single client arrives in an empty queue, there is no concurrence and the waiting time is zero. In such conditions, the service rate μ, i.e. the server's maximum throughput in terms of requests processed per second, equals $\frac{1}{\overline{R}}$, where $\overline{R}$ is the mean response time. Assuming $K = 1$, the first estimation of $\hat{C}_{max}$ equals μ.

With an M/G/K model, the rate of request arrivals converges to $K * \mu$. If the SUT becomes saturated, then the previous assumption on K is confirmed. BaaSP stops load injection and returns the number of active virtual users of the latest step completed without saturation. But, when $\hat{C}_{max}$ is reached without saturating the server, the assumed value of K is incremented, and the assumption on $\hat{C}_{max}$ is upgraded to $K * \mu$, with $K = 2, 3, 4 \ldots$ for subsequent iterations.

When BaaSP upgrades the assumed value of K, the workload increase towards the new target $\hat{C}_{max}$ is split into a number of steps, determined by a BaaSP parameter in the benchmark policy: the *fineness factor* f. The *injection step* is the number of new virtual users to add to go for the next step. The injection step equals $\frac{\hat{C}_{max}}{f*\lambda}$, where λ is the mean request throughput issued by each virtual user. Greater values for f will give more accurate results but will result in longer experience time.

4.3   Dynamic Injector Provisioning

As shown for the BaaSP architecture (Fig. 2), all injector VMs are equipped with monitoring probes. The InjectorsSaturationController is configured with one or more saturation policies based on information gathered by the monitoring probes. As presented above, a saturation policy takes the form of a threshold policy. For example, the CPU load of the injector VM should be below 100%. Thus, the InjectorsSaturationController periodically compares the information it receives with saturation policies. When a policy is violated, a new injector VM will be added. The injection provisioning protocol is summarized in Fig. 4 and can be interpreted as follows:

(a) The InjectorsSaturationController asks the Deployer to create a new injector VM. The InjectorsSaturationController then disables its saturation detection process (to avoid further new additions before the current one has been treated).
(b) The Deployer asks the IaaS (cloud) to start a new VM.
(c) The VM is equipped with a deployment agent which informs the Deployer that it is started.
(d) The Deployer sends its configuration to the new injector.
(e) The injector registers its configuration by contacting the Supervisor.
(f) The Supervisor integrates the new injector configuration in its injector list and forwards this configuration to its inner component. The Supervisor then requests that the injectors added start their load injection (by setting the SUT URI). The Supervisor also informs the InjectionController of the presence of a new injector. The InjectionController registers the new injector and dispatches the number of vUsers equally between injectors.
(g) Finally, the InjectionController tells the InjectorsSaturationController to re-enable its saturation detection process.

This protocol was successfully applied in several use cases, which are presented in the next section.

4.4   BaaSP Cost Benefit

As we mentioned in Section 1, one of the main contribution of our platform is the reduction of the cost of the test over the cloud (in terms of VMs uptime)

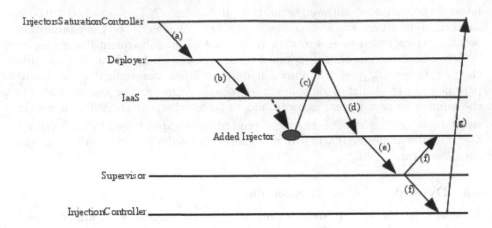

Fig. 4. Injector VM addition process

compared to a statically provisioned testing. The cost of running BaaSP in a commercial cloud (such as Amazon EC2) includes several parameters: the number of VM, their uptime, their type, outgoing network traffics, the number of IO operations, etc. Therefor, modeling the cost of the test should consider different circumstances, including the location of the injection system towards the SUT. We limit our evaluation to one circumstance: the SUT and BaaSP are on the same cloud. For comparison, we also consider that the static load injection tool runs in the same cloud as the BaaSP and they use the same type of VM. With statically provisioned injectors, the number of injector VMs is constant throughout the test. For our comparison, we assume that this number is the total number of VM instantiated by the BaaSP (i.e. the tester choose exactly the right maximum number of VM, which is extremely unusual). The cost of the test in this case (noted Cost0) can be calculated by the following formula:

$Cost_0 = nbInjVM * TestUpTime * Cost_{tu}$ (Equation 1),
where $nbInjVM$ is the total number of injector VMs, $TestUpTime$ is the duration of the test, and $Cost_{tu}$ is the cost of running a VM in the cloud for a given unit of time.

With scalable injector provisioning, the execution time of the i-th injector VM is about $\frac{TestUpTime*(nbInjVM-i+1)}{nbInjVM}$. Thus, the cost of a test in this case is $Cost_{BaaSP} = [\sum_{i=1}^{nbInj} \frac{TestUpTime*(nbInjVM-i+1)}{nbInjVM}] * Cost_{tu}$, which corresponds to $Cost_{BaaSP} = [\frac{TestUpTime*(nbInjVM+1)}{2}] * Cost_{tu}$ (Equation 2).

Regarding (Equation 1) and (Equation 2), **the cost of the test is halved when using our platform**. Notice that the evaluation of $Cost_0$ is the most optimistic one since we don not consider the possible repetitions of the test to determine the appropriate workload. Also we assume that the tester in that case does not overestimate the number of VMs required for the test.

5 BaaSP Use Cases: Benchmarking a JEE Application

We tested how well our solution could determine the bottleneck tiers of a JEE application, and tune it to improve performance.

5.1 Experimental Context

System Under Test. We tested RUBiS [1], a JEE benchmark which implements an auction web site modeled on eBay. It defines interactions such as registering new users, browsing, buying and selling items. This application is deployed on a load-balanced architecture composed of virtual machines providing the following middleware: Apache Tomcat (7.0) as servlet container, and a MySQL server (5.1.36) to host auction items (about 48 000 items). We used a HAProxy load balancer in front of Tomcat servers when several Tomcat servers were tested. The MySQL-Proxy load balancer was also used. To remain within the allowable page length for this article, this paper oly presents experimental results for browsing requests. Fig. 5 summarizes the architecture of these applications.

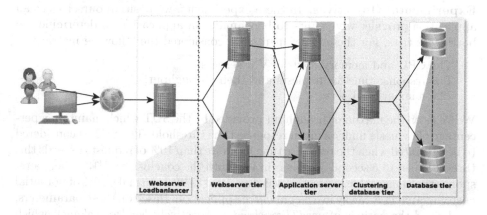

Fig. 5. Architecture of a JEE application

Cloud Environment. Our experiments were carried out using the Grid'5000 [10] platform, which is composed of clusters in different areas of France. We used two Grid'5000's clusters (Chinqchint and Chicon) to deploy the SUT and the injection platform separately. The two clusters run OpenStack [11] and Xen hypervisors (version 3.2) to set up a virtualized cloud providing VMs with configurations similar to the Amazon EC2 [12] Small one. All VMs run the same operating system as the nodes which host them: Linux Ubuntu 10.0.4 distribution with a 2.6.30 kernel, over a gigabit connection. Fig. 6 summarizes the cloud environment configuration.

	Cluster Chinqchint, Represents the SUT cloud	Cluster Chicon, Represents the injector cloud
Model	SGI Altix Xe 310	IBM e Server 326m
CPU	Intel Xeon E5440 QC 2.83 GHz / 4 MB / 1333 MHz (2cpus, 4cores/cpu)	AMD Opteron 285 2.6 GHz / 1 MB / 800 MHz (2cpus, 2cores/cpu)
Memory	8 GB	4 GB
Network	cards Myri-10G (10G-PCIE-8A-C) Gigabit Ethernet	Myri-10G (10G-PCIE-8A-C) Gigabit Ethernet
Storage	SATA 2(driver: ahci)	SATA 2(driver: sata_nvw)
OS	Linux Ubuntu 10.0.4 distribution with a 2.6.30 kernel	
IaaS	OpenStack (StackOps), version 0.4-b1262-d20120223	
	Xen version 3.2, Credit scheduler, network in bridge mode	
Deployed Servers	RUBiS severs	BaaSP with injectors
	The two sites are linked with 10Gb/s dark fibers	
VMs	3Gb of disk, 1740Mb of Memory, 1 vcpu	

Fig. 6. Configuration of our experimental cloud platform (Grid'5000)

Experimental Objectives. In these experiments, we position ourselves as an application provider who wants to benchmark an application to determine the bottleneck tiers. For these experiments, we considered the following metrics:

- The CPU and memory loads of VM servers;
- The response time for requests and their throughput;
- The number of vUsers.

We focus on the maximal throughput provided by the SUT which maintain a percentage of requests under a given response time threshold. The SUT is considered to be saturated when the response time for more than 10% of requests exceeds this threshold (set to 5 seconds). This is in line with the conclusion of [13],where a response time longer than 5 seconds was described as likely to make 10% of potential customers navigate away in a e-commerce application. Based on these parameters, we defined the notions of *goodThroughput* (respectively *badThroughput*), which represents the throughput of requests below the threshold (respectively above the threshold). The throughput metric determines the capacity of the RUBiS application while ensuring an SLO response time. In addition to throughput, we considered the number of vUsers causing SUT saturation. The response time metric in these experiments was computed with a +-30ms margin error; for throughput, the margin of error was +-10req/s. The last metric we assessed was the cost of the experiment. Our solution, based on dynamic injector provisioning, was compared to a static injectors provisioning solution.

Configuration. The servers were configured with default values, with one exception. The JVM of the Tomcat server was configured to avoid invocation of the garbage collector during experiments. The RUBiS servlets handling injected requests manage a JDBC connexion pool. The size of this pool is equal to the sum of *max_connections* configured for the MySQL servers.

The Deployer system is deployed on a VM on the Chicon cluster, while other BaaSP components (SutSaturationController, InjectorsSaturationController, InjectionController, and CLIF) are all deployed on a single Small VM. Each CLIF injector is equipped with a CPU probe and deploys automatically (when requested) on a separate Small VM. The InjectorsSaturationController is configured to detect injector saturation when CPU load reaches 100% (using the mean from 50 statistical values). The InjectionController uses a ramp up and stabilization time (about 35 seconds) when adding vUsers.

5.2 Detecting Bottleneck Tiers.

For this experiment, all RUBiS servers were deployed on Small VMs.

MySQL. The first bottleneck tier was the one limiting application performance (maximum throughput in our case). To identify this tier, we tested a RUBiS configuration comprising a Tomcat server linked to a MySQL server. The results of this experiment, performed using BaaSP, using up to 3 injector VMs and with about 250 vUsers are shown in Fig. 7. It is clear that the MySQL VM CPU reaches 100% at 380s (Fig. 7(a)), while the Tomcat VM CPU load is negligible (close to 1%). In terms of memory load, neither VM becomes saturated (Fig. 7(b)). The maximum throughput for the application (about 180 req/s) is shown to be achieved when the CPU load of MySQL VM reaches 100%. In fact, the throughput increases until 380s, and remains constant for the remainder of the experiment, whereas the number of vUsers continues to increase (Fig. 7(c)). For the response time (Fig. 7(d)), there is no badThroughput until the MySQL VM CPU reaches 100% (time 380s, curve "Good SLA"). After this time, some requests take more than 10s to execute (curve "Bad SLA"). This causes the SUTSaturationController to terminate the experiment. **In conclusion, the bottleneck tier is MySQL and its bottleneck resource is the CPU**.

To check that the BaaSP effectively detects the bottleneck tier of the SUT, we performed the same experiment without BaaSP. To do that, we use a former version of the CLIF tool which allows the tester to design the workload he wants to submit (a function of the number of vUsers over the time). Based on the results of the first experiment with BaaSP, we design a workload which follows the shape of the one generated by the BaaSPs InjectionController component. Notice that in a normal situation, the tester should test several workload to determine the appropriate shape. In order to show that the saturation point determined by BaaSP is correct (about 180 req/s), we run the test until the SUT trashes and observe this point is met or exceed. To prevent a lack of injector VMs, we statically provision up to 50 VMs. Fig. 8 shows the last results of this experiment after several attempts. Fig. 8 (a) shows that the application trashes with more than 25000 vUsers. The maximum throughput (the saturation point) is the same as in the previous experiment (180 req/s) with BaaSP. About 50% of requests took more than 20000 ms to treat (Fig 8 (b)) with more than about 4500 vUsers.

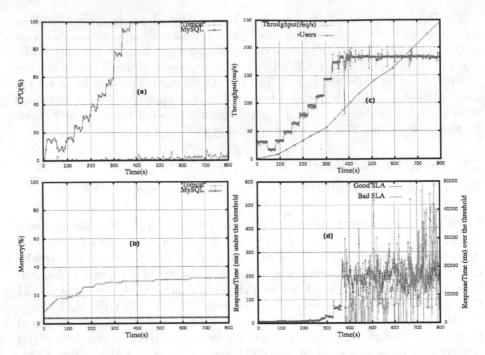

Fig. 7. Bottleneck tier detection: the MySQL server is CPU-bound. (a) Server CPU load, (b) Server memory load, (c) Application throughput, and (d) application response time (below and above the threshold)

Tomcat. MySQL is the first bottleneck tier; in this step, we determined the saturation point for the Tomcat server (i.e., how many replicated MySQL servers are needed to make Tomcat into the bottleneck tier). To do this, the experiment was repeated varying the number of MySQL servers. Experiments were stopped when the SUT's capacity (maximum throughput) in the current experiment (running n MySQL servers) was the same as in the previous experiment (running n-1 MySQL servers); n-1 MySQL servers are therefore required to saturate the Tomcat tier. This was performed for one (Fig. 9(a)) and two (Fig. 9(b)) Tomcat instances.

With one Tomcat instance (Fig. 9(a)) 18 instances of MySQL fully saturate the Tomcat tier. Up to 14 injector VMs were dynamically provisioned as necessary to complete this experiment. Plotting the CPU and memory loads for different servers in these experiments reveals Tomcat as the first bottleneck tier, with a CPU load of 100% (Fig. 10).

With two Tomcat instances (Fig. 9(b)) the Tomcat tier became saturated with 30 MySQL instances (with 25 injector VMs required to perform the test). Note that even when the number of Tomcat instances is doubled, the number of MySQL instances needed to saturate the Tomcat tier does not increase proportionally. Indeed, the application's performance is not doubled either. This is also the case when MySQL instances are doubled.

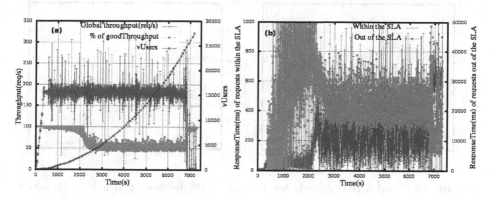

Fig. 8. Experiments without BaaSP: the application trashes with over 25000 vUsers, we observe the same saturation point as with BaaSP

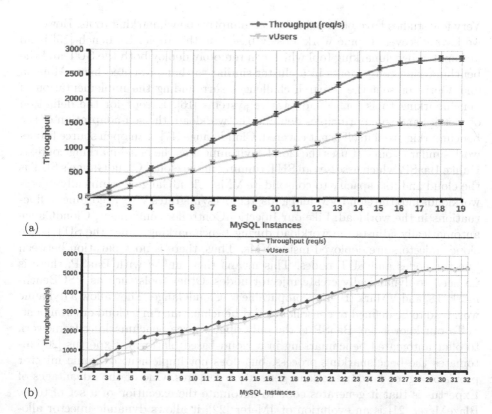

Fig. 9. How many instances of MySQL makes Tomcat the bottleneck tier with one (a) and two (b) Tomcat instances?

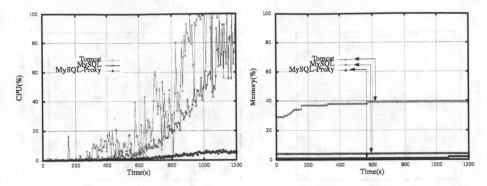

Fig. 10. CPU and Memory loads for Tomcat, MySQL-Proxy and a MySQL server when assessing 19 MySQL instances

6   Related Work

Very few studies have been published on adaptive benchmarking tools. However, we have discovered some work loosely based on this topic. Unibench [15] is an automated benchmarking tool which can remotely deploy both the SUT and the benchmarking components in a cluster similar to that presented here. Almeida and Vierra present the research challenges surrounding the implementation of benchmarking tools for self-adaptative systems [16]. Except for the definition of metrics and some principles defining the workload, the self-adaptation of the benchmarking tool itself is not covered. CloudGauge [17] is an open source framework similar to ours. It uses the cloud environment as the benchmarking context. Unlike BaaSP, which assesses an SUT running in the cloud, CloudGauge's SUT is the cloud and its capacity to consolidate VMs. CloudGauge dynamically injects workloads into the cloud VM and adds/removes/migrates VMs according to fluctuations in the workload. Like our InjectionController component, CloudGauge automatically adjusts the workload during benchmarking. Since the SUT is the cloud, injectors are deployed inside VMs. Thus, there is no separation between injector nodes and SUT nodes. This means that, unlike with BaaSP, there is no need to dynamically create injector nodes. Other tools such as VSCBenchmark [18] and VMark [19] are comparable to CloudGauge. They allow a dynamic workload to be defined to consolidate VM benchmarking in a cloud environment.

To our knowledge, BaaSP is the only open source benchmarking framework to offer automated benchmarking in a cloud-based platform. Expertus [20] automates the benchmarking process, but does not implement dynamic injector provisioning, or automated load generation features. One of the advantages of Expertus is that it generates code to automate the execution of a set of tests. BlazeMeter [21] is an evolution of JMeter [22], it allows dynamic injector allocation and de-allocation in the cloud to reduce the cost of tests. As this tool is proprietary, no technical or scientific description is available, making comparisons difficult. NeoLoad [23] is similar to BlazeMeter, it allows deployment of injectors in a cloud environment to benchmark an application. New injectors can be integrated throughout the benchmarking process. However, this integration must be initiated by the administrator through planning. Unlike BaaSP, NeoLoad does not include an automated injector saturation detection component.

7   Conclusion

This paper explores Cloud Computing features to facilitate application benchmarking and to test scalability. Load testing solutions can be provided on-demand in the cloud and can benefit from self-scalability.

We describe a Benchmark-as-a-Service platform that provides a number of benefits in terms of self-traffic generation, reduced cost and resource savings. Traffic is generated automatically without tester intervention, as with non-cloud-based BaaSP. The traffic-generating algorithm uses statistical formulas based on the computed response time and throughput of the SUT. The self-scalability of the platform facilitates benchmarking and reduces reduces the cost for lengthy campaigns. In fact, it requires no static provisioning, which can become prohibitive in terms of human and hardware resources. Experiments on the RUBiS benchmark show how BaaSP determines the bottleneck tiers of a JEE application. The same experiments done by hand without BaaSP show the same results, but with more hardware resources used after several attempts.

We next plan to add auto-scalability to the RUBiS benchmark and to enhance our Benchmark-as-a-service platform to report the resource provisioning of the self-scalable RUBiS itself.

Acknowledgment. This work is supported by the French Fonds National pour la Societe Numerique (FSN) and Poles Minalogic, Systematic and SCS, through the FSN Open Cloudware project.

References

1. Amza, C., Cecchet, E., Chanda, A., Cox, A.L., Elnikety, S., Gil, R., Marguerite, J., Rajamani, K., Zwaenepoel, W.: Specification and implementation of dynamic web site benchmarks. In: IEEE Annual Workshop on Workload Characterization, Austin, TX, USA, pp. 3–13 (2002)
2. Dillenseger, B.: CLIF, a framework based on fractal for flexible, distributed load testing. In: Annals of Telecommunications, vol. 64(1-2), pp. 101–120. Springer, Paris (2009)
3. Bruneton, E., Coupaye, T., Leclercq, M., Quema, V., Stefani, J.-B.: An Open Component Model and Its Support in Java. In: Crnković, I., Stafford, J.A., Schmidt, H.W., Wallnau, K. (eds.) CBSE 2004. LNCS, vol. 3054, pp. 7–22. Springer, Heidelberg (2004)
4. Harbaoui, A., Salmi, N., Dillenseger, B., Vincent, J.: Introducing Queuing Network-Based Performance Awareness in Autonomic Systems. In: Proceedings of the International Conference on Autonomic and Autonomous Systems, Cancun, Mexico, pp. 7–12 (2010)

5. Kleinrock, L.: Queueing Systems. Wiley-Interscience, New York (1975) ISBN 0471491101
6. Stewart, W.: Introduction to the Numerical Solution of Markov Chains. Princeton University Press, Princeton (1994) ISBN 0691036993
7. Jain, R.K.: The Art of Computer Systems Performance Analysis: Techniques for Experimental Design, Measurement, Simulation, and modelling. John Wiley and Sons, Inc., Canada (1991) ISBN 0471503363
8. Oracle, Java Message Service, (October 2012), http://docs.oracle.com/cd/E19957-01/816-5904-10/816-5904-10.pdf
9. Kephart, J.O., Chess, D.M.: The Vision of Autonomic Computing. Computer 36(1), 41–50 (2003)
10. Grid'5000: a scientific instrument designed to support experiment-driven research (October 2012), https://www.grid5000.fr/mediawiki/index.php/Grid5000:Home
11. Openstack web site (October 2012), http://openstack.org/
12. Amazon Web Services, Amazon EC2 auto-scaling functions (October 2012), http://aws.amazon.com/fr/autoscaling/
13. Simic, B.: The performance of web applications: Customers are won or lost in one second. A. R. Library (2008)
14. Wang, Q., Malkowski, S., Jayasinghe, D., Xiong, P., Pu, C., Kanemasa, Y., Kawaba, M., Harada, L.: The impact of soft resource allocation on n-tier application scalability. In: Proceedings of the 2011 IEEE International Parallel & Distributed Processing Symposium, Washington, DC, USA, pp. 1034–1045 (2011)
15. Rolls, D., Joslin, C., Scholz, S.-B.: Unibench: a tool for automated and collaborative benchmarking. In: Proceedings of the IEEE International Conference on Program Comprehension, Braga, Portugal, pp. 50–51 (2010)
16. Almeida, R., Vieira, M.: Benchmarking the resilience of self-adaptive software systems: perspectives and challenges. In: Proceedings of the International Symposium on Software Engineering for Adaptive and Self-Managing Systems, Waikiki, Honolulu, HI, USA, pp. 190–195 (2011)
17. El-Refaey, M.A., Rizkaa, M.A.: CloudGauge: a dynamic cloud and virtualization benchmarking suite. In: Proceedings of the IEEE International Workshops on Enabling Technologies: Infrastructures for Collaborative Enterprises, Larissa, Greece, pp. 66–75 (2010)
18. Jin, H., Cao, W., Yuan, P., Xie, X.: VSCBenchmark: benchmark for dynamic server performance of virtualization technology. In: Proceedings of the International Forum on Next-Generation Multicore/Manycore Technologies, Cairo, Egypt, pp. 1–8 (2008)
19. Makhija, V., Herndon, B., Smith, P., Roderick, L., Zamost, E., Anderson, J.: VMmark: a scalable benchmark for virtualized systems, Technical Report VMware-TR-2006-002, Palo Alto, CA, USA (September 2006)
20. Jayasinghe, D., Swint, G.S., Malkowski, S., Li, J., Park, J., Pu, C.: Expertus: A Generator Approach to Automate Performance Testing in IaaS Clouds. In: Proceedings of the IEEE International Conference on Cloud Computing, Honolulu, HI, USA, pp. 115–122 (June 2012)
21. BlazeMeter, Dependability benchmarking project (October 2012), http://blazemeter.com/
22. The Apache Software Foundation, Apache JMeter (October 2012), http://jmeter.apache.org/
23. Neotys, NeoLoad: load test all web and mobile applications (October 2012), http://www.neotys.fr/

Ditto – Deterministic Execution Replayability-as-a-Service for Java VM on Multiprocessors

João M. Silva[1], José Simão[2,3], and Luís Veiga[1,2]

[1] Instituto Superior Técnico - ULisboa
[2] INESC-ID Lisboa
[3] Instituto Superior de Engenharia de Lisboa (ISEL)
joao.m.silva@ist.utl.pt, jsimao@cc.isel.ipl.pt, luis.veiga@inesc-id.pt

Abstract. Alongside the rise of multi-processor machines, concurrent programming models have grown to near ubiquity. Programs built on these models are prone to bugs with rare pre-conditions, arising from unanticipated interactions between parallel tasks. Replayers can be efficient on uni-processor machines, but struggle with unreasonable overhead on multi-processors, both concerning slowdown of the execution time and size of the replay log. We present Ditto, a deterministic replayer for concurrent JVM applications executed on multi-processor machines, using both state-of-the-art and novel techniques. The main contribution of Ditto is a novel pair of recording and replaying algorithms that: (a) serialize memory accesses at the instance field level, (b) employ partial transitive reduction and program-order pruning on-the-fly, (c) take advantage of TLO static analysis, escape analysis and JVM compiler optimizations to identify thread-local accesses, and (d) take advantage of a lightweight checkpoint mechanism to avoid large logs in long running applications with fine granularity interactions, and for faster replay to any point in execution. The results show that Ditto out-performs previous deterministic replayers targeted at Java programs.

Keywords: Deterministic Replay, Concurrency, Debugging, JVM.

1 Introduction

The transition to the new concurrent paradigm of programming has not been the easiest, as developers struggle to visualize all possible interleavings of parallel tasks that interact through shared memory. Concurrent programs are harder to build than their sequential counterparts, but they are arguably even more challenging to debug. The difficulty in anticipating all possible interactions between parallel threads makes these programs especially prone to the appearance of bugs triggered by rare pre-conditions, capable of evading detection for long periods. Moreover, the debugging methodologies developed over the years for sequential programs fall short when applied to concurrent ones. Cyclic debugging, arguably the most common methodology, depends on repeated bug reproduction

D. Eyers and K. Schwan (Eds.): Middleware 2013, LNCS 8275, pp. 405–424, 2013.
© IFIP International Federation for Information Processing 2013

to find its cause, requiring the fault to be deterministic given the same input. The inherent memory non-determinism of concurrent programs breaks this assumption of fault-determinism, rendering cycling debugging inefficient, as most time and resources are taken up by bug reproduction attempts [1]. Furthermore, any trace statements, added to the program in an effort to learn more about the problem, can actually contribute further to the fault's evasiveness. Hence, cyclic debugging becomes even less efficient in the best case, and ineffective in the worst.

Memory non-determinism, inherent to concurrent programs, results from the occurrence of data races, i.e., unsynchronized accesses to the same shared memory location in which at least one is a write operation. The outcomes of these races must be reproduced in order to perform a correct execution replay. In uniprocessors, these outcomes can be derived from the outcomes of a much smaller subset of races, the synchronization races, used in synchronization primitives to allow threads to compete for access to shared resources. Efficient deterministic replayers have been developed taking advantage of this observation [2–5].

Replaying executions on multi-processors is much more challenging, because the outcomes to synchronization races are no longer enough to derive the outcomes to all data races. The reason is that while parallelism in uniprocessors is an abstraction provided by the task scheduler, in multi-processor machines it has a physical significance. In fact, knowing the task scheduling decisions [6, 7] does not allow us to resolve races between threads concurrently executing in different processors. Deterministic replayers have difficulties with unreasonable overhead when applied in this context, as the instructions that can lead to data races make up a significant amount of the instructions executed by a typical application. Currently there are four distinct approaches to deal with this open research problem, discussed in Section 2. Even using techniques to prune the events of interest, long running applications can make the log of events grow to an unmanageable size. To avoid this, a checkpointing mechanism can also be used to transparently save the state of the program, with the events before the checkpoint truncated from the log. The last saved state, may be potentially smaller than the original untruncated log, and can also be used as a starting point for a future replay allowing for a faster replay solution.

In this paper, we present Ditto, our deterministic replayer for unmodified user-level applications executed by the JVM on multi-processor machines. It integrates state-of-the-art and novel techniques to improve upon previous work. The main contributions that make Ditto unique are: (a) A novel pair of logical clock-based [8] recording and replaying algorithms. This allows us to leverage the semantic differences between load and store memory accesses to reduce trace data and maximize replay-time concurrency. Furthermore, we serialize memory accesses at the finest possible granularity, distinguishing between instance fields and array indexes; (b) Reduced trace and log space. We use a constraint pruning algorithm based on program order and partial transitive reduction to reduce the amount of trace data on-the-fly and a checkpointing mechanism to employ in long running applications; (c) A trace file optimization that highly reduces the size of logical clock-based traces; Though we discuss and implement Ditto in the context of a JVM runtime, its underlying techniques may be directly applied to other high-level, object-oriented runtime platforms, such as the Common Language Runtime (CLR).

We implemented Ditto on top of the open-source JVM implementation Jikes RVM (Research Virtual Machine). Ditto is evaluated to assess its replay correctness, bug reproduction capabilities and performance. Experimental results show that Ditto consistently out-performs previous state-of-the-art deterministic replayers targeted at Java programs in terms of record-time overhead, trace file size and replay-time overhead. It does so across multiple axes of application properties, namely number of threads, number of processors, load to store ratio, number of memory accesses, number of fields per shared object, and number of shared objects.

The rest of the paper is organized as follows: Section 2 describes some instances of related work; Section 3 explains the base design and algorithms of Ditto; Section 4 presents fundamental optimizations; Section 5 discusses some implementation related details; Section 6 presents and analyzes evaluation results; and Section 7 concludes the paper and offers our thoughts on the directions of future work.

2   Related Work

Deterministic replayers for multi-processor executions can be divided into four categories in terms of the approach taken to tackle the problem of excessive overhead. Some systems replay solely synchronization races, thus guaranteeing a correct replay up until the occurrence of a data race. RecPlay [3] and JaRec [4] are two similar systems that use logical clock-based recording algorithms to trace a partial ordering over all synchronization operations. RecPlay is capable of detecting data races during replay. Nonetheless, we believe the assumption that programs are perfectly synchronized severely limits the effectiveness of these solutions as debugging tools in multi-processor environments.

Researchers have developed specialized hardware-based solutions. FDR [9] extends the cache coherence protocol to propagate causality information and generate an ordering over memory accesses. DeLorean [10] forces processors to execute instructions in chunks that are only committed if they do not conflict with other chunks in terms of memory accesses. Hence, the order of memory accesses can be derived from the order of chunk commits. Though efficient, these techniques have the drawback of requiring special hardware.

A more recent proposal is to use probabilistic replay techniques that explore the trade-off between recording overhead reduction through partial execution tracing and relaxation of replay guarantees. PRES partially traces executions and performs an offline exploration phase to find an execution that conforms with the partial trace and with user-defined conditions [11]. ODR uses a formula-solver and a partial execution trace to find executions that generate the same output as the original [12]. These techniques show a lot of potential as debugging tools, but are unable to put an upper limit on how long it takes for a successful replay to be performed, though the problem is minimized by fully recording replay attempts.

LEAP is a relevant Java deterministic replayer that employs static analysis, to identify memory accesses performed on actual thread-shared variables, hence reducing the amount of monitored accesses [13]. Because LEAP recording algorithm associates access vectors to fields, it can not distinguish accesses to the same field of different objects. In workloads where there are many objects of a single type but they are not shared among threads, this will diminish the concurrency of the recording and replaying mechanisms. ORDER [14] is, like Ditto, an object centric recorder. From a design point of view, ORDER misses support for online pruning of events and a checkpoint mechanism for faster replay. Regarding current implementation, the baseline code base (Apache harmony) is now deprecated, while Ditto was developed in a research oriented, yet production-like quality JVM, that is widely supported by the research community.

Deterministic replay can also be used as an efficient means for a fault-tolerant system to maintain replicas and recover after experiencing a fault [15, 16].

3   Ditto – System Overview

Ditto must record the outcomes of all data races in order to support reproduction of any execution on multi-processor machines. Data races arise from non-synchronized shared memory accesses in which at least one is a write operation. Thus, to trace outcomes to data races, one must monitor shared memory accesses. The JVM's memory model limits the set of instructions that can manipulate shared memory to three groups: (i) accesses to static fields, (ii) accesses to object fields, and (iii) accesses to array fields of any type.

In addition to shared memory accesses, it is mandatory that we trace the order in which synchronization operations are performed. Though these events have no effect on shared memory, an incorrect ordering can cause the replayer to deadlock when shared memory accesses are performed inside critical sections. They need not, however, be ordered with shared memory accesses. In the JVM, synchronization is supported by synchronized methods, synchronized blocks and synchronization methods, such as `wait` and `notify`. Since all these mechanisms use monitors as their underlying synchronization primitive, their acquisitions are the events that Ditto intercepts. For completeness, we also record values and orderings of external input to threads, such as random numbers and from other library functions, while assuming the content of input from files is available.

3.1   Base Record and Replay Algorithms

The recording and replaying algorithms of Ditto rely on logical clocks (or Lamport clocks) [8], a mechanism designed to capture chronological and causal relationships, consisting of a monotonically increasing software counter. Logical clocks are associated with threads, objects and object fields to identify the order

Algorithm 1. Load wrapper	**Algorithm 2.** Store wrapper
Parameters: f is the field, v is the value loaded	**Parameters:** f is the field, v is the value stored
1: **method** WRAPLOAD(f,v)	1: **method** WRAPSTORE(f,v)
2: MONITORENTER(f)	2: MONITORENTER(f)
3: $t \leftarrow$ GETCURRENTTHREAD()	3: $t \leftarrow$ GETCURRENTTHREAD()
4: TRACE($f.storeClock$)	4: TRACE($f.storeClock, f.loadCount$)
5: $f.loadCount \leftarrow f.loadCount + 1$	5: $clock \leftarrow$ MAX($t.clock, f.storeClock$) $+ 1$
6: **if** $f.storeClock > t.clock$ **then**	6: $f.storeClock \leftarrow clock$
7: $t.clock \leftarrow f.storeClock$	7: $f.loadCount \leftarrow 0$
8: **end if**	8: $t.clock \leftarrow clock$
9: $v \leftarrow$ LOAD(f)	9: STORE(f,v)
10: MONITOREXIT(f)	10: MONITOREXIT(f)
11: **end method**	11: **end method**

between events of interest. For each such event, the recorder generates an order constraint that is later used by the replayer to order the event after past events on which its outcome depends.

Recording: The recorder creates two streams of order constraints per thread – one orders shared memory accesses, while the other orders monitor acquisitions. The recording algorithm for shared memory accesses was designed to take advantage of the semantic differences between load and store memory accesses. To do so, Ditto requires state to be associated with threads and fields. Threads are augmented with one logical clock, the thread's clock, incremented whenever it performs a store operation. Fields are extended with (a) one logical clock, the field's store clock, incremented whenever its value is modified; and (b) a load counter, incremented when the field's value is loaded and reset when it is modified. The manipulation of this state and the load/store operation itself must be performed atomically. Ditto acquires a monitor associated with the field to create a critical section and achieve atomicity. It is important that the monitor is not part of the application's scope, as its usage would interfere with the application and potentially lead to deadlocks.

When a thread T_i performs a load operation on a field f, it starts by acquiring f's associated monitor. Then, it adds an order constraint to the trace consisting of f's store clock, implying that the current operation is to be ordered after the store that wrote f's current value, but specifying no order in relation to other loads. Thread and field state are then updated by incrementing f's load count, and the load operation itself performed. Finally, the monitor of f is released. If T_i instead performs a store operation on f, it still starts by acquiring f's monitor, but follows by tracing an order constraint composed of the field's store clock and load count, implying that this store is to be performed after the store that wrote f's current value and all loads that read said value. Thread and field states are then updated by increasing clocks and resetting f's load count. Finally, the store is performed and the monitor released. Algorithms 1 and 2 list pseudo-code for these recording processes.

Unlike memory accesses, performed on fields, monitor acquisitions are performed on objects. As such, we associate with each object a logical clock. Moreover, given that synchronization is not serialized with memory accesses, we add

Algorithm 3. Recording monitor acquisition operations

Parameters: o is the object whose monitor was acquired
1: **method** AFTERMONITORENTER(o)
2:     $t \leftarrow$ GETCURRENTTHREAD()
3:     TRACE($o.syncClock$)
4:     $clk \leftarrow$ MAX($t.syncClock, o.syncClock$)+1
5:     $o.syncClock \leftarrow clk$
6:     $t.syncClock \leftarrow clk$
7: **end method**

Algorithm 4. Replaying load memory access operations

Parameters: f is the field whose value is being loaded into v and is protected by a monitor
1: **method** WRAPLOAD(f,v)
2:     $t \leftarrow$ GETCURRENTTHREAD()
3:     $clock \leftarrow$ NEXTLOADCONSTRAINT(t)
4:     **while** $f.storeClock < clock$ **do**
5:         WAIT(f)
6:     **end while**
7:     $v \leftarrow$ LOAD(f)
8:     $t \leftarrow$ GETCURRENTTHREAD()
9:     **if** $f.storeClock > t.clock$ **then**
10:         $t.clock \leftarrow f.storeClock$
11:     **end if**
12:     $f.loadCount \leftarrow f.loadCount + 1$
13:     NOTIFYALL(f)
14: **end method**

a second clock to threads. When a thread T_i acquires the monitor of an object o, it performs Algorithm 3. Note that we do not require a monitor this time, as the critical section of o's monitor already protects the update of thread and object state.

Consistent Thread Identification: Ditto's traces are composed of individual streams for each thread. Thus, it is mandatory that we map record-time threads to their replay-time counterparts. Threads can race to create child threads, making typical Java thread identifiers, attributed in a sequential manner, unfit for our purposes. To achieve the desired effect, Ditto wraps thread creation in a critical section and attributes a replay identifier to the child thread. The monitor acquisitions involved are replayed using the same algorithms that handle application-level synchronization, ensuring that replay identifiers remain consistent across executions.

Replaying: As each thread is created, the replayer uses its assigned replay identifier to pull the corresponding stream of order constraints from the trace file. Before a thread executes each event of interest, the replayer is responsible for using the order constraints to guarantee that all events on which its outcome depends have already been performed. The trace does not contain metadata about the events from which it was generated, leaving the user with the responsibility of providing a program that generates the same stream of events of interest as it did at record-time. Ditto nonetheless allows the original program to be modified while maintaining a constant event stream through the use of Java annotations or command-line arguments, an important feature for its usage as a debugging tool.

Replaying Shared Memory Accesses: Using the order constraints in a trace file, the replayer delays load operations until the value read at record-time is available, while store operations are additionally delayed until that value has been read as many times as it was during recording, using the field's load count.

This approach allows for maximum replay concurrency, as each memory access waits solely for those events that it affects and is affected by.

When a thread T_i performs a load operation on a field f, it starts by reading a load order constraint from its trace, extracting a target store clock from it. Until f's store clock equals this target, the thread waits. Upon being notified and positively re-evaluating the conditions for advancement, it is free to perform the actual load operation. After doing so, thread and field states are updated and waiting threads are notified of the changes. Algorithm 4 lists pseudo-code for this process. If T_i was performing a store operation, the process would be the same, but a store order constraint would be loaded instead, from which a target store clock and a target load count would be extracted. The thread would proceed with the store once f's store clock and load count both equaled the respective targets. State would be updated according to the rules used in Algorithm 1. Replaying monitor acquisitions is very similar to replaying load operations, with two differences: (i) a sync order constraint is read from the trace, from which a target sync clock is extracted and used as a condition for advancement; and (ii) thread and object state are updated according to the rules in Algorithm 3.

Notice that during replay there is no longer a need for protecting shared memory accesses with a monitor, as synchronization between threads is now performed by Ditto's wait/notify mechanism. Furthermore, notice that the load counter enables concurrent loads to be replayed in an arbitrary order, hence in parallel and faster, rather than being serialized unnecessarily.

3.2   Wait and Notify Mechanism

During execution replay, threads are often forced to wait until the conditions for advancement related to field or object state hold true. As such, threads that modify the states are given the responsibility of notifying those waiting for changes. Having threads wait and notify on the monitor associated with the field or object they intend to, or have manipulated, as suggested in Algorithms 1-2 and 3, is a simple but sub-optimal approach which notifies threads too often and causes bottlenecks when they attempt to reacquire the monitor. Ditto uses a much more refined approach, in which threads are only notified if the state has reached the conditions for their advancement.

Replay-time states of fields and objects are augmented with a table indexed by three types of keys: (i) load keys, used by load operations to wait for a specific store clock; (ii) store keys, used by store operations to wait for a specific combination of store clock and load count; and (iii) synchronization keys, used by monitor acquisitions to wait for a specific synchronization clock. Let us consider an example to illustrate how these keys are used. When a thread T_i attempts to load the value of a field f but finds f's store clock lower than its target store clock (tc), it creates a load key using the latter. T_i then adds a new entry to f's table using the key as both index and value, and waits on the key. When another thread T_j modifies f's store clock to contain the value tc, it uses a load key (tc) and a store key $(tc, 0)$ to index the table. As a result of using the load key, it will retrieve the object on which T_i is waiting and invokes `notifyAll` on it. Thus, T_i is notified only once its conditions for proceeding are met.

3.3 Lightweight Checkpointing

For long running applications, and especially those with fine-grained thread interactions, the log can grow to a large size. Furthermore, the replay can only be necessary to be done from a certain point in time because the fault is known to occur only at the end of execution. Ditto uses a lightweight checkpointing mechanism [17] to offer two new replay services: (i) replay to most recent point before fault; (ii) replay to any instant M in execution. Checkpoint is done recording each thread stack and reachable objects. In general, the checkpoint size is closely related to the size of live objects, plus the overhead of booking metadata necessary for recovery. While the size of live objects can remain consistent over time, the log size will only grow. Regarding scenario (i), replay starts by recovering from the last checkpoint and continues with the partial truncated log. So, the total recording space is $sizeof(lastCheckpoint) + sizeof(truncatedLog)$ which is still bounded to be smaller than $2 * sizeof(checkpointSize)$, since we trigger checkpointing when the log reaches a size close to the total memory used by objects (90%). In scenario (ii), replay starts with the most recent checkpoint before instant M (chosen by the user), and the partial log collected after that instant. In this case, the total recording space is $N * sizeof(checkpoint) + N * sizeof(truncatedLog)$, where N is the number of times a checkpoint is done. In this case there is a trade-off between overhead in execution time and granularity in available replay start times [17]. Even so, the total recording space is bounded to be smaller than $2 * N * sizeof(checkpoint)$.

3.4 Input Related Non-Deterministic Events

Besides access to shared variables, another source of non-determinism is the input some programs use to progress their calculus. This input can come from information asked to the program's user or from calling non-deterministic services, such as the current time or the random number generator. All such services are either available through the base class library or calls using the Java Native Interface. Each time a call is made to a method that is a source of input non-determinism (e.g. `Random.nextInt`, `System.nanoTime`), the result is saved in association with the current thread. If the load/store is made over a shared field, the replay mechanism will already ensure the same thread interleaving as occurred in the recording phase. Regarding non shared fields, the replay of deterministic information can occur in a different order than the one of the original execution. This is not a problem since the values are affiliated with a thread and are delivered using FIFO order during each thread execution.

4   Additional Optimizations

4.1   Recording Granularity

Ditto records at the finest possible granularity, distinguishing between different fields of individual instances when serializing memory accesses. Previous
deterministic replayers for Java programs had taken sub-optimal approaches:
(i) DejaVu creates a global-order [2]; (ii) LEAP generates a partial-order that distinguishes between different fields, but not distinct instances [13]; and (iii) JaRec
does the exact opposite of LEAP [4]. The finer recording granularity maximizes
replay-time concurrency and reduces recording overhead due to lower contention
when modifying recorder state. The downside is higher memory consumption associated with field states. If this becomes a problem, Ditto is capable of operating
with an object-level granularity.

Array indexes are treated like object fields, but with a slight twist. To keep
index state under control for large arrays, a user-defined cap is placed on how
many index states Ditto can keep for each array. Hence, multiple array indexes
may map to a single index state and be treated as one program entity in the
eyes of the recorder and replayer. This is not an optimal solution, but it goes
towards a compromise with the memory requirements of Ditto.

4.2   Pruning Redundant Order Constraints

The base recording algorithm traces an order constraint per event of interest.
Though correct, it can generate unreasonably high amounts of trace data, mostly
due to the fact that shared memory accesses can comprise a very significant
fraction of the instructions executed by a typical application. Fortunately, many
order constraints are redundant, i.e., the order they enforce is already indirectly
enforced by other constraints or program order. Such constraints can be safely
pruned from the trace without compromising correctness. Ditto uses a pruning
algorithm that does so on-the-fly.

Pruning order constraints leaves gaps in the trace which our base replay algorithm is not equipped to deal with. To handle these gaps, we introduce the
concept of free runs, which represent a sequence of one or more events of interest
that can be performed freely. When performing a free run of size n, the replayer
essentially allows n events to occur without concerning itself with the progress
of other threads. Free runs are placed in the trace where the events they replace
would have been.

Program Order Pruning: Consider the recorded execution in Figure 1(a), in
which arrows represent order constraints traced by the base recording algorithm.
Notice how all dashed constraints enforce orderings between events which are
implied by program order. To prune them, Ditto needs additional state to be
associated with fields: the identifier of the last thread to store a value in the field,
and a flag signaling whether that value has been loaded by other threads. Potential load order constraints are not traced if the thread loading the value is the

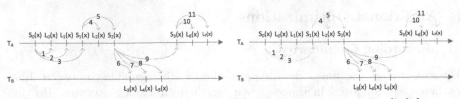

(a) Order constraints traced by base recording algorithm.

(b) Pruning constraints implied by program order.

Fig. 1. Example of Ditto's constraint pruning algorithm

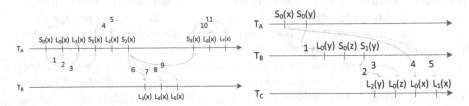

Fig. 2. Pruning constraints implied by previous constraints

Fig. 3. Example of partial transitive reduction

one that wrote it. Thus, constraints 1, 2, 4, 10 and 11 in Figure 1(a) are pruned, but not constraint 6. Similarly, a potential store order constraint is not traced if it is performed by the thread that wrote the current value and if that value has not been loaded by other threads. Hence, constraints 3 and 5 are pruned, while 9 is not, as presented in Figure 1(b). Synchronization order constraints are handled in the same way as load operations, but state is associated with an object instead of a field.

Partial Transitive Reduction: Netzer introduced an algorithm to find the optimal set of constraints to reproduce an execution [18], which was later improved upon in RTR [19] by introducing artificial constraints that enabled the removal of multiple real ones. Ditto does not directly employ any of these algorithms for reasons related to performance degradation and the need for keeping flexibility-limiting state, such as Netzer's usage of vector clocks, requiring the number of threads to be known a priori. Instead, Ditto uses a novel partial transitive reduction algorithm designed to find a balance between trace file size reduction and additional overhead.

Transitive reduction prunes order constraints that enforce orderings implicitly enforced by other constraints. In Figure 1, for example, T_B performs three consecutive load operations which read the same value of x, written by T_A. Given that the loads are ordered by program order, enforcing the order $S_2(x) \rightarrow L_3(x)$ is enough to guarantee that the following two loads are also subsequent to $S_2(x)$. As such, constraints 7 and 8 are redundant and can be removed, resulting in the final trace file of Figure 2 with only 2 constrains.

To perform transitive reduction, we add a table to the state of threads that tracks the most recent inter-thread interaction with each other thread. Whenever a thread T_i accesses a field f last written to by thread T_j (with $T_i \neq T_j$), f's store clock is inserted in the interaction table of T_i at index T_j. This allows Ditto to declare that order constraints whose source is T_j with a clock lower than the one in the interaction table are redundant, implied by a previous constraint. Figure 3 shows a sample recording that stresses the partial nature of Ditto's transitive reduction, since the set of traced constraints is sub-optimal. Constraint 4 is redundant, as the combination of constraints 1 and 2 would indirectly enforce the order $S_0(x) \rightarrow L_0(x)$. For Ditto to achieve this conclusion, however, the interaction tables of T_B and T_C would have to be merged when tracing constraint 2. The merge operation proved to be too detrimental to efficiency, especially given that the benefit is limited to one order constraint, as the subsequent constraint 5, similar to 4, is pruned. In summary, Ditto is aware of thread interactions that span a maximum of one traced order constraint.

4.3   Thread Local Objects and Array Escape Analysis

Thread Local Objects (TLO) static analysis provides locality information on class fields, that is, it determines fields which are not involved in inter-thread interactions, aiming to save execution time and log space. The output of this kind of analysis is a classification of either thread-local or thread-shared for each class field. We developed a stand-alone application that uses the TLO implementation in the Soot bytecode optimization framework[1] to generate a report file that lists all thread-shared fields of the analyzed application. This file can be fed as optional input to Ditto, which uses the information to avoid intercepting accesses to thread-local fields.

TLO analysis provides very useful information about the locality of class fields, but no information is offered on array fields. Without further measures, we would be required to conservatively monitor all array fields accesses. Ditto uses, at runtime, information collected from the just-in-time compiler to do escape analysis on array references and avoid monitoring accesses to elements of arrays declared in a method whose reference never escapes that same method. This analysis, although simple, can still avoid some useless overhead at little cost. Nonetheless, there is a lot of unexplored potential for this kind of analysis on array references to reduce recording overhead which we see as future work.

4.4   Trace File

Ditto's traces are composed of one order constraint stream per record-time thread. Organizing the trace by thread is advantageous for various reasons. The first is that it is easy to intercept the creation and termination of threads. Intercepting these events is crucial for the management of trace memory buffers, as

---

[1] http://www.sable.mcgill.ca/soot/

they must be created when a thread starts and dumped to disk once it terminates. Moreover, it allows us to place an upper limit on how much memory can be spent on memory buffers, as the number of simultaneously running threads is limited and usually low. Other trace organizations, such as the field-oriented one of LEAP [13], do not benefit from this – the lifetime of a field is the lifetime of the application itself. A stream organized by instance would be even more problematic, as intercepting object creation and collection is not an easy task.

The trace file is organized as a table that maps thread replay identifiers to the corresponding order constraint streams. The table and the streams themselves are organized in a linked list of chunks, as a direct consequence of the need to dump memory buffers to disk as they become full. Though sequential I/O is generally more efficient than random I/O, using multiple sequential files (one per thread) turned out to be less efficient than updating pointers in random file locations as new chunks were added to it. Hence, Ditto creates a single-file trace.

Given that logical clocks are monotonically increasing counters, they are expected to grow to very large values during long running executions. For the trace file, this would mean reserving upwards of 8 bytes to store each clock value. Ditto uses a simple but effective optimization that stores clock values as increments in relation to the last one in the stream, instead of as absolute values. Considering that clocks always move forward and mostly in small increments, the great majority of clock values can be stored in 1 or 2 bytes.

5   Implementation Details

Ditto is implemented in Jikes RVM, a high performance implementation of the JVM written almost entirely in a slightly enhanced Java that provides "magic" methods for low-level operations, such as pointer arithmetic [20]. The RVM is very modular, as it was designed to be a research platform where novel VM ideas could be easily implemented and evaluated. This was the main reason we developed Ditto on it.

The implementation efforts were done in two main sub-systems: threading and compiler. Regarding the threading system, each Java thread is mapped to a single native thread. This is relevant to Ditto, as it means scheduling decisions are offloaded to the OS and cannot be traced or controlled from inside the RVM. As a consequence, Java monitors are also implemented with resort to OS locking primitives. Regarding the compiler, Jikes RVM does not interpret bytecode; all methods are compiled to machine code on-demand. The VM uses an adaptive compilation system in which methods are first compiled by a fast baseline compiler which generates inefficient code. A profiling mechanism detects hot methods at runtime, which are then recompiled by a slower but much better optimizing compiler. This compiler manipulates three intermediate representations (IR) on which different optimizations are performed. The high-level IR (HIR) is very similar to the bytecode instruction set, but subsequent IRs are closer to actual processor ISAs.

Intercepting Events of Interest: Implementing Ditto in Jikes RVM required intercepting the events of interest through hooks in the thread management subsystem and the addition of instrumentation phases to the compilers. Moreover, mechanisms were added to manage thread, object and field states. A drawback of Jikes being written in Java is that it uses the same mechanisms for executing as the application. As such, when intercepting events, we must ignore those triggered by the VM. Depending on the event, the VM/application distinction is done using either static tests that rely on package names, or runtime tests that inspect the Java stack.

Ditto intercepts thread creation, both before and after the launch of the native thread, and thread termination, mainly for the purpose of initializing and dumping trace memory buffers. The thread creation hooks are also used to enter and exit the critical section protecting replay identifier assignment. If the event occurs in the context of a synchronized method or block, Ditto simply replaces the usual method used to implement the monitor enter operation with a wrapper method during compilation. Monitor acquisitions performed in the context of synchronization methods like `wait` or `notify` are intercepted by a hook in the VM's internal implementation of said methods. To avoid costly runtime tests, call sites are instrumented to activate a thread-local flag which lets Ditto know that the next executed synchronization method was invoked by the application. Events triggered through the JNI interface are also intercepted by a hook inside the VM, but they require a runtime test to ascertain the source, as we do not compile native code.

During method compilation, accesses to shared memory are wrapped in two calls to methods that trace the operation. Instrumentation is performed after HIR optimizations have been executed on the method, allowing Ditto to take advantage of those that remove object, array or static field accesses. Such optimizations include common sub-expression elimination and object/array replacement with scalar variables using escape analysis, among others.

Threading and State: Thread state is easily kept in the VM's own thread objects. Object and field states are kept in a state instance whose reference is stored in the object's header. After modifying the GC to scan these references, this approach allows us to create states for objects on-demand and keep them only while the corresponding object stays alive. Ditto requires the trace file to be finalized in order to replay the corresponding execution. When a deadlock occurs, the JVM does not shutdown and the trace memory buffers are never dumped, leaving the trace in an unfinished state. The problem is solved by adding a signal handler to Jikes which intercepts `SIGUSR1` signals and instructs the replay system to finish the trace. The user is responsible for delivering the signal to Jikes before killing its process if a deadlock is thought to have been reached.

Trace File: In Section 4 we described the way thread order constraint streams are located in the trace file using a combination of table and linked list structures. Structuring the streams themselves is another issue, as Ditto's recording algorithm generates three types of values that must be somehow encoded in the stream: (i) clock increment values; (ii) free run values; and (iii) load count values. Furthermore, the clock value optimization, also presented in Section 4, makes value sizes flexible, requiring the introduction of a way to encode this information as well.

The three kinds of values are encoded using the two most significant bits of each value as identification metadata. However, adding two more bits for size metadata would severely limit the range of values that each entry could represent. Moreover, it is usual for consecutive values to have equal size, leading to a lot of redundant information if the size is declared for each individual entry. Taking these observations in mind, we introduce meta-values to the stream which encode the size and number of the values that follow them in the stream. The meta-values take up two bytes, but their number is insignificant in comparison to the total amount of values stored in the trace. Ditto uses a VM's internal thread whose only purpose is to write trace buffers to disk. By giving each thread two buffers, we allow one buffer to be dumped to disk by the writer thread while the other is concurrently filled. In most cases, writing to disk is faster than filling a second buffer, allowing threads to waste no time waiting for I/O operations.

6   Evaluation

We evaluate Ditto by assessing its ability to correctly replay recorded executions and by measuring its performance in terms of recording overhead, replaying overhead and trace file size. Performance measurements are compared with those of previous approaches, which we implemented in Jikes RVM using the same facilities that support Ditto itself. The implemented replayers are: (a) DejaVu [2], a global-order replayer; (b) JaRec [4], a partial-order, logical clock-based replayer; and (c) LEAP [13], a recent partial-order, access vector-based replayer. We followed their respective publications as closely as possible, introducing modifications when necessary. For instance, DejaVu and JaRec, originally designed to record synchronization races, were extended to deal with all data races, while LEAP's algorithm was extended to compress consecutive accesses to a field by the same thread, absent in available codebase. Moreover, our checkpoint for instant replay is deactivated for fairness.

We start by using a highly non-deterministic microbenchmark and a number of applications from the IBM Concurrency Testing Repository[2] to assess replay correctness. This is followed by a thorough comparison between Ditto's runtime performance characteristics and those of the other implemented replayers. The results are gathered by performing a microbenchmark and recording executions of selected applications (because of space constraints) from the Java Grande and DaCapo benchmark suites. All experiments were conducted on a 8-core 3.40Ghz Intel i7 machine with 12GB of primary memory and running 64-bit Linux 3.2.0. Baseline version of the Jikes RVM is 3.1.2. Ditto's source will be available in the Jikes RVM research archive.

---

[2] https://qp.research.ibm.com/concurrency_testing

Replay Correctness: In the context of Ditto, an execution replay is said to be correct if the shared program state goes through the same transitions as it did during recording, even if thread local state diverges. Other types of deterministic replayers may offer more relaxed fidelity guarantees, as is the case of the probabilistic replayers PRES [11] and ODR [12].

We design a microbenchmark to produce a highly erratic and non-deterministic output, so that we can confirm the correctness of replay with a high degree of assurance. This is accomplished by having threads randomly increment multiple shared counters without any kind of synchronization, and using the final counter values as the output. After a few iterations, the final counter values are completely unpredictable due to the non-atomic nature of the increments. Naively re-executing the benchmark in hopes of getting the same output will prove unsuccessful virtually every time. On the contrary, Ditto is able to reproduce the final counter values every single time, even when stressing the system by using a high number of threads and iterations. The microbenchmark will also be available in the Jikes RVM research archive. Regarding the *IBM concurrency testing repository*, it contains a number of small applications that exhibit various concurrent bug patterns while performing some practical task. Ditto is capable of correctly reproducing each and every one of these bugs.

6.1 Performance Results

After confirming Ditto's capability to correctly replay many kinds of concurrent bug patterns, we set off to evaluate its performance by measuring recording overhead, trace file size and replaying overhead. To put experimental results in perspective, we use the same performance indicators to evaluate the three implemented state-of-the-art deterministic replay techniques for Java programs: DejaVu (Global), JaRec, LEAP.

Microbenchmarking: The same microbenchmark used to assess replay correctness is now used to compare Ditto's performance characteristics with those of the other replayers regarding recording time, trace size and replaying time, across multiple target application properties: (i) number of threads, (ii) number of shared memory accesses per thread, (iii) load to store ratio, (iv) number of fields per shared object, and (v) number of shared objects, (vi) number of processors.

The results are presented in Figures 4 and 5. Note that graphs related to execution times use a logarithmic scale due to the order of magnitude-sized differences between replayers' performance, and that in all graphs lower is better.

Figure 4 shows the performance results of application properties (i) to (iii). Record and replay execution times grows linearly with the number of threads, with Ditto taking the lead in absolute values by one and two orders of magnitude, respectively. As for trace file sizes, Ditto stays below 200Mb, while no other replayer comes under 500Mb. The maximum is achieved by LEAP at around 1.5Gb. Concerning the number of memory access operations, the three indicators increase linearly with the number of memory accesses for all algorithms. We attribute this result to two factors: (i) none of them keeps state whose complexity

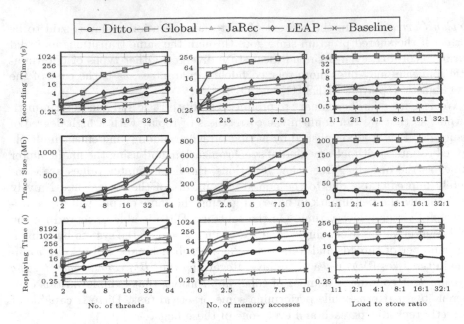

Fig. 4. Recording time, trace size and replaying time as a function of the number of threads, accesses per thread (x10^6) and load:store ratio

increases over time, and (ii) our conscious effort during implementation to keep memory usage constant. Ditto is nonetheless superior in terms of absolute values. Finally, regarding the load and store ratio, Ditto is the only evaluated replayer that takes advantage of the semantic differences between load and store memory accesses. As such, we expect it to be the only system to positively react in the presence of a higher load:store ratio. The experimental results are consistent with this, as we can observe reductions in both overheads and a very significant reduction of the trace file size.

Figure 5 shows the performance results of application properties (iv) to (vi). Stressing the system with an increasing number of fields per object, property (iv), and number of shared objects, property (v), is crucial to measure the impact of Ditto's recording granularity. Ditto and LEAP are the only replayers that improve performance (smaller recording and replaying times) as more shared fields are present, though Ditto has the lowest absolute values. This result is due to both replayers distinguishing between different fields when serializing events. However, LEAP actually increases its trace file size as the number of fields increases, a result we believe to be caused by their access vector-based approach to recording.

Regarding the number of shared objects, JaRec is the main competitor of Ditto as they are the only ones that can distinguish between distinct objects. LEAP's offline transformation approach does not allow it to take advantage from this runtime information. Although JaRec is marginally better than Ditto past the 64 object mark, it fails to take advantage of the number of shared objects during the replay phase.

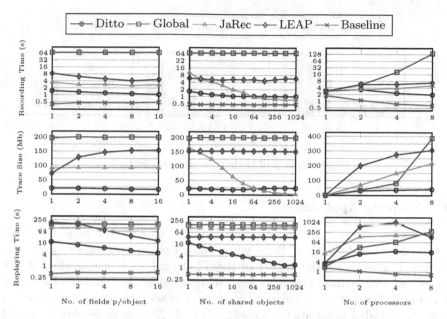

Fig. 5. Recording time, trace size and replaying time as a function of the number of fields per object, shared objects and processors

Concerning the number of processors, the experimental results were obtained by limiting the JikesRVM process to a subset of processors in our 8-core test machine. Ditto is the only algorithm that lowers its record execution time as the number of processors increases, promising increased scalability to future deployments and applications in production environments. Additionally, its trace file size increases much slower than that of other replayers and the replay execution time is three orders of magnitude lower than the second best replayer at the 8 processor mark.

Effects of the Pruning Algorithm: To assess the effects of Ditto's pruning algorithm we modified the microbenchmark to use a more sequential memory access pattern in which each thread accesses a subset of shared objects that overlaps with that of two other threads. Figure 6 shows the trace file size reduction percentage, the recording speedup and the replaying speedup over the base recording algorithm from applying program order pruning only, and program order pruning plus partial transitive reduction. The results clearly demonstrate the potential of the algorithm, reducing the trace by 81.6 to 99.8%. With reductions of this magnitude, instead of seeing increased execution times, we actually observe significant drops in overhead due to the avoided tracing efforts.

Looking at the results of all microbenchmark experiments, it is clear that Ditto is the most well-rounded deterministic replayer. It consistently performs better than its competitors in all three indicators, while other replayers tend to overly sacrifice trace file size or the replay execution time in favor of recording efficiency.

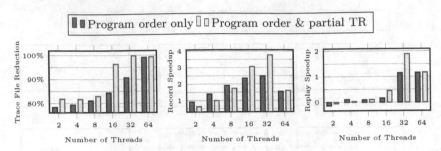

Fig. 6. Effects of Ditto's pruning algorithm

6.2   Complete Applications

In this section we use complete applications to compare the execution time overhead and the log size of Ditto when compared to other state of the art replayers. Furthermore, the impact of the TLO analysis is also evaluated. All applications were parametrized to use 8 threads (i.e. the number of cores of the available hardware). From the the *Java Grande benchmark*[3] we selected the multi-threaded applications, namely: (a) MolDyn, a molecular dynamics simulation; (b) MonteCarlo, a monte carlo simulation; and (c) RayTracer, a 3D ray tracer. Table 1 reports on the results in terms of recording overhead and trace file size. Considering them, two main remarks can be made: Ditto's record-time performance is superior to that of competing replayers, and the trace files generated by Ditto are insignificantly small. The result suggests that the static analysis can be further improved to better identify thread-local memory accesses, which represents a relevant future research topic.

From the *DaCapo*[4] benchmark, we evaluate the record-time performance of Ditto and the other replayers using the lusearch, xalan and avrora applications with the large set. The results are shown in Table 1 and highlight an interesting observation: for applications with very coarse-grained sharing, as is the case of lusearch and xalan, Ditto's higher complexity is actually detrimental. The lack of stress allows the other algorithms to perform better in terms of recording overhead, albeit generating larger trace files (with the exception of JaRec). Nonetheless, Ditto's recording overhead is still quite low.

7   Conclusions and Future Work

We presented Ditto, a deterministic replay system for the JVM, capable of correctly replaying executions of imperfectly synchronized applications on multiprocessors. It uses a novel pair of recording and replaying algorithms that combine state-of-the-art and original techniques, including (a) managing differences between load and store memory accesses, (b) serializing events at instance field

---

[3] http://www.epcc.ed.ac.uk/research/java-grande
[4] http://dacapobench.org

Table 1. Record-time performance results for representative Java workloads

	Ditto		Global		JaRec		LEAP	
	Overhead	Trace	Overhead	Trace	Overhead	Trace	Overhead	Trace
MolDyn	2831%	239Kb	>181596%*	>2Gb*	3887%	188Mb	>13956%*	>2Gb
MonteCarlo	390%	248Kb	79575%	1273Mb	410%	0.39Kb	10188%	336Mb
RayTracer	4729%	4.72Kb	>164877%*	>2Gb*	5197%	21Mb	>9697%*	>2Gb*
lusearch	4.56%	3Kb	1.89%	288 Kb	2.26%	3Kb	0.69%	564Kb
xalan	5.23%	6kb	4.52%	475Kb	2.71%	0.2Kb	2.73%	485Kb
avrora	378%	22Mb	2771%	565Mb	372%	23Mb	–*	>2Gb*

* Current implementation cannot deal with trace files over 2 GB.

granularity, (c) pruning redundant constraints using program order and partial transitive reduction, (d) taking advantage of TLO static analysis, escape analysis and compiler optimizations, and (e) applying a simple but effective trace file optimization. Ditto was successfully evaluated to ascertain its capability to reproduce different concurrent bug patterns and highly non-deterministic executions. Performance results show Ditto consistently outperforming previous Java replayers across multiple application properties, in terms of overhead and trace size, being the most well-rounded system, multicore scalable and leveraging checkpointing and restore capabilities. Evaluation results suggest that future efforts to improve deterministic replay should be focused on improving static analysis to identify thread-local events.

Acknowledgments. This work was partially supported by national funds through FCT – Fundação para a Ciência e a Tecnologia, projects PTDC/EIA-EIA/113613/2009, PTDC/EIA-EIA/102250/2008, PEst-OE/EEI/LA0021/2013 and the PROTEC program of the Polytechnic Institute of Lisbon (IPL)

References

1. Lu, S., Park, S., Seo, E., Zhou, Y.: Learning from mistakes: a comprehensive study on real world concurrency bug characteristics. SIGOPS Oper. Syst. Rev. 42, 329–339 (2008)
2. Choi, J.D., Srinivasan, H.: Deterministic replay of java multithreaded applications. In: Proceedings of the SIGMETRICS Symposium on Parallel and Distributed Tools, SPDT 1998, pp. 48–59. ACM (1998)
3. Ronsse, M., De Bosschere, K.: Recplay: a fully integrated practical record/replay system. ACM Trans. Comput. Syst. 17, 133–152 (1999)
4. Georges, A., Christiaens, M., Ronsse, M., De Bosschere, K.: Jarec: a portable record/replay environment for multi-threaded java applications. Softw. Pract. Exper. 34, 523–547 (2004)
5. Dunlap, G.W., Lucchetti, D.G., Fetterman, M.A., Chen, P.M.: Execution replay of multiprocessor virtual machines. In: Proceedings of the Fourth ACM SIG-PLAN/SIGOPS International Conference on Virtual Execution Environments, VEE 2008, pp. 121–130. ACM (2008)
6. Russinovich, M., Cogswell, B.: Replay for concurrent non-deterministic shared-memory applications. In: Proceedings of the ACM SIGPLAN 1996 Conference on Programming Language Design and Implementation, PLDI 1996, pp. 258–266. ACM (1996)

7. Geels, D., Altekar, G., Shenker, S., Stoica, I.: Replay debugging for distributed applications. In: Proceedings of the Annual Conference on USENIX 2006 Annual Technical Conference, p. 27. USENIX Association (2006)
8. Lamport, L.: Time, clocks, and the ordering of events in a distributed system. Commun. ACM 21, 558–565 (1978)
9. Xu, M., Bodik, R., Hill, M.D.: A "flight data recorder" for enabling full-system multiprocessor deterministic replay. In: Proceedings of the 30th Annual International Symposium on Computer Architecture, ISCA 2003, pp. 122–135. ACM (2003)
10. Montesinos, P., Ceze, L., Torrellas, J.: Delorean: Recording and deterministically replaying shared-memory multiprocessor execution efficiently. In: Proceedings of the 35th Annual International Symposium on Computer Architecture, ISCA 2008, pp. 289–300. IEEE Computer Society (2008)
11. Park, S., Zhou, Y., Xiong, W., Yin, Z., Kaushik, R., Lee, K.H., Lu, S.: Pres: probabilistic replay with execution sketching on multiprocessors. In: Proceedings of the ACM SIGOPS 22nd Symposium on Operating Systems Principles. SOSP 2009, pp. 177–192. ACM (2009)
12. Altekar, G., Stoica, I.: Odr: output-deterministic replay for multicore debugging. In: Proceedings of the ACM SIGOPS 22nd Symposium on Operating Systems Principles, SOSP 2009, pp. 193–206. ACM (2009)
13. Huang, J., Liu, P., Zhang, C.: Leap: lightweight deterministic multi-processor replay of concurrent java programs. In: Proceedings of the Eighteenth ACM SIGSOFT International Symposium on Foundations of Software Engineering,l FSE 2010, pp. 207–216. ACM (2010)
14. Yang, Z., Yang, M., Xu, L., Chen, H., Zang, B.: Order: object centric deterministic replay for java. In: Proceedings of the 2011 USENIX Conference on USENIX Annual Technical Conference, USENIXATC 2011, Berkeley, CA, USA. USENIX Association (2011)
15. Bressoud, T.C., Schneider, F.B.: Hypervisor-based fault tolerance. ACM Trans. Comput. Syst. 14, 80–107 (1996)
16. Napper, J., Alvisi, L., Vin, H.M.: A fault-tolerant java virtual machine. In: DSN, pp. 425–434. IEEE Computer Society (2003)
17. Simão, J., Garrochinho, T., Veiga, L.: A checkpointing-enabled and resource-aware java virtual machine for efficient and robust e-science applications in grid environments. Concurrency and Computation: Practice and Experience 24(13), 1421–1442 (2012)
18. Netzer, R.H.B.: Optimal tracing and replay for debugging shared-memory parallel programs. In: Proceedings of the 1993 ACM/ONR Workshop on Parallel and Distributed Debugging, PADD 1993, pp. 1–11. ACM (1993)
19. Xu, M., Hill, M.D., Bodik, R.: A regulated transitive reduction (rtr) for longer memory race recording. In: Proceedings of the 12th International Conference on Architectural Support for Programming Languages and Operating Systems, ASPLOS-XII, pp. 49–60. ACM (2006)
20. Alpern, B., Attanasio, C.R., Barton, J.J., Burke, M.G., Cheng, P., Choi, J.D., Cocchi, A., Fink, S.J., Grove, D., Hind, M., Hummel, S.F., Lieber, D., Litvinov, V., Mergen, M.F., Ngo, T., Russell, J.R., Sarkar, V., Serrano, M.J., Shepherd, J.C., Smith, S.E., Sreedhar, V.C., Srinivasan, H., Whaley, J.: The jalapeño virtual machine. IBM Syst. J. 39(1), 211–238 (2000)

DynaSoRe: Efficient In-Memory Store
for Social Applications

Xiao Bai[1], Arnaud Jégou[2], Flavio Junqueira[3], and Vincent Leroy[4]

[1] Yahoo! Research Barcelona
xbai@yahoo-inc.com
[2] INRIA Rennes
arnaud.jegou@inria.fr
[3] Microsoft Research Cambridge
fpj@apache.org
[4] University of Grenoble - CNRS
vincent.leroy@imag.fr

Abstract. Social network applications are inherently interactive, creating a requirement for processing user requests fast. To enable fast responses to user requests, social network applications typically rely on large banks of cache servers to hold and serve most of their content from the cache. In this work, we present *DynaSoRe*: a memory cache system for social network applications that optimizes data locality while placing user views across the system. DynaSoRe storage servers monitor access traffic and bring data frequently accessed together closer in the system to reduce the processing load across cache servers and network devices. Our simulation results considering realistic data center topologies show that DynaSoRe is able to adapt to traffic changes, increase data locality, and balance the load across the system. The traffic handled by the top tier of the network connecting servers drops by 94% compared to a static assignment of views to cache servers while requiring only 30% additional memory capacity compared to the whole volume of cached data.

1   Introduction

Social networking is prevalent in current Web applications. Facebook, Twitter, Flickr and Github are successful examples of social networking services that allow users to establish connections with other users and share content, such as status updates (Facebook), micro-blogs (Twitter), pictures (Flickr) and code (Github). Since the type of content produced across application might differ, we use in this work the term *event* to denote any content produced by a user of a social networking application. For this work, the format of events is not important and we consider each event as an application-specific array of bytes.

A common application of social networking consists of returning the latest events produced by the connections of a user in response to a read request. Given the online and interactive nature of such an application, it is critical to respond to user requests fast. Therefore, systems typically use an in-memory

D. Eyers and K. Schwan (Eds.): Middleware 2013, LNCS 8275, pp. 425–444, 2013.

store to maintain events and serve requests to avoid accessing a persistent, often slower backend store. Events can be stored in the in-memory store in the form of materialized views. A view can be producer-pivoted and store the events produced by a given user, or it can be consumer-pivoted and store the events to be consumed by a given user (*e.g.*, the latest events produced by a user's connections) [16]. We only consider *producer-pivoted views* in this work.

When designing systems to serve online social applications, scalability and elasticity are critical properties to cope with a growing user population and an increasing demand of existing users. For example, Facebook has over 1 billion registered and active users. Serving such a large population requires a careful planning for provisioning and analysis of resource utilization. In particular, load imbalance and hotspots in the system may lead to severe performance degradation and a sharp drop of user satisfaction. To avoid load imbalances and hotspots, one viable design choice is to equip the system with a mechanism that enables it to dynamically adapt to changes of the workload.

A common way to achieve load balancing is to randomly place the views of users across the servers of a system. This however incurs high inter-server traffic to serve read requests since the views in a user's social network have to be read from a large amount of servers. SPAR is a seminal work that replicates all the views in a user's social network on the same server to implement highly efficient read operations [15]. Yet, this results in expensive write operations to update the large amount of replicated views. Moreover, SPAR assumes no bounds on the degree of replication for any given view, which is not practical since the memory capacity of each individual server is limited. Consequently, it is very important to make efficient utilization of resources.

In this work, we present *DynaSoRe* (Dynamic Social stoRe), an efficient in-memory store for online social networking applications that dynamically adapts to changes of the workload to keep the network traffic across the system low. We assume that a deployment of DynaSoRe comprises a large number of servers, tens to hundreds, spanning multiple racks in a data center. DynaSoRe servers create replicas of views to increase data locality and reduce communication across different parts of data centers. We assume a realistic tree structure for the networking substrate connecting the servers and aim to reduce traffic at network devices higher up in the network tree.

Our simulation results show that with 30% additional memory (to replicate the views), DynaSoRe reduces the traffic going through the top switch by 94% compared to a random assignment of views and by 90% compared to SPAR. With 100% additional memory, DynaSoRe only incurs 2% of the total traffic with the random assignment, significantly outperforming SPAR which incurs 35% of the traffic with the random assignment.

Contributions. In this paper, we make three main contributions:

- We propose *DynaSoRe*, an efficient in-memory store for online social applications, which dynamically adapts to changes of the workload to keep the network traffic across the system low.

- We provide simulation results showing that DynaSoRe outperforms our baselines, random assignment and SPAR, and that it is able to reduce the amount of network traffic across the system.
- We show that DynaSoRe is especially efficient compared to our baselines when assuming a memory budget, which is an important practical goal due to cost of rack space in modern data centers.

Roadmap. The remainder of this paper is structured as follows. We specify in Section 2 the model and requirements of an efficient in-memory store. We present the design of DynaSoRe in Section 3 and evaluate it in Section 4. We discuss related work in Section 5 and present our conclusions in Section 6.

2   Problem Statement

2.1   System Model

DynaSoRe is a scalable and efficient distributed in-memory store for online social applications that enable users to produce and consume events. We assume that the social network is given and that it changes over time. The events users produce are organized into *views*, and the views are producer-pivoted (contain the events produced by a single user). A view is a list of events, possibly ordered by timestamps. DynaSoRe supports `read` and `write` operations. A `write` request from user u of an event e writes e to the view of u. A `read` request from user u reads the views of all connections in the social network of u. This closely follows the Twitter API. According to Twitter, status feeds represent by far the majority of the queries received[1]. Consequently, the benefits of DynaSoRe (that are only measured with the read/write operations) are significant even in a complete social application that also supports other kinds of operations.

DynaSoRe spans multiple servers, as the views of all users cannot fit into the memory of a single server. Distributing the workload across servers is critical for scalability. Our applications reside in data centers. Servers inside a data center are typically organized in a three-level tree of switches, which has a core tier at the root of the tree, an intermediate tier, and an edge tier at the leaves of the tree [1,7,8] as shown in Figure 1. The core tier consists of the top-level switch (ST), which connects multiple intermediate switches. The intermediate tier consists of intermediate switches (SI) and each of them connects a subset of racks. The edge tier consists of racks and each rack is formed by of a set of servers connected by a rack switch (SR). The network devices, *i.e.*, switches at different levels of the tree architecture, only forward network traffic. The views of users are maintained in the servers (S), connected directly to rack switches. The servers have a bounded memory capacity and we established its capacity by the number of views it can host. We use b to denote the number of bytes we use for a view. Brokers (B) are also servers connecting directly to rack switches and they are in charge of reading and writing views on the different servers of the data center.

---

[1] http://www.infoq.com/presentations/Twitter-Timeline-Scalability

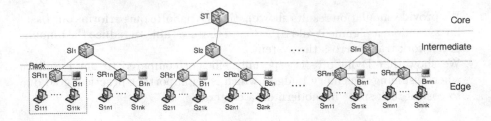

Fig. 1. System architecture of DynaSoRe

Note that DynaSoRe could be deployed on several data centers by adding a virtual switch representing communications between data centers, which would then be minimized by DynaSoRe . In practice, Web companies such as Facebook do not have applications deployed across data centers. Instead, they replicate the content of each data center through a master/slave mechanism[13]. Thus in this work we focus on the case of a single data center.

In the system, events are organized in views and stored as key-value pairs. Each key is a user id and the value is the user view comprising events the user has produced. This memory store is back-ended by a persistent store that ensures data availability in the case of server crashes or graceful shutdowns for maintenance purposes. We focus in this work on the design of the memory store and a detailed discussion of the design of the persistent store is out of scope.

2.2   Requirements

To provide scalable and efficient `write` and `read` operations, DynaSoRe provides the following properties: locality, dynamic replication, and durability.

Locality. A user can efficiently read or write to a view if the network distance between the server executing the operation and the server storing the view is short. As one of our goals is to reduce the overall network traffic, we define the network distance between two servers to be the number of network devices (*e.g.*, switches) in the network path connecting them. DynaSoRe ideally ensures that all the views related to a user (*i.e.*, her own view and the views of her social connections) are placed close to each other according to network distance so that all requests can be executed efficiently. This requires flexibility with respect to selecting the server that executes the requests and the servers storing the views.

Dynamic replication. Online social networks are highly dynamic. The structure of the social network evolves as users add and remove social connections. User traffic can be irregular, with different daily usage patterns and flash events generating a spike of activity. Adapting to the behavior of users requires a mechanism to dynamically react to such changes and adjust the storage policy of the views impacted, for both number and placement of replicas. One goal for DynaSoRe is to trace user activity to enable an efficient utilization of its memory budget through accurate choices for the number and placement of replicas. Such a replication policy needs also to consider load balancing and to satisfy the capacity constraints of each server.

Durability and crash tolerance. We assume that servers can crash. Missing updates because of crashes, however, is highly undesirable, so we guarantee that updates to the system are durable. To do this, we rely upon a persistent store that works independently of DynaSoRe. Updates to the data are persisted before they are written to DynaSoRe to guarantee that they can be recovered in the presence of faulty DynaSoRe servers. Since we replicate some views in our system, copies of data might be readily available even if a server crashes. In the case of a single replica, we need to fetch data from the persistent store to build it. In both cases, single or multiple replicas, crashes additionally require live servers to dynamically adjust the number of replicas of views to the new configuration.

2.3   Problem Formulation

Given the system model and requirements, our objective is to generate an assignment of views to servers such that *(i)* each view is stored on at least one server and *(ii)* network usage is minimized. The first objective guarantees that any user view can be served from the memory store. We eliminate the trivial case in which the cluster does not have the storage capacity to keep a copy of each view. DynaSoRe is free to place views on any server, as long as it satisfies their capacity constraints. Any available space can be used to replicate a view and optimize the second objective. We define the amount of extra memory capacity in the system as follows : Given V the set of views in the system, and b the amount of memory required to store a single view, the system has $x\%$ extra memory if its total memory capacity is $(1 + x/100) \times |V| \times b$. To reduce network traffic, we need to assign views to servers such that it reduces the number of messages flowing across network devices. Note that a message between servers reaching the top switch also traverses two intermediate switches and two rack switches. Consequently, minimizing the number of messages going through the top switch is an important goal to reduce network traffic.

We show in Section 4 that DynaSoRe is able to dynamically adapt to workload variations and to use memory efficiently. In this work, we focus on the mechanisms to distribute user views across servers and on the creation and eviction of their replicas. Although important, fault tolerance is out of the scope of this work and we discuss briefly how one can tolerate crashes in Section 3.3.

3   System Design

In this section, we present the design of DynaSoRe. We first present its API, followed by the algorithm we use to make replication decisions. We end this section with a discussion on some software design issues.

3.1   API

DynaSoRe is an in-memory store used in conjunction with a persistent store. The API of DynaSoRe matches the one used by Facebook for memcache [13]. It consists of a `read` request that fetches data from the in-memory store, and a `write` request that updates the data in the memory store using the persistent store. Consequently, DynaSoRe can be used as a drop-in replacement of memcache to cache user views and generate social feeds.

Read(u, L): u is a user id and L is a list of user ids to read from. For each id u' in L, it returns $view(u')$.

Write(u): u is a user id. It updates $view(u)$ by fetching the new version from the persistent store.

3.2   Algorithm

Overview. DynaSoRe is an iterative algorithm that optimizes view access locality. DynaSoRe monitors view access patterns to compute the placement of views and selects an appropriate broker for executing each request. Specifically, DynaSoRe keeps track, for each view, the rates it is read and written, as well as the location of brokers accessing it. When DynaSoRe detects that a view is frequently accessed from a distant part of the cluster, consuming large amounts of network resources, it creates a replica of this view and places it on a server close to those distant brokers. This improves the locality of future accesses and reduces network utilization. Similarly, when a broker executes a request, DynaSoRe analyzes the placement of the views accessed, and selects the closest broker as a proxy for the next instance of this operation.

Routing. DynaSoRe optimizes view access locality by placing affine views on servers that are close according to network distance, and replicating some of the views on different cluster sub-trees to further improve locality. Using such tailored policies for view placement requires a routing layer to map the identifiers of requested views to the servers storing them.

Brokers. Each request submitted to DynaSoRe is executed by a broker. A request consists of a user identifier and an operation: `read` or `write`. DynaSoRe creates, for each user, a read proxy and a write proxy, each of them being an object deployed on a broker. The motivation of using two different proxies per user stems from the fact that they access different views. The write proxy updates the view of a user, while the read proxy reads the views of a user's social connections. These views may be stored in different parts of the cluster. Allowing DynaSoRe to select different brokers gives it more flexibility and impacts network traffic. The mapping of proxies to brokers is kept in a separate store and is fetched by the front-end as a user logs in. Once a front-end receives a user request, it sends it to the broker hosting the proxy for execution.

Routing policy. When multiple servers store the same view, the routing layer needs to select the most appropriate replica of the view for a given request. The routing policy of DynaSoRe favors locality of access. Following the tree structure of a cluster, a broker selects, among the servers storing a view, the closest one, *i.e.* the one with which it shares the lowest common ancestor. This choice reduces the number of switches traversed. When two replicas are at equal distance, the broker uses the server identifier to break ties.

Routing tables. The write proxy of a user is responsible for updating all the replicas of her view and for storing their locations. Whenever a new replica of the view is created or deleted, the write proxy serves as a synchronization point and updates its list of replicas accordingly.

The read proxy of a user is in charge of routing her read requests. To this end, each broker stores in a routing table, for every view in the system, the location of its closest replica according to the routing policy described earlier. The routing table is shared by all the read proxies executed on a given broker. The write proxy of a view is also responsible for updating the routing tables whenever a view is created or deleted. As the routing policy is deterministic, only brokers affected by the change are notified.

Servers also store some information about routing. Each view stores the location of its write proxy, so that a server may notify a proxy in case of an eviction or replication attempt of its replica. When several replicas of a view exist, each replica also stores the location of the next closest replica. Both information are used to estimate the utility of a view that will be described in Section 3.2.

Proxy placement. To reduce the network traffic, the proxies should be as close as possible to the views they access. Whenever a request is executed, the proxy uses the routing table to obtain the location of the views and execute the operation. As a post-processing step, the proxy analyzes the location of these views and computes a position that minimizes the network transfers. Starting at the root of the cluster tree, the proxy follows, at each step, the branch from which most views were transferred, until it reaches a broker. If the obtained broker is different from the current one, the proxy migrates to the new broker for the next execution of this request. In the case of a write proxy, this migration involves in sending notification messages to view replicas.

Access Statistics. To dynamically improve view access locality, DynaSoRe gathers statistics about the frequency and the origin of each access to a view. This information is stored on the servers, along with the view itself. The origin of an access to a view is the switch from which the request accessing this view comes. Consequently, two brokers directly connected to the same switch correspond to the same origin. The writes to a given view are always executed in the location of its write proxy. However, reads can originate from any broker in the cluster. This explains why their origins should be tracked.

To reduce the memory footprint of access recording, DynaSoRe makes the granularity coarser as the network distance increases. Considering a tree-shaped topology, a server records accesses originating from all the switches located between the server and the top switch, as well as their siblings. For example, in Figure 1 the server S_{111} records the accesses originating from the switches SR_{11} (the accesses from the local broker) to SR_{1n} and from SI_2 to SI_m instead of an individual record for every switch. In this way, in a cluster of m intermediate switches and n rack switches per intermediate switch, every replica records maximum $m - 1 + n$ origins instead of $m \times n$ origins. While significantly reducing the memory footprint, this solution does not affect the efficiency of DynaSoRe. The algorithm still benefits from precise information in the last steps of the convergence, and relies on aggregated statistics over sub-trees for decisions about more distant parts of the cluster.

DynaSoRe is a dynamic algorithm that is able to react to variations in the access patterns over time. We use rotating counters to record the number of accesses to views. Each counter is associated to a time period, and servers start updating the following counter at the end of the period. For example, to record the accesses during one day with a rotating period of one hour, we can use 24 counters of 1 byte. The number of counters, their sizes and their rotating periods can be configured depending on the reactivity we expect from the system, the accuracy of the logs and the amount of memory we can spend on it. It is possible to compress these counters efficiently. For instance, one may decrease the probability of logging an access as the counter increases to account for more accesses on 1 byte. One may also store these counters on the disk of the server to enable asynchronous updates of the counters. These optimizations are out of the scope of this work, and in the remainder of this paper we assume that the size of the counters is negligible with respect to the size of the views.

Storage Management. A DynaSoRe server is a in-memory key-value store implementing a memory management policy. A server has a fixed memory capacity, expressed as the number of views it can store. DynaSoRe manages the servers as a global pool of memory, ensuring that the view of each user is stored on at least one server. Each server stores several views, some of them being the only instance in the system, while others are replicated across multiple servers and therefore optional. The objective of DynaSoRe is to select, for each server, the views that will minimize network utilization, while respecting capacity constraint. We assume that the events generated by users have a fixed size, such as those of Twitter (140 characters). Heavy content (*e.g.*, pictures, videos, etc.) are usually not stored in cache but in dedicated servers.

View utility. Each server maintains read and write access statistics for the views it stores, as described in Section 3.2. Using these statistics, DynaSoRe can evaluate the utility of a view on a given server, *i.e.*, the impact of storing the view on this server in terms of network traffic. DynaSoRe uses the statistics about the origins of read requests to determine which of them are impacted by the view. It then computes the cost of routing them to the next closest replica instead of this server, which represents the read gains of storing the view on the server.

Algorithm 1. Estimate Profit

1: **function** ESTIMATE PROFIT(logs, server, nearest)
2:      serverReadCost ← 0
3:      nearestReadCost ← 0
4:      **for all** < $source, reads$ >∈ logs.reads() **do**
5:          serverReadCost + = reads · COST(source, server)
6:          nearestReadCost + = reads · COST(source, nearest)
7:      serverWriteCost ← writes · COST(broker, server)
8:      serverProfit ← nearestReadCost − serverReadCost − serverWriteCost
9:      **return** serverProfit

The traffic generated by write requests represents the cost of maintaining this view, and is subtracted from the read gains to obtain the utility. The details of the utility computation are presented in Algorithm 1. The utility of a view is positive if its benefits in terms of read requests locality outweighs the cost of updating it when write requests occur. The goal of DynaSoRe is to optimize network utilization. Hence, views with negative utility are automatically removed.

Replication of views. Servers regularly update the utility of the views they store and use this information to maintain an admission threshold so that a sufficient amount (*e.g.,* 90%) of their memory is occupied by views whose utility is above the admission threshold. If less memory is used, the admission threshold is 0. These admission thresholds are disseminated throughout the system using a piggybacking mechanism. Each broker maintains the admission threshold of the servers located in its rack, and transmits the lowest threshold to other racks upon accessing them. Thus, each server receives regular updates containing the lowest access threshold in other racks. A replica of a view on a given server serves either the brokers of the whole cluster, when this is the unique replica, or the brokers of a sub-tree of the cluster, when multiple replicas exist. Upon receiving a request for a view, a server updates its access statistics and evaluates the possibility of replicating it on another server of this sub-tree. This procedure is detailed in Algorithm 2. The utility of the replica is computed by simulating its addition on one of the servers, following the approach described previously. If the utility exceeds the admission threshold of the server, a message is sent to the write proxy of the view to request the creation of a replica.

When no replicas can be created, the server attempts to migrate the view to a more appropriate location. The computation of the utility of the view at the new location is slightly different from the replication case, since it assumes the deletion of the view on the current server and therefore generates higher scores. Algorithm 3 details this procedure. The migration of the view is subject to the admission threshold. Using the admission threshold avoids the migration of views rarely accessed to servers with high replication demand.

Eviction of views. To easily deploy new views on servers, DynaSoRe ensures that each server regularly frees memory. When the memory utilization of a server exceeds a given threshold (*e.g.,* 95%), a background process starts evicting the views that have the least utility. Views that have no other replica in the system have infinite utility and cannot be evicted. Since multiples servers could

---

Algorithm 2. Evaluate Creation of Replica

```
1: procedure EVALUATE CREATION OF REPLICA(logs)
2:     newReplica ← ∅
3:     bestProfit ← 0
4:     for all < source, reads >∈ logs.reads() do
5:         profit ← ESTIMATE PROFIT(logs, source, this)
6:         threshold ← ADMISSION THRESHOLD(source)
7:         if profit > threshold & profit > bestProfit then
8:             newReplica ← LEAST LOADED SERVER(source)
9:             bestProfit ← profit
10:    if newReplica ≠ ∅ then
11:        SEND(newReplica) to broker
```

---

try to evict the different replicas of the same view simultaneously, DynaSoRe relies on the write proxy of the view as a synchronization point to ensure at least one replica remains in the system. Servers typically manage to evict a sufficient amount of views to reach 95% capacity. One exception happens when the full DynaSoRe cluster reaches it maximum capacity, in which case there is no memory left for view replication. This proactive eviction policy decouples the eviction of replicas from the reception of requests, thus ensuring that memory can be freed at any time even when some replicas do not receive any requests.

3.3 Software Design

Durability. DynaSoRe complies with the architecture of Facebook, and relies on the same cache coherence protocol [13]. When a user writes an event, this command is first processed by the persistent store to generate the new version of the view of a user. The persistent store then notifies DynaSoRe by sending a **write** request to the write proxy of the user, which fetches the new version of the view from the persistent store and updates the replicas. The persistent store logs **write** requests before sending them, so they can be re-emitted in case of a crash. If a server crashes, the views can be safely recovered from the persistent store. Also, frequently accessed views are likely to be already replicated in the memory of other servers, allowing faster recovery and avoiding cache misses during the recovery process. We have chosen this design because memory is limited, and replicating frequently accessed views leads to higher performance compared to replicating rarely accessed views for faster recovery. However, if a large amount of memory is available, DynaSoRe can also be configured to keep multiple replicas of each view on different servers. In that case, the threshold for infinite utility is set to the minimum number of replicas and recovery is fully performed from memory. The state of brokers and the location of the proxies of users are persisted in a high performance disk-based write-ahead log such as BookKeeper [10], so that the setup of DynaSoRe is also recoverable.

Cluster Modification. The configuration of the cluster on top of which DynaSoRe is running may change over time. For example, the number of servers allocated to DynaSoRe can grow as the number of users increase. There are three different ways a server can be added to the system:

Algorithm 3. Compute Optimal Position of Replica

```
 1: procedure COMPUTE OPTIMAL POSITION OF REPLICA(logs)
 2:     nearest ← NEAREST REPLICA
 3:     bestPosition ← this
 4:     bestProfit ← ESTIMATE PROFIT(logs, this, nearest)
 5:     for all < source, reads >∈ logs.reads() do
 6:         profit ← ESTIMATE PROFIT(logs, source, nearest)
 7:         threshold ← ADMISSION THRESHOLD(source)
 8:         if profit > bestProfit & profit > threshold then
 9:             bestPosition ← LEAST LOADED SERVER(source)
10:             bestProfit ← profit
11:     if bestProfit < 0 then
12:         SEND(removeThis) to broker
13:     else
14:         if bestPosition ≠ this then
15:             SEND(bestPosition, removeThis) to broker
```

1. The additional server is added into an existing rack. In this case, the new server will become the least loaded server in the rack, and all the new replicas deployed into this rack are stored in this new server until it becomes as loaded as the other servers in the rack.

2. A new rack is added below an existing intermediate switch. The same reasoning for the previous case applies here. The new rack is automatically used to reduce the traffic of the top router.

3. A new branch is added to the cluster by adding a new intermediate switch. In this case, DynaSoRe has no incentive to add data to the new servers since no requests will originate from there. When adding a new branch to the data center, we consequently need to move some views and proxies onto the new servers to bootstrap it. This procedure is, however, not detailed in this paper.

Removing servers on the other hand requires the views hosted by the servers to be relocated. Before removing a server, the views that have no other replica should be moved to a near server. The views that exist on multiple servers can simply be deleted as DynaSoRe will recreate them if needed.

Managing the Social Network. As described earlier, DynaSoRe does not maintain the social network, and instead receives the list of users from which data need to be retrieved when executing a **read** request. Consequently, the only direct impact of a modification to the social network is the modification of the list of views accessed by reads. The addition of a link between users u_1 and u_2 increases the probability to have either u_2's view replicated near u_1's read proxy, or u_1's read proxy migrated closer to a replica of u_2's view. DynaSoRe adapts to the modifications to the social network transparently, without requiring any specific action. When a new user enters the system, DynaSoRe needs to allocate a read proxy, a write proxy, and a view on a server for this user. The server chosen is the least loaded one at the time of the entrance of the user, and the two proxies are selected to be as close as possible to this server.

4   Evaluation

4.1   Baseline

Random In-memory storage systems, such as Memcached and Redis, rely on hash functions to randomly assign data to servers. This configuration is static in the sense that it is not affected by the request traffic. For this scheme, the proxies of a user are deployed on the broker located in the same rack in which the user view is located. This is the simplest baseline we compare against, as it ignores the topology of the data center, the structure of the social graph, and does not leverage free memory through replication.

METIS Graph data can be statically partitioned across servers using graph partitioning. This leverages the clustering properties of social graphs and increases the probability that social friends are assigned to the same sever. We rely on the METIS library to generate partitions, and randomly assign each of them to a server. The read and write proxies of users are deployed on the broker located in the rack hosting their view. This solution does not take into account the hierarchy of the cluster, and does not perform replication. It also does not handle modifications to the social graph, and needs to re-partition the whole social graph to integrate them.

Hierarchical METIS We improve the standard graph partitioning to account for the cluster structure. We first generate one partition for each intermediate switch, and then recursively re-partition them to assign views to rack switches and then servers. Compared to directly partitioning across servers, this solution significantly reduces the network distance of views of social friends assigned to different servers.

SPAR SPAR [15] is a middleware that ensures the views of the social friends of a user are stored on the same server as her own view. SPAR assumes that it is always possible to replicate a view on a server, without taking into account memory limitations. We adapt SPAR to limit its memory utilization. The views of the friends of a user are copied to her server as long as storage is available. When the server is full, these views are not replicated. Similarly to the graph partitioning case, the proxies of a user are located in the rack hosting her view.

4.2   Datasets

Social Graphs. We evaluate the performance of DynaSoRe by comparing it against our baselines on three different social networks (summarized in Table 1):
- a sample from the Twitter social graph from August 2009 [3]
- a sample from the Facebook social graph from 2008 [17]
- a sample from the LiveJournal social graph [2]

Request Log. In this section, we rely on two different kinds of request logs for our experiments, a synthetic one and a real one. The real one is obtained from Yahoo! News. We discuss the logs we used in more details below.

Table 1. Number of users and links in each dataset

	# users	# links
Twitter	1.7M	5M
Facebook	3M	47M
LiveJournal	4.8M	69M

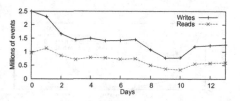

Fig. 2. Number of reads and writes in the Yahoo! News Activity dataset

Synthetic logs. Huberman et al. [9] argue that the read and write activity of users in social networks is proportional to the logarithm of their in and out degrees in the social graphs. Silberstein et al. [16] observe that there are approximately 4 times more reads than writes in a social system. Using this information, we create a random traffic generator matching these distributions and obtain, for each social graph, a request log. We additionally assume that each user issues on average one write request per day and that requests are evenly distributed over time. Compared to real workloads, these synthetic workloads show low variation, which enables DynaSoRe to accurately estimate read and write rates.

Real user traffic. Yahoo! News Activity is a proprietary social platform that allows users to share (**write**) news articles, and view the articles that their Facebook friends read (**read**). We use a two-week sample of the Yahoo! News Activity logs as a source of real user traffic in the experiments. We focus in this experiment on users who performed at least one read and one write during the two weeks. This selection results in a dataset of 2.5M users with 17M writes and 9.8M reads. Figure 2 depicts the distribution of read and write activities per day. Users can consult the activity of their friends both on the Yahoo! website, or on Facebook. In the latter case, the reads are not processed by the Yahoo! website and do not appear in the log, which explains the prevalence of writes in our dataset. Because we do not have access to the Facebook social graph, we map the users of Yahoo! News Activity to the users in the Facebook social graph presented in Section 4.2. We rank both lists of users according to their number of writes and their number of friends, respectively, and connect users with the same rank. Because the Facebook social graph has more users, we only consider the first 2.5 million users according to the number of friends.

4.3   Simulator and Cluster Configuration

We implement a cluster simulator in Java to evaluate the different view management protocols on large clusters. The simulator represents all the servers and network devices in order to simulate their message exchanges and measure them. The virtual data center used in our experiment is composed of a top switch, 5 intermediate switches, each connected to 5 rack switches, for a total of 25 racks containing 10 machines each. In every rack, 1 machine is broker while the 9 others are servers to store views. Servers keep view access logs using a sliding counter of 24 slots shifted every hour. After each shift, the replica utility is recomputed and

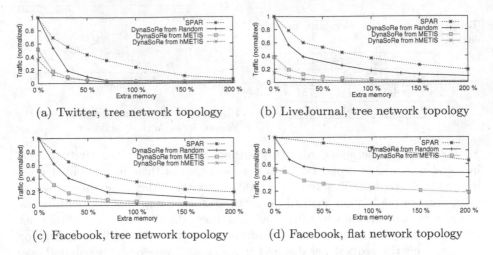

(a) Twitter, tree network topology   (b) LiveJournal, tree network topology

(c) Facebook, tree network topology   (d) Facebook, flat network topology

Fig. 3. Top switch traffic with varying memory capacity

the server's admission threshold is updated. Each server has the same memory capacity, and the total memory capacity is a parameter of each simulator run. Finally, we assume that each application message, *i.e.*, `read`, `write` request and their answer, is 10 times longer than a protocol message. In fact, most protocol messages do not carry any user data and are therefore much smaller.

4.4   Initial Data Placement and Performance

The random placement and graph partitioning approaches produce static assignments of views to servers, which persists during the whole experiment. SPAR places views as the structure of the social network evolves. We first create one replica for each user, and we simulate the addition of all the edges of the social graph to obtain the its view placement. Once the memory of all servers has been used, the view layout remains constant. For DynaSoRe, the system is deployed on an existing social platform and uses this configuration as an initial setup. It then modifies this initial view placement by reacting to the request traffic.

We consider three different view placement strategies when initializing DynaSoRe: Random, METIS and hierarchical METIS (hMETIS). Using the synthetic request log, we evaluate the performance of each system after convergence, *i.e.*, once the content of the servers stabilizes. Figures 3a, 3b and 3c depict the traffic of the top switch for the 3 different social graphs. The traffic is normalized with respect to the traffic of Random. On the x-axis, we vary the extra memory capacity of the cluster. $x = 0\%$ means the capacity matches exactly the space required to store all the views without replication. With $x = 100\%$ memory capacity doubles, so the algorithms can replicate views up to 2 times on average.

Considering the initial data assignment ($x = 0\%$), we can clearly see that graph partitioning approaches (METIS and hMETIS) outperform Random data placement. Furthermore, hierarchical partitioning leads to a two-fold improvement over standard clustering. These results are expected: partitioning increases the probability that views of social friends will be stored on the same rack, which reduces the traffic of the top switch upon accessing them. hMETIS further improves this result by taking into account the hierarchy of the cluster. Thus, when the views of 2 friends are not located on the same rack, they are likely to be communicated through an intermediate switch rather than the top switch.

As we increase the memory capacity, both DynaSoRe and SPAR are able to replicate and move views. Yet, the results indicate that DynaSoRe is much more efficient than SPAR for using the available memory space. For example, in the case of Twitter, with 30% memory in addition to the amount of data stored, SPAR reduces the traffic by 42% compared to a Random, while DynaSoRe reduces it by 80%. These figures also demonstrate the importance of the initial data placement in the case of DynaSoRe. As DynaSoRe relies on heuristics to place views in the cluster, a good initial placement allows it to converge to better overall configurations, while a random placement converges to slightly worse performance. As the amount of available memory further increases, the performance of DynaSoRe converges and part of the memory remains unused. Indeed, DynaSoRe detects that replicating some views does not provide an overall benefit, since the cost of writing to the extra replicas outweighs the benefits of reading them locality, which induces higher network traffic.

Table 2 and Table 3 present the average switch traffic at the top, intermediate, and rack levels for two memory configurations. We normalize the traffic value by the equivalent switch traffic using Random. DynaSoRe is initialized using hMETIS. Note that network traffic drops more significantly for the top switch which is the most loaded with Random. As fewer requests access different racks, rack switches also benefit from DynaSoRe, but to a lesser extent. Comparing absolute values, the traffic of the top switch almost drops to the level of a rack switch. Ultimately, DynaSoRe is able to relax the performance requirements for top and intermediate switches.

Figure 4 shows the traffic on the top switch for the Facebook graph using the real user traffic extracted from Yahoo! News Activity. For space reasons, we only display the performances achieved by SPAR and DynaSoRe starting from the placement generated by Random and METIS with 50% extra memory. The figure shows the evolution of the traffic over time, and we can see that the traffic on the top switch follows the request pattern observed in Figure 2. This figure shows that DynaSoRe is able to converge to an efficient view placement configuration,

Table 2. Switch traffic, 30% extra memory **Table 3.** Switch traffic, 150% extra mem.

	Facebook	Twitter	Live J.		Facebook	Twitter	Live J.
Top switch DynaSoRe	.07	.06	.04	Top switch DynaSoRe	.01	.01	.01
Top switch SPAR	.65	.55	.60	Top switch SPAR	.24	.11	.26
Inter switch DynaSoRe	.14	.11	.08	Inter switch DynaSoRe	.03	.02	.02
Inter switch SPAR	.77	.61	.70	Inter switch SPAR	.39	.13	.37
Rack switch DynaSoRe	.60	.59	.57	Rack switch DynaSoRe	.54	.53	.53
Rack switch SPAR	.94	.84	.90	Rack switch SPAR	.77	.60	.75

even in the case with high variance traffic. DynaSoRe still clearly outperforms the baseline, confirming the results obtained with the synthetic logs. Our results (not shown here for space reasons) show that the performance of DynaSoRe is consistently better (3 times when starting from Random, 9 times when starting from METIS) than Random independently of the traffic variation, confirming the robustness of DynaSoRe under high traffic.

4.5   Behavior in Flat Network Topologies

The results presented above assume a tree topology for the network of the data center. This setup is common in data centers, hence DynaSoRe was specifically tailored for it. For the sake of fairness (as the baselines are designed without considering any network topology of data centers), we also evaluate DynaSoRe on a flat network topology. In this case, all of the 250 servers act as both caches and brokers, and are directly connected to a single switch. This configuration is similar to the one used to evaluate SPAR in [15]. Figure 3d shows that the performances of DynaSoRe and SPAR on the Facebook social graph using the synthetic request logs. Given that DynaSoRe was specifically tailored to tree topologies, the performance gap between DynaSoRe and SPAR is not as large as that presented in Figure 3c. DynaSoRe still clearly outperforms SPAR, in particular in the configurations of low memory, thanks to its better replication policy. In the remainder of the evaluation, we focus on the tree network topology.

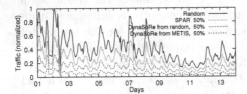

Fig. 4. Top switch traffic with Yahoo! News Activity requests, Facebook

Fig. 5. Flash event: Addition of 100 followers, Facebook, 30% extra memory

4.6   Flash Events

Online social networks are often subject to flash events, in which the activity of a subset of users suddenly spikes. To evaluate the reactivity of DynaSoRe, we simulate a sudden increase of popularity of some users, and measure the evolution of their number of replicas and the number of requests each of them processes. More precisely, at time $t = 2$ days in the simulation run, we randomly select a user and make this user popular by adding 100 random followers to read her view. Five days later ($t = 7$ days) all these additional followers are removed. We repeat this experiment 100 times on the Facebook dataset with a 30% extra memory capacity. We present the average results in Figure 5.

At the beginning of the experiment, the user is not particularly active, and has 1.15 replicas on average. As new followers arrive, DynaSoRe detects that the number of reads of the view increases, and starts replicating it on other servers. DynaSoRe stabilizes in a configuration close to 5 replicas for this view. Given that the users reading this view are selected at random, they originate from all racks of the cluster and DynaSoRe generates a replica per intermediate switch. After replication, the average number of reads per replica is very close to the initial situation. The utility of replicas is high enough to be maintained by the system, but additional replicas do not pass the admission threshold. At the end of this period, the number of reads per replica drops sharply. DynaSoRe is able to detect and adjust the utility of the replicas, which leads to their eviction before the end of the following day. These results illustrate DynaSoRe's ability to react quickly to flash events, and evict replicas once they become useless.

4.7 Convergence Time

SPAR and the three static approaches to assign views only require the social graph to determine the assignment of views. They do not react dynamically to traffic changes, and consequently, they do not require any time to converge as long as the social graph is stable. For DynaSoRe, however, it is important to evaluate the convergence time, using both stable synthetic traffic and real traffic. Before converging to a stable assignment, DynaSoRe replicates views regularly. This traffic of replicas generates messages that also consume network resources. Once the system stabilizes, the overhead of system messages becomes negligible.

Figure 6a shows the traffic of the top switch when running DynaSoRe on the Facebook social graph using synthetic traffic with an extra memory of 150%. We separate the application traffic and the system traffic to study the convergence of DynaSoRe over time (x axis). After a few hours of traffic, DynaSoRe has almost reached its best performance, starting both from a random placement and from a placement based on graph partitioning. The amount of system messages sent by the protocol rapidly drops and reaches its minimum after one day. Note that less memory capacity makes the time to converge shorter, since DynaSoRe performs fewer replication operations. Figure 6b displays the results of the same experiments executed using the real request trace from Yahoo! News Activity. As the workload presents more variation, DynaSoRe does not fully converge, and the system traffic remains at a noticeable level as views are created and evicted. The request rate of the real workload is lower than the synthetic one, which explains the slower convergence: DynaSoRe is driven by requests. Initializing DynaSoRe using graph partitioning, however, induces an initial state that is more stable, allowing the system traffic to remain low. Despite slower convergence, the application traffic still reaches its best performance after one day.

5 Related Work

DynaSoRe enables online data placement in in-memory store for social networking applications. We review in this section related work on in-memory storage systems, offline data placement algorithms, online data placement algorithms, and discuss their differences with DynaSoRe.

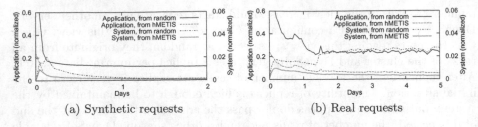

(a) Synthetic requests   (b) Real requests

Fig. 6. Top switch traffic over time, Facebook, 150% extra memory

In-memory Storage. RAMCloud [14] is a large-scale in-memory storage system that aggregates the RAM of hundreds of servers to provide a low-latency key-value store. RAMCloud does not currently implement any data placement policy, and could benefit from the algorithms used in DynaSoRe. RAMCloud recovers from failures using a distributed log accessed in parallel on multiple disks. This is similar to write-ahead logging approach described in Section 3.3 and could be also used in DynaSoRe.

Offline Data Placement. Curino *et al.* describe Schism [4], a partitioning and replication approach for distributed databases to minimize the amount of transactions executed across multiple servers. Schism uses an offline standard graph partitioning algorithms on the request log graph to assign database tuples to servers. DynaSoRe is an online strategy, creating and placing views dynamically. As a consequence, it is much easier to react to changes in access patterns that frequently occur in social applications. DynaSoRe benefits from graph clustering techniques similar to those used in Schism to generate more effective initial placement of views for faster convergence to ideal data placement.

Zhong *et al.* consider the case of object placement for multi-object operations [19]. Using linear programming, they place correlated objects on the same nodes to reduce the communication overhead. However, this solution focuses on correlation and does not take access frequencies into account. It does not account for the hierarchy of network either.

Duong *et al.* analyze the problem of statically sharding social networks to optimize read requests [5]. They demonstrate the benefits of social-network aware data placement strategies, and obtain moderate performance improvements through replication. Nonetheless, these results are limited by the absence of write requests in the cost model. In addition, it only supports static social networks and does not account for network topology.

There are a few graph processing engines [6,12,18] that split graphs over several machines using offline partitioning algorithms. Messages exchanged between partitions are the results of partial computations, which can be further reduced through the use of combiners. While these approaches lead to important gains, they cannot be applied to all kind of requests, and they mostly benefit long computational tasks rather than low latency systems considered in this paper.

Online Data Placement. SPAR [15] is a middleware for online social networking systems that ensures that the server containing the view of a user also contains those of her friends. This favors reads, but sacrifices writes as all the replica of a user's view need to be updated. Similar to DynaSoRe, SPAR uses an online algorithm that reacts to the evolution of the social network. The main differences between SPAR and DynaSoRe stems from the assumption on the storage layer. SPAR assumes that storage is cheap enough to massively replicate views, up to 20 times for 512 servers, largely exceeding fault tolerance requirements. DynaSoRe is much more flexible, and operates at a sweet spot, trading a small storage overhead for high network gains. By default, DynaSoRe does not guarantee that each view is replicated multiple times, and relies on the stable storage to ensure durability. Yet, DynaSoRe can be configured to provide an in-memory replication equivalent to SPAR, as explained in Section 3.3.

Silberstein *et al.* propose to measure users' events production and consumption rates to devise a push-pull model for social feeds generation [16]. The specialized data transfer policy significantly reduces the load of the servers and the network. DynaSoRe is inspired by this work and also relies on the rates of reads and writes of events to decide when to replace views. However, DynaSoRe addresses different problem and focuses on determining where to maintain the views, which will lead to performance gain in addition to this approach.

DynPart [11] is a data partitioning algorithm triggered upon inserting tuples in a database. DynPart analyzes requests matching a tuple and places the tuple on the servers that are accessed when executing these requests. While DynPart handles insertion of data, it never reverts previous decisions and therefore cannot deal with new requests or changes in request frequency. Social networks are frequently modified, leading to different requests, and are subject to unpredictable flash events. For these reasons, DynaSoRe is a better fit for social applications.

6 Conclusion

Adapting to workload variations and incorporating detail of the underlying network architecture are both critical for serving social networking applications efficiently. Typical designs that randomly and statically place views across servers induce a significant amount of load to top tiers of tree-based network layouts. DynaSoRe is an in-memory view storage system that instead adapts to workload variations and uses the network distance between servers to reduce traffic at the top tiers. DynaSoRe analyzes request traffic to optimize view placement and substantially reduces network utilization. DynaSoRe leverages free memory capacity to replicate frequently accessed views close to the brokers reading them. It selects the brokers that serve each request and places them close to the views they fetch according to network distance. In our evaluation of DynaSoRe, we used different social networks and showed that with only 30% additional memory, the traffic of the top switch drops by 94% compared to a static random view placement, and 90% compared to the SPAR protocol.

Acknowledgement. This work was supported by the LEADS project (ICT-318809), funded by the European Community, the Torres Quevedo Program from the Spanish Ministry of Science and Innovation, co-funded by the European Social Fund; and the ERC Starting Grant GOSSPLE number 204742.

References

1. Al-Fares, M., Loukissas, A., Vahdat, A.: A scalable, commodity data center network architecture. In: Proceedings of SIGCOMM, pp. 63–74 (2008)
2. Backstrom, L., Huttenlocher, D., Kleinberg, J., Lan, X.: Group formation in large social networks: membership, growth, and evolution. In: Proceedings of SIGKDD, pp. 44–54 (2006)
3. Cha, M., Haddadi, H., Benevenuto, F., Gummadi, K.P.: Measuring User Influence in Twitter: The Million Follower Fallacy. In: Proceedings of ICWSM (2010)
4. Curino, C., Jones, E., Zhang, Y., Madden, S.: Schism: a workload-driven approach to database replication and partitioning. In: Proceedings of the VLDB Endowment, vol. 3(1-2), pp. 48–57 (2010)
5. Duong, Q., Goel, S., Hofman, J., Vassilvitskii, S.: Sharding social networks. In: Proceedings of WSDM, pp. 223–232 (2013)
6. Gonzalez, J.E., Low, Y., Gu, H., Bickson, D., Guestrin, C.: Powergraph: Distributed graph-parallel computation on natural graphs. In: Proceedings of OSDI (2012)
7. Greenberg, A., Hamilton, J.R., Jain, N., Kandula, S., Kim, C., Lahiri, P., Maltz, D.A., Patel, P., Sengupta, S.: Vl2: a scalable and flexible data center network. In: Proceedings of SIGCOMM, pp. 51–62 (2009)
8. Hoelzle, U., Barroso, L.A.: The Datacenter as a Computer: An Introduction to the Design of Warehouse-Scale Machines. Morgan and Claypool Publishers (2009)
9. Huberman, B.A., Romero, D.M., Wu, F.: Social networks that matter: Twitter under the microscope. First Monday 14(1) (2009)
10. Junqueira, F.P., Kelly, I., Reed, B.: Durability with bookkeeper. ACM SIGOPS Operating Systems Review 47(1), 9–15 (2013)
11. Liroz-Gistau, M., Akbarinia, R., Pacitti, E., Porto, F., Valduriez, P.: Dynamic workload-based partitioning for large-scale databases. In: Liddle, S.W., Schewe, K.-D., Tjoa, A.M., Zhou, X. (eds.) DEXA 2012, Part II. LNCS, vol. 7447, pp. 183–190. Springer, Heidelberg (2012)
12. Malewicz, G., Austern, M.H., Bik, A.J.C., Dehnert, J.C., Horn, I., Leiser, N., Czajkowski, G.: Pregel: a system for large-scale graph processing. In: Proceedings of SIGMOD, pp. 135–146 (2010)
13. Nishtala, R., Fugal, H., Grimm, S., Kwiatkowski, M., Lee, H., Li, H.C., McElroy, R., Paleczny, M., Peek, D., Saab, P., Stafford, D., Tung, T., Venkataramani, V.: Scaling memcache at facebook. In: Proceedings of NSDI, pp. 385–398 (2013)
14. Ongaro, D., Rumble, S.M., Stutsman, R., Ousterhout, J., Rosenblum, M.: Fast crash recovery in ramcloud. In: Proceedings of SOSP, pp. 29–41 (2011)
15. Pujol, J.M., Erramilli, V., Siganos, G., Yang, X., Laoutaris, N., Chhabra, P., Rodriguez, P.: The little engine(s) that could: scaling online social networks. In: Proceedings of SIGCOMM, pp. 375–386 (2010)
16. Silberstein, A., Terrace, J., Cooper, B.F., Ramakrishnan, R.: Feeding frenzy: selectively materializing users' event feeds. In: Proceedings of SIGMOD, pp. 831–842 (2010)
17. Wilson, C., Boe, B., Sala, A., Puttaswamy, K.P., Zhao, B.Y.: User interactions in social networks and their implications. In: Proceedings of Eurosys, pp. 205–218 (2009)
18. Yang, S., Yan, X., Zong, B., Khan, A.: Towards effective partition management for large graphs. In: Proceedings of SIGMOD, pp. 517–528 (2012)
19. Zhong, M., Shen, K., Seiferas, J.: Correlation-aware object placement for multi-object operations. In: Proceedings of ICDCS, pp. 512–521 (2008)

O^2SM: Enabling Efficient Offline Access to Online Social Media and Social Networks

Ye Zhao[1], Ngoc Do[1], Shu-Ting Wang[2], Cheng-Hsin Hsu[2], and Nalini Venkatasubramanian[1]

[1] Department of Information and Computer Science, University of California, Irvine, USA
[2] Department of Computer Science, National Tsing Hua University, Hsin-Chu, Taiwan

Abstract. In this paper, we consider the problem of efficient social media access on mobile devices, and propose an Offline Online Social Media (O^2SM) Middleware to: (i) rank the social media streams based the probability that a given user views a given content item, and (ii) invest the limited resources (network, energy, and storage) on prefetching only those social media streams that are most likely to be watched when mobile devices have good Internet connectivity. The ranking scheme leverages social network information to drive a logistic regression based technique that is subsequently exploited to design an utility based content prefetching mechanism. We implemented O^2SM and a corresponding app, oFacebook, on Android platforms. We evaluated O^2SM via trace data gathered from a user study with real world users executing oFacebook. Our experimental results indicate that O^2SM exhibits superior viewing performance and energy efficiency for mobile social media apps; its lightweight nature makes it easily deployable on mobile platforms.

1 Introduction

The last few years have witnessed the wild success of social networks and social media sites such as Facebook, Twitter, LinkedIn, Google+, and Instagram – communications using these networks have indeed become a part and parcel of our lives today. With the growing popularity of mobile communications, users connect to these social networks using mobile devices (e.g., smartphones, tablets) and expect to derive the same experience no matter how and where they connect. A market study reports that 37% of users accessing rich content, e.g., video, audio, and images, on PCs have switched to mobile devices; moreover, 55% of smartphone users use Facebook on their smartphones [4]. Another survey, done in Canada, shows that 61% of users access Facebook through mobile devices [1]. These market reports indicate that social media streams, carrying rich content, have become key aspects of how people view information and how society interacts today. However, several challenges arise in enabling rich social media on mobile devices including: (i) sporadic network availability causing intermittent access (ii) bandwidth limitations in shared wireless media, and (iii) high access cost from volume driven dataplans – all of the above result in degraded user experience and limit the exchanges of social media information on mobile devices.

A simple approach to cope with intermittent Internet access is to share or download social media streams when possible, as if they were traditional media streams from content providers, such as Netflix and Hulu. However, there are key differences between

D. Eyers and K. Schwan (Eds.): Middleware 2013, LNCS 8275, pp. 445–465, 2013.

social media and traditional media streams that makes best effort downloads have inferior performance in our case:

- **Personalized preferences:** The demands of traditional media streams are dictated by global popularity (e.g., movies, television), whereas access to rich social media streams are driven by user preferences and content characteristics. Therefore, traditional one-size-fits-all, popularity based content ranking mechanisms do not work for social media streams.
- **Dynamic, variable size contents:** Compared to traditional media, social media sharing is exemplified by more dynamic uploads (by users); the average size of content that is shared during an update is also smaller than that of media content providers. For example, it is reported that majority of YouTube videos are shorter than 10 mins, while traditional video servers offer up to 2-hour videos [30].
- **Sporadic viewing situations:** Dynamic uploads by social network users and asynchronous access (by their friends) result in sporadic access patterns, e.g., users checking Facebook updates at a cafeteria line. Unlike media downloads where the item of interest can be pre-specified by the users, users may wish to view newly uploaded content in new situations, including those where mobile Internet access is unavailable, intermittent, or expensive (e.g., on a bus/train).

Today, the social media mobile applications (apps), such as mobile Facebook [2], are simple client side implementations that work as dedicated social media browsers. In the absence of connectivity at the time users wish to use the apps, users do not have access to up-to-date social media content. In this paper, we consider the problem of efficient social media access on mobile devices and develop solutions to make the mobile social media experience seamless, personalized, and effective. We achieve this by: (i) *ranking* the social media streams based the probability that a given user views a given content item, and (ii) investing the limited resources (network, energy, and storage) on *prefetching* only those social media streams that are most likely to be watched when mobile devices have good Internet connectivity.

A comprehensive solution for these two tasks must account for multiple factors including network conditions, content characteristics, device status, and users' social networks. These factors are typically outside the purview of content providers (e.g., current network conditions for a particular user) or the app at the user side (e.g., characteristics of a specific content item). We develop a mobile middleware system that bridges the device OS and network environment to various social networking apps, such as Facebook, Google+, LinkedIn, and Twitter to determine what content to prefetch and when. Such a middleware approach allows us to: (i) reuse key techniques and implementations across multiple devices/users (ii) make better prefetch decisions based on global information, and (iii) control the overhead due to data transfers and environmental sensing. Note that the proposed schemes are designed to work in tandem with user driven navigation of social media content (e.g., through mobile Facebook) and not replace them. In fact, we envision that users can provide feedback on relevance of the content through existing well known frontends (such as mobile Facebook).

The key contributions of this paper are as follows:

- We design a comprehensive *Offline Online Social Media (O^2SM)* middleware to enable accessing social media on mobile devices with intermittent Internet access.

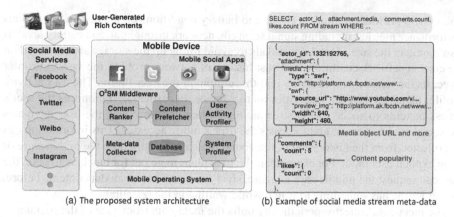

(a) The proposed system architecture   (b) Example of social media stream meta-data

Fig. 1. The proposed system architecture and an example of social media stream metadata

- We develop, implement, and evaluate novel algorithms for content ranking and prefetch planning to optimize the user experience of mobile social apps. The proposed techniques are theoretically grounded using machine learning and optimization based approaches.
- We implement a mobile middleware system and a concrete app, oFacebook (offline Facebook), to automatically prefetch user-generated contents in social media streams to provide mobile users uninterrupted access to social networks.
- We conduct a user study using oFacebook to collect trace data from 10 users, to determine how users access media information on Facebook via mobile devices. We perform extensive trace-driven simulations to evaluate the proposed middleware.

To the best of our knowledge, O^2SM is the first system that enables a systematic, automated approach for viewing relevant and up-to-date social media in an offline manner.

2   System Architecture

Fig. 1(a) presents the architecture of our proposed middleware, O^2SM that bridges the mobile OS and social network apps running on a user's mobile device. O^2SM systematically detects user-generated rich content from the mobile user's social media streams (e.g., fresh photos or videos posted by the user's friends), and intelligently prefetches contents in order to cope with intermittent Internet access. The choice of what to prefetch and when is crucial since the mobile device is limited in resources, such as battery level and storage space - in the social media context, it is imperative that the mobile user's demands and preferences are taken into consideration while selectively downloading content. Furthermore, energy efficient download is also a must in order to achieve good user experience, e.g., overly-aggressive prefetching decisions may drain the device battery , which prevents the user from using his or her phone for necessary daily activities.

The O^2SM middleware consists of five components: (1) *system profiler*, (2) *user activity profiler*, (3) *meta-data collector*, (4) *content ranker*, and (5) *content prefetcher*.

The system profiler monitors network and battery conditions on the device via various performance metrics, including signal strength, network throughput, and battery level. It also monitors the size of total downloads to avoid filling up the storage space. Based on the current network conditions and past history of network profiles, the system profiler forecasts the network connectivity and throughput in the near future. The user activity profiler monitors the user's activities on the device. In particular, it monitors the user's access patterns to social media streams, e.g., when and how long the user navigates the social media streams, and forecasts the user's future accesses. This information can be collected from the history log of the social media apps built atop the middleware or upon explicit user input. For example, if the user plans to go out for lunch in an hour, the user can request the middleware to aggressively prefetch social media contents before, so that he/she has something to watch while waiting in the restaurant.

The meta-data collector periodically pulls the meta-data from each of the social media streams to get updates of new rich contents since the last pull. This is done when the network is available and the remaining battery level is above an operational threshold, which is configurable by the user. The meta-data is usually small in size. Fig. 1(b) shows an example meta-data request and its JSON responses for a media content using Facebook Query Language (FQL) [3]. Our experiments show that the average meta-data size is around 700 bytes per content, and is negligible when compared with the typical data size of 140 KB of a photo or that of 3 MB of a 1.5-minutes video. The collected meta-data is saved onboard the meta-data database for later processing.

To support intelligent content prefetching, the content ranker invoked by the content prefetcher queries the database on fresh content items that have not been downloaded by the system as yet, and predicts the probability the user would view them. The ranking algorithm is based on social relations between entities in the social networks, user interests and content popularity. The ranked contents are fed to the content prefetcher to make decisions on which contents to prefetch and when to prefetch. The crux of this component is a cost-benefit driven prefetch scheduling algorithm which aims to maximize the overall prefetching gain (benefit-cost) by intelligently selecting contents to download and scheduling their download time. This is achieved by carefully taking into account the variations in the sizes of the contents (from content meta-data), their expected probability of being watched (from the content ranker), predicted network conditions such as the network connectivity and bandwidth (from the system profiler), as well as predicted user activity such as when the user will navigate his/her social media streams (from the user activity profiler). Once the contents are scheduled for downloads, they are inserted into a download queue. The downloader downloads the contents in the queue based on their scheduled times.

3   Social Media Content Ranking Component

Given resource constraints at mobile devices, a method to efficiently rank social media contents based on their importance is critical. Prefetching all media contents that accompany heavy multimedia objects, e.g., images or videos, could not only be harmful to user, when he or she is in need of phone battery to survive in daily work, but also waste resources if the downloaded contents are not later viewed by user. This section is dedicated to present the background and our approach to develop a ranking system that works efficiently for mobile devices and scalably against the arrival of new contents.

Background: Traditional ranking systems can be classified into three categories: (1) content based approaches [5, 9, 12], (2) collaborative filtering approaches [7, 20, 27], and (3) social network based approaches [19, 21, 25]. Content based approaches [5, 9, 12] rank media contents using the correlation between the attributes of media content, such as descriptions, keywords, tags, images, and video features (e.g., colors), and user preferences. The basic process here matches up the attributes of the user profile (with preferences,interests), with the attributes of contents. The performance of this category is limited by dictionary-bound relations between the keywords obtained from users and the descriptions of media contents. More comprehensive feature extraction (e.g., image and video analysis) is expensive and hence not supported by most social media.

Collaborative filtering approaches [7, 20, 27] recommend media contents by first calculating the similarity between all users in the system based on their previous ratings of media contents. Ratings are, for example, represented using numeric scores from 1 to 5 and similarity is estimated using heuristic measures, such as the well known cosine function. The system, then, projects a ranking a user is likely to give a piece of recommended content by aggregating the ratings of the user's k nearest neighbors on the content. Collaborative filtering approaches are useful for highly sparse data where the matrix (ratings) is partially missing. Issues for these approaches include *cold start*, i.e., all ratings are missing, and high computation complexity, i.e., a large number of users and contents involves an inference process, that is critical due to limited resources on mobile devices.

The last category ranks social media contents via social networks. Social networks are characterized by heterogeneous entities, e.g., contents, users, and social relations. Recent studies [19, 21, 25] exploit relations among entities to recommend contents. For example, a user is likely to view contents generated by friends, whom the user interacts with frequently over social networks. The approaches in this category fit our system's goals best because they could utilize the underlying social relations captured in our system. However, while the intuitions are appealing, a direct application of the existing techniques to our system is not easy. For example, the work in [19] is based on a social graph to evaluate social relations among entities, and works only for a fixed set of entities. It requires rebuilding the social graph and recalculation of weights when new contents arrive, which happens frequently in our system. Extensions to the collaborative filtering concept [21, 25] by employing relations to estimate similarity have been studied, they suffers from high computation complexity that are unsuitable to mobile deployment.

Our Approach: We inherit the spirit of the social network based recommendation systems [19, 21, 25] to rank social media contents based on social relations and interactions, but targets to work efficiently on mobile devices and be scalable to the arrivals of new contents. Besides, we take user-poster interests and content popularity into account to improve the ranking accuracy. In some sense, user-poster interests and content popularity can be considered as indirect content based features because they capture user preferences and content impacts on viewers. The main design principles for the ranking

Table 1. Representation of user interactions

Interaction Type	Explanations
Post(u, f)	User u writes a post on poster f's Wall page, tags f in a photo, a video or an album of images.
Post(f, u)	Vice versa.
Comment(u, f)	User u comments on a post from f, or on a tag of a photo, a video or an album from f.
Comment(f, u)	Vice versa.
Like(u, f)	User u likes a post uploaded by f, or an image, a video or an album tagged by f, or u likes a comment from f.
Like(f, u)	Vice versa.
Message(u, f)	User u sends a private message to f.
Message(f, u)	Vice versa.

component in our mobile system are *light weight* and *fast provisions of ratings on newly incoming contents.*

Our approach first identifies and constructs social based features that can infer user-content interactions. We then employ a supervised learning approach to predict the probability of a social media content viewed by a user. In this paper, we develop our ranking component to support content ranking on Facebook, but the approach is general enough to be readily applied to other social networks, e.g., Twitter as presented in [13].

We construct the following features to capture the underlying social relations. Let u be a user with a friend f. Table 1 presents key interaction types between u and f.

1. **Post interactions**: This feature captures the interactions between the user and a friend of the user via posts on their social media sites, e.g., Facebook Wall page. It is clear that u is likely more interested in f's posts if interaction between u and f is high. We use the total number of interactions between u and f to quantify this feature. Post interactions include post(u, f), post(f, u), comment(u, f), comment(f, u), like(u, f), and like(f, u) as shown in Table 1. In Facebook, a user can post message on his or her friend's Wall page or tag the friend in a photo. A Twitter user can retweet an interesting message or @reply a tweet from some person the user follows. All of these are considered post interactions. Some social networks, for example Facebook, allow users to subscribe or like a page (e.g., a soccer club like Manchester United or a university like Harvard University). Any updates from the page will be sent to the subscribers similar to those from a friend. For simplicity, we consider a page as a friend of u.

2. **Private message exchange**: Different from post interactions, which may be available in public, private messages are only available to the recipients. We use the total number of messages sent and received between user u and friend f of u to quantify the feature (i.e., message(u, f) and message(f, u) in Table 1). The higher number of exchanged messages, the higher the interaction level between u and f and higher the probability that u views f's posts. In Facebook, users can send and receive private email-like messages l to and from their friends (and even strangers).

Twitter and Weibo users can communicate with each other through direct messages with a limited number of characters.

In addition to the above features, we extract and represent two others features - the level of interest of a user u has to a specific friend f, and the popularity of a post.

1. **User interest w.r.t to a friend**: We measure the interest of u w.r.t to a friend f of u by the number of view clicks to contents posted by f. The higher number of view clicks indicates a higher interest level of u to f.
2. **Post popularity**: A post from friend f,with a high number of comments and likes, is likely interesting because it receives high attention from many viewers. It is therefore likely to be interesting to u even the viewers are not u's friends. We thus employ the number of comments and likes in a post to predict the viewing probability.

In order to predict the probability a content is viewed by a user, we employ a well-known supervised learning algorithm - logistic regression classifier. Logistic regression is an additive model used to predict the probability of a discrete event given a set of explanatory variables. It weights the impact of all constructed features with estimated coefficients. In the literature, the logistic regression has been used for prediction, such as friendship strength prediction [16]. We are the first applying the logistic regression to predict the probability of user-content interactions based on the social networks.

Now we describe how to apply the logistic regression to our content ranking component. The logistic regression in the training process learns a model of the form:

$$p(y_i|x_i) = \frac{1}{1 + e^{-(c_0 + \sum_1^n c_j x_i^j)}}, \tag{1}$$

where x_i is a vector of the features $(x_i^1, ..., x_i^n)$ described above for content i, and y_i is 1 if the user clicks to view content i. Otherwise, y_i is 0. The model is represented by a vector of coefficients c, in which c_0 is not multiplied with any feature and added to the vector as noise. In the training process, the model is learned by maximizing the log-likelihood of the logistic regression model. A well-known approach for the maximization problem is a trust region Newton method [18]. The resulting model is then used to evaluate the viewing probability for a newly arriving media content by simply applying Eq. (1) to the features of the new content. In the evaluation section, we will show that the training process that calculates the model parameters for our ranking component is indeed light weight and fast. This technique is attractive in our setting since the processing of newly arriving contents essentially reduces to that of applying Eq. (1). Furthermore, the simplicity of the scheme lends itself to be easily deployed on mobile devices.

4   Ranking-driven Social Media Prefetching

Prefetching social media contents has received attention at CDNs. [29] considered the problem of efficient geo-replicating contents across multiple data-centers spread around the world. However, little research has been done for prefetching social media contents to mobile clients. Mobile prefetching is an increasingly relevant topic of

---

Algorithm 1. Prefetch Scheduling

Step 1-Read Unviewed Ranked Contents:
read the list of unviewed ranked contents output from the Content Ranking component.
Step 2-K Slot-ahead Forecast:
forecast the network conditions and user context for the next K slots.
Step 3-Offline Online Social Media Prefetch Scheduling (O²SMPS):
formulate an O²SMPS problem using a cost/benefit analysis to decide which contents to
download in each of the next K slots.
Step 4-Contents Download:
sequentially download contents that are scheduled for the current slot.

---

research. Techniques have been developed for determining when to prefetch based on
network conditions such as WiFi and cellular signal strength [10, 26, 28]. Minimizing
energy consumption during prefetching is critical for mobiles - studies [6, 11] indicate
that WiFi is typically more efficient than cellular networks, and techniques to aggregate
multiple data transfers to save energy have been developed. [8, 17] exploit social networks to assist prefetching video prefixes. In general, prefetching has been explored in
client-server and peer-to-peer settings using factors such as energy, transfer volume and
user preferences.

Much of the earlier work focuses on what to prefetch and does not explicitly account for whether the prefetched content is consumed or not. A more comprehensive
prefetching scheme must incorporate *which* items to prefetch for maximum benefit. [31]
observes that users tend to launch a fairly fixed sequence of the apps, and user locations
have a strong correlation with app usage so a decision engine was proposed to determine
which apps to prefetch. In contrast to the above approaches, we propose a comprehensive scheme that exploits the previously described ranking mechanism to determine
what to prefetch and develops a efficient scheduling technique for *when* to prefetch.

The O²SM prefetcher divides time into *prefetching period* or slot (e.g., 15 minutes),
say $T_{prefetch}$, and runs the prefetch scheduling algorithm at the start of every slot. The
algorithm selects a number of contents for download in each prefetching period optimizing for large time-scale prefetching. Algorithm 1 shows the flow of the scheduling
algorithm. The goal of the algorithm is to provide the best viewing experience when
the user navigates his/her social media streams, while keeping the prefetching cost low.
The O²SM prefetcher strives to balance the potential benefit of prefetching against its
cost: Since the prefetching benefit is different for different contents and the prefetching
cost of the same content varies over time when network condition changes, the prefetch
scheduling algorithm determines what to download and when to download by formulating a *Offline Online Social Media Prefetch Scheduling (O²SMPS)* problem. In the
following sections we describe the cost/benefit modeling and the O²SMPS problem in
details, and discuss the forecasting techniques used in our system.

4.1   Cost/Benefit Modeling

Let $I = \{i_1, i_2, \ldots, i_{|I|}\}$ be the list of ranked contents and q_i is the likelihood of
content i will be viewed by the user. We evaluate the cost/benefit of content prefetching

in the next K slots to determine the best prefetching time by forecasting the network conditions and user activity in the future. Let $t = 1, 2, \cdots, K$ be the slotted time for the next K prefetching slots. The system monitors the use of the 3G and WiFi network interfaces for Internet access. Let $p_{wifi}(t)$ be the probability that the device uses the WiFi interface for data transfer at slot t, and $bw_{wifi}(t)$ is the corresponding download bandwidth. Similarly, $p_{cell}(t)$ and $bw_{cell}(t)$ are the probability and bandwidth for the 3G interface at slot t. The system also predicts how likely the user will actively navigate his/her social media streams. Let $p_{nav}(t)$ denote the predicted likelihood that the user may become active at slot t. We discuss the network and user activity profiling and prediction techniques in the Sec. 4.2.

Inspired by [14], we estimate the cost and benefit of prefetching each content along three dimensions: *viewing performance*, *energy use*, and *data plan use*. We consider two costs involved in prefetching: the *energy cost* and the *cellular data plan cost*. The cost for prefetching a content may vary over time when the network conditions change. Formally, we define the estimated cost of prefetching a content i at slot t_{pre} as:

$$C(i, t_{pre}) = w_e \times C_{Energy}(i, t_{pre}) + w_d \times C_{cell}(i, t_{pre}),$$

where w_e and w_d are weighting coefficients for energy and cellular data consumption respectively. The coefficients are configurable to the user. For instance, if the user uses an unlimited cellular data plan so that the cellular data usage is not a concern, then w_d can be set to zero. On the other hand, if the user is discreet about energy use, he may prefer a large value for w_e.

The benefit of prefetching is threefold: the *viewing performance benefit*, the *energy benefit* and the *cellular data plan benefit*. The viewing performance benefit comes from the improved user experience when the user views a prefetched content. The energy and the data plan benefits are the saves in the energy use and data plan use that would be otherwise consumed when the user views the content. Clearly, the benefit depends on: (i) probability of the content to be viewed and (ii) network condition at the time when the user navigates the streams. Formally, we define the estimated benefit to prefetch a content i in case the user navigates his/her social media streams in slot t_{nav} as:

$$B(i, t_{nav}) = B_{view}(i, t_{nav}) + w_e \times B_{energy}(i, t_{nav}) + w_d \times B_{cell}(i, t_{nav}).$$

We next define $B_{energy}(\cdot)$. We adopt the energy models developed by PowerTutor [32]. For downloading a content under WiFi at slot t, the energy cost is modeled as $e_{wifi}(i, t) = c_{wifi} \times \frac{s_i}{bw_{wifi}(t)}$, where c_{wifi} is a power coefficient for WiFi interface. For downloading under 3G, the energy cost is $e_{cell}(i, t) = c_{cell} \times \frac{s_i}{bw_{cell}(t)} + e_{tail}$, where c_{cell} is a power coefficient for 3G and e_{tail} is an estimated 3G tail energy cost. Since contents are prefetched in batches, to estimate the tail energy cost we let $e_{tail} = c_{tail} \times \frac{T_{tail}}{l_{avg}}$ where c_{tail} is the power coefficient for 3G tail energy, T_{tail} is the typical 3G tail time (usually > 10 seconds), and l_{avg} is the history average of the number of contents downloaded in a batch by the prefetcher. To predict the 3G tail energy consumption for on-demand fetches from the user, we let $e_{tail} = c_{tail} \times \min(T_{inactive}, T_{tail})$ where

$T_{inactive}$ is the history average of the idle period between two consecutive content requests from the user. Then, the expected energy to download a content i at slot t is:

$$E(i,t) = \frac{p_{wifi}(t)}{p_{wifi}(t) + p_{cell}(t)} \times e_{wifi}(i,t) + \frac{p_{cell}(t)}{p_{wifi}(t) + p_{cell}(t)} \times e_{cell}(i,t).$$

Since the prefetching energy cost $C_{energy}(i, t_{pre}) = E(i, t_{pre})$, the energy benefit becomes $B_{energy}(i, t_{nav}) = q_i \times E(i, t_{nav})$, which takes the probability of the content to be viewed into consideration.

We define $B_{cell}(\cdot)$ in a similar way. The expected cellular data plan use for downloading a content i at t is:

$$D(i,t) = \frac{p_{cell}(t)}{p_{wifi}(t) + p_{cell}(t)} \times s_i.$$

Therefore, the data plan cost $C_{cell}(i, t_{pre}) = D(i, t_{pre})$ and data plan benefit $B_{cell}(i, t_{nav}) = q_i \times D(i, t_{nav})$.

The viewing performance benefit is considered as the granted feasibility for offline access if the user desires to view a content when he/she doesn't have network access. On the other hand, if the user checks the content when he/she has network access, the benefit is the hidden latency of the on-demand content downloading/buffering. Assume the download bandwidth at the time when the user requests the content is bw, the hidden latency can be formulated as $d(i) = \frac{\min(s_i, s_{max})}{bw}$, where s_{max} is the maximum playback buffer size for videos, or $s_{max} = s_i$ for non-video content. Then, taking into account the viewing probability of the content as well as the predicted network conditions, for any time slot t_{nav} that the user may actively navigate social media contents, the expected viewing performance benefit for prefetching content i is:

$$B_{view}(i, t_{nav}) = p_{wifi}(t_{nav}) \times q_i \times d_{wifi}(i, t_{nav}) + p_{cell}(t_{nav}) \times q_i \times d_{cell}(i, t_{nav})$$
$$+ w_{off} \times (1 - p_{wifi}(t_{nav}) - p_{cell}(t_{nav})) \times q_i,$$

where $d_{wifi}(i, t_{nav})$ and $d_{cell}(i, t_{nav})$ are the predicted hidden latency under WiFi and 3G respectively, and w_{off} is a relative benefit weight of viewing offline to viewing online, that can be customized by the user.

4.2   O²SMPS Problem

The O²SMPS problem maximizes the prefetching gain as the benefit minus cost, by allocating contents for downloads in each of the next K slots. We define a prefetch scheduling matrix, $Z = \{z_{i,k}\}$, where $z_{i,k} \in \{0,1\}$, such that $z_{i,k} = 1$ if download content i at slot k and $z_{i,k} = 0$ otherwise. Furthermore, let $y_i(k)$ be another 0-1 variable that indicates whether a content i *has been* downloaded before slot k. It is easy to see that $y_i(1) = 0$ and $y_i(k) = \sum_{l=1}^{k-1} z_{i,l}$ under the constraint that $\sum_{k=1}^{K} z_{i,k} \leq 1$, i.e., a content can not be scheduled for download more than once.

To be useful, a content must be prefetched before the user checks his/her social media streams. Taking into account $p_{nav}(t)$, i.e., the likelihood that the user may actively navigate social media contents at each of the K slots, we can calculate an *expected prefetch scheduling benefit* for any scheduling $Z = \{z_{i,k}\}$ as:

$$Benefit(Z) = p_{nav}(1) \times \sum_{i=1}^{|I|} (B(i,1) \cdot y_i(1))$$
$$+(1 - p_{nav}(1))p_{nav}(2) \times \sum_{i=1}^{|I|} (B(i,2) \cdot y_i(2))$$
$$+ \cdots + \prod_{k=1}^{K-1} (1 - p_{nav}(k))p_{nav}(K) \times \sum_{i=1}^{|I|} (B(i,K) \cdot y_i(K)),$$

where each term on the right side of the equation specifics the expected prefetching benefit if the next time when the user navigates his/her social media streams is at the kth slot. On the other hand, the *expected prefetch scheduling cost* for the prefetch scheduling Z is:

$$Cost(Z) = \sum_{i=1}^{|I|} \sum_{k=1}^{K} C(i,k) \cdot z_{i,k}.$$

Now we formally define the O^2SMPS problem as:

maximize $Benefit(Z) - Cost(Z)$ (2a)

subject to $\sum_{i=1}^{|I|} s_i \cdot z_{i,k} \leq T_{prefetch} \cdot bw(k)$ $k = 1, \ldots, K$;   (2b)

               $\sum_{k=1}^{K} z_{i,k} \leq 1$ $k = 1, \ldots, K$;   (2c)

               $z_{i,k} \in \{0,1\}$ $i = 1, \ldots, |I|; k = 1, \ldots, K$,   (2d)

where (2b) specifies that the total amount of data can be downloaded in a prefetching slot is constrained by the average download bandwidth in the slot.

The above problem can be reduced to a Generalized Assignment Problem (GAP) [23] that assigns $|I|$ items to K bins and the value of each item varies for different bins it puts in. The problem is known to be NP-hard, and its efficient approximation algorithms has been studied extensively in literature. In this work, we adopt the polynomial-time algorithm by Martello and Toth [22] that provides an approximate solution to the problem under the overall time complexity of $O(K|I|logK + |I|^2)$.

The algorithm has two phases. The first phase tries to provide a reasonably good assignment uses a measure of the *desirability* of assigning content i to slot t, say $g_{i,t}$. It iteratively considers all the unassigned contents, and picks the content with the maximum difference between the largest and second largest $g_{i,t}$ to get assigned first. The intuition is such content is most *critical* since failing to assign it into its best slot will negatively impact the overall performance most. We let $g_{i,t} = \frac{f_{i,t}}{s_i}$, where $f_{i,t}$ is the gain of assigning content i to slot t derived from F, and s_i is the size of the content. So $g_{i,t}$ is a measure of the *unit gain* of the content i in slot t. In the second phase, once all contents have been assigned, the solution is improved through local exchanges. Readers are referred to [22] for the algorithm details.

Forecasting Network Connectivities and User Activity. The prefetcher relies on two predictions for each of the prefetching slots to make scheduling decisions: (a) a network prediction in terms of the connectivity probability distribution vector $\overline{p_{net}}(k) = [p_{wifi}(k), p_{cell}(k), (1 - p_{wifi}(k) - p_{cell}(k))]$ as well as the bandwidth vector $\overline{bw}(k) = [bw_{wifi}(k), bw_{cell}(k), 0]$; and (b) a user activeness prediction as the likelihood $p_{nav}(k)$ that the user might navigate his/her social media streams in the slot.

Because people are creatures of habit, many existing profiling and forecasting techniques (e.g., location-based or time series prediction) can be used by both prediction problems to achieve highly accurate predictions. A notable technique is Bread-Crumbs [24], which is a location-based prediction scheme. It tracks the movement of the mobile device and utilizes a simple Markov model to generate connectivity forecasts. Their evaluation results indicate a very good accuracy. The technique requires the location information either from the device's GPS or techniques like Place Lab [15] where the device has to communicate with a remote server to extract its location information from the information of its current WiFi access point and cellular towers. To mitigate this constraint, we applied a another simple Markov model based technique when the location information is not generally available.

We use a time-dependent Markov model for forecasting. The technique is applied to both network connectivity and user activity forecast. To forecast network connectivity, the states of the Markov model are *WiFi*, *cellular* and *offline*. To forecast user activeness, the states are *active* and *inactive*. The transition matrix depends on the time of the day. Since the prefetch schedule is slotted, say N slots a day, we maintain the same number of transition matrix to capture the probability of a transition from a state at slot t to a state at slot $t + 1$. For each state in the model and time boundary between slots, the prediction component updates the corresponding Markov transition matrix whenever the model is in the state and transitions to another or the time is moved to a new slot. The future predictions can then be made from the trained transition matrix. For example, let $A(k)$ be the transition matrix for transition from slot k to slot $k+1$, given the network connectivity at slot k as $\overline{p_{net}}(k)$, we can approximate the network connectivity $k + 1$ and slot $k + 2$ as $\overline{p_{net}}(k)A(k)$ and $\overline{p_{net}}(k)A(k)A(k + 1)$ respectively. Meanwhile, the average bandwidth vector $\overline{bw}(k)$ can be easily derived for each time slot.

5   System and Application Implementation

As a proof-of-concept, we implemented O^2SM as a userspace Java library targeted at the Android platform. Our initial prototype supports prefetching of social media streams from Facebook. In the future, we will extend the system for Instagram and Twitter streams as well. Fig. 2 depicts the implemented system that includes two layers, the O^2SM middleware and *oFacebook* app.

The middleware layer runs as a service on Android, which contains two main threads, one to collect the meta-data for the social media stream and the other to prefetch media contents. Once the user logs into his/her Facebook account, collection of meta-data from newly uploaded contents is initiated. The prefetching thread implements the utility based prefetch algorithm discussed earlier - in principle, we can plug in alternate

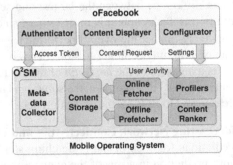

Fig. 2. The proposed system's implementation

prefetch techniques (e.g., prefetch all etc.). The middleware can also fetch media contents on-demand when it receives requests from the oFacebook app.

(a)   (b)   (c)

Fig. 3. Snapshots of the oFacebook app: (a) show a video content, (b) show an album content, and (c) set configuration parameters. App link: http://www.ics.uci.edu/~dsm/oFacebook.

The oFacebook app (see Fig. 3) is implemented on top of the O^2SM middleware. The oFacebook app begins with the user logging into Facebook through its *Authenticator* component. Once the user is logged in and authenticated, the metadata is obtained, content ranked and downloaded, he/she can interact with the downloaded social media stream, e.g., view a photo, watch a video, see comments and likes. Content items are downloaded through the middleware either on-demand or via prefetching. The oFacebook app captures metrics(e.g., user clicks to view) and passes this to the middleware to learn how the user accesses the Facebook content - this will help the improve the ranking process with use. The oFacebook app also provides interfaces to change system settings (network and battery) through its *Configurator* component.

In our implementation, O^2SM stores the prefetched contents in local storage so that they can be accessed later via social media applications. The identifiers of the contents are their original URLs; if the same content is referred by multiple social media streams (e.g., a YouTube video is posted to both the user's Facebook and Twitter account), only one copy is prefetched and stored locally. This is realized by implementing a *get(URL)* API that the SM app calls to access a specific content. If the content has been prefetched, the content data is returned to the SM app; otherwise, the middleware fetches the content using the on-demand fetcher module. All prefetched contents will be purged after a specific period (configurable by user) to save storage - the default value is one week. A *mark(URL)* API allows a user to permanently store a downloaded content, and a *unmark(URL)* API to cancel a previous mark.

6   Performance Evaluations

To gain better understanding of the performance of the proposed system and algorithms, we conducted a trace-driven evaluation. We distributed the oFacebook app to 10 participants located in America, Asia and Europe to run for 10 days from May 15th to 24th,

2013, and collected trace data to drive simulations to test the different algorithms. The users were asked to accept the terms of services agreeing to let us store and send logs for evaluation purposes. To secure the participants' data, we did not log any private content or person such as user names, message content, post descriptions and photo/video URLs. We represent Facebook users by hashed user ids and represent Facebook contents and multimedia objects (i.e. photos and videos) by hashed object ids using an one-way hash-code function to prevent the trace back to the original information. The participants use our system similarly to the standard mobile Facebook app: they install the system through an Android executable file (.apk), login to Facecbook with their Facebook account, and enjoy the downloaded Facebook newsfeed stream through a Facebook-similar navigation GUI. In the measurement version distributed in the user study, the ranker predicts a viewing probability of 1 for all posted content; the prefetching thread simply downloads all media contents - this allows us to measure user-content interaction behavior without bias. Some information collected in the collected log traces is listed:

- *Content*: information on social media contents such as created time, author id, number of likes and comments, multimedia file size. (There are 12,596 contents collected in 10 days for all users. The maximum number of contents for a single user is 3,919 while the minimum number is 130.)
- *user Activity*: the time and content id when users click to view contents. (A single participant clicks 693 times on average to view the downloaded contents. The maximum ratio of the number of views to the number of contents for a single user is 95% while the minimum ratio is 17%.)
- *Friend*: the ids of friends of users. (A single user has 310 friends on average. The maximum number of friends a user has is 503 while the minimum number is 75.)
- *System*: information on the current network (e.g., connected or not, WiFi or cellular networks, signal strength, and etc) and battery (e.g., charging or not, battery level, and etc).

6.1 Integrated System Evaluations

We have implemented a trace driven simulator in Java to drive the evaluation of the proposed system. The simulator implements a time slotted system, and runs simulations for each of the ten users for a simulated time of 10 days using their own trace data. The simulator reads (a) the newsfeed stream trace to generate content items that arrive into the system; (b) the network trace for the network condition at the simulated time; and (c) the user activity trace for the viewing activity at the simulated time. Moreover, the Power-Tutor energy model is implemented in the simulator to evaluate energy consumption for content downloads. The contents derived from the trace data are ranked by the proposed ranking technique. See Section 6.2 for a more detailed evaluation of our ranking scheme.

Since the middleware is intended to support multiple social media applications at the same time, the content/data load is expected to be higher than that from the trace where only one social media source is considered. To gain a better understanding of the performance of each prefetching algorithm under a much higher data load, we have implemented a synthetic stream generator to provide synthetic social media stream input to the simulator. The synthetic stream generator uses a Poisson model to generate social media contents that arrives to the system. Each social media content has a type and size that are drawn randomly from the collected trace data. We consider a parameter r, "video ratio", to control the probability of drawing a video over an image in each synthetic content. Moreover, to emulate the ranking on synthetic contents, the generator assigns a viewing probability to each item using a uniform-random distribution. To emulate actual user viewing behavior on the ranked and downloaded content, we label content as viewed, again, using a uniform random distribution. Consequently, about 50% of the content will be considered as viewed, this yields an accuracy of 75% for the emulated ranker (closely matches results from trace data).

Besides the synthetic stream generator, we also implemented a synthetic network connectivity simulator to produce synthetic network connectivity. The purpose the synthetic simulation is to evaluate the system under different network environments that are not covered by the trace data. The network connectivity simulator is implemented using a Markov model with three states: "WiFi connectivity", "Cellular connectivity" and "no connectivity". State transitions occur every 15 minutes following the specified transition probability. The bandwidth of each state follows a Gaussian distribution, except for the "no connectivity" state whose bandwidth is always zero.

We consider the following performance metrics in our evaluation:

- *energy consumption*: which has 2 aspects: (a) prefetch energy consumption for contents that are prefetched and (b) on-demand fetch energy consumption for contents not prefetched, but requested.
- *prefetch energy per hit*: which is evaluated as the total prefetch energy over the number of prefetched contents being viewed by the user; since not all the prefetched contents are viewed, this metrics serves as an indication of both prefetch accuracy and prefetch energy efficiency.
- *on-demand fetch delay*: which is the downloading delay from on-demand fetching contents if they are not prefetched by the time they are viewed; since this metric aims to examine the latency that the user will experience for viewing unprefetched contents, we also considered the difference for fetching photos and videos in the simulator; For photo fetching, the delay is the latency for downloading the entire content. For video fetching, the delay is the latency for downloading the first 1 MegaByte considered as the playback buffer size.
- *cellular data consumption*: which is the amount of data downloaded through the 3G/4G interface.

We compared our proposed prefetch scheduling algorithm with two baseline approaches. The "Aggressive" scheme periodically reads all feeds that arrive to the system but have not been downloaded, ordered from the newest to oldest, and sequentially downloads them whenever the network is available. The "Aggressive(Rank)" algorithm takes into account the content rank derived from the ranking algorithm. It periodically reads the most recent 100 feeds that have not been downloaded, but only downloads contents whose predicted viewing probability is larger than 50% (i.e. considered more likely to be viewed). Besides the baseline prefetching approaches, we also consider the conventional scenario of social media access where no prefetching is used in order to demonstrate the prefetching benefit.

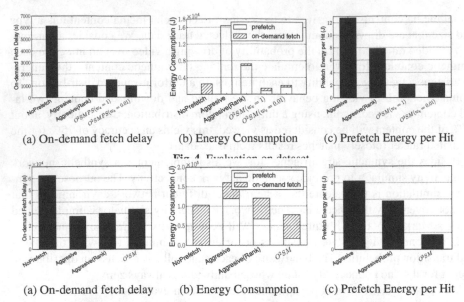

(a) On-demand fetch delay   (b) Energy Consumption   (c) Prefetch Energy per Hit

Fig. 5. Evaluation using synthetic contents where 50% are viewed

Experimental Results. Figure 4 reports the comparative performance of the O^2SM system with baseline schemes under purely trace based evaluations. We make several observations. All prefetching approaches are able to significantly improve a user's viewing experience by reducing the on-demand fetch delay for content viewing (Fig. 4a). The "'Aggressive'" approach improves the user's viewing experience to the most extent, by downloading every content possible. However, its prefetch energy consumption is significantly high (Fig. 4b). On the other hand, by taking into account the viewing prediction from the ranking technique, the "'Aggressive(Rank)'" and O^2SM algorithms provide much better energy efficiency by selectively downloading contents. Comparing the two we can see that while both algorithms provide a similar viewing experience improvement(Fig. 4a), the O^2SM algorithm uses only around 1/4 of the prefetch energy of the "'Aggressive(Rank)'" algorithm (Fig. 4b and Fig.4c) by intelligently scheduling the download when there are good connectivity.

We also evaluated the O^2SM algorithm under different values of the w_e parameter, which indicates the significance of the energy evaluation in the cost/benefit analysis. We can see that with larger w_e, the algorithm is more conservative on prefetching. It achieves less energy use but results in less improved viewing performance because fewer contents are downloaded. One way to take advantage of the effect of the parameter setting is to let the system adaptively adjust the parameter value base on the current battery level. For example, we can adapt w_e to a lower (higher) value when the battery level is high(low)to enable more(less) aggressive prefetching and tradeoff viewing performance for energy conservation. We also tested the impact of the forecast range of network conditions and user activities on the performance of the O^2SM algorithm. We observe that when the forecast range is larger, the algorithm performs marginally better and achieves lower on-demand fetch delay and lower prefetch energy for a useful prefetch.

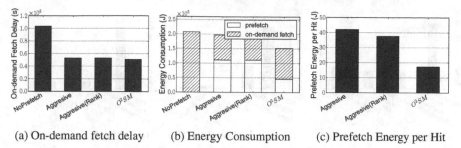

(a) On-demand fetch delay   (b) Energy Consumption   (c) Prefetch Energy per Hit

Fig. 6. Evaluation using synthetic contents where 100% are viewed

To gain a better understanding of the performance of each algorithm under high content/data loads especially when the network resources are not enough to ensure the prefetch of all contents, we evaluated them through synthetic simulation using the synthetic stream generator. The generator injects feeds into the system with Poisson mean rate of 1 feed per 5 minute, and the video ratio is 0.33, i.e. 1/3 of all the feeds generated are video feeds. We still use the trace data for network conditions.

Results in Fig. 5 show that under high content/data load, the "Aggressive" algorithm performs poorly; the high energy cost incurred (Fig. 5b and 6b) does not lead to a better viewing performance (Fig. 5a and 6a). This is because the aggressive scheme wastes network and energy resources on content that will not be viewed. On the other hand, O^2SM exhibits the best energy efficiency of all techniques: it also has the lowest total energy consumption and "prefetch energy per hit". We also evaluated the scenario where all contents will be viewed by the user. In this case, all content must be prefetched, and selective downloads based on rank will not help prefetch performance. The results are shown in Fig. 6. We observe that O^2SM can still improve prefetch energy performance by scheduling contents downloads when the mobile device has good network connectivity.

Since none of the users in our trace data have a 3G/4G data plan, to validate the system under cellular network connectivity we further evaluated the algorithms under synthetic network connectivity generated by the network connectivity simulator. The transition matrix for the network connectivity is randomly created, however, with the probability from any state to "cellular connectivity" larger than 50%. We still used the trace data for contents generated in the simulation. Fig. 7 shows the simulation results using synthetic network connectivity. We observe that by adjusting the w_d parameter, O^2SM adjusts the cellular data plan use to improve prefetch performance, while keeping a low prefetch energy cost.

6.2 Evaluations on the Content Ranker

We evaluate our ranking approach with Facebook data collected from the user study by employing 5-fold cross validation. Here, we randomly partition our data sets into 5 equal size subsets. Among the 5 subsets, 4 are used for training and the last subset is used for testing. This process is repeated 5 times, each time choosing one different set for testing. We report the ranking component's performance with two metrics that are widely used in designing recommendation systems: (i) the Receiver Operator

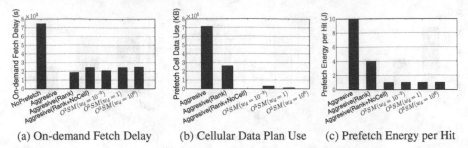

(a) On-demand Fetch Delay   (b) Cellular Data Plan Use   (c) Prefetch Energy per Hit

Fig. 7. Evaluation using synthetic network connectivity

Characteristic (ROC) curve and (ii) the area under the ROC curve (AUC). The ROC curve compares the number of contents that are viewed by user (i.e., positives) and correctly predicted to be viewed (i.e., true) with the number of contents that are not actually viewed (i.e., negatives) but incorrectly predicted (i.e., false). The ROC graph is plotted on two axes where the Y axis depicts true positive rate, which is equal to the number of correctly predicted positives divided by the number of positives, and the X axis shows false positive rate, which is the number of wrongly predicted negatives divided by the number of negatives. Intuitively, points in the upper left in the graph indicate better performance . The second metric, AUC, is a measure for the effectiveness of diagnostic tests; it is interpreted as the expected true positive rate, averaged over all false positive rates. An AUC that is closer to 1 indicates a higher accuracy. AUC is known to be a good metric to indicate accuracy for data set with skewed distributions.

Fig. 8a shows the AUCs for 10 participants. Our ranking component achieves high performance with the average accuracy of 71.7% (ranging from 81% to 62%). A random ranking in which contents are predicted randomly to be viewed or not be viewed (i.e., flip a coin) would yield 50% AUC. In Fig. 8b, we plot the ROC curves for three users 4, 5, and 7, whose AUC is the best, good and worst among the set of the participants respectively, to illustrate further the AUC results. The line of the circles in Fig. 8b represents the random ranking's performance. The ROC curve results for the users are consistent to the AUCs reported in Fig. 8a. For example, it is shown that the curve of user 4 with the highest AUC indeed dominates in Fig. 8b, and is much higher than the random ranking's line.

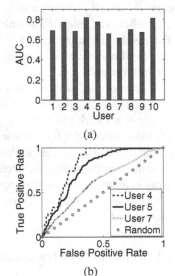

Fig. 8. Evaluations on the content ranker: (a) AUC for all users, (b) the ROC curve for three users

We further show the running time of the training process. Since the whole data set is from our 10-day experiment, the data for the training process includes 8-day contents (we use the 5-fold cross validation). We use a DELL laptop with a dual core 1.8 Ghz CPU and 4 GB RAM running on Windows 7, and employ MATLAB (its logistic regression libraries are glmfit and glmval) to train and extract the learning model. The average running time to come up with a model is only 0.006

seconds while the maximum running time measured is 0.138 seconds. These results indicate that our ranking component is very efficient to mobile devices. Note that we do not need to train the model frequently, but run it once per day with a data set of the most recent 10 days to update the model with the current behaviors of the user.

We argue (and our results indicate) that the integrated system is inherently scalable for the following reasons. Since it is designed as a system that executes primarily on the user device (with little interaction between users for operation), we can scale to an arbitrarily large number of users (limited only by the network and OSN provider). Secondly, the ranking scheme, as illustrated is inherently low-overhead (avg. running time of 0.006 secs) and can scale well both in terms of the social network size and the number of content items that they upload - in general, the ranking overhead is minuscule compared with the download/prefetch overhead for the rich content. Finally, since the purpose of the system is to prefetch for future viewing, the sub-second latency has little to no impact on viewing delay.

7 Concluding Remarks

In this paper, we designed and developed an offline and online social media middleware system that prefetches media contents from online social networks for mobile users who suffers from interruptions from the Internet. Our system is equipped with two main components, media content ranker and prefetcher. Future work includes further research on cross social media networks, i.e., systems support multiple social networks. We also intend to explore the use of in-network resources, e.g., brokers/clouds, for storage and complex content ranking mechanisms. Eventually, the merge of social media/network and mobile computing will enable sharing and access of personalized content from multiple sources. This paper is an enabling step in that direction.

References

1. Canada-new media trend watch long-haul, http://tinyurl.com/bv6p7mp
2. Facebook mobile app., https://www.facebook.com/mobile/
3. F.Q.L., https://developers.facebook.com/docs/reference/fql/
4. Ndp report, http://tinyurl.com/d3xq7dy
5. Ahn, J., Brusilovsky, P., Grady, J., He, D., Syn, S.: Open user profiles for adaptive news systems: Help or harm? In: 16th International Conference on World Wide Web, pp. 11–20 (2007)
6. Balasubramanian, N., Balasubramanian, A., Venkataramani, A.: Energy consumption in mobile phones: a measurement study and implications for network applications. In: 9th Internet Measurement Conference, pp. 280–293 (2009)
7. Cacheda, F., Carneiro, V., Fernandez, D., Formoso, V.: Comparison of collaborative filtering algorithms: Limitations of current techniques and proposals for scalable, high-performance recommender systems. ACM Transactions on the Web 5, 2 (2011)
8. Cheng, X., Liu, J.: Nettube: Exploring social networks for peer-to-peer short video sharing. In: INFOCOM 2009, pp. 1152–1160 (2009)

9. Chu, W., Park, S.: Personalized recommendation on dynamic content using predictive bilinear models. In: 18th International Conference on World Wide Web, pp. 691–700 (2009)
10. Devlic, A., Lungaro, P., Kamaraju, P., Segall, Z., Tollmar, K.: Energy consumption reduction via context-aware mobile video pre-fetching. In: IEEE International Symposium on Multimedia, pp. 261–265 (2012)
11. Gautam, N., Petander, H.,, N.J.: A comparison of the cost and energy efficiency of prefetching and streaming of mobile video. In: 5th Workshop on Mobile Video, pp. 7–12 (2013)
12. Gemmis, M., Lops, P., Semeraro, G., Basile, P.: Integrating tags in a semantic content-based recommender. In: ACM Conference on Recommender Systems, pp. 163–170 (2008)
13. Gilbert, E.: Predicting tie strength in a new medium. In: ACM Conference on Computer Supported Cooperative Work, pp. 1047–1056 (2012)
14. Higgins, B., Flinn, J., Giuli, T., Noble, B., Peplin, C., Watson, D.: Informed mobile prefetching. In: 10th International Conference on Mobile Systems, Applications and Services, pp. 155–168 (2012)
15. LaMarca, A., Chawathe, Y., Consolvo, S., Hightower, J., Smith, I., Scott, J., Sohn, T., Howard, J., Hughes, J., Potter, F.: Place Lab: Device positioning using radio beacons in the wild. In: 3rd International Conference on Perasive Computing, pp. 116–133 (2005)
16. Leskovec, J., Huttenlocher, D., Kleinberg, J.: Predicting positive and negative links in online social networks. In: 19th International Conference on World Wide Web, pp. 641–650 (2012)
17. Li, Z., Shen, H., Wang, H., Liu, G., Li, J.: Socialtube: P2P-assisted video sharing in online social networks. In: INFOCOM 2012, pp. 2886–2890 (2012)
18. Lin, C., Weng, R., Keerthi, R.: Trust region newton method for large-scale logistic regression. The Journal of Machine Learning Research 9, 627–650 (2008)
19. Liu, D., Ye, G., Chen, C., Yan, S., Chang, S.: Hybrid social media network. In: 20th ACM Internatioanl Conference on Multimedia, pp. 659–668 (2012)
20. Ma, H., King, I., Lyu, M.: Effective missing data prediction for collaborative filtering. In: 30th International Conference on Research and Development in Information Retrieval, pp. 39–46 (2007)
21. Ma, H., Zhou, D., Liu, C., Lyu, M.R., King, I.: Recommender systems with social regularization. In: 4th ACM International Conference on Web Search and Data Mining, pp. 287–296 (2011)
22. Martello, S., Toth, P.: An algorithm for the generalized assignment problem. In: Operations Research (1981)
23. Martello, S., Toth, P.: Generalized assignment problems. In: 3rd International Symposium on Algorithms and Computation, pp. 351–369 (1992)
24. Nicholson, A., Noble, B.: BreadCrumbs: Forecasting mobile connectivity. In: 14th International Conference on Mobile Computing and Networking, pp. 46–57 (2008)
25. Noel, J., Sanner, S., Tran, K., Christen, P., Xie, L., Bonilla, E., Abbasnejad, E., Penna, N.: New objective functions for social collaborative filtering. In: 21st International Conference on World Wide Web, pp. 859–868 (2012)
26. Rahmati, A., Zhong, L.: Context-based network estimation for energy-efficient ubiquitous wireless connectivity. IEEE Transaction on Mobile Computing 10, 54–66 (2011)
27. Sarwar, B., Karypis, G., Konstan, J., Riedl, J.: Item-based collaborative filtering recommendation algorithms. In: 10th International Conference on World Wide Web, pp. 285–295 (2001)
28. Schulman, A., Navda, V., Ramjee, R., Spring, N., Deshpande, P., Grunewald, C., Jain, K., Padmanabhan, V.: Bartendr: A practical approach to energy-aware cellular data scheduling. In: 16th International Conference on Mobile Computing and Networking, pp. 85–96 (2010)

29. Traverso, S., Huguenin, K., Trestian, I., Erramilli, V., Laoutaris, N., Papagiannaki, K.: Tail-gate: Handling long-tail content with a little help from friends. In: 21st International Conference on World Wide Web, pp. 151–160 (2012)
30. Xu, C., Dale, C., Liu, J.: Statistics and social networking of youtube videos. In: 16th International Workshop on Quality of Service, pp. 229–238 (2008)
31. Yan, T., Chu, D., Ganesan, D., Kansal, A., Liu, J.: Fast app launching for mobile devices using predictive user context. In: 10th International Conference on Mobile Systems, Applications, and Services, pp. 113–126 (2012)
32. Zhang, L., Tiwana, B., Dick, R., Qian, Z., Mao, Z., Wang, Z., Yang, L.: Accurate online power estimation and automatic battery behavior based power model generation for smartphones. In: IEEE/ACM/IFIP International Conference on Hardware/Software Codesign and System Synthesis, pp. 105–114 (2010)

AnonyLikes: Anonymous Quantitative Feedback on Social Networks

Pedro Alves and Paulo Ferreira

Instituto Superior Técnico - ULisboa / INESC-ID
pedro.h.alves@gmail.com, paulo.ferreira@inesc-id.pt

Abstract. Social network applications (SNAs) can have a tremendous impact in raising awareness to important controversial topics such as religion or politics. Sharing and liking are powerful tools to make some of those topics emerge to a global scale, as already witnessed in the recent Tunisian and Egyptian revolutions.

However, in several countries the simple act of liking an anti-government article or video can be (and has already been) used to pursue and detain activists. Therefore, it is of utmost relevance to allow anyone to anonymously "like" any social network content (e.g. at Facebok) even in presence of malicious administrators managing the social network infrastructure.

We present anonyLikes, a protocol which allows SNAs users to "like" a certain post (e.g., news, photo, video) without revealing their identity (even to the SNA itself) but still make their "like" count to the total number of "likes". This is achieved using cryptographic techniques such as homomorphic encryption and shared threshold key pairs. In addition, the protocol ensures all other desirable properties such as preventing users from "liking" a particular post more than once, while preserving anonymity.

The anonyLikes protocol is fully implemented using Facebook as an example and can be easily used by developers (e.g. Facebook itself or other social network applications and infrastructures) to provide an alternative "like" button called "anonyLike".

1 Introduction

Social network applications (SNAs) have achieved massive popularity in recent years, with Facebook leading the way with its 900 million users[1], but also Twitter and Linkedin both with 200 million each.[2]

These applications allow people all over the world to connect each other at an unprecedented scale. Although these connections are primarily being established to share media and keep in touch with friends, family and colleagues, they are also being used to raise awareness and coordinate large communities around important topics, such as the political status of some countries. For example, Egyptian activist Wael Ghonim credited Facebook with the success of the Egyptian people's uprising, in particular for its key

---

[1] http://www.statisticbrain.com/facebook-statistics/
[2] http://blog.linkedin.com/2013/01/09/linkedin-200-million/,
http://mashable.com/2012/12/18/
twitter-200-million-active-users/

D. Eyers and K. Schwan (Eds.): Middleware 2013, LNCS 8275, pp. 466–484, 2013.

role in organizing the most important protest on January 25th.[3] During the revolution, hundreds of thousands of Egyptians used Facebook to post, like and share news and videos, raising global awareness about what was going on in the country.

However, that didn't prevent Wael Ghonim from being arrested for 12 days, shortly after the protest.[4] Like Wael, many activists suffered from their activities on social networks - Egypt and several other countries have been reported to track down activists on social networks[5] to the point where bloggers died while in custody for their anti-government articles.[6]

We present AnonyLikes, a protocol which allows SNAs users to promote/raise awareness to certain content (news, links, photos or videos which we will refer generically as posts through the rest of the paper) without revealing their identity (even to social networks administrators). Even though social networks typically go to great length to protect the privacy of their users, they still have to abide by the legislation of each country and may be forced to reveal internal data to governmental agencies under a court order.[7] Even if that doesn't happen, there are still (less legal) ways to get access to data, either by employing hackers[8] or by tapping into internal disgruntled employees who have access to the social network database. Even under these potential attacks, AnonyLikes always guarantees the anonymity of the users who have "liked" some content. Our protocol uses cryptographic techniques (see below) to guarantee the privacy of the "like" activity (i.e., the information that an user "liked" a given post) even with access to the SNA's database.

Our interaction model is similar to the one already existent and to which users are accustomed - a "like button", which can be embedded into a blog or news site, associated with a given post along with the number of "likes" already submitted by other users. Note that we will use the term "like" for the rest of the paper as a generic verb to denote an action that increases awareness of a certain post (it could also be "share", "retweet", "reblog", etc.).

Despite similarities with the existing interaction models (in particular, Facebook) AnonyLikes is, in fact, a completely different protocol whereby messages exchanged with the social network server are encrypted in such a way that:

– it is not possible to ascertain which post each user "liked";
– it is possible to know how many people "liked" a certain post.

---

[3] http://www.huffingtonpost.com/2011/02/11/
egypt-facebook-revolution-wael-ghonim_n_822078.html.
[4] http://www.huffingtonpost.com/2011/02/07/
wael-ghonim-google-exec-egypt-protests_n_819438.html
[5] http://readwrite.com/2011/06/15/the_arab_spring_a_status_
report
[6] http://readwrite.com/2011/04/12/bahraini_blogger_dies_in_
custody
[7] http://www.theregister.co.uk/2012/06/11/woman_wins_landmark_
trolling_case_against_facebook/
[8] http://www.guardian.co.uk/media/2013/jan/31/
new-york-times-hacking-china-cybercrime

This is achieved using a combination of homomorphic encryption [23] and shared threshold key pairs: [11]:

- Users can "like" anything from an almost unlimited set of posts, i.e there is no limit to the set of posts a user can "like";
- The period during which users can "like" is unlimited, i.e.there is no closing date after which a post can no longer be "liked".

In summary, the requirements that guide the design of the anonyLikes protocol are the following:

- **R1**: Users should be able to "like" a given post;
- **R2**: Only authenticated users can "like";
- **R3**: It must not be possible for anyone (including the social network infrastructure, e.g., facebook.com) to know a certain user "liked" a particular post;
- **R4**: "Liking" a post must have an effect (even though not immediate) on the number of "likes" (count) of that post and that effect must be visible to everyone;
- **R5**: It must not be possible for someone to "like" a particular post more than once;
- **R6**: The user interaction must be similar to the one already existent in major social network applications such as Facebook and Twitter (in particular, concerning usability and performance).

Note that we cannot guarantee that the social network infrastructure servers (simply referred as SNA-server from now on) don't add fake "likes" to a given post (although this already happens today), i.e., it doesn't artificially increment the "likes" count. However, the SNA-server cannot ignore *true* "likes" without raising suspicion since R4 mandates that the "like" action must have an effect on "likes" count.

In summary, the contributions of this work are:

- A protocol (AnonyLikes) that allows social network users to provide quantitative feedback (e.g., "like" on Facebook) about a certain post without revealing their identity, even to the SNA-server itself. Using this protocol, social networks are still able to calculate the sum of feedback (e.g., the number of people that "liked" a given post on Facebook) while preventing multiple "likes" from the same user.
- A reference implementation of the AnonyLikes protocol for Facebook "likes" that can easily be used by Facebook itself or that can serve as the basis for other social network implementations.

The remainder of this paper is organized as follows. The next section presents the AnonyLikes protocol. After that, we describe the implementation of the prototype. Section 4 presents an evaluation of the protocol regarding three aspects: Usability, Probabilistic Duplicates Detection, and Performance. Finally, Sections 5 and 6, present relevant related work and draw some conclusions, respectively.

2 Protocol

The anonyLikes protocol can be applied to any social network that has the concept of quantitative feedback, i.e., that features an action that increments a number associated

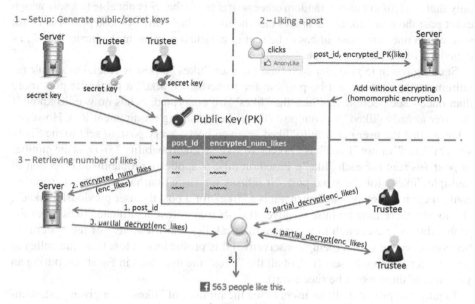

Fig. 1. The 3 steps of the AnonyLikes protocol

with a post. For example, in Facebook and Tumblr, that action is "like", in Twitter is "retweet", etc. The general idea (see Figure 1) is to encrypt the "likes" with a key that is shared among the social network and a set of independent entities (e.g., NGOs) so that none of these entities alone can decrypt it. By using a special property of the encryption algorithm, the SNA-server is able to sum the number of "likes" of a given post without having to decrypt them (i.e., the sum is also encrypted). When the user wants to know how many "likes" are associated with a given post, it coordinates all the entities to jointly decrypt the sum. We now present the details of this protocol.

The anonyLikes assumes a SNA-Server S (e.g., hosted at facebook.com) and a set of Trustees T_i (e.g., public national institutes, NGOs, etc.). Clients exchange encrypted messages with S and communicate with T_i to decrypt such messages (in particular, the number of "likes" of a given post).

There is an initial setup process where a shared threshold key pair is generated across S and all T_i. The generated public key will be published and used to encrypt all the "like" messages. Each entity (S and T_i) stores its part of the private key (also called shadow). To decrypt such messages (or, better said, the result of operations on those messages), a certain number of T_i (depending on the threshold) must collaborate, i.e., S alone is not be able to decrypt them.

After the setup stage, the social network is ready to accept "like" messages. A "like" message is a tuple $(post\_id, like)$, where $post\_id$ is a unique identifier of the post, and $like$ is an integer telling whether the user "liked" that post (value=1) or not (value=0). On each one of these messages, the $like$ value is encrypted with the previously generated public key and the tuple is then sent to S. Note that, since the $post\_id$ is sent in cleartext, the client cannot send only the posts the user "likes"; it has to also send posts the user didn't "like". So, every time a user "likes" a given post, the client sends not only that *post_id* but also n random other *post_ids*, so that S is not able to know which exact post the user "liked". S knows that the user "liked" one of those posts but is not sure which one. The *post_id* has to be sent in cleartext to prevent duplicate "likes", as explained in the next paragraph.

Sending multiple *post_ids* each time the user "likes" a post is crucial to satisfy requirement R5 (it must not be possible for someone to "like" a particular post more than once - see Section 1). Since the "likes" are encrypted, S has no way to know if the user already "liked" a given post (therefore satisfying requirement R3). However, it knows that the user *potentially* "liked" a given post - every *post_id* sent to the SNA-server ("liked" or not "liked") is a potential "like" with probability $1/n$ (n is the number of *post_ids* sent for each "like"). Based on this, S applies a probabilistic detection of multiple "likes" for the same post - it refuses *post_ids* that has already received because there is a high probability that it is a "like" for a post the user previously "liked". Obviously, there may be false positives (i.e., S may refuse legitimate "likes") but the probability is low enough to guarantee the usability and usefulness of the system. In Section 4, we show that (being conservative) this probability is less than one collision per year for Facebook users (i.e., of all the "likes" the user does in Facebook during an year, one of them won't be successful).

Finally, the protocol allows users to see the number of "likes" of a given post, without knowing who did each individual "like". This is possible thanks to the additive homomorphic properties of an ElGamal variant known as exponential ElGamal [9]. In exponential ElGamal, it is possible to add two encrypted messages, without having to decrypt them first, and the decryption of the encrypted sum equals the sum of the decrypted values. S applies this property by adding each encrypted "like" (remember that the "like" value is either 1 or 0) with the already existent encrypted sum of that *post_id* (or zero if it is the first). When a user retrieves the number of "likes" of a given post, it is actually retrieving the encrypted sum associated with that post. The client is responsible for coordinating with the necessary number of Trustees (based on a pre-defined threshold) in order to decrypt that sum using their part of the private key.

2.1 Phases of the Protocol

We now detail the three phases of the protocol (setup, "liking" a post, and retrieving the number of "likes"), starting with a brief summary of the cryptographic building blocks (ElGamal cryptosystem, homomorphic encryption, threshold ElGamal, and zero knowledge proof) which are used by the protocol.

Cryptographic Building Blocks

ElGamal. The anonyLikes protocol relies on the ElGamal cryptosystem [14]. ElGamal works in the $\mathbb{Z}_p^*$ subgroup G_q of order q, where p and q are large primes such that $p = 2q + 1$. A secret key $x \in \mathbb{Z}_q$ is selected and the corresponding public key $y = g^x \mod p$ is computed. A message $m \in G_q$ is encrypted by selecting a random integer value $r \in \mathbb{Z}_q$, and constructing the following pair $(\alpha, \beta) = (g^r \mod p, my^r \mod p)$. Decryption is computed as $m = \alpha^{-x}\beta$.

February 8th, 2013
10:48 AM ET

👍 AnonyLike

563 people like this.

Egypt's corruption woes

By **Sahar Aziz** and **Derek Clinger**, Special to CNN

Editor's note: Sahar Aziz is president of the Egypti
Association and a fellow at the Institute for Socia
Derek Clinger is a Law Clerk at the Egyptian Ame
The views expressed are their own.

Upon taking office, President Mohamed Morsy vow
Egypt. Indeed, corruption was among the first issu

Fig. 2. Example of a post with the associated anonyLike button and the number of (anonymized) people that "liked" that post

Homomorphic Encryption. We say that ϵ is a $(\oplus, \otimes)$-homomorphic encryption scheme if for any instance E of the encryption scheme, given $c_1 = E_{r1}(m_1)$ and $c_2 = E_{r2}(m_2)$, there exists an r such that $c1 \otimes c2 = E_r(m1 \oplus m2)$. This property is crucial in the anony-Likes protocol to calculate the number of "likes" (sum) of a given post without having to decrypt individual "like" messages. The ElGamal cryptosystem satisfies this property for multiplication operations, so we need to use a variant known as exponential ElGamal [9] that satisfies this property for additive operations, i.e. $c1 * c2 = E_r(m1 + m2)$.

Threshold ElGamal. The goal of a threshold scheme for public-key encryption is to share a private key among a set of receivers such that messages can only be decrypted when a substantial set of receivers cooperate [11]. In the anonyLikes protocol, the receivers are called *Trustees*. The main steps of a threshold system are: (i) a *key generation* step to generate the private key jointly by the receivers, and (ii) a *decryption* step to jointly decrypt a ciphertext without explicitly reconstructing the private key. More details about both steps applied to the ElGamal cryptosystem can be found in Cramer[9].

Zero Knowledge Proof of Validity. In the anonyLikes protocol, each "like" message contains a set of tuples $(post\_id, E(like))$, where $like$ can be either 0 or 1. S needs to make sure that $like$ has indeed one of those two values without revealing the exact value. This is accomplished by attaching to each tuple a proof of validity (see Cramer[8] for more details).

Setup. The setup phase occurs only once before the system is made available to the public in general. Its primary goal is to generate a keypair responsible for the encryptions/decryptions that occur in the other phases of the protocol.

S and all T_i create a shared threshold ElGamal key pair $(\epsilon_{pk}, \epsilon_{sk1}, \epsilon_{sk2}, ..., \epsilon_{skn})$. ϵ_{pk} is published on S's site and S and each T_i hold its part of the secret key.

"Liking" a Post. This phase occurs when the user clicks the "AnonyLike" button that is associated with a given post (see Figure 2). All "likes" have to be authenticated, so if the user has not previously authenticated himself on S he will be redirected to do so, prior to submitting the "like" message. We now detail all the steps since the user clicks the "AnonyLike" button until the SNA-server responds with a successful message.

1. User U clicks the AnonyLike button associated with a given post identified by P_{like}, using the client software (e.g., browser).
2. The client software randomly chooses n other posts P_i that: (1) have occurred recently (w.r.t. the age of the post being "liked"); (2) are from the same topic (based on hashtags, labels and words within the post) and (3) are public (i.e., not confined to posts from friends). These three restrictions increase the difficulty for an attacker to guess P_{like} from the several P_i. If it simply chose posts regardless of their age or topic, the attacker could guess that the most recent or relevant P_i would be the one with the "like" (and this would be correct in the vast majority of cases). Also, choosing only posts from friends would hugely reduce the set of posts from which to draw the random ones so we use only public posts (which is usually the case for the political/ideological posts that motivated this article).
3. The client software creates a message M containing the tuple $(P_{like}, E_{\epsilon pk}(1))$ and a set of n tuples $(P_i, E_{\epsilon pk}(0))$, $1 <= i <= n$. This means the software encrypts "1" for the post the user "likes" and "0" for the others. The position of the P_{like} tuple in the message is random (its index is obtained from a random number generator).
4. The client software sends this message to S (remember that U has already been authenticated in S) plus a set of proofs $Proof_i$ (one for each tuple) that will be used to verify that they contain valid "like" values.
5. S uses $Proof_i$ to verify that the "like" value for each post is either 0 or 1 (without having to decrypt it).
6. S updates the vector of *potencial* "likes" of this user $V_u = (P_0, ..., P_n)$. This vector contains all P_i that ever came in a message associated with this user. If any P_i contained in the message already exists in V_u, the SNA-server S returns an error. This is to probabilistically prevent duplicated "likes" from the same user for the same post.
7. S updates its *LikesStats* table $(P_i, E_{\epsilon pk}(\text{num\_likes}))$ for every P_i in the message using the additive property of homomorphic encryption, without having to decrypt the tuples in the message. This table stores the total number of "likes" of every post in the system, encrypted by ϵ_{pk}. M can now be discarded.
8. S responds to the client software with a success message.

Note that, steps 5 and 6 prevent the submission of multiple "likes" for the same post (requirement R5). In addition, step 7 guarantees that the "like" has an effect on the number of "likes" of the associated post while still preventing S from knowing which particular post the user "liked".

Retrieving the Number of "Likes". This phase is responsible for retrieving the number of users that already "liked" a given post, as shown in Figure 2. Usually, this is calculated by the SNA-server but, in anonyLikes, the SNA-server has no way of knowing this number since it is encrypted with a shared key that is distributed among a set of trustees (generated on the previously mentioned setup phase). Therefore, the client software assumes the role of coordinating with the Trustees to decrypt that number.

1. The client software asks S for the number of "likes" of a given post P_i;
2. S searches its *LikesStats* table for P_i and gets the corresponding $E_{\epsilon pk}(\text{num\_likes})$;

3. S partially decrypts the num_likes - $D_{\epsilon sk1}(E_{\epsilon pk}(\text{num\_likes}))$ and returns this to the client;

4. The client software sends $D_{\epsilon sk1}(E_{\epsilon pk}(\text{num\_likes}))$ to several T_i (previously chosen by the user or random) until it is fully decrypted. Supposing we had 2 Trustees (T_1 and T_2), the final decrypted num_likes would be the result of

$$D_{\epsilon sk_{T_2}}(D_{\epsilon sk_{T_1}}(D_{\epsilon sk_{SNA-Server}}(E_{\epsilon pk}(\text{num\_likes}))))$$

5. Finally, the client software shows the user the number of "likes".

3   Implementation

To evaluate the anonyLikes protocol, we developed three components: the SNA-server component, the trustee component and the client component. We used these components to implement a web application that provides an interface showing several random posts from Facebook (10 in the current implementation) along with an anonylikes button and the anonymized number of people that "liked" each one of such posts.

Due to the non-anonymous nature of Facebook, it is not possible to implement this protocol on top of their API.[9] For example, to use the API for submitting a "like", the application has to provide the user who is "liking", therefore preventing any kind of anonymization. Nothe that, using the same (fake) user for all "likes" doesn't work because Facebook prevents more than one "like" from the same user. Our SNA-server component is therefore a simplified replica of Facebook with some adaptations to allow the implementation of the anonyLikes protocol. This component can be the basis for adaptations implemented by Facebook itself, should it decide to use the anonyLikes protocol in the future.

Table 1 shows the responsibilities of each component. Note that the encryption/decryption operations are all performed by the client component. We now look into detail on each of such components.

3.1   SNA-Server Component

The SNA-server component is responsible for: (i) coordinating the distributed generation of the threshold shared key, (ii) receiving encrypted "like" messages, and (iii) providing the encrypted sum of "likes" that will be used to show how many people "liked" a given post. It is implemented as a Python/Django application and its source code is fully available at https://bitbucket.org/anonymousJoe/anonylikes. AnonyLikes reuses some code that was adapted from the Helios system [1] as it provides the implementation of some of the cryptography functions needed (and the code is open-source).[10].

The SNA-server connects to a MySQL database with 3 tables: (i) PublicKey - contains the public key used to encrypt "likes"; (ii) LikesStats - contains tuples ($post\_id$, $encrypted\_num\_likes$), and (iii) PotentialLikesUser - contains all the $post\_ids$ that each user has potentially "liked".

---

[9] http://developers.facebook.com/docs/reference/api/publishing/
[10] Available at https://github.com/benadida/helios-server

Table 1. Responsibilities of each anonyLikes component

Comp.	Responsibilities	Impl.
SNA-Server	Generate public key	Django/
	Coordinate generation of shared secret key	Python
	Store secret key (SNA-server part)	
	Receive encrypted "Likes"	
	Provide encrypted sum of "Likes"	
Trustee	Store secret key (trustee part)	Bottle/
	Provide decrypting factor	Python
Client	Retrieve random posts	Browser/
	Encrypt "likes"	Javascript
	Send encrypted "Likes"	
	Receive encrypted sum of "Likes"	
	Get decryption factors	
	Decrypt sum of "Likes"	

Several actions in the SNA-server must be previously authenticated. We delegate the authentication on Facebook using their OAuth implementation.[11] If the user is not already authenticated in our SNA-server, he is redirected to Facebook where he is asked if he wants to login into AnonyLikes and provide his basic information and email (see Figure 3).

Generation of the Shared Key. The generation of the shared key among all the Trustees is partially executed in the browser and partially executed in the SNA-server. The SNA-server starts by generating the public key and its part of the secret key. Then, each Trustee opens the *Trustee setup* page using a browser to locally generate its part of the secret key. This generation is performed in the browser using a Javascript implementation of the ElGamal cryptosystem. Each Trustee stores locally the generated secret key which is then cleared from the browser's memory. Throughout the whole process, the secret key never leaves the Trustee's computer.

Receiving Encrypted "Likes". The SNA-server provides a REST endpoint to receive encrypted "like" messages. Although programmers can use this endpoint directly, we also provide an embeddable html/javascript that can easily be included on any site to add an "AnonyLike" button (see Figure 2). In this case, all the encryption and communication is automatically handled by the embedded javascript code.

This endpoint verifies that all the encrypted "likes" contained in the message are valid "likes" (i.e., contain the value 0 or 1) using a Zero Knowledge Proof Verification algorithm (already mentioned in the Section 2). Then, for each one, it adds it (using ELGamal homomorphic additive properties) to the existing number of "likes" associ-

---

[11] http://developers.facebook.com/docs/concepts/login/

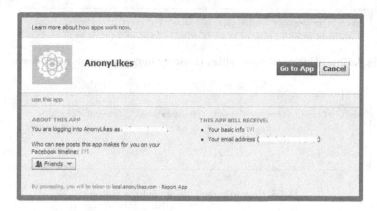

Fig. 3. Users login into AnonyLikes through Facebook

ated with that post using the LikesStats table. Finally, it updates the PotentialLikesUser table with all the *post_ids* contained in the message.

Providing the Encrypted Sum of "Likes". The SNA-server provides a REST endpoint that responds with the number of "likes" of a given post. This is a simple query to the LikesStats table. Since the SNA-server has one part of the shared secret key, it just partially decrypts the number of "likes" before returning it to the client.

3.2 Trustee Component

The trustee component is responsible for storing its part of the shared secret key and, based on that, providing the decryption factor through a REST endpoint. It is implemented as a Bottle server (very lightweight application server that runs Python) that is easily installed on any hosting provider. This component should be installed by each Trustee on a server of his choice. The url of such servers must be made public, so that clients can choose among all the Trustees the ones that will be contacted to get the decryption factor.

3.3 Client Component

The client component is where the encryption/decryption takes place using a Javascript implementation of the ElGamal cryptosystem. Since the Javascript technology is too slow for certain heavy operations such as generating randomness and modular exponentiation, Java is utilized for such computation, using an applet running in the browser.

We now detail two important aspects of the Client component implementation: how to embed the "anonyLike" button, and how to retrieve random posts to go along the *real* post (i.e the one "liked").

Embedding the "Anonylike" Button. The client component consists of a javascript file (anonyLikes.js) and several cryptographic libraries (e.g., elgamal.js). For convenience, programmers only have to import anonyLikes.js as depicted in Figure 4 and all

```
<script data-main="/anonyLikes.js" src="/static/require.js"></script>
```

Fig. 4. How to include the anonylikes javascript library and all its dependencies

```
<div class="anonylike-button" data-post-id="34435556_546456">
    <!-- anonyLikes.js will fill this space with the anonyLikes
         button and the number of people who liked it -->
</div>
```

Fig. 5. How to embed the anonylikes button

the required cryptographic libraries are automatically loaded. Then, programmers have to insert HTML code similar to Figure 5 in the place where they want the "anonyLike" button to show up. anonyLikes.js inserts html code inside that $< div >$ to show the button and the number of people that already "liked" that post. This is very similar to how the original Facebook "like" button is embedded, so it is easy to include anonyLikes on any site.

Retrieving Random Posts. Another important aspect of the Client component implementation is obtaining n random recent posts to go along the "liked" post (recall that the message sent to the SNA-server contains the $post\_id$ the user "liked" plus n random $post\_id$s the user didn't "like"). This operation is performed by the browser using AJAX calls to the Facebook's API. Since Facebook's API only provides a service to search for posts, we get random posts by issuing random queries and getting the first result. This operation (obtaining n random posts) is executed in the background as soon as the page loads to minimize the time spent after clicking the "anonyLike" button (see next section). The user usually clicks the "anonyLike" button after reading/watching the post, which takes sufficient time for the background job to finish retrieving n random posts.

4   Evaluation

In this section, we present the response to the following questions that are crucial to the success of anonyLikes:

– Usability - Can we satisfy requirement R6 (The user interaction must be similar to the one already existent in major social network applications such as facebook and twitter)?
– Duplicates Detection - Does our probabilistic duplicates detection mechanism (necessary for requirement R5) affect the user experience?
– Performance - Is the performance of our prototype adequate to user expectations (requirement R6)?

Table 2. Some statistics on Facebook usage

Total users	1.060 billion
Average daily "likes"	2.7 billion
Average daily "likes" per user	2.5 "likes"
Number of "likes" per year	912 "likes"
Total number of location-tagged posts	17 billion

4.1 Usability

The AnonyLikes behavior is very similar to the original Facebook "like" behavior from the user's perspective. As can be seen in Figure 2, the look of both the button and number of users who already "liked" is very similar to the original one. From the programmer's perspective it is also very similar as programmers only need to import one javascript library (see Figure 4) and define the placeholder where the button will show up (see Figure 5).

So, from a usability point of view, the anonyLikes functionality is as easy as the original Facebook "like" functionality (which is already used by millions).

4.2 Probabilistic Duplicates Detection

The anonyLikes protocol relies on the assumption that it is highly unlikely that a user will "like" one of the random posts that is sent along the "liked" one. This assumption is the basis for duplicate "like" detection: if the user "likes" a post that he has already *potentially* "liked", the SNA-server will not accept that action because it will assume that the user is "liking" the same post twice.

The actual probability of such occurrence is calculated taking into account three variables: M being the total number of posts on Facebook (the universe from which to grab the random posts); n being the number of $post\_ids$ that are sent within each message ($n - 1$ random posts plus the "liked" one), and L being the number of "like" messages the user sends per year. Thus, the probability of getting a collision per year is:

$$Pr_{collision} = \frac{Ln}{M} \tag{1}$$

In Table 2 we show some stats on Facebook.[12] Unfortunately, the total number of posts is not available (only the total number of location-tagged posts) so we will assume 17 billion as the total number of posts which is clearly a conservative assumption, given that many posts are still not location-tagged. We are also making the very conservative assumption the total number of posts is constant per year.

With these numbers, we can now calculate the $Pr_{collision}$ (per year), using $n = 20$:

$$Pr_{collision} = \frac{912 * 20}{17.000.000} = 0,1\% \tag{2}$$

---

[12] http://expandedramblings.com/index.php/
by-the-numbers-17-amazing-facebook-stats/

Table 3. Average time spent on getting random posts from Facebook

Type	n	Avg. Time (s)
Sequential	4	6.5
	6	8.5
	12	18.3
	18	26.9
Parallel	4	2.0
	6	2.0
	12	3.8
	18	5.4

We can see that, even with our very conservative assumptions (we believe that this probability is much lower), the user will have approx. one collision per year (0,1% of 912 posts). We believe that this is an acceptable collision rate; obviously, developers can use higher n values to further decrease the number of collisions, although doing so will also impact the performance of the application as explained in the next section.

4.3 Performance

There are three steps in the anonyLikes protocol that may take long enough to affect the usability: (i) retrieving n random posts; (ii) encrypting the message with the "likes", and (iii) decrypting the number of "likes". Their duration is related to CPU consumption and time spent on network calls. We measured each of these steps.

Retrieving n Random Posts. To retrieve n random posts we issue n AJAX calls to Facebook's search API. We experimented with two different approaches: (i) sequential - we make (synchronously) AJAX calls sequentially, and (ii) parallel - we make all AJAX calls in parallel and wait until all of them finish. Using the Chrome browser connected to the Internet through a regular domestic 6 Mb/s Cable connection (a common scenario), we achieved the results shown in Table 3.

As expected, the parallel approach is much faster as the browser establishes multiple connections with Facebook. However, per the HTTP specification, browsers put a cap on the maximum number of connections to the same host (this cap is browser dependent). In Chrome (the browser that was used for these tests) the cap is 6 connections and that is the reason why the time to get 4 random posts is equal to the time needed to get 6 random posts.

Even if we set n to be 18, and given the fact that we start fetching random posts as soon as a page loads, we find 5.4 seconds to be a reasonable time that doesn't affect the usability because the user will generally take longer to read the page content before clicking the "anonyLike" button.

Encrypting "Like" Messages. To measure the time spent on the ElGamal encryption algorithm, we used both Chrome and Firefox browsers running on a Intel Core i7 Processor (4 cores) at 2.2Ghz (Windows 8). We experimented several values for n

Table 4. Average time spent encrypting the number of "likes" (ms)

Operation	Chrome	Firefox
Encrypt "likes" ($n = 6$)	1366	1324
Encrypt "likes" ($n = 12$)	2742	2461
Encrypt "likes" ($n = 20$)	4584	3968

Table 5. Average time spent on getting and decrypting the number of "likes"

Operation	Avg. time (ms)
Getting encrypted num of "likes" from SNA-server	19
Getting decryption factor from one trustee	79
Decryption in the browser (Javascript)	30
Total (with three trustees)	286

(number of random posts that go along the "liked" post) since this affects directly the encryption time.

We can see in Table 4 that, although the ElGamal encryption is a heavy operation, it consumes an acceptable amount of time. We can also see that Firefox is slightly faster than Chrome but the difference is very small. To improve the user experience, we use a similar technique to what we used for retrieving random posts (see previous subsection): start encrypting the "like" as soon as the page loads so that when the user clicks the button it is (hopefully) already encrypted and the user only has to wait for the SNA-server to respond. If the user takes longer than 10 secs to read the page, it is long enough to *hide* the 5.4 secs retrieving random posts (as shown in previous section) plus 4 secs encrypting; thus, the "like" will have already been encrypted before the user reads the page; otherwise he will have to wait a few seconds (during which a progress dialog is shown).

Decrypting the Number of "Likes". Decrypting the number of "likes" involves three steps: (i) getting the encrypted number of "likes" from the SNA-server; (ii) getting the decryption factors from each trustee; (iii) use the decryption factors to decrypt the number of "likes".

We can see that the time spent is split between network calls and CPU consumption. To measure this operation, we used a Chrome browser running on a Intel Core i7 Processor (4 cores) at 2.2Ghz (Windows 8). We used three Trustees and both the SNA-Server and the Trustees were in the same machine as the browser (localhost). Since we cannot control the real network bandwidth that will be available to anonyLikes clients, we measured this operation on the localhost. This way, we could understand how long the SNA-server takes to respond with the encrypted number of "likes" (step i), and how long each trustee takes to respond with the decryption factor (step ii). Table 5 shows the results. We can see that the whole operation is very fast (almost unnoticeable by the user) with most time spent in getting the decryption factors from each trustee. Obviously, the more trustees needed to decrypt the message, the longer it will take.

We believe that three trustees is a reasonable number of trustees in a real-world scenario (regarding the risk of collusion) but there is nothing in anonyLikes preventing any other number of trustees. We have performed the same performance tests (as above) with five and seven trustees and the whole operation is very fast as well (424 ms and 552 ms, respectively).

5   Related Work

AnonyLikes is motivated by the recent use of SNAs as a vehicle for activism and can be related to previous work done in the area of electronic voting (considering a vote to be similar to a "like"). Therefore, we present related work pertaining both areas.

5.1   Activism and Privacy on Social Networks

The role of social networks during major political transitions such as the ones witnessed in Tunisia, Egypt and Iran have raised interest on the research community in recent years [20,2,24]. For example, the series of uprisings transforming the Arab world (the so-called "Arab Spring") following the Tunisian revolution in January 2011 made extensive use of SNAs coupled with mobile technology enabling citizens to create communities bounded together by a common goal [22]. Also, some studies have shown the impact of SNAs on civic activism (activism not targeted towards a government) such as the Mexican Drug War [21]. These forms of activism all share concerns regarding the privacy of the people involved, since the targeted entity (e.g., government, drug cartel) can repress them by arresting, torturing and even killing.

To prevent these forms of repression, activists have to take special measures to protect themselves. They use pseudonyms instead of real names on their SNA accounts [24]. However, using pseudonyms has several disadvantages: (1) people don't trust pseudonyms as much as real names; (2) pseudonyms can be used by the government to post misleading activist content; (3) given enough history, it is possible to associate pseudonyms with real identities [4].

More experienced users also hide their IP address (which can be used to identify them by their location) when making connections with SNAs using proxy servers or public hotspots [24]. However, this technique relies on technological know-how that the majority of the users don't have. One interesting (and effective) measure taken by the authorities to suppress and obstruct the information flow between local internet activists is to reduce the speed of data transfer on the local ISP (Internet Service Provider) thus increasing the time to upload video materials to Facebook accounts. Activists get around this restriction by sending the material abroad via email in low resolution to be uploaded from there.

The use of pseudonyms raises a fundamental question: "can I trust this person?". For example, Monroy-Hernandez [21] presents the difficulty on asserting the credibility of information as one of the main conclusions of his work on the role of SNAs in Mexican Drug War. One important technique outlined in his work is to test reproducibility - if the same fact is present in posts coming from multiple disparate sources, than it must be true. Based on this, some people have created special well-known Facebook accounts to which everyone can send messages. If a lot of messages contain the same fact, that fact is published on this account.

The anonyLikes protocol is designed to protect the privacy of content "likers" and not so much the content creators. However, it can also help anonymized (through pseudonyms) content creators to get credibility through the amount of quantitative feedback their posts receive. Although not guaranteed, a post "liked" by thousands of users is more credible than a post "liked" by only a few. By protecting the privacy of the "likers", this effect may be more visible on these environments.

5.2 Electronic Voting

Electronic voting has been a research topic for over 25 years [3,7]. Today, there is a consensus on the minimum set of properties that these systems should satisfy [16]:

- **Accuracy**: (1) it is not possible for a vote to be altered, (2) it is not possible for a validated vote to be eliminated from the final tally, and (3) it is not possible for an invalid vote to be counted in the final tally.
- **Democracy**: (1) it allows only eligible voters to vote, and (2) it ensures that eligible voters vote only once.
- **Privacy**: (1) neither authorities nor anyone else can link any ballot to the voter who cast it, and (2) no voter can prove that he voted in a particular way.
- **Verifiability**: anyone can independently verify that all votes been counted correctly.

Note that when compared to our scenario of supporting anonymous "likes" in social networks, there are some relevant differences: i) users can "like" anything from an almost unlimited set of posts while in elections there is a small limited set of candidates from which to choose from, and ii) the period during which users can "like" is unlimited, while in an election there is not a point in time when the election is closed and the number of votes revealed; this is also related to the fact that, while on elections it is not possible to know intermediary results (i.e., to know the current vote count before the voting period ends) in SNAs it is possible (and desirable) to know the current number of "likes" at any time.

Regarding the accuracy property, the anonyLikes protocol cannot ensure that it is not possible to inject fake "likes". However, it ensures that a "like" cannot be transformed into a "non-like" (since what is stored is the number of "likes" and not the individual "like"). AnonyLikes also satisfies the democracy and privacy properties but does not satisfy the verifiability property. However, since users expect to see an immediate increase on the number of "likes" after their action, it would be very difficult to alter (adding or decreasing) the "likes" count without raising suspicions. This derives from the fact that in anonyLikes, the effect of a "like" must be visible to everyone (requirement R4).

Voting protocols can be categorized into three main categories accordingly to their cryptographic primitives: mixnets [5,17], blind signatures [15,16] and homomorphic encryption [3,9].

Mixnets create a robust anonymous channel by having encrypted votes going through a collection of servers whose task is to shuffle them. To ensure that mix-servers do not drop or replace votes, the servers must provide proofs of correct operation. One example of mixnets applied to elections is the scheme proposed by Lee [18] consisting on four steps. First, each voter prepares a first ballot by encrypting his vote. The ballot is then sent to a tamper-resistant randomizer (TRR) for randomization. Second, the TRR randomizes the first ballot with re-encryption to produce a final ballot. Third, the TRR also produces a Designated Verifier Re-encryption Proof (DVRP) to prove the correctness of re-encryption to the voter. The final ballot and the DVRP are then sent to the voter. Finally, the voter checks the DVRP, then signs and submits the final ballot if the check is accepted. A general criticism of mixnets is that the proofs of correction can be complex, cumbersome and inefficient [15].

Blind signatures [6] are a class of digital signatures where a message gets digitally signed without giving any knowledge about the message to the signer. This is similar to putting a document and a sheet of carbon paper in a sealed envelope that somebody signs on the outside. After removing the envelope we get the signed document. Applying this technique to electronic elections, voters obtain a blind signature on their ballot from an administrator which is then submitted to a voting bulletin board. The bulletin board will only accept votes signed by the administrator. This protocol has the advantages of simplicity and low computational cost. The problem is that the submission of votes to the bulletin board must use an anonymous channel which is hard to achieve. Frequently, this anonymous channel is implemented using mixnets but if a mixnet is available a blind signature is not required anymore.

Regarding SNAs, blind signatures have been used to design a privacy-enhanced variant of Twitter, where the content, hashtags and follower interests are encrypted and thus not visible to the Twitter server [10]. However, this mechanism doesn't provide anonymous quantitative feedback (e.g., number of retweets).

In a homomorphic encryption-based [23] voting scheme, votes are added while encrypted, so no individual vote ever needs to be revealed. In order to ensure that the private decryption key of the election is not used to decrypt an individual vote, a threshold encryption scheme must be applied to distribute the key among several authorities in such a way that multiple authorities have to combine their shares in order to use it. Although computationally expensive, this scheme has the big advantage of not requiring an anonymous channel. In fact, voters may openly authenticate themselves to the voting servers. Since the anonyLikes protocol is to be used in large-scale through the Internet channel (increasing the complexity of creating an anonymous channel), we chose homomorphic encryption as the underlying scheme for the anonyLikes protocol.

Homomorphic encryption has already been proposed as privacy-preserving mechanism for SNAs. For example, Domingo-Ferrer [12] proposes a system that uses homomorphic encryption to preserve the privacy of social network relationships when accessing a resource. It has also been used to preserve privacy when finding friends within a certain geographical distance [13] and matching personal profiles [19] among others.

To the best of our knowledge, anonyLikes is the first protocol to apply homomorphic encryption (or any cryptographic technique whatsoever) to quantitative feedback in social networks.

6   Conclusions

Quantitative feedback on SNAs has been shown to have profound impact on several forms of activism, by raising awareness and giving voice to important and sensitive topics in environments that otherwise constrain freedom of speech. Examples of such environments are countries with authoritarian governments and cities controlled by drug cartels. In these environments, people are afraid to use SNAs to promote their causes as they can be subject to retaliations from the targeted entities.

In this paper, we propose anonyLikes, a protocol that enables SNAs users to give quantitative feedback without revealing their identity, even to the social network infrastructure itself. This protocol employs strong cryptographic techniques (homomorphic encryption, shared threshold key pairs) to guarantee the privacy of the users. In particular, what is stored on the SNA-server is not individual "likes" but rather the count of "likes" on any given post. Moreover, that count is encrypted in such a way that several entities (trustees) must collaborate to decrypt it (i.e., it is not possible for a single entity to decrypt it).

We are able to *probabilistically* prevent duplicated "likes" without breaking user's privacy by mixing the real "like" with several fake "likes" (i.e. by sending several post_ids for which the SNA-server doesn't know if they have been "liked" or not). This effectively prevents duplicated "likes" but can wrongly prevent a legitimate "like" although this happens only once per year on average. We believe we have achieved an acceptable tradeoff between privacy and usability.

We have implemented the anonyLikes protocol within a Facebook replica, using an interaction model very similar to Facebook: developers can easily embed an "anony-Like" button next to any content (blog post, video, etc.). The same mechanism also displays the current number of "likes" of that post. This implementation is publicly available and can be used by any SNA developer wishing to support privacy-preserving quantitative feedback.

Finally, we evaluated the performance of the system and found that it can be implemented today without breaking user expectations for this kind of applications. Moreover, since the performance is tied to CPU speed, it will tend to improve in the upcoming years with advances in processor technology.

Acknowledgments. This work was partially supported by national funds through FCT – Fundação para a Ciência e a Tecnologia, under projects Pest-OE/EEI/LA0021/2013 and PTDC/EIA-EIA/113993/2009.

References

1. Adida, B.: Helios: Web-based open-audit voting. In: USENIX Security Symposium, pp. 335–348 (2008)
2. Al-Ani, B., Mark, G., Chung, J., Jones, J.: The Egyptian blogosphere: a counter-narrative of the revolution. In: Proceedings of the ACM 2012 Conference on Computer Supported Cooperative Work (2012)
3. Benaloh, J.: Verifiable secret-ballot elections. PhD thesis, Yale University (1987)
4. Beresford, A., Stajano, F.: Location privacy in pervasive computing. In: IEEE Pervasive Computing (2005)

5. Chaum, D.: Untraceable electronic mail, return addresses, and digital pseudonyms. Communications of the ACM 24(2), 84–90 (1981)
6. Chaum, D.: Blind signatures for untraceable payments. In: Advances in Cryptology: Proceedings of Crypto (1982)
7. Chaum, D.: Elections with unconditionally-secret ballots and disruption equivalent to breaking RSA. In: Günther, C.G. (ed.) EUROCRYPT 1988. LNCS, vol. 330, pp. 177–182. Springer, Heidelberg (1988)
8. Cramer, R., Damgård, I.B., Schoenmakers, B.: Proof of partial knowledge and simplified design of witness hiding protocols. In: Desmedt, Y.G. (ed.) CRYPTO 1994. LNCS, vol. 839, pp. 174–187. Springer, Heidelberg (1994)
9. Cramer, R., Gennaro, R., Schoenmakers, B.: A secure and optimally efficient multi-authority election scheme. European Transactions on Telecommunications 8(5), 481–490 (1997)
10. Cristofaro, E.D., Soriente, C.: Hummingbird: Privacy at the time of twitter. In: 2012 IEEE Symposium on Security and Privacy (SP), vol. 1692, pp. 285–299 (2012)
11. Desmedt, Y.G., Frankel, Y.: Threshold cryptosystems. In: Brassard, G. (ed.) CRYPTO 1989. LNCS, vol. 435, pp. 307–315. Springer, Heidelberg (1990)
12. Domingo-Ferrer, J., Viejo, A., Sebé, F., González-Nicolás, U.: Privacy homomorphisms for social networks with private relationships. Computer Networks 52(15), 3007–3016 (2008)
13. Dong, W., Dave, V., Qiu, L., Zhang, Y.: Secure friend discovery in mobile social networks. In: 2011 Proceedings IEEE INFOCOM, pp. 1647–1655 (April 2011)
14. El Gamal, T.: A public key cryptosystem and a signature scheme based on discrete logarithms. In: Blakely, G.R., Chaum, D. (eds.) CRYPTO 1984. LNCS, vol. 196, pp. 10–18. Springer, Heidelberg (1985)
15. Fujioka, A., Okamoto, T., Ohta, K.: A practical secret voting scheme for large scale elections. In: Zheng, Y., Seberry, J. (eds.) AUSCRYPT 1992. LNCS, vol. 718, pp. 244–251. Springer, Heidelberg (1993)
16. Joaquim, R., Ferreira, P., Ribeiro, C.: EVIV: An end-to-end verifiable Internet voting system. Computers & Security 32, 170–191 (2013)
17. Juels, A., Catalano, D., Jakobsson, M.: Coercion-resistant electronic elections. In: Proceedings of the 2005 ACM Workshop on Privacy in the Electronic Society, pp. 61–70 (2005)
18. Lee, B., Boyd, C., Dawson, E., Kim, K., Yang, J., Yoo, S.: Providing receipt-freeness in mixnet-based voting protocols. In: Lim, J.I., Lee, D.H. (eds.) ICISC 2003. LNCS, vol. 2971, pp. 245–258. Springer, Heidelberg (2004)
19. Li, M., Cao, N., Yu, S., Lou, W.: FindU: Privacy-preserving personal profile matching in mobile social networks. In: 2011 Proceedings IEEE INFOCOM, pp. 2435–2443 (April 2011)
20. Lotan, G., Graeff, E., Ananny, M., Gaffney, D., Pearce, I., Boyd, D.: The Revolutions Were Tweeted: Information Flows During the 2011 Tunisian and Egyptian Revolutions. International Journal of Communication 5, 1375–1406 (2011)
21. Monroy-Hernández, A.: The new war correspondents: he rise of civic media curation in urban warfare. In: Proceedings of the 2013 ACM Conference on Computer Supported Cooperative Work, pp. 1443–1452 (2013)
22. Olaore, O.: Politexting: Using Mobile Technology to Connect the Unconnected and Expanding the Scope of Political Communication. In: Information Systems Educators Conference 2011 ISECON Proceedings, pp. 1–8 (2011)
23. Rivest, R.: On data banks and privacy homomorphisms. Foundations of Secure Computation 4(11) (1978)
24. Wulf, V., Misaki, K., Atam, M.: On the ground' in Sidi Bouzid: investigating social media use during the tunisian revolution. In: Proceedings of the 2013 ACM Conference on Computer Supported Cooperative Work, pp. 1409–1418 (2013)

Peer-to-Peer Keyword Search: A Retrospective

Patrick Reynolds[1] and Amin Vahdat[2]

[1] GitHub, Inc.
[2] University of California, San Diego and Google, Inc.

Abstract. Peer-to-peer systems have been an exciting area of research. Challenges in building them have included scalability, reliability, security, and—of particular interest to these authors—search functionality. This paper surveys some of the history of the field, looks at the lasting impacts of peer-to-peer research, and provides at least one view of where we go from here.

1 Introduction

2001 was an exciting time for research on peer-to-peer systems. Napster [38] had recently been shut down for abetting widespread copyright violation [18]. Gnutella [41] and Freenet [9,10] survived but used completely unstructured overlays that compromised performance and search completeness. Other peer-to-peer systems reused Napster's ideas or Gnutella's protocol, and these too were eventually shut down [25,34,35,55]. Peer-to-peer systems needed both better protocol design and applications other than file sharing.

Chord [46], CAN [39], Pastry [43], Tapestry [57], and Kademlia [36] collectively introduced the idea of structured, decentralized overlay networks. The abstraction they implemented was a distributed hash table, or DHT, which mapped fixed-size, opaque keys to arbitrary values. All of the DHTs were efficient, requiring just $O(\lg n)$ operations to look up a key in an n-node system.

Soon after, distributed file systems like the Cooperative File System (CFS) [14] and PAST [15] were built on top of DHTs. At least initially, however, neither the DHTs nor the distributed file systems provided any search functionality.

In 2002, we set out to design a complete, efficient keyword search service [40] for applications based on DHTs.

This paper revisits our original paper, surveys other interesting research on peer-to-peer keyword searching, examines the state of peer-to-peer technologies today, and identifies some of the lasting impacts that peer-to-peer networks have had.

1.1 A definition

In 2001 as well as today, the definition of a peer-to-peer system is a fuzzy one. The most prominent distinguishing characteristic of a peer-to-peer system is that nodes owned by individuals make up the bulk of both the consumers (clients)

D. Eyers and K. Schwan (Eds.): Middleware 2013, LNCS 8275, pp. 485–496, 2013.
© IFIP International Federation for Information Processing 2013

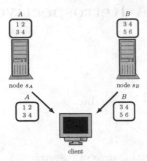
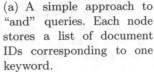
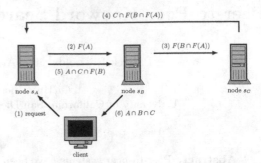

(a) A simple approach to "and" queries. Each node stores a list of document IDs corresponding to one keyword.

(b) Bloom filters help reduce the bandwidth requirement of "and" queries. $F(A)$ is a Bloom filter representing the set A, and $B \cap F(A)$ is the set of all elements from B that matched the Bloom filter $F(A)$.

Fig. 1. Adding a Bloom filter to DHT search

and providers (servers) of the service. A peer-to-peer service generally uses bandwidth, storage, and/or CPU time provided by users of the service. Further, a robust peer-to-peer service should be decentralized enough that no administrator can disable the system.

Some prominent peer-to-peer services, including Napster, Skype prior to 2012, and all BitTorrent search pages, rely on centralized components that can or could be administratively disabled. We still consider them peer-to-peer services, albeit ones with room for improvement.

2   Efficient Peer-to-Peer Searching

A good peer-to-peer search feature needs to be decentralized, efficient, and complete. Early peer-to-peer systems were not. Napster's search feature was centralized, which made it unscalable and easy to shut down. Gnutella's search feature was both inefficient and incomplete: it flooded queries throughout the network up to a fixed number of hops away from the requester, limited by a time-to-live (TTL) value. It could not locate any resources beyond that number of hops. Early DHTs did not provide search at all.

2.1   Our Contribution

The simplest implementation of keyword search on a DHT uses an *inverted index*, as shown in Figure 1(a). The DHT maps each keyword to a list of document IDs, corresponding to the documents that contain the keyword. A client performing a search for one keyword retrieves the list of document IDs associated with that keyword. To perform a conjunctive ("and") query of multiple keywords, the client

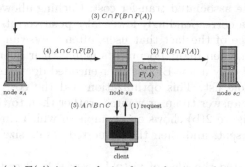 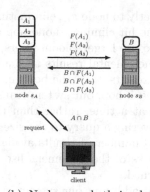

(a) $F(A)$ is already in the cache at node s_B

(b) Nodes send their data one chunk at a time until the desired intersection size is reached

Fig. 2. Caching and incremental results

retrieves the list of document IDs for each keyword and locally calculates the intersection. This approach is clearly decentralized and complete, but it is not especially efficient. If the user searches for keywords that individually appear in many documents but that rarely appear together, then downloading the entire list of document IDs for each word is wasteful.

Our paper proposed three optimizations to this simple approach: Bloom filters, caching, and incremental results. For these to work, we changed the protocol from Figure 1(a) so that intersections are calculated within the DHT, as shown in Figure 1(b). In this revised protocol, the client sends the entire query—e.g., "efficient AND network AND protocols"—to the node hosting the first keyword. That node sends the remaining words in the query, along with a list of document IDs for the first keyword, to the node responsible for the second keyword. This second node calculates the intersection between the second keyword's set of document IDs and the set of document IDs it received from the first node. Forwarding continues in this fashion until all keywords have been considered (all sets of document IDs have been intersected), at which point the last node sends the final list—IDs of the documents containing all the keywords—back to the client.

Bloom filters [5,19,37] are a compact but lossy way to represent membership in a set. They answer the question "Is element x in the set," occasionally returning false positives—a value of "true" even when x is not in the set. In our search system, we used them as a compact way to represent the set of document IDs for documents that contain a given keyword. Instead of transferring entire lists of document IDs, the system transferred Bloom filters representing those lists.

Caching reduces both network traffic and latency by avoiding the transfer of information that has been used recently. Our system cached Bloom-encoded lists of document IDs corresponding to a given keyword. Figure 2(a) shows an example where node s_B already has the Bloom filter $F(A)$; the client sends the query directly to node s_B, eliminating one hop and the cost of transferring $F(A)$. Each cache hit eliminates one hop and the associated transfer cost. Caching allowed us to use larger Bloom filters, with a correspondingly lower false-positive rate.

Incremental results take advantage of the fact that users often only want a few results—say, the best ten—even when many documents match their query. At each hop, our system transferred only a few Bloom filter-encoded document IDs at a time, rather than the whole list. This optimization tied the cost of answering a query to the size of the answer the user wanted, rather than to the total number of results available. Figure 2(b) shows an example in which three chunks of the document list A are sent, and then the requested result size is reached.

In addition, our system incorporated the idea of virtual hosts [14]. Peer-to-peer systems are often heterogeneous in their capabilities: nodes differ in their available CPU power and network capacity. Assigning more-capable nodes a larger number of virtual hosts allowed us to take advantage of their additional capacity.

We measured the effectiveness of our optimizations using a corpus of 105,593 HTML documents and a trace of 95,409 web searches. For each query, we calculated the number of bytes transferred and the total time for the system to satisfy the query. Taken together, our optimizations reduced the time to answer a query by about an order of magnitude.

2.2   Similar Work

Other research projects tackled the problem of peer-to-peer keyword search differently. This section explores three of those systems.

PIER. PIER [26] implements relational queries on top of a DHT, scalable to at least thousands of nodes. Relations composed of tuples are stored in the DHT; each tuple is stored according to its namespace and primary key. Joins are performed by retrieving the relevant relations with multicast queries, then storing them back in the DHT in temporary relations keyed (in the DHT) by the appropriate column for the join. Joins based on Bloom filters are provided, as well, to reduce the number of tuples that must be transferred to temporary tables.

PIER provides expressiveness well beyond keyword-index systems, and it can easily be used to implement keyword queries. However, we believe that the number of nodes involved in each query and the number of bytes transferred among those nodes will be much higher than in a purpose-built keyword-search system.

PlanetP. PlanetP [13] is a file sharing system built with an emphasis on searchability. Each node in the system hosts the documents its user wishes to share, as opposed to a DHT where those documents would be copied onto unrelated nodes. Each node builds an inverted index of the keywords in the documents it shares, then computes a Bloom filter to represent the set of keywords found in at least one document on that node. All nodes in the system flood their Bloom filters to all other nodes, then gossip updates as the Bloom filters change. When a user wants to perform a query, PlanetP uses the Bloom filters to figure out which remote nodes to contact. The false-positive aspect of Bloom filters adds an essentially harmless probability that some nodes will be contacted and return zero results.

OverCite. OverCite [47] is a distributed version of CiteSeer, which is a library and search engine for scientific research papers. OverCite distributes responsibility for storing, indexing, and searching papers among all participating nodes using a DHT. The responsibility for indexing those documents is divided among k partitions; the nodes responsible for a partition in the DHT index the documents contained in the partition. The rationale for using partitions is to avoid making every search query a broadcast. Each partition is $1/k$ the size of the full index and is replicated n/k times, so each node must store $1/k$ of the total index and will receive $1/n$ of the query load. Two additional optimizations are proposed: replicating author and title metadata to all nodes, and replicating common search terms on all nodes. Both optimizations allow certain queries to be answered by a single node, rather than sending each query to k nodes to cover all partitions.

3 Where We Are Now

Fifteen years have passed since Napster was released, and ten years have passed since the first peer-to-peer search papers were published. Where are we now?

Very few prominent Internet services or businesses use peer-to-peer systems. The most successful peer-to-peer system by far is file sharing, accounting for 10% to 20% of traffic during peak hours, on fixed (not mobile) networks [52]. The only other peer-to-peer system that is a household name in the U.S.—clearly a subjective distinction on our part—is Spotify. Skype used to rely on a peer-to-peer overlay but no longer does. Peer-to-peer networks are also popular for live and on-demand video streaming services in China.

Spotify's network is a hybrid of client-server and peer-to-peer protocols [29]. Each client keeps a persistent connection open to a Spotify server, through which it can browse available content, learn about other clients currently online, and receive the first fifteen seconds of any song where low latency is required. Desktop (not mobile) clients retrieve full songs directly from other clients whenever possible. Clients form an unstructured overlay network and use flooding queries with a TTL of two to search for songs.

Spotify's central servers make the peer-to-peer protocol simpler by providing lists of online clients and by providing a backstop data source for content not present within two overlay hops. The peer-to-peer network offloads the majority of song download traffic.

Skype originally used peer-to-peer technology to provide a user directory and NAT traversal [45]. Audio and video streams and chat messages go directly from one user to another whenever possible. Each *supernode* maintains a list of logged-in users and a current IP address for each one. Supernodes also assist in routing calls and chat messages to clients whose device is suspended or behind a firewall. In 2012, Skype moved all supernode functionality off of end-user PCs and onto dedicated *mega-supernodes* in data centers run by Microsoft [23, 24].

Two large, live-video streaming services in China, PPS.tv (PPStream) and Funshion, use peer-to-peer technology. PPStream uses the DONet protocol, which is an unstructured, mesh-style multicast [8, 56]. Funshion is based on BitTorrent [20].

3.1 Disadvantages of Peer-to-Peer Systems

From the perspective of running an Internet service, peer-to-peer systems couple some desirable properties with some serious challenges. The most appealing property of a peer-to-peer system is that it lets a business use customers' bandwidth and computing resources without paying for them. However, in most cases, the challenges overwhelm this potential cost savings:

- Most last-mile connections have asynchronous bandwidth, heavily favoring downloads over uploads. A bandwidth-limited peer-to-peer service like file sharing or video streaming must therefore find many uploaders for each downloader.
- End-user network connections, especially when geographically distant from each other, have roughly 1,000 times lower bandwidth and 1,000 times higher latency than connections within a data center.
- Using customers' computers in unexpected ways can lead to bad publicity.
- Peer-to-peer services require users to download and install software, which providers must write and maintain for each target platform. An unmodified web browser can access centralized services, but it cannot access peer-to-peer services.
- Customers turn off their computers more often than data centers do.
- Mobile devices, which account for a rapidly increasing fraction of Internet traffic [52], magnify all of these issues: they are battery- and CPU-constrained, their bandwidth is usually slower and often metered, and they cannot run the same client software as desktop PCs.
- Customer-owned nodes are not trustworthy.
- Services with data retention or wiretap requirements will likely find it easier to comply with the law if infrastructure is centralized [21].

Some of the limitations of customer-owned computing resources, particularly security and reliability, can be overcome with software, at a cost of additional redundancy and complexity. Others, including poor network connectivity and customers' aversion to installing additional software, are more stubborn. Overall, the risks and costs of harnessing customer-owned resources are almost always higher than the risks and costs of running services in professionally managed data centers.

Further, hosted computing, storage, and bandwidth resources have gotten dramatically cheaper per unit in the last decade [54]. Utility computing, both infrastructure as a service (IaaS) and platform as a service (PaaS), allows new Internet services to start out cheaply with just a fraction of a single server, without relying on peer-to-peer systems. Both Amazon and Google offer a resource-limited tier of hosting services for free. At this point, even cash-strapped startups favor starting new Internet services in data centers.

Web search in particular is a service that favors data centers over peer-to-peer systems. Our test corpus contained 105,593 documents, while Google's contains around fifty billion. A fully featured web search service does things like spelling suggestions, autocomplete, instant search, location awareness, and personalization that are not amenable to caching or representation in Bloom filters. Our and others' search protocols mask wide-area bandwidth and latency constraints well enough for the demands of a file-sharing service, perhaps, but not well enough to be competitive with a modern search engine built with dedicated computing resources.

3.2 Advantages of Peer-to-Peer Systems

In spite of the challenges, the most popular file-sharing services still use peer-to-peer systems [2, 11, 30, 52]. We believe that this fact is due almost entirely to censorship resistance. No matter how widely replicated an infrastructure-based service is, it is still vulnerable to a well placed letter, phone call, domain seizure, or DMCA takedown notice. Peer-to-peer systems have proven far more resilient. In 1993, John Gilmore said, "The Net interprets censorship as damage and routes around it" [17]. Peer-to-peer systems codify that ideal in software.

Much of the censorship exercised against web sites and peer-to-peer systems is copyright related. Publishers of movies, songs, books, and software, among others, hope to preserve their ability to charge for each copy made of their copyrighted works. However, censorship happens for other reasons, too. For example:

- **Political** - In 2008, both the McCain [53] and Obama [16] campaigns had political messages removed due to DMCA takedown notices. Also in 2008, during the South Ossetia War, the nation of Georgia blocked all websites with addresses ending in .ru [7].
- **Moral** - Russia has instituted an unpublished blacklist of sites relating to drugs, suicide, or pornography [3]. The United Kingdom is creating its own list, currently optional but enabled by default, to restrict access to pornography; web forums; information about violence, terrorism, and eating disorders; and "esoteric material" [27].
- **Security** - Volkswagen successfully sued to censor research about vulnerabilities in its keyless entry systems [49]. Life science researchers have instituted policies for censoring themselves when research seems to pose more risk than social good [44].
- **Competitive** - Universal Music Group briefly had Megaupload's "Mega Song" removed from YouTube, despite not having any copyright claim against it [33].

- **Suppressing criticism** - KTVU used DMCA takedown requests to remove copies of a newscast in which its anchor read obviously fake and offensive names for the pilots of Asiana flight 214 [28].
- **Accidental** - The U.S. Immigration and Customs Enforcement (ICE) accidentally took down the hip-hop music blog `dajaz1.com` for a year before returning it without explanation [32]. YouTube's Content ID system automatically flags videos for possible removal, but it often flags videos that do not contain copyrighted content or that might qualify as fair use [12]. While attempting to prevent unauthorized distribution of Windows 8 and Office, Microsoft has accidentally requested that Google remove links to the BBC, Wikipedia, and OpenOffice, among others [50, 51].

In each case, censorship was possible because a small number of administrative entities—ISPs, domain registrars, YouTube, research conference organizers, etc.—could be compelled to block or remove the content. Peer-to-peer systems provide an alternative distribution channel for content when censors get too heavy handed.

Formal peer-to-peer systems are not the only way that the Internet routes around censorship. Content that is small and not obviously offensive or copyright-infringing will often end up widely distributed and widely mirrored if someone tries to censor it. Far more people know what Barbara Streisand's house looks like, how badly the Suburban Express bus company treats its customers, and how to 3D print a gun than would have if interested parties had not attempted to censor that information [4, 22, 42]. In a sense, technology news sites, parodies, memes, and web forums act like an informal peer-to-peer network when they mirror content in this fashion.

3.3 Impacts

Several ideas from peer-to-peer systems have found their way into systems that are not strictly peer-to-peer. Most large-scale Internet services are geographically distributed, self-organizing, and resilient. Some systems, including the Cassandra database and the Tahoe-LAFS file system, explicitly incorporate DHTs [1, 48].

BOINC—the computing platform that runs SETI@home [6]—runs primarily on end users' computers, much like a peer-to-peer system. Unlike nodes in a peer-to-peer system, nodes in BOINC are only servers and do not consume the service that other nodes provide. Also, nodes are centrally managed rather than self-organizing. However, like a peer-to-peer system, BOINC successfully deals with malicious participants and harnesses spare CPU cycles.

4   Where We Go from Here

We believe that peer-to-peer systems continue to have both technical and social value. They may be a good way for modestly funded research groups to bootstrap an Internet service. They provide a stress test for new protocols, because protocols and techniques that work within the resource and security constraints of a peer-to-peer system will often work even better in a centralized system. Finally, of course, they provide outstanding resistance to censorship, in a way that commercial and centrally managed services cannot.

To that end, we believe the most important focus areas in peer-to-peer research are:

- **Security** - Services that become popular, or that host content that someone wishes to censor, become the target of attacks. Attackers may disrupt routing or searching, or they may intercept or modify content. Peer-to-peer systems have to deal with the possibility that nodes are Byzantine faulty [31].
- **Anonymity** - If the main use case for peer-to-peer systems is distributing censored content, then participants might need to remain anonymous when publishing or retrieving that content. Providing anonymity in a robust, efficient way could provide immense social value.
- **Searchability** - Simply put, we cannot read what we cannot find. BitTorrent users currently rely on centralized, commercial web sites to map keywords to document identifiers. Eventually, whether through legal changes or technical attacks, these sites will probably get shut down. Existing and new peer-to-peer search technologies should be applied to ensure that users can find content.

In 2013, as in 2001, peer-to-peer networking remains an exciting, fruitful area of research.

References

1. The Apache Cassandra Project, http://cassandra.apache.org/ (accessed August 16, 2013)
2. Ares, http://aresgalaxy.sourceforge.net/ (accessed August 16, 2013)
3. Russia internet blacklist law takes effect. BBC News (October 2012)
4. US government orders removal of Defcad 3D-gun designs. BBC News (May 2013)
5. Bloom, B.H.: Space/time trade-offs in hash coding with allowable errors. Communications of the ACM 13(7), 422–426 (1970)
6. BOINC, http://boinc.berkeley.edu/ (accessed August 16, 2013)
7. Reporters Without Borders War still having serious impact on freedom of expression (October 2010), http://bit.ly/14mTqDm (accessed August 16, 2013)
8. Chen, S., Huo, L., Fu, Q., Guo, R., Gao, W.: FBSA: a self-adjustable multi-source data scheduling algorithm for P2P media streaming. In: Sebe, N., Liu, Y., Zhuang, Y.-t., Huang, T.S. (eds.) MCAM 2007. LNCS, vol. 4577, pp. 325–333. Springer, Heidelberg (2007)
9. Clarke, I.: A distributed decentralised information storage and retrieval system. Master's thesis, University of Edinburgh (1999)
10. Clarke, I., Sandberg, O., Wiley, B., Hong, T.W.: Freenet: A distributed anonymous information storage and retrieval system. In: Proceedings of the ICSI Workshop on Design Issues in Anonymity and Unobservability (2000)
11. Cohen, B.: Incentives build robustness in BitTorrent. In: Proceedings of the Workshop on Economics of Peer-to-Peer Systems, vol. 6, pp. 68–72 (2003)

12. Content ID disputes - YouTube,
    https://www.youtube.com/yt/copyright/content-id-disputes.html
    (accessed August 16, 2013)
13. Cuenca-Acuna, F.M., Peery, C., Martin, R.P., Nguyen, T.D.: PlanetP: Using gossiping to build content addressable peer-to-peer information sharing communities. In: Proceedings of the International Symposium on High Performance Distributed Computing (HPDC), pp. 236–246 (2003)
14. Dabek, F., Frans Kaashoek, M., Karger, D., Morris, R., Stoica, I.: Wide-area cooperative storage with CFS. In: Proceedings of the ACM Symposium on Operating Systems Principles (SOSP) (October 2001)
15. Druschel, P., Rowstron, A.: PAST: A large-scale, persistent peer-to-peer storage utility. In: Proceedings of Hot Topics in Operating Systems (HotOS), pp. 75–80. IEEE (2001)
16. Eggerton, J.: NBC, Obama campaign spar over YouTube video (October 2008), http://bit.ly/13GPgWW (accessed August 16, 2013)
17. Elmer-Dewitt, P.: First nation in cyberspace. TIME International (December 1993)
18. Evangelista, B.: Napster files for bankruptcy. San Francisco Chronicle (June 2004)
19. Fan, L., Cao, P., Almeida, J., Broder, A.: Summary cache: A scalable wide-area web cache sharing protocol. In: Proceedings of ACM SIGCOMM, pp. 254–265 (1998)
20. Funshion online - about us, http://www.funshion.com/english/about_us.html
    (accessed August 16, 2013)
21. Gallagher, R.: Skype won't say whether it can eavesdrop on your conversations. Slate (July 2012)
22. Gallagher, S.: Express to Internet hate: Bus company threatens redditor with lawsuit. Ars Technica (April 2013)
23. Gillett, M.: What does Skype's architecture do? (July 2012),
    http://blogs.skype.com/2012/07/26/what-does-skypes-architecture-do/
    (accessed August 16, 2013)
24. Goodin, D.: Skype replaces P2P supernodes with Linux boxes hosted by Microsoft. Ars Technica (May 2012)
25. Healey, J.: StreamCast's undoing (May 2008),
    http://opinion.latimes.com/bitplayer/2008/05/streamcasts-und.html (accessed August 16, 2013)
26. Huebsch, R., Hellerstein, J.M., Lanham, N., Loo, B.T., Shenker, S., Stoica, I.: Querying the Internet with PIER. In: Proceedings of the International Conference on Very Large Data Bases (VLDB), pp. 321–332 (2003)
27. Killock, J.: Sleepwalking into censorship (July 2013),
    https://www.openrightsgroup.org/blog/2013/sleepwalking-into-censorship
    (accessed August 16, 2013)
28. Kravets, D.: Local newscast uses DMCA to erase air crash reporting blunder (July 2013),
    http://www.wired.com/threatlevel/2013/07/youtube-newscast-asiana/
    (accessed August 16, 2013)
29. Kreitz, G., Niemelä, F.: Spotify—large scale, low latency, P2P music-on-demand streaming. In: Proceedings of the IEEE International Conference on Peer-to-Peer Computing (P2P), pp. 1–10. IEEE (2010)
30. Kulbak, Y., Bickson, D.: The eMule protocol specification. eMule project (2005),
    http://emule-project.net
31. Lamport, L., Shostak, R., Pease, M.: The Byzantine generals problem. ACM Transactions on Programming Languages and Systems (TOPLAS) 4(3), 382–401 (1982)

32. Lee, T.B.: ICE admits year-long seizure of music blog was a mistake. Ars Technica (December 2011)

33. Lee, T.B.: UMG claims right to block or remove YouTube videos it doesn't own. Ars Technica (December 2011)

34. Leeds, J.: Grokster calls it quits on sharing music files. New York Times (November 2005)

35. Liang, J., Kumar, R., Ross, K.W.: The KaZaA overlay: A measurement study. In: Proceedings of the IEEE Annual Computer Communications Workshop, pp. 2–9. IEEE (2004)

36. Maymounkov, P., Mazières, D.: Kademlia: A peer-to-peer information system based on the XOR metric. In: Druschel, P., Kaashoek, M.F., Rowstron, A. (eds.) IPTPS 2002. LNCS, vol. 2429, pp. 53–65. Springer, Heidelberg (2002)

37. Mullin, J.: Optimal semijoins for distributed database systems. IEEE Transactions on Software Engineering 16(5), 558–560 (1990)

38. Napster, http://opennap.sourceforge.net/napster.txt (accessed August 16, 2013)

39. Ratnasamy, S., Francis, P., Handley, M., Karp, R., Shenker, S.: A scalable content-addressable network. In: Proceedings of ACM SIGCOMM (2001)

40. Reynolds, P., Vahdat, A.: Efficient peer-to-peer keyword searching. In: Endler, M., Schmidt, D.C. (eds.) Middleware 2003. LNCS, vol. 2672, pp. 21–40. Springer, Heidelberg (2003)

41. Ripeanu, M.: Peer-to-peer architecture case study: Gnutella network. In: Proceedings of the International Conference on Peer-to-Peer Computing, pp. 99–100. IEEE (2001)

42. Rogers, P.: Streisand's home becomes hit on Web. Mercury News (January 2003)

43. Rowstron, A., Druschel, P.: Pastry: Scalable, decentralized object location, and routing for large-scale peer-to-peer systems. In: Guerraoui, R. (ed.) Middleware 2001. LNCS, vol. 2218, pp. 329–350. Springer, Heidelberg (2001)

44. Selgelid, M.J.: Governance of dual-use research: an ethical dilemma. Bulletin of the World Health Organization (June 2009)

45. Skype FAQ: What are P2P communications? https://support.skype.com/en/faq/FA10983/what-are-p2p-communications (accessed August 16, 2013)

46. Stoica, I., Morris, R., Karger, D., Frans Kaashoek, M., Balakrishnan, H.: Chord: A scalable peer-to-peer lookup service for Internet applications. In: Proceedings of ACM SIGCOMM (2001)

47. Stribling, J.: OverCite: A cooperative digital research library. Master's thesis, Massachusetts Institute of Technology (2005)

48. Tahoe-LAFS, https://tahoe-lafs.org (accessed August 16, 2013)

49. Torchinsky, J.: VW demands British court censor scientific paper about car security (July 2013), http://bit.ly/1c75SPx (accessed August 16, 2013)

50. Microsoft DMCA notice mistakenly targets BBC, Techcrunch, Wikipedia, and U.S. govt (October 2012), http://bit.ly/QVArtf (accessed August 16, 2013)

51. Microsoft censors OpenOffice download links (August 2013), http://bit.ly/1a5Tu1J (accessed August 16, 2013)

52. Sandvine Inc. ULC. Global Internet phenomena report, 1H (2013)

53. von Lohmann, F.: McCain campaign feels DMCA sting (October 2008), https://www.eff.org/deeplinks/2008/10/mccain-campaign-feels-dmca-sting (accessed August 16, 2013)

54. Web hosting now vs 10 years ago (February 2008),
    http://royal.pingdom.com/2008/02/19/web-hosting-now-vs-10-years-ago/
    (accessed August 16, 2013)
55. Woody, T.: The race to kill Kazaa. Wired (February 2003)
56. Zhang, X., Liu, J., Li, B., Yum, T.-S.P.: CoolStreaming/DONet: a data-driven
    overlay network for peer-to-peer live media streaming. In: Proceedings of IEEE
    INFOCOM, vol. 3, pp. 2102–2111. IEEE (2005)
57. Zhao, B., Kubiatowicz, J., Joseph, A.: Tapestry: An infrastructure for fault-tolerant
    wide-area location and routing. Technical Report UCB/CSD-01-1141, Computer
    Science Division (EECS), University of California, Berkeley (2001)

Author Index